From Warwick XMAS (2017).

THE BUMPER BOOK

OF THINGS THAT NOBODY KNOWS

Also by William Hartston

How to Cheat at Chess

The Penguin Book of Chess Openings

Soft Pawn

The Ultimate Irrelevant Encyclopedia

The Kings of Chess

Chess – The Making of the Musical

The Drunken Goldfish and Other Irrelevant Scientific Research

How was it for you, Professor?

The Guinness Book of Chess Grandmasters

Teach Yourself Chess

Teach Yourself Better Chess

*The Book of Numbers: The Ultimate Compendium
of Facts About Figures*

Mr Hartston's Most Excellent Encyclopedia of Useless Information

Forgotten Treasures: A Collection of Well-loved Poetry (Vols 1, 2 and 3)

The Things That Nobody Knows

Even More Things That Nobody Knows

THE BUMPER BOOK

OF THINGS THAT NOBODY KNOWS

1001 MYSTERIES OF LIFE, THE UNIVERSE AND EVERYTHING

WILLIAM HARTSTON

Atlantic Books
London

This collection first published in hardback in Great Britain in 2017
by Atlantic Books, an imprint of Atlantic Books Ltd.

The Things That Nobody Knows first published in Great Britain
in 2011 by Atlantic Books.

Even More Things That Nobody Knows first published in Great Britain
in 2015 by Atlantic Books.

1 2 3 4 5 6 7 8 9

A CIP catalogue record for this book is available from the British Library.

Hardback ISBN: 978-1-78649-074-2
E-book ISBN: 978-1-78649-075-9

Printed in Great Britain

Atlantic Books
An Imprint of Atlantic Books Ltd
Ormond House
26–27 Boswell Street
London
WC1N 3JZ

www.atlantic-books.co.uk

PREFACE

When Atlantic Books approached me in 2010 and asked if I could write a book containing 501 things that nobody knows, I was delighted to accept the challenge. Paradoxically, I had often felt that we learn more by thinking about the things we don't know than the things that we do. It's also much more fun. 501 unanswered questions later, *The Things That Nobody Knows* was born.

Three years later, they asked if I could do 501 more, which led to *Even More Things That Nobody Knows*, confirming that there is no limit to human ignorance. The book you are now reading comprises all the items from the earlier two books with one small amendment. Looking through the contents of both books, I found only one question that had been definitively answered and if you turn to item 200 from *The Things That Nobody Knows*, you will see what it is. On the plus side, this reduces the total number of Things That Nobody Knows listed in these pages from 1002 to 1001, which is a much more pleasing number. I hope you enjoy or are enlightened by at least some of them.

William Hartston
Cambridge 2017

PART 1

THE THINGS THAT NOBODY KNOWS

How can we remember our ignorance,
which our growth requires, when we are
using our knowledge all the time?

Henry David Thoreau (1817–62)

CONTENTS

INTRODUCTION

Ignorance, Fruit-Fly Genitalia and the End of the World

There are known knowns. These are things we know that we know. There are known unknowns. That is to say, there are things that we now know we don't know. But there are also unknown unknowns. These are things we do not know we don't know.

Donald Rumsfeld, 12 February 2002

The trouble with people like Donald Rumsfeld is that they give ignorance a bad name. The US Secretary of State for Defense was generally derided when he made the clumsy statement quoted above, but he was just trying to remember a line from Confucius quoted by Henry David Thoreau in *Walden* (1854):

To know that we know what we know, and that we do not know what we do not know, that is true knowledge.

With the wisdom of Confucius supporting him, Thoreau went on to ask:

How can we remember our ignorance, which our growth requires, when we are using our knowledge all the time?

While Rumsfeld was simply categorizing different levels of not knowing, Confucius and Thoreau had a much more positive approach to ignorance, an approach that provides the basic *raison d'être* of this book. I come to praise ignorance, not to bury it; for there is no better key to understanding the vast and ever-growing expanse of human knowledge. The topics covered in the forthcoming pages are exactly what the book says on the cover: things that nobody knows. Many people, when I have mentioned the title of the book, have unjustifiably assumed it to be another of those not-many-people-know-that collections of useless information. It isn't. There may be a great number of such intriguing facts here, but they are only included when they are crucial to explain what nobody at all knows, and why nobody knows it.

More than three hundred years ago, the French philosopher and mathematician Blaise Pascal likened our knowledge to a sphere which, as it grows larger, inevitably increases the area with which it comes into contact with the unknown. Henry Miller put this more succinctly in *The Wisdom of the Heart* (1941):

> *In expanding the field of knowledge we but increase the horizon of ignorance.*

This book is a guided tour around Miller's horizon of ignorance.

When listening to scientists or other experts talking about the latest advances in their fields, I have always found it more intriguing, and generally more enlightening, when they get on to the subject of the things they don't know. Rumsfeld's known unknowns are what determines the direction of future research – and that is what makes ignorance so exciting.

According to a recent estimate in the on-line Ulrichsweb periodicals directory, there are around 300,000 academic journals currently being published around the world. These may come out weekly, monthly or less frequently, but the total number of issues of all these journals in any year must be over 3 million, and with an average in the region of ten papers in each journal, each reporting a previously unknown result, that adds up to over 30 million additions to our knowledge every year, which is around one every second. There has to be a vast amount of ignorance out there to keep all those journals in material, and the things that nobody knows that I have identified in the pages that follow only scratch the surface.

I ought now to write something about ontology, epistemology, Karl Popper's concept of falsifiability, Thomas Kuhn's paradigm shifts and everything else that contributes to our ideas of reality, knowledge and what is knowable, but there will be plenty of time for that sort of thing later when we get on to the subject of philosophical unknowns. There is, however, just one more subject that I want to mention: fruit-fly penises.

Male fruit flies have tiny hooks and spines on their penises, the function of which – until recently – nobody knew. The standard way to resolve such a question would be to shave these bristles off and see what effect this had on the sex life of the subject. In the case of fruit-fly penises, however, the bristles are so small they can only be seen under a microscope, and even the best scalpel is too clumsy an instrument to attempt to use as a razor. At the end of 2009, however, researchers at the University of California published a paper describing a method of shaving fruit-fly penises with a laser. Not only could they shave off the bristles, but they could even perform the task with such accuracy that only the top third of each bristle was trimmed. By comparing the sexual exploits of unshaven, partially shaven, and totally shaven fruit flies, they could then tell everyone what they wanted to know. Answer: the sole role of the hooks and spines is to act as biological Velcro and keep the male fruit fly attached to the female during sex.

And until the paper was published, that is probably something that even Donald Rumsfeld did not know that he did not know.

After toying with various ways of organizing the material, I finally decided to settle for the most systematically arbitrary of all: alphabetical order by subject. Where appropriate, I have included cross-references to related topics at the end of the subject sections. These are introduced by the words 'see also', followed by the name(s) of the related subject or subjects and the numbers of the relevant unknowns. There are also cross-references embedded within the body of the entries, directing the reader to other entries that shed further light on the topic under scrutiny.

Before diving into the deep end of our pool of ignorance, I cannot resist concluding this introduction with an example of a question we know we can't answer – at the time of writing, anyway. The question is

Will the world end in 2012?

More precisely, the question is whether the world will end on 21 December 2012, a date supposedly predicted by the ancient Mayans. The calculation is based on the Mayan Long Count Calendar, which must be the most complex way of counting our days that humanity has ever devised. Rather than expressing a date in three figures, as the day, month and year (originally chosen to correspond to the period of rotation of the Earth, and the orbits of the Moon around the Earth and the Earth about the Sun), the Mayans used five figures from interwoven counting systems. There were 20 days (called K'in) in a Winal, 18 Winal in a Tun, 20 Tun in a K'atun, 20 K'atun in a B'ak'tun. A Long Count ended after 13 B'ak'tun. Multiply all these together, and you get 1,872,000 days in a Long Count, after which it starts again. That's just over 5,128 solar years, and since the Mayan calendar began on 11 August 3114 BC, the calculations mean that it will reach its end on 21 December 2012 (remember there was no year zero in our calendar).

Actually the Mayans did not predict the End of the World on that date, nor even a great cataclysm, and some say the date had no more significance than any 1st of January, but it's a good excuse for a blockbuster movie, and NASA has been plagued with phone calls from people who believe in it, some even saying that they are contemplating suicide to avoid the horrors that the End of the World may bring.

So the good news is that the world will probably not end in 2012, but we shall definitely know whether the prediction is correct on 22 December of that year.

To be conscious that you are ignorant
is a great step to knowledge.

Benjamin Disraeli, *Sybil* (1845)

AARDVARKS

1. Is the aardvark the closest living relative of a creature from which all mammals evolved?

In 1999 scientists sequenced and analysed the complete mitochondrial DNA of the aardvark, an unprepossessing, somewhat comical ant-eating creature from Africa, whose name is Afrikaans for 'earth pig'. The results showed that the aardvark may be the closest living relative of the ancient ancestor of all the placental mammals – that is, all mammals, including ourselves, apart from marsupials and the egg-laying monotremes (such as the duck-billed platypus). Surprisingly, the genetic make-up of the aardvark is closer to that of the elephant than the South American anteater, which shares its taste in food and its general appearance.

Research suggests that the chromosomes of the aardvark have undergone relatively little change since placental mammals first evolved over 100 million years ago, but how close the first placental mammal was to the aardvark of today is unknown.

Our knowledge can only be finite, while our ignorance must necessarily be infinite.

Sir Karl Popper (1902–94)

AMERICA

2. Who were the first people to populate America and how did they get there?

Until very recently, the so-called Clovis people were thought to have been the original human inhabitants of the Americas and thus the ancestors of all later indigenous people in both North and South America. The Clovis people were named after the town of Clovis in New Mexico where evidence of their existence was first detected by archaeologists in the 1930s. A distinctively shaped spear point found there became the identifying feature of the Clovis culture, and similar items were later found in many other places. The most generally held theory was that the Clovis people had come from Asia some 13,000 years ago, during the last Ice Age, following herds of animals across the land bridge that then connected Siberia to Alaska. The newcomers went on to establish the first human settlements in North America.

The 'Clovis first' theory, has periodically been disputed by claims of finds that may indicate a pre-Clovis population. Most recently, a large hoard of tools and artefacts was unearthed in Texas which appear to date back to 15,500 years ago, some 2,500 years before the Clovis people are thought to have arrived. Furthermore, the existence of huge ice sheets in North America at the time would have made travel by land from Asia unlikely, and the supporters of a pre-Clovis theory suggest that the original inhabitants arrived by sea, probably from Polynesia, arriving in South America and spreading north.

3. Who is America named after: Amerigo Vespucci or Richard Amerike?

For several hundred years, it has been generally assumed that America was named after the navigator Amerigo Vespucci, who in 1499 sailed from Italy on a voyage of discovery to what is now known as Brazil. The earliest known use of the word 'America' is on a 1507 map by Martin Waldseemüller (→ CARTOGRAPHY 70), a map based mainly on information supplied by Vespucci. Yet there is no evidence that Vespucci himself ever claimed to have given the continent its name, and it is known that in later editions of the map, Waldseemüller tried to change the name to *Terra Incognita* ('unknown land').

From the 1960s, however, evidence began to accumulate in support of an alternative theory regarding the origin of the name 'America'. It all began with the discovery of trading records concerning a Welsh merchant, Richard ap Meryk, who had anglicized his name to Richard Amerike on setting up business in Bristol in the late fifteenth century. Salt cod, in those days, was big business, and the Bristol fishermen brought a good deal of it from Iceland until that trade was stopped by the king of Denmark in 1475. They then sought out new fishing grounds, and the records support the idea that they found what they were looking for off the coast of Newfoundland. This discovery, naturally enough, they kept secret, but Amerike is known to have been a major supporter of John Cabot's voyage of discovery to North America in 1497.

It is now known that both Columbus and Vespucci had copies of Cabot's map. The only question is whether Cabot had already named the new land after his sponsor Amerike. Intriguingly, one more piece of the jigsaw has been wedged in to fit that theory: Amerike's coat of arms. This coat of arms includes stars and stripes, and his supporters say that it inspired the American flag. That is possible, but unlikely: the stripes on Amerike's version are vertical, not horizontal; there are only three stars; and as well as red, white and blue, his coat of arms includes a prominent element of mustardy yellow.

4. Did the Chinese discover America before Christopher Columbus?

In 2002 the retired British submarine commander Gavin Menzies published a best-selling book entitled *1421: The Year China Discovered the World*, in which he argues that Chinese explorers not only reached America long before Columbus, but also discovered Australia, New Zealand and Antarctica – and even circumnavigated the globe a century before Magellan. His claim is that fleets of massive junks under the command of the eunuch-admiral Zheng He performed all these feats at the behest of the Chinese emperor. Although some historians denounce his claims as pure fiction, with no evidence to back them, Menzies says they explain some early European maps that appear to give accurate details of lands that were supposedly undiscovered at the time.

In 2006 a map was unveiled in Beijing that had recently been discovered in an antiques shop. The map included Chinese characters stating it was drawn by Mo Yi Tong and copied from a map made in the 16th year of the reign of the Emperor Yongle, which was 1418. This map included Australia and other lands supposedly unknown at the time. Three years later, in 2009, some more Chinese maps came to light. These claimed to be copies of fifteenth-century originals, and had been collected by the late Dr Hendon Harris Jr, who in 1973 had published a book on discoveries supposedly made by early Chinese mariners. Harris went much further than Menzies, suggesting that the Chinese had reached the Americas around 2200 BC and were the ancestors of the Native Americans.

5. What happened to Virginia Dare, the first English child born in the New World, and the Lost Colony of Roanoke Island?

Virginia Dare, born on 18 August 1587, was the first child born in the Americas to English parents, Eleanor and Ananias Dare. She was born into the colony established that year on Roanoake Island, in what is now North Carolina. The settlers, who were sponsored by Sir Walter Raleigh, were led by Virginia's maternal grandfather, John White. Not long after Virginia was born, the colonists ran short of food, and White returned to England seeking fresh supplies and support. But when he returned three years later, the entire colony had disappeared. Before White's departure, the colonists had agreed to carve a cross if they were in distress or under attack, or, if they decided to move the settlement, they were to carve the name of their new location. White found no cross, just the letters 'CROATOAN'. Croatan Island, not far from Roanoke, was the home of the friendly Croatan tribe, but with the onset of equinoctial storms, White was obliged to return to England without ever establishing the fate of his granddaughter, or any of the other settlers.

Theories to account for the disappearance of the colonists range from drowning, cannibalism and Spanish aggression to peaceful assimilation into the local tribes, but their exact fate remains uncertain. The Lost Colony DNA Project is currently trying to compare the DNA of relatives of the Roanoake colonists with DNA taken from people with Native American ancestry to try to determine whether the colonists died out completely, or 'went native' and interbred with the local people.

6. How did Davy Crockett die?

As everybody knows, Davy Crockett died heroically fighting the Mexicans under Santa Anna at the Battle of the Alamo in 1836. Or did he? There are two very distinct versions of Crockett's death:

(i) According to a black slave named Ben who cooked for Santa Anna's forces, Crockett's body was found at the Alamo, surrounded by at least sixteen Mexican corpses, with Crockett's knife deeply embedded in one of them. That seems to tally with the usual story.

(ii) According to other accounts of the battle, around half a dozen Texans surrendered to the Mexicans and were promptly executed by Santa Anna. Some say that Crockett was among them. This version is supported by the memoirs of a Mexican officer named José Enrique de la Peña, who asserted that Crockett did not die in the battle. The authenticity of these memoirs has been disputed.

7. Did Custer's Last Stand ever really take place?

What really happened on 25 June 1876 at the Battle of the Little Bighorn, where General George Custer and his men were wiped out by Chief Crazy Horse and his Sioux braves? The usual tale highlights Custer's heroism when, heavily outnumbered, he and his men shoot their horses and pile them into a barricade (leave out the shot horses if this is being filmed for purposes of family entertainment) and withstand the Red Indian hordes until they are all killed. Since all Custer's 210 men were wiped out, however, all accounts of his Last Stand have come from the other side, and all the early accounts were made at a time of delicate negotiations between the Sioux and the US government, when there were advantages to be seen in portraying Custer in as heroic a light as possible.

Investigations of what is now known as Custer Hill have led to strong disagreement about what happened. The large number of bodies found there, together with other evidence, has been taken by some to support the story of the barricade and the hopeless but heroic Last Stand. Analysis of the positions of spent cartridge cases, however, has suggested to some a picture of men in a panic, running and shooting wildly in all directions, including into the air and into the ground. Later accounts by participants on the winning side have also suggested that it was all over quite quickly, 'in the time it takes a hungry man to eat a meal', as one is quoted as saying.

ANCIENT HISTORY

8. Did Atlantis ever exist?

In the fourth century BC, the Greek philosopher Plato wrote of the lost city of Atlantis, an island that 'disappeared into the depths of the sea in a single day and night'. He placed it somewhere around the Straits of Gibraltar, and the legend of Atlantis has been with us ever since. Historians have generally given little credence to the tale, pointing out that the invention of imaginary cities was a common literary device of Plato's time – but that has never stopped speculation and occasional expeditions in search of Atlantis.

In 2009 there was a report of images of a vast rectangular grid on the Atlantic seabed, which Atlantis-lovers saw as evidence of a lost city. Unfortunately, closer examination suggested that the grid was an image created by the ship that conducted the survey. More credible was a recent survey by archaeologists and geologists of the marshlands of the Doñana Park near Cadiz, Spain, using deep-ground radar, digital mapping and underwater technology. This revealed what could be a city buried in mud by a tsunami. That interpretation is reinforced by the discovery of sites said to be 'memorial cities' built by the survivors. This is hardly the city under the sea described by Plato, but he places its destruction at around 10,000 years before his own time, so the Spanish site, which dates from 6000–5000 BC, could be the origin of the Atlantis legend, even if it was several thousand years later than Plato's estimate.

9. What did the people of the Magdalenian culture, who lived in Western Europe around 15,000 years ago, do with the cups they made from human skulls?

In the fifth century BC the Greek historian Herodotus, in his description of the Scythians who lived on the far side of the Black Sea, relates how they drank from the skulls of their enemies. There have been similar accounts from other cultures, but there was little material evidence until archaeologists investigating Gough's Cave, a Palaeolithic (Old Stone Age) site in Somerset, uncovered fragments of both human and animal bones – including forty-one pieces of human skull. These pieces, when pieced together, were found to be from half a dozen individuals, and showed what the researchers described as 'meticulous shaping of cranial vaults': the skulls had been worked into the shape of cups. However, the archaeologists were unable to tell whether these 'cups' were actually used for drinking, or whether they played a part in some other ceremony, such as a burial ritual.

10. What did the Minoans call themselves?

From around the twenty-seventh to the fifteenth century BC, the Minoans on the island of Crete were one of the world's most advanced civilizations. Their buildings, their art (which influenced that of both Greece and Egypt) and their ability to recover from natural disasters such as earthquakes and volcanic eruptions all attest to a high level of organization and administration. Yet their ethnic origins and language remain unknown, and their writings, in the script known as Linear A, have yet to be deciphered. All of which contribute to the fact that we do not even know how they referred to themselves. It was certainly not 'Minoan', a term invented by the

British archaeologist Sir Arthur Evans after the mythical King Minos of Crete, who kept the Minotaur in his labyrinth – a story possibly inspired by the elaborate cellars of the Palace of Knossos, which Evans excavated in the early years of the twentieth century.

See also WRITING SYSTEMS 494

11. Who was the victor at the Battle of Kadesh?

The Battle of Kadesh, fought around 1274 BC, was one of the greatest battles of history, and was said to have involved more chariots than any other battle, before or since. Kadesh is also the first major battle for which we have detailed accounts from both sides. In fact, it could be said that we know almost everything about the Battle of Kadesh except who won.

The battle was fought between the armies of the Pharaoh Ramses II of Egypt and Muwatallis, king of the Hittites. After misjudging the closeness of the Hittite forces, Ramses allowed his own troops to become split, leaving him vulnerable to a sudden ambush by the Hittites. By his own account, he was on the verge of defeat when reinforcements arrived and drove off the enemy. Both sides then retreated and a truce was signed shortly thereafter.

For the rest of his long reign, Ramses proclaimed Kadesh as a great Egyptian victory, while the Hittites were firmly convinced they had won the battle. Archaeological investigations have failed to produce evidence to support either side's claim.

12. Did the Hanging Gardens of Babylon ever exist?

According to legend, the Hanging Gardens of Babylon, one of the Seven Wonders of the Ancient World, were built around 600 BC by King Nebuchadnezzar II of Babylon for his wife, Amytis of Media, in Iran, who was pining for the trees and plants of her homeland. The Gardens were written about and highly praised by Greek historians of the first century BC, which was about a hundred years after they were said to have been destroyed in an earthquake. The earlier Greek historian Herodotus, who lived in the fifth century BC, is said to have included the Hanging Gardens in his own list of the Seven Wonders, but this list has not survived and there is no definite reference to the Gardens in any of his known writings. Curiously, neither is there any known reference to them in Babylonian writings of the time.

Since the site of Babylon was rediscovered in the nineteenth century, archaeological excavations have produced some evidence that match parts of some descriptions of the Hanging Gardens, but none of this evidence is sufficient to confirm their existence. One suggestion is that the Gardens never existed, but were just intended as a poetic device. Another suggestion is that they did exist, but were in Nineveh, not Babylon, having been built by Sennacherib of Assyria in the seventh century BC. The oldest of the Seven Wonders would then have been a confused amalgamation between Sennacherib's real gardens and Nebuchadnezzar's mythical version.

13. What caused the collapse of many civilizations around the eastern Mediterranean between the late Bronze Age and early Iron Age?

Between around 1200 and 1150 BC, as iron began to replace bronze as the favoured material for tools and weaponry, a number of civilizations around the Eastern Mediterranean suffered cataclysmic declines from which they never recovered.

In Greece, the great stone palaces of the Mycenean culture were all destroyed, in Egypt the period of the New Kingdom came to an end as the country reeled under foreign invaders such as the mysterious 'Sea Peoples', while in the Near East the Hittite empire fell apart, and cities across the region were sacked or burnt to the ground. Various causes, both natural and human, may have lain behind such widespread collapse. There is some evidence of prolonged drought, and of earthquakes and volcanic activity, while some scholars have suggested that mass migrations (possibly connected with climate change) combined with the new iron-based weapons technology may have led to a heightened mood of militarism and a desperate drive for conquest. Or it could be simply that the civilizations that had emerged in the region over the previous two millennia had sown the seeds of their own downfall by becoming too complex to be sustained by the existing systems of rule and administration.

14. What was the original purpose of Stonehenge?

About 5,000 years ago, on Wiltshire's windswept Salisbury Plain, the ancient inhabitants of Britain built a henge, a simple structure consisting of a bank, a ditch and some diggings known as the Aubrey holes. These holes, named after their discoverer, the seventeenth-century antiquarian John Aubrey, are round pits in the chalk, each about 1 metre (3 ft) wide and 1 metre deep, with flat bottoms. Together they form a circle some 87 metres (284 ft) in diameter. Some cremated human bones have been found in the chalk.

The construction was then abandoned for about a thousand years until 2150 BC, when some eighty-two massive bluestones from the Preseli Mountains in southwest Wales were erected on the site. The stones, weighing up to 4 tonnes, would have had to travel some 380 km (240 miles) from their original location, and much research and speculation has been spent on the question of how they were moved. The most likely method involved moving the stones on boats by river and sea, and then using rollers to move them across land. It has also been suggested that the stones may have been transported from Wales by the ice sheets thousands of years earlier, during the last Ice Age.

But what was it all for? It has been suggested that Stonehenge was a temple, or an astronomical observatory, or a centre of healing, or a place of human sacrifice – but with little known about the life or beliefs of the pre-Celtic inhabitants of these islands, there are few clues to go by.

15. What was the origin of the 260-day Tzolk'in calendar of the Mayans?

We have already encountered the ancient Mayan calendar in connection with whether the world will end in 2012 (→ INTRODUCTION), but the reasons behind its complex interweavings of numerical patterns are almost unfathomable. The combination of two different types of week, one of 13 days, the other of 20, to give a 260-day cycle running in conjunction with the 365-day year, is particularly baffling. The commonest – but by no means satisfactory – explanation offered is that the numbers 13 and 20 appear to have held some special significance for the Mayans.

It has been suggested that the 13-day week may relate to the lunar calendar, being the period between a new moon and a full moon. The trouble with this theory is that it doesn't add up, as it would give a lunar month of 26 days instead of the more accurate figure of 29. Supporters of the theory respond by saying that you can enjoy the full moon on the day before and the day after too, so the full cycle is 13 days from new to full, 3 days of full-moon watching, then 13 days of a waning moon. Hey presto: 29. But even the Mayans must have felt there was something unsatisfactory about a 13-day lunar week, with the phases of the Moon starting 3 days later every cycle.

As for the 260-day cycle, one suggestion is that it is the period of human gestation, or at least the time between the first missed period and childbirth. Yet there is no evidence to suggest that Mayan midwives had a large influence on the calendar system.

16. Where did the Etruscans come from?

The Etruscans – the ancient inhabitants of Tuscany – were a major power in central Italy from the beginning of the Iron Age to the early days of the Roman empire. Indeed, it was the Etruscans who were largely responsible for turning the small village of Ruma on the banks of the River Tiber into the mighty city we know as Rome. Yet where the Etruscans came from has been a matter of dispute for more than two millennia. The ancient Romans maintained that their origins lay in Asia Minor; the ancient Greeks, on the other hand, believed they were an indigenous Italian race. The Etruscans themselves left no literature, no religious texts nor any other clues as to their origins, apart from some items found in graves and tombs. What little remains of their language makes it clear that it is not Indo-European – indeed, no similarity has been detected with any known language, alive or dead.

17. When did humans discover that the Earth is round?

'They all laughed when Christopher Columbus said he thought the Earth was round.' Those lyrics from the Ira and George Gershwin song have a good deal to answer for. By the time of Columbus, we had known for around two thousand years that the Earth was round. The Greek mathematician Pythagoras postulated a spherical Earth in about 600 BC and another Greek, the astronomer Eratosthenes, may not have been far out in his calculation of the radius of the Earth around 240 BC – and from that time, no reputable Greek thinker ever suggested that the Earth was anything but round. A few eccentric early Christian theologians reverted to a Flat Earth theory, on the grounds that the Greeks were pagans and therefore must be wrong, but they were always very much in the minority.

The ancient Greeks themselves disagreed as to who was the first to confirm the shape of the Earth, and we lack sufficient knowledge of the astronomical techniques of the ancient Greeks to make any kind of informed speculation. According to Diogenes Laertius, writing in the third century BC, Pythagoras was the first to write of a spherical Earth; according to Theophrastus, it was the philosopher Parmenides in the fifth century BC; and according to Zeno, it was the poet Hesiod around the start of the seventh century BC. However, none of these writers inform us of the grounds on which they make their claims.

18. What is the story behind the thousands of huge jars at the Plain of Jars in Laos?

In north-central Laos, in the province of Xieng Khouang, thousands of huge prehistoric stone jars have been found at about ninety sites, with between one and four hundred jars at each site. Each jar is up to 3 metres (10 ft) in height and about 1 metre (3 ft) in diameter.

When the jars were first investigated in the 1930s, they were thought to be connected to burial practices, as they were similar to other jars found in Indo-China that had definitely been used for that purpose, but no human or animal remains were ever found in or near the Laotian jars. A local belief is that the jars were used for brewing alcohol, but there is no evidence to support that idea. The jars also seem to be designed to be fitted with lids, and although such lids have been found nearby, no jar has been discovered with the lid in place. Even the age of the jars is unknown, though they are thought to date from the Iron Age, some time between 500 BC and AD 500.

19. What was the cause of death of Alexander the Great?

Alexander III of Macedon was undoubtedly among the most successful military commanders of all time. By the age of thirty, after a ten-year series of campaigns against the Persians and others, he had created one of the largest empires in history. But before his thirty-third birthday, he was dead.

All we know of his death, which occurred in Babylon in June 323 BC, is that it followed an intense fever, and that two days before he died, his soldiers marched past him in tribute as he waved silently. Later Greek and Roman historians, rather like a good many modern journalists, were disinclined to let the facts get in the way of a good story, and came up with a number of different scenarios to account for his death.

Plutarch mentions a fever, which he says developed a fortnight earlier after Alexander had dinner with one of his admirals and then indulged in a drinking session with a friend. Diodorus says he died in agony after drinking a large bowl of wine in honour of Hercules. Others suggest that he was poisoned by Antipater, one of his own generals, who had recently been dismissed as viceroy of Macedonia. Antipater's son Iollas was Alexander's wine-pourer, so would have had both the motive and the opportunity.

A less dramatic explanation is that Alexander died from a combination of heavy drinking and a series of wounds sustained in battle, while one more recent suggestion is that he was poisoned by excessive amounts of the hellebore in the medication he took for his injuries. Death by natural causes from diseases such as typhoid, malaria and West Nile fever are also possible. The latest theory, proposed in 2010, is that Alexander's symptoms – which included not only fever, but also excruciating pains in his liver and his joints, and loss of the power of speech – were consistent with poisoning by calicheamicin, a highly toxic substance produced by certain soil bacteria. Calicheamicin is found in the River Mavronéri in the Peloponnese, a river that the ancient Greeks identified with the River Styx, the mythical entrance to the Underworld, whose waters were said to be deadly poisonous.

20. Were any of the crystal skulls in museums made in ancient times?

The release in 2008 of the film *Indiana Jones and the Crystal Skull* renewed public interest in such skulls, examples of which are on display in some of the world's most reputable museums. Said to have been produced by the long-lost Mesoamerican civilizations of the Aztecs or the Mayans, and believed by some to possess mystical properties, the skulls caught the imagination of the New Age movement in the 1960s – and this no doubt boosted the already flourishing trade in fake relics allegedly from pre-Columbian times, a trade that has gone on since at least the middle of the nineteenth century.

Attempts to date the crystal skull in the British Museum have been made at various times since 1950, and in 1996 a joint study of the BM skull and a similar one in the possession of the Smithsonian Institution in Washington, DC, revealed tool marks that must have been made by a jeweller's wheel – a tool unknown to the Aztecs or Mayans, and which only appeared much later in Europe. The BM consequently reclassified their skull, which they had acquired in 1897, as 'old' rather than 'ancient'.

Whether any of the skulls in other museums or in private hands are genuine antiquities remains an open question.

ANTARCTICA

21. Who was the first person to set foot on Antarctica?

The ancient Greeks named the Arctic after *arktos*, the Greek word for 'bear', referring to the Great Bear constellation, Ursa Major, which is seen in the northern sky. With admirable logic, they called the other end of the globe *Antarktike*, because it was opposite (*anti-*) the Arctic. In the eighteenth and early nineteenth centuries, hundreds of expeditions sailed south for the purpose of fishing or exploration, until the ice stopped them making further southward progress. It was only with the United States Exploring Expedition of 1838–42, led by Charles Wilkes, that the existence of land beneath the ice was confirmed and Antarctica was shown to be a true continent.

The first person to set foot on that land after Wilkes had confirmed its existence may have been a member of the crew on an expedition led by the French explorer and sea captain Jules-Sébastien-César Dumont d'Urville; this may have occurred on 20 January 1840. There is some evidence, however, that the American sealer John Davis may have set foot on the Antarctic Peninsula in 1821, but even he was not sure whether he landed on the continent itself or a nearby island, and the precise location of his landing was not properly recorded. There are similar doubts about the location of the 1840 landing by d'Urville's expedition.

22. What creatures live in Lake Vostok in Antarctica?

Around 4 kilometres (2.5 miles) below the surface of the Antarctic ice lies Lake Vostok, the largest of the subglacial lakes of the southern continent. It has lain hidden for at least 14 million years and possibly twice as long. Its existence was not even suspected until 1967, and not confirmed until 1993. Not even a water sample has been extracted from it, but a Russian team has been drilling through the ice and almost reached the lake when the weather forced them to give up in February 2011. When the coldest season is over, however, drilling will resume and we may soon learn the nature of the life-forms that have grown in this vast but isolated lake, which measures 250 by 50 kilometres (150 by 30 miles). The results will be of particular interest to scientists looking for life elsewhere in the Solar System, as the conditions in Lake Vostok are thought to be similar to those found on some of the moons of Jupiter and Saturn.

Quite apart from the possibility of the discovery of new life-forms in Lake Vostok, there is another huge unanswered question about the lake.

23. What is the cause of the huge imbalance in the Earth's magnetic field to the north of Lake Vostok in Antarctica?

Following the confirmation of the existence of Lake Vostok, a good deal of research on its size and nature was conducted by means of radar, either from the air or on the ground. These surveys revealed the unexpected existence of tidal currents and pockets of warm water, and these suggested both geothermal activity and more than one subterranean source for the waters of the lake. The most surprising discovery was made in 2003, when a large discrepancy was found in the Earth's magnetic field over a considerable area of the lake. The difference between the measured value and the expected value is much greater than can be explained by normal daily variations of the field, and the discovery was seized upon by conspiracy theorists to support a wide range of increasingly bizarre ideas.

Some said the disparity was evidence of a secret city beneath the Antarctic ice. Could it be, the conspiracy theorists speculated, the lost city of Atlantis (→ ANCIENT HISTORY 8), or a US or Russian nuclear facility, or a crashed spacecraft – or even 2 million descendants of Nazis who had fled there after the Second World War?

The most likely explanation, however, is that the disparity is evidence of a thinning of the Earth's crust beneath the waters of the lake caused by unexplained geological factors in the planet's distant past. The project of drilling down to the lake's surface has already taken more than fifteen years, and we may have to wait some time before finding out what is going on at the bottom of the lake, whether it is Atlantis, a Nazi colony, alien activity – or just an interesting piece of geology.

See also CARTOGRAPHY 71

See also PENGUINS 359

ANTHROPOLOGY

24. Is there any biological reality to the idea of different human races?

As our knowledge of genetics has grown, the concept of 'race' in human beings has become ever more difficult to define. Before we knew about evolution and genes, it seemed obvious that human beings belonged to various different races. You only had to look at them. As we learned about genes controlling different aspects of a person's appearance, however, the idea of 'race' became ever more difficult to sustain as a biological reality rather than a social construct or a pseudo-scientific attempt to justify xenophobic prejudice. From the genetic point of view, physical differences such as skin colour or hair texture are very superficial.

Recently, there have been attempts to justify a scientific concept of race based on the idea of breeding communities that remain essentially isolated from other such communities and therefore may develop their own genetic strains over a large number of generations. Opponents of that idea, however, suggest that interbreeding has always taken place, and any idea of 'pure' races evolving would have been scuppered by the historical movements of populations.

25. Why do Native Americans have grooves on the backs of their teeth?

For more than a century, American dentists have commented on a curious feature found in those of Native American descent: their front teeth have grooves on their backs. Such a characteristic has also been identified in Siberians, which has been taken to support the theory that the early inhabitants of North America arrived during the last Ice Age from Asia across a land bridge to Alaska (→ AMERICA 2). It is still very much an open question how and when this tooth-ridge evolved and what evolutionary advantage it could possibly have conferred .

26. Why are West Indian men three times as likely as white Englishmen to contract prostate cancer?

Many recent studies have confirmed that the incidence of prostate cancer and the associated mortality rate among Afro-Caribbeans is significantly higher than in other groups. Some recent research has extended its scope to show that African-Americans and men in West African nations historically associated with the transatlantic slave trade also have high rates of prostate cancer, suggesting that there is a genetic predisposition to it among these groups. Other research – in Guadeloupe, Martinique, Jamaica and elsewhere – has put the blame on diet or on pesticide use.

27. Did the Dogon people of Mali possess inexplicable astronomical knowledge?

From the 1930s until the 1950s, the French anthropologist Marcel Griaule studied the Dogon people of Mali and in 1946 reported that they apparently possessed extraordinary astronomical knowledge, mostly relating to the star Sirius. According to Griuale, they knew it was part of a binary star system whose companion took 50 years to complete an orbit. Sirius, however, is extraordinarily faint, and its companion star is a white dwarf which is completely invisible to the human eye, and whose existence has only been confirmed by mathematical calculations of the orbit of Sirius. The Dogons also apparently knew about the rings of Saturn and the moons of Jupiter.

More recently, doubt has been cast on the Dogons' astronomical knowledge, with another researcher suggesting that they are very vague about which star they are referring to. All the same, Griaule's accounts remain perplexing.

If they really did know about Sirius, there are two theories, one considerably more probable than the other. The first suggests that the Dogon learnt about it from alien visitors, presumably from Sirius. The more likely explanation is that they gleaned the information from a team of astronomers who visited Mali in 1893 to see a solar eclipse.

28. What happened to the Khazars?

We have already mentioned the unexplained disappearance of numerous civilizations at the end of the Bronze Age (→ ANCIENT HISTORY 13). A more recent mystery concerns the fate of the Khazars. The Khazars were an agglomeration of various nomadic peoples, who, between the sixth and eleventh centuries AD, coalesced to create one of the largest states in Eurasia, extending across the steppes of southern Russia from the Aral Sea in the east to the Black Sea in the west, and south across the Caucasus to the borders of what are now Turkey and Iran. Towards the end of this period, the might of the Khazar empire was sapped by battles with Svyatoslav of Kiev, then with the Mongol hordes, and their power faded away. Yet over the next two centuries, reports of Khazarian communities and individuals showed that the people had survived, if not their empire.

Many of these reports were from Jewish sources, which is not surprising, as Khazar royalty and most of its aristocracy had converted to Judaism in the eighth century. As a result, various writers (notably Arthur Koestler in his 1976 book *The Thirteenth Tribe*) have speculated that Jewish communities in both Russia and Poland may have descended from the Khazars. This theory has yet to be supported by genetic evidence (→ JUDAISM 253–4).

ARMADILLOS

29. Why do nine-banded armadillos suffer from leprosy?

It is often stated that the nine-banded armadillo is the only animal other than the human that can suffer from leprosy. That is not quite true, as mice and rhesus monkeys have also been infected with leprosy, but the armadillo is certainly the most useful experimental animal for leprosy research, as up to 5 per cent of wild armadillos are thought to suffer from the disease. They are thus not only a valuable source of the bacteria that cause the disease, but also useful subjects for testing possible drugs and vaccines. The question as to why humans and armadillos should have evolved to share a particular susceptibility to the disease may possibly be illuminated when the complete genome of the nine-banded armadillo is unravelled.

AUSTRALIA

30. When did human beings first reach Australia?

The history of *Homo sapiens* – modern humans – is generally believed to have begun in Africa around 200,000 years ago, before our species gradually spread across the rest of the world. We know that the ancestors of the modern Aborigines first reached Australia from Asia, but there is still a large discrepancy between various estimates as to when this happened. The earliest human remains in Australia are from a site at Lake Mungo, New South Wales, and have been dated to around 50,000 years ago. Caution has been expressed about this figure, however, as some say that the carbon-dating techniques used are unreliable beyond 40,000 years.

Rocks bearing Aboriginal art have been dated even earlier, to 60,000 years ago, but with equal caution, and claims of 70,000 years have been made for a discovery of Aboriginal tools. It has even been suggested that an increase in the extent of fires in Australia 120,000 years ago is evidence of human activity at that time.

An associated problem is the question of *how* the first Australians reached their destination. The usual explanation involves a land bridge from Asia to the prehistoric continent of Sahul, formed by what are now Australia and New Guinea. The existence of a land bridge, however, is difficult to reconcile with the lack of similarity between animal species in Australasia and Southeast Asia (the so-called Wallace Line, dividing the fauna of the two regions, cuts through the islands of the Indonesian archipelago). Furthermore, the date at which the land bridge disappeared may not tally with the time the first Australians arrived – so they may have arrived by sea.

31. What killed off the giant kangaroo in Australia?

The giant kangaroo, which was up to 3 metres (10 ft) tall and weighed around 200 kg (450 lb), became extinct around 45,000 years ago, which tallies quite well with theories regarding the date that humans first arrived on the continent (→ 30). A natural conclusion is that the animal was simply hunted to extinction. An alternative theory blames climate change, pointing out that many other large Australian species, including 2-tonne wombats and 5-metre (16 ft) land crocodiles, died out before humans are thought to have arrived on the scene. According to this theory, it was drought that killed off the giant kangaroo.

In 2009, however, an analysis of the teeth of giant kangaroos revealed traces of drought-resistant plants, which was taken by some to point the finger back at humanity, as the animal had evidently adapted to climate change.

32. Why does Australia have so many venomous animals?

It is said that seven of the world's ten most venomous snakes are to be found in Australia. Fortunately, the snakes tend to avoid people and there has not been a death from snakebite in Australia for many years. On the other hand, box jellyfish, stonefish, and both funnel web and redback spiders *do* continue to kill people. All of which raises the question as to why so many species have evolved a deadly weapon against humans in a continent in which the human population has always been very sparse.

In the seas around Australia, the fatal attractions include the long tentacles of the box jellyfish whose powerful venom may cause excruciating pain and even death from cardiac arrest. The blue-ring octopus is another of the world's most toxic sea creatures: although only the size of a golf ball, it delivers a venom that paralyses its victim, with no known antidote. Perhaps most painful of all, however, is the stonefish, which lurks at the bottom of reefs, disguised as a rock.

Back on land, apart from the snakes, Australia offers the funnel web and redback spiders, of which the latter are known to have developed an unpleasant habit of nesting under lavatory seats. Thanks to the development of anti-venoms, deaths from spider bites are now very rare, but that does not alter their level of toxicity.

Snakes in India or scorpions in Mexico may be responsible for far more human fatalities, but the wide variety of fauna with anti-human capabilities in Australia is remarkable.

BATS

33. What is it like to be a bat?

In 1974 the American philosopher Thomas Nagel wrote a paper with this question as its title, and his essay has since become one of the most widely cited papers in any discussion of consciousness. Nagel argues that mental activity cannot be explained in terms of a physical process without losing the subjective experience. There can never be an objective account of a conscious experience. Or, to put it another way, only a bat can know what it is like to be a bat.

BEES

34. Why have half the honeybee colonies in the USA and Europe collapsed since 2006?

In Europe, it is known as honey-bee-colony depopulation syndrome, while in America they call it colony collapse disorder. Whatever the name, the result is the same: previously thriving colonies of honeybees can suffer catastrophic collapse. Since 2006, Europe and the USA have lost around half of their honeybees, and nobody quite knows why. Mites, parasites, fungi, pesticides or viruses could be to blame; even GM crops have been accused, and recent research has identified a parasite and a fungus that appear to have been present in all collapsed colonies; but the precise cause is still unknown.

35. How do bumblebees manage to fly?

Until 1996, bumblebees posed a big problem to the science of aeronautics, The problem was raised at the University of Göttingen in Germany in the 1930s, when a calculation was made that showed that according to everything that was known at the time, there was no way a bumblebee's wings, flapping at the rate they do, could possibly produce enough lift to enable the bumblebee to fly. Its body weight was simply too high to be kept airborne.

In 1996 researchers in Cambridge seemed to have found the solution. By building a model of a flying insect and analysing the forces acting on it, they discovered a previously unknown source of lift, created by vortices of air trapped around the creature's body. For some years, this allowed bumblebees to buzz around in peace, in the knowledge that their flight was scientifically possible after all. In 2001, however, Michael Dickinson and James Birch of the University of California came up with a more detailed picture of air flow over an insect wing, and in so doing cast renewed doubt on the possibility of bumblebee flight. After creating a robotic fruit fly that was more sophisticated than the Cambridge bumblebee, they concluded that the vortices identified in the earlier work could not explain the mystery of bumblebee flight after all.

Ever more complex models of flying insects followed, but there is still a discrepancy between theory and practice, possibly due in part to a difficulty in accurately simulating the rotation of an insect's wings during flight. A recent study compared the actual ability of bumblebees to lift weights with theoretical predictions of how much they could carry. While the latest models stated that a bumblebee should be able to lift its own body plus an additional 53 per cent of its own weight, the experiments showed that the weight-lifting abilities of bees are 18 per cent better than predicted. So there are clearly some aspects of a bee's flying ability that we still do not properly understand.

36. Do bumblebees have personalities?

The question of whether animals have personalities has been intriguing a number of researchers in recent years, and a flurry of papers have reported that creatures such as spiders, squid, blue tits and social bees have all shown behaviour indicating that individuals possess something analogous to human personality. For the purpose of these experiments, 'personality' is equated with 'individual-specific consistency in their behaviour across time and context'. In other words, if an animal shows an identifiably different behaviour to another of its species in response to a similar situation, and that difference is maintained over time, then the animal has a personality.

In 2010, researchers at London University reported the results of experiments to monitor the reactions of bumblebees when they encountered flowers of a colour they had not previously seen. Using artificial flowers with sucrose solutions at their centres, the researchers measured the time bees spent foraging at each flower. As is generally the case with animals encountering something new, they spent longer investigating the strangely coloured flowers, either out of interest (neophilia) or suspicion (neophobia), but the overall results fell short of confirming that bumblebees have personalities. In that respect, the experiments started well by showing that individual bees showed differing behaviours towards the new plants, but those differences were not exhibited consistently over an extended period: 'We conclude that for the neophilia/neophobia paradigm used here, bumblebee foragers do not fulfil the criteria for animal personality in the common sense of the term. Instead their behavioural response to novelty appears to be plastic, varying on a day to day basis.'

More research is clearly needed.

37. What information do bees obtain from watching the waggle dance of others, and how do they obtain it?

Ever since Karl von Frisch began to decipher the dance language of honeybees – for which he received a Nobel prize in 1973 – work has continued to understand this means of communication. We now know that the choreography of a bee's 'waggle dance' contains information about the direction, distance and quality of a food source. The dance starts with a run forwards, during which the bee conveying the information waggles its posterior and buzzes, then it turns right, returns along a semicircular path to its starting place, runs forwards again, then turns left and again returns in a semicircle. This figure-of-eight manoeuvre is repeated many times.

The direction of the initial forward run indicates the angle between the Sun and the food source, while the speed of the dance indicates its distance. Thanks to recent research, we know that European bees can communicate with Asiatic bees of the same species, though the Asiatic bees tend to get distances wrong until they get used to their visitors. We also know that when deprived of sleep, bees can still communicate distance accurately, but their indications of direction become unreliable.

What we do not know is how this information (and how much of it) is picked up by the other bees that are present when the dance is being performed. Besides the choreography, the dancing bee also buzzes and emits chemicals, which may be smelt by other bees. Experiments with robotic bees seem to suggest that the dance is enough, but other experiments seem to confirm that sound and chemistry also play a part. Doubt has also been cast on how accurately the audience perceive the intentions of the dancer, or whether there is still a strong hit-and-miss element in their attempts to follow instructions.

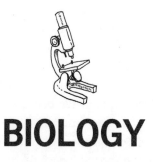

BIOLOGY

38. What is life?

Poets, theologians and scientists have all pondered this question at length, but none has come up with a totally convincing answer. From a scientific point of view, the question is how atoms and molecules of hydrogen, carbon, oxygen and other elements combine to form living plants, microbes, animals, human beings and everything else in the living world, which utilize energy and energy-giving items in their environment to grow and reproduce, and which after death turn back into inorganic material from which new generations may be formed. What is the literally vital (from the Latin *vita*, 'life') element that gives something life? Or, as the great Austrian physicist Erwin Schrödinger put it in his 1944 book *What is Life*, 'How can the events in space and time which take place within the spatial boundary of a living organism be accounted for by physics and chemistry?'

The subsidiary question, known as Schrödinger's paradox, is how life apparently manages to circumvent the second law of thermodynamics. According to that law, all closed systems – whether we are talking about the motion of the molecules of a gas in a test tube, or the collisions between balls on a snooker table, or the behaviour of the entire solar system – approach a state of maximum disorder. Without any external input, the energy within a system will tend to diffuse and disperse, causing all apparent order and organization to decrease. By contrast, life can only function if chemical elements form themselves into ordered structures that maintain their integrity. A living organism obtains energy from food or light and utilizes that energy to maintain a highly ordered state. Organisms are organized. Living organisms may decay and die just as inorganic materials corrode and crumble; the difference is that a living organism may leave behind the seeds from which a new generation will emerge. Once life appears, it seems to have a tendency to spread, bringing order rather than the increasing disorder predicted by the second law of thermodynamics. The only answer must be that life is not a closed system. The increase of order inside an organism must be more than balanced by an increase in disorder in the universe as a whole.

39. What causes ageing?

The search for an elixir of life that would negate or reverse the ageing process has occupied philosophers, alchemists and snake-oil salesmen for centuries, but there cannot be much hope of finding one until we know why organisms grow old and die. Since the 1980s, there has been a breakthrough in the understanding of the biology of ageing involving research into the function and operation of the strings at the ends of DNA molecules, called telomeres. With each reproduction of a cell, the telomere string has been found to grow shorter, thus acting as a sort of counter for the number of times the cell has reproduced. When the telomere has shortened to nothing, the cell stops reproducing and dies.

The optimists might say that all we need to achieve eternal youth is to find a way of resetting the telomere counter, or modifying the DNA in a manner that would stop the telomere-shortening process. An enzyme called telomerase is known to have such a function, and a good deal of research is being conducted to try to discover a method of turning that to youth-giving advantage. The question remains as to how telomeres evolved in the first place. One can only wonder whether, before telomeres appeared on the scene, all living organisms were immortal, unless some external event brought their lives to an end.

40. What causes a living cell to die?

Besides the telomere-related ageing process, cells die for two main reasons: necrosis (corresponding to illness or injury) or aptosis (an inevitable, biologically pre-programmed cell death). Aptosis, which has been described as a 'suicide mechanism', occurs as a response to signals that may come from outside (extracellular) or inside the cell itself (intracellular), and each of these types of signal may take many forms.

What links all the different reasons for cell death, and why cells need to undergo a constant process of reproduction and death anyway, are still unknown.

41. How do different cells know where to go during the development of an embryo?

A human body is made of around 100 trillion cells of about two hundred different types. All this begins with the fertilization of a single egg cell, which then divides and continues dividing, leading to the creation of innumerable cells. Our DNA may include the instructions for undifferentiated cells to turn into the right types in the right proportions to build the human body, but how do those cells, once formed, know where to go? What tells the cells designed to form the feet to head for one end of the building site, while the brain cells go to the other end?

Current research on this question concentrates on substances called morphogens, which influence both cell differentiation and cell position in the embryo. Some morphogens have been identified, but knowing *what* is responsible for giving cells their sense of direction is not the same as knowing *how* this information is put into operation.

42. How does the body regulate blood supply to its cells?

Cells need a blood supply in order to survive. The blood carries nutrients to the cells and carries away waste products, not directly but by filtering into the so-called interstitial space between blood capillaries and cells. The regulation of blood vessels is affected by a protein called VEGF (vascular endothelial growth factor), which comes in many different forms, some pro-angiogenic (encouraging the growth of blood cells) some anti-angiogenic (inhibiting it). If we could fully understand how VEGF works, that might supply us with a way of turning off the blood supply to cancerous tumours and starving them of the nutrients they need to survive.

43. Why do cancerous tumour cells migrate to different parts of the body?

Cancer results from a single cell that is genetically damaged and as a consequence undergoes a process of uncontrolled division and growth. Not only does it not know when to stop growing, but parts of the original cancerous growth, or primary tumour, may break off, travel through various routes to different parts of the body, and modify themselves into forms that can grow in the new environment as secondary tumours. If we knew the cause and mechanics of this modification process, we might be able to prevent secondary tumours from forming.

Beware of false knowledge; it is more dangerous than ignorance.

George Bernard Shaw (1856–1950)

44. Why can some creatures, such as salamanders, regrow lost limbs while others, such as humans, cannot?

Salamanders, flatworms and a number of other creatures can easily regrow lost body parts, including organs, muscle and nerves. Human regenerative capabilities, on the other hand, are much more limited: we can grow new skin and nerves, but an entire arm or leg is out of the question. Yet we know the body must possess the information needed to grow limbs, or it could not have done so during the embryonic stage.

Research on creatures that can regrow limbs, together with research on embryonic development, has identified the proteins responsible, as well as some of the genes that turn them on and off. One theory is that the key to regeneration lies in reproducing the conditions in the amniotic fluid during the development of an embryo. Indeed, some regeneration has been reported in mice with missing limbs that have been fitted with sleeves containing the right ingredients. Another theory holds that at an early stage of evolution, we all possessed the ability to regrow lost limbs, but while salamanders and worms have kept it, humans and other mammals have lost this ability, possibly through the development of a sophisticated immune system that prevents it from operating. The key to regeneration, if this is the case, would lie in unblocking the mechanism that stops this regenerative ability from functioning after the body is first formed.

45. Is there any hope that the people who have had their bodies – or just heads – cryogenically frozen may one day live again?

Cryonics is the procedure whereby a person's body (or just their head or brain) is frozen at death, the person concerned hoping that in the future they may be revived and cured. The number of people – mostly, if not all, Americans – who have undergone this procedure is estimated to be between 75 and 200. These figures include some who defrosted and had to be buried after the companies that froze them failed financially.

But is there any hope that such a procedure might work? Critics of cryonics, when it was first introduced in the early 1960s, very reasonably objected that the procedure involved the formation of ice crystals, which would cause irreparable damage to tissues, particularly in the brain. To prevent such injuries, the freezing technique was later improved by pumping the body full of cryoprotectants – chemicals such as the natural antifreeze found in various Arctic and Antarctic insects, fish, amphibians and reptiles.

On the general topic of resuscitation, there are two main schools of thought:

On the one hand, there is the argument that when you're dead you're dead, and nothing can change that. Since US law only permits the freezing of a body after death has occurred, that would rule out any chance of resuscitation.

On the other hand, sixty-one scientists signed an open letter in 2010 saying that in their view 'Cryonics is a legitimate science-based endeavour' and that 'there is a credible possibility that cryonics performed under the best conditions achievable today can preserve sufficient neurological information to permit eventual restoration of a person to full health'.

That 'credible possibility' could, of course, just mean that we know so little now about how the brain stores its information and memories that we don't know how much is irrevocably destroyed by death and the freezing process. If we do not know how something works or what has stopped it working, there is a credible possibility that we might one day find out and be able to mend it.

See also DNA 132–4, EVOLUTION 182–6

For lust of knowing what should not be known,
We take the golden road to Samarkand.

James Elroy Flecker (1884–1915)

BIRDS

46. Why do so many birds fly into windows?

According to Daniel Klem, who is probably the world's greatest authority on birds flying into windows, at least 225 species of birds have been seen flying into windows in the USA and Canada, and his estimate for the number of birds killed by flying into glass is somewhere between 100 million and 1 billion a year. Some say that birds fly into windows because they see the reflections of trees and grass in the glass; others say they are attacking their own reflection, which they see as another bird that needs to be chased from their territory. But however you (or the bird) looks at it, such birds clearly do not have the ability to perceive or understand reflections. In many ways, a bird's eye is a far more sophisticated and intricate organ than a human eye, yet we have no problem with glass or mirrors. A reflection-detection gene would have great survival value in the bird world, but as glass windows have only been in widespread use for a few hundred years, perhaps evolution has not had time to catch up. On the other hand, hedgehogs in the north of England have been observed scurrying across motorways instead of curling up in front of motor vehicles and being squashed, so life-saving evolutionary changes do sometimes happen relatively quickly.

We may, however, be on the verge of some interesting discoveries about the visual abilities of birds, thanks to research into our next unknown...

47. Do migrating birds use the Earth's magnetic field to navigate?

The question of how migrating birds find their way has long been a puzzle, but the idea that the Earth's magnetic field plays a part has been around for a long time. Only recently, however, has an explanation been offered as to how this might work. The key is the discovery of proteins called cryptochromes, which have been found to be sensitive to the extremely weak variations in the Earth's magnetic field. The theory is that if birds' eyes contained cryptochromes, they could 'see' the Earth's magnetic field and steer by it. As long as they do not fly into any windows on the way.

48. How much do chickens communicate with each other by clucking?

Researchers in Australia have claimed that chickens can convey at least twenty types of message in their clucking behaviour. Not only that, but their communication is sophisticated and involves high-level decision-making. Using an animated CGI rooster and monitoring hens' responses to its clucks and movements, Chris Evans and K-lynn Smith of Macquarie University, New South Wales, drew the conclusion in 2009 that chickens can effectively talk to each other. Not only do they have different clucks to warn other chickens of different types of predator, such as hawk or fox, but their clucking also gives information about the quality of food they have found. Most intriguing of all, it was found that roosters alter their food clucks according to who is listening. If there is a hen nearby, they squawk about the food as part of a courtship display, but if a larger male is in the vicinity who might steal the food, they keep quiet and rely on gestures to lure the hen to the dinner table. However, the limitations of what chickens can say, and the matter of whether it can be called language, are still open questions.

49. Why do birds interrupt each other's songs?

There are three main theories about why birds sometimes start singing before another bird has finished its own song. Some researchers have argued that it's an aggressive signal; some have said that it's a signal, but not necessarily aggressive; while others maintain that it just happens and doesn't mean anything at all. Whether a bird is interrupting another or merely joining in a duet may, of course, be difficult to determine. It is known, however, that zebra finches only sing duets with each other after they have become a couple.

See also DODOS 135, PENGUINS 359, SEX 417

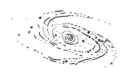

BLACK HOLES

50. What happens at the centre of a black hole?

In 1931 the Indian physicist Subrahmanyan Chandrasekhar calculated that when a high-mass star collapses, the gravitational pull of its mass can be enough to compact it into an ever smaller space until it has shrunk to nothing, but a nothing of huge mass. In other words, it has a radius of zero and infinite density. Furthermore, its gravitational pull will be so great that anything – even light itself – within a certain distance (later called the event horizon) will be sucked in and never escape.

The whole concept seemed so preposterous to some astronomers that they refused to accept it, but later observations confirmed Chandrasekhar's theory, and his infinitely tiny yet infinitely mighty masses were dubbed 'black holes' (despite long resistance by the French, as the term, when translated into their language, means something rude).

Black holes are now accepted as part of the cosmological landscape, but the infinite density at their centres continues to pose problems. According to Einstein's theory of general relativity ($\rightarrow$ EINSTEIN 165), at the centre of a black hole space-time curvature becomes infinite and the pull of gravity is infinitely strong. Mathematically, the centre of a black hole is a singularity where space and time break down – as do the laws of physics themselves.

51. Which came first: black holes or galaxies?

Black holes have an important role to play in our theory of the formation of the universe. As more black holes were discovered, it was noticed that many galaxies had one at their centre – raising the question of whether the black hole had played a role in the formation of the galaxy itself. The standard picture once accepted by most astrophysicists had the Big Bang creating vast amounts of gases and energy; the gases then coalesced into the solid matter from which stars were formed; the stars then arranged themselves in galaxies through gravitational pull; and black holes were formed by stars burning out and collapsing. But recently a new possibility has been raised: was it in fact the black holes that had provided the gravitational pull to attract the stars and keep them in their galactic formation?

In 2009 astronomers in California estimated the mass of black holes in galaxies 12 billion light years away. Comparing the mass of a black hole with the total mass of its galaxy revealed a significantly higher figure than had been obtained for closer galaxies. Since the measurements, because of the distance, relate to a situation that pertained 12 billion years ago, and black holes cannot diminish in size, the Californian team concluded that the other galaxies must have grown around the black holes at their centres. As Christopher

Carilli of the National Radio Astronomy Observatory put it: 'Black holes came first and somehow – we don't know how – grew the galaxy around them.' The study, however, only took in four galaxies, and other astronomers have suggested that they may not be typical and that no clear conclusions can be drawn.

52. Why is the Sun moving so fast?

We all know that the Moon orbits the Earth about once a month and that the Earth orbits the Sun once a year, but it is easy to forget that the Sun is itself orbiting the centre of the Milky Way galaxy, moving at a speed of about 220 km (135 miles) per second in an orbit that takes about 240 million years to complete. The problem is that according to everything we know about the Milky Way and the laws of planetary motion devised by the German mathematician Johannes Kepler (1571–1630), the speed of the Sun ought to be only 160 km (100 miles) per second.

The Sun is not the only star moving at a speed different from that predicted. Accounting for such discrepancies, both in the Milky Way and other galaxies, is one of the major problems in cosmology.

Observations from the Hubble telescope have suggested a strong relationship between the rotational speed of stars and the mass of the black hole at the centre of their galaxy, but the reasons for this are unknown. A disc of dark matter (→ COSMOLOGY 107) at the edge of the galaxy could explain it, but another possible explanation involves a change in the laws of physics for objects on a galactic scale.

53. How many black holes are there in the Milky Way?

Until the early years of the present century, the existence of a black hole at the centre of the Milky Way was a matter for speculation. But as the evidence of its gravitational influence grew, the presence of a super-massive black hole at the heart of the Milky Way became undeniable. In recent years it has been located in the constellation of Sagittarius, and its mass estimated at 2 or 3 million times that of our Sun.

In 2009 a team of Harvard astrophysicists researching the early universe suggested that there could be hundreds of black holes in the Milky Way, the result of collisions with other galaxies a long time in the past. The Harvard team said that as their theory was a new one, nobody had been looking for such objects – and without the usual shining star cluster around a black hole, their proposed black holes would be 'all but impossible to find'.

BOUDICCA

54. Where did Boudicca fight her last battle with the Romans?

There is an oft-repeated story dating back to the 1930s that Boudicca, the queen of the Iceni who rose up against the Roman conquerors of Britain, is buried underneath a platform at King's Cross Station in London (though different accounts give different platform numbers). Whether this story was originally a hoax or based on a misunderstanding of a place name is unknown. The site of King's Cross used to be the village of Battle Bridge, but the word 'battle' in that name is thought to be a corruption of 'broad ford' rather than referring to any specific battle.

Leicestershire, Warwickshire, Essex and Northamptonshire have been suggested as possible locations of Boudicca's final defeat by the Romans, in AD 60 or 61. But all these surmises appear to be based not on any hard evidence for a particular location, but rather on the assumption that her army would have retreated north from London by the Roman road known as Watling Street.

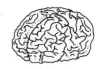

THE BRAIN

Let's admit it: we just don't know how brains work. Ever since thinkers started pondering the question, there has been a tendency to adopt the latest technological ideas to try to explain mental processes. The ancient Greeks saw the brain as an elaborately engineered plumbing system; much later, in the early twentieth century, it became an electrical circuit; and most recently the brain has been compared with a highly complex computer network. Every theory seemed to explain some aspects of brain function while ignoring others, yet ever since the seventeenth-century French philosopher René Descartes, and perhaps for even longer, one question has remained a matter of intense debate among philosophers and every type of neuroscientist:

55. How are the mind and the brain connected, if at all?

The brain, as we see it, is an organ for receiving and processing information. We can now look at individual neurons (nerve cells) in the brain and watch them working. Thanks to highly sophisticated brain-scanning methods, we can watch a brain as its owner thinks and see which parts are active. To some extent, we can therefore discern the mechanics of mental processes. But while we are thinking, we may know what we are thinking about; we have subjective experiences connected to those thoughts; we may even decide what we want to think about. This subjective side of our mental activity is called the mind (which is closely related to, though not identical with, the concept of consciousness). How we see the mind–brain relationship essentially comes down to two (or possibly three) choices:

(i) All events in the brain operate in accordance with the same laws of physics, so the brain completely determines all our behaviour, including subjective experiences. The mind, in other words, is just part of the brain.

(ii) The mind is a higher level process than the brain. It may both influence and be influenced by what goes on in the brain, but is a radically different type of process.

(iii) Subjectivity is just an illusion, so there's no mind–brain problem anyway.

This problem cannot be resolved until we know a great deal more about how the brain functions and what consciousness really is.

56. Will it ever be possible to read someone else's thoughts by examining their brain?

Shortly after the discovery in the early 1950s of the DNA double helix and the associated information-carrying messenger-RNA molecules, there was hope in some quarters that this would lead to an understanding of how the brain functions. In particular, some scientists thought that memories or new concepts or any other new piece of information corresponded with a newly formed RNA molecule in the soup of brain chemicals. If this was right, it should be possible, the theory went, to extract information from one animal's brain and inject it into another animal of the same species. Several experiments – with fish, worms, rats and other creatures – were performed to test the theory. Sadly, before any strong conclusions could be drawn, our understanding of the way RNA works made it clear that codifying memories could not be part of its function and the memory-transfer experiments stopped.

Quite how knowledge resides in the brain is still an open question. Individual neurons may be stimulated to produce specific mental responses, but it could be, depending on one's answer to the previous question, that what we think of as knowledge is just the mind's way of interpreting a neuron and the links called synaptic pathways that lead from one neuron to another.

Perhaps one day a complete map of the 100 billion or so neurons plus the trillions of synapses in an individual's brain will tell us everything we need to know about what they are thinking. But for the time being at least, we can't tell what someone is thinking by examining their brain activity. But if we cannot read what a brain is thinking by monitoring it with scientific equipment, we might ask whether it is possible through some sort of direct brain-to-brain exchange of information – which bring us to the next question:

57. Is telepathy possible?

Since the nineteenth century, a vast number of experiments have been conducted to test whether mind-reading is a reality. Rationalists point to the many hoaxes and frauds in this area, and to the fact that, even when an apparently well-designed experiment has given a result significantly supporting the telepathy hypothesis, such experiments have always proved impossible to repeat reliably. Parapsychologists, on the other hand, tend to assert that while no individual proof of telepathy has ever been demonstrated, the large number of published studies supporting it taken as a whole cannot be explained away as mere chance or, indeed, by any means other than accepting that some degree of telepathy has taken place. During the Cold War years, both the Soviet and US military intelligence organizations believed so much in the possibility of telepathy that they expended a great deal of energy in experiments in 'remote viewing' (not to mention trying to kill goats by staring at them), but the results were, to say the least, unconvincing.

58. Why have human brains been getting smaller for the past 20,000 years?

The first human beings of the genus *Homo* evolved over 2 million years ago. *Homo sapiens* has been around for some 200,000 years. Examination of skull sizes in the fossil record show that for nearly all of human history our skull sizes have been increasing. That appears to make sense. Bigger brains, at least in relation to body size, seem to indicate greater processing capacity and a higher level of intelligence. Yet in the past 20,000 years, comparisons of cranial capacity show that our brains have been getting smaller. This is difficult to explain, though several theories have been advanced, including the following:

(i) Our brains may have got smaller overall, but certain parts of the brain, such as the cerebellum (which controls motor movement coordination), have grown. The result is a smaller but more efficient brain.

(ii) Larger brains may not always be a sign of intelligence. Wolves have larger brains than dogs and are better at problem-solving, while dogs are better at carrying out learned tasks. Early humans may have had more problems to solve.

(iii) We are getting stupider.

Further research is clearly needed.

59. Why do people with more friends have larger amygdala?

The amygdala, two almond-shaped portions of the brain deep in the temporal lobes, is the part of the brain responsible for emotions. The size of the amygdala has been associated, both in humans and other primate species, with the size of an individual's social circle. Indeed, in a paper published at the end of 2010, it was reported that amygdala size correlates with the number of 'friends' people have on Facebook.

Whether increased social activity leads to growth of the amygdala or a large amygdala encourages social activity is unclear. There is also the question to what extent the number of a person's Facebook 'friends' tallies with their number of real friends, and also the question of how either of these numbers relates to the intensity of their social calendar.

60. How can a single brain cell hold the concept 'Brad Pitt and Jennifer Aniston', while remaining unresponsive to each of the individuals involved?

In 2005 Rodrigo Quian Quiroga of the California Institute of Technology in Pasadena published research that has raised all sorts of questions about how the brain works. Studying epileptic patients who had been implanted with devices to monitor brain-cell activity, he was able to detect individual neurons that became active in response to the patient seeing pictures of well-known people. In one patient, he identified a cell that only responded to pictures of Bill Clinton. Another had a Jennifer Aniston cell, and so on. Most remarkably, however, he found one case of a neuron that responded to pictures of Brad Pitt and Jennifer Aniston together, but remained inactive when the patient was looking at either Brad Pitt or Jennifer Aniston alone.

The idea of a 'grandmother cell' was coined in 1959 by the neurobiologist Jerome Lettvin to mock the suggestion that a single cell could be responsible for identifying an individual person. Nobody now believes that the elimination of one neuron could cause us to forget dear old Granny, but Quiroga's research clearly demonstrates hitherto unsuspected complexity in what information a single cell may hold. However, whether the Pitt + Aniston cell can be reprogrammed to become a Pitt + Jolie cell, as the leading man changes partners, is unknown.

61. Are sex and violence linked in human brains as they seem to be in mice?

According to a report published in 2011, experiments on mice have identified a small cluster of brain cells that come to life when the mouse is fighting, and also when it is having sex. When these cells are stimulated in a male mouse, it will attack any other male that comes near – even if the other male has been castrated or anaesthetized, which is normally enough to make another male mouse ignore it. The stimulated mouse will also attack females, but only if he is not already mating with them. On one occasion the male concerned even attacked a stuffed laboratory glove.

The results seemed to show that sex and violence are linked in the mouse's brain. 'I think there's every reason to think that this would be true in humans,' said David Anderson, one of the researchers responsible for the finding. As someone once asked, 'Are you a man or a mouse?' Perhaps, as far as sex and violence are concerned, it could be too close to call.

62. How do general anaesthetics work?

Well, they consist of a cocktail of drugs that put you to sleep, relax your muscles and prevent you from feeling anything – and you don't remember anything, unless something goes terribly wrong. We all know that, but quite how they do the job so well is still not completely understood. The general view is that general anaesthetics operate directly on the central nervous system to inhibit synaptic transmission, in other words, they interfere with the way neural impulses are transmitted between adjacent neurons. This results in a general loss of consciousness that affects sensory awareness in all forms and in all parts of the body. Yet the precise biochemistry behind the whole process has yet to be explained.

63. Are cell phones bad for us – or might they be good for brain function?

Ever since mobile phones became popular in the early 1990s, there have been concerns, and scare stories, about them being a health risk and even a possible cause of brain cancer. Research has failed to confirm these dangers, but in February 2011 a study was published claiming to show that spending 50 minutes with a cell phone at one's ear *does* change brain-cell activity.

Specifically, the researchers found that glucose metabolism, which is a general sign of brain activity, increases in the area of the brain closest to the phone's antenna. The significance of this, the researchers and other experts have said, has yet to be assessed. As we all know, spending fifty minutes sitting next to someone who has a cell phone at his ear can also be a stressful experience, but that is another matter.

See also CONSCIOUSNESS 101–5, LANGUAGE 255, MEMORY 288–95

BRUSSELS

64. What is the origin of the small boy depicted in the Mannekin Pis statue in Brussels?

One of the most popular tourist attractions in Belgium is the statue in Brussels known as *Mannekin Pis* ('little man pee'), depicting a naked little boy urinating into a fountain. The sculpture was designed by Jerome Duquesnoy and dates back to 1618 or 1619, though it replaced an earlier similar statue that may have dated back to the fourteenth century. Yet the reason for the little boy's quaint pose, in either the original or its replacement, is buried beneath piles of myth.

One story is that the statue celebrates an incident in which the little boy put out a fire by peeing on it, thus saving a king's castle from burning down. A similar tale has the little boy urinating on the fuse of explosives left at the city walls by an invading force.

Another version says the statue is of the infant Duke Godfrey III of Leuven, who is said to have urinated on enemy troops from a position high in a tree where he had been lifted in a basket to keep him safe from the battle.

Or you may prefer the tale of a rich merchant whose son went missing and who vowed to commission a statue of the boy exactly as he was found.

BUTTERFLIES

65. How do monarch butterflies know where to go on their long migrations?

The monarch butterfly is an extraordinary creature. Each year, beginning in August, vast numbers of them begin a migratory flight from Canada and the north of the USA to Mexico. The journey, which takes two to three months, covers between about 3,000 and 5,000 km (2,000–3,000 miles). It is possible that none of the butterflies that embark on the journey reach the destination: monarchs are prolific and fast breeders, and the butterflies that arrive in Mexico in the autumn may be three or more generations separated from those that began the migration at the end of summer.

As many as 300 million monarchs may eventually spend the winter in Mexico, of which around half will have died before the flight back in spring. Then once again the two- or three-month flight may involve three or more generations, before the monarchs reach their summer home. Unanswered questions remain: when they emerge from their chrysalises, how do the young butterflies know where they are on the migration route, and what cues do they pick up from their environment to show them the way ahead?

66. If you teach a caterpillar something, will the butterfly it turns into retain that knowledge?

Earthworms have been taught to turn one way or the other in a T-shaped enclosure. Just place food at one end or the other of the top bar of the T and the creature will learn. It is reasonable to assume that caterpillars would be similarly easy to teach. But what, if any, of this training would be carried over when the caterpillar metamorphoses into a butterfly? Does a left-turning caterpillar turn into a leftwards-flying butterfly?

As the main task of the caterpillar brain must be to keep its body working satisfactorily, it must be radically different from the butterfly brain, which has a totally different set of bodily priorities. But even though the caterpillar's brain turns to soup as it metamorphoses into a butterfly, it would be interesting to know if anything in the caterpillar's mental life is carried through to its role as a butterfly. No research seems to have been done in this intriguing field.

The sum part of ignorance that we arrange and classify we give the name knowledge.

Ambrose Bierce (1842–1913)

CANNIBALISM

67. Was cannibalism ever a normal human practice?

In William Arens's 1979 book *The Man-Eating Myth: Anthropology and Anthropophagy*, the author argues that throughout the ages people have spread tales of anthropophagy (i.e. cannibalism) in order to discredit their enemies and establish their own cultural superiority. He concluded that cannibalism was never a widespread practice, and that accounts of it are generally steeped in racism and are over-dependent on hearsay evidence. In the opposite corner are Daniel Diehl and Mark P. Donnelly, who in their 2006 work, *Eat Thy Neighbour: A History of Cannibalism*, insist that the practice was widespread in ancient times.

68. Did our Stone Age ancestors eat their own dead?

Almost all cultures include horror stories of flesh-eating ogres in their myths, but convincing evidence of widespread cannibalism among ancient peoples is very rare. In the 1990s a team of French and American archaeologists began investigating a 100,000-year-old Neanderthal site in a cave at Moula-Guercy close to the River Rhône in southern France. In 1999 they reported that they had found human bones from which the flesh had been removed in the same way that the Neanderthals butchered animal meat. This appeared to suggest cannibalism, but the archaeologists could not say whether this was part of a ritual, or an act of desperation at a time of famine, or whether it was standard practice among the Neanderthals of the time.

In 2009 a much larger collection of butchered human bones was found in the village of Herxheim in southwestern Germany. This appeared to present much clearer evidence of everyday cannibalism – and among modern humans, for these remains date from the early Neolithic period, between 7,000 and 7,500 years ago. Researchers concluded that over a period of a few decades, people at this site ate hundreds of their fellow humans.

Some archaeologists suggest that the evidence points not to cannibalism, but to a ritual practice in which bodies that had previously been buried were disinterred, dismembered and the flesh removed, before being reburied. To the sceptics, scratch marks on bones do not necessarily mean that our ancestors were cannibals.

69. Were the Anasazi people of the American Southwest cannibals?

In 2001 in New Orleans the Society of American Archaeology held a symposium under the title 'Multidisciplinary Approaches to Social Violence in the Prehispanic American Southwest'. Under the cloak of that academic title lay one simple question: Did the Anasazi, who were the ancestors of the Pueblo Indians of the southwestern USA, routinely eat each other, roasted or boiled, in the period between AD 900 and 1200?

There are two sides to the debate, dubbed 'the bleeding hearts' and 'the rip-their-hearts-out' factions by the Colorado archaeologist Steven Lekson. The pro-cannibalism faction cited the usual evidence – cut marks, abrasions and marks that human bones and cooking pots could have left on each other. The anti-cannibalism faction proposed various alternative theories, suggesting that the bodies may have been prepared by reburial, or may have been preyed upon by wild animals, or might even have been the corpses of executed witches. The matter may only ever be resolved if archaeologists discover either a recipe book from the period or a well-preserved body with human flesh in its stomach.

CARTOGRAPHY

70. How did Martin Waldseemüller know about the Pacific Ocean for his 1507 map of the world?

In 1507 the German cartographer Martin Waldseemüller (→ AMERICA 3) published his *Universalis cosmographia secundum Ptholomaei traditionem et Americi Vespucii aliorumque lustrationes* ('The universal cosmography according to the tradition of Ptolemy and the voyages of Amerigo Vespucci and others'), a map that charted the New World discoveries begun by Christopher Columbus. His map depicted not only the east coast of the Americas, as explored by the early navigators, but for the first time showed the hitherto unmapped ocean later to be known as the Pacific. Yet the Spanish explorers Ponce de León and Vasco Núñez de Balboa did not set eyes on the Pacific Ocean until 1512 or 1513, at least five years after Waldseemüller's map. There had, of course, been speculation that America was a new continent and not, as Columbus had thought, the other side of Asia, but some of the distances measured on the map are uncannily accurate. Either Waldseemüller knew something that we do not know he knew, or he made a very lucky guess.

71. How did the Piri Reis map of 1513 give such an accurate picture of Antarctica?

Discovered in an old library in Turkey in 1929, this map drawn on gazelle skin was the work of Piri Reis, a famous Ottoman admiral, geographer and cartographer of the sixteenth century. Piri Reis – more properly Haci Muhiddin Piri oglu Haci Mehmed

– acknowledged his debt to various extant maps – some even then a thousand years old – in the collection of the Imperial Library of Constantinople, to which his rank gave him access. Remarkably, the Piri Reis map shows not only the western coast of Africa and the eastern coast of South America, but also the northern coast of Antarctica – in perfect detail. Even more extraordinarily, he shows the coastline of the land beneath the ice, though geological evidence shows that the latest this could have been charted in an ice-free state is 4000 BC, if not even earlier. So who made the map from which Piri Reis obtained his information – and where and when can it have been made?

It's because someone knows *something* about it that we can't talk about physics. It's the things that nobody knows about that we can discuss. We can talk about the weather; we can talk about social problems; we can talk about psychology; we can talk about international finance… so it's the subject that nobody knows anything about that we can all talk about!

Richard Feynman (1918–88)

CATS

72. Why are female cats right-pawed and tom cats left-pawed?

In 2009, scientists at Queen's University, Belfast published the results of a study on paw preference in cats. When cats are playing with a fishing-rod toy, the scientists found that they were equally likely to use either left or right paw, but when posed with the more complex task of getting food from a glass jar, male cats were found to show a strong preference for using their left paw, while females used their right.

In humans, left-handedness has been associated with the hormone testosterone (which has been used to explain why more men than women are left-handed). Exposure to testosterone has also been shown to result in a female cat changing her paw preference from right to left. Scientists do not yet know why the hormone has this effect, or whether it is testosterone that is responsible for the initial handedness.

See also HANDEDNESS 222–4

73. What colour was Christopher Smart's cat Jeoffry?

While incarcerated in London's St Luke's Hospital for Lunatics between 1757 and 1763 with only his cat for company, the poet Christopher Smart wrote a poem of over 1,200 lines called *Jubilate Agno* ('Rejoice in the Lamb'), of which 74 lines are devoted to his pet. Beginning with the words 'For I will consider my Cat Jeoffry', he extols the cat's personal and religious virtues at great length.

After Smart was released from St Luke's, he quickly ran into debt and died in a debtors' prison. What became of the cat is not known, and he never told us what colour it was. More than one recent publication of the full poem, however, include illustrations depicting Jeoffry as a marmalade cat. This has no doubt been prompted by Smart's line 'For he is of the tribe of Tiger', although this might equally suggest a tabby. Smart may simply be comparing his small feline with the fearsome big cat of the forests of southern Asia, or even using 'tribe of Tiger' simply to mean the cat family – rather than telling us Jeoffry had black and orange stripes.

CHEMICAL ELEMENTS

74. Can untriseptium, aka the theoretical element 137, aka feynmanium, ever exist?

When in 1869 Dmitri Mendeleyev presented to the Russian Chemical Society his periodic table of the chemical elements, he showed how they could be listed by their atomic number (which turned out to be equal to the number of protons in their nucleus) and in groups that shared similar, recurring properties. His table had certain gaps, which he believed would be filled by the discovery in the future of hitherto unknown elements, whose properties he successfully predicted. Some ninety elements occur naturally; those of greater mass are highly unstable and radioactive, and can only be created for very short periods in the laboratory. In recent years elements have been synthesized with atomic numbers up to 118.

The great US physicist Richard Feynman, who died in 1988, once pointed out that according to a simple interpretation of theories proposed by Niels Bohr and Paul Dirac, no element with an atomic number greater than 137 can exist, because the mathematics would then give a speed for its electrons greater than that of light, which is impossible. For that reason element 137, or untriseptium, is also known as feynmanium. Attempts to synthesize it, however, have so far failed.

> I can live with doubt, and uncertainty, and not knowing. I think it's much more interesting to live not knowing than to have answers which might be wrong.

Richard Feynman (1918–88)

75. Does californium exist naturally on earth?

As mentioned above, when in 1869 Dmitri Mendeleyev presented his periodic table of the chemical elements, he posited the existence of hitherto unknown elements and predicted what properties such elements would have. In many cases, these unknown elements tallied with unexplained lines in the solar spectrum ($\rightarrow$ THE SUN 455), which gave some hints to researchers as to how they might synthesize such elements. As scientists began to understand the concept of radioactive decay – by which one atom could change into another – they developed methods of encouraging the formation of the missing items in Mendeleyev's table. One such item was the new element discovered at the University of California in 1950, and shortly afterwards named in honour both of that university and of the State of California.

Californium has atomic number 98, and has been found to have a number of applications, from the treatment of cancer to the start-up processes of nuclear reactors. Around twenty isotopes of californium have been discovered, all highly radioactive, but with

56

half-lives (the average time they take to decay) varying from a few minutes to 898 years.

Since californium has been detected in the spectrum of the Sun, and it is known to be formed by the effect of nuclear radiation on other atoms, it may well have been present on Earth in the early days of the planet, but taking less than a thousand years to decay, it could not have survived since then. The question of whether any californium is still being produced naturally on Earth is still unanswered. It has been found in the radioactive dust after nuclear explosions, and it is thought that minute amounts may be produced by nuclear reactions in uranium ores. Such traces of californium as have been found so far, however, have all been near facilities that use synthetic californium for medical or prospecting purposes, so presumably were man-made.

76. How far can the periodic table extend beyond the 118 known elements?

Although the Dirac and Bohr equations suggest that no element with an atomic number greater than 137 can exist (→ 74), they do not take relativity into account. Some calculations have suggested that the elements end at atomic number 139, while others suggest they may theoretically extend up to 173. Of the 118 known elements, of which the latest, rather unimaginatively named ununoctium, or one-one-eight, was identified in 2002 and synthesized in 2006, only numbers 1 to 94 are known to occur naturally on earth. Of those, only about eighty are considered stable, while the others decay radioactively over timescales varying from minutes to billions of years. Even some of the elements generally considered stable are thought to decay eventually, though the process may take considerably longer than the universe has been in existence.

The trouble with the heavier elements is that the repulsion forces between the protons tend to overwhelm the strong nuclear force binding the atom together. For this reason, the atom, often created under extreme conditions of temperature or pressure, only exists for the tiniest fraction of a second. We do not know what possible limits there may be to determine whether it can exist at all.

CHIMPANZEES

77. Why do ambidextrous chimpanzees eat fewer termites?

A good deal of recent research has shown that many chimpanzees in the wild as well as in captivity show a preference for using one hand over the other. This has raised some curious anomalies. On the admittedly simplistic principle of two hands being better than one, one might expect ambidextrous chimps to be the most successful, and that indeed seems to be the case in some trials, yet when it comes to fishing out termites with a twig and eating them, ambidextrous chimps have been found to end up with smaller meals than their right-handed or left-handed colleagues.

One suggestion is that ambidextrous chimps end up with two hands that both perform normal tasks adequately, while the others have one hand that is rather weak or clumsy and the other that is very good, and which is therefore better suited to specialist tasks such as fishing for termites with a twig. Before we can claim to understand the problems of the ambidextrous chimp, a good deal more research is needed comparing the performances in a wide variety of tasks of ambidextrous and non-ambidextrous chimps.

78. Why don't chimpanzees ask questions?

The argument over whether non-human primates can develop language skills has raged for almost half a century, since researchers started to teach chimpanzees sign language. The most celebrated chimps in that respect were Washoe (1965–2007) and Nim Chimpsky (1973–2000), the latter being punningly named after the US philosopher Noam Chomsky, who wrote extensively on language. Each developed a vocabulary of over a hundred signs, which it was claimed they manipulated in ways that indicated genuine linguistic ability.

Some observers, however, maintained that all the chimps were doing was exhibiting conditioned responses and selecting the appropriate signs they had learned. These sceptics were not convinced this constituted evidence of thought being put into words.

While Washoe, Nim Chimpsky and other chimpanzees did seem able to understand variations in word order and to manipulate signs in a way that could be taken to indicate a form of communication, one curious linguistic ability has remained absent in our primate cousins: they do not seem to be able to ask questions. Why they have this particular linguistic block has not been explained.

See also DISEASE 126, DOGS 136

This gray spirit yearning in desire to follow knowledge like a sinking star beyond the utmost bound of human thought.

Alfred, Lord Tennyson (1809–92)

CHRISTIANITY

79. Was there ever a real Holy Grail?

The Holy Grail is a sacred but elusive object that figures in Christian and literary tradition. It is said to be the cup or bowl used by Jesus at the Last Supper, and is believed to have miraculous powers. In the Middle Ages the Holy Grail played an important part in the Arthurian cycle of legends, first being mentioned in a poem by Chrétien de Troyes entitled *Perceval, le Conte du Graal* (*Perceval, the Story of the Grail*), written between 1180 and 1191. Shortly afterwards, Robert de Boron gave the Grail added significance and mystery in his poem *Joseph d'Arimathe*, in which Joseph of Arimathea (who in the Gospels gives up his tomb for the burial of Jesus) is given the Grail by an apparition of Christ himself, and then uses it to collect drips of Christ's blood when he is taken down from the Cross.

As more than a millennium divides the Crucifixion and the first reference to the Grail, it looks very much like a myth, but several churches hold artefacts held to possess certain Grail-like characteristics. The most significant of these is the Holy Chalice in Valencia Cathedral, Spain, a vessel that has been the official papal chalice of many popes and which was used by Pope Benedict XVI during a mass held in the cathedral in 2006. It was given to the cathedral by King Alfonso V of Aragon in 1436, but was supposedly brought to Spain by St Lawrence in the third century. Some archaeologists have dated the chalice to the first century AD, and many Christian historians say that, of all the various artefacts claimed to be the Holy Grail, this particular vessel is most likely to be the genuine article.

80. How did the image of a man become imprinted on the Turin Shroud?

The Shroud of Turin is a much-revered piece of ancient linen cloth kept in Turin Cathedral, Italy. On the Shroud can be seen the image of a man, traditionally said to be an impression of the body of Christ after he had been taken down from the Cross. The Shroud has posed its mysteries for so long that there is even a word for its scientific study: sindonology (from the ancient Greek word *sindon*, meaning a burial cloth). Yet even the most diligent sindonologists would admit that certain aspects of this holy relic are baffling.

The Shroud has been well documented since the fourteenth century, though whether it dates from that period or truly is the cloth in which Christ's body was wrapped after the Crucifixion is still a matter of dispute. After intense debate, small samples of the cloth were made available for carbon-dating in 1988 and the results suggested, with a 95 per cent degree of certainty, that it dated from between 1260 and 1390. Subsequently, however, both the testing methods and the nature of the sample tested have been questioned. There is some evidence that the fabric sample may not have been typical of the original cloth as a whole but the result of later repair or tampering.

Whatever the date of the cloth, the origins of the image on it are a complete mystery. Signs of injury to the body imprinted on it are consistent with what is known of crucifixion methods at the time of Christ – but this knowledge would not have been available in the fourteenth century. The image also becomes clearer when viewed as a photographic negative, yet it dates from long before photography. Finally, no attempt to reproduce such an image on cloth has ever succeeded.

81. Was the patron saint of Ireland a Scot or a Welshman?

St Patrick is the patron saint of Ireland, but the only reliable details of his life consist of two letters known to have been written by him, and they are rather short on facts. He gives his place of birth as Banna Venta Berniae in Britain, which some maintain is in southwest Scotland, just over the border from Carlisle, and others have placed in Wales. He was kidnapped by pirates and taken to Ireland at the age of sixteen, but subsequently escaped and returned home, before going back to Ireland to spread the word of Christ. He died in AD 493 on 17 March, according to the old Irish annals, but even that is not entirely certain, as until recently it was generally believed that St Patrick had died in 420.

There are similar gaps in our knowledge of the identities of many popular saints, including St George and St Valentine.

82. Did the early Christians have a hand in writing the Dead Sea Scrolls?

In the winter of 1946–7, a Bedouin shepherd made an astonishing discovery when he accidentally fell into a cave near the ruins of Khirbet Qumran on the northwest shore of the Dead Sea. As he clambered out, he brought with him a handful of ancient scrolls. Over the next few years, many more scrolls were recovered from this and a number of other nearby caves. They were found to date from between 150 BC and AD 70, and contained 972 texts from, and commentaries on, the Jewish Bible, written in Hebrew, Aramaic and Greek. By far the oldest original Biblical texts, the Dead Sea Scrolls immediately attained a religious and mystical significance that added to the debate over their origins, translations and relevance.

The most natural conclusion concerning their origins was that they were sacred texts of the Essenes, a devout Jewish sect of the period who Pliny had said lived on the west side of the Dead Sea. Since 1990, however, alternative theories of the scrolls' origins have been proposed. Further archaeological evidence from Qumran, together with analysis of the content of the scrolls, has suggested to some that they may have been written not by the Essenes, but by another Jewish sect in Qumran; or they may have been compiled in Jerusalem, then later taken to the Qumran caves for safe-keeping. Other scholars have taken a fragment of St Mark's Gospel in the scrolls as evidence that some of the texts may have been written by early Christians.

83. Who wrote the New Testament Gospels?

Nobody is sure when the Gospels of Matthew, Mark, Luke and John were written, or by whom, but most agree that the Gospel of Mark was the first to be written, around AD 65; Mathew and Luke followed shortly after, perhaps between AD 65 and 70; while John is thought to be the last, dating from around AD 100. These conclusions are largely derived from analysis of the texts, with both Matthew and Luke quoting extensively from Mark, while John recounts different events in a different style. But who were Matthew, Mark, Luke and John?

The author of Matthew is traditionally identified with the tax collector mentioned in Matthew 9:9 (also known as Levi), but if that is the case, and he was so strongly connected with Jesus, why does he rely so heavily on the writings of Mark?

Mark himself was not an apostle but an associate of the apostle Paul for a short time, though some authorities insist that his Gospel is more closely based on the preaching of Peter.

The Gospel of Luke is thought to have been written by the same person as the Book of Acts, for one follows the other in a natural way, and both are addressed to a Roman named Theophilus. Apart from that, all we seem to know about Mark is that he was a doctor.

The authorship of St John's Gospel is the most mysterious of all, and the text never even mention's John's name. The reference to 'the disciple that Jesus loved' in John 13:23 is generally taken to refer to the author of the Gospel, but that doesn't help us identify him. It is generally accepted, however, that he wasn't the same John who wrote the Book of Revelation. *That* John had his visions of the Apocalypse on the Greek island of Patmos, and is known as St John the Divine.

See also JESUS CHRIST 249–51

CLEOPATRA

84. What did Cleopatra look like?

The Greek historian Plutarch, in describing the great Egyptian queen who lured both Julius Caesar and Mark Antony into her bed, wrote that 'her beauty… was in itself not altogether incomparable, nor such as to strike those who saw her; but her conversation had an irresistible charm'. The Roman historian Cassius Dio, on the other hand, says: 'She was a woman of surpassing beauty.'

On a more specific point, the seventeenth-century French philosopher and mathematician Blaise Pascal, in his *Pensées*, wrote: 'Cleopatra's nose, had it been shorter, the whole face of the world would have been changed.' We should remember, however, that at the time, large noses were seen as a symbol of strength. Sadly we are unable to check this, as most of the statues of Cleopatra have had their noses knocked off. In any case, portrayals of Cleopatra in statues and on coins are highly inconsistent. According to a study at Nottingham University in 2007, based on her face on a coin, Cleopatra was a pointy-nosed, thin-lipped woman with a jutting jaw.

85. Did Cleopatra really die of a snake bite, or was she poisoned?

According to the Greek historian and philosopher Strabo, who lived at the same time as Cleopatra, Cleopatra took her own life either by applying a poisonous ointment or by allowing herself to be bitten by an asp, a small, venomous snake. Later Roman writers chose the asp version, some even upping it to two asps. They all agreed that she was bitten on the arm, but Shakespeare added a bit of drama by having her clasp the asp to her breast.

Other historians, however, have suggested that this is all romantic nonsense and that her Roman vanquisher Octavius (later the Emperor Augustus) had her killed. The latest diagnosis, offered by the German historian Christoph Schaefer in 2010, concludes that a snake could not have caused the slow and pain-free death reported, and that the fatal cocktail she took most likely consisted of a mixture of hemlock, wolfsbane and opium.

> Woe unto you, lawyers! For ye have taken away the key of knowledge.
>
> The Gospel of Luke 11:52

86. Where are Cleopatra and Mark Antony buried?

The final resting places of both Cleopatra and her lover Mark Antony are unknown. According to Plutarch, Octavius allowed them to be buried together, but there are no known accounts of where the burial took place. Various sites around Alexandria have offered hope to archaeologists that the tomb may be found, but excavations have so far failed to reveal the secret.

CLIMATE

87. How much of the current climate change is due to greenhouse gases?

In the 1970s, following a number of very cold winters, there was a flurry of panic suggesting the approach of a new ice age and blaming it on greenhouse gases. When these gases accumulate in our atmosphere, they have two effects. One is a warming effect, in which they act like a duvet and stop the Earth's radiated heat from escaping into the atmosphere. The other is a cooling effect, in which the gases act as a barrier to the Sun's rays. At the time, because it had been so cold, it was assumed that the cooling effect was greater than the warming.

Now, thanks to proper scientific investigation, we know that the warming effect is greater, which is why there is so much current activity dedicated towards cutting greenhouse-gas emissions in order to combat global warming. Yet even if we accept that warming is taking place, the precise contribution of greenhouse gases is difficult to assess. We are, after all, still coming out of the Little Ice Age that brought extremely cold spells of weather at various periods between about 1550 and 1850. Quite how much of the current climate change is just a continuation of the post-Little-Ice-Age warming-up process, and how much is due to greenhouse gases is unclear.

88. How much of the current climate change is due to human activity?

One of the vogue words of the moment is 'anthropogenic', meaning 'It's all our fault'. Yet even if we just consider the warming caused by increased greenhouse-gas levels, it is difficult to assess the human contribution with any confidence of accuracy. Burning fossil fuels certainly contributes to increasing CO_2 levels, but carbon dioxide is far from being the only, or even the worst, of the greenhouse gases. Other leading offenders include water vapour, which has its origins in a number of natural processes, and methane (→ PLANTS 385), which may have the strongest effect on climate of any greenhouse gas.

Human farming practices certainly contribute to the production of methane, via the burping of cows and sheep. But we should not forget the world's 250 trillion termites, whose remorseless chomping also makes a significant contribution.

COFFEE

89. Who invented the coffee grinder?

The coffee plant is native to Ethiopia, but the first evidence of coffee beans being turned into a beverage comes from fifteenth-century Yemen. The fashion for this black, bitter drink spread across the Middle East and the Mediterranean, reaching Europe in the late sixteenth century. Although hand-operated spice mills had been in use since the 1400s, coffee beans continued to be ground using the more basic technology of mortar and pestle, or by millstones. Even as late as 1620, when the Pilgrim Fathers sailed for America on the *Mayflower*, all they brought with them for grinding coffee was an adapted mortar-and-pestle device.

In the 1660s a certain Nicholas Book, 'living at the Sign of the Frying Pan in St Tulies Street' in London, publicized himself as the only man known to make mills that could grind coffee to powder, but he was not necessarily the inventor of the machine he manufactured. The first US patent for a coffee grinder was issued in 1798 to Thomas Bruff of Maryland, who, when he was not grinding coffee, was Thomas Jefferson's dentist.

90. Does drinking coffee make us more alert?

The presence of caffeine in coffee has given the beverage an enduring reputation as a stimulant. However, research published in 2010 suggests that we may all have been mistaken. In the experiment the subjects, who included both coffee-drinkers and non-coffee-drinkers, were all asked to avoid caffeine for 16 hours. They were then given either a caffeine capsule or a placebo, and later a slightly higher dose or another placebo. Subjects then took a personality test to measure their emotional state and alertness.

The results showed that caffeine did not improve the alertness of either group, though some of the non-coffee-drinkers reported headaches and showed increased anxiety. Heavy coffee drinkers who had been given placebos, however, showed a lower level of alertness and also reported headaches.

The results seemed to show not that coffee makes us more alert, but that a lack of coffee makes coffee-drinkers less alert. A coffee-drinker's morning cup only serves to counteract the caffeine withdrawal symptoms that have built up overnight. The effects of caffeine seem to be more complex than had been thought.

91. Why does caffeine destroy the regularity of spiders' webs?

In the early 1950s the Swiss pharmacologist Peter Witt began a fascinating series of experiments on the changes in the pattern of spiders' webs when the creatures spinning them were under the influence of drugs. Different drugs produced different deformities in web pattern, and Witt developed the theory so well that he could identify which drug the spider had taken from a few simple measurements of the resulting web.

By the 1990s the idea had been taken up by others, including NASA, and various experiments showed that in general the more toxic a drug was, the greater the distortion produced in the web pattern. To the surprise of researchers, however, the most devastating effect on web pattern was produced by caffeine. The web produced by the caffeine-fed spider lost all regularity and looked like just a haphazard collection of strands.

The psychiatric literature contains many accounts of caffeine-induced psychosis in people with particular sensitivity to its effects. It may be that a similar effect serves to wreck spiders' webs.

See also SPIDERS 446

First come I; my name is Jowett.
There's no knowledge but I know it.
I am Master of the college:
What I don't know isn't knowledge.

Henry Charles Beeching (1859–1919).
('Jowett' was Benjamin Jowett, influential Master of Balliol College, Oxford, and a translator of Plato.)

COMPOSERS

92. At what speed did J.S. Bach intend his compositions to be played?

Until the German inventor Johann Nepomuk Maelzel patented the metronome in 1815, composers could only give vague guidance on the speed at which their compositions should be performed. However, the early metronomes, although useful in ensuring regularity of tempo, were not that accurate in delivering a specified number of beats per minute. Whether such regularity is a boon or an unwanted intrusion on a performer's interpretative freedom has always been a matter of debate. The nineteenth-century German composer Johannes Brahms, for example, was quoted as saying: 'I am of the opinion that metronome marks go for nothing. As far as I know, all composers have, as I, retracted their metronome marks in later years.'

Before the advent of the metronome, composers used Italian terms such as *allegro* ('lively'), *lento* ('slow') and *andante* (literally 'going, moving', i.e. at a walking pace) to convey their intentions, while Handel frequently used the term *tempo ordinario*, suggestive of some sort of 'standard' speed. Bach never used that phrase, but some have suggested that the time signatures of his compositions, such as 3/4 or 3/8, were intended to give information on the basic tempo. Others believe that Bach was perfectly happy for performers to choose their own tempi, and his use of the usual Italian terms was an indication only of the relative speeds of one section compared with another. The American 'Bach tempo scientist' Cory Hall, for example, has concluded that *allegro* should be twice as fast as *lento*, and that *moderato* should be exactly midway between them.

To appreciate the freedom some performers feel in interpreting Bach's tempi, one has only to compare Glenn Gould's 1955 recording of the Goldberg Variations with his 1981 version: the opening aria in the later recording is played at half the speed of the earlier version. Who can tell which Bach would have preferred? Maybe he would have loved them both – or maybe he would have been quite horrified.

93. Who wrote the libretto for Haydn's *Creation*?

In 1795, near the end of Joseph Haydn's second visit to London, the violinist and impresario Johann Peter Salomon gave him the libretto in English of an oratorio on the subject of the Creation. Haydn, whose English was not good, had it translated into German by Baron Gottfried van Swieten, from which it seems to have been translated back into English. The original version, a lengthy poem entitled *The Creation of the World* based on texts from Milton's *Paradise Lost* and the Bible, is now lost, and Haydn later said that he could not remember the name of the author.

The music was written to be performed either in English or in German, and when the work was first published, both versions were given. The English version, however, came in for a great deal of criticism. For example, the poet Anna Seward (the so-called Swan of Lichfield), wrote in 1802: 'It is little wonder that the words translated from the German almost literally into English, should be neither sense nor grammar, nor that they should make wicked work with Milton.' Here is an example of the English libretto Seward so abhorred:

Now vanish before the holy beams
the gloomy dismal shades of dark;

the first of days appears.
Disorder yields to order the fair place.
Affrighted fled hell's spirits black in throngs;
down they sink in the deep of abyss
To endless night.

It is now impossible to tell whether the stilted language and grammar are the fault of the unknown English author of *The Creation of the World*, or whether they should be blamed on whoever it was who translated Swieten's German back into English.

94. Why did Schubert leave his Eighth Symphony unfinished?

Franz Schubert died in 1828 at the tragically early age of thirty-one, so it is hardly a surprise that he left much work incomplete, but his great Unfinished Symphony is still a puzzle. (What is surprising and hugely impressive is that, like Mozart, he wrote so much in such a short life.) Schubert began work on his Symphony No. 8 in B Minor in 1822 and wrote two movements, both fully scored for orchestra, together with the piano score of a third movement, a scherzo, of which the first two pages only were completed for orchestra – and that is all. At the time it would have been conventional for a symphony to have four movements, but there is no evidence that Schubert even started work on a finale, despite the fact that he lived for another six years, during which he completed a great deal of work, including the whole of his Ninth Symphony.

To add to the mystery, Schubert gave the incomplete score to his friend Anselm Hüttenbrenner in 1823, who did not reveal its existence until thirty-seven years after Schubert had died. Why Hüttenbrenner waited so long – and why certain pages appear to have been torn from the manuscript after the beginning of the scherzo – have given rise to a certain amount of speculation. The completed movements received their first performance in Vienna in 1865, with the last movement of the composer's Third Symphony tagged on as a finale.

Various theories have been put forward as to why Schubert failed to complete the work: he intended to complete it later; he did complete it, but the original score went missing; or he simply ran out of inspiration. A number of attempts have been made in modern times to complete the symphony, some inspired by the competition the Columbia Gramophone Company held in 1928 to mark the centenary of Schubert's death.

95. Did Schubert die of syphilis?

The official cause of Franz Schubert's early death was typhoid fever, yet there has long been a theory that the true cause was syphilis. The composer is thought to have contracted the disease from a prostitute in 1822 (though the sex of the prostitute has always been a matter for speculation), but he was supposedly cured in 1824. When Schubert's body was disinterred in 1863 (and again in 1888), to 'secure the mortal remains against further decay', it is said to have shown little sign of tertiary syphilis. However, the symptoms shown by the composer shortly before his death are consistent with mercury poisoning, and at the time mercury was often given as a treatment for syphilis.

96. Who was the woman Beethoven addressed as 'My Immortal Beloved'?

When Ludwig van Beethoven died in 1827, some letters were found among his effects, scrawled in pencil and clearly never delivered. Dated 6 July and 7 July, and believed to have been written in 1812 (though the year is not specified on the letters), they are addressed to 'My angel, my all, my very self' and 'My Immortal Beloved', and consist of an outpouring of passion.

'Oh, where I am, you are with me – I will see to it that you and I, that I can live with you.' he writes. 'No other woman can ever possess my heart – never – never... Oh God, why must one be separated from her who is so dear?' He ends, 'Oh, do continue to love me – never misjudge your lover's most faithful heart.' Nobody knows who was the intended recipient of all this passion, or why Beethoven never sent the letter. However, the wording of the letter suggests a relationship of long standing, and the 'Immortal Beloved' has been identified with a number of different women.

The favourite candidate is Josephine Brunsvik, with whom the composer had been passionately involved over a long period and to whom he had written more than a dozen other love letters. But several others also enter the frame. There was Josephine's cousin Giulietta Guicciardi, with whom Beethoven had also fallen in love and to whom he had given free piano lessons, and to whom he had also dedicated the 'Moonlight' Sonata; there was Josephine's sister Thérèse von Brunsvik; there was the Countess Marie Erdödy; there was his doctor's daughter, Therese Malfatti; there was the young singer Amalie Sebald. And there were others. For such a faithful lover, Beethoven certainly had plenty of immortal beloveds to choose from.

97. Beethoven's 'Für Elise' is one of the most popular pieces of piano music of all, but who was Elise?

The delightfully simple piano piece called 'Für Elise' ('for Elise') was composed by Beethoven around 1810, so what could be more natural than for the forty-year-old composer to have written it for the beautiful eighteen-year-old woman he had just fallen in love with and later proposed to?

The only problem with that theory is that her name wasn't Elise, but Therese. Nevertheless, Therese Malfatti, the daughter of Beethoven's doctor, has until recently been the prime suspect as the dedicatee of 'Für Elise' – and has also been suggested as Beethoven's

'Immortal Beloved' (→ 96). There is even a story that Beethoven got so drunk the night he intended to perform the piece and then ask for Therese's hand in marriage that the dedication 'Für Therese' that he scrawled on the manuscript he gave her was so illegible that it was later misread as 'Für Elise' – and the name stuck. One nineteenth-century German musicologist claimed to have seen the manuscript among the possessions Therese left at her death, but this manuscript has never been sighted again.

Recently, however, a real Elise has entered the reckoning. Elisabeth Röckel, a singer and pianist, was close to both Beethoven and his friend and colleague, the brilliant Austrian pianist and composer Johann Nepomuk Hummel. She married Hummel, but Beethoven's affection was apparently undiminished. And in 2009 the Berlin musicologist Klaus Martin Kopitz announced that his researches revealed that she was known to her circle of friends as Elise.

Others, however, have pointed out that Elise was a very common name at the time, and that Beethoven was constantly falling in love with young women.

98. Did Tchaikovsky really die of cholera?

Perhaps no other composer's death has elicited such controversy as that of Pyotr Ilyich Tchaikovsky, on 6 November 1893. The official diagnosis was cholera, but even that has given rise to conflicting theories:

(i) His death was an accident, caused by inadvertently drinking a glass of unboiled tap-water during a cholera epidemic in 1893.

(ii) He drank the tap-water deliberately in suicidal despair at his homosexuality.

(iii) The tap-water was just a convenient excuse: he actually contracted cholera from a male prostitute.

(iv) He was obliged to drink the tap-water by a 'court of honour' of his fellow alumni of the St Petersburg Imperial School of Jurisprudence, as punishment for his homosexuality.

Some have rejected the cholera theory entirely, noting that the normal quarantine regulations were not followed after his death and his body was not sealed in a zinc coffin. Instead, the composer died of arsenic poisoning, either administered by himself or by one of his doctors on the orders of Tsar Alexander III after Tchaikovsky had seduced one of his sons.

At least some of the mystery might be cleared up if Tchaikovsky's body were to be exhumed and tested for arsenic, but this is unlikely to happen. As the authoritative *New Grove Dictionary of Music and Musicians* (2001) comments, 'We do not know how Tchaikovsky died. We may never find out... '

99. What was the enigma behind Elgar's *Enigma Variations*?

There are two main theories about the enigma behind Edward Elgar's *Enigma Variations*, described by the composer as 'variations on an original theme for orchestra', and first performed in 1899. The first holds that the enigma in question is the identity of a person, while the second maintains that it is a musical theme that is implied, but never heard.

If it is a person, attention has concentrated on the thirteenth variation, which is identified only by three asterisks – in contrast to the others, which are all given sets of initials that readily identify a number of Elgar's friends and the composer himself. The main candidates put forward for Variation 13 are both ladies whose identities Elgar might have thought it delicate not to reveal. One is Helen Weaver, to whom Elgar had been engaged for eighteen months in 1883–4 before she emigrated to New Zealand; the other is Lady Mary Lygon, who sailed for Australia at about the time Elgar was writing the *Enigma Variations*. In either case, his inclusion of quotations from Felix Mendelssohn's concert overture *Calm Sea and Prosperous Voyage* in the variation might seem appropriate.

Elgar himself hinted at the other theory, stating that in addition to the theme that starts the work, on which the fourteen variations are based, 'through and over the whole set another and larger theme "goes" but is not played'. 'Auld Lang Syne', Mozart's 'Jupiter' Symphony, Bach's *Art of Fugue*, 'Rule Britannia' and 'Twinkle, Twinkle Little Star', among many others, have all been authoritatively claimed as the missing theme.

The most imaginative suggestion, however, is that the enigma is the mathematical value of π which, to three decimal places, is equal to 3.142. The evidence proposed in support of this is that the first four notes of the entire piece are notes 3, 1, 4 and 2 in the G minor scale, the key of the opening andante. In addition, Elgar marked off the first six bars of the piece with a double bar line, which supporters of the π theory claim is a deliberate ruse to draw attention to the fact that those six bars contain twenty-four black notes (all crotchets and quavers, with no 'white' minims), supposedly representing the 'four-and-twenty blackbirds baked in a pie'. He also referred to a 'dark saying' at the heart of the enigma, and what can be darker than black-note blackbirds baked in a π?

There is much pleasure to be gained from useless knowledge.

Bertrand Russell (1872–1970)

100. Would the world have come to an end if Scriabin had not cut himself shaving?

Alexander Scriabin – composer of such works as the orgasmic *Poem of Ecstasy* and inventor of the so-called 'Mystic Chord' – died on 27 April 1915 from septicaemia (blood poisoning), which developed after he cut a boil on his lip while shaving. At the time, the monomaniacal Russian – who once expressed the desire to 'possess the world as I possess a woman' – was working on a composition called *Mysterium*, a vast synaesthetic extravaganza involving the senses of sight and smell as well as hearing. Regarding this grandiose project, Scriabin proclaimed:

> *There will not be a single spectator. All will be participants.*
> *The work requires special people, special artists and a completely*
> *new culture. The cast of performers includes an orchestra, a*
> *large mixed choir, an instrument with visual effects, dancers,*
> *a procession, incense, and rhythmic textural articulation. The*
> *cathedral in which it will take place will not be of one single type*
> *of stone but will continually change with the atmosphere and*
> *motion of the Mysterium. This will be done with the aid of mists*
> *and lights, which will modify the architectural contours.*

It was to be performed in the foothills of the Himalayas in India, would last seven days and would, Scriabin believed, be followed by the end of the world and the replacement of humans by 'nobler beings'.

He was probably wrong, but we cannot be absolutely sure that we were not all saved by a shaving cut.

See also MURDER 322, MUSIC 327–8, 330

CONSCIOUSNESS

101. What is the difference between 'mind' and 'consciousness'?

The terms 'mind' and 'consciousness' have been used by philosophers, psychologists, neurologists and others for so long that distinctions between them have become hopelessly blurred. Some writers use the words almost interchangeably, some try to define them as totally distinct, others allow varying degrees of overlap. The general consensus, though, is that 'consciousness' is the state of mind that recognizes one's own existence, while 'mind' is the set of mental processes that the brain uses to process information and sensory input. Whether consciousness is entirely included in mind, however, is unclear. The American neuroscientist Antonio Damasio, in his book *Self Comes to Mind* (2010), describes consciousness as 'mind with a twist… since we cannot be conscious without having a mind to be conscious of'. Others, however, have suggested that one can lose one's mind without losing consciousness.

Until we know much more about how the brain works, it seems doubtful whether we can even define the terms sufficiently precisely to talk of the difference between mind and consciousness.

See also BRAIN 55

102. Are animals conscious?

Some would argue that language is necessary before a creature can be considered conscious. That argument seems to boil down to saying consciousness demands talking to yourself – and you can't talk to yourself without language. So if you don't believe that animals have language, they can't be conscious.

More generally, consciousness is sometimes viewed as a specifically human attribute that emerged at a particular point in our evolution and may even be taken as a characteristic of humanity itself.

A growing viewpoint sees consciousness not as an attribute that you either have or you don't, but as a factor that may be possessed in varying degrees by any creature that possesses feelings and emotions. The neuroscientist Antonio Damasio characterizes the two ends of the scale of consciousness as 'core consciousness', which is the basic sense of the here and now, and 'autobiographical consciousness', which brings in not only the present, but also a full sense of identity involving the past and the hoped-for or expected future.

Pet-lovers, of course, will say that all the above is nonsense and that Fido has feelings, and displays loyalty and love and intelligence, and that he has a mind of his own, and of course he's conscious or he wouldn't now be asking to be taken for a walk.

103. Can robots become self-aware?

The debate over artificial consciousness is similar to the arguments surrounding artificial intelligence: there is a weak version and a strong version. The weak hypothesis is that machines or robots could be programmed to behave in a manner that simulates conscious behaviour indistinguishable from that of humans. Just as computers are now being programmed to pass the 'Turing Test' of being able to respond to questions in a way that fools people into thinking they are human, there is good reason to suppose that with improving technology, computers will one day be able to pass some kind of 'Turing Consciousness Test'. But if all they are doing is carrying out programmed instructions, that, in the opinion of many, cannot count as consciousness.

The strong hypothesis is that as advances are made in data analysis, processing speeds, computational methods and decision-making techniques, true consciousness will inevitably emerge.

The debate is strongly connected to the question of whether mind and consciousness (→ 101) are a direct consequence of physical and chemical processes in the brain (→ BRAIN 55).

104. For how long does a severed head stay conscious?

Immediately after Charlotte Corday (→ FRENCH HISTORY 190) had been guillotined for the murder of the French Revolutionary leader Jean-Paul Marat in 1793, the executioner, a man named Legros, picked up her head and slapped it on the cheek. According to witnesses, an expression of 'unequivocal indignation' came over her face, which also reddened at the insult. Legros was imprisoned for three months for this breach of guillotine etiquette, but whether Mademoiselle Corday was aware of what was happening is still a matter of dispute.

Hers is one of several cases of guillotine victims supposedly showing signs of consciousness after their heads had been severed. In one instance, a gruesome experiment was carried out in which a dog's blood was pumped into the victim's severed head some time after execution, supposedly inducing twitching and movements of the lips. That and most other such cases can be explained as muscle spasms, which are purely mechanical movements rather than evidence of consciousness.

Medical evidence suggests that after sudden cardiac arrest, unconsciousness occurs within five to fifteen seconds, but brain death takes between four and six minutes. That would have allowed Corday and other guillotine victims a few seconds to have been aware of what had happened to them, but not for the face to redden in annoyance, as the blood supply would have been cut off. Some maintain, however, that the trauma of decapitation induces immediate unconsciousness. France continued to use the guillotine as a method of execution until 1977, since when controlled experimentation on this topic has proved tricky.

105. Can any part of our consciousness survive death?

For the past decade, Dr Sam Parnia of Southampton University has been studying so-called 'Near Death Experiences' (NDEs), in which patients who have suffered cardiac arrest have, after resuscitation, told of lucid visions, during which they have frequently reported information that they supposedly could not have obtained from their locations on hospital beds. In 2008 he launched the AWARE (AWAreness during REsuscitation) study, in which images were projected above hospital beds that could not be seen from the position of the patient. Accounts of NDEs from the patients are to be correlated with details of the images to look for evidence that consciousness has, in some way, left the body and explored its surroundings.

Writing in 2008, the scientist and parapsychology researcher Dr Sue Blackmore stated: 'If human consciousness can really leave the body and operate without a brain then everything we know in neuroscience has to be questioned.' She welcomed Dr Parnia's research as a scientific attempt to investigate matters usually left to philosophers and theologians.

COSMOLOGY

The development of our understanding of the way the universe works is perhaps the greatest intellectual achievement of humanity. Thanks to our understanding of the laws of physics, we can obtain precise information about stars and galaxies so far distant that even the light from them takes billions of years to reach us. Newton's laws of motion, modified by Einstein's theory of relativity, enable us to work out their mass, and analysis of the spectrum of the light we receive from them gives us information about their chemical composition.

Considering the fact that the human brain necessarily evolved with the prime purpose of improving our chances of survival in competition with other creatures on the plains of Africa, it is remarkable how flexible its thinking power has become. Even though we may have detected the galaxy now known as Abell 1835 IR1916, which is 13.2 billion light years away, there is, however, still a great deal we do not know, between here (→ EARTH 141–50) and the furthest reaches of the universe.

106. Where have all the neutrinos gone?

Ever since the British physicist J.J. Thomson discovered the electron in 1897, it has become increasingly difficult to keep pace with the proliferation of fundamental particles. In the good old days of ignorance, atoms were supposedly indivisible – indeed, the word itself comes from an ancient Greek word meaning 'that which cannot be divided'. The discovery of the electron was followed by the realization that most of the mass of the atom was in a tiny central nucleus, around which the electrons oribited. The nucleus turned out to be made up of protons (discovered in 1919) and neutrons (discovered in 1932). Yet as if splitting the atom into protons, neutrons and electrons was not enough, electrons proved to be just one of a number of different particles called leptons, while we now know that protons and neutrons are themselves made up of smaller particles, called quarks. Another class of particle, called gauge bosons, also play a role in the atom. But more of that later, for the question of neutrinos is what is bothering us at the moment.

Neutrinos are very like electrons, but without any electric charge. They whizz along at close to the speed of light, and hardly interact with anything. Every second, trillions of neutrinos pass through us and we do not even notice. Their existence was first postulated in 1930 as a means of accounting for the apparent loss of energy and momentum when an atomic nucleus decays. But it was not until 1956 that a neutrino was finally detected experimentally.

Finding a balance between theory and experiment, however, has proved even more elusive. The number of neutrinos produced by atomic reactions in the Sun ought to be predictable from measurements of the energy received, yet the number of neutrinos detected falls well short of the prediction. That disparity could be accounted for if there are different types of neutrino, some with mass and some not. But how many types are there? Measurements of energy from the Sun and other cosmic forces give us one answer, direct detection of neutrinos suggests another, while the so-called 'Standard Model' of particle physics gives a third. It has been suggested that the elusive 'dark matter' that seems to hold the universe together (→ COSMOLOGY 107) may consist of neutrinos, but until we have reconciled the question of the number of neutrino types, we remain in the dark about their role in dark matter – which brings us to the next question…

107. What is dark matter, and where does it come from?

In his hugely influential work *The Structure of Scientific Revolutions* (1962), the American physicist and philosopher Thomas Kuhn drew a distinction between science's usual plodding pace of advance, involving incremental additions to the body of knowledge, and the occasional revolutionary 'paradigm shift' that necessitates tearing down and replacing the established theories with something radically different. Copernicus's ideas about the Solar System, Newton's laws of gravity and motion, Einstein's theory of relativity and the entire field of quantum mechanics are examples of such paradigm shifts. Kuhn suggested these upheavals are precipitated as much by social, cultural and historical factors as they are by purely scientific ones.

Some moments in scientific history, however, seem particularly ripe for a paradigm shift, when the old theories are finding it more and more difficult to explain new observations, and the entire structure of current assumptions is beginning to creak at the joints. Astronomy and cosmology are now going through such a phase, though the roots of this revolution go back more than seventy-five years.

In 1934 the Swiss astronomer Fritz Zwicky discovered something inexplicable about the orbital speed of clusters of galaxies. The motion of such clusters must be determined by gravity, but there simply was not enough known mass in the clusters to account for the gravitational attraction that clearly existed. In fact, the amount of observable matter in one cluster was out by a factor of more than one hundred. To get around this anomaly, Zwicky came up with the radical idea of 'dark matter', which could not be seen and did not interact with electromagnetic radiation but had mass and therefore exerted a gravitational pull. This dark matter inhabited what had previously been thought of as empty space – which is therefore not empty at all.

Zwicky's idea was difficult to test as his dark matter was, almost by definition, undetectable. So the theory remained in the background until the 1990s, when more and more observations appeared to challenge the existing theory and demand the existence of dark matter. Not only was dark matter necessary to explain the rotation of galaxies as we currently see them, it was also needed to explain how the galaxies formed in the first place. As our picture grew of what must have happened in the first instant after the Big Bang when matter itself began to be formed, it became increasingly clear that the entire universe would not have held together without the existence of dark matter. Indeed, it seemed that dark matter must account for around 80 per cent of the matter in the universe, if not more.

In December 2009 researchers involved in the Cryogenic Dark Matter Search at Stanford University announced that they might have detected direct evidence of dark matter (though they admitted there was a 23 per cent chance it was something else). But what dark matter is and where it came from still remain a mystery – though perhaps not quite such a mystery as the next question...

108. What is dark energy and where does it come from?

In 1998 our view of the universe began to get even weirder when measurements from distant galaxies led to the conclusion that they were moving away from us faster than had previously been suspected. The conclusion was inescapable: not only is the universe expanding, but its rate of expansion is increasing. This was similar to the problem that had caused Einstein to introduce his 'cosmological constant' almost a century ago ($\rightarrow$ EINSTEIN 164) – although his intention in so doing was to keep the universe in a steady state. Einstein's gravitational theory became tidier when it became accepted that the universe was not in a steady state, but rather expanding, making the cosmological constant unnecessary. But nothing had predicted an accelerating rate of expansion.

Einstein's theories, however, once again came to the rescue. Just as his famous $E = mc^2$ had shown an equivalence between matter and energy, it was reasoned that there must be a similar equivalence between dark matter and dark energy. The expansion rate of the universe could then be accounted for by the pull of dark energy. Quite where all this dark energy comes from is just as much of a mystery as dark matter, but the latest estimate is that the entire mass-energy of the universe consists of 72.8 per cent dark energy, 22.7 per cent dark matter and only 4.6 per cent what we think of as ordinary matter – which is therefore not ordinary at all, but rather rare, consisting of less than one-twentieth of the entire universe.

109. What is the true value of the Hubble constant?

In the 1920s the American astronomer Edwin Hubble came up with a simple law giving the relationship between the velocity V at which distant galaxies are moving away from us and their distance D from the Earth:

$$V = H_o D$$

The term H_o is known as the Hubble constant, and the rate at which the universe is expanding depends on its value. The age of the universe also depends on the Hubble constant, as Hubble's equation also allows us to run the expansion backwards to determine when everything in the universe was in the same place and the Big Bang (which was also Hubble's idea) happened.

The velocity of galaxies may be determined from the red shift in the light we receive from them, but we can be less sure in our measurements of their distance, which accounts for the fact that different values have been given for H_o. The recent discovery of an accelerating rate of expansion of the universe also suggests that the Hubble constant may not be constant after all, and astronomers have taken to calling it the 'Hubble parameter' instead.

Current measurements of H_o suggest that the universe is between 13.64 and 13.86 billion years old, but that could change as our theories of variations of H_o over time are modified.

110. Are there galaxies so far away, and moving away from us so fast, that we can never know they exist?

Putting Hubble's law and Einstein's special relativity together tells us that not only are some galaxies moving away from us at close to the speed of light, but that space itself is expanding, making their apparent speed of recession greater than that of light. Pursuing this idea leads to the concept of an 'observable universe' about 46 billion light years across. This raises the question of whether there could be galaxies ever further away, moving away from us faster than light itself, from which the light has not had time to reach us since the Big Bang itself – and never will have enough time to do so.

111. Has the speed of light always been the same?

Much of Einstein's theory of general relativity relies on the speed of light in a vacuum being a fundamental constant, unchanged by place or over time. That theory is consistent with many measurements and observations over a long period, but it has been suggested that some of the anomalies outlined above could be accounted for by variations in the speed of light over the life of the Universe. No experimental evidence has yet been found to support that idea, but some scientists are considering it to be a possibility...

112. Is the speed of light now the same everywhere?

...and even if the speed of light has always been the same in our corner of the universe, a variance in its value in distant galaxies could also account for discrepancies between theory and measurement.

113. What was the so-called 'WOW!' signal detected on 15 August 1977 by scientists searching for extraterrestrial intelligence?

On 15 August 1977 Dr Jerry R. Ehman, working on the Search for Extra-Terrestrial Intelligence (SETI) project at Ohio State University, picked up a radio signal that was quite unlike anything expected from outer space. Thirty times louder than normal background sounds, it lasted for 72 seconds. Seeing the computer printout giving details of the signal, Ehman just circled the anomalous details – which bore all the hallmarks of an artificially generated signal – and wrote the word 'WOW!' by them. The signal was never repeated, or anything similar picked up.

Some have seen this one signal as evidence of intelligent life elsewhere in the universe. Others have suggested it was simply a signal originating on Earth that had been reflected back by a piece of space debris. But the WOW! signal has never been explained.

114. What is the cause of gamma ray bursts, a phenomenon that could be devastating for our planet?

From billions of light years away, flashes of gamma rays, probably associated with massive explosions in distant galaxies, have reached Earth, lasting anything between a few milliseconds and several minutes. A burst is followed by an afterglow, and is estimated to release as much energy as the Sun will give out in its entire lifetime. Because of their huge power, gamma ray bursts (GRBs) are thought to be associated with such cataclysmic galactic events as supernovae, which occur when a high-mass star collapses to form a neutron star or a black hole.

All GRBs so far detected have originated outside our own galaxy, the Milky Way – which may be fortunate as it has been suggested that any GRB in our galaxy and beamed in our direction would release enough electromagnetic energy to extinguish all life on Earth. No GRB has yet been connected to a specific supernova event that might have caused it, and no one has yet explained the mechanism by which GRBs are generated.

See also BLACK HOLES 50–3, EINSTEIN 164, THE MOON 311–12, PHILOSOPHY 367, PLANETS 374–81, THE SOLAR SYSTEM 436–9, THE SUN 454–5, THE UNIVERSE 458–66

Science is the belief in the ignorance of experts.

Richard Feynman (1918–88)

DINOSAURS

The problem with dinosaurs is that they lived a very long time ago – between 250 million and 65 million years ago – and the vast majority of our knowledge of them is based on fossilized bones and skeletons, which are all that have survived the ravages of time.

115. Were the dinosaurs cold-blooded, like all today's reptiles?

Until the 1970s the view that dinosaurs, like other reptiles, were cold-blooded was almost unquestioned. Cold-bloodedness (something of a misnomer) means that an animal has a variable body temperature, which it has to control by external means (such as basking in the sun to warm up). In contrast, warm-blooded animals, such as birds and mammals, maintain a constant body temperature using internal thermoregulation mechanisms.

Since the 1970s, some palaeontologists have pointed to a number of factors that suggest dinosaurs may have been warm-blooded after all. Unlike modern reptiles, which either crawl or walk with their limbs extended out to the side, one of the main groups of dinosaurs walked with their limbs directly beneath their bodies, like birds and mammals. Dinosaurs also had large ribcages that could have held mammal-like hearts and lungs, and their bones had channels for rapid blood circulation similar to those found in the bones of warm-blooded animals. Supporters of cold-blooded dinosaurs, however, argue that in the largest dinosaurs a warm-blooded metabolism would be likely to cause internal overheating and immediate death.

A recent study, however, has suggested that the bigger a dinosaur was, the warmer its blood, suggesting that the question may have no single answer.

116. Why were some dinosaurs so large?

Dinosaurs were, on average, much larger than any land animals seen today. Several theories have been put forward to explain this:

(i) During the era of the dinosaurs, the Earth was covered by such lush vegetation that even the largest plant-eaters had no problem finding enough food. This being the case, the bigger the animal the greater the evolutionary advantage, as large size is a good defence against being killed and eaten by one's carnivorous colleagues. In a sort of arms race, the carnivores grew big for the same reason: the bigger they were, the bigger the prey they could take on.

The suggestion that large vegetarian dinosaurs were better equipped to reach the higher branches of plants is less convincing, as there is no reason to believe there was a shortage of food at the time.

(ii) Those who believe that dinosaurs were cold-blooded maintain that is why they were so big: cold-blooded creatures with greater mass are better able to maintain constant body temperature, warming up during the day and cooling slowly at night. In smaller cold-blooded creatures, the larger ratio of surface area to mass may have made this more difficult in the prevailing climatic conditions.

(iii) Those who believe that dinosaurs were warm-blooded also claim that is a factor in their large size. They point out that the uninsulated skin of dinosaurs was a source of heat loss, and the lower ratio of surface area to mass in larger dinosaurs would have protected them from the chilling effects that would have been dangerous to a warm-blooded creature.

To conclude: large size may have kept cold-blooded creatures cool, or it may have kept warm-blooded creatures warm...

117. What was the lifespan of dinosaurs?

To answer this question, we need to know two things about the remains of a dinosaur. Firstly, how old was it when it died? And secondly, did it die of old age? Although we can sometimes tell from evidence of injury that a dinosaur met a violent end, it is generally impossible to answer either of these questions.

Estimates of the lifespan of dinosaurs are therefore based on what we know, from the evidence of present-day animals, of the connection between size and lifespan and the possible role of metabolism. Calculations based on these factors have resulted in estimates from a respectable 75 years to an awesome 300 years for the lifespans of dinosaurs – a very broad range indeed.

118. What colours were dinosaurs?

Until recently, we knew nothing of the skin of dinosaurs. Depiction of their colour was left to the imagination of illustrators, who tended to go for a mixture of the green of lizards and the grey or murky brown of elephants and rhinos. In 2009, however, remnants of skin and 'proto-feathers' were found on dinosaur remains in China. These, and certain other features of dinosaur remains, have encouraged a belief that both skin and 'proto-feathers' were part of the creature's display mechanism to improve its breeding prospects.

Whether dinosaurs of the opposite sex liked bright colours is a matter for pure speculation, but at least the find has encouraged illustrators to open their palettes to a more striking and dazzling range in recent years.

> The fundament upon which all our knowledge and learning rests is inexplicable.
>
> Arthur Schopenhauer (1788–1860)

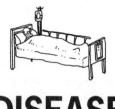

DISEASE

119. What was sweating sickness?

Sweating sickness, also known as the 'English sweate', was a highly virulent disease that struck England in a series of epidemics between 1485 and 1551, after which it apparently vanished, with the last recorded case in 1578. The onset of symptoms was sudden and dramatic, starting with anxiety, followed by violent cold shivers, giddiness, headache and excruciating pains in the neck, shoulders, arms and legs, with severe fever and great exhaustion. Death often occurred within hours. Its virulence was described by Dr John Caius in *A Boke or Counseill Against the Disease Commonly Called the Sweate, or Sweatyng Sicknesse* (1556). In this, Caius reports that the disease

> *immediately killed some in opening their windows, some in playing with children in their street doors, some in one hour, many in two it destroyed, & at the longest, to they that merrily dined, it gave a sorrowful supper. As it found them so it took them, some in sleep some in wake, some in mirth some in care, some fasting & some full, some busy and some idle, and in one house sometime three sometime five, sometime seven sometime eight, sometime more some time all, of the which, if the half in every town escaped, it was thought great favour.*

At this distance of time, there is little prospect of scientists ever establishing the causative organism, although it was clearly some kind of infection.

120. What is the cause of autism?

The condition (or set of conditions) known as autism was only named in 1943, and is still a long way from being understood. Characterized mainly by impairments in social interaction and communication, autism is seen by some as a distinct mental disorder and by others as an extreme point on a spectrum that begins with the mildly obsessive condition known as Asperger's syndrome. Some suggest that autism should not be treated as a disorder at all, but merely as an extreme but acceptable point in the range of normality.

Studies have shown that autism has a strong genetic component, with several genes identified as playing a possible part, though no single gene appears to be responsible for autism on its own. An imbalance in the brain's production of certain hormones has also been associated with the condition, while some blame post-natal factors, such as diet, medication or some other external factor.

It seems increasingly clear that autism is due to a complex set of distinct causes that may be connected – but which are not necessarily so. There is still much unravelling to be done.

Must helpless man in ignorance sedate
Roll darkling down the torrent of his fate?

Samuel Johnson (1709–84)

121. Why are engineers more likely to have autistic children and grandchildren than non-engineers?

To test the theory that autism has a genetic component, in 1997 the British psychologist Simon Baron-Cohen and others compared the family histories of children with autism. Their findings showed that in a sample of 919 families with a child with autism, 28.4 per cent had either a father or grandfather who was an engineer, compared with only 15 per cent of families without autism. Later studies also showed that students of mathematics and physics were more likely to have autism in their families than students of subjects demanding a high degree of social understanding. Perhaps social interaction is simply too fuzzy or too imprecise a skill to catch the interest of the methodical autistic brain.

122. Is there a connection between cholesterol intake and arteriosclerosis?

Cholesterol is an essential component of cell membranes in mammals, and also plays a part in various metabolic processes. But eating a diet rich in such things as cheese, eggs and fatty meat can lead to high levels of cholesterol in the blood. There is no doubt that arteriosclerosis (a build-up of calcium on the insides of artery walls) and atherosclerosis (a similar build-up of fats) are linked to high levels of cholesterol in the blood and lead to heart attacks. But whether the diseases are caused by high cholesterol intake is still open to question. An alternative view is that the diseases themselves interfere with the body's mechanism for breaking down cholesterol, and thus it is the diseases that are responsible for the cholesterol build-up, and not the other way round.

There is a (no doubt apocryphal) story of an American who heard that the incidence of heart disease in the USA is far greater than in Japan, where the diet is low in cholesterol. But there is also a low level of heart disease in France, where cholesterol intake is as high as anywhere (think of those 246 varieties of cheese). The American concluded that the cause of heart disease was not cholesterol but speaking English. He was probably wrong about English, but he could have been right about cholesterol.

123. What causes eating disorders?

Behavioural, biological, biochemical, emotional, psychological, interpersonal and social factors have all been blamed for eating disorders such as bulimia and anorexia nervosa, but even cases with apparent physical causes still pose many questions. In some individuals, a relationship has been shown between eating disorders and chemicals in the brain that control hunger, appetite and digestion, but whether it is the eating disorder that causes the chemical imbalance or vice versa is unclear. Eating disorders have also been frequently found to run in families, raising questions of a possible genetic component.

124. What causes pimples and acne?

Pimples occur when a pore or hair follicle collapses in on itself and blocks the secretion from the sebaceous gland of sebum, an oily secretion that lubricates the hair and skin. The trapped sebum builds up into an oily spot. Various factors have been identified as causes of pimple formation, such as poor diet (including vitamin deficiency), hormonal imbalance (which is why teenagers are particularly prone to spots) and stress. What is not clear is why one sebaceous gland should give rise to a pimple while another does not.

125. Why are some babies born prematurely?

Around 7 per cent of babies in the UK are born prematurely (before the thirty-seventh week of pregnancy). Estimates in the USA vary between about 8 and 12 per cent. Various causes have been identified, including multiple pregnancy, pre-eclampsia (high blood pressure usually associated with problems in the placenta), haemorrhage, illness in the mother, foetal abnormality and cervical incompetence (premature widening of the cervix). In around 40 per cent of cases, however, the cause is unknown. But given that the immediate cause of a woman going into labour at full term is also unknown, this is perhaps not surprising.

126. How did AIDS and HIV originate?

The first reference to acquired immune deficiency syndrome, abbreviated to AIDS, in medical literature was in 1982. The disease had first been identified among gay men, but was later also found in other groups, such as haemophiliacs (who depend on frequent blood transfusions) and intravenous drug users. Cases of the disease itself are thought to date back to the mid-1970s, and by the mid-1980s it had spread to every continent except Antarctica. The discovery in 1983 of the human immunodeficiency virus (HIV), which is now generally accepted as the cause of AIDS, gave direction to a search for the origins of the disease.

In 1999 a type of simian immunodeficiency virus (SIV) that was very similar to HIV was found in a frozen sample of blood taken from a captive chimpanzee that had originated in West Africa. Tracing back the origins of that SIV virus led to the conclusion that it had come from two other strains of SIV and had at some point crossed species from chimps to humans. How it did so has been the subject of diverse theories:

(i) It may have spread to humans through the killing and eating of chimpanzees.

(ii) It may have entered through cuts into the blood stream of hunters who had killed the chimpanzees.

(iii) It may have been spread through the testing of an oral polio vaccine that had been cultivated in cells from the kidneys of chimpanzees.

Conspiracy theorists (with no tangible evidence) have also suggested that AIDS may have been part of a secret CIA project, either deliberately designed to wipe out gay men, or as a general biological weapon.

127. Where does the ebola virus live between human outbreaks?

Ebola is one of the most contagious and virulent diseases known to medical science. It can be transmitted by no more than a handshake, and once infected the victim suffers massive internal bleeding, as the walls of the blood vessels are destroyed. There is no known cure, and between 50 and 90 per cent of those infected die.

The first identified outbreak was in 1976 in Sudan and in a nearby region of Zaire. The disease is named after the Ebola River Valley in the Democratic Republic of the Congo (formerly Zaire). Others followed, but nobody knew where the virus lurked between human outbreaks. Bats have long been suspected, as they have frequently been found at the site of ebola outbreaks. Insects, birds and non-human primates, which are all known to have died from the disease, have also fallen under suspicion.

As with AIDS, it has been suggested that human epidemics have begun with the eating of diseased bush meat (as the flesh of hunted wild animals is known in Africa). However, since ebola is as quickly fatal to other primates as it is to humans, it seems unlikely that they are a reservoir for the virus between outbreaks. The search for its hiding place continues.

128. Why has the incidence of asthma in humans increased so much in recent decades?

World Health Organization studies report significant increases in the incidence of asthma in a number of different countries over recent decades. The rate among US children increased from 3.6 per cent in

1980 to 9 per cent in 2001, while the rate in Switzerland increased from 2 per cent around thirty years ago to 10 per cent today. This may partly be due to an improvement in diagnosis rates. From 1930 until 1950, asthma was officially considered a psychosomatic illness and treated as a psychological rather than a medical ailment. On the other hand, asthma has long been associated with allergic conditions, which may be exacerbated by inner-city living, which is on the increase. Other environmental and genetic factors are also known to be involved, but the reasons for the worldwide increase in the disease are not fully understood.

129. Does cold weather increase your chance of catching a cold?

This is a question on which we seem to be constantly changing our minds. Before we understood about germs, the accepted folk wisdom was that cold weather brought colds. That view was then dismissed as an old wives' tale, and the increased prevalence of colds in winter was explained by the fact that people spend more time indoors during cold weather, thus increasing their chance of catching an infectious disease from somebody else.

In 2005, however, an interesting experiment was performed at the Common Cold Research Centre in Cardiff in which ninety people immersed their feet in a bowl of ice-filled water for twenty minutes, while a control group kept their feet in an empty bowl for the same period. Over the next five days, 29 per cent of the group who had had their feet in icy water developed cold symptoms, compared to only 9 per cent of the control group.

The explanation seems to be that coldness may not cause the common cold, but it may decrease the body's resistance by reducing the supply of white blood cells – a primary defence against the various viruses that cause the common cold. But since the specific viruses responsible for the common cold have not been identified, we cannot be sure of that.

130. Can you catch a cold by kissing?

It used to be thought that kissing was an effective way of spreading colds, but an experiment conducted at the University of Wisconsin in 1984, in which people without colds kissed people with colds, resulted in only one in thirteen of the healthy kissers catching the disease. The official line since then has been that cold viruses are not carried on the lips or in the saliva, but live in the mucus in the nose. So kissing is fine, but Eskimo-style nose-rubbing is out.

On the other hand, close contact with a sufferer has always been held to carry the risk of catching a cold, as the virus may easily be transferred from nose to hand or into the air. So kissing is only all right if you can do it without being in close contact with the person kissed – particularly, one might think, close contact with any part of the anatomy near their nose.

131. Will disease ever be eradicated?

We have eradicated smallpox. We may be on the verge of eradicating polio. We are on the point of eradicating rinderpest in cattle. We thought we were well on the way to eradicating tuberculosis, until the emergence of drug-resistant strains. So will we ever eradicate all diseases? There seems to be no reason in principle why we should not, one day, develop a way of eliminating all the things that interfere with the functioning of the human body, unless, of course, disease is in some way essential to the continuing existence of the human race. After all, if being disease-free is an evolutionary advantage, which we might naively assume to be the case, then why have we not evolved that way? The disease-creating organisms always seem to be one step ahead of us in the evolution game.

See also ANTHROPOLOGY 26, ARMADILLOS, 29, BIOLOGY 43, COMPOSERS 95, 98, FOOTBALL (AMERICAN) 187, GARLIC 205, MEDICINE 282–7, THE MIDDLE AGES 303, SMOKING 434–5

DNA

The discovery by Francis Crick and James D. Watson in 1953 of the double-helix structure of the DNA (deoxyribonucleic acid) molecule has proved to be one of the most far-reaching in the history of science. Darwin's theory of evolution and the science of genetics had already been with us for many years, but the discovery of the double helix showed how genetic information is encoded at the molecular level. The DNA of each individual organism provides a unique blueprint for that organism, as well as the information that makes it the species it is. Every organism has a copy of its unique DNA in every one of its cells. As the genotypes of more species and more individuals are unravelled, we are able to answer more and more questions regarding the origins and relationships of different organisms. But the explosion of information this has provided has created a vast cloud of unanswered questions, of which the following are perhaps only the most basic.

132. Is all life DNA-based?

Every independent life form so far encountered in the universe is DNA-based. Even viruses, which can only survive by invading a host cell, are based either on DNA or the closely related RNA. DNA (deoxyribonucleic acid) contains the genetic instructions for the development and functioning of all organisms, from the humblest plant or microbe to the human being. If there is another way for life to function, we haven't found it yet. Or if we have found it, we haven't recognized it, perhaps because it is so different from us. If DNA is essential for life of any form, then the question we have to ask is: What is it about DNA that makes it so special?

133. Why do some highly evolved complex organisms have less DNA in their genome than simpler organisms?

All the information needed to make a human being, or any other living thing, is contained in his, her or its genome, which comprises the entirety of the organism's hereditary information and which is encoded in its DNA. Long stretches of the genome form the heritable units known as genes, and our genes are transmitted to us on our chromosomes (organized structures of DNA and protein found in each cell). So one might think that the human being – the most complex organism we know – ought to have a longer genome, and more genes and chromosomes, than anything else.

Far from it. The human genome consists of about 3 billion pairs of bases consisting of the structural units known as nucleotides. Just to read out the human genome would take about nine or ten years without stopping. Pretty complex, you might think, but the microscopic *Amoeba dubia* has a longer genome than us, as do the lungfish and the Easter lily.

So what about our genes? Well, we have about 25,000 genes, which is about the same number as mustard grass and not that many more than a roundworm. Finally, how do we score on chromosomes? We have a respectable 46 chromosomes (23 pairs), but carp have 104 – and even some species of potato have 48.

It may be that the organisms mentioned above need all their genetic material, but much of it may simply represent redundant leftovers from a long evolutionary process.

134. Why does the vast majority of information in our DNA appear to have no function?

As far as we can tell, the main role of DNA is to provide the information needed to construct the large variety of proteins required to build our bodies and keep them functioning. Yet it has been estimated that as little as 2 per cent of our DNA has that function. The rest used to be known as 'junk DNA', with the implication that it was like the lines of code in a lazy computer program that had been overwritten by later instructions but never removed.

More recently, attention has focused on segments of this apparently 'junk' DNA that seem to have the function of determining when genes are turned on and off. It may turn out that much of our genome has such a controlling function, or it may turn out that much of it really is junk – a no longer wanted genetic inheritance from a distant past.

See also EGYPTOLOGY 162, EVOLUTION 182–6, GENETICS 206–14, MOZART 315, PALAEONTOLOGY 355–6, PROTEINS 393, 395

DODOS

135. Is the dodo extinct?

The dodo is generally believed to have become extinct soon after 1662, when the last known specimen of this large flightless bird was sighted on the Indian Ocean island of Mauritius. Natural history, however, is littered with examples of species that have, as it were, come back from the dead. In 1938, for example, fishermen off the coast of South Africa netted a large, primitive-looking fish. This turned out to be a coelacanth, a species that had supposedly died out 65 million years ago. So what is the chance that a dodo is still around somewhere?

In 2010 the journal *Nature*, under the title 'Should we be trying to save the dodo?', reported a new statistical technique to estimate the chance of saving threatened species, or finding living examples of species thought to be extinct. The technique is based on a formula into which are entered the dates of the last ten confirmed sightings of the animal, and from this it calculates the chance that a live specimen is still lurking undiscovered somewhere. When the dodo's details are entered, it comes up with the answer that the probability that the dodo lives on is 3.07×10^{-6} – or about three chances in a million.

DOGS

136. Why are dogs even more likely to catch yawning from humans than other humans are?

A fascinating experiment was conducted at London University in 2008 to determine whether human yawning is contagious to dogs. Of the twenty-nine dogs in the study, twenty-one yawned after watching the researcher yawn. That represents 72 per cent of the sample catching the yawn, compared with only 45 per cent (or in some studies 60 per cent) reported in humans, and 33 per cent in chimpanzees. Furthermore, when the humans just opened their mouths, none of the dogs yawned, suggesting that only true yawns are contagious.

137. Are dogs psychic?

In 1983 the academic parapsychologist Helmut Schmidt performed an experiment in which a dog was rewarded with chocolates whenever a human subject made a correct guess in a test of extrasensory perception. The dog, which was described as a 'supposedly non-psychic' miniature dachshund, was thus motivated to try to influence the man's performance. The man's performance did indeed improve during the course of the experiment, but the dog was found to do even better when rewarded for making its own correct choices in an ESP experiment without having a human as an intermediary. It was concluded that further research was needed.

In 1999 Dr Rupert Sheldrake published a book entitled *Dogs That Know When Their Owners Are Coming Home and Other Unexplained Powers of Animals*, in which he presented case studies of dogs that apparently showed signs of knowing, at a distance, the movements of their owners. A number of academics have indicated that they are unconvinced.

138. Do dogs distinguish rational from irrational acts?

This question formed the title of a paper in 2010, which reported two experiments to determine whether dogs were more likely to follow directions given to them in a rational manner than those delivered in an irrational way. In the first experiment, humans pointed with their legs in the direction in which food could be found. Some of the humans had their hands occupied, which made pointing with their legs a rational act, others had free hands, which made pointing with the legs irrational (or at least unnatural). The second experiment involved trained dogs demonstrating a task that involved operating a lever. The natural doggy way to pull the lever would be to use the mouth, but the trained dogs did it with a paw, either when their mouths were holding a ball, making the use of the paw rational, or when their mouths were empty, making the paw-use supposedly irrational. The experimenters concluded that 'our results suggest that dogs do not distinguish rational from irrational acts', which contradicted the conclusions of earlier experimenters. So the question is still open.

See also THE BRAIN 58, CONSCIOUSNESS 102

DRUIDS

139. What did the ancient Druids believe?

Between 200 BC and AD 200, various Greek and Roman writers described the Druids, who to them appeared as a mysterious priestly class with great influence in Britain, Ireland and Gaul. Julius Caesar wrote that they acted as judges in Gaul, and were highly respected as intermediaries between men and gods, but all he mentions regarding their doctrine is that they believed in reincarnation – the transmigration of souls. The Druids themselves left no written records. What we do know about the Druids is that they had nothing to do with Stonehenge – a much earlier structure (→ ANCIENT HISTORY 14). The connection between the two was not made until the 17th century – and the 'Ancient Druid Order', far from being ancient, was not founded until 1717.

140. Did the Druids use a 'wicker man' to burn human sacrifices alive?

Julius Caesar also says that the Druids indulged in human sacrifice, the victims usually being criminals but sometimes innocent people. However, history is littered with examples of such allegations, intended to give the impression that the people one wishes to conquer are utterly barbarous, and in need of a civilizing hand. In Caesar's account, the victims were burned alive in a large wooden effigy, known in recent times as the 'wicker man' (as popularized in the cult 1970s film of that name). In another account, also from the first century BC, the Greek historian Diodorus Siculus, reports that the Druids made their human sacrifices by plunging a dagger into the victim's chest and forecasting the future from the way his legs twitched.

There is no archaeological evidence of wicker men, and evidence of human sacrifice is strongly disputed.

THE EARTH

141. What causes ice ages on Earth?

Over the last 2 or 3 billion years, geological evidence tells us that there have been at least five ice ages on Earth, but we do not really understand the mechanics of what causes them. One factor must be the amount of heat we receive from the Sun, which varies according to slight changes in the Earth's orbit and the angle between the Earth's axis of rotation and the plane of its solar orbit. Other factors may also affect the energy emitted by the Sun, but we do not know what they are. Another factor is the gravitational pull of other planets on the Earth's orbit, and there has also been a suggestion that the temperature on Earth may be affected by changing temperatures of the space through which its orbit takes it.

Around 1940 the Serbian geophysicist and engineer Milutin Milanković studied changes in the Earth's orbit and showed that it underwent various potentially climate-changing wobbles with periods of 21,000 years, 26,000 years and 41,000 years, now known as the Milanković cycles, which must have something to with the

Earth's periodic ice ages, though they fail to fit perfectly with the geological data.

There is also the question of continental drift and plate tectonics, which by varying the relative positions and areas of sea and land influence how much solar heat the planet retains at its surface, because sea is slower to warm and slower to cool than land. Greenhouse gases may also have played a role. It has been suggested, for example, that gases emitted by widespread volcanic eruptions 630 million years ago may have been largely responsible for the end of one ice age.

To complicate matters further, there are also glacial periods within each ice age, during which the ice sheets advance and recede. For the past 11,000 years or so, we have been in an interglacial period, with the ice sheets generally receding, but from around 1350, temperatures began to fall until the start of the seventeenth century, bringing a 'little ice age' that lasted until the early nineteenth century, a chilly period which nobody can completely explain.

142. Why did the Earth's temperature rise dramatically about 55 million years ago?

At the very end of the Palaeocene era, 55 million years ago, there was a climatic anomaly known as the Palaeocene–Eocene thermal maximum. Ocean surface temperatures worldwide shot up by between five and eight degrees Celsius and stayed that way for a few thousand years. In the Arctic, it heated up even more, to an estimated 23°C. The main effects of such warming would have been an expansion of the water in the oceans, changing the planet's ratio of sea to land. There would also have been a marked effect on the species of marine life. Geological evidence and the fossil record both confirm that such changes happened, as do chemical analyses of molecules found in the fossil shells of primitive creatures. But nobody knows what caused the huge temperature change.

143. What caused the so-called 'Tunguska event' above Russia in 1908?

On 30 June 1908 a massive explosion – about a thousand times more powerful than the atom bomb that destroyed Hiroshima – occurred in the sky near the Tunguska River in a remote part of Siberia. Hundreds of academic papers have been written on the subject, yet we are still not sure what it was. Some suggest a comet or asteroid that vaporized in the Earth's atmosphere, but it left no evidence or even a crater. Eye-witness accounts, however, told of a column of blue light almost as bright as the Sun moving across the sky, followed by a sound like heavy artillery fire. According to one account it was as if 'the sky split in two'. Seismic stations across Eurasia registered a huge explosion, while the atmospheric shock wave was detected as far away as the UK. Later investigators established that over 2,000 square km (800 square miles) of forest were flattened, with some 80 million trees knocked over by the blast. There were also numerous holes in the ground that were at first thought to be meteor craters, but no traces of meteors, or anything else from whatever exploded, have ever been found.

144. Why did the Earth's thermosphere collapse so badly in 2008–9?

Way above the Earth's surface, at a height of between 90 and 500 km (55 and 300 miles), lies the thermosphere, the highest level of the Earth's atmosphere. The thermosphere traps ultraviolet radiation from the Sun and its temperature increases the higher you get, unlike the other three atmospheric levels (the troposphere, stratosphere and mesosphere), which get colder with height.

In 2008–9, however, the thermosphere showed a dramatic shrinkage, which has not been explained. It is known that an increase in carbon dioxide in the atmosphere can reduce the size of the thermosphere; it is known that a decrease in solar activity can also have that effect; but calculations taking both of those into account still leave at least 60 per cent of the shrinkage unexplained. There is clearly some aspect of the Sun's influence on Earth that we do not understand.

145. What is the cause of the so-called flux transfer events that open a magnetic portal between the Earth and Sun, and why do these portals open every eight minutes?

Enveloping the Earth, some 70,000 km (43,000 miles) above the planet's surface, is a region of space called the magnetosphere. Only discovered in 1958 by the *Explorer 1* space probe, the magnetosphere (which isn't a sphere at all, but more of a teardrop shape) is formed by the action of the Earth's magnetic field on the free ions from the ionosphere (a part of the uppermost layer of the atmosphere) and electrons from the solar wind. Its magnetic forces, in fact, act as a protective shield against the potential ravages of the solar wind. Every eight minutes, however, a portal opens in the magnetosphere that allows high-energy particles from the Sun to flow through to the Earth. This is known as a flux transfer event, but no one yet knows what causes them or why they happen every eight minutes.

146. What was the history of the Earth before the break-up of the super-continent Pangaea?

When in 1912 the German meteorologist Alfred Wegener proposed that the Earth had once consisted of a single super-continent, the idea was greeted with great scepticism. The hypothetical continent was not even given a name until 1926, when a conference on Wegener's theory of continental drift came up with the name of Pangaea (from the Greek for 'all land') and dubbed the ocean that surrounded it Panthalassa (meaning 'all sea'). Suspicion of Wegener's theory diminished as the fossil evidence accumulated, and was entirely vindicated in the 1960s, when plate tectonics provided a plausible mechanism not only for continental drift, but also for seismic activity and volcanism. But what the Earth was like before Pangaea remains a matter for speculation.

One theory, supported by some geological evidence, is that the planet goes through a cycle in which, over a period of between 300 and 500 million years, super-continents form and then break up. But what the map of the Earth looked like during these earlier cycles, if they indeed occurred, remains largely a matter of guesswork.

147. What is the Earth's core made of?

Considering how much we now know about the rest of the universe, we know surprisingly little about what goes on deep inside our own planet. We can calculate, from our knowledge of the strength of the Earth's gravitational pull, what its mass must be; we can measure directly the density of the material near the surface of the Earth; and we can deduce from those figures that the inside of the Earth must be much denser than the part we know.

Apart from that, our main evidence of the nature of the Earth's core has come from the analysis of seismic waves caused by earthquakes. Unexpected patterns in the readings of seismographs at different places on the Earth's surface indicated that the waves were meeting some obstruction in their passage, and that is what led to the current picture of a solid inner core with a radius of about 1,220 km (760 miles), surrounded by a liquid core extending to around 3,400 km (2110 miles) from the Earth's centre.

Considerations of density and examination of meteorites thought to have formed in the same way as our planet have led to the conclusion that the inner core is composed mainly of iron and nickel, but it seems generally agreed there are also other elements there, at present unidentified. In 2006, after examining the composition of meteorites believed to be similar to the 'planetesimals' that crashed together to form the Earth billions of years ago, the Australian geologist Bernard Wood concluded that 99 per cent of the Earth's gold is missing, and that it must have sunk to the core, which must also contain most of the Earth's platinum. All we have to do to find out is to drill down about 5,000 km (3,000 miles).

148. What is the temperature at the centre of the Earth?

In Dante's *Inferno*, at the centre of the Earth lies Cocytus, a frozen lake that forms the ninth and lowest circle of Hell where traitors such as Judas are punished for all eternity. Satan himself is trapped at its centre, his constant tears freezing as they add to the icy lake.

This picture of the centre of the Earth is not supported by scientific opinion, but there is still considerable discrepancy in estimates of the temperature at the centre of the Earth, which vary between about 4,000 and 7,000°C. These estimates are based on calculating the melting point of iron at the boundary of the inner and outer core, at the huge pressure known to exist at the Earth's centre.

149. When will the next mass extinction take place on Earth?

Fossil records indicate that there have been five major extinctions on Earth in the last 500 million years, each resulting in the extinction of more than half the life forms on the planet. The most recent was about 65 million years ago and resulted in the extinction of the dinosaurs.

There is a good deal of evidence that that extinction was caused by the impact of an asteroid, though alternative explanations include climate change caused by volcanic eruptions, the evolution of mammals that ate dinosaur eggs, and a change in plant-life resulting in the herbivorous dinosaurs becoming fatally constipated. The cause of the other mass extinctions is unknown, which makes it difficult to estimate when the next one will be. Potential causes of future extinctions include human-generated environmental change, energy bursts from outside our galaxy, climate change that is outside our control, and stray asteroids crashing into the Earth. In any case, the Sun, as it burns out in about another 5 billion years, will explode into a red giant and engulf the Earth, though at the current rate of one mass extinction every 100 million years, we will have had about fifty mass extinctions before then anyway.

150. Did life on Earth come from outer space?

The fossil record indicates that life on Earth began around 3.5 billion years ago, a relatively short time after the planet was formed 4.6 billion years ago. Doubts have been cast on whether this is long enough for the complex molecules that are necessary for life to have formed from carbon, oxygen, hydrogen and nitrogen. At around the same time as life on Earth first appeared, our planet was subjected to the 'Late Heavy Bombardment', when the Earth and Moon were battered by large numbers of rocks from space. Since the universe had been around for some 9 billion years before the Earth was formed, there would have been plenty of time for the so-called 'prebiotic molecules', or even basic life forms, to have appeared elsewhere, and these could have been dumped on Earth by meteorite strikes. This theory is called exogenesis (meaning 'birth from outside'), but would need good evidence of life elsewhere in the universe to support it.

See also ANCIENT HISTORY 17, CLIMATE 87–8, EVOLUTION 182, THE PLANETS 375, THE SOLAR SYSTEM 439, WATER 470

The learning and knowledge that we have, is, at the most, but little compared with that of which we are ignorant.

Plato (424/3 BC–348/7 BC)

EARTHQUAKES

151. What is the nature of the forces that drive the movement of the Earth's tectonic plates?

Until the early twentieth century, it was generally believed that the world as we know it was quite literally set in stone. The planet might once have been a mass of gases and molten rock, but everything had now cooled down, leaving us with the unchanging land and sea as we now see it. In 1912, however, the German meteorologist Alfred Wegener came up with the theory of 'continental drift'. He proposed that the Earth had once consisted of the oceans and a super-landmass that he called Pangaea, which had split up to form the continents as we now know them (→ THE EARTH 146). Wegener also maintained that this process continues to this day – the continents are still on the move. Wegener's theory provided an explanation as to why similar or identical fossils and rock types are found in places far apart from each other – but he had no explanation of what was making the continents move.

In the 1960s the theory of continental drift was supported by a new and wider-reaching theory: that the lithosphere, the outer rocky shell of the planet comprising the crust and the upper mantle, is made up of a number of vast and mobile 'tectonic' plates. There are roughly seven major plates and seven minor plates, depending how you count them, and the lithosphere they make up sits on top of the asthenosphere, a hotter and therefore more plastic and movable layer of the Earth's mantle. Where plates are moving away from each other, new lithosphere is formed by molten rock rising from the asthenosphere below. This process is called sea-floor spreading, and accounts for the mid-ocean ridges found in the Atlantic, Pacific and Indian Oceans. At other boundaries, one plate is sliding under another, and part of the lithosphere, as it is pushed deeper, heats up and melts. There are also boundaries where the plates simply slide (or grind) past each other, with lithosphere being neither created nor destroyed.

Studies of where earthquakes and volcanic activity occur, together with aerial mapping of the sea floor, confirmed the theory, and demonstrated that it is the movement of the plates that causes these geological disturbances. Yet there is still argument about what is driving the movement of the plates.

One theory is that heat from the Earth's core causes convection currents in the asthenosphere, which lead to movement in the tectonic plates. Recent imaging of the internal structure of the Earth, however, has failed to identify the convection cells that would support this theory. Instead, plumes or channels of heat have been suggested, but they too have not been confirmed.

Another theory is that tectonic movement is at least in part gravity-driven as molten rock beneath the ocean cools and solidifies at the edge of plates, becoming more dense and slipping down beneath the neighbouring plate, causing further movement.

A third theory claims that the Earth's rotation and tides exert a force on the Earth's crust, which brings about movement of the tectonic plates.

Perhaps the answer is a combination of all of these, to one degree or another.

152. How do animals predict earthquakes?

Accounts of animals apparently predicting earthquakes have been known since ancient times. In 373 BC Greek historians recorded that rats, snakes and weasels deserted the city of Helice in large numbers just days before a devastating quake took place. Fish moving violently, chickens that stop laying eggs and bees leaving their hives have also been reported, while elephants in Sri Lanka and Thailand in 2004 were reported to have saved people from the devastating Boxing Day tsunami, caused by a vast undersea earthquake, by carrying them to higher ground. Studies in the USA have reported increased incidence of lost pet reports in local newspapers just before seismic activity.

So what are these animals picking up that our seismographs are missing? If we knew the answer to that, we would be better at predicting earthquakes ourselves.

See also THE EARTH 147, THE PLANETS 375

EASTER ISLAND

153. How did the Easter Islanders move their large Moai statues across the island?

When the Dutch explorer Jacob Roggeveen became the first European to land on the remote Easter Island in the southeastern Pacific Ocean, on Easter Sunday 1722, he and his crew were astounded to find the huge statues known as Moai. Later investigations have revealed 887 of these statues, which are up to 10 metres (33 ft) tall and weigh up to 86 tonnes. Carbon-dating indicates they were carved between the thirteenth and seventeenth centuries, generally out of volcanic rock from a crater known as Rano Raruka. But how did the islanders move these massive statues, sometimes to places many kilometres away? The local belief was that divine intervention enabled the statues themselves to walk to their destinations. Putting that to one side, there remain three main theories:

(i) The islanders used wooden rollers, dragging the statues across them with ropes.

(ii) They used wooden sledges, perhaps mounted on wooden rollers, to carry the statues.

(iii) They attached ropes around the necks and bodies of the statues and waddled them upright across the terrain, one step at a time.

The first two theories were originally discounted, as there were no trees growing on the island when Roggeveen landed, but later investigations of pollen deposits indicated that severe deforestation had taken place before 1650, and that there was probably no shortage of trees when the statues were made. All the same, attempts to move the statues by any of the suggested methods have been generally unconvincing.

154. How do we decipher the Rongorongo script found on stone and wood carvings from Easter Island?

In the nineteenth century, around two dozen wooden tablets were found on Easter Island bearing inscriptions in an unknown form of hieroglyphics. They were first mentioned in 1864 in an account by the French-born friar Eugène Eyraud, who was based in Chile and became the first European to live with the Easter Islanders. Eyraud mentioned hundreds of tablets, but by the time they came to be investigated by others in 1868, all but twenty-four had vanished.

Many of the symbols used on the surviving tablets look like people or animals, and alternate lines seem to be written upside down, but all attempts to decipher the tablets, or even to confirm that Rongorongo (which means 'lines for chanting') is a language, have failed. Its lack of similarity to any other known script suggests that it may have been one of the very few independent inventions of a writing system in the history of humankind.

Eyraud died of tuberculosis in 1868. He is thought by some to have brought the disease to Easter Island, where it wiped out around a quarter of the population.

Knowledge and timber shouldn't be much used till they are seasoned.

Oliver Wendell Holmes (1809–94)

155. What happened to the civilization that erected the Easter Island statues?

Even before the Europeans brought disease and the slave trade to Easter Island, the native population had undergone a severe decline. In the early seventeenth century, the population is estimated to have been about 15,000. A century later, it was down to under 3,000. Deforestation, possibly connected with the arrival of the Little Ice Age around 1650, internal wars and even cannibalism have been blamed for the population decrease, but no convincing evidence has been given for any of these having such a dramatic effect.

According to oral tradition, there were once two classes on the island known as the Long Ears (because of their extended ear lobes) and the Short Ears. The Long Ears are said to have enslaved the Short Ears and forced them to carve the Moai statues, but one night the Short Ears rose in revolt and killed all the Long Ears. That would account for the sudden cessation of statue-building, which left many Moai unfinished, but no evidence has been offered to support the legend.

ECONOMICS

Economists are notorious for not knowing things, or at least for not reaching precise conclusions. After eighty years and hundreds of books and papers on the subject of the Great Depression in the USA, for example, economists are still arguing about what its primary causes were. So to be kind to economists, I have decided to include just two examples of economic uncertainty.

156. What is the relationship between money supply and inflation?

Vast acreages of books and papers have been written on this, but basically it all comes down to the 'equation of exchange' proposed by the American economist Irving Fisher in 1911:

$$MV = PT$$

Where M is the amount of money, V is the velocity of circulation, P is price and T is transactions.

To see what this means, and why it's likely to be true, we need to look at what each means in a little more detail. If we take P to be a measure, such as the retail price index, of how much things cost, and T as the number of things people buy in a year, then PT will reflect the total amount they spend. On the left-hand side of the equation, M is the total amount of money sloshing around in the economy, and V is the number of times each unit of money is utilized in a financial transaction. So MV once again equals the total amount spent.

Now some people say that all the money in circulation is being used all the time, even if it's just being used to accumulate interest, and consumer demand for goods doesn't change much, so V and T remain more or less constant, which means that P, the measure of average prices, must be proportional to M, the money in circulation. Prices go up when the money supply is increased and fall when it is cut. QED on all counts.

Of course it's nowhere near as simple as that, as there are a handful of different definitions of money supply, according to whether they include credit and other notional borrowings and financings as well as printed banknotes. There is also a debate on whether to include values of investments and stock prices in the calculation of P, not to mention the continuing problems of arriving at a precise definition of V.

All the same, in the European and Japanese economies of the twentieth century, and also to a lesser extent in the US economy, there does seem to have been a correlation between money supply and interest rates, which are strongly linked to inflation. Since 1995, however, this correlation has been distinctly less convincing.

An economist is an expert who will know tomorrow why the things he predicted yesterday didn't happen today.

Lawrence J. Peter (1919–90)

157. Why are monkeys as irrational as humans in their economic behaviour?

Since 2005, research at Harvard and Yale Universities has demonstrated surprising similarities between the economic decisions taken by monkeys and people. The research began with experiments on tamarin and capuchin monkeys in which they were given tokens they could exchange for food. It quickly became clear that the concept of 'money' was something the monkeys could pick up without difficulty, and once this was established, their reactions to economic change could be tested.

In one early experiment, the monkeys were 'sold' portions of different types of vegetables and fruit at various prices, and when their shopping behaviour had settled, the prices were effectively changed by doubling the size of apple portions that could be purchased for one token. Under such circumstances, economic theory would predict that more apples would be sold and less money spent on, for example, grapes and melon. Not only did the monkeys follow this general behaviour, but their change in shopping patterns was found to be within 1 per cent of the change predicted by economic theory.

That set the stage for an even more interesting set of experiments to see how monkeys behave in a situation in which human behaviour is irrational. The human version is based on two games:

In Game One you are given $100 and told that you must make a choice. Your option is either to toss a coin and be given an extra $100 if it lands heads, but nothing if it is tails, or you can dispense with the coin-tossing and just be given another $50.

In the first case, you end up with $200 or $100, with equal probability; in the second, you end up with $150, come what may. So both are worth $150 on average and, in pure economic terms, there is nothing to choose between them. Yet when people are offered this choice, most of them are found to take the extra $50 and settle for a certain $150 rather than take the risk of ending up with only $100.

Game Two is essentially the same, but presented in a different way: you start with $200, but now the coin toss will either leave your money intact or lose you $100, while the other option is to hand back $50 and dispense with the coin-tossing. Again, you end up with $200 or $100 in the first option or a certain $150 in the second. But in this case, most people opt for the coin toss, apparently at least to give themselves a chance of hanging on to all their money.

Since the two games are mathematically identical, the differing behaviour by humans is not easy to explain. Interestingly, however, capuchin monkeys have been found to show precisely the same irrationality. In their case, there was no coin-tossing, but an experiment was designed with grapes to produce an analogous pair of games involving making a choice between which of two salesmen they bought grapes from.

In the first experiment, each salesman offered a plate containing two grapes. One always delivered both grapes when the money token was handed over; the other added one grape half of the time, but the other half of the time took one away. The monkeys preferred to do business with salesman number one.

In the second experiment, the salesmen both offered three grapes. Salesman one, however, always removed one of the grapes before handing the plate over; salesman two sometimes handed over all three grapes, but sometimes removed two of them. This time, the monkeys went for salesman two.

Whether this is evidence of a type of mental irrationality that monkeys and humans have shared since the two lines of primate began to diverge some 350 million years ago, or whether there are different reasons behind similar irrationalities is unclear.

Real knowledge is to know the extent of one's ignorance.

Confucius (551–479 BC)

EGYPTOLOGY

158. Were human sacrifices made at royal tombs in ancient Egypt?

Excavating the 5,000-year-old tomb of Pharaoh Aha-Mena in 1899–1900, the pioneering British archaeologist Flinders Petrie reported the discovery of an area to the east of the royal tombs he called the Great Cemetery of the Domestics. This consisted of thirty-four smaller graves, which he believed contained the remains of the pharaoh's servants. One theory is that they were put to death by poisoning at the time of the pharaoh's funeral, so that they could continue to serve him in the afterlife.

There is also some evidence that criminals or others may have been put to death during funerals as a sacrifice to the gods. While both these theories are consistent with an interpretation of inscriptions and also with some human remains found in the tombs, other explanations are also possible.

159. Where was the Land of Punt and where is the lost capital of Itj-Tawi?

During the Fifth Dynasty, around 2500 BC, Pharaoh Sahure organized an expedition to the Land of Punt, which was apparently very rich in commodities such as gold and ivory that were highly prized in Egypt. Several more expeditions to Punt are well documented over the next thousand years, but its location is never made clear. Some historians place it in East Africa, others in Arabia.

Another lost location is the capital city of Amenemhat I who was the first pharaoh of the Twelfth Dynasty, ruling from 1991 to 1962 BC. It is said that when he came to power he founded a new capital, which he named Itj-Tawi, 'the one that seizes the two lands'. It is thought to have been near the village of el-Lisht, where he built his pyramid, but no trace of this capital city has ever been found.

160. Was the labyrinth at Heracleopolis a myth or a reality?

Heracleopolis is the Greek name of Henen-nesut, which was the capital of Lower Egypt. According to the Roman writer Pliny the Elder, there was a vast labyrinth at Heracleopolis, said to contain forty shrines and many pyramids and temples to all the Egyptian gods. In 1940 a British archaeological team was reported to have discovered the labyrinth, but one of the team members fell ill and another disappeared, after which the excavation had to be abandoned. The location of the labyrinth remains a mystery – if it indeed existed in the first place.

161. What happened to Nefertiti?

Nefertiti, whose bust in the Egyptian Museum in Berlin may be the most copied ancient Egyptian relic after the mask of Tutankhamen, was the 'Great Royal Wife' (i.e. the principal consort) of Akhenaten, who ruled from around 1379 to 1362 BC. However, after about fourteen years of his reign, all references to her vanish. She may have died of plague, which was sweeping through Egypt at the time, or she may have ruled Egypt as Neferneferuaten after Akhenaten's death. More than one mummy has been identified with Nefertiti, but in all cases the evidence is very weak.

Knowledge comes, but wisdom lingers.

Alfred, Lord Tennyson (1809–92)

162. How did Tutankhamen die and who were his parents?

In 1922 the English archaeologist Howard Carter and his sponsor Lord Caernarvon made an astonishing discovery in Egypt's Valley of the Kings: it was not just the tomb of an Egyptian pharaoh, but uniquely one that had escaped the attentions of grave-robbers. The pharaoh in question was Tutankhamen, who ruled from around 1333 to 1323 BC, and thanks to his glorious funeral mask and the other beautiful artefacts found in his tomb, Tutankhamen has become the most famous of all ancient Egyptians. Yet until recently we knew almost nothing about him. He was about 1.675 metres (5 ft 7 in) tall, had large front teeth with an overbite, came to the throne at the age of nine or ten, and died at eighteen.

A computerized tomography scan in 2005 showed that he had broken his leg shortly before his death and that it had become infected, while DNA analysis in 2010 showed traces of malaria in his body. Either of those would have been enough to account for his early death, though signs of injuries detected in X-rays of his mummy together with evidence of possible plotting against him have led to some speculation that he may have been assassinated.

The DNA analysis also confirmed that Tutankhamen's father was the mummy known as KV55 and his mother was KV35, known as 'the Younger Lady'. There is much support for the view that KV55 was the pharaoh Amenhotep IV, who adopted the name Akhenaten, and that KV35 was his wife and sister, whose name is unknown. However, the identification of these two mummies has been disputed. We do, however, know that Tutankhamen's wet nurse was called Maia.

163. Did Egyptians really wear perfumed cones of fat on their heads at special events?

In Egyptian art, women, and sometimes men, are frequently depicted with strange conical structures balanced on their heads.

The usual explanation is that these were cones of fat that had been impregnated with perfume. As the event progressed the fat would melt, so releasing its perfumes on the wig or hair of the wearer.

However, in the absence of evidence either of greasy wigs or the means of attaching these fat cones to the wearer's head, some have suggested that the depiction of these cone-headed people was merely an artistic device to suggest good cheer, nice smells and riches sufficient to buy perfume.

See also MEDICINE 287, MURDER 316, PYRAMIDS 396–8, SPHINX 440–4

EINSTEIN

164. Was Einstein right about the cosmological constant?

When Albert Einstein proposed his theory of general relativity in 1916, he was concerned that the mathematics behind it suggested that gravity would cause the universe to contract and eventually to collapse in on itself. At the time, Einstein shared the general belief that the universe was unchanging in size, so to make his theory fit that idea, he introduced the notion of a 'cosmological constant' (→ COSMOLOGY 108). This allocated a density and pressure to empty space, so reducing the effect of gravity.

In 1929 the American astronomer Edwin Hubble made careful measurements that showed that other galaxies are moving away from ours, and that the universe is not unchanging in size, but actually expanding. Faced with the evidence, Einstein described the cosmological constant as the 'biggest blunder' of his life, yet recent developments in cosmology suggest that he may have been right after all – for established ideas run into problems when considering where the universe came from and where it is going. We may now be agreed that everything started with a Big Bang, but we cannot explain what held the universe together for long enough after that bang for matter to form and eventually coalesce into the stars and galaxies we now know. We can also calculate how old the universe is, based on the distance light has travelled since then. But we cannot explain why similar calculations seem to make some stars older than the universe itself. Einstein's cosmological constant may explain both these anomalies, and experiments now in progress at the Large Hadron Collider (LHC) at CERN in Switzerland may confirm that he was right after all. Einstein's 'biggest blunder' may yet come to the rescue of cosmologists.

165. If time and space are as inextricably linked as Einstein seemed to demonstrate, why is time so different from the other dimensions?

Einstein's idea of the space-time continuum is one of the most powerful and profound scientific ideas of all time. Writing of the unsustainability in his new physics of the concept of 'now', he said: 'It appears therefore more natural to think of physical reality as a four-dimensional existence, instead of, as hitherto, the evolution of a three-dimensional existence.' Einstein's theory of relativity had shown that time itself moves at different rates for different observers, and this had made it necessary to see the world as embedded in a four-dimensional space-time continuum, rather than three dimensions moving forwards in time.

But if time is on a some sort of a par with the other dimensions, why does it seem so different, and why can't we travel backwards in time?

Einstein later wrote that 'the separation between past, present and future is only an illusion, although a convincing one' – which is why this is such a difficult concept for us poor time-bound creatures to come to terms with.

166. What were the jokes that Einstein told his parrot?

In 2004 a sixty-two-page diary was found at Princeton University, covering the period from October 1953 up to Einstein's death in April 1956. It had belonged to Johanna Fantova, who was a close friend of Einstein in his final years. As well as recording Einstein's thoughts on physics and the politics of the time, Fantova recounts how, on his seventy-fifth birthday, Einstein was given a parrot. The great man decided the bird was depressed, and tried to cheer it up by telling it bad jokes. But what those jokes were, the parrot never divulged.

Education is a progressive discovery of our own ignorance.

Will Durant (1885–1981)

167. What were Einstein's last words?

Einstein died in hospital at Princeton, New Jersey, on 18 April 1955. Before he passed away, he uttered a few sentences in German. Unfortunately, the nurse attending him at the time did not speak the language, so his last words are lost. He did, however, scrawl down a few words: 'Political passions, once they have been fanned into flame, exact their victims…' The writing then trailed away.

See also BLACK HOLES 50, COSMOLOGY, 107–8, 110–11

ENGLISH HISTORY

168. Did King Arthur ever exist?

The earliest known mention of the legendary British leader known as Arthur dates back to the *Historia Brittonum* ('history of the Britons'), written in the ninth century, probably by a Welsh monk known as Nennius. Arthur only merits one paragraph in this chronicle, which does, however, list the twelve great battles he is supposed to have fought in the fifth or sixth century against the Saxon invaders. Details of these battles, such as Mons Badonicus (in which the Britons decisively defeated the Saxons at an unknown location), tie in with other historical accounts of the time. However, the earliest account of Mons Badonicus, that written by the sixth-century monk Gildas in his *De Excidiu et Conquestu Britanniae* ('on the ruin and conquest of Britain'), does not mention Arthur.

Arthur makes some brief appearances in accounts dating from the tenth and eleventh centuries, but it was the *Historia Regum Britanniae* ('history of the kings of Britain') by the twelfth-century Welsh cleric Geoffrey of Monmouth that fleshed out the story, providing the earliest known mentions of Merlin, Guinevere, Lancelot and the sword Excalibur. The earlier references had only identified Arthur as *dux bellorum* – a sort of warlord or military commander – but Geoffrey of Monmouth made him a king.

Probably inspired by Geoffrey of Monmouth, French literary romances of the twelfth and thirteenth centuries embellished the story even further, adding, for example, Arthur's legendary castle at Camelot. By the time Thomas Malory wrote *Le Morte d'Arthur* in the late fifteenth century, the Arthurian legend in its familiar form, complete with knights and Round Table, was firmly established. How much any of this tallies with the original Arthur, or whether Geoffrey of Monmouth made it all up rather than relying on now lost historical sources as he claimed, is a matter of pure speculation.

169. Why did the seventh-century Anglo-Saxons bury a longboat at Sutton Hoo, which was found with no human remains inside?

In 1939 a longboat 27 metres (almost 90 ft) in length was found buried at Sutton Hoo in Suffolk. It was one of the most magnificent and perplexing archaeological finds ever made in Britain. Inside the boat the archaeologists found golden artefacts and other precious treasures, but no human remains. The site was known as a cemetery, dated to the sixth and early seventh centuries, but this burial of a treasure-filled ship was unlike anything else. Two theories have been put forward to account for the absence of a body: either a body was originally buried with the ship, but it had been completely dissolved by chemicals in the soil; or the tomb was an early cenotaph to commemorate a powerful dignitary of the time. In either case, the person concerned is thought to have been Raedwald, a powerful East Anglian king of the seventh century. But whether he was buried with the ship or not may also be a secret that has dissolved into the soil.

170. When Edward the Confessor died in 1066, did he really say to Harold Godwinson 'I commend my wife to your care and with her my whole kingdom'? If so, what did he mean by it?

On his deathbed in the early days of 1066, King Edward the Confessor is alleged to have said those words to Harold Godwinson, apparently in contravention of his earlier promise to make William of Normandy his heir. Harold was promptly crowned king of England, but nine months later lost his life at the Battle of Hastings.

Did King Harold and his supporters invent Edward's supposed deathbed words? The earliest source appears to be the *Vita Ædwardi Regis* ('life of King Edward'), completed around 1067 and commissioned by Edward's wife, Edith of Wessex (whose marriage to Edward the Confessor was childless). Edith, the daughter of Godwin, Earl of Wessex, was Harold's sister.

Or did Edward in fact speak those words, intending only that Harold should look after the kingdom until William arrived to accede to the throne? As Edward's final illness was described as a 'malady of the brain' (most probably either a brain haemorrhage or some other form of stroke), we might also ask whether Edward was coherent enough to make his wishes clear.

171. What was the fate of Hereward the Wake?

Hereward the Wake ('the watchful one') was an Anglo-Saxon warrior who in 1070 led a revolt in the fens of East Anglia against the Norman takeover of England. He seems to have had a rebellious streak from his youth, having been exiled at the age of eighteen for disobeying his father. The anti-Norman revolt collapsed following the capture in 1071 of Hereward's base on the Isle of Ely. Hereward escaped by water, but what happened to him subsequently is more a matter of legend than fact. Some say his resistance continued and he was killed by Norman knights; others hold that he was pardoned by William the Conqueror and lived the rest of his life in peace; and the final possibility is that he never received a pardon but disappeared once more into exile and obscurity. The romanticization of his life and legend in Charles Kingsley's 1865 novel *Hereward* turned him into an archetypal English hero for the Victorian schoolroom.

172. Was the bricklayer Richard of Eastwell the illegitimate son of Richard III?

Richard III is known to have had at least two illegitimate children. There was John of Gloucester, who was appointed Captain of Calais in 1485 by his father as 'our dear bastard son', and there was Katherine Plantagenet, whose marriage in 1482 to the Earl of Pembroke was financed by the king. But there is a great mystery surrounding a third alleged illegitimate offspring, Richard of Eastwell.

Apart from a burial record for 'Rychard Plantagenet' in the parish records at Eastwell, Kent, in 1550, there is no hard evidence in support of the claim, but a number of circumstantial factors give it some credibility.

In 1546 Sir Thomas Moyle, Speaker of the House of Commons, was having some building work carried out on his property. When the workmen took a break, he noticed that while the other workers chatted and drank, one old bricklayer sat on his own reading a book in Latin. Sir Thomas went to talk to the man and gained his confidence, after which the man told his story. He had, he said, lived with a Latin schoolmaster until he was fifteen or sixteen, and did not know who his parents were, but a distinguished gentleman visited four times a year and paid for his upkeep. At the age of sixteen he was taken by the gentleman to Bosworth Field, where the forces of Richard III faced those of the would-be usurper, Henry Tudor. The boy was introduced to the king, who told him he was his son, and that he would acknowledge him if he won the battle. If he lost, the king advised the boy to conceal his identity forever. Richard was killed, Henry took the throne, and the boy fled to London, where he was apprenticed to a bricklayer.

Impressed with the tale, Sir Thomas Moyle allowed the man to live on his estate until his death. This was the story, at any rate, included by the English antiquary Francis Peck in his *Desiderata Curiosa*, a two-volume miscellany published in 1732 and 1735.

173. Was Amy, the wife of Robert Dudley, Earl of Leicester, killed so that Dudley could marry Queen Elizabeth I?

Elizabeth I was in love with Robert Dudley; Dudley was married to Amy Robsart; Amy died from a broken neck at the age of twenty-eight, her body being found at the foot of a short flight of stairs at Cumnor Place, near Oxford in 1560. The official inquest returned a verdict of 'misfortune', but the rumour at the time was that the 'misfortune' had been engineered by William Cecil, adviser to the queen, or by Dudley himself. The tragedy was subsequently fictionalized by Sir Walter Scott in his novel *Kenilworth* (1821). In this, Amy is the victim of a complex plot of deceit by Leicester's villainous steward, Varney. At the end of the novel, while Leicester entertains Elizabeth at Kenilworth, Varney engineers Amy's death at Cumnor Place, where she falls through a trapdoor.

In the mid-1950s a theory was proposed that Amy Dudley suffered from breast cancer, which could have weakened her spine, causing it to snap after a short fall. More recently, the rediscovery of the findings of the inquest has shown that the evidence could support either a fall or a more violent end.

174. Was the Gunpowder Plot an elaborate government conspiracy?

When Guy Fawkes was stopped, in the nick of time, from blowing up the Houses of Parliament in 1605, the case against the plotters looked clear-cut. It was without doubt a revolt by English Catholics against the anti-Catholic measures of King James I, whom they planned to assassinate, possibly with the idea of installing his daughter, Princess Elizabeth, as a Catholic queen (although she was not a Catholic).

That is all, no doubt, true. But there are several elements of the plot and its foiling that have suggested to many that there may be more to the story – and that Guy Fawkes and his colleagues may have been set up in an elaborate government sting, probably concocted by Robert Cecil, the king's ferociously anti-Catholic chief minister. Much of this conspiracy theory centres on a letter received by Lord Monteagle warning him to stay away from the House on the day the explosion was planned. The letter came from his cousin Francis Tresham, one of the plotters, who, it is said, may have been a double agent working directly for Cecil. Cecil's motive, according to this theory, was simply to discredit the Catholics in as dramatic a manner as possible. Otherwise, the theorists ask, how were the plotters able to rent a house so near to Parliament, how did they acquire so much gunpowder with such apparent ease, and – most of all – how did they manage to smuggle it into the cellar of the House of Lords?

175. Was James de la Cloche the illegitimate son of Charles II, as he claimed?

In 1862 the British historian Lord Acton received documents from Jesuit archives in Rome telling the extraordinary tale of James de la Cloche. The story begins in 1646, when the future King Charles II of England, then only in his teens, visited Jersey. Here he had an affair with Lady Marguerite de Carteret, as a result of which he fathered a son known as James de la Cloche.

The documents include three letters from Charles, which acknowledge that he was the father and relate how he granted James an annuity of £500 a year as long as he remained in London and practised the Protestant faith. James, however, went to Rome and joined a Jesuit seminary. He may even have acted as the king's secret and unofficial ambassador to the Vatican when Charles was contemplating converting to Rome (which, in fact, he only did on his deathbed, in 1685).

All mention of James de la Cloche in Rome ceases abruptly in 1668, but the following year a man calling himself James Stuart arrived in Naples, with the story that he was the illegitimate son of Charles II. He died in 1669, and in his will included a specific request to Charles II to grant his son a principality.

Whether James de la Cloche and James Stuart were the same person, whether either was the natural son of Charles II, and whether the letters de la Cloche showed to the Jesuits were forgeries are all still unknown. If the whole thing was fabricated, it must rank James de la Cloche as one of the greatest confidence tricksters in history.

See also ANCIENT HISTORY 14, BOUDICCA 54, DISEASE 119, THE MIDDLE AGES 298–300, 304, MURDER 319–19, 321, 324, SEX 421

ENGLISH LANGUAGE

The English language has its roots in Anglo-Saxon (known to scholars as 'Old English'), which emerged from the languages of the Germanic invaders who began to take over the country after the Romans left in the fifth century AD. But English is far from a 'pure' language, and is full of words that can be traced to Latin, Greek and Norman French, and also a great range of other languages, from Arabic ('alcohol', 'algebra', 'algorithm') and Hindi ('pyjamas', 'jodhpurs', 'bungalow') to Inuit ('anorak', 'kayak') and Australian Aboriginal ('boomerang', 'kangaroo'). Etymological research has usually been able to track the origins of any given word. The older ones can be linked by sound or spelling to the languages they came from, while the newer ones can be tracked back to their first appearances in print. Yet there are 1,098 words listed in the *Oxford English Dictionary* as 'origin unknown', and another 206 with 'origin obscure'. The examples that follow scarcely scratch the surface of our linguistic ignorance.

176. Why did jazz musicians in the 1920s start referring to an engagement as a 'gig' – and why is their music called 'jazz' anyway?

'Gig' is such a recent addition to our language that you would have thought someone would know how it started, yet the *Oxford English Dictionary* simply says 'origin unknown', before listing its earliest known uses, from 1926 and 1927, both in *Melody Maker*.

Another 'origin unknown' word is 'jazz' itself, which the *OED* suggests may be related to the word 'jasm', which is an alternative to 'jism', meaning energy or vitality. But what about the origin of those words? The *OED* again just says 'unknown', but they have been linked to Mandinki, a language of West Africa, the ancestral home of many African-Americans: in Mandinki the word *jasi* means to act in a bizarre or unusual manner, and more generally, along the West African coast, *jazz* meant 'hurry up', and the word was adopted into Louisiana Creole with this meaning, whence (some propose) it came to be applied to the fast, syncopated music popular in New Orleans at the end of the nineteenth century. This 'jazz' music made its first appearance in New York in 1915, introduced by Freddie Keppard's Original Creole Band, and made a more lasting impact with the arrival in 1917 of Nick LaRocca's Original Dixieland Jazz Band.

177. Where did the word 'bloke' come from as a slang term for a man?

The word 'bloke' has been used to mean a man or fellow for at least 150 years, and in the earlier years of the twentieth century it was used specifically to refer to a ship's captain. The nearest the *Oxford English Dictionary* can come to suggesting an origin is to cite an unlikely suggestion that it may somehow be connected to a Romany (and originally Hindi) term for a man: *loke*.

178. Where did the word 'posh' come from?

It has long been claimed that the word 'posh' derives from an acronym printed on the more expensive tickets issued by P&O in the glory days of the great ocean-going liners. 'Posh', it is claimed, stands for 'Port Out, Starboard Home', indicating the side of the ship on which the wealthier passengers would be allocated a cabin on the outward and return journeys in order to get the best of the sun (if sailing across the North Atlantic from Britain to America), or in order to be shaded from the fierce heat of the sun (if sailing from Britain to India, in the days of the British Raj).

The trouble is that nobody has ever produced one of these fabled tickets, and until one turns up, lexicographers will remain highly sceptical. Other theories include a borrowing from the Romany word *posh*, meaning a half, which was used for a halfpenny, then to money in general, whence it could have come to denote anyone rich. Or it may simply come from a quick and lazy way to say 'polished'. Finally, some claim it comes from a character called Murray Posh in George and Weedon Grossmith's comic novel *The Diary of a Nobody* (1888–9), who is described as 'quite a swell'.

179. What was the origin of the phrase 'rule of thumb'?

Did carpenters in the distant past use the length of the top joint of their thumb as a measure, equal approximately to one inch? If so, the word 'rule' in the phrase 'rule of thumb' refers to the use of the thumb as a ruler. Or does the phrase refer to the practice among brewers of using their thumbs to test the temperature of the fermenting liquid? Or does the phrase refer to a medieval by-law, which permitted men to beat their wives, but only with a stick no thicker than their thumbs? The latter explanation is very popular among amateur lexicographers, but there no evidence at all to support it. In fact, that explanation was offered first in the 1970s, while the phrase has been in use at least since the 1690s.

180. What was the origin of the phrase 'the full Monty'?

For an expression that has only come into common use comparatively recently – especially after the release of the film *The Full Monty* in 1997 – the origin of the phrase is curiously obscure. Some say it is simply a corruption of 'the full amount'. Others claim that it is a reference to the hero of El Alamein, Field Marshal Bernard Montgomery (1887–1976), affectionately known to his men as 'Monty', and that the phrase refers either to his full chest of medals, or to his liking for a full English breakfast. Others again suggest that the phrase might be a reference to full three-piece suits sold by the tailor Montague Burton (1885–1952), or to bets placed at the famous casino in Monte Carlo, or to full bales of wool from Montevideo.

A combination of the field marshal and the tailor seems the most likely, though who came first is anyone's guess.

181. How did the game of golf get its name?

There is a popular tale, for which there is no supporting evidence whatsoever, that the first golf club displayed a sign saying 'Gentlemen Only, Ladies Forbidden', giving rise to an acronym by which the game became known. That is almost certainly entirely apocryphal. The earliest known appearance of the word 'golf' was in an act of King James II of Scotland in 1457 banning the game, and this was centuries before people began to form words from initial letters. Indeed, the earliest citation for the word 'acronym' in this sense in the *Oxford English Dictionary* dates back only to 1943. Perhaps the 'Gentlemen Only' sign was advanced as a derivation because nobody seems to have come up with any other convincing explanation. The Scots word *gowf* means a blow or slap, but it seems more likely that the word in this sense came from the game rather than the other way round. There is also a Dutch word *kolf*, meaning a club or bat, which may have something to do with it, but no link has ever been established.

While we are on the subject of false acronyms, perhaps I should also mention that there is no evidence that those accused of certain immoral acts ever had 'For Unlawful Carnal Knowledge' stamped on their charge sheets.

EVOLUTION

182. How did life on Earth begin?

Our planet has been in existence for about 4.6 billion years, and for about the last 3.5 billion years there has been some sort of life on it. Even the simplest life forms that have been detected, however, are remarkably complex organisms, and the idea that they could have arisen by chance arouses very different reactions, even among scientists. Some say there's no real problem, as there are hundreds of billions of galaxies, each with hundreds of billions of stars, so even events that seem impossibly unlikely are still quite likely to have happened somewhere in the universe.

Others insist that the simplest life forms must themselves have evolved from simpler self-replicating molecules (such as DNA), and there is currently a good deal of research aimed at creating such organisms in the laboratory. This could provide evidence that such events could have happened in the conditions on the early Earth.

183. How did complex cells evolve from simple ones?

In 1952 Stanley Miller and Harold Urey at the University of Chicago performed an experiment showing that amino acids, which have been called the 'building blocks of life', could have formed spontaneously from inorganic chemicals thought to have been present in the Earth's atmosphere almost 4 billion years ago. While essential to life, however, amino acids cannot themselves be considered life forms. They are the components of proteins, a wide range of even more complex molecules which – along with nucleic acids (such as DNA), carbohydrates and lipids – are essential to the structure and function of the living cell as we know it today. But what form the first truly living things took is still a matter of speculation.

The most likely candidates are prokaryotes, simple single-celled organisms such as bacteria, which do not have a nucleus. Their name comes from the Greek karyon, meaning 'kernel', and pro-, 'before' or 'prior'. The name distinguishes them from the far more complex eukaryotic (the prefix eu- meaning 'true' or 'good') cells, as found in the group of more evolved unicellular organisms known as protists (including, for example, amoebae and single-celled algae), together with plants, fungi and animals. Although both types of cell are DNA-based, their structures and mode of functioning are very different, which makes it difficult to see how eukaryotic cells could have evolved from prokaryotic ancestors. The most plausible suggestion is that groups of prokaryotic cells may have joined together in symbiotic (mutually supportive) colonies, from which the eukaryotic cells developed. The process may even have started with one cell eating another. Yet it is unlikely that we will ever be able to produce any incontrovertible evidence that such a process actually took place.

184. Which came first, the gene or the protein?

The very basis of life as we know it consists of amino acids organized into proteins, whose construction is mediated by the nucleic acids DNA or RNA. But the nucleic acids are themselves synthesized through processes involving proteins. So proteins and DNA (which carries genetic information) appear to be inseparable, yet they are too distinct to have evolved together.

One theory, known as the RNA-world hypothesis, is that life on Earth began with organisms based on RNA (ribonucleic acid), from which DNA and genes evolved, which gave rise to proteins. In contrast, the iron-sulphur-world theory proposes that the earliest life comprised a very simple form of metabolism, without genetics, that occurred on the surface of minerals through complex chemical reactions fuelled by volcanic activity. These early cells could then have evolved into proteins, from which the nucleic acids and genes emerged.

185. Who or what was LUCA (the Last Universal Common Ancestor)?

Just as the name 'Mitochondrial Eve' has been given to the most recent woman whom all people on Earth can claim as a direct ancestor, the acronym LUCA has been bestowed on the hypothetical living organism much further back in time from which all organisms now alive descended. Since the genetic code was first deciphered in the 1960s, we have come to realize that all cellular life has a great deal in common. All life stores its genetic information on DNA, in packets called genes, which contain the recipes for making RNA and proteins.

If everything living operates under the same rules, it seems reasonable to assume that way back it all stemmed from the same common ancestor, and the last such ancestor must have been around after DNA had evolved, but long before life forms split into the myriad variants we see today, from bacteria to plants, reptiles, mammals and humans.

186. Has evolution in general been a gradual process, or have species evolved by sudden jumps between periods of stasis?

There are two theories about the pace at which the evolutionary process works. Darwin's own conception was that it is gradual and going on all the time; small changes in organisms build up over long periods into big ones. One objection to that idea, however, was the absence in the fossil record of evidence of the intermediate forms that would substantiate this gradualist theory. Darwin himself was troubled by these evolutionary missing links, though others have argued that the fossil record should be expected to have a great deal missing, as fossilization is something that only happens by chance, when conditions are appropriate.

In 1972, however, the American palaeontologists Stephen Jay Gould and Niles Eldredge proposed a theory they called 'punctuated equilibrium', which proposed that species tend to remain the same for long periods, then change with a sudden jerk. Furthermore, Gould and Eldredge maintained that such changes do not occur in the mainstream population, where interbreeding is likely to nullify rather than encourage changes, but on the fringes of a population, where a group with the modified gene live in relative isolation, allowing the genetic change to be preserved, if it is better suited to survival than the older genetic make-up. While evidence has been found in the fossil record of some examples that appear to conform to the patterns of punctuated equilibrium, it is by no means clear whether such patterns are normal or only of rare occurrence. Those who believe such patterns are rare hold to the theory called 'punctuated gradualism', which maintains that generally speaking the process of evolution is slow and gradual, but every now and again it speeds up rapidly.

See also DNA 132–4, GENETICS 206–14, GIRAFFES 215–16,
HUMAN EVOLUTION 237–41

FOOTBALL (AMERICAN)

187. To what extent are American footballers and dwarfs prone to chronic traumatic encephalopathy (CTE)?

CTE is a neurodegenerative disease caused by repeated trauma to the head. However, its symptoms – which may include tremors, speech problems and dementia – usually occur only many years after the injuries. Signs of CTE were first observed in boxers about eighty years ago, and was associated with being 'punch drunk', but more recently it has been observed in American footballers – and in a dwarf who had participated in dwarf-throwing contests, in which he had been knocked out on a dozen occasions.

Yet nobody knows why symptoms take so long to appear, or how many hits to the head, or how hard those hits need to be, for a person to develop CTE. Nor is it known if there are other causes besides blows to the head.

> There are many things of which a wise man might wish to be ignorant.
>
> Ralph Waldo Emerson (1803–82)

FRENCH HISTORY

188. Who was the Man in the Iron Mask?

From his arrest under the name Eustache Dauger in 1669 until his death in 1703 (when he was known as Marchioly), the identity of this prisoner of Louis XIV was kept a secret. Nobody was even allowed to see his face, which was kept hidden behind an iron mask. It has even been suggested that he was James de la Cloche, the alleged illegitimate son of Charles II (→ ENGLISH HISTORY 175). Did all who knew who he was take the secret with them to their graves, neither writing it down nor telling anyone? Over three hundred years later, we seem no nearer solving the mystery. Films have been made and books written in which a number of candidates have been put forward, but no real evidence has been found.

Voltaire suggested that the man in the iron mask was an older, illegitimate brother of Louis XIV; the historian Hugh Ross Williamson thought he might have been the king's natural father; but such claims that the prisoner had royal blood have been disputed on the grounds that he applied to work as valet to the prison governor, which would have been a very un-royal task. Others have proposed General Vivien de Bulonde, who, when fighting the Austrians, incurred the king's wrath by ordering a hasty withdrawal of the troops under his command. But given the prisoner was prevented from talking to or meeting anyone other than one guard at the jail, and that all his clothes and belongings were destroyed when he died, only circumstantial evidence has been offered for any of these candidates – who represent only a handful of those who have been suggested over the centuries.

Perhaps somewhere, in an old library in France, there is a forgotten slip of paper containing the answer to this mystery. The vital clue may not exist or may never be found, but it could turn up tomorrow.

189. Did anyone ever say 'Qu'ils mangent de la brioche'?

That line – so often attributed to Marie Antoinette, wife of Louis XVI, and most commonly translated as 'Let them eat cake' – seems to have its origins in Jean-Jacques Rousseau's *Confessions*, which were written in the late 1760s, when Marie Antoinette was still a teenaged Austrian archduchess living in Vienna. Rousseau says they were spoken by 'a great princess' on hearing that the peasants had no bread, but he does not specify who this princess was.

Louis XVIII, in his memoirs, describes the line as an old legend, and says that within his family it was usually attributed to Maria Theresa, wife of Louis XIV. Those memoirs, however, were written after Rousseau's *Confessions*, which may have influenced his thoughts.

The connection with Marie Antoinette no doubt came about through her growing unpopularity in the years leading up to the French Revolution, a time when her opponents would gladly have seized upon Rousseau's story and attached her name to it. But where Rousseau got it from is not known.

190. What colour was Charlotte Corday's hair?

Charlotte Corday, who was guillotined in 1793 (→ CONSCIOUSNESS 104) for the assassination of the radical Jacobin leader Jean-Paul Marat, became a martyr and heroine of the Girondists, the moderate party during the French Revolution. But what colour was her hair?

Of the many paintings of her, most were done posthumously and portray her as dark-haired, but in some portraits done from life, she is depicted as a brunette. Her passport, however, describes her hair colour as chestnut, while a crime scene painting done by Jean-Jacques Hauer shortly after the murder shows her as fair-haired. It has been suggested, however, that for the purposes of that painting, Hauer wished to portray her as vain and aristocratic, so made her look as though she had powdered her hair.

191. Who was the first person to cross the Pont Julien?

The Pont Julien near Lacoste, a picturesque mountain village tucked away in the Vaucluse department of southeast France, is a rare example of a Roman bridge dating back to the 1st century BC. The bridge was closed to traffic in 2005, when the last person to cross it was Finnbar Mac Eoin, author of *Two Suitcases and a Dog*. A plaque on the bridge marks the event, saying: 'We do not know who was the first person to cross, but an Irishman was the last.'

See also THE MIDDLE AGES 298–300, MURDER 320

FUNDAMENTAL PARTICLES

192. Is there hope for the theory of super-symmetry?

Physicists have long been searching for a 'Theory of Everything' that will explain in a coherent way all the forces that hold the universe together. Despite the development of quantum mechanics and the theory of relativity, the search seemed to be getting no further, but one of the latest candidates is string theory, of which we shall have more to say later (→ PHYSICS 369, QUANTUM PHYSICS 401).

One of the predictions of string theory, however, is that at higher energy levels we should start to see evidence of a symmetry in the elementary particles. Known as super-symmetry (or SUSY for short), the theory gives every particle that transmits a force (a boson) a partner particle that makes up matter (a fermion), and vice versa. The trouble is that none of the predicted particles was ever detected until the Large Hadron Collider at CERN in Switzerland came up with its convincing evidence for the Higgs boson. Before that, even some fervent supporters of SUSY were beginning to suggest that it may have to be abandoned. Even with the discovery of the Higgs, a great deal of evidence is still lacking, but hope for SUSY has now been rekindled.

193. Are quarks made of even smaller particles?

The Greeks had a word for a fundamental particle: they called it an atom, which meant indivisible. In 1897 the English physicist J.J. Thompson discovered the electron, showing that atoms were divisible after all. Later, it was found that the electrons were in orbit round a tiny nucleus, constituting most of the mass of the atom and comprising particles called protons and neutrons. Then, in 1964, the American physicist Murray Gell-Mann proposed that protons and neutrons were made up of even smaller particles, which he dubbed quarks (borrowing a word from James Joyce's novel *Finnegans Wake*). There are six different types, or 'flavours', of quark, known by the rather picturesque names of up, down, top, bottom, strange and charm, none of which can exist on their own, but which combine in various ways to form other particles. But whether the search for smaller and smaller particles will stop with the quark, nobody can say.

194. Do protons decay into quarks, which could then form other fundamental particles?

As mentioned above (→ 192), for many decades the Holy Grail of physics research has been the search for a 'Theory of Everything', bringing together the four fundamental forces governing the behaviour of matter. These are electromagnetism, the strong force (which holds elementary particles together to form atoms and molecules), the weak force (which is responsible for radioactive decay), and gravity.

As the Theory of Everything seemed to grow ever more elusive, the search was narrowed to finding a 'Grand Unified Theory' (GUT) that would explain the first three of these forces, leaving out the problem of gravity, which is a very much weaker force than the other three, although it works over great distances. With the development of the quark-based 'Standard Model' of particle physics, several GUTs have been proposed and their predictions tested experimentally.

One such prediction concerns the transformation of protons into neutrons and vice versa. This has been observed experimentally in free neutrons and protons, which are not bound to other particles in an atomic nucleus, but the bound versions are highly stable. In fact, the theories predict a decay process with a half-life of about 10^{32} years. That's about the age of the universe, with another 22 zeroes added to the end. Experiments to detect signs of such a process taking place have yet to produce any evidence supporting it.

195. What will the discovery of the Higgs boson lead to?

When this book first came out in the autumn of 2011, this item read: 'Does the Higgs boson exist?' However, in July 2012, scientists at the Large Hadron Collider at Cern in Switzerland announced the discovery of a particle that, with '99 per cent certainty' they believed to be the elusive Higgs boson. Later the same month, they upgraded their confidence to 99.99 per cent. But now that we know the Higgs exists, the question remains: So what?

The Higgs boson was the one remaining particle predicted by the so-called Standard Model that had remained unconfirmed. Then Standard Model describes all particles in terms of matter and force. Matter is made from a class of particles called fermions, which may be either quarks or leptons, and force is accounted for by another class of particles: bosons.

Quarks and leptons each come in six forms, held together by four types of boson. The fifth boson, named after the English physicist Peter Higgs who first proposed its existence in the 1960s, is believed to be what gives particles their mass and is therefore the key to the transformation of energy into matter in the first fraction of a second after the Big Bang.

What happens now, however, is a matter of pure speculation. When Quantum Mechanics was first developed, nobody had any idea of what it would lead to. So much modern technology, from the development of transistors to the fine-tuning of televisions, from ultra-accurate atomic clocks to nanotechnology depend on quantum theory. No doubt the Higgs boson will be found to have practical applications, but nobody yet seems to have any idea what they might be.

196. Where does the discovery of the Higgs boson leave the standard model?

Many physicists were hoping that the Higgs would not be discovered because of perceived inadequacies in the Standard Model. Its discovery has confirmed the Model, yet this does not account for gravity or offer any explanation for the dark matter and dark energy (→ COSMOLOGY 106–8) which are thought to account for over 95 per cent of the mass of the universe. If the Higgs turns energy into mass, does it have a role in the evolution of dark matter?

197. Why do some particles have mass, while others have none?

According to current theory, photons, which are particles of light, have no mass, while other particles, such as electrons and quarks, do have mass. Quite what the difference is, and why there is a difference at all, is unknown. According to supporters of the Higgs boson theory, a 'Higgs field' permeates the entire universe and interacts with mass-less particles to give them mass. This is another problem that the Large Hadron Collider may throw light on. But whether that light can be transformed into mass is another matter.

See also QUANTUM PHYSICS 399–407

GAMES

198. How did the children's string game of cat's cradle spread to so many different cultures?

The game of cat's cradle, played by two people and involving the manipulation of loops of string held around the fingers, clearly has a long history. It has been found among diverse populations around the world, with several anthropologists reporting attempts to teach it to children in isolated communities to gain their trust and friendship, only to discover that they already knew it.

Everyone from the Inuit of the Arctic to tribes in sub-Saharan Africa seems to know cat's cradle, but whether it was invented independently by a number of cultures or has one origin from which it spread throughout the world is unknown. Even the origin of its name is disputed. Some say that it is a corruption of 'cratch-cradle' (i.e. manger-cradle), but the *Oxford English Dictionary* describes that as a 'guess' that is 'not founded on facts'. The earliest known use of the name in English dates from 1768, but the game itself is probably much older.

199. What was the fifth card in Wild Bill Hickok's fatal hand besides the aces and eights?

When Wild Bill Hickok was shot in the back of the head on 2 August 1876 while playing poker in Saloon No. 10 at Deadwood, South Dakota, it was widely reported that he was holding two pairs, of aces and eights. Those cards are even known as 'Dead Man's Hand', but there are five cards in a poker hand, so what was the other one?

The earliest known account of the hand came many years later from Ellis Pierce, the town barber, who was called to prepare the body for burial. He told of the aces and eights, but did not mention the fifth card. The modern No 10. Saloon, built in the image of the original where Wild Bill was shot, displays the hand on its wall – with the fifth card as the nine of diamonds. The Adams Museum, however, also displays the hand, with the queen of hearts as the fifth card, while the five of diamonds, jack of diamonds and queen of clubs have also been claimed as the fifth card.

There is, of course, the possibility that only four cards had been dealt and the deal was interrupted when Hickok was shot...

200. Is there a sudoku puzzle with sixteen numbers in the initial set-up with a unique solution?

SOLVED! No there isn't! In 2012, three mathematicians from Cornell University in New York proved by an exhaustive computer search that a 16-number sudoku does not exist. This is the only one of the 1002 original Things That Nobody Knows questions that has now been definitively answered.

201. Can bacteria solve sudoku puzzles?

In an extraordinary experiment at the University of Tokyo in 2010, *E. coli* bacteria were shown to be able to solve simple sudoku-like puzzles. The experiment involved sixteen types of modified *E. coli* bacteria, each of which was given a distinct genetic identity according to the square it had been assigned in a four-by-four grid. The bacteria were also designed to be able to adopt one of four 'colours'. Some of the bacteria were allocated colours; others were left to determine their own.

By means of RNA, the bacteria could transmit their position and colour details to each other. Additional programming of the genes prevented the bacteria whose colour had not been assigned from adopting the same colour as any other in the same row, column or two-by-two block as itself. In other words, the same rules as sudoku. The experiment showed not only that the bacteria choose the right colours to complete the grid, but that they 'solve' all the squares at the same time.

The researchers say that by expanding these principles to eighty-one types of bacteria, a full nine-by-nine grid could be solved. But that has yet to be confirmed in practice.

202. What is the result of a chess game if both sides play perfectly?

With best play, the game of noughts-and-crosses (tic-tac-toe in the USA) should end in a draw, as it is not difficult to demonstrate. In the more complex game of Connect Four, it was shown by exhaustive analysis in 1974 that the first player can force a win. The still more challenging game of gomoku (five in a row) was solved by computer in 1994, showing that the first player may again force a win with best play. But what about chess?

Results from international tournaments have supported the general view that White, who moves first, has an advantage, with results for White around 2 or 3 per cent ahead of Black. With around 10^{120} possible chess games (which is significantly more than the number of atoms in the universe, estimated at around 10^{80}), a complete analysis of chess is currently impossible. Whether White's advantage is enough to win, or whether Black can defend himself, or whether indeed with best play Black should actually win, at present appear to be unfathomable questions.

203. How many guesses does it take to win at Mastermind?

The game of Mastermind is a simple but tantalizing exercise in deduction in which one player places four pegs in a row from a set containing six colours and the other player, who cannot see the pegs, has to guess the colour of each of the concealed pegs. After each try, the guessing player is told how many pegs he has identified correctly and how many are the right colour but in the wrong place. The game continues until a correct guess is made.

Detailed analysis has shown that the guesser can always succeed in at most five moves, and that the average number required is 4.478. The unsolved question, however, is what happens if all the guesses have to be made right at the start, without waiting for the replies?

A set of six guesses is known that guarantee that the answers will allow the guesser to work out the other player's peg formation. If the colours are identified by the numbers 1, 2, 3, 4, 5, 6, just ask about (1, 2, 2, 1), (2, 3, 5, 4), (3, 3, 1, 1), (4, 5, 2, 4), (5, 6, 5, 6) and (6, 6, 4, 3) and the replies will let you work out the answer on your seventh try. However, no one has been able to work out whether this set of six can be reduced to five.

The greatest enemy of knowledge is not ignorance, it is the illusion of knowledge.

Stephen Hawking (b.1942)

GARLIC

204. Why are vampires supposed to be repelled by garlic?

The legend that garlic has the power of fending off vampires may have been popularized by Bram Stoker's novel *Dracula*, published in 1897, but it is much older than that. In Romania in particular, where much of Transylvania is now located, garlic has long been held as an effective way of warding off evil and curing disease. The practice of smearing corpses with garlic, or leaving cloves of garlic in their orifices in order to prevent evil spirits entering and to keep vampires away has also been recorded.

Some connect the garlic/vampire myth with the fact that mosquitoes are repelled by garlic. The idea that a measure to protect against one biting, disease-spreading creature was put into service against another is not totally convincing, however, as mosquitoes were only shown to spread various diseases (such as malaria and yellow fever) in the later nineteenth century. Whether the irritation of their bite alone was enough for them to be compared to Count Dracula is arguable. Garlic has long had the reputation of being health-giving, but no convincing explanation has been offered as to why it should be so repellent to vampires.

205. Does eating garlic reduce the rate of cancer and flu?

The belief that garlic is effective against a number of diseases goes back at least to the ancient Egyptians around 1500 BC. In the Middle Ages people used it in an attempt to ward off the plague, and it was given to soldiers in both World Wars in the belief that it prevented gangrene.

Over the past decade, much research has gone into the question of whether garlic has a beneficial effect against cancer, and a large number of studies have reported a positive result. Many of these, however, are based on population studies, comparing garlic consumption with cancer figures; others are based on laboratory tests on animals; and many are based on the injection of chemicals derived from garlic.

The jury is still out on the question of whether eating garlic has the desired effect, and if so, how much one ought to eat. Equally unproved by scientific studies is the reputation garlic vodka has in Russia as a way of preventing or treating flu.

GENETICS

206. How is the blueprint of the genetic code translated into building instructions through which a body is formed?

Thanks to the pioneering work of Crick and Watson (→ DNA) and the many who followed, we now know the alphabet of genetics and the details of what it spells out in the human genome. We know the genome comprises a vast string of nucleotides that come in four varieties known as A, C, T and G, which in various combinations provide the code of individual genes. We have identified the genes associated with certain characteristics and ailments, and we know that the same genes may be responsible for different but related parts in the construction of different organisms. But how does it all work? How is the genetic code read during the process of growth, and how do certain strings lead to the development of certain proteins, or blue eyes, or a susceptibility to a particular disease? We know the letters; we are beginning to pick up some of the words; but the whole process of how this is turned into a living creature is a mystery.

207. How can we predict how a gene will function?

Scientists have had great success in identifying the genes that are associated with certain functions or characteristics, but the reverse process is a very different matter. It's a bit like having a dictionary that translates English into Chinese, and trying to find a particular Chinese word in it. If that word is very similar to one that has been encountered before, you have grounds for making a good guess, but a radically new string of Chinese ideograms can pose impossible problems.

In the same way, if a string of nucleotides represented by the letters A, C, T and G is very similar to a known gene, then its function will probably be similar too. But when it bears only a small resemblance to anything seen before, we have no way of knowing what part of the body it controls or what its effect might be.

208. How do genes affect behaviour?

Long before we knew about the genetic code, and even before Darwin's theory of evolution, it was known that we inherit characteristics from our parents or more distant ancestors. Yet while the science of genetics has thrown much light on the inheritance of physical characteristics, the inheritance of behavioural characteristics has proven much more difficult to explain.

The long-running argument on the relative effects of nature and nurture on an individual's development has never been totally settled, but many studies on twins have shown that the development of attitudes, intelligence and certain personality factors all have at least a component of heredity in them. It may be that the balance of brain chemicals that can affect behaviour is directly controlled by genetic factors, but many behavioural factors are the result of a conscious decision-making process. The manner in which genes can affect such processes, or the extent to which they might do so, has yet to be discovered.

209. How do the various parts of an animal's body know when to stop growing?

Somehow, our cells (and those of every other living thing) read the genetic information from our DNA, transcribe it and copy it to messenger-RNA. The RNA is read by the next stage in the production line, which is the ribosome that uses the RNA information to produce sequences of amino acids, which in turn assemble into proteins. The RNA sequence even tells it when to stop. But the stopping instruction only refers to the end of an individual protein. How the machinery knows it has come to the end of a bone, or a nose, or a leg – and it is therefore time to stop – is another matter entirely.

210. Why don't identical twins suffer from the same genetic diseases?

Until recently, 'identical twins' were thought to have absolutely identical genes, so if one suffered from a disease that was known to be genetically transmitted, the other ought to have it too. If that was not the case, then the only available explanation was that environmental factors must be playing a part in causing the gene to do its worst, or to prevent it from so doing.

Recently, however, it has become increasingly clear that identical twins may not be genetically identical at all. A study of nineteen pairs of identical twins revealed variations in their DNA caused either by missing segments or segments that had been copied several times. The double-helix structure of DNA ensures a mechanism for repairing such errors, but for some reason it does not always operate, resulting in small differences.

Apart from copying errors, there is also something called 'gene over-expression', the situation when a gene produces more RNA and more protein than it ought to. Gene over-expression has also been identified in identical twins who do not share a genetic disease, leading to the suggestion that the over-expressed gene is responsible for causing the disease gene to come into action. But we do not know how or why.

211. Is there a genetic key that can switch off ageing in humans?

Genetic modification performed on certain living things has succeeded in doubling their lifespan or more. This has been successfully done with yeast, worms and mice. What causes the ageing factor in humans is not properly understood and a number of different factors are thought to be involved, but genes seem to play a significant part. In the organisms mentioned above, a factor was identified that turned age-regulated genes on and off. There is good reason to believe that something similar will one day be found in humans – although at this stage it is not possible even to guess the extent to which it may prolong life.

212. Does experience create a mechanism whereby genes may be turned on and off?

The idea of the French naturalist Jean-Baptiste Lamarck (1744–1829) that acquired characteristics can be inherited has been discredited since Darwin's day. But there is growing evidence for a sophisticated new theory called epigenetics, which brings back the idea of experience affecting aspects of our genetic make-up.

The basic idea behind epigenetics is not that experience can change our DNA, but that it may affect the activation of certain genes or of certain proteins associated with DNA. In some cases, the theory maintains, this may also result in the inheritance of whatever characteristic has been changed. Studies in different parts of the world have suggested that starvation, toxins and stress may all have genetic effects that last several generations.

213. How do bacteria swap genes?

Genes may pass from one generation of humans to the next, but recent discoveries have shown that bacteria have another way of doing it. Called 'horizontal gene transfer', it involves a bacterium picking up genetic information from near relatives, which may include genes that enable the bacteria to withstand antibiotics. This may help explain how bacteria are able to adapt so quickly to new environments, but how the transfer takes place has not yet been discovered.

214. Is the human genome inherently unstable and therefore bound to lead to our extinction?

The evolutionary history of the human genome has displayed its wonderful pliability, which has enabled us to change, adapt, survive and take control, to a large extent, of our environment. That same pliability, however, has fostered the parallel evolution of diseases and other life-threatening factors of ever-increasing sophistication and potential danger. A study of the extinction of other species over the ages shows that some have fallen prey to environmental change, natural disasters or similar external factors, but others have just died out, the seeds of their own extinction being apparently sown in their own genetic make-up. Will the human race go the same way?

See also AARDVARKS 1, DNA 132–4, EVOLUTION 182–6, HUMAN BEHAVIOUR 235, HUMAN EVOLUTION 237–41

GIRAFFES

215. Why do giraffes have long necks?

The old theory was that giraffes with long necks had an evolutionary advantage as they could reach the leaves that were higher in trees after the lower leaves had been eaten. There are at least three arguments against this theory, Firstly, when the long neck of the giraffe was evolving, the Earth was covered with lush vegetation and there would have been no leaf shortage at low levels. Secondly, giraffes are fussy eaters and go for certain types of leaf rather than the highest ones. Lastly, giraffes tend to eat with their necks held horizontally, not stretching upwards.

Alternative theories that have been suggested are that long necks evolved to improve a giraffe's ability to look for predators; that long necks evolved as a sexual signal; or that giraffes evolved long legs to help them run faster, and long necks then became necessary to reach to ground level to drink.

A detailed examination of all these theories, however, reached the conclusion that there was insufficient evidence to support any of them.

216. Why are so many male giraffes homosexual?

Several studies of animal sexual behaviour have remarked on the frequency of homosexual relations between male giraffes. One study even reported that over a period of observation of giraffe sexual behaviour, 94 per cent of activity was between two males, 5 per cent was male–female and 1 per cent female–female.

While some have pointed out the potential evolutionary advantage of a gay gene, in that it may provide additional male help in the family in looking after children, the gay giraffe figure is surprisingly high.

See also SLEEP 428

THE GREEKS

217. How did Socrates make a living?

Considering the huge influence of Socrates on the subsequent course of Western philosophy, it is remarkable how little we know about the fifth-century BC Athenian thinker. Almost all we do know comes from the philosophical writings of his followers Plato and Xenophon and the comic plays of Aristophanes. Nobody bothered with a biography. Socrates himself did not even write down his own ideas, for which we rely largely on Plato's *Dialogues*. Yet how much of these are Plato's own thoughts put into Socrates' mouth and how much was genuine Socratic wisdom has long been argued.

On the matter of what Socrates did for a living, we face not so much a lack of information as a good deal of evidence that he did nothing. In Plato's *Apology*, Socrates cites his poverty as evidence that he is not a teacher. Xenophon also has him denying that he ever accepted payment for his teachings and quotes him as saying that he devotes himself entirely to discussing philosophy. Later writers said that he followed his father's profession of stonemasonry, but no evidence has been found to support that assertion. Socrates did, however, marry the much younger Xanthippe, who bore him three sons, so he must have had some sort of income to support them.

What we do know is that he annoyed the Athenian establishment so much that in 399 BC he was tried and found guilty of atheism and corrupting the youth of the city. As a result he was sentenced to kill himself by drinking hemlock.

> I know nothing except the fact of my ignorance.
>
> Socrates

218. Did Pythagoras ever exist?

We may not know much about Socrates, but we know even less about the person who gave his name to the famous theorem about the square of the hypotenuse (→ THE UNIVERSE 461). The Pythagorean school of philosophy – which proposed that number and ratio underlay the workings of the universe – flourished as a secret sect in the late sixth century BC, but nothing was written about Pythagoras himself until hundreds of years later.

The lack of information may have been due, in part at least, to the secrecy of the brotherhood and the cult it spawned – whose followers believed, among other things, in the transmigration of souls and the sinfulness of eating beans. Some have suggested that there never was a man called Pythagoras, but that he was a fictional figurehead in whose name the theories and discoveries of the brotherhood could be issued.

219. What was the secret behind the Greeks' use of fire as a weapon?

Towards the end of the seventh century AD, the Byzantine empire, centred on the predominantly Greek-speaking city of

Constantinople, introduced a new secret weapon, used both on land and at sea. Described as 'liquid fire', it was projected from siphons on enemy positions or ships, bursting into flames on contact and being notoriously difficult to extinguish. Fire had long been used in battle, but this 'Greek fire', as it became known, was far fiercer than anything that had previously been seen, causing panic and destruction wherever it was used. The secret behind the weapon was passed from one Byzantine emperor to the next for centuries.

Even when siphons and samples of the flammable material and even entire fire ships were captured by enemies, attempts to reproduce the secret formula failed, and neither the principal chemicals in the composition of Greek fire nor the alleged 'secret ingredient' it contained were ever discovered. By the early thirteenth century the use of Greek fire as a weapon had faded away. Perhaps the formula had been lost, or perhaps its makers could no longer obtain the required ingredients.

See also ANCIENT HISTORY 17, 19, VENUS DE MILO 467

HAIR

220. Why do we have pubic hair?

There are several theories:

(i) Pubic hair evolved as a way of signalling our sexual maturity to members of the opposite sex.

(ii) It provides protection for a delicate part of our anatomies.

(iii) The hair helps the body retain the pheromones produced by our glands to signal to the opposite sex and entice them to reproduce. In other words, the hair is good because it makes us smellier.

221. Why does the hair on our heads grow so long?

From an evolutionary point of view, our ability to grow our hair so long seems strange. The common ancestor we share with the other apes is generally assumed to have been hairy. In the course of our evolution away from our ape relatives, we have gradually shed most of our body hair. Yet on our heads the hair grows much longer than that of any other ape, or indeed almost any other mammal. Most of the rest of the hair on our bodies grows to a certain length then falls out, which is the way most mammal hair behaves, yet on our heads, and even on men's chins, it may grow to a length of a metre or more.

Once again, sexual selection has been offered as an explanation, but whether it is the beauty of the long hair, or the belief that it signals some sort of fitness, or the smells it may retain, is not specified.

It is impossible to make people understand their ignorance; for it requires knowledge to perceive it and therefore he that can perceive it hath it not.

Jeremy Taylor (1613–67)

HANDEDNESS

222. Is it true that most, if not all, polar bears are left-handed?

Open almost any book of trivia and you will find the following claim: All polar bears are left-handed. You will also, in all probability, read that 'A duck's quack doesn't echo', which is complete nonsense, but has been copied by so many indiscriminate trivia peddlers from other dealers in junk factoids that the sentence now racks up 'about 226,000' hits on Google. By contrast, the left-handed polar bear statement scores only 'about 90,000', but the jury is still out on the matter.

The anthropologist Richard Nelson, who spent a year in the 1960s living in an Inuit (Eskimo) community in the village of Wainwright in the north of Alaska, just inside the Arctic Circle, reported the advice he had received to dive to your right if attacked by a charging polar bear:

> *Inupiaq elders say polar bears are left-handed, so you have a slightly better chance to avoid their right paw, which is slower and less accurate. I'm pleased to say I never had the chance for a field test. But in judging assertions like this, remember that Eskimos have had close contact with polar bears for several thousand years.*

It has been suggested that the story of the left-handed polar bear may have had its origins in an account by an Inupiaq elder who saw one polar bear using its left paw, from which he generalized. There is also an often repeated claim that polar bears, when hunting seals, cover their black noses with their right paws in order to conceal their presence against the snowy background while leaving their dominant left paws free to swipe the seal when close enough. That too is based solely on anecdotal evidence.

Sadly, however, there is a great lack of proper scientific investigation of these matters. The paper most often quoted to counter the left-handed polar bear claim is a 2004 study into limb fractures of captive polar bears. In this, the author notes that more injuries occur to the right limbs than the left limbs, from which she draws the tentative conclusion that polar bears use their right limbs more than their left. One might, however, draw the opposite conclusion by suggesting that they are more likely to damage their right limbs because they are more adept at using their left paws. In any case, the number of polar bears in the study was too small to draw strong conclusions.

It is surely time for the scientific and Inuit communities to join forces to resolve this matter. A proper study of handedness in polar bears is long overdue.

223. What proportion of walruses are left-flippered?

In 2003 a team of researchers led by Nette Levermann of the University of Copenhagen, filmed the feeding behaviour of walruses. After dividing the film into 20-second sections, they examined each segment for preferential use of right or left flipper in collecting molluscs and cleaning them before eating. Their results showed that in 89 per cent of the segments in which a flipper is being used, it was the right flipper. This result was widely reported, but with differing interpretations. Some said that all walruses are right-flippered and use that flipper 89 per cent of the time; others said that 89 per cent of walruses are right-flippered, which is much the same ratio as right-handed humans.

To find out which interpretation is correct, I contacted Nette Levermann. She said she didn't know. She was not even sure how many walruses she and her team had filmed, but it was at least five and all were male. Examination of the bones in walrus flippers, however, supports the view that walruses are predominantly right-flippered.

224. What evolutionary advantages arise from right- or left-handedness in humans?

About 90 per cent of humans are right-handed; most of the rest are left-handed, as ambidexterity is rare. Yet why we should have evolved to prefer one hand over the other is difficult to explain. It may have something to do with the use of tools and the acquisition of specialist abilities where there could be advantages in having one hand doing delicate work and the other relegated to basic jobs such as holding or pushing. Or it could have something to do with the development of hemispheric differences in the brain, with certain activities performed by the left-brain and others by the right-brain. Such asymmetric brain development would be expected to lead to differing hand preferences. Yet all such explanations are no more than speculations.

225. Is handedness in some way connected to the acquisition of language skills?

Whatever the reason for having a dominant hand, the next natural question is to ask why most humans favour right over left. Again lateral asymmetry in the brain has been invoked, with the suggestion that right-handedness may be connected with the acquisition of language, as we know that the language centres of the brain are usually on the left side, and the left side of the brain controls the right hand.

In 2011 the psychologist Dr Gillian Forrester published the results of detailed observations of hand usage by a family of gorillas.

While they tended overall to use their two hands equally for tasks she classified as 'social interaction' (such as scratching their head, patting a friend on the back or mothering), they were more likely to use their right hands for inanimate targets (such as using objects and eating or preparing food).

Previous studies on great apes had not identified any consistent population-wide bias for one hand or the other outside humans. The new study, Forrester suggests, may offer evidence that a preference for the right hand in specific tasks may have been the first step in evolving left-brain language skills. 'The basic hierarchy of steps required to make and use tools could be akin to providing us with the scaffolding to build a syntax for language,' she says.

However, while around 10 per cent of people are left-handed, only 5 per cent have their language skills on the right side of their brain. So whether left-handers are right- or left-brained for language skills seems to be equally likely.

See also CATS 72, CHIMPANZEES 77

HUMAN BEHAVIOUR

226. Why do people blush?

We know that blushing is strongly connected to adrenaline. Heightened emotions lead to increased adrenaline levels, which cause the chemical transmitter adenylyl cyclase to send signals to the veins in our face, increasing the blood flow and making us blush. That is a fair answer to the mechanics of blushing, but does not tell us why we blush. What is the evolutionary advantage of having a sympathetic nervous system that tells other people when we are feeling embarrassed? Why is it mainly our faces that blush (though blushing has also been observed to a lesser extent on the neck, chest and even legs)? And why should blind people blush more than sighted people, as some experimental evidence seems to suggest?

227. Why do people cry at emotional times?

Tears come in three basic varieties: there are basal tears, which moisten the eye and protect it; there are reflex tears, which are shed to flush out the eye when it becomes irritated; and most puzzling of all are the emotional tears that flow when we are happy, sad, in pain, or otherwise overcome with strong feelings.

Chemical analysis has shown that emotional tears are higher than the other types in manganese, which is known to be connected with temperament, and prolactin, a hormone that regulates milk production. The natural painkiller leucine enkephalin is also found in tears. Crying may thus help to balance the body's stress levels and provide relief by preventing build-ups of these chemicals, and they may somehow be connected with the reduction of pain. Why this should all happen through tears rather than any of the other, probably more efficient, ways the body has of producing beneficial chemicals and expelling unwanted by-products has not been established.

228. Why do we yawn?

Why we yawn, why other people yawning makes us yawn, and why our yawning makes dogs yawn (→ DOGS 136) are very puzzling questions. One theory is that it has something to do with gasping for oxygen and that it may be a relic from a stage in prenatal development connected to the breathing process. However, experiments in which subjects have been given different amounts of oxygen to breathe have shown no difference in their yawning behaviour, so a need for oxygen seems unlikely to be a cause. Another theory is that it may be caused by a gene that had something to do with the gills of the fish-like creatures from which we are all descended.

One idea that has been supported by experiments is that yawning may help to cool the brain or the body. It has been demonstrated that budgerigars yawn more in a warm room than in a cold one, and that they yawn most of all during periods when the temperature is rising. Human yawning also changes with temperature: people holding a cold pack to their foreheads yawn less than those holding a warm pack. Whether that shows yawning to be a cooling mechanism, however, is arguable.

229. Why do we kiss?

The Austrian psychoanalyst Sigmund Freud (1856–1939) said that kissing has its origins in breast-feeding, specifically the pouting movements that a baby's lips makes when searching for a nipple. Some suggest that it goes back to a time when mothers would chew food for their babies and deliver it mouth-to-mouth.

Another theory is that kissing is part of a tasting and smelling ritual that is useful in selecting a mate. The scent glands on a person's face may help a person select the partner with whom they will have the healthiest offspring. Another idea is that kissing may be a way of demonstrating one's good intentions and earning trust. Just as stroking instead of hitting demonstrates goodwill and sensitivity, kissing instead of biting may give a positive message.

Yet none of this explains why certain cultures, such as Australian Aborigines or the inhabitants of certain South Pacific islands, never kissed until the Europeans arrived and taught them how. Even the Chinese did not habitually indulge in kissing to any great extent until recently. Whether kissing is something in our genes, developed through evolution, or whether it is learned behaviour is still passionately debated.

230. What was the origin of laughter?

Anatomically, laughter is caused by the epiglottis constricting the larynx, but why should our epiglottis constrict our larynx when we are amused, or tickled, or happy, or experiencing a release of tension? Research with bonobos (pygmy chimpanzees from West Africa) shows a strong similarity between the laughter of tickled bonobo infants and the laughter of human babies, and this supports the view that laughter emerged very early in human evolution, before our ancestors diverged from the apes around 4 million years ago. It has recently been suggested that laughter emerged as the communication skills of the brain were evolving. Even before we began to talk, laughter enabled entire groups to share a good feeling, so it may have been one of our earliest social skills. Confirming such a theory, however, is far from easy.

231. Why are we ticklish?

Laughing when tickled is a strange mixture of physiological and psychological responses. Generally speaking, it is the most sensitive areas of the body that are the most likely to be ticklish – but this is not always the case. Feet, for example, are usually more ticklish than hands, even though they are less sensitive. There also seems to be an element of surprise needed for tickling to work properly, which may explain why we cannot tickle ourselves. As with laughter, it has been suggested that tickling is a form of communication, but recent research has suggested that ticklishness may not be confined to humans and apes, and that the vocalizations of tickled rats have a lot in common with those of tickled human babies, which is very difficult to reconcile with any psychological theories of tickling.

232. Why do people like music?

'As neither the enjoyment nor the capacity of producing musical notes are faculties of the least use to man in reference to his daily habits of life, they must be ranked among the most mysterious with which he is endowed.' So wrote Charles Darwin in *The Descent of Man* (1871). In the century and a half that has passed since Darwin made that comment, the mystery of music has scarcely diminished at all.

Music of some sort seems to have existed in every known human culture throughout every age, which leads to the almost inescapable conclusion that an ear for music and a love of music are innate human traits that must have developed at some stage of our evolution long ago. For the 'music gene' to have survived and become so prevalent, it must be beneficial either to survival or to our ability to reproduce. To argue the first case, one would have to show that an appreciation of music somehow made humans better suited to cope with their environment; in the second case, one would need to show that being musical improves a human's chances of finding a mate and/or having healthy offspring.

Some have speculated that the rhythms and varying pitches in music may have a physical effect through setting up sympathetic resonances in the body, but there are no precise suggestions as to how this might work. Darwin thought it so unlikely that music gave any biological advantage that he concluded that it must be some sort of mating display, comparable to birdsong. Others, however, have found that analogy highly unconvincing. The French anthropologist Claude Lévi-Strauss wrote in 1971: 'Although ornithologists and acousticians agree about the musicality of the sounds uttered by birds, the gratuitous and unverifiable hypothesis of the existence of a genetic relation between birdsong and music is hardly worth discussing.' Nevertheless, the idea of music having its origins as a form of sexual display has attracted growing interest in recent years, and when opponents have cited the early death of so many pop stars as an argument against any supposed evolutionary advantage of musicality, supporters of the theory have insisted that the existence of groupies lends weight to its claim to be useful for reproductive success.

In that respect, an analogy between the evolution of human musicality and peacock's tails has been suggested. The peacock's proud display of its tail feathers is a potent display of its strength and masculinity, so females pick the males with the best tails. This not only strengthens the survival value of the good-tail gene, but also favours the peahens who go for males with big tails. The importance of the tail display thus grows, to a point where huge tails are in danger of becoming an encumbrance. In a similar fashion, musical production and musical appreciation feed on one another, leading to ever greater complexity in music and the development of different types of music in different cultures. A tenuous argument perhaps, but probably the best alternative to Darwin's dismissal of musicality as a complete mystery.

233. Why does heat make people aggressive?

For more than a century, a wide range of studies have confirmed that people think and act more aggressively when they are hot. Analysis of violent crime statistics shows higher rates during hot weather than when it is cold, while experiments with subjects in temperature-controlled rooms show that those in the hot rooms have more violent and aggressive thoughts than those who are kept chilled.

Yet other experiments, as well as common experience, indicate that being hot makes people lethargic and lacking energy. This is highly paradoxical: aggression and violence demand energy, so how is it that the same thing can lead to a decrease in energy but an increase in aggression? This sort of question continues to leave students of human behaviour hot and bothered.

234. Does birth order affect personality development?

Writing in 1908, the Austrian psychologist Alfred Adler asserted that birth order played a significant role in determining personality. Firstborn children, he claimed, would have a greater chance of growing up to become leaders, thanks to their being the oldest in the family and having the responsibility of looking after their younger siblings. They would also be more likely to suffer from neuroses and even substance addiction, caused by their feeling of abandonment when the parents started lavishing attention on a younger child.

For similar reasons, Adler said that the middle child in a three-child family would grow up to be the most well balanced and have the greatest chance of success in life, while the youngest would have poor social relationships and be the most likely to take risks, thanks to having been spoiled by his or her parents.

Adler (a second child) did not produce any research to support these assertions, which he felt sure must be true because they fitted with the Freudian model of personality development. A large number of studies have been done over the past hundred years or so to test Adler's claims, but the results have varied greatly, some producing no correlations whatsoever between birth order and personality factors, others producing support for the beliefs, and a few producing results in the opposite direction from those predicted.

Even those who agree that birth order *does* have effects on personality development are unclear to what extent this is due to parental behaviour towards their offspring or whether some of it might be due to an innate predisposition the child is born with.

What wonder grows where knowledge fails.

Tacitus (*c.* AD 55–c.117)

235. Are humans attracted most to those with a dissimilar genetic makeup?

Choosing a mate can be a problem. On the one hand, it seems best to look for someone like yourself: you will be more likely to empathize with them, less likely to argue, and will, therefore, probably stay together longer. On the other hand, someone just like you is going to have the same weaknesses, making them unable to provide the things that you are least able to do for yourself, leaving the pair of you ineffective in facing the world as a two-person team. Evolutionarily, two sets of dissimilar genes are also more likely to lead to healthy offspring and to maintain genetic diversity in the species as a whole.

Research published in 2009 seems to confirm that for mandrills (baboon-like monkeys, and thus related to ourselves), opposites do indeed attract. The sense of smell is thought to play a large part in mandrill mate-selection, with male mandrills rubbing their chests on trees to release odour from a scent gland. A group of genes called the major histocompatibility complex (MHC) helps to build proteins involved in the body's immune system and also affects body odour by interacting with bacteria on the skin. Female mandrills seem most attracted to males whose smell is least similar to their own, which leads to greater genetic variability in the MHC and therefore produces offspring with a stronger immune system. Female mandrills also tend to mate with as many males as possible, though they show a greater chance of having their eggs fertilized by males who differ from them genetically. If their eggs have a way of rejecting sperm with similar genetic make-up to their own, it would further increase the likelihood of healthy offspring.

We may know more about the mating strategies of mandrills than that of humans, but recent research has shown that men are more attracted to women who are ovulating and that women using contraceptive pills are more likely to favour more effeminate men, while those not on the pill go for butch, muscular types. Since contraceptive pills have been shown to mask a woman's natural smell, it has been suggested that they may be making it more difficult for people to sniff out the right partners.

236. How do we judge whether a picture of a human face is male or female?

One of the things humans are extraordinarily good at is judging whether a picture of a face is that of a man or a woman. Even when the picture is cropped and edited to remove all obvious gender-linked cues such as hair length and make-up, we can usually tell whether it is a man or a woman. For decades, computer programmers have been trying to get machines to do the same thing. A recent paper on the subject mentioned a whole range of techniques and technologies that have been tried, such as principal component analysis, independent component analysis, support vector machines, image intensity. Whatever it is that we do when we see a face, it probably does not include any of the above techniques, but it reaches a decision with great accuracy and speed. Perhaps if we knew how we did it, we would be able to program computers to do it too.

See also GENETICS 208, SLEEP 428–9, 431–2

It is a very sad thing that nowadays there is so little useless information.

Oscar Wilde (1854–1900)

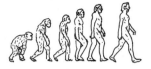

HUMAN EVOLUTION

237. Were the dwarf people of Flores in Indonesia a different species from *Homo sapiens*?

In 2003, on the Indonesian island of Flores, palaeontologists found fossil skeletons of humans who were only 1 metre (3 ft) tall, and who had very small brains. The remains have been dated to between 38,000 and 18,000 years ago, which makes them difficult to fit into the generally accepted picture of human evolution. The genus *Homo* is thought to be between 2.3 and 2.4 million years old. The bipedal *Homo erectus* emerged around 1.5 million years ago, followed by *Homo neanderthalensis* (Neanderthal man) about half a million years ago (→ PALAEONTOLOGY 355–6), while the recent arrival, *Homo sapiens* (modern humans), has been around for only about 200,000 years. Whether Neanderthals and modern humans are both descendants of *Homo erectus*, however, is an open question, and there is still some doubt about whether *Homo neanderthalensis* died out completely, or whether there was some interbreeding with our ancestors – in which case there is still some Neanderthal in our genes.

The fact that the Indonesian 'dwarf' people – known to science as *Homo floresiensis* and to the tabloids as 'hobbits' – are of such recent date poses a real puzzle. The existence of quite sophisticated tools with the fossils suggest that *Homo floresiensis* may have been a subspecies of *Homo sapiens*, yet the considerable difference in height suggests that it was a separate species. There is also the question of how such tools could have been designed by creatures with such small brains. Brain size isn't everything, though. The cranial capacity, and hence brain size, of *Homo neanderthalensis* was as large or even larger than that of *Homo sapiens*. And yet the technologies of the latter, even in its early days, were considerably more sophisticated. Then there is one final question that has not been entirely resolved. While some scientists are adamant that *Homo floresiensis* constitutes a separate species, or at least sub-species, others argue that they are merely specimens of *Homo sapiens* who suffered from a genetic growth disorder.

Interestingly, the island of Flores is also one of the locations where the fossils of dwarf elephants have been found, but the question of a relationship between dwarf elephants and dwarf humans is something beyond even the unknowingness of this book.

238. Why does *Homo sapiens* have forty-six chromosomes while the other great apes have forty-eight?

Somewhere in our evolutionary past, we seem to have lost a pair of chromosomes. Alone among the great apes, humans have forty-six chromosomes arranged in twenty-three pairs, while all the others have forty-eight. Anti-evolutionists have cited this as evidence that apes and humans cannot have had a common ancestor, but in fact the very opposite is true. Chromosome number 2 in humans is almost identical to two ape chromosomes, known as 2p and 2q, spliced together, which strongly suggests that at some stage in our evolution the chromosomes became fused.

Presumably this splicing would have first occurred in a single pre-hominid individual. Under normal circumstances, there would have been a very high likelihood that such a drastic genetic mutation would have died out, but since the fused chromosome of the new model contained all the genetic information of the old, it would still have been able to reproduce with its forty-eight-chromosome neighbours.

The mystery is how the forty-six-chromosome version became a dominant new species. If the fusing together of two chromosomes was not an important part of our transition from ape to human, then one would expect both forty-six-chromosome and forty-eight-chromosome varieties of human to exist today, but if it was a vital change, then what was it about the fusion process that made such a big difference?

239. What is the role of art in human evolution?

Over 17,000 years ago the Cro-Magnons – some of the earliest examples of modern humans in Europe – were responsible for creating a stunning display of cave paintings at Lascaux in France. Many of these paintings are clearly identifiable as animals of the time; some are humans; very few if any are plants or landscapes. The real puzzle, however, is why the Cro-Magnons made these paintings at all.

The usual justification for art of any type is that it is a form of communication; any work of art embodies a crystallization of ideas or emotions or even a broad view of the world into a physical object that others may perceive and share. Yet language is thought to have developed long before the Lascaux paintings, so why invent pictures to communicate when words can do the job already?

The painters at Lascaux were not alone among prehistoric artists. Carvings by Australian Aborigines have been dated to roughly the same period, while a Siberian rock carving of what looks like a man on skis having sex with an elk is thought to date from around 5000 BC.

So what was it all for? Some have suggested that all artistic abilities have evolved as part of sexual selection ($\rightarrow$ HUMAN BEHAVIOUR 232); others maintain that art, particularly the ability to draw likenesses of things encountered in the real world, has been an essential component of the evolution of self-awareness and consciousness. One might say it comes down to what you think the Siberian was trying to tell others when he carved that picture in 5000 BC. Was it 'Come and have a good time with me – just look at this if you don't believe me,' or was it 'Bet you can't guess what I was doing this afternoon; look, I'll draw it for you.'

240. Are humans getting cleverer?

According to the New Zealand academic James Flynn, people are getting cleverer. The 'Flynn effect', as it is called, is based on findings in many different parts of the world that people's average scores on intelligence tests have been steadily on the increase. This improvement seems to have been going on since the earliest days of intelligence testing, but whether it reflects an increase in intelligence is highly debatable.

The idea of IQ testing is to measure 'crystalline intelligence', which is the type of pure intelligence supposed to underlie any particular application that requires mental ability. Supporters of Flynn would say that our ancestors, even as recently as our grandparents or parents, had lower crystalline intelligence than we do, though their practical skills may have been just as good. Others, however, would say that all that has happened is that we have become more culturally attuned to intelligence testing, and that IQ tests have become more and more a practical application of an ability that we are all learning at school.

241. Has human evolution stopped?

In 2002 there was an interesting debate held at the Royal Society of Edinburgh under the title 'Is Evolution Over?' The event showed that leading scientists had very different views on the matter, and nothing has happened in the years since that debate to bring us anywhere nearer an answer. There are three main points of view:

(i) Of course evolution is not over. Humans are becoming brighter, healthier and living longer than ever before and evolution is continuing just as it always has.

(ii) Yes, we are living longer, but this is due to increases in our medical knowledge, which is actually working against natural selection. A few generations ago, rates of child mortality were high, which eliminated unfit genes from the gene pool. Now almost everyone (in the Western world at least) survives into adulthood, when they reproduce and their genes, however unfit, live on. Evolution has therefore stopped.

(iii) Actually it's even worse than that. Because of medicine, books, computers and all sorts of other inventions, humans now rely on machines and the ideas of others to give themselves an easy life. A few decades ago, when it was observed that the pigeons in London's Trafalgar Square seemed to be getting weaker and less healthy, part of the blame was put on the tourists who fed the birds, and their tendency to give preferential treatment to injured or unhealthy-looking specimens. Physical unfitness thus came to have positive survival value. The 'evolution is going backwards' school of thought would argue that something similar is happening to the human race.

See also GENETICS 208, 210–2, 214, HAIR 221, HANDEDNESS 224

INSECTS

242. How do fruit flies smell the difference between hydrogen and deuterium?

This may sound rather an esoteric question, but it has important implications for the question of how our sense of smell works. The traditional theory of olfaction is that molecules of a smelly substance dock into receptor proteins in the olfactory membranes, rather like a key into a lock. The docking can only happen if the shape of the odorant matches that of the cavity in the protein; if they fit together, a neural signal is sent to the brain, identifying the smell.

The difference between deuterium and hydrogen, however, is not in the shape of the molecules. Deuterium is an isotope of hydrogen with a proton and a neutron in its atomic nucleus, where hydrogen has only a proton. Their chemical properties are almost identical, and their docking abilities into olfactory receptor proteins ought to be the same. Yet results published in 2011 showed that fruit flies can be trained to distinguish between versions of a fragrant molecule made with hydrogen and those containing deuterium. They can even be trained, by being given mild electric shocks, to avoid either the deuterium-based or the hydrogen-based products.

This result has been seized on by proponents of a new theory of smell that says it is not the shape of a molecule that our receptor proteins respond to, but their rate of vibration. Deuterium atoms, being heavier than hydrogen atoms, vibrate more slowly, but whether that is what the flies are sensing, and whether the human sense of smell works in the same way, are open questions.

243. Why do male crickets that grow up listening to other crickets have better immune systems and bigger testicles than those that don't?

Research at the University of California published in 2010 has shown that the development of crickets is affected by the extent to which they hear other crickets chirping while they are growing up. At first, this was noticed in relation to the size of the cricket community in which they live, but later experiments comparing crickets maturing in a soundproof environment with those that could hear the outside world confirmed that it was hearing the chirping that made all the difference. Specifically, it was discovered that crickets growing up in silence had weaker immune systems than those that grew up hearing chirping. Later, it was also found that the reproductive systems of those in the soundproof crèche were smaller than those in the noisy world.

This does not make bad sense: the extent to which they hear other crickets would under normal circumstances be a good guide to how many other crickets are in the neighbourhood. The more crickets there are around, the more likely a specific cricket is to meet others and catch a disease from them. Also the more other crickets are around, the more chance there is to find others to mate with. So more chirps means more disease and more mating, hence demanding a better immune system and bigger testicles. How auditory signals become translated into such physical changes, however, has yet to be explained. Crickets, incidentally, hear through vibration receptors on the front of their legs.

244. Do flies have free will?

Theologians and philosophers have argued about free will for centuries, but in 2007 scientists reached the conclusion that free will does exist – for fruit flies, at least. The experiment on which this conclusion was based involved a fly glued to a board by its head and with its wings and legs tethered. The tethers were attached to sensitive equipment which could record the strains being applied by the fly to its restraints. The entire apparatus was placed in a draught-free environment so that no external forces were acting on the fly.

The argument was that if the fly was merely a creature that responded automatically to stimuli, the pattern of its tugging should be repetitive or random. Analysis of the tugs of its legs and the flaps of its wings, however, revealed a changing but non-random pattern. In some sense the fly was therefore 'deciding' what to do in a way the experimenters said exhibited free will.

The argument about human free will is certain to go on, but it will now be more difficult to say that humans have free will and flies do not.

See also BEES 34–7, BUTTERFLIES 65–6

INVENTIONS

We know that Adolphe Sax invented the saxophone and that Christopher Cockerell invented the hovercraft, but there are a vast number of inventions, from the abacus to the zip, for which the original inventor's name is lost or credit for the invention is disputed. It would be easy to fill this book with such things, but we must make do with just a handful of examples in honour of all lost and disputed innovators.

245. Who invented the pencil?

Around the middle of the sixteenth century, a graphite mine was discovered high in the hills of Cumbria, England. The substance was not known at the time to be a form of compressed carbon, but it was quickly recognized by local farmers to be very useful for marking sheep. For that purpose, the graphite was cut into sheets from which rods were sliced. Such rods were originally wrapped in string or sheepskin, but later inserted into hollowed-out wooden holders.

Before that time, artists had used similar rods made of lead, which were referred to as 'pencils' from the Latin word for a little tail. (The word 'penicillin', so-called for the tail-like strands of the fungi from which it comes, has the same derivation.) Since graphite was originally thought to be a form of lead, the newly invented tools were called 'lead pencils' – and the name has stuck.

Incidentally, the first person to patent a pencil sharpener was John Lee Love of Massachusetts in 1897.

246. Who invented the screw?

We know that the English instrument-maker Jesse Ramsden invented the first satisfactory screw-cutting lathe in 1770, and that in 1797 Henry Maudslay produced an improved version that allowed mass-production of accurately made screws. However, metal screws and nuts to fit them had been made from the fifteenth century, and wooden screws had been used in wine or olive oil presses for centuries before that.

In ancient Greece, Archimedes had invented a 'screw' for lifting water, but we have no idea who borrowed the screw-shape idea from him to produce a screw that could fasten things together.

247. Who invented the potato peeler?

Even the inventor of the first potato peeler may not have realized that he or she had invented the potato peeler. Most of the early patents for such devices describe themselves as 'apple peelers' or 'vegetable parers', though to modern eyes they may look like potato peelers. The real trouble, though, is that the invention of the potato peeler almost certainly pre-dates the issuing of patents.

The first apple peeler patented in the USA, for example, dates back to Moses Coates in 1803, but no patents were issued before 1790, and instruments with similar functions were almost certainly in use at that time. The *Oxford English Dictionary* gives no citation for uses of the term 'potato peeler' until 1869.

248. Who invented skateboards?

Skateboarding first became a craze in 1963–4 when the first competitions were held and shops experienced huge demand for these platforms on roller-skate wheels. The idea seems to have begun in the 1950s, when Californian surfers latched onto the idea of surfing the streets. Yet nobody knows who started it. Perhaps several people came up with the idea at the same time – certainly several have claimed to be the original inventor, but no convincing evidence has ever been presented.

See also COFFEE 89

JESUS CHRIST

249. What did Jesus do between his childhood years and his late twenties?

Apart from a brief passage in Luke (2:41–52), when the twelve-year-old Jesus goes missing on a trip in Jerusalem and is found in the Temple debating with the elders, there is no reference to anything Jesus did from shortly after his birth until the ministry of his final few years. All Luke tells us is that after he was found in the Temple, Jesus went back to Nazareth with his parents and was submissive to them and increased in wisdom and stature. Considering the dramatic account of his birth, at which he was hailed as the promised Messiah, this is a huge and puzzling gap in the story.

250. Where was Golgotha, the site of Jesus' crucifixion?

According to the New Testament, the crucifixion took place at Golgotha, a name deriving from an Aramaic word meaning 'place of the skull'. Some have suggested this was a hill whose shape was reminiscent of a skull; others suggest it was believed to be the burial place of the skull of Adam. When St Jerome translated the relevant passage into Latin in the fourth century, he used the phrase *Calvariae Locus*, meaning 'place of the skull', and it is from this that the English name 'Calvary' derives. But where was it?

John's Gospel tell us that Jesus' body was carried only a short distance before it was placed in the tomb. This suggests that the site was probably near a cemetery.

Hebrews 13:12 says that the site was 'outside the city gate', but does not specify which gate, while Matthew tells us it was near a road that carried a lot of foot traffic.

The site on which the Church of the Holy Sepulchre was built satisfies all these requirements, but it is only one of several that do so, and Biblical historians are divided in their views as to whether it is in the right place.

251. How tall was Jesus?

Estimates for Jesus' height vary between about 1.38 and 1.85 metres (4 ft 6 in and 6 ft 2 in), which is about as wide a range as one could wish not to have. According to the first-century Jewish-Roman historian Josephus, he was three cubits tall, but there is a good deal of argument about the size of a cubit (→ OLD TESTAMENT 339). The common cubit is generally thought of as 46 cm (18.5 in), which gives us the 1.38 m figure, but there is also the 'royal cubit' measuring about 53 cm (21 in), which would give a height nearer 1.59 m (5 ft 3 in), which was about the average adult male height of the time. On the other hand, measurements based on the image on the Shroud of Turin (→ CHRISTIANITY 80) have led to estimates between 1.75 m and 1.85 m (5 ft 10 in and 6 ft 2 in). There is no mention of Jesus' height in the Gospels, which suggests to some commentators that his height must have been around average.

JUDAISM

252. What happened to the Ark of the Covenant, or was it always mythical?

The idea of the Ark of the Covenant runs through the Jewish Bible with impressive consistency. This casket, in which Moses was said to have been given the Ten Commandments, and which in some versions also contains Aaron's rod and a jar of manna, appears first in the Book of Exodus, and then many times in Deuteronomy, Joshua, Judges, I Samuel, II Samuel, I Kings, I Chronicles, II Chronicles, Psalms and Jeremiah, as well as turning up again in the New Testament in Hebrews and Revelation. All of these attest to the great power of the Ark – not so far different from what Indiana Jones experienced in *Raiders of the Lost Ark*, in fact.

Mere repetition, however, does not make it true, and the Ark has been sought in vain for two millennia, with a multitude of myths locating it in a number of widely separated places in Asia, the Middle East, Europe and Africa. In 2008 Tudor Parfitt published *The Lost Ark of the Covenant*, a book that tells the tale of the author's researches into a clan in Zimbabwe called the Lemba, who claimed to be a lost tribe of Israel. In their myths, their ancestors brought the Ark of the Covenant to Africa from Jerusalem. The claims of the Lemba were generally viewed with intense suspicion until an examination of their genes revealed a marker they shared with a group of Jews.

Following the leads in the Lemba myths, Parfitt discovered an ancient wooden box with certain similarities to the Biblical Ark. Carbon dating revealed this as having been made in the fourteenth century AD, suggesting to Ark-believers that it was a direct copy of the original made when the true Ark destroyed itself.

253. How did the Jewish people split into Ashkenazim and Sephardim?

Following the conquest of the kingdom of Israel by the Assyrian empire around 720 BC, many Jewish people dispersed throughout the Middle East and North Africa. The Jewish-Roman wars and persecution by various Roman emperors led to the exile of the remaining Jews from Judaea in the second century AD and further dispersion. This diaspora led to the formation of small, initially isolated Jewish communities throughout the known world, which eventually coalesced into two main groups: the Ashkenazim, essentially comprising the European Jews, and the Sephardim, who were the Asian Jews.

That, at least, is the traditional explanation of both religious and cultural differences between the groups, as well as their general appearance. Yet recent genetic studies have produced a number of surprises. While confirming that both groups had the same origin, analysis of the DNA of both Ashkenazi and Sephardic Jews has revealed an unexpected degree of similarity. Many Jewish communities were thought to have been founded by converts to the faith; that view is not supported by genetic analysis. In particular, the role of the Khazars (→ ANTHROPOLOGY 28) in the development of Judaism in Eastern Europe is left in great doubt by genetic evidence.

As more and more studies of the gene pools of various Jewish communities are completed, a growing picture is emerging of their relationship to one another and the extent of intermarriage between existing communities. In some cases, this confirms historical views, in other cases it seems to contradict them. The jigsaw of the Jewish diaspora is far from complete.

254. What happened to the Lost Tribes of Israel?

Now here is a Biblical mystery that modern science really is beginning to throw some light on. According to the Book of Genesis, the twelve sons of Jacob fathered the twelve tribes of Israel, which settled on the two sides of the Jordan River. After the death of King Solomon, the tribes of Judah and Benjamin formed the Southern Kingdom of Israel, the other ten tribes the Northern Kingdom. In 722 BC the Assyrians conquered the Northern Kingdom and much of the Southern, and sent the ten tribes into exile.

That, in a contentious nutshell, is the story behind the Ten Lost Tribes of Israel. Some accounts speak of a total of thirteen tribes, as Joseph's two sons are said to have split into two tribes, while others hold that the tribe of Levi, whose members were to be the priests, had a different status from the others. But however one counts them, there has long been a mystery about what happened to the Ten Lost Tribes.

Genetic studies of Jewish populations in various parts of the world are beginning to piece together the picture. The priestly origin of the tribe of Levi seems to be confirmed by the existence of a so-called 'Cohanim' gene, which has been found in members of the priestly class (and those named Cohen) in many different Jewish communities. Scientific studies have shown that the Lemba tribe of Zimbabwe, who claim to be descended from one of the Lost Tribes (→ JUDAISM 252), began to diverge genetically from Middle-Eastern Jews around the time of the Assyrian conquest of Israel.

The first pieces of the genetic jigsaw are in place. Whether the final picture will reveal twelve tribes, which date back to around three thousand years ago as the Biblical story suggests, is an intriguing question.

See also OLD TESTAMENT 339–43

LANGUAGE

255. At what point did early humans begin to use language?

Somewhere in the long history of human evolution, we began to talk to each other, but estimates of when that point came vary vastly. Some say that it began with the emergence of *Homo erectus* around 2 million years ago; others say that the shape of the ears of *Homo heidelbergensis*, dated to about half a million years ago, show that he was the first to speak; while the most conservative view is that proper language did not come into being until *Homo sapiens sapiens*, the truly modern human, came into existence 200,000 years ago.

The main reason for the great disparity is the underlying question of what we mean by language. Vocal communication is generally taken as the start of language (as written communication seems to demand conceptual skills of a higher order), but a high level of structure is needed before such behaviour can be called 'language'. Birds and animals, for example, have been shown to have vocabularies consisting of a number of 'words' or grunts with different meanings, but this is hardly language.

Whether such squawks and grunts developed seamlessly into language as we now know it, or whether an evolutionary change was responsible for the introduction of syntax and the level of abstraction that exists in all human languages, is an open question.

256. Did Neanderthals talk to each other?

Until the 1980s the popular image of Neanderthal man was that of a great, unkempt, low-foreheaded, lumbering creature who uttered nothing but grunts. In 1983 that view changed with the discovery of a Neanderthal hyoid bone in a cave in Israel. The hyoid is a small bone that connects the muscles of the tongue and the larynx, thus giving the possibility of the articulation of a wide range of sounds that had previously been impossible. Lumbering, unkempt and low-foreheaded he may have been, but Neanderthal man had the physical means of talking much as modern humans do today. Since analysis of the ears of his predecessor, *Homo heidelbergensis*, had already shown that early humans had the acoustic apparatus needed to distinguish a wide range of sounds, Neanderthal man began to look like a good candidate for the first talker.

In his 2006 book *The Singing Neanderthals*, the palaeontologist Steve Mithen has developed this theory to suggest that language developed from song, and that the Neanderthals were the first to make that transition. He even coined a word for their humming language, which he called 'hmmmmm' because it would have been 'holistic, manipulative, multi-modal, musical and mimetic'. 'Hmmmmm' could also be taken as the reaction expressed by others in the field to this intriguing theory.

257. Who were the speakers of Proto-Indo-European?

In the late eighteenth century the English scholar and philologist Sir William Jones commented on the similarity between certain words in Sanskrit, one of the ancient languages of India, and their equivalents in classical Latin and Greek. Ever since then, interest has focused on the supposed common root of all the languages of the so-called Indo-European family, which includes not only most of the European languages, from Gaelic and Greek to Spanish and Swedish, but also many languages in India and Iran. Around half the world's population are now thought to be native speakers of languages that developed from a Proto-Indo-European root, though no records of this root language survive. Indeed, it is thought to have been purely a spoken language, never written, but the question of who spoke it is also unanswered.

By 3000 BC Proto-Indo-European (PIE) had begun to diverge into other languages, but what happened before that, and where PIE came from in the first place, is a matter of pure speculation. Precise suggestions for the time of its origin range between 4000 BC and 7000 BC, but some have suggested that the birth of PIE was several millennia earlier than that. Where did it start? Armenia, Eastern Europe, India, Northern Europe and Anatolia have all been suggested, but it is little more than educated guesswork. All we do know, from the words and sounds shared by many languages that developed from PIE, is that they probably used solid wheels without spokes, travelled in boats, had snow in winter and worshipped a sun god.

258. Where did the Basque language come from?

Basque is a real linguistic mystery. Spoken by around 650,000 people in northern Spain and southwestern France, it appears to be related to no other language. The Basque region is surrounded by an area dominated by Romance and other Indo-European languages, to which it bears no similarity. The general conclusion is that Basque is the last survivor of a language group that pre-dated Indo-European, and that somehow the Basques were ignored by the Romans as their military and linguistic conquests spread through Europe.

Another theory is that the Basque people and their language came to the region from somewhere further east, after the fall of the Romans. Having nothing to compare it with, however, the history of the Basque language has been impossible to trace with any degree of confidence.

259. Is an infant's ability to learn language in some way pre-programmed into his or her brain?

From the 1950s onwards, the American linguist-philosopher Noam Chomsky developed a theory that language skills are innate in humans; in other words, that we are genetically pre-programmed with a capacity for learning languages. In Chomsky's model we are all born with a 'language organ' in the brain that has evolved for the specific task of learning and using language. While we acquire a specific language early in life from our parents or those around us, we are all equipped with the same mental skills for what he called 'universal grammar', which includes the concepts of syntax and the principles of communication skills that underlie all languages.

Chomsky supported his theories with evidence from the formation of human speech organs, the speed with which children acquire their mother tongue, the arguably unique language skills of humans, and studies of the mistakes made by children in their early efforts at speech. When a child says something in a logical but ungrammatical way – such as arguing with anyone who says 'Chomsky wrong' by saying 'No Chomsky wrong' instead of 'Chomsky not wrong' – Chomsky would, after patting the child on the head, no doubt commend her use of universal grammar while waiting to acquire the specific syntactical rules of English.

Attempts to isolate this 'language organ' or to draw up the rules of universal grammar, however, have not made much progress. Opponents of Chomsky's innatist theory would deny that language is so special. Our brains have an undeniable ability to recognize patterns and form concepts, and that, they would contend, is enough to explain language acquisition.

260. To what extent does language influence thought?

One of the most intriguing and contentious debates in twentieth-century linguistics centred on the Sapir-Whorf hypothesis. This was something of a misnomer, as the anthropologist Edward Sapir had little to do with it, while Benjamin Lee Whorf was a Massachusetts fire inspector who only dabbled in linguistics as an amateur. What's more, the whole thing wasn't really a hypothesis in the first place.

Now known by the more academically respectable title of 'the principle of linguistic relativity', the idea comes in two varieties. In the strong version, language totally determines thought, and linguistic categories limit and determine cognitive categories. In the weak version, language and linguistic categories influence thought and some kinds of non-linguistic behaviour.

Whorf gave these ideas great popularity in an article in 1940 in which he mentioned the number of words Eskimos allegedly had for snow. Looking for an example of language influencing perception, he listed seven different types of snow for which he maintained there were different Inuit words. It is highly doubtful, however, that he ever knew a single word in any Eskimo dialect, or that he had ever met an Eskimo. Nevertheless, the idea caught the public imagination, and, thanks to this article, Eskimo words for snow rapidly became the standard example of the Sapir-Whorf hypothesis, with the number of such words apparently increasing every time it was mentioned.

The Scottish-born US linguist Geoffrey Pullum gave a hilarious account of the Eskimo snow-word inflation in *The Great Eskimo Vocabulary Hoax and Other Irreverent Essays on the Study of Language* (1991). He ends the title essay with an account of his own actions on hearing a lecturer perpetrate the 'Eskimological falsehood', and tells the reader what to do if it should happen to them:

I just held my face in my hands for a minute, then quietly closed my binder and crept out of the room.

Don't be a coward like me. Stand up and tell the speaker this: C.W. Schultz-Lorentzen's Dictionary of the West Greenlandic Eskimo Language (1927) gives just two possibly relevant roots: qanik, meaning 'snow in the air' or 'snowflake', and aput, meaning 'snow on the ground'. Then add that you would be interested to know if the speaker can cite any more.

For the record, the strong principle of linguistic relativity has been generally abandoned after research has shown that people's perception of colour differences appears not to be influenced by the words for colours in their language. But the extent to which the weak principle applies is still a matter of debate.

See also ENGLISH LANGUAGE 176–81, WRITING SYSTEMS 493–5

MAGNETISM

261. What is the cause of the Earth's magnetic field?

Ever since the Chinese watched the behaviour of slivers of lodestone in bowls of water over a thousand years ago, we have been aware of the Earth's magnetism. Around 1600 the English physicist William Gilbert showed that this magnetism comes from the Earth itself, and some two hundred years later, the German scientist Carl Friedrich Gauss showed that the source of this magnetism is right at the centre of our planet. Quite what causes it, however, has remained a challenging problem.

In 1939 the US physicist Walter Elsasser proposed the idea of a dynamo mechanism caused by convection currents in the molten iron of the Earth's core combined with the Earth's own rotation, but his theories never quite tallied with our knowledge of convection and our growing understanding of the composition of the Earth's core. In 2007 another US scientist, J. Marvin Herndon, proposed that a uranium-based natural nuclear reactor at the Earth's centre could be a possible source for the magnetic field, and the dynamo and geo-reactor theories have been fighting it out ever since.

Whichever theory wins the argument, it will also have to answer this question:

262. Why does the Earth's magnetic field sometimes flip, changing North and South Poles around?

Every million years or so, the North and South Magnetic Poles switch, and the Earth's magnetic field is reversed. That is the astounding conclusion drawn from the analysis of igneous rocks. Such rocks, formed from the molten state, contain indicators of the magnetic field at the time of their solidification. These magnetic 'fossils' indicate that reversals of the Earth's magnetic poles have occurred, but no one has yet established how this change occurs, or how long it takes for the change to be accomplished.

263. What effect would a flipping of the planet's magnetic poles have on life on Earth?

The short answer is that we haven't the faintest idea. We know the Earth's magnetic field plays a part in protecting us from solar radiation, and there is no reason to believe that would change if the poles were reversed, but what would happen during the period of reversal, which some suggest could last for 5,000 years, is completely unknown.

There is also the matter of those birds and animals that make use of the magnetic field for purposes of navigation. Whether a slow change in the field would fatally confuse such creatures, and whether the time frame of magnetic flipping would allow an evolutionary change to take place that would provide the necessary adjustment, are interesting questions.

As for human beings, since we no longer use the Earth's magnetism to steer ships, it is quite likely that we would not even notice. That is, if any of us are still around when it next happens.

See also BIRDS 47

MAMMALS

264. What is the relationship between the size of a mammal and the amount of food it requires?

Pound for pound, large animals need less food than small animals. It has been said that this is because small animals run around more, and therefore need more energy. Since the reason given for them running around is to search for food, this looks like a rather circular argument. A more sensible suggestion was made by the German biologist Max Rubner in 1883, who suggested that a large proportion of a mammal's energy requirement came from its need to maintain a constant body temperature. Since heat is constantly being lost through the skin, he proposed that the minimum energy requirement should be proportional to the mammal's surface area.

As mass (m) is proportional to volume, which is proportional to the cube of linear dimensions, while surface area is proportional to the square of linear dimensions, Rubner proposed that the basal metabolic rate (BMR) ought to be proportional to $m^{2/3}$.

That calculation, however, was mainly theoretical, and work in the 1930s and 1940s produced figures based on experiments with living animals suggesting that 2/3 was too small an exponent in the equation and that BMR is proportional to $m^{3/4}$, a figure that appeared to tally well with a famous 'mouse-to-elephant curve' produced by the biologist Samuel Brody at the University of Missouri in 1945, giving the BMR of a wide range of mammals.

Subsequently, the 3/4 figure was generally accepted until a paper in 2003 cast doubt on the earlier research, suggesting that it was weighted heavily in favour of domestic pets and laboratory animals, which would be expected to be less active than specimens in the wild. After adjustment for these factors, the figures seemed to support the earlier 2/3 figure again, so we would have to say that the jury is still out.

265. How far can rats count?

This matter has been hotly debated since the 1970s, and a series of experiments have been designed to test rats' counting abilities. An early experiment had rats running round a course and being rewarded when they did so, except on every fourth run. Results showed that the rats were slower on the non-rewarded runs, apparently showing that they could count up to three. But were the rats really counting, or going by the amount of time it took to run the course three times?

In 1983 H. Davis and J. Memmott performed an experiment giving a fixed number of electric shocks to rats over a variable time period, to see if they could count the number and then realize they were safe. Their conclusion was that 'rats may be taught to count, but such behaviour is highly unnatural and may be blocked or overshadowed by more salient sources of information'. Later the same year, however, the Japanese scientists H. Imada, H. Shuku and M. Noriya performed a similar experiment and concluded that 'there was no evidence that rats could count'.

The general opinion now seems to be that rats *can* count, but that they are extremely reluctant, and will do so only if all else fails. Getting them to count numbers greater than five may be more than they are willing to tolerate. Ants, on the other hand, seem to be very good at counting and can even do simple sums. Their ability to count their walking paces was demonstrated in an experiment on Sahara ants in 2006 in which some ants were fitted with stilts and others had half their legs amputated. Results of experiments published in 2011, meanwhile, revealed ants' arithmetic ability by showing how they can assess optimal routes to find food in a maze.

266. Why do zebras have stripes?

Charles Darwin and Alfred Russel Wallace, nineteenth-century contemporaries and co-founders of the theory of natural selection, argued about this. Wallace said that zebras' stripes made them harder for predators to detect at dusk, when the zebras went to drink. Darwin said that was nonsense, and that the stripes would have provided no protection at all – but he did say he thought they were beautiful.

Other suggestions are that the stripes act as camouflage in long foliage; that stripes confuse predators, who find it difficult to identify the vulnerable young zebra in a mass of stripes; that stripes are a sort of barcode enabling zebras to recognize one another; that black-and-white stripes in general act as a warning signal; that stripes make it difficult for predators to tell where the animal's outline ends; or that black stripes and white stripes absorb different amounts of solar radiation, so setting up a cooling convection system on the animal's skin.

See also PANDAS 357

267. Why do reindeer eat hallucinogenic mushrooms?

There are numerous accounts of animals, from shrews to elephants, gorging themselves on fermenting fruit and displaying symptoms of drunkenness as a result, but there has been little evidence that such animals deliberately get drunk. In the Christmas 2010 edition of the *Pharmaceutical Journal* the deputy editor, Andrew Haynes, wrote of the passion reindeers show for fly agaric – the *Amanita muscaria* mushroom – which is renowned both for its toxicity and for its psychedelic properties. Reindeer have long been known to hunt specifically for this type of mushroom, and Haynes suggests that they deliberately consume a mind-altering substance in order to escape the tedium of the long winter nights. That would imply that reindeer have a level of consciousness and self-awareness rather higher than we generally give them credit for. It might also, as Haynes suggests, give credence to the view that Santa's reindeer really could fly.

268. What do sheep see in other sheep than enables them to recognize each other?

Research has shown that sheep can not only distinguish between other sheep from pictures of their faces, but can remember the faces of fifty other sheep for up to two years. They can also recognize a picture in profile of another sheep's face when they have previously only seen it from the front. Given the choice between a picture of a sheep that is experiencing stress and an unstressed sheep, they will also tend to choose the unstressed one. Mother ewes, however, have difficulty recognizing their own lambs at a distance when the appearance of the head region is altered with the use of coloured dyes.

None of which tells us what is going through the sheep's mind when it looks at these pictures, or what characteristics in a sheep's face it uses in order to make such discriminations.

269. Do monkeys change their behaviour when they know they are being watched?

We are all liable to act differently if we know we are being watched, but do monkeys change their behaviour if they know humans are watching them? The question is important for research into animal behaviour, and a partial answer was given in a paper in 2010. By comparing the movements of a group of capuchin monkeys that knew experimenters were watching them with the movements of a group that were being tracked by radios in their collars, researchers were able to show that 'Capuchins did not move faster, stop to rest less frequently, or display higher levels of activity when they were being followed compared to when they were alone.' They may, however, have changed their behaviour in more subtle ways, or be behaving atypically because they were wearing radio-collars, or because they were already habituated to the experimenters.

See also AARDVARKS 1, ARMADILLOS 29, BATS 33, CATS 72–3, CHIMPANZEES 77–8, DOGS 136–8, GIRAFFES 215–16, PANDAS 357–8, SLEEP 430, SQUIRRELS 453

MARINE LIFE

270. Do fish feel pain?

The question of whether animals in general feel pain dates back to the seventeenth-century French philosopher René Descartes, who was firmly of the opinion that they did not. Animals, he said, lack consciousness so cannot be aware of pain. As our understanding of fish physiology has grown, however, it has become increasingly clear that a fish's response to pain may not be so different from that of a human. When fish are subjected to physically damaging experiences, their bodies respond in ways analogous to those of humans, as does their behaviour. In the late 1990s it was even discovered that fish possess nociceptors in their skin, the pain-detectors that transmit messages to the brain when injury occurs.

So the fish's body responds to the pain, and the fish brain knows about it, but whether the fish itself knows it is in pain may be another matter. Pro-fishing scientists argue that it is the highly developed neocortex of our brain that is responsible for our being conscious of a feeling of pain and other conscious emotions and sensations. The fish brain does not have a neocortex, so if it does experience pain, it must do so in a way that is different from humans. So to answer the question, we would have to know what it is like to be a fish, which may be even more difficult to answer than what it's like to be a bat (→ BATS 33).

271. Where does the nautilus lay its eggs in the wild?

There is hardly any creature known to science that is more mysterious than the nautilus, a relative of the octopus, possessed of numerous tentacles and a coiled shell. These ancient sea creatures, according to the fossil record, have hardly changed in the last 500 million years. They live at depths of around 300 metres (1000 ft), coming up to about 100 m (300 ft) to feed, which they only have to do about once a month. The nautilus moves by a sort of jet propulsion, sucking in water and expelling it at high pressure. Almost blind, they locate food and potential mates by smell or other chemical cues. Some nautilus eggs have been found attached to rocks at their feeding depths, but whether that is their normal egg-laying behaviour is unknown. Like so much else in the depths of our oceans, the nautilus is a mystery. We do not know how long they live; we do not know how long they take to reach maturity after hatching; no single nautilus in the wild has ever been tracked from birth to death. We do not even have any idea of how many nautiluses there are in the oceans, or whether they ought to be classified as endangered. Knowing where they lay their eggs would be a very useful place to start for increasing our knowledge of these elusive creatures.

272. Where in the sea do giant squid live?

The nautilus, however, only gets the silver medal for aquatic mystery. In terms of human ignorance, it comes in some way behind the giant squid. In the ancient world, both Aristotle and Pliny the Elder wrote about these creatures, but the scientific community did not fully accept their existence until the late eighteenth century. Since then, around six hundred specimens have been found, almost all dead. Many had been washed ashore, some were floating in the ocean, others were found in the stomachs of sperm whales.

The first time a live specimen was filmed was in 2001, and the first to be photographed in deep water was in 2004. On the rare occasions when a live giant squid has been captured, it has not survived.

We do not know how many species of giant squid there are: estimates vary between one and twenty. We do not know how they mate. We do not know how big they can grow; corpses and captured specimens suggest that a body length of 5 metres (16 ft) is rarely exceeded, though alleged and probably exaggerated sightings have claimed lengths up to 20 metres (65 ft), including tentacles. We do not know how long they live. We do not know where they live, but they have been found in the Atlantic, Pacific and Southern Oceans.

The even bigger, and just as mysterious, colossal squid has only been sighted off Antarctica. With fewer than ten specimens ever having been found alive or dead, estimates of the size of the colossal squid have been based mainly on tentacles and beaks found in the stomachs of whales, but a recent colossal squid corpse was found with eyes 27 cm (11 in) across, which are the largest eyes ever seen in an animal. And they may well have been larger still when the animal was alive. A maximum length (including tentacles) of 12–14 metres (40–45 ft) is generally thought likely.

273. Why do narwhals have spiral tusks?

Imagine a cross between a unicorn and a whale and you have the narwhal. Or a male narwhal at any rate, for only the males possess the long, straight tusk that extends from its upper left jaw in a left-handed spiral. Females may have shorter tusks. In rare cases, narwhals develop two tusks, but when they do, they both spiral in the same direction.

Darwin was fascinated by the narwhal's tusk, as it seemed to serve no useful purpose. Narwhals have very rarely been seen using it in a fight, or to break ice, or as a tool for feeding purposes. The only suggestion that Darwin and others have made is that it is a secondary sexual characteristic. Whether female narwhals go for a male with a long tusk has yet to be confirmed, but males have been observed rubbing their tusks together in an activity called 'tusking', which is thought to be part of a ritual establishing and maintaining social dominance.

274. Why do whales strand themselves on beaches?

Why single whales, or entire pods numbering in their dozens, strand themselves on beaches and die is one of the great puzzles of the animal world. This happens to around two thousand whales every year, and although a variety of explanations have been suggested, nothing is known for sure. Here are a few of the suggestions:

(i) It all starts when a single sick or injured whale swims into shallow waters. It is then followed by members of its pod, who refuse to abandon it. They are all then trapped by falling tides.

(ii) Their guidance systems are disrupted by naval sonar, or by weather conditions, or by variations of the Earth's magnetic field, or by disease.

(iii) Undersea seismic activity creates currents that lead the whales astray.

In 2000 the US Navy did admit responsibility for intense underwater sonar waves that may have led to the stranding of whales of several species in the Bahamas, but many such strandings are not linked to any known sonar activity.

275. Are jellyfish colour-blind?

Box jellyfish are very active and agile swimmers, and are good at avoiding obstacles on the seabed. This isn't perhaps so surprising as they do have twenty-four eyes. These come in four types, and research in 2007 revealed that it was the lower lens eyes, one of the four types, that are responsible for obstacle avoidance.

The jellyfish detect plants and other potential obstacles by the visual contrast between the object and its surroundings. The question was whether the visual contrast involves intensity or colour. As it turned out, the strength of the jellyfish's response to an obstacle was found to depend only on intensity contrast. According to the researchers this 'fits with our other data which strongly suggest that the jellyfish are, in fact, colour-blind'.

276. How intelligent are dolphins?

The belief that dolphins are highly intelligent all began with measurements of brain size. Large animals, of course, tend to have larger brains than small animals, so the view was taken that what mattered was the 'encephalization quotient' (EQ), which is the ratio of actual brain size to predicted brain size for an animal of the same mass. Cats have an EQ of 1, rabbits and rats 0.4, and chimpanzees between 2.2 and 2.5. At the top of the scale come humans, with an EQ of around 7.5, while bottlenose dolphins come second at 5.6.

This seemed to confirm that dolphins are pretty smart, but in 2006 Paul Manger, a researcher at Witwatersrand University in South Africa, came up with an alternative hypothesis: the dolphin does not use most of its brain for thinking, but rather for thermoregulation. Dolphins are, after all, warm-blooded creatures living in cold waters, which get even colder when they dive. Maintaining their body temperature is vital and the dolphin brain might not be so much a thinking organ as a glorified thermostat.

At the start of 2010, scientists in the USA declared that dolphins should be treated as 'non-human persons' in view of their intelligence. Their argument, based on brain size, is less convincing than behavioural evidence would have been. Dolphins have, after all, been observed to do some very clever things, such as recognizing themselves in mirrors, holding sponges over their noses to protect themselves from spiny fish, and teaching tricks learned from humans to other dolphins – all types of behaviour once thought to be exclusive to the great apes.

277. Can lobsters recognize other lobsters by sight?

For some years, it has been known that lobsters can recognize each other by smell. Lobsters tend to urinate most when they are aggressive, and when two lobsters fight, both remember the smell of the other's urine. If the same lobsters encounter each other again, the one that lost the fight will avoid any altercation with the lobster that beat him, while the winning lobster will be eager to fight again. Since lobsters have poor vision and fights tend to take place in the murky depths of the sea, it is hardly surprising that smell rather than vision is the dominant sense. More recently, however, the question has been raised as to whether lobsters know each other's faces.

In order to answer this question, researchers at the University of Florence, Italy, placed ninety-eight lobsters bought in a local fish market in a tank divided by a variety of partitions. These partitions could be opaque, transparent, perforated (to allow the transmission of smells) or unperforated. The results showed that when lobsters could see each other, they started bumping against the divider aggressively, but when they could not see each other, they hardly moved at all, whether or not they could smell the others. When the partitions were removed, the lobsters that had previously seen each other started fighting or actively avoiding each other, while the others adopted a more investigatory approach.

The conclusion was that lobsters can recognize by sight when another lobster is around, but whether they can recognize a particular lobster they have met before by sight alone is still an open question.

See also THE PLANETS 377

MATHEMATICS

278. Are there any odd perfect numbers?

A perfect number is defined as an integer that is equal to the sum of its proper divisors. The first perfect number is 6, as the divisors of 6 are 1, 2 and 3, and 6 = 1+2+3. The next perfect number is 28 (as 1+2+4+7+14 = 28), and the next two after that are 496 and 8,128. All these were known to the ancient Greeks, but it was not until 1456 that a fifth perfect number, 33,550,336, was discovered.

In the eighteenth century the Swiss mathematician Leonhard Euler proved that every even perfect number has the form $2^{p-1}(2^p -1)$, where p is a prime number. The five examples above are given by the values 2, 3, 5, 7 and 13 for p. It is not known, however, whether there are infinitely many perfect numbers, or whether there are any odd perfect numbers. The best we can say is that if there is an odd perfect number, it must have at least 1,350 digits.

279. Are pi and e absolutely normal numbers?

To explain what this is about, let's start with the first thirty digits in the value of pi (π):

π = 3.141592653589793238462643383327...

Now it has long been known that this decimal expansion goes on forever and does not endlessly repeat the same string of digits. But the question of whether it is 'normal' or 'absolutely normal' depends on the relative number of occurrences of each digit in the expansion. So let's count how many times each of the digits from 0 to 9 occurs. There are no zeroes, two 1s, four 2s, seven 3s, three 4s, three 5s, three 6s, two 7s, three 8s, and three 9s, but if we went on and extended the value of pi to a hundred or a thousand or a million places or more, we would find that the numbers of each digit become closer to each other. Not only that, but if we counted the number of times the sequences '11' or '90' or '47' or any other two-digit number appears, they too would be roughly equal. And the same would be true of any other number of digits.

Any infinite decimal that has the property that any string of digits is as likely to occur as any other string of the same length is called a 'normal' number.

The above example, however, was linked to the decimal expansion for pi; that is, the one based on our usual counting system to base ten. What about the binary pi:

π = 11.0010010000111111011010101000100010000101...?

Does that have the same number of 1s as 0s, and the same number of 00s as 01s or 10s or 11s? And what if we had used base three, or four, or some other number?

Any number that displays the quality of being normal in any

system we choose is called 'absolutely normal'. The funny thing is that although mathematicians have proved that almost all numbers (in a very precisely defined sense of 'almost all') are absolutely normal, we can hardly give an example of any of them. Nor is there any known method of determining whether a given number, such as pi or *e*, the base of natural logarithms, is absolutely normal.

280. What is the answer to the Collatz problem (or Syracuse algorithm)?

Think of a number. If it is even, halve it; if it is odd, multiply it by three and add one. Then apply the same process to the result and keep on doing so. So if we start with 11, for example, the sequence goes: 11 - 34 - 17 - 52 - 26 - 13 - 40 - 20 - 10 - 5 - 16 - 8 - 4 - 2 - 1 - 4 - 2 - 1... and then keeps repeating 4 - 2 - 1. The conjecture is that whatever number you start with, it always ends up at this 4 - 2 - 1 sequence. Every number so far checked has eventually reached that end, but there is no known proof that all numbers do so.

Warning: It is known that if there is any number that does not eventually fall into the 4 - 2 - 1 pattern, then it must have at least nineteen digits, so don't waste your time looking for a smaller one.

281. Does P = NP?

In 2000 the Clay Mathematics Institute in Cambridge, Massachusetts, issued a list of seven Millennium Prize Problems comprising what they considered to be the most important unsolved questions in mathematics. A correct solution to any of them will win a prize of $1 million. So far, only one has been solved, and the mathematician responsible turned down the prize. The P = NP conjecture is one of the six remaining problems. Being at a stratospheric level of mathematics, none of the Clay problems are easy to explain, but here is an idea of what P = NP is all about.

It is all to do with the time it takes a computer to find the answer to a question. Suppose we wanted to know what is the longest word in this book. All a computer would have to do is look at each word in turn, count how many letters it has, and see whether it is longer than the longest one it has previously encountered. The number of operations the computer has to execute would be roughly proportional to the number of words in the book, which we shall call N. Other more difficult problems might require a number of operations proportional to N^2 or N^3 or some other power of N. Those would be much bigger numbers than N, but all such powers soon become insignificant, as N grows, when compared with 2^N.

If a problem can be solved with a number of operations given by powers of N, it is said to be solvable in polynomial time; if it needs 2^N operations, it takes exponential time. The implications for computing can be very important. If N = 100, for example, and our computer can perform 100 operations a second, then it will take just over a minute and a half to complete N^2, and almost three hours for N^3, but 2^N would take it longer than the universe has been in existence.

So back to the P = NP problem, in which the right-hand represents all the problems whose answers can be found in polynomial time, while the left-hand side is all the problems whose answers could be checked in polynomial time. There is a big difference between finding and checking an answer. Finding the factors of a large number can be a very tedious and time-consuming process. Checking that two particular numbers are the factors you seek is easy: you just multiply them together.

There are many such problems with easy-to-check answers, but where only exponential-time computational methods are known for finding those answers in the first place. If P = NP is correct, then there must be a polynomial-time method that nobody has thought of yet. And in some cases, that would be worth a million dollars of anyone's money.

See also GAMES 203, NUMBERS 337, PRIME NUMBERS 390–2

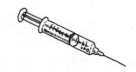

MEDICINE

282. Does the placebo effect exist, and if so what causes it?

Ever since the eighteenth century, the medical effect of placebos has been remarked upon. In recent times, acceptance of the 'placebo effect' has been sufficiently widespread to ensure that any test of a new drug will include a group of subjects given, in place of the drug being tested, a placebo – something that looks just like the genuine drug but has no physiological effect. More often than not, the placebo will be found to have had a beneficial effect on a number of patients. In the original clinical trials of Viagra as a treatment for erectile dysfunction, for example, around 25 per cent of the subjects who had been given a placebo reported significant improvement (compared with over 70 per cent for those who took the real drug, which accounts for its immediate popularity).

In recent years, however, several studies have cast doubt on the placebo effect, with suggestions that its potency may be limited to ailments with a psychological or subjective side to them, such as those involving the patient's perception of pain. When a physiological effect is associated with taking a placebo, it may be connected to the production in the brain of dopamine, which is known to be associated with a feeling of well-being. Curiously, the medical profession has always been hostile to the idea of faith healing, yet the effect of faith to a believer ought to be very similar to that of a placebo on someone who thinks he is being given medicine.

The whole picture, however, has been thrown into additional confusion by a recent report of a trial in which patients suffering from irritable bowel syndrome were given placebos and told that they contained no drugs of any use whatsoever. And they still reported improvement in their condition. So placebos seem to work even if you know they are placebos. Whether belief in the placebo effect is necessary for them to work, however, requires further research.

283. Is there any scientific basis for homeopathy?

Can a solution of some ingredient have beneficial effects even if that solution has been diluted to a degree at which not a single molecule of the ingredient is still present? That idea, enshrined in homeopathic theory and practice, has been roundly condemned as preposterous by mainstream medical practitioners and scientists, while studies have repeatedly reported that homeopathic treatments achieve no better results that placebos. Yet the homeopathic industry continues to thrive, and both practitioners and many of their patients insist that it works.

From a strict scientific point of view, the case for homeopathy must be considered unproven, yet in 2010 a Nobel prize-winning scientist announced a finding that was seized upon by the homeopathic brigade as supporting their claims. Luc Montagnier, the French virologist who won the 2008 Nobel prize for physiology or medicine for linking the HIV virus to AIDS, reported a series of experiments investigating the electromagnetic properties of highly diluted biological samples. He found that small DNA fragments caused identifiable electromagnetic signals in aqueous solutions in which they were dissolved, and those signals continued to be detected even after the solution had been diluted to a very high degree. He suggested that subatomic structures were created in the water that persisted even when the substance that created them was removed.

Professor Montagnier did not mention homeopathy in his report, but supporters of alternative medicine claimed that it vindicated all they had been saying about water having a memory, and that

Montagnier had now explained just how homeopathy works.

Or it might just be the placebo effect.

284. Why does honey help wounds heal?

As long ago as two thousand years before the discovery of bacteria, honey was used to treat wounds infected by them. The Greek physician Pedanius Discorides praised honey as 'good for all rotten and hollow ulcers', but like many other folk remedies, honey was for a long time treated with great suspicion by the medical profession. As recently as 1976 its use was described as 'worthless but harmless' in an editorial in *Archives of Internal Medicine*. Since then, however, a good deal of individual case studies and research have supported the view that wounds treated with honey may, in many cases at least, heal more quickly than those treated with antibiotics. But it is still not clear how the honey treatment works.

Part of the effect may be due to honey being a supersaturated sugar solution. This means it contains very little water, so treating a wound with honey may help absorb moisture from the wound, denying the bacteria the water they need to survive.

Some studies, on the other hand, have shown that honey can be more effective when diluted. This seems to be because of an enzyme in honey that releases hydrogen peroxide, which is known to have an antibacterial effect. The antiseptic effect of the alkaline hydrogen peroxide occurs only when the natural acidity of honey itself is diluted and neutralized by body fluids. Yet the acidity of honey may also play a part in the fight against bacteria.

All these effects sound rather basic compared with the sophistication of antibiotics, and it seems likely that honey possesses some other healing component that has not been identified. The honey from manuka trees in New Zealand seems particularly potent as an antibacterial agent, but because we do not know what ingredient is responsible, the hypothetical molecule is simply called by the registered trade mark 'Unique Manuka Factor'.

285. Why don't the immune systems of pregnant women reject their foetuses?

Our auto-immune systems are designed to reject foreign tissues. That is the perennial problem of transplant surgery: the host body naturally rejects the transplanted organ unless drugs are given to suppress the rejection mechanism. But if the immune system reacts so violently towards foreign bodies, why do pregnant mothers not reject their foetuses? After all, half the genes of the foetus come from the father and are responsible for the creation of proteins that one would expect the mother's body to recognize as not part of her.

One theory holds that the placenta provides a barrier to keep the immune cells from getting at the foetus; another idea is that the foetus itself somehow has a way to hide the proteins it produces from the mother's immune system. Yet no one has come up with a precise idea of how either of those would work. Research with pregnant mice has supported a third idea: that the foetus itself produces an enzyme that inhibits the development of immune cells. This enzyme may create a 'no-auto-immune zone' to protect the mouse foetus from the mother's natural defence mechanism.

Whether this also happens in humans has yet to be confirmed, but it is already clear that the auto-immune system is even more sophisticated and complex than had previously been thought.

286. What molecular mechanisms are responsible for the association of obesity with certain types of cancer?

There is a great deal of evidence that obesity is linked to increased rates of certain types of cancer. One study has even claimed that 25 per cent of all cancer cases worldwide are due to excess weight and a sedentary lifestyle. But we have almost no idea why being too fat should lead to cancerous growths.

Since obesity is known to be linked to diabetes, which seems to be caused by the effect of excess fat on the body's insulin production, something similar may be contributing to the cancer link, but whether it is insulin-related, or related to some other substance, or whether fat has an effect on the mechanism that causes cancer-causing genes to come into operation, are all questions that need a good deal of further research.

287. Are mummies good for you?

From the twelfth to the eighteenth centuries, 'powdered mummy' was a common item sold by apothecaries across Europe. The Science Museum in London even has an exhibit that it describes as 'Green cylindrical wooden herb box with lid to contain mummia (powdered mummy), now empty, European, 1601–1800'.

Originally, the use of powdered mummy as a drug was inspired by the supposed curative powers of bitumen, which it was incorrectly thought was used by the Egyptians in the mummification process. Egyptian mummies were seen as a cheap source of bitumen, which was even responsible for their name: *mummiya* was a Persian term for bitumen.

At some point in the Middle Ages people got the wrong end of the mummified stick and started to believe that the supposed medicinal properties of the powder were due to its having been a living body. This belief resulted in the appearance of medicinal recipes asking for the dried body of a hanged man, or some similarly gruesome ingredient.

In the eighteenth century, physicians began to lose faith in powdered mummy and the item, once so popular, faded from apothecaries' lists. No controlled studies have ever been performed, as far as is known, to test whether powdered mummy is good for you, with or without bitumen.

See also DISEASE 119–31

MEMORY

288. How and where are memories stored in the brain?

In the 1920s the American psychologist Karl Lashley conducted a famous experiment to determine where memories are stored in a rat's brain. After teaching the rat to run through a maze, he cut out a bit of its brain to see if he could excise the memory. But as long as the rat was still functioning, it always seemed to remember what it had learnt, whichever part of the brain he cut out. His conclusion was that memories are not stored in any particular place, but are spread around all areas of the brain.

According to current theory, memories are created in the hippocampus and later transferred to the frontal lobes, but we still need the frontal cortex and the hippocampus to retrieve them. The whole business of laying down a memory, putting it away somewhere safe and retrieving it at a later date is clearly extraordinarily complex, and made all the more so by the realization that every time you recall a memory, you create a new memory of having recalled it. So whether a memory exists in a particular place in the brain seems almost as doubtful as Lashley thought, though one cannot help feeling that it must be somewhere.

289. What form do memories take in the brain?

In the 1960s, when the recent discoveries of DNA and RNA were seen as the potential answers to everything we needed to know about life, there was a theory that each new memory corresponded to the creation of a new RNA molecule. Among the experiments designed to test the theory were various attempts to extract memories from the brain of a rat or goldfish and transfer them physically to another individual of the same species. There was even one famous experiment in which a flatworm was taught something, then minced and fed to another worm to see if knowledge was edible. Even though the results of some of these experiments seemed to confirm the RNA theory of memory, the whole idea was soon quietly abandoned, though recent research suggests it may not have been totally misguided. Memories are now seen as having something to do with the creation of new synapses joining certain neurons (nerve cells) in the brain, or the strengthening of existing synapses. Such synaptic alterations require the creation of new RNA and proteins in the hippocampus, and experiments with mice have shown that when RNA synthesis is stopped, it has an adverse effect on the subject's ability to consolidate memories.

But we still don't know what memories look like.

290. What is the difference between the way the brain stores long-term and short-term memories?

The division of memory into short-term and long-term has been with us since the nineteenth century, and offers a very plausible model for the way we experience memory. The idea that thoughts are held for a brief time in short-term memory while we decide whether to retain them in long-term memory or let them fade away is enticing. Yet opinions are divided on whether there really are two different types of memory – and if there are, what the difference is. Attempts to identify a boundary between the two types of memory have been inconclusive.

What you don't know would make a great book.

Rev. Sydney Smith (1771–1845)

291. By what mechanism do we recall past memories?

In the 1960s researchers performed an intriguing experiment on goldfish. The fish was placed in a T-shaped tank and taught to swim up to the crossbar, then turn in a particular direction. This is simply accomplished by placing food at one or other end of the crossbar. Before the experiment begins, however, some alcohol is added to the water.

When the goldfish, by now a bit tipsy, has learnt which way to turn, it is sobered up by being placed in clean water. Further experiments show that it is now liable to have forgotten what it learnt. But put it back into alcoholic water and it will remember it again. Humans have shown a similar tendency: learn something when you are drunk and you may forget it when you sober up. Next time you get drunk, however, it may well all come back to you.

These are examples of memory being context-dependent, which supports a theory of memory recall known as 'encoding specificity'. A memory, under this theory, is not stored in isolation but together with the situation in which it was formed.

The other main theory is that recalling a memory is a two-stage process, first involving search and retrieval, then recognition. That at least would explain why recognizing something you have seen before is a much easier process than recalling what it looked like: recognition only involves one of the two stages of recall.

In either case, the mechanism by which it all happens has yet to be discovered.

292. Is consciousness a high-level consequence of memory in all its forms?

Consciousness involves being aware that I exist and knowing who I am, or at least having some sense of identity. You could say that our sense of identity is nothing more than the total of all our memories, and the knowledge that we exist is provided by the constant flow of experiences and sensations into our short-term memory. So you could say that consciousness is a direct consequence of all our memories.

On the other hand, you could say that computers have memories, but don't have consciousness. Perhaps consciousness is what gives human memory its unique quality.

See also CONSCIOUSNESS 101–5

293. Is there any hope of discovering how memories work with our current understanding of physics, or does an entire new level of physics need to be discovered?

As was mentioned in the introduction to the section on the brain, there has been a tendency throughout the history of science to explain the brain's functioning by analogy with the latest technology, whether that is plumbing or electronic computers. In his 1989 book *The Emperor's New Mind*, Sir Roger Penrose suggests that certain aspects of our mental functioning – notably the problem of consciousness – may not be explicable by our current understanding of physics. When we cannot say how memories are stored, where they are stored, how they are retrieved or what form they take, it strongly suggests that the real problem is a lack of understanding of the physical processes involved in the brain. Penrose proposes a hypothesis in which quantum mechanics somehow plays a role. However, some philosophers argue that memory and consciousness are by their very nature subjective, and thus not entirely amenable to mechanistic explanations.

294. Why can we not remember anything of our earliest years, when it is clear that babies have good working memories?

What is your earliest memory? For most people, the first thing they can remember dates from the age of about three, but babies can remember faces and have an amazing capacity to learn things, which involves having a memory. So what happens to all the memories of our infant years?

Could it be that the acquisition of language alters the way we remember things, almost as though our brains have been reprogrammed with a new operating system that can no longer consciously access the older memories of our infant years? And if we do remember things from infancy, how can we tell whether we are remembering them or remembering what we were told about them by our mothers, or remembering a misremembered version of it from our slightly later years?

295. Is there truly any such thing as a 'memory', or is it just a convenient human construct, a catch-all term for a wide variety of mental activities that we do not understand?

I can remember that the Battle of Hastings was in 1066; I can remember what I had for breakfast this morning; I can remember seeing the Northern Lights in Iceland thirty-five years ago. Yet these memories are of very different types: the first is a firm memory of a fact, and the other two are personal experiences, one much more recent than the other. My memory of breakfast is probably fairly accurate, as it was not very long ago and has not had the opportunity to fade or change, but my memory of the Northern Lights has been accessed many times and probably changed a little every time. It is not so much a single 'memory' as the amalgamation of all the memories I have had of that event over several decades all merged and blurred into a single entity.

Studies of people's recollections of their youth have shown that such 'memories' can be wildly at variance with the historical facts. You think you are remembering something, but what you recall is a reconstruction of an embellishment of a version of something you thought you remembered. And that, more often than we would like to admit, is what a 'memory' really is.

THE MIDDLE AGES

296. Why did the Danes turn into Viking pirates?

From the late eighth century, the previously stay-at-home people of Scandinavia embarked on a period of dramatic expansion – raiding, looting, colonizing and trading from Russia and Constantinople in the east, to Spain and North Africa in the south and Iceland and Greenland in the west. They even reached as far as Newfoundland and Labrador in North America, centuries before Cabot and Columbus rediscovered the New World.

What brought about this huge change in culture? There are three main theories:

(i) It was all prompted by the desire of Charlemagne, king of the Franks from 768 and emperor of the Romans from 800, to impose Christianity by force. The battle between the forces of Christendom and Norse paganism had already been raging for almost a century, so the Viking expansion may have been motivated by a desire to protect the pagan Norse culture and to wreak revenge on Charlemagne.

(ii) It was all caused by a population boom that left the Norse people with insufficient agricultural land to feed their growing numbers. With their nautical skills already highly developed, taking to the high seas was an easier option than clearing the forests to the east.

(iii) There was a long-term European economic slump caused by the fall of the Roman Empire and the rise of Islam, both of which events had led to a decline in international trade. The Viking expansion was driven by a need to open up new markets.

None of these sets of circumstances completely accounts for the vast extent of the Viking expansion, but any of them might have planted the seeds for an era of successful belligerence.

297. Who invented firearms?

Gunpowder is thought to have been invented by the Chinese in the ninth century, possibly by Daoist monks looking for an elixir of eternal life. Its use in weaponry, particularly firebombs, began shortly afterwards, but the earliest account of firearms – guns – dates from the twelfth century. A sculpture from that period found in a cave in Sichuan shows a man carrying a type of primitive cannon known as a bombard, with flames and a cannonball emerging from its mouth. The oldest surviving cannon of this type has been dated to 1288. The unanswered question is who first had the idea of using the explosive power of gunpowder to propel metallic projectiles at an enemy. All we know is that he was probably Chinese, lived around the twelfth century, and invented something that led to the arms industry as we know it today.

298. How many Normans invaded England in 1066?

For one of the most significant events in British history, we have remarkably few precise details about the Battle of Hastings. Perhaps that is not surprising when our main source is a lengthy embroidered cartoon (the Bayeux Tapestry), which was probably not completed until eleven years later. Even the story about King Harold being killed by an arrow in his eye is very much disputed.

As to the size of the armies, the English are thought to have numbered 7,000–8,000, but there are no reliable sources for the size of the army of William the Conqueror. Most writers believe it was about the same size as the English army, but attempts to give a more precise figure have varied between 4,000 and 20,000.

299. Did the so-called Malfosse Incident really happen during the Norman Conquest, and if so, where?

At least five chroniclers of the eleventh and twelfth centuries mention an incident that supposedly took place at a site known as Malfosse ('evil ditch'). Their accounts differ in various ways, but tell a similar tale of the Norman pursuit of desperate English troops in the closing stages of the Battle of Hastings.

The English have decided to make a last stand at Malfosse where a ditch, or some other natural formation, offers them an advantage. The Normans are led by Eustace of Boulogne and William himself, and the two are conferring. An English soldier, either wounded or playing dead on the battlefield, sees the two French knights deep in discussion. He gets to his feet and hits one of the knights with a stone between the shoulder-blades with such force that blood pours out of his mouth and nose and he is carried away badly wounded.

French accounts of the battle omit any reference to the incident, which if it happened would have been a narrow escape for William. At least five possible sites have been suggested for Malfosse, but nothing has been found to confirm the incident.

300. Where was the Bayeux Tapestry made?

The Bayeux Tapestry, which is not a tapestry at all but a piece of embroidery, is thought to have been completed in 1077, and is our main source of information about the Battle of Hastings eleven years earlier. But who commissioned the Bayeux Tapestry, who did the embroidery and where it was made have long been disputed.

French tradition holds that it was commissioned by Queen Matilda, wife of William the Conqueror, and made by herself and her ladies in waiting. Others say that it was commissioned by Bishop Odo, William's half-brother, which might help explain why it was found in Bayeux Cathedral in Normandy, which was built for Odo.

Experts in historical embroidery, however, have suggested that the style and expertise of the Tapestry suggest English not French origins, and the style of lettering in the Latin words it displays again point to England as the source. In particular, the letter U always appears as V, which was much more the English style.

Since the earliest known reference to the Tapestry is in an inventory of Bayeux Cathedral from 1476, the first four hundred years of its history are lost. Until that gap is filled we will have to continue to guess where the elaborate stitching began.

301. Where is Genghis Khan's grave?

When the great Mongol emperor Genghis Khan died in 1227 at the age of about sixty-five, he was buried, according to tradition and his expressed wishes, in an unmarked grave in a secret location. So secret, in fact, that according to legend his funeral escort killed anyone they encountered, including the slaves who built the tomb, and on their return were themselves killed. Some say that a river was diverted over the site, while another story is that horses trampled the land and trees were planted to hide the grave. Whatever the secrecy measures were, they certainly seem to have worked, for the site of Genghis Khan's grave is still unknown.

While we are on the subject, the manner of his death is also the subject of various different stories. One such tale concerns a princess captured as war booty from battles with the Tangut in China. The princess is said to have concealed a pair of pliers in her vagina, and these damaged Genghis Khan so badly that he died of the injuries. That might at least explain why he wanted his grave kept secret, but the tale is generally held to have been invented by his Mongolian rivals.

302. Did Marco Polo reach China, or was his account of that land all made up?

The Venetian merchant Marco Polo (1254–1324) was undoubtedly one of the great travellers of the Middle Ages. His book *Il Milione* (known in English as *The Travels of Marco Polo*) was a medieval best-seller, translated into many languages, yet there are some aspects of his account that suggest that he may not have travelled as far as he claimed. In particular, his writings about China have been cited as evidence that he was merely recounting tales told to him by others, rather than narrating his personal experiences.

For example, his account, while detailed in some respects, fails to mention Chinese calligraphy, or chopsticks, or tea, or foot binding, or even the Great Wall. What is more, no mention of Marco Polo has been found in Chinese records of the time, despite his claim to have served as a special emissary for Kublai Khan, the Chinese emperor. All the same, Marco Polo was the first European to mention tigers, the imperial Chinese postal system, Japan, and the Grand Canal linking Beijing to Hangzhou.

On his deathbed, Marco Polo is said to have been urged by a priest to confess that he had made up much of his book. In reply, he is reputed to have said, 'I have not told half of what I have seen.'

303. What was the cause of the Black Death?

In the middle of the fourteenth century, the Black Death is thought to have killed around half of Europe's population and reduced the world population by about 20 per cent. Yet we cannot be sure what caused it, or even what it was. Until recently it was generally assumed that the Black Death was a form of bubonic plague, similar to that which caused epidemics in European cities in the seventeenth century. But since the beginning of the twenty-first century, following studies of detailed contemporary accounts of the Black Death, doubts have been expressed as to whether it really was bubonic plague. While the symptoms were in many ways similar, the Black Death struck at different times of the year, and had a different fatality rate and differing levels of recurrence and periods between outbreaks, from those experienced during the later epidemics of bubonic plague. Its contrasting behaviour in cities and rural communities also seemed to differ from the behaviour of bubonic plague. This led several researchers to suggest alternatives, such as a form of haemorrhagic fever (similar to ebola) or even anthrax, as the main cause of the Black Death.

In 2010, however, a detailed analysis of the DNA found in the teeth of bodies found in medieval plague pits found evidence of a bacterium associated with bubonic plague. If that is true, there is still the question of how the disease was transmitted to humans. We know that bubonic plague can be carried by the fleas that live on rats. Outbreaks of the Black Death, however, are known to have occurred in areas too hot for fleas to survive – but that is also true of nineteenth-century epidemics of bubonic plague in China, India and the Middle East. Yet the pustules or buboes of nineteenth-century victims of bubonic plague appeared mainly in the groin, where fleas are known to bite. In the case of the Black Death, the buboes frequently appeared also on the armpits and neck, which are distinctly less popular feeding grounds for fleas. Finally, it had been suggested that outbreaks of bubonic plague were linked to a decrease in the rat population, which forces the fleas to jump to humans to find other feeding grounds. No such changes in the rat population have been identified in connection with the Black Death.

304. Who was Perkin Warbeck?

Perkin Warbeck (1474–99), pretender to the throne of England, is one of the most mysterious characters in English history. Claiming to be Richard of Shrewsbury, Duke of York – the younger son of Edward IV, who was believed to have died in the Tower of London

(→ MURDER 321) – he made several attempts to seize the throne from Henry VII. He was officially recognized as Richard of Shrewsbury by Margaret of York, sister of Edward IV, though it is unclear whether this was because she believed him or because she saw him as a useful political ally.

When he was captured by the king's forces, he made a confession in which he gave details of his Flemish origins, and claimed to have learnt English in Ireland. As this confession was given under duress, it is considered nothing more than a fabrication concocted in an attempt to avoid the death penalty.

In appearance, Perkin Warbeck was said to have resembled Edward IV, leading some to speculate that he may have been the king's illegitimate son, or even the prince he had claimed to be. Perkin Warbeck was hanged in 1499 and his body sent for dissection. As nothing of him remains, even DNA testing cannot solve this mystery.

See also ENGLISH HISTORY 169–172, MURDER 317–19, 321, POPES 387–8

MODERN HISTORY

305. Who is the soldier buried in the Tomb of the Unknown Warrior in Westminster Abbey?

There is only one tombstone in London's Westminster Abbey on which it is forbidden to walk. That stone bears a plaque with a long inscription beginning with the words:

BENEATH THIS STONE RESTS THE BODY OF A BRITISH
WARRIOR UNKNOWN BY NAME OR RANK BROUGHT
FROM FRANCE TO LIE AMONG THE MOST ILLUSTRIOUS
OF THE LAND.

This is the tomb of the Unknown Warrior.

The idea for such a memorial began in 1916, when an army
chaplain, the Reverend David Railton, saw a grave in France marked
with a wooden cross and the words 'An Unknown British Soldier'.
Railton wrote to the Dean of Westminster in 1920 proposing that
an unidentified British soldier, killed in the war that had just
finished, should be brought from France and given a state funeral
in Westminster Abbey.

The idea was approved and a selection of unidentified bodies
were exhumed from various battlefields and brought to a chapel in
France. Each was on a stretcher and was covered by a British flag. A
British brigadier general then chose one of the bodies, not knowing
which battlefield any of them had come from, and that body was
brought to London to be buried as the Unknown Warrior. The other
bodies were taken away for reburial.

306. How did Amelia Earhart die?

On 2 July 1937 the pioneering American pilot Amelia Earhart went
missing on a flight over the Pacific. Neither she nor her navigator
Fred Noonan was ever seen again, and their plane has never been
found. She was declared legally dead on 5 January 1939. Becoming
the first woman to fly solo across the Atlantic in 1932 had earned
Earhart unique celebrity status around the world, and news of her
disappearance was met with grief and a determination to find out
what had happened. All that we are left with, however, are a few pieces
of disputed evidence and a large number of speculative theories.

The most likely explanation is that her plane, a Lockheed Electra,
ran out of fuel and her attempt to land it on the small airstrip on

tiny, remote Howland Island, near where her last message came from, failed owing to faulty navigational equipment. The plane crashed into the sea and Earhart and Noonan drowned.

Another popular theory is that they crashed not in the sea off Howland Island but about 350 miles away on Gardner Island (now Nikumaroro in Kiribati). In 1940 a British colonial officer found a skeleton on Gardner Island which he believed to be that of a woman, together with an item of aircraft equipment. The bones were sent to Fiji where, after an examination, they were declared to be those of a short male. A more recent examination of the data, however, concluded that they were from a tall white female of Northern European ancestry. Unfortunately this was based only on bone lengths, as the bones themselves had long before gone missing in Fiji.

In 2010 another group of researchers found what they thought were bones from a human finger on Nikumaroro. DNA analysis was inconclusive, but suggested that they might be from a human or a sea turtle. Other artefacts have been found on Nikumaroro, which may have come from a plane similar to Earhart's Electra.

A rather more outlandish theory is that Earhart and Noonan crashed on an island occupied by the Japanese and were executed as spies. Some take this theory seriously, despite the fact that it is similar to the plot of a 1943 film called *Flight for Freedom*, in which a character reminiscent of Earhart undertakes a spying mission against the Japanese.

307. Did Hitler ever issue written orders for the 'Final Solution' – the extermination of the Jews of Europe?

The 'Final Solution' seems to have been such a clear and universally accepted plank of Hitler's policy that it seems unthinkable that no such order was given, yet no documentary proof has ever been unearthed. The Nazi propaganda minister Joseph Goebbels alludes in his diary to the Führer making his objectives clear on the matter, but despite a great deal of research, no written orders have been found. Perhaps none were given; perhaps all traces of them were destroyed; perhaps they will turn up tomorrow.

308. What happened to the Amber Room?

In 1716 King Wilhelm I of Prussia gave a fabulous gift to his ally, Tsar Peter the Great of Russia. Built between 1701 and 1709, it was a complete room decorated with amber panels backed with mirrors and gold leaf. Known as the Amber Room, it was eventually set up in the Catherine Palace near St Petersburg, and covered an area of some 55 square metres (600 sq ft).

The Amber Room remained much admired and generally undisturbed until the German invasion of the Soviet Union in 1941. The Russians tried to disassemble it but the material proved too fragile. The Germans, however, managed to do so safely, and in October 1941 the Amber Room was brought to Königsberg Castle in Prussia in twenty-seven crates.

Early in 1945, crates were again seen leaving Königsberg Castle, but no information exists on what was in them. Later the city of Königsberg (now Kaliningrad in the Russian Federation) was heavily bombed by the British and the castle was destroyed by the Russians. The Amber Room has never been seen again, though rumours of the discovery of hiding places or signs of gold and/or amber continue to surface every few years.

309. Who was the man whose body was washed up on Somerton Beach in Australia in 1948 in the so-called Tamam Shud case?

At 6.30 a.m. on 1 December 1948, a man was found dead at Somerton Beach in Adelaide, Australia. Apart from being dead, he appeared to be in fine condition and aged about forty-five. Close examination revealed that all identifying labels had been removed from his clothes. Neither his fingerprints nor dental records matched anything in Australia, and when the search was extended worldwide, it didn't help. An autopsy revealed internal abnormalities, including a grossly extended spleen, which were thought to be consistent with poisoning, but no traces of any known poison were found.

An appeal for possible sightings of the man in Adelaide before his death led to the discovery of a brown suitcase that contained more clothes with labels removed and a jacket that had been made in America. A hidden pocket was found stitched into his trousers which contained a piece of paper apparently torn from a book containing the words 'tamam shud'.

Thanks to good literary detective work, the words were recognized as a Persian phrase that appears at the end of Edward Fitzgerald's translation of the *Rubáiyát* of Omar Khayyám. The phrase means 'ended'. The very book the words had been torn from was later found, thrown on the back seat of an unlocked car shortly before the man's death. The book was examined and found to be a very rare edition of the work. It also contained what looked like a coded message, which nobody has yet been able to crack. All attempts to identify the man have also come to nothing.

310. What proportion of all the people who have ever lived are alive today?

It is frequently claimed by lovers of useless information that half the people who have ever lived are alive today. That is complete nonsense, but even estimating the correct figure is not easy. Before the middle of the nineteenth century, accurate population figures were not known for large areas of the world. We know that the population rose above 7 billion in 2011; it reached 6 billion in 1999, 5 billion in 1987, and is estimated to have first passed the billion mark in 1804.

Around the birth of Christ, the world population is thought to have been about 200 million, but before that everything is guesswork; and even if we only go back as far as the evolution of modern man, *Homo sapiens sapiens*, we have at least 200,000 years of humans to count.

Making certain assumptions about population growth, and assuming there was no great population explosion or disaster we do not know about, then it has been estimated that the total number of humans who have ever lived is about 110 billion, of whom just over 6 per cent are alive today. But we will probably never know the true figure.

THE MOON

311. Did the Moon split from Earth after a massive collision?

We know that the Moon has remained relatively unchanged over the past 2.5 billion years, but how it came into being is still not known for sure. There are four theories concerning its origin.

(i) It may have formed from coalescing gas and dust at the same time as the Earth.

(ii) It may have been an asteroid that came close to Earth and was captured by the Earth's gravitational pull.

(iii) It may have spun off from Earth during the early period of our planet's formation.

(iv) It may have been formed from rock and debris from Earth that was knocked off in a collision with another planet about the size of Mars.

Generally, the last of these theories is thought to be the most probable, but we cannot be certain. It would at least account for the fact that the Moon always has the same side facing Earth: its pattern of rotation would have been inherited from that of its mother planet.

312. What, if anything, caused the Moon's Linné Crater to change its appearance in the mid-nineteenth century?

Among the features on the surface of the Moon is a beautiful bowl-shaped crater that is named after the great Swedish zoologist and botanist Carl Linnaeus. The Linné Crater, which is only about 10 million years old (very young for such a crater), began to attract considerable attention in 1866 when the German astronomer Johann Schmidt claimed to have detected a change in its appearance.

Schmidt, the director of the Athens Observatory, was a highly respected scientist who had a particular interest in and expertise regarding the Moon, of which he was preparing a map that was better than anything previously seen. For several decades, great interest centred on the shape-changing crater, though the general conclusion was that Schmidt's observation was caused by his optical instruments rather than the crater itself.

More recently, further changes have been observed at Linné, and these have been put down to 'residual outgassing' (i.e. the emission of a gas), which could distort the appearance of the crater. Schmidt's 1866 observations could have been caused by an unusual increase in the amount of gas produced. So something may be going on at Linné that needs explaining after all.

See also WATER 471

'Beauty is truth, truth beauty,' – that is all
Ye know on earth, and all ye need to know.

John Keats (1795–1821)

MOZART

313. What was the cause of Mozart's death?

Wolfgang Amadeus Mozart suffered from so many illnesses during his lifetime (1756–91) that it is difficult to tell what killed him at the tender age of thirty-five. According to his death certificate, he died from 'severe miliary fever', but 'miliary' just means small bumps on the skin, so is more a description of the symptoms than a diagnosis of the disease.

Mozart's wife Constanza is said to have spoken of his suspicions that he had been poisoned, which contributed to the persistent suggestion that the Italian composer Antonio Salieri was responsible for his rival's death (a rumour that inspired a verse drama by Alexander Pushkin, an opera by Nikolai Rimsky-Korsakov and Peter Shaffer's play and film *Amadeus*). But according to the medical evidence, poisoning is unlikely. If Mozart was poisoned, the most likely suspect is not Salieri but the proprietary medicines containing antimony that Mozart took for other real and supposed illnesses. He was quite a hypochondriac.

One recent study concluded that the most likely diagnosis was rheumatic fever. Another declared that it was probably a streptococcal infection known locally as *Wassersucht* leading to an acute nephritic syndrome caused by post-streptococcal glomerulonephritis. Or kidney failure, as you and I would call it.

314. How much of Mozart's *Requiem* did Mozart actually write?

The anonymous stranger who commissioned Mozart's *Requiem* towards the end of the composer's life is now known to have been Count Franz von Walsegg, who is thought to have adopted the subterfuge in order to pass off the work as his own. When Mozart died with the *Requiem* unfinished, it was completed by his friend and colleague Franz Xaver Süssmayr and delivered to Walsegg, but how much of the final score was genuine Mozart and how much is attributable to Süssmayr has never been satisfactorily sorted out.

The original autograph manuscript clearly shows the Introit in Mozart's hand, together with much of the Kyrie and Dies Irae, and the vocal parts of the offertory. Süssmayr spoke of 'scraps of paper', now lost, for much of the remainder of the composition, though he later claimed that the Sanctus and Agnus Dei were all his own work.

Ten years younger than Mozart, Süssmayr may have been his student and certainly worked as his copyist. He went on to a reasonably successful career as a composer himself, particularly of church music and opera, but never produced anything remotely as impressive as Mozart's *Requiem*.

315. Is the skull displayed at the International Mozarteum Foundation in Salzburg really that of Mozart?

In 1902 the International Mozarteum Foundation in Salzburg was presented with an intriguing if somewhat macabre gift: Mozart's skull. Or that at least was what it purported to be, and the story it came with provided some corroboration.

The usual romanticized account of Mozart's body being tossed into a paupers' mass grave on a stormy night has not stood up to examination, and the accepted view is that he was buried in a wooden coffin in a grave with four or five other people, which was the normal middle-class custom in Vienna at the time. A few years later, the bones were dug up to enable the plot to be used by others, which was also normal practice. The story behind the Mozarteum skull is based on an account of Joseph Rothmayer, one of the original gravediggers, who said that he attached a wire round the neck of Mozart's body so that he would be able to identify it. When the bodies were dug up in 1801, Rothmayer said he took the skull away with him, and that was the skull presented a century later to the Mozarteum.

In 2006, to celebrate the 250th anniversary of Mozart's birth, DNA studies were commissioned to compare the bones in the skull with samples taken from thigh bones of two skeletons in the Mozart family grave. Not only did these analyses not solve the problem, they even introduced another one. For not only was Mozart's skull found to show no relationship to the others, but the others showed no relationship to each other. At least one of them must therefore have not been a Mozart, raising the question of the identity of the uninvited corpse in the family vault. The skull, in fact, may be the only true Mozart in the trio. The DNA test was therefore ruled inconclusive.

MURDER

316. Was Pharaoh Ramses III assassinated?

Ramses III ruled Egypt for thirty-one years around 1170 BC and has been described as the last of the great pharaohs. But he ruled at a time of great turmoil, beset by wars and economic difficulties –

indeed, his inability to pay his workmen led to the earliest general strike in known history. Yet that was not the reason for the plot to assassinate him.

That such a plot existed is made clear by a set of trial documents that led to thirty-eight people being sentenced to death. It all began with a squabble between two of his wives over which of their sons would succeed Ramses, but it developed into a major conspiracy involving state officials, army personnel, scribes and even members of the royal harem.

Ramses died before the sentences were carried out, but whether the assassination plot had succeeded is unclear. His mummy shows no obvious wounds, and no traces of poison or snakebite were found, both of which have been suggested as causes of his death. However, his mummy was equipped with an amulet to protect him from snakes in the afterlife.

317. Who killed Edward the Martyr in 978?

Edward the Martyr had a short but troubled life. The eldest son of King Edgar, he came to the throne of England in 975 when he was only about thirteen years old. His reign began with the inauspicious sighting of a comet, continued with a famine, and ended three years after it had begun when he was murdered at Corfe Castle in Dorset. According to the *Anglo-Saxon Chronicle*, he was buried without honours or ceremony.

Some say his murder was organized by his step-mother Ælfthryth, whom he was visiting at Corfe; some say the man behind it – who was also at Corfe – was Edward's younger half-brother Ethelred (the Unready – but ready enough to take the throne when Edward was dead); some say that Edward's uncontrolled rages had upset so many people that anyone could have killed him. The version given by William of Malmesbury, writing two centuries later, asserts that Ælfthryth:

allured him to her with female blandishment and made him
lean forward, and after saluting him while he was eagerly
drinking from the cup which had been presented, the dagger of an
attendant pierced him through.

William's contemporary, Henry of Huntingdon, says that it was Ælfthryth who wielded the knife. But William and Henry were writing at such a remove from the events that they describe that they cannot be judged reliable.

318. Was Godwin, father of King Harold II, poisoned?

Thanks to his political skills, Godwin, Earl of Wessex, was probably the most powerful man in England when Edward the Confessor came to the throne in 1042. Even though Godwin was widely held responsible for the murder of Edward's brother, Alfred the Atheling, Edward was content to marry Godwin's daughter to cement his ties with the powerful earl. But since Edward had taken a vow of celibacy, nothing much came of the union. No children, anyway.

As usual for any medieval power behind the throne, Godwin accumulated enemies, and his situation was not helped when his son Swegen was outlawed in 1046 for seducing the Abbess of Leominister. Relations with Edward deteriorated, Godwin even at one stage raising an army against the king. That particular dispute was settled without bloodshed, but when Godwin died at a banquet at Winchester in 1053, there were two very different accounts of what happened.

The *Anglo-Saxon Chronicle* relates how Godwin suddenly sank against his footstool, speechless and helpless. He was carried into the king's chamber, where he lingered on for several days, still immobile and unable to speak, until he finally died.

The Norman version, however, written long after the event, tells of Godwin holding up a piece of bread and denying to the king that he had had a hand in his brother's death: 'God forbid that I should swallow this morsel, if I have done anything which might tend either to his danger or your disadvantage.' He then popped the bread – which in some versions of the story is a communion wafer – into his mouth and choked to death.

Suspicious circumstances, one might say, in either case.

319. Was William Rufus murdered?

On 2 August 1100 King William II of England – known as William Rufus, probably because of his ruddy complexion – went out hunting in the New Forest and was shot through a lung with an arrow. His companions said it was just a hunting accident, made worse when the king fell onto the arrow after the shot, driving it further into his body. He died shortly afterwards, and his body was left on the spot as those who had been with him fled to make preparations for the succession.

The main suspect – if it was not an accident – has always been Walter Tirel, possibly acting for William's brother Henry, who succeeded him as Henry I. But no charges were ever laid, let alone any conviction achieved. Yet even the accounts that say it was an accident (for example, William of Malmesbury writing c.1125 and Orderic Vitalis c.1135) say that it was Tirel's arrow that killed the king. William Rufus did, however, have many enemies, notably in the Church, especially after Anselm, Archbishop of Canterbury, had been forced into exile.

320. Was Agnès Sorel, mistress of Charles VII of France, murdered?

Agnès Sorel (1421–50) was Charles VII's favourite mistress. She bore him three daughters and was pregnant with the fourth when she died suddenly at the age of twenty-eight. The immediate diagnosis was dysentery, but a forensic examination of her disinterred remains in 2005 revealed that the cause of death was mercury poisoning.

In the fifteenth century, mercury was commonly used in cosmetic preparations or to treat certain diseases, so an innocent explanation is not ruled out. Both Charles's son, the future Louis XI, and one of his ministers, Jacques Coeur, might have stood to gain from Agnès Sorel's removal, but there is no direct evidence against either.

Charles VII himself was evidently not too inconvenienced by her death, as he swiftly recruited her cousin, Antoinette de Maignelais, to take over her role in his bed.

321. Were the Princes in the Tower murdered, and if so, by whom?

When Edward IV of England died in April 1483, his brother Richard, Duke of Gloucester, was named 'Lord Protector of the Realm' for the late king's son and obvious successor, the twelve-year-old Edward V. Eager to assume power, Richard had both the royal princes – Edward and his younger brother Richard of Shrewsbury (→ THE MIDDLE AGES 304) – declared illegitimate by Parliament on the grounds of doubts about the legality of the marriage between Edward IV and their mother, Elizabeth Woodville.

In the run-up to Edward's coronation, the young princes were staying at the Tower of London, then simply a royal residence. They were seen playing in the grounds in the summer of 1483, but were never seen again. In 1674, during renovations at the Tower, the skeletons of two children were found under a staircase, but no identification was possible and they were reburied. In 1933 the grave was again opened, but once more, no identification was possible.

Next time, perhaps they will use DNA testing – but there are no plans for another exhumation.

322. Who murdered Jean-Marie Leclair?

Jean-Marie Leclair the Elder (1694–1764) was a renowned violin virtuoso and one of the leading French composers of his time, specializing in works for the violin, though he also wrote one opera. He was also employed as premier dancer and ballet master in Turin and, moving between that city and Paris, he was celebrated as the most travelled French musician of his age.

Shortly after the break-up of his second marriage, Leclair bought a small house in Paris, and it was here that he was found dead in October 1764. He had been stabbed in the back. Suspicion fell on his ex-wife and his nephew, but no evidence was ever found to implicate them, or a rival musician, which seemed the only other likely possibility. The murderer or murderess was never discovered.

323. Who killed Mary Rogers, whose death inspired Edgar Allan Poe to write his second detective story?

In 1841 Edgar Allen Poe (→ WRITERS 486–7) wrote 'The Murders in the Rue Morgue', which is often acknowledged as the first detective story. The following year he wrote his second detective story, 'The Mystery of Marie Rogêt', but this time there was a big difference: it was very closely based on a real event.

Mary Rogers's body had been found floating in the Hudson River on 28 July 1841, bearing signs of having been severely battered. Finger-sized marks on her neck were taken as an indication that she had been strangled. She was about twenty-one years old.

Before her death she had been employed in a tobacconist's shop in New York – largely because her great beauty was such a draw for customers. Among those who purchased their smoking requisites from the 'Beautiful Cigar Girl' (as she became known) were the writers James Fenimore Cooper, Washington Irving and, according to some accounts, Edgar Allan Poe himself.

Mary's death was seized upon by the newspapers as a sensational crime mystery. Over the following months several arrests were made, but all suspects were soon released. Increasingly bizarre stories began to circulate: that she had been killed by her fiancé; that she had died as the result of an unsuccessful abortion; that the body was not that of the Beautiful Cigar Girl at all. One later writer even named Edgar Allan Poe as a possible suspect. The case has never been solved.

324. Who was Jack the Ripper?

Between August and November 1888 five women were violently killed in London's East End. The bodies were slashed and mutilated. A further six murders, both before and after this period, were linked to those five, though differences in method raised doubts that they were by the same killer. Nearly all the victims were prostitutes. A letter to the police, purportedly from the murderer but probably a fake, was signed 'Jack the Ripper'. The name stuck.

The case has fascinated both professional and amateur sleuths ever since, and over a hundred potential suspects have been named, ranging from the writer Lewis Carroll and the painter Walter Sickert to Prince Albert Victor, Duke of Clarence and son of the future King Edward VII. Yet all we know is that the killer may have possessed medical knowledge and may have been left-handed. Even those facts, however, are disputed.

325. Who killed Lizzie Borden's parents?

An otherwise unremarkable New England spinster has been immortalized in a rhyme chanted by generations of American girls as they spin a skipping rope for their playmates to jump over:

> Lizzie Borden took an axe,
> Gave her mother forty whacks.
> When she saw what she had done
> She gave her father forty-one.

In fact Lizzie Borden was acquitted of the hatchet murders of her father and stepmother on 4 August 1892 in Fall River, Massachusetts.

The jury reached their verdict after only an hour and a half's deliberation. But if Lizzie Borden did not deliver the fatal whacks, who did? Later writers have speculated that the maid or Lizzie's half-brother may have had motives to kill the Bordens, but neither was ever charged or apparently even suspected at the time. Lizzie died in 1927, aged sixty-six and worth around a million dollars. She left $500 in perpetual trust for the care of her father's grave.

326. Who killed Edwin Drood?

Edwin Drood is engaged to Rosa Bud, but Rosa is also loved by her choirmaster, John Jasper, who is Drood's uncle. Then Neville Landless arrives from Ceylon and also falls in love with Rosa. He takes an intense dislike to Edwin, who disappears under mysterious circumstances.

So, in the most cramped of nutshells, runs the plot of Charles Dickens's final novel, *The Mystery of Edwin Drood*, left incomplete at his death in 1870. The trouble is that Dickens never got round to revealing who killed Edwin Drood, or what role was played in his disappearance by the mysterious stranger, Dick Datchery.

Various attempts have been made to finish the story, including one by an American spiritualist who claimed to be in touch with the spirit of Dickens himself. In 1914 the Dickens Fellowship in London staged a trial of John Jasper, who had always been considered the most likely murderer, with G.K. Chesterton as the judge. When the jury returned a verdict of manslaughter, Chesterton ruled that the mystery of Edwin Drood was insoluble and fined everyone, except himself, for contempt of court.

When ignorance gets started it knows no bounds.

Will Rogers (1879–1935)

MUSIC

327. Who composed the song 'Greensleeves'?

There has long been a rumour that Henry VIII composed 'Greensleeves', but where this idea came from is anyone's guess. The style of the music was not known in England at the time, and although the king was an accomplished musician and is known to have written many songs, none of his known work is similar to 'Greensleeves'.

A ballad named 'Green Sleeves' was registered at the London Stationers' Company in 1580, and the song was included in a book dated 1584, in which it is described as a 'new tune'. Since Henry VIII died in 1547, his involvement seems unlikely.

While we are on the subject of anachronisms, it is perhaps worth mentioning that Shakespeare, in *The Merry Wives of Windsor*, has Falstaff exclaim: 'Let the sky rain potatoes! Let it thunder to the tune of "Greensleeves"!' The play is set around 1400, long before potatoes were brought from the New World to England.

328. Who wrote the music and who wrote the words for the British national anthem?

'God Save the Queen' (or 'King') has never formally been adopted as the British national anthem, but has filled that role in the life of the nation since 1745, when it was first performed in public at the Theatre Royal in Drury Lane. Both the tune and the words, however, are much older than that. The music has been attributed to England's greatest composer, Henry Purcell (1659–95), and the French composer Jean-Baptiste Lully (1632–87), among others. Another strong candidate is an earlier English composer, John Bull, who wrote a keyboard piece strikingly similar to the anthem in 1619.

The words are even older, but may have come together from various traditional sources. The phrase 'God save the king' was a watchword of the Royal Navy in the mid-sixteenth century, eliciting the response 'Long to reign over us'. The earliest known version of music and lyrics together in a form similar to the one used today was published in 1745 in the *Gentleman's Magazine*. This version began with the words 'God save Great George Our King' – George II's place on the British throne then being under threat from the Jacobite Rebellion led by Prince Charles Edward Stuart.

329. Who wrote the words to 'Happy Birthday to You'?

In 1893 the American sisters Patty and Mildred Hall wrote a tune that has been described as the most recognized song in the English language. It was written for children, and the original words were not 'Happy birthday to you' but 'Good morning to you'.

The 'Happy birthday' lyrics to the same tune first appeared in print in 1912, but are thought to be even older. Whether the adaptation was made by the Hall sisters, their students, or someone else entirely is unknown. The song was not copyrighted until 1935.

330. Who wrote the music for 'The Battle Hymn of the Republic'?

In the 1850s there was a popular Methodist campfire song in America known either as 'Say Brothers, Will You Meet Us' or 'Canaan's Happy Shore'. The first of those lines was sung three times followed by the words 'On Canaan's happy shore'. There followed a chorus beginning with the words 'Glory, glory, hallelujah!'

In 1861 a new version of the song appeared, with the same chorus but with the lyrics known as 'John Brown's Body' (referring to the abolitionist John Brown, who in 1859 had been hanged for his part in an anti-slavery revolt). Finally, in 1862, in the second year of the American Civil War, Julia Ward Howe published the version entitled 'The Battle Hymn of the Republic'.

The original tune is usually attributed to William Steffe, but it seems likely that he did no more than take a song that already existed in the folk tradition and arrange it for a Methodist song book, around the mid-1850s. Composition of the 'John Brown' version, with music for the verse as well as the chorus, was also claimed by Thomas Brigham Bishop, a Maine songwriter, bandleader and Union soldier, but he admitted that he was building on a traditional tune.

Others too have claimed authorship of the music, but perhaps that highly successful and prolific composer known as 'Traditional' ought to get the credit.

331. Where is the body of Glenn Miller?

On 15 December 1944 a plane took off in terrible weather from an RAF base near London to take Glenn Miller to join his band in Paris. According to the official story, neither the plane nor Miller nor his companions were ever seen again. Investigations into what happened have led to a number of theories, of which the following are only a small sample.

(i) Miller's plane was bombed or shot down by the Germans.

(ii) Miller's plane, flying low, was hit by bombs ditched by a British plane returning after a raid on Germany.

(iii) The plane crashed on the French coast, but the accident was covered up by the general who had ordered the flight to go ahead despite the wretched weather. This version was put forward in 1999 by a veteran army chaplain from the unit that claimed to have found the plane and the bodies.

(iv) Miller arrived safely in Paris, where he was killed in a brawl in a brothel. This version was given by a German journalist in 1997 who claimed he had been told the story by German intelligence experts.

See also COMPOSERS 92–100, ENGLISH LANGUAGE 176, HUMAN BEHAVIOUR 232, MURDER 322, MUSICAL INSTRUMENTS 332–4

MUSICAL INSTRUMENTS

332. Who invented the violin?

We know that the ancient Chinese and Japanese both had the idea of stringing horse hair over a box and rubbing it to make music, and that Leonardo da Vinci produced plans for a keyboard instrument that played notes by drawing a bow across strings. We can also date the appearance of the four-string violin more or less as we now know it to the early or mid-sixteenth century in Italy. We know that this four-string version developed from a three-stringed predecessor and that its design was perfected by Andrea Amati, grandfather of Nicolò Amati, the great seventeenth-century violin maker. But the identity of the first person to come up with the idea of the fourth string is lost in musical history.

333. What is responsible for the extraordinary sound quality of Stradivarius violins?

In Italy in the seventeenth and eighteenth centuries, a number of instrument makers – notably Nicolò Amati, Antonio Stradivari or Stradivarius, and various members of the Guarneri and Guadagnini families – produced cellos and violins that give a richer and more pleasing tone than anything we can make today, despite all the advantages of modern technology. So what was their secret?

Some have put it down to the climatic conditions in Italy at the time, which they contend produced the perfect wood for musical instruments. Some say it is what the makers did with the wood, such as soaking it in water or treating it for woodworm. Some say it is simply the weathering of the material over the centuries that gives the sound quality, and that the instruments probably did not sound so good when they were made. Some say it was the secret recipe of the varnish; some say it was simply the meticulous craftsmanship. Some say it was a combination of all the above.

Recent scientific tests, using X-ray spectroscopy to identify the elements in substances applied to the wood, have failed to reveal the secret. The only advance in knowledge has been a negative finding: there was nothing special at all in the varnish Stradivarius used. It was just the same combination used by other makers of that era: an application of linseed oil, followed by an oil resin containing red iron oxide and other common crimson pigments. Whatever the secret was, though, the result sounds wonderful.

334. What is responsible for the extraordinary sound quality of the banjo?

The characteristic twang of a banjo has fascinated acoustic engineers for years. The sound comes from vibration of the strings and a circular membrane, each of which set off sympathetic vibrations in the others, and this sympathetic feedback continues. Recent efforts to analyse the sound and produce computerized acoustic models of the banjo sound have made some progress, but a computer-banjo still does not quite sound like the real thing.

NUMBERS

335. Why in The *Hitchhiker's Guide to the Galaxy* did Douglas Adams choose 42 as the answer to Life, the Universe and Everything?

Adams was frequently asked this question and gave various different answers, all boiling down to basically: 'No reason at all.' 'I just wanted an ordinary, workaday number, and chose 42,' he once said. 'It's an un-frightening number. It's a number you could take home and show to your parents.'

Others have suggested that it's a pun on the song title 'Tea For Two': for tea, two. Yet the origins may have lain deep in Adams's subconscious when he was working as an extra in some management training videos made by John Cleese's Video Arts company. One such video featured Cleese as a bank teller having great difficulty adding up a column of numbers. At the end of the film, Cleese finally reaches the answer and triumphantly declares 'It's 42!' At that moment, the man walking across the back of the scene is none other than Douglas Adams.

It has also been pointed out that 9 × 6 does equal 42, just as the Earth computer claimed, as long as you are working in base 13. Adams, however, strongly denied that this had anything to do with it, saying: 'I may be a sorry case, but I don't write jokes in base 13.'

336. Why does the number 42 crop up so often in the works of Lewis Carroll?

In *Alice in Wonderland*, Lewis Carroll refers to 'Rule 42: All persons more than a mile high to leave the court', while the price on the Mad Hatter's hat is 10s 6d, which is 126 pence, or 3 × 42. The first edition of the book had 42 illustrations by John Tenniel.

In *The Hunting of the Snark* the Baker has 'forty-two boxes, all carefully packed, / With his name painted clearly on each'. The poem also refers to a Rule 42: 'No one shall speak to the Man at the Helm.'

Why was Carroll so fond of the number 42? When not writing for children, he was the Reverend Charles Lutwidge Dodgson, a Cambridge mathematics don with a keen interest in comparative religion. It has been pointed out that there is a Hindu goddess with 42 arms, and that there were originally 42 Articles of the Church of England before they were cut down to 39. Or Carroll may have identified it, just as Douglas Adams claims to have done (→ 335), as a nice un-frightening number you could take home to your parents.

337. Is the 196-algorithm true for the number 196?

Think of a number with at least two digits; reverse it; add the two numbers together. If the answer is palindromic (i.e. reads the same forwards as backwards), then stop. Otherwise, repeat the process of reversal followed by addition. To give a couple of examples:

42 + 24 = 66, which is palindromic.

87 + 78 = 165; 165 + 561 = 726; 726 + 627 = 1,353; 1,353 + 3,531 = 4,884.

It has been conjectured that whatever number you start with, you will always eventually reach a palindromic answer, but it may take some time. Starting with the number 187, for example, you do not reach the goal until the answer is 8,813,200,023,188.

The reason this is known as the 196-algorithm is that nobody knows if it is true for the number 196. If it does end up with a palindromic number, it has been shown that the number will have at least 300 million digits. But nobody has succeed in proving, for 196 or any other number, that the process will never reach the desired goal.

LEARNING, *n.* The kind of ignorance distinguishing the studious.

Ambrose Bierce (1842–1913), *The Devil's Dictionary*

338. Why is 666 the 'number of the beast'?

In the King James Bible, the Book of Revelation (13:18) has the following passage: 'Let him that hath understanding count the number of the beast: for it is the number of a man; and his number is six hundred threescore and six.'

But why 666? Various explanations have been given using arithmetic codes to translate names into numbers and identifying beastly characteristics in a variety of people from the Emperor Nero (renowned persecutor of the early Christians) to Napoleon and Kaiser Wilhelm II of Germany. But none of these theories satisfactorily explains why 666 was chosen.

It is the number you get if you add together all of the Roman number symbols – D, C, L, X, V and I – but if that is the reason, then why not include M and arrive at 1,666?

The question is further muddied by recent research suggesting a transcription error and that the real number of the beast is not 666 but 616 – but that is just as difficult to justify.

See also MATHEMATICS 278–80

OLD TESTAMENT

339. How long was the cubit mentioned in the account of the dimensions of Noah's Ark?

When the Lord told Noah to make an ark of gopher wood, He specified that 'the length of the ark shall be three hundred cubits, the breadth of it fifty cubits, and the height of it thirty cubits' (King James Bible, Genesis 6:15). Noah must have known what God was talking about, because he did not then ask whether the Lord was referring to an Egyptian royal cubit, a Roman cubit, a Persian cubit or a Sumerian cubit, all of which could refer to different lengths – a state of affairs that has led to disagreements about anything measured in cubits ever since (→ JESUS CHRIST 251).

Traditionally, a cubit was the distance between a man's elbow and the tip of his outstretched middle finger. It was also frequently defined as a fixed number of 'palms', which were the breadth of a hand, but the number of palms in a cubit might vary between six and nine, and in most cases the cubit defined in this way was longer than that given by the other definition of elbow to middle finger.

340. What were the names of the women on Noah's Ark?

The Book of Genesis lists four women on the Ark: the wives of Noah and of his sons Shem, Ham and Japheth. But we are not told the names of any of them. Other ancient scribes do suggest names for them, but no two writers agree, and around ten sets of names, often widely differing from each other, have been offered. The one thing we can be reasonably certain of, contrary to the beliefs of 12 per cent of Americans surveyed in 1997, is that Joan of Arc was not Noah's wife.

341. Did the flood that resulted in the formation of the Black Sea inspire the story of Noah?

There are two rival theories concerning the formation of the Black Sea. The older theory is that over the past 30,000 years or so, water has flowed between the Aegean and Black Seas, sometimes in one direction, sometimes the other, but gradually raising the water level in the latter. The other theory, first proposed in 1997, is of a massive flood around 5600 BC caused by the waters of the Aegean overflowing and spilling over the Bosporus at a rate about two hundred times greater than today's flow of water over Niagara Falls. The result was the formation of the Black Sea and the flooding of a vast area of land, causing at least displacement and probably disaster for all the peoples of the region.

Memories of such a cataclysmic event could, it has been suggested, have led to the story of Noah's Flood – a story that is by no means unique in Middle Eastern mythology, paralled in other sources such as the *Epic of Gilgamesh* from Mesopotamia. Scientific examination of Black Sea sediments has not yet either confirmed or refuted the hypothesis of a sudden flood, but a link to the Noah story would be even more difficult to establish.

342. Was the Exodus of the Israelites mythological or historical?

There are so many independent references to the Exodus in the Old Testament and other ancient texts that it is difficult to dismiss the story as pure myth. Those seeking a historical background for the events described in the Book of Exodus and the next three books of the Old Testament point to the late Bronze Age collapse of various civilizations in the eastern Mediterranean (→ ANCIENT HISTORY 13) and a number of examples of Egypt expelling certain peoples from its lands. The massive eruption of the volcanic island of Thera around 1600 BC has also been cited as a possible explanation of the plagues of Egypt and the crossing of the Red Sea.

Yet the account in Numbers of 600,000 men and their women and children being led across the wilderness by Moses does not tally with what we know of contemporary population figures, either in Egypt at the time of the supposed departure of the Israelites or in the promised land of Canaan at the time of their arrival. The figure must be at best an exaggeration or mistranslation. No archaeological evidence has been found in support of the Exodus story, though a number of sites have been excavated along the supposed route.

It seems reasonable, therefore, to conclude that the story of the Exodus is a blend of religious and historical elements, though we cannot be sure of the factual basis of the latter.

343. Who wrote the Old Testament Psalms?

The Book of Psalms contains 150 items, of which 73 are ascribed to David. However, these ascriptions in ancient texts are thought by some scholars to be unreliable, having been added long after the psalms were written. Another view is that the word ascribing them to David did not mean 'by David' but 'of David', meaning only that he collected together the works of various ancient psalmists. Analysis of the language used in the psalms has also been taken by some scholars to suggest that they were written over a long period, and were not all by the same hand.

The names of Asaph and the 'Sons of Korah' also appear in ascriptions, as do those of Henan, Ethan, Solomon and Moses. As with much else in the Old Testament, we do not know who the author was and do not have enough samples from known writers to be able to undertake a proper textual analysis.

See also JUDAISM 252, 254

OLM

344. How does the olm live for so long, and why doesn't it seem to age?

The olm, or proteus, is a blind wormlike amphibian around 20 to 30 cm (8 to 12 in) long that lives in underground caves in the karst region of the northern Balkans. Its eyes are undeveloped but have some sensitivity to light, while its senses of hearing and smell are good. The remarkable thing about the olm is that, according to a recent estimate, it may live for a hundred years, which is far longer than one would expect from its size. Even more remarkable is the fact that – according to recent examinations of specimens over the age of sixty – they show no physical signs of ageing. The olm can also live for up to ten years without food. Whether the absence of sunlight from its habitat contributes to its health and longevity is a matter for further research.

> All you need in this life is ignorance and confidence, and then success is sure.
>
> Mark Twain (1835–1910)

PAINTING

345. What happened to Leonardo da Vinci's lost masterpiece, *The Battle of Anghiari*?

In 1504 Leonardo da Vinci was commissioned to paint a battle scene in the Hall of the Five Hundred at the Palazzo Vecchio in Florence. Michelangelo was to paint a different battle scene on the opposite wall. It was the only time the two men worked on the same project, and it was to be Leonardo's largest work.

We have a good idea of the magnificence of the work from the artist's numerous preliminary sketches and from the copy of the central section made in the following century by the Flemish master Peter Paul Rubens, with its splendid depiction of men on horseback in the midst of the fury of battle. But Leonardo's original is lost. Sometime in the mid- to late sixteenth century, the Hall of the Five Hundred was enlarged and the painting was lost. Some think it may still be hidden behind later frescoes on the wall, and that perhaps one day it will be revealed again.

346. Did Leonardo da Vinci leave a coded message in microscopic letters in the eyes of the *Mona Lisa*?

Dan Brown's best-selling 2003 book *The Da Vinci Code* may have been fiction, but in December 2010 members of Italy's National Committee for Cultural Heritage claimed to have discovered what may be a true da Vinci code. Apparently, if you hugely enlarge images of the eyes of the *Mona Lisa*, letters and numbers can be detected within them. These can only be seen with the aid of a microscope, but the researchers say the right eye clearly shows the letters LV, which could stand for Leonardo da Vinci, while the left eye also has symbols, but they are rather blurred and it is difficult to make out what they are. The number 72, or it may be L2, is in the bridge in the background. The researchers had been prompted to examine the painting closely after coming across a fifty-year-old book in an antique shop, which indicated that such symbols might exist.

347. Who was the model for the *Mona Lisa*?

There has always been some doubt over the identity of the model in Leonardo's *Mona Lisa*, but the general opinion has always been that she was Lisa Gherardini, wife of Francesco del Giocondo, the silk merchant who commissioned the painting. This was apparently confirmed in 2005 when a note was found in the margin of a book written in 1503, identifying her as the model.

In February 2011, however, another theory emerged. Not only was it not Lisa Gherardini, it was not even a woman. Comparing the face in the painting with other faces appearing in Leonardo's oeuvre, it was suggested by the Italian art historian Silvano Vinceti that it was in fact the face of Gian Giacomo Caprotti, known as Salai, an attractive male apprentice of Leonardo's who is thought to have also been his lover. Supporters of Vinceti's theory also referred to the mysterious microscopic coded letters (→ 346) in the portrait's eyes, one of which is said to be an S, possibly standing for Salai.

Not to be outdone, in May 2011 supporters of the traditional Lisa Gherardini theory announced that they were close to identifying her burial place, and when they do so they hope to exhume the bones, find the skull, and from that recreate what she looked like.

348. Who was the subject of Albrecht Dürer's sketch entitled *Head of a Negro*, and what was Dürer's relationship to him?

Dürer's marvellous 1508 portrait known simply as *Head of a Negro* was drawn right at the beginning of the transatlantic slave trade, a time when black men were not often seen in Europe other than at ports (mostly in Spain and Portugal), where they would have been en route to America. Yet Germany, where Dürer lived and spent most of his time, had no such ports. Perhaps the rarity of the subject was what prompted Dürer's desire to draw the man, but if the subject was indeed a slave, how did he come to be sitting for Dürer, and if he wasn't a slave, then who was he?

In the art of the time, black faces were common in paintings of the Adoration of the Magi, but rare in other works, particularly portraits. In his journal, Dürer mentions meeting an African woman in Antwerp, in the house of the Portuguese trade commissioner. This woman was the subject of his portrait known as *The Negress of Brandon*, but Dürer's meeting with her took place in 1521, long after he sketched his *Head of a Negro*. The identity of the subject of the latter picture is still a complete mystery.

349. Which of Rembrandt's supposed self-portraits were actually painted by Rembrandt?

The seventeenth-century Dutch master Rembrandt van Rijn painted more self-portraits than any other major artist, but there is a debate over the precise number. The problem is that the paintings that have been classified as Rembrandt self-portraits come in three categories: the paintings Rembrandt executed himself; the forgeries; and the paintings that were executed, copied or completed by his students. The first two categories are clear enough, but the last creates a good deal of room for argument and confusion. At one time, about ninety paintings were thought to be authentic Rembrandt self-portraits; now the estimates vary between thirty and eighty.

Interestingly, New York Customs records show that 9,482 alleged Rembrandts were imported to the USA between 1800 and 1850. The worldwide figure for works confirmed as genuine Rembrandts is now down to around three hundred, though new discoveries continue to be made. In 2008 a newly authenticated Rembrandt self-portrait sold for £2.2 million ($4.5 million at the time) at auction. The auction house had thought it to be a fake and had estimated that it would fetch £1,500.

350. How did Caravaggio die?

Apart from being a great artist, Michelangelo Merisi da Caravaggio was a notorious brawler and trouble-maker. Jailed several times and exiled from Rome for killing a man in a fight, he was even expelled as official painter to the Order of the Knights of Malta as 'a foul and rotten member'.

Caravaggio died at the age of thirty-eight in 1610, supposedly of a fever, but since several attempts had previously been made on his life, one of which is said to have left him disfigured, foul play cannot be ruled out. In 2010, bones found by Italian researchers at a church in Tuscany were identified 'with 85 per cent certainty' as those of Caravaggio. Investigations suggested sunstroke, infected wounds and lead poisoning, possibly from the lead in his paints, as possible causes of death.

Ignorance more frequently begets confidence than does knowledge. It is those who know little, and not those who know much, who so positively assert that this or that problem will never be solved by science.

Charles Darwin (1809–1882)

PALAEONTOLOGY

351. What explains the 'Cambrian explosion', when a vast number of species of plants and animals appeared around 530 million years ago?

When Charles Darwin proposed his theory of evolution, one of his biggest problems came in accounting for the Cambrian explosion. Evolution ought, according to Darwin, have been a slow process, yet the fossil record seemed to indicate that over a few million years, which is a very short period in evolutionary terms, a large number of species of both animals and plants came into existence. When the Cambrian period began 570 million years ago, most organisms were single-celled creatures. Then suddenly a large range of multicellular organisms evolved, resulting in something much more like life as we know it today. There are several suggestions to account for this:

(i) The fossil record gives an incorrect picture, as something may have happened in the Precambrian era that prevented fossils from being laid down.

(ii) There's nothing wrong with the fossils. It's just that for some reason we have failed to find those in the period just before the Cambrian.

(iii) Some vital change occurred in the evolution of living organisms in the early Cambrian that gave a huge advantage to multicellular creatures, enabling them to evolve in great numbers.

(iv) Something in the climate, atmosphere or elsewhere in the environment changed the nature of what types of creature were best fitted to survive.

Since 1980 more Precambrian fossils have been unearthed that support the view that the Cambrian explosion may not have been as explosive as had been thought, but it is still difficult to explain in standard evolutionary terms.

352. How did the creatures of Madagascar get there?

Around 75 per cent of the animal species in Madagascar are found nowhere else on Earth. The fossil record has never supported a case for a slow, separate evolution on Madagascar itself, so the belief has generally been that the creatures of Madagascar must have come from the African continent long ago, either by a land bridge or carried over by ocean currents on rafts of matted vegetation.

The land-bridge theory runs into the evidence that different species arrived at different times over some 40 million years. If there was a land bridge, one would expect them to have wandered across over a relatively brief period rather than having the ancestors of shrews and hedgehogs waiting some 25 million years after lemur-like creatures had crossed. Yet the raft theory runs counter to our knowledge of ocean currents around Madagascar, knowledge that makes it unlikely that anything drifted over from Africa.

In 2010, however, a paper in *Nature* reported research supporting the view that the currents round Madagascar may have changed both in speed and direction some 23 million years ago, which was about the time new species ceased to arrive on the island. Measuring the strength of prehistoric ocean currents is a tricky business, however, and it may be that this has to remain a theory.

353. Why did mammoths become extinct?

Numerous theories have been put forward:

(i) The last mammoths froze to death in Siberia at the onset of the last ice age (Victorian theory).

(ii) Climate change and disease are the most probable causes of the mammoths' extinction (Penn State University research, 2008).

(iii) Humans hunted the mammoths to extinction (research in Madrid, 2008).

(iv) Humans hunting mammoths was not the main problem. It was human over-hunting of other animals and possibly the over-consumption of certain plants, which in turn caused major disruption to the entire ecosystem, leading to the extinction of many species (research at UCLA and Oregon State University published in 2010).

(v) Mammoth extinction was caused by the milder climate leading to a growth in trees, which increased the shade and took nutrients from the soil, both of which led to a severe decrease in the growth of the vegetation the mammoths needed to survive (research in Alaska, 2006).

(vi) Mammoth extinction was a consequence of a large change in the Earth's fauna about 13,000 years ago (conclusion of a study of fossilized mammoth dung in Wisconsin, 2009).

354. Did our *Australopithecus afarensis* ancestor known as Lucy walk on the ground or swing from the branches of trees?

Australopithecus afarensis lived between 3.9 and 2.9 million years ago, which is at least a million years before *Homo erectus*, but which of them was the first to be truly bipedal continues to be a source of debate. The discovery of *Australopithecus* footprints in 1978 demonstrated that they certainly did walk upright at least some of the time, but studies of their bones offer conflicting information.

The curvature of the fingers and toes is similar to that of modern apes and suggests that the ability to grasp branches and climb was important to them. On the other hand (or more accurately foot), the absence of an abductable (grasping) big toe – an absence shared by modern humans – suggests that their feet were used more for walking than swinging from branches. Their pelvic formation has also been cited as evidence for a bipedal gait. We do not even know if they lived most of the time in trees or on the ground.

355. Did Neanderthals have furry coats of hair?

We know, from their fossil skeletons, that Neanderthals (→ HUMAN EVOLUTION 237) were shorter than us, had bigger noses and projecting brows and not much in the way of chins. But they did have bigger brains than we do. We also know that they shared an ape-like ancestor with us, but one of the troubles with skeletons is that they have no hair. So we do not know whether Neanderthals were furry like apes or relatively hairless like modern humans.

According to DNA research, Neanderthals had a similar distribution of hair colours to our own. Or, as one somewhat dubious newspaper report of 2008 put it: 'European Neanderthals had ginger hair and freckles.' Less eye-catching reports suggested that about 1 per cent of Neanderthals had ginger hair.

When, in the course of our evolution, we lost most of our body hair, or why we did so, are unknown. One recent suggestion is that parents put their furriest babies to death through a desire to distance their species from other mammals, so passing on less hairy genes. But whether this happened (if it happened at all) before or after the Neanderthals is a matter of pure speculation.

356. Did Neanderthals have music?

DNA research has shown that Neanderthals possessed the FOXP2 gene, which is thought to play a vital part in the acquisition and use of language, so they may have been the first humans to talk to each other, or at least to grunt in an intelligible manner (→ LANGUAGE 237). There is another theory, however, that language began with music and that human speech began with something closer to birdsong. So it is possible that the Neanderthals communicated musically and, thanks to the FOXP2 gene, this evolved into language.

PANDAS

357. Why are pandas black and white?

Almost everything we said about zebras (→ MAMMALS 266) applies equally to pandas, except that pandas have no predators, so the idea that their colouring acts as a warning to other species is even less convincing. It has been suggested that the stark black-and-white markings do act as a kind of warning – a territorial warning to other pandas to keep away. It has also been suggested that the colouring enables pandas to see each other more distinctly and helps them in their search for a mate.

358. How does a female panda choose which of her cubs to bring up and which to abandon?

Pandas give birth to one, two or sometimes three cubs, but they will never care for more than one. In the event of multiple births, the mother will select one cub to look after and abandon the others, which soon die. This would make sense if she always abandoned the weaker cubs, which many have assumed is what happens, but there is no evidence to support that theory, nor are there any other findings to suggest what the mother panda is looking for when she makes her selection.

PENGUINS

359. What is the penguin population of Antarctica?

In April 2011 the US National Oceanic and Atmospheric Administration published a report linking variability in the amount of Antarctic krill with a decline in penguin population. Both krill harvesting and a decline in krill put down to global warming seemed to be depriving penguins of one of the major items in their diet. Several publications seized on this report to assert that penguin numbers had decreased by 50 per cent or more, and that the survival of baby penguins had been affected still more. Yet the original paper had taken pains to avoid making claims about the entire Antarctic penguin population, the authors making it clear that their figures related only to certain species of penguin (of which there are seventeen in all in the Antarctic) and to certain closely monitored breeding colonies.

Scientists at the British Antarctic Survey have been more wary. Addressing the question of whether penguin populations are declining, they say: 'Some species are but others are not – it depends where you look.' Adélie penguin populations have fluctuated, they say, while chinstrap penguins have decreased significantly, and gentoo numbers have risen.

On their website, the Antarctic explorers Guillaume and Jennifer Dargaud are even more explicit about how little we know:

> *Many parts of Antarctica, including some of the shores, have never been explored, so the precise number of penguins is unknown. Evaluations have been done by counting manually the*

penguin populations in some areas and extrapolating to the entire continent... But keep in mind that these are highly inaccurate statistics, most colonies not having been visited for decades, and many more having never received a visit.

The definitive Antarctic penguin census has clearly not yet been undertaken.

See also SEX 417

PHILOSOPHY

The entire subject of philosophy might be considered to consist of the things we do not know. What follows is just a small selection of the sort of unanswered questions philosophers love to think about.

360. Do we have free will?

The problem as to whether or not we have free will – a question that both philosophers and theologians have struggled with for centuries – boils down at its simplest to the compatibility or otherwise between free will and determinism. The theological version comes down to a discussion of the nature of God's omniscience. If God is omniscient, the argument goes, then He knows everything about the past, present and future, including all the decisions we, His creations, are going to make. Our actions are therefore predetermined and we don't really have free will at all.

Such an argument, however, does not require the existence of God. The scientific version is based on the idea that the universe runs according to immutable laws. Every particle in the universe is governed by these laws, whether we know them or not, so all our actions must be the result of them and thus predetermined. The biological version of the same argument would include our genetic make-up and experiences, which determine other aspects of our behaviour and the choices we think we are making.

See also INSECTS 244

361. Is free will an illusion caused by quantum uncertainty?

When the laws of quantum mechanics were discovered in the 1920s, they gave us a new way of approaching the question of free will. Suddenly, at a subatomic level, we found ourselves facing a level of indeterminacy quite foreign to the rigid picture painted by classical physics. According to the 'uncertainty principle' enunciated by the German theoretical physicist Werner Heisenberg, it was impossible to determine the position and velocity of a particle at the same time, thus making it impossible to predict its future. Furthermore, according to quantum theory, particles could be in two different places at the same time and a cat could be both dead and alive (→ QUANTUM PHYSICS 401). This idea led to the idea of parallel universes, encompassing all the possibilities of quantum uncertainty.

Advocates of free will might claim that that is what they have been saying all along. When we make a choice, we are just steering ourselves in the direction of a chosen universe. Deniers of free will could equally say that all quantum uncertainty has done is to introduce a predictable randomness into physical laws, and the existence of that randomness is what makes us think we have the ability to make choices.

362. Does a cause necessarily precede its effect?

From Aristotle in ancient Greece to the eighteenth-century Scottish philosopher David Hume and beyond, the very idea of causality seemed to insist that cause precedes effect. Hume even began his definition of of 'a cause' by describing it as 'an object precedent and contiguous to another'. Only in the mid-twentieth century did philosophers begin to ask whether this was indeed necessary.

The standard argument against cause coming later than effect is similar to the argument against travelling backwards in time: if A causes B, but B precedes A, then what happens if, after B has occurred, we do something to stop A happening?

There are two obvious ways around that dilemma. One is to say that if A is truly the cause of B, then you would find it impossible to stop A from happening once B had occurred. The other is to say that stopping A does not cause a logical dilemma. B can still happen without A. All we have done is change the cause of B.

For the past fifty years, physicists have conjectured the existence of certain particles, called tachyons, that can travel faster than light – which would mean they could travel backwards in time. And that would mean that their future (from the perspective of our time frame) could affect their past.

Not long before writing this, I overheard a conversation in which a family were discussing what the date was going to be on the following Monday. 'It's definitely the 21st,' one lady said, 'because Tuesday is Geoffrey's birthday, and that is the 22nd.' That seemed to settle the matter for me: if Monday is the 21st because Tuesday is the 22nd, then the effect has preceded the cause. Some philosophers, however, would disagree.

363. What is knowledge?

Plato said that for something to be considered 'knowledge' it must satisfy three criteria: it must be justified, true and believed. For more than two thousand years, philosophers have been arguing about whether he was right. Take, for example, the following scenario:

A celebrity is involved in a road accident and a newspaper publishes a report based on incorrect evidence that he has been killed. Someone reads this report just before jetting off on holiday to an out-of-the-way location where international news is hard to come by. A week later, the celebrity dies of his injuries. Does the holidaymaker know that he is dead? He believes it, because he read it in the paper. It is now true (though it wasn't when he read it). It is justified, because it was a reputable paper that doesn't often make such mistakes.

You could say it all hangs on what one means by 'justified', and that is basically what philosophers have been arguing about all this time.

364. Is the self identical with the body?

This is one of the 'Fourteen unanswerable questions' of Buddhist philosophy that the Buddha himself refused to answer. It is the question of whether the self is eternal and unchanging, as the eternalists believe, or whether it dies with the body, as the materialists claim. It is said in Buddhist scripture that considering such matters is a waste of time, so we shall move on to the next item without further ado.

365. Is colour a product of the mind or an inherent property of objects?

The Austrian physicist Erwin Schrödinger once wrote: 'The sensation of colour cannot be accounted for by the physicist's objective picture of light-waves.' We have such a vivid perception of the concepts we call 'red', or 'blue' or 'yellow' that it is difficult to think of them as merely ranges on a scale of wavelengths of light.

There are, of course, many things in everyday experience to which we can assign figures on a precise scale: temperature, or length, or weight, for example. Yet we can tell whether one thing is hotter than another, or bigger or heavier. Without specialized knowledge of light frequencies, however, we would be hard pressed to put colours in the right order without relying on the ROYGBIV of the rainbow. Even with that help, however, we would not claim to perceive red and violet as at opposite ends of a scale.

Some of the things we experience are subjective (philosophers use the term 'qualia' for such things), some are objective. Colours fall in between: they are our subjective experiences of an objective phenomenon. Whether they exist at all or only in our minds is a difficult question to answer.

366. When is a heap not a heap?

This is known as the Sorites paradox, from the Greek word for 'heap', and it is attributed to the Greek philosopher Eubulides of Miletus (flourished fourth century BC), whose argument went as follows:

If you remove one grain of sand from a heap of sand, it will still be a heap of sand.

A million grains of sand is a heap.

So if we remove the grains one by one, it will always still be a heap.

Eventually all the grains will be gone. So even when we have no sand at all, it is still a heap.

There is a similar argument about the hairs on the head of a non-bald man.

Bertrand Russell tried to get round this paradox by saying that all natural language is vague, but when so much of philosophy depends on the precise use of language, that does seem a bit of a cop-out.

367. Is the number of stars in our galaxy odd or even?

Even the ancient Greek philosophers said that we can never know the precise answer to that one. It used to be cited as an example of a question to which a precise answer existed, but which we can never know. Actually it's an even more difficult question than the Greeks imagined, as we would have to decide whether to include white dwarfs and black holes and other types of collapsed stars, and what to do with the stars that are thousands of light years away, so may seem to be there, but could have collapsed ages ago.

According to a recent estimate, there are about 200 billion stars in the Milky Way and about 100,000,000,000,000,000,000,000 stars in the universe. But at the end of 2010, astronomers reported that we may have got it wrong and that there could be three times as many. If we are not even sure whether the figure is 1 followed by 23 zeroes or 3 followed by 23 zeroes, the chance of ever knowing whether the precise answer is odd or even is pretty slim.

368. Do coincidences happen more often than they ought to?

The Swiss psychologist Carl Jung (1875–1961) had a belief in the inherent connectedness of things, maintaining that the world is well ordered, with events propelled to move in a coherent direction by the 'collective unconscious'. At the heart of his ideas is the concept he called 'synchronicity', which he conceived as a connecting process that did not rely on cause and effect.

Coincidence-mongers love collecting and pointing out the remarkable coincidences that happen to themselves and others, some of which seem mind-boggling in their unlikelihood.

Cold rationalists argue that we all lead very rich lives, with thousands of things happening to us every day that offer coincidence opportunities. What would really be remarkable would be if surprising coincidences did not happen from time to time. But measuring the precise frequency with which coincidences happen and calculating whether they happen more often than they ought is not an easy task.

There is a famous list of supposedly mystical coincidences linking the assassination of Abraham Lincoln and that of John F. Kennedy. Both had seven-letter surnames; both were shot from behind on a Friday; both were elected in years ending -60; both were succeeded by men named Johnson who were born in years ending -08; Lincoln was in Ford's Theatre, Kennedy in a Ford convertible; and so on and so on. But there are always plenty of coincidences to be found if you are looking for them.

See also BATS 33, THE GREEKS 217–18, INSECTS 244, REALITY 408–411

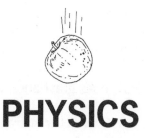

PHYSICS

369. Why is gravity so much weaker than the other fundamental forces of physics?

There are four fundamental forces that hold the universe together. We are all familiar with the electromagnetic force from our experience of magnetism and electricity; we may have heard of the strong nuclear force, which is what holds protons and neutrons so firmly together inside the atomic nucleus; and if we have delved into quantum theory, we may have run into the weak nuclear force, which acts on subatomic particles and is responsible for nuclear decay. However, even the weak nuclear force – which is only a millionth of the strength of the strong nuclear force – is a giant compared with the fourth force, the force of gravity.

If you measure the gravitational force between two particles, you need to add 30 zeroes to it to get an approximation of the weak nuclear force. This is a big problem for any physicist looking for a theory of everything.

String theory is the nearest anyone has come so far. By seeing our three-dimensional world as a slice, or 'brane', in a ten-dimensional universe, a reconciliation of the forces can be obtained. This views gravity as a force acting through all ten dimensions, of which we perceive only a feeble three-dimensional effect, while the other forces act only in our three dimensions. It all comes down to the difference between 'open strings', which are the fundamental ten-dimensional vibrating squiggles of string theory, and 'closed strings', which are the same thing, but with the ends joined together to form a loop.

Some physicists, however, think that adding another seven dimensions to the universe is inventing rather a big sledgehammer just to crack the puny nut of gravity.

370. How does gravitation work?

Newton saw gravity as a force between two objects. Einstein saw it as a consequence of the warping of the space-time continuum caused by mass. Newton believed that gravity was instantaneous. Einstein posited the existence of 'gravitational waves', moving at the speed of light. Recent experiments seem to have confirmed Einstein's view, but what his gravitational waves consist of and how they are propagated remains a mystery.

371. Is cold fusion possible?

In March 1989 Martin Fleischmann and Stanley Pons of the University of Utah reported an experiment which, if it was correct, could have changed the world. What they announced was the detection of the results of nuclear fusion in an experiment conducted at room temperature. Previously fusion had only been seen to occur at enormously high temperatures. If Pons and Fleischmann were right, their discovery could lead to an almost inexhaustible source of cheap energy.

Other scientists rushed to repeat the experiment and verify the results, but with no success. By the end of 1989 there was a heavy cloud of distrust surrounding the idea of cold fusion, and much criticism was being flung at Pons and Fleischmann for alleged experimental errors.

Yet despite this denunciation by many in the scientific community, various teams have continued to pursue the Holy Grail of cold
fusion, and there continue to be sporadic reports of claims that the
results of nuclear fusion have been detected in experiments at room
temperature. Some still clearly believe that it may be theoretically
possible.

372. Can solar energy be converted into a practical fuel?

The Sun, though clearly a massive potential source of energy, cannot
be used for the vast majority of our energy needs. The trouble is
the intermittent nature of solar energy as far as we on Earth are
concerned, together with the problems of storing it for later use.
Solar panels may be good at heating our homes during the day, and
the heat may to some extent be stored in hot-water tanks, but in
general the best thing that can be done with excess energy captured
by solar panels is to feed it into the electricity grid.

Solar-powered cars have been developed, but at best they require
an alternative source of energy to be used when it is not sunny. The
most practical idea at present seems to be a battery-powered car
that can be recharged with solar energy – but in practical terms the
best this can offer is to extend the range of the car   beyond that
offered by the battery. A car that replaces conventional fuels with
solar power but still performs equally well is still a long way off.

373. Is there a limit to how fast humans can run?

A hundred years ago, the world record for the men's 100 metres
was 10.6 seconds. Sprinters have slowly but surely chipped away at
the record, which now stands – as of July 2011 – at 9.58 seconds (a
time achieved by Usain Bolt in August 2009). Given our mass, leg
length, muscle power and other physical factors, there must be a
theoretical maximum speed at which humans can run, but what
is it?

How much of the improvement has come through the creation of faster running tracks or better shoes and how much is due to stronger and better-trained athletes is arguable, but biostatisticians have used the 100-metre record data to attempt to predict the limits of human running speed.

Until recently, a smooth curve seemed to fit the data linking world 100-metre records to the year they were set. Gradually declining but flattening out, this resulted in a prediction of about 9.45 seconds as the ultimate humans could hope to achieve. Then along came the Jamaican sprinter Usain Bolt, who broke the world record three times in 2008 and 2009, sending the actual data plummeting below the smooth curve that had been predicted. It should have been another twenty or thirty years before such times had been reached.

The biostatisticians have gone back to their computers, but with the smoothness of the curve now badly dented, all bets are now off.

See also EINSTEIN 164–7, FUNDAMENTAL PARTICLES 192–7, MAGNETISM 261–3, QUANTUM PHYSICS 399–407

THE PLANETS

374. How did the planets form?

Astronomers believe they have a pretty good idea of how the Solar System formed. It began around 4.6 billion years ago in a huge cloud of gas and dust, most probably thrown out by the massive explosive force of a supernova somewhere else in the galaxy. The gravitational pull of this massive dust cloud attracted more material, eventually causing the cloud to collapse in on itself. Since angular momentum has to be conserved, its rotational speed increased, causing the cloud to flatten out into a disc around a very dense core.

This core eventually coalesced into the Sun, while some of the dust particles at the end of the disc were flung out into space, eventually becoming the planets – again formed by the clumping caused by the mutual gravitational pull of the particles. This explains why the planets are all to be found in more or less the same plane, which is that of the original disc.

Yet the theory still leaves much unanswered. How did the discs of both the Sun and the planets take on their present almost spherical shape? How did they lose the massive angular momentum they once had? And while it is easy to accept that dust particles clump together to form rocks in space, it is not known how these rocks stick together and build up into planets. This last question may hold the key to understanding why some stars have planetary systems and others do not.

Until these questions are answered, we cannot really say we understand how the planets were formed.

375. Is there still volcanic and tectonic activity on Venus?

Venus, which in many ways is the planet most similar to Earth, has more volcanoes than any other planet in the Solar System. An active volcano was recently identified on one of Venus's moons, yet whether any of Venus's own 1,600 or so major volcanoes is still active is unknown. In 2010, temperature readings from the surface of Venus were reported to suggest the presence of three active volcanoes, which could be continuing the process of resurfacing the planet with lava.

The underlying question is whether Venus is a totally dead clump of rock (like our Moon) or whether it is still active and in the process of formation (like our own Earth). It would help if we knew whether

Venus had active tectonic plates or whether its surface is one solid piece, but again there is considerable dispute over what lies beneath the planet's crust. As of now, the Earth is still the only planet in the Solar System that is definitely known to possess tectonic plates.

376. Why does Venus rotate in the wrong direction, and why does it turn so slowly?

Looking down on the plane of the orbits of the planets around the Sun, all but one of them are rotating in the same direction on their own axis. This is the same direction of rotation as their own orbit around the Sun. The exception is Venus, whose own rotation about its axis is retrograde – in the opposite direction to its solar orbit. It is also very slow: a day on Venus (the period of rotation on its own axis) is longer than a Venusian year (the period of its orbit around the Sun).

We do not know why this is so. If, as is generally thought likely, all the planets were formed in the same way in the same era in the development of the Solar System, they would all be expected to rotate in the same direction. Venus's rotation may have been slowed by the effect of the tides in its dense atmosphere, but a complete reversal seems to need a different explanation.

377. Are there fish on the moons of Jupiter?

The European Space Agency and NASA are currently collaborating on a mission that involves two craft in orbit around Jupiter's largest moons, Europa and Ganymede, both of which are thought to have large underground oceans. The presence of water in its liquid state always raises the possibility of the presence of life, so these two moons now top the list of extraterrestrial locations in the Solar System where life might be found. Failing that, they could offer prospects of being habitable.

In 2009 the Arizona scientist Richard Greenberg raised the possibility of fish-like creatures living in the oceans of Europa. As he says, there is no evidence at present of any life in these oceans, but the conditions are thought to be similar to those that led to life on Earth, and if this proves to be the case, he estimates there could be not just microscopic organisms but 3 million tonnes of fish swimming around.

378. What is the explanation for the Great Red Spot on Jupiter?

The biggest storm in the Solar System has been raging for at least the last 347 years on Jupiter, the system's largest planet. This storm is so huge that three Earths could fit within its area, and its winds have been measured at 614 km/h (384 mph). Visible from Earth through a telescope, it appears as a Great Red Spot, the name by which it has always been known since it was discovered in the mid-1660s. Yet nobody knows why it is red, nor what caused it. One suggestion is that its tornado-like power is constantly swirling up dust and debris from the planet's surface or from elsewhere in Jupiter's atmosphere, though what lends it its bright red colour and what gives it its energy are both unknown.

In 2000 a half-size version of the Great Red Spot was spotted on Jupiter. It started out white, then turned brown, and in 2006 became the same red as its big brother, so became affectionately known as Red Spot Jr.

379. Why is Jupiter's Great Red Spot shrinking?

Big though it is, the Great Red Spot used to be bigger. Over the course of the twentieth century, it lost half its size, and between 1996 and 2006 its area diminished by a further 15 per cent or so. The reason for the decrease is unknown, though it has been suggested that it may have something to do with the Jovian equivalent of global warming and climate change.

380. What happened to the WD5 asteroid that came close to colliding with Mars in January 2008?

In November 2007 astronomers detected an asteroid 50 metres (160 ft) across, which was estimated to have a one in twenty-five chance of colliding with Mars. By January 2008 the odds had lengthened considerably, and it eventually passed Mars at a distance equivalent to about 6.5 times the radius of the planet. Even so, that is near enough for the gravitational pull of Mars to have had a significant effect on the asteroid's path, which explains why tracking it became impossible and it was soon lost. A larger planet, such as Jupiter, might well have exerted a pull strong enough to fling the asteroid right out of the Solar System, but Mars is thought too small to have such an effect and so WD5 may well still be somewhere in the vicinity of the Earth and Mars. The relatively small size of WD5 makes it difficult to detect, and we are unlikely to see it again unless it passes close to Earth.

381. Is there, or has there ever been, life on Mars?

In 1996 analysis of a meteorite that had fallen in Antarctica about 13,000 years ago revealed traces of fossils of bacteria that suggested there may have been primitive life on Mars 4 billion years ago. An unnamed source at NASA described the finding as 'arguably the biggest discovery in the history of science'.

In recent years, space probes have produced increasing evidence that there was once water on Mars. In 2008 ice was found, showing that water is still present on the planet, and in 2009 and 2010 it was claimed that liquid water had been identified, all of which appeared to confirm that there were, and still are, the conditions to support life on Mars. In 2009 methane was discovered in the planet's thin atmosphere, raising the possibility that the gas could have been produced from a biological source.

Where this Martian water came from and how long it has been

there, however, are still puzzling scientists, and firm evidence of life, either now or in the past, is still absent.

See also THE EARTH 141–50, THE SOLAR SYSTEM 436–9

PLANKTON

382. Why are there so many different species of plankton?

From the point of view of evolution, plankton pose a bit of a problem. Under the standard evolutionary model, when two related species are competing for the same resource, the stronger should prevail and the other become extinct. The only important things plankton have to compete for are light and nutrients, yet for some reason a vast number of different species have evolved. This is all the more puzzling as their main contribution to the marine ecosystem seems to be to prop up the bottom of the food chain and be eaten by other species.

The two main theories to account for this suggest either that there are plenty of delicate environmental facts such as current and water turbulence that may have led to the emergence of different species, or that the fact that many plankton eat other plankton may be combined with the constant variation of environmental conditions to ensure that there is no point of equilibrium between the various species, and so evolution continues to drive diversification.

PLANTS

383. Where did flowers come from?

'The rapid development, as far as we can judge, of all the higher plants within recent geological times is an abominable mystery.' So wrote Charles Darwin in a letter to the botanist Joseph Dalton Hooker in 1879.

According to the fossil record as Darwin saw it, after mosses, ferns, conifers and other varieties of green plant had been around for a couple of hundred million years or so, flowering plants suddenly appeared about 130 million years ago, and very rapidly diversified into something similar to the wide range of species we know today.

Much recent research has gone into examining the DNA of a plant called *Amborella trichopoda*, which is found in the rain-forests of New Caledonia in the Southwest Pacific. With tiny greenish-yellow flowers and red fruits, it is thought to be the missing link between the gymnosperms (primitive plants without flowers) and angiosperms (flowering plants), and a direct descendant of the very first flowering plant. Its genome may help to identify how flowering plants came into existence, but their remarkably fast proliferation and diversification are likely to remain 'an abominable mystery' for some time.

384. What determines the height to which different plants grow?

Plants can be classified as either 'determinate' or 'indeterminate', according to whether they grow to a specific size then stop, or continue growing as long as they receive nutrients. In some plants, genes have been identified that come into play to stop growth when a certain criterion is reached, but there seems to be no single gene producing that function for all plants.

To add to the confusion, several plants, such as the tomato, have both determinate and indeterminate varieties. We have not yet identified the mechanism, when determinate and indeterminate varieties are crossed, that dictates which of the two growth patterns the hybrid will follow.

385. Do plants generate methane, and if so, how do they do it?

In 2006 a discovery was announced that threatened to overturn a whole range of beliefs concerning the role of plant life in the Earth's biosphere. Researchers at the Max Planck Institute in Heidelberg, Germany, were monitoring emissions from leaves and trees in laboratory conditions designed to be similar to those the plants would encounter in the open air. Much to their surprise, they detected a significant amount of methane in the emissions, where none had been expected, and the amount of methane increased when there was more sunlight and when the air was warmer.

This finding, if true, would necessitate a radical reassessment of our view of the effects of plant life on global warming. We know that plants absorb carbon dioxide, which is a greenhouse gas – which is why they are valued in the fight against global warming – but if plants also emit methane, which has a greater warming effect than carbon dioxide, they could be net contributors to the problem, rather than a method of combating it.

The German researchers estimated that plants could be responsible for 10 to 30 per cent of all methane emissions. Yet others were unconvinced. In oxygen-starved environments, such as swamps or rice paddies, methane emissions are common, yet the production of methane in oxygen-rich conditions requires considerably more energy and it was unclear where that energy would come from.

Three years later, another theory emerged: that the plants were not creating methane, but merely absorbing it from the soil and releasing it again through their leaves. For the time being, however, the question of the role of plants in methane production is still open.

386. How does the growth of trees reflect changes in climate?

Until recently, the width of tree rings had been taken as a good indication of climate. Indeed, the whole science of dendroclimatology sprang from that observation, and much of the historical data on global warming has been obtained from the study of tree rings. Research published in 2007, however, indicated a discrepancy between the climate record as indicated by reconstruction from tree-ring data and temperatures actually recorded.

Whether this anomaly is specific to the high northern latitudes where the data came from, or whether it indicates a more general problem, is unclear. As the researchers said, 'The causes, however, are not well understood and are difficult to test due to the existence of a number of co-varying environmental factors that may potentially impact recent tree growth.' In other words, it's a bit more complex than had been thought.

The greater our knowledge increases, the greater our ignorance unfolds.

John F. Kennedy (1917–63)

POPES

387. Was there ever a real Pope Joan?

Separating myth from fact in tales about the papacy in the Dark Ages can be very difficult, but there can scarcely be any tale more unlikely than that of Pope Joan. The tale concerns a learned and religious woman who disguised herself as a man, rose in the hierarchy of the Roman Catholic Church and was elected pope in 853. After two years in the papacy, she is said to have given birth while riding a horse. There are different versions of what happened to her after that: some say, for example, that she was killed by an angry mob, while others say she repented and lived out the rest of her days in obscurity.

Most early references to Pope Joan (or Joanna) date from the thirteenth century, though a disputed mention of her exists in a ninth-century document in the form of a footnote – although this may have been added later. Her existence seems to have been widely believed in throughout the Middle Ages, though most historians and religious scholars nowadays dismiss it as a myth.

388. Were medieval popes examined on a toilet-lid-like chair to establish their masculinity?

One of the consequences of the Pope Joan story, whether it was true or false, concerned a marble chair with a large, toilet-like hole in its seat. This was said to have been a part of the papal enthronement, when the pope-elect had to sit on the seat naked from the waist down, while cardinals filed past, either peering or feeling to confirm his masculinity. When satisfied, they are supposed to have incanted the line: '*Testiculos habet et bene pendentes*' in confirmation of his having passed the inspection.

This procedure is said to have been instituted in the fifteenth century in response to the widespread belief in the Pope Joan story. The truth of such a papal testing chair does not, of course, require Pope Joan to have existed, merely that people, including the cardinals, believed that she had existed. Such a chair, however, has never been produced, and in 1601 Pope Clement VIII declared the whole Pope Joan story to be a myth. Whether his *testiculos* had been pronounced *bene pendentes* before his enthronement is not recorded.

PRAYER

389. Does prayer work?

While it can hardly be denied that prayer can have a beneficial effect on the person praying, the question of whether it can influence external events has long been debated. Since the nineteenth century, many experiments have been conducted, often involving patients in hospitals, to test the efficacy of prayer. Typically one group of patients will have a team of religious people praying for their recovery, while another group will not. None of the patients or the hospital staff know who is in which group. Some experimenters have claimed their results show that prayer works; others have said it makes no difference whatsoever.

Since the gods of most religions would not play ball with experimenters trying to prove or disprove their existence by such crude means, some less obvious method of testing the efficacy of prayer is required it we are to have any hope of answering the question.

PRIME NUMBERS

390. Is there an infinite number of twin primes?

Twin primes are sets of two consecutive odd numbers that are both prime: for example, 3 and 5, 17 and 19, and 569 and 571. Such pairs have been found in which the consecutive primes each contain thousands of digits – but the question of whether there is an infinite number of such pairs is still unanswered. Euclid proved that there are infinitely many prime numbers, but twin primes are a different matter entirely.

391. Is every even number greater than two the sum of two primes?

Known as the Goldbach conjecture, this question was raised in correspondence between the German mathematician Christian Goldbach and the great Swiss mathematician and physicist Leonhard Euler in 1742. In response to one query about prime numbers from Goldbach, Euler said that it followed from every even integer being the sum of two primes, and he added 'I regard this as a completely certain theorem, although I cannot prove it.' In the centuries since, nobody else has been able to prove it either. Its truth has, however, been verified for all numbers with seventeen or fewer digits.

392. Is the Riemann hypothesis correct?

This is another of the Clay Institute prize questions (→ MATHEMATICS 281), worth a million dollars to anyone who proves it. The German mathematician Bernhard Riemann formed his hypothesis as long ago as 1859, but understanding it is difficult if you do not have a degree in analytic number theory. So let's just try to give an idea what it is about.

A century before Riemann, Leonhard Euler (him again) had been looking at the curious distribution of prime numbers – perhaps even while he was trying to solve the Goldbach conjecture (→ 391) – and in that connection invented a function (that's a sort of equation) whose value, for any given number, gave some information about the number of prime numbers smaller than any given number.

Riemann went further, extending Euler's function beyond the real numbers to the complex numbers, that is to say numbers of the form $x + iy$, where i is the imaginary number defined as being equal to the square root of -1. (I told you it was tricky.)

Riemann called his equation the zeta function, and the question that intrigued Riemann was what values of x and y made it equal to zero, for those values had an important part to play in the distribution of the primes. There were some obvious zeroes, but all the non-obvious ones seemed to be arranged on a particular line.

Riemann conjectured that all its non-trivial zeroes were on that line, and that is now known to be true for the first few billion of them. If the Riemann hypothesis is true, a whole lot of other results about prime numbers will follow, but nobody has yet succeeded in proving it, or finding a zero that is not on the magic line.

PROTEINS

393. What determines the way a polypeptide – a chain of amino acids – folds into the three-dimensional structure of a protein?

Thanks to the discovery of the DNA double helix, we are beginning to understand how a living organism assumes the form it does. The genetic code contains the recipes for amino acids, which are strung together to form polypeptides, with in turn fold up to form proteins, each of which has a specific job to do in the growth of cells.

There is one vital gap in our understanding of this process, however, which is in the folding procedure. A polypeptide is just a string of amino acids, like the beads on a necklace. This string must fold itself in the right manner into the three-dimensional shape of a protein. If it is folded in the wrong way, the resulting protein may not work and stands a good chance of being toxic. So where does the organism get the folding plans from?

The polypeptide seems to know what to do, yet it contains only the amino acids, which seem unlikely to contain all the rules needed for all their numerous applications.

394. Why are amino acids always left-handed, and sugars always right-handed?

All organic chemical compounds contain carbon atoms, which bond with other organic molecules to form the more complex molecules that constitute the basic structures of life. Sometimes the manner in which the molecules bond together allows, in theory, two different forms, which are known as left-handed and right-handed. These terms are given according to the way polarized light passes through the compound, rotating either in a right-handed or left-handed way.

It turns out that almost all our amino acids are left-handed and almost all our carbohydrates, included sugars, are right-handed. There seems no reason why we could not use right-handed amino acids or left-handed sugars, but we don't. Somewhere in the evolution of life itself, one form was ditched in favour of the other. But we do not know when this happened, or why.

395. How do proteins find their partners?

Interactions between proteins are at the heart of the life-building process, which means that a protein must have a way of finding the protein with which it is to interact, or to identify the string of the DNA code that is responsible for that protein. No one has yet discovered by what process it manages to locate the right partner in the massive stream of DNA data.

THE PYRAMIDS

396. Are the Pyramids of Giza sequenced in line with stars?

Did the Egyptians build the pyramids wherever there was room and wherever they felt like it, or was there a plan behind their placement? In 1994 Robert Bauval and Adrian Gilbert published *The Orion Theory*, which contended that the positions of the three largest pyramids at Giza were chosen to match the three stars in Orion's Belt. The pyramids are almost equally spaced, with the third just off to the side of the line of the other two. The three stars have exactly the same formation. Not only that, but the relative sizes of the pyramids almost exactly match the relative brightnesses of the stars.

Other correlations were also found between certain aspects of the pyramid constructions and various stars. There are, however, a very large number of stars in the sky, and some sort of coincidence might only be expected. Critics of the Orion theory have also suggested that the supposedly significant orientations may not have existed at the time the pyramids were built.

397. How were the pyramids of ancient Egypt built?

Every year or so, a new article appears in a newspaper or journal that claims to have 'solved the problem that has baffled archaeologists for centuries' and then proceeds to explain the latest theory of how the Egyptians built the pyramids. And they all give different answers. Building the pyramids was a phenomenal achievement. The Great Pyramid of Cheops consists of 2.3 million limestone blocks weighing roughly 7 million tonnes, and for four thousand years after it was built it remained the tallest building in the world. Even with a workforce that has been estimated to consist of 20,000 men, hacking these blocks from a quarry, dragging them to the building site (for the Egyptians did not use wheels) and lifting them to the top of this massive structure would have been an awesome task.

There is some evidence that ramps were used to lift the blocks to progressively higher levels, but the Egyptians left no written accounts of how they did it, or how the architect achieved such precision with such a huge workforce to command. So any explanation comes down in the end to an explanation of how they *might* have done it. Assuming, of course, that the pyramids were not built by extraterrestrials, as some have claimed.

398. When and why did the era of pyramid building begin and end?

The Egyptians are thought to have built pyramids as tombs for their rulers on and off for around a thousand years, from about 2700 BC until about 1700 BC, with the pyramid-building industry at its peak from 2575 to 2150 BC. In all, around 135 Egyptian pyramids are known, and they are thought by many to have been conceived as a way of ensuring the pharaoh's successful transition into the afterlife. The orientation of the hidden chambers in certain pyramids towards a dark part of the night sky has even suggested to some that they may have been conceived as some sort of launch pad into immortality.

Yet where these beliefs came from and why the pyramid building stopped are unknown. Belief in an afterlife and the rituals associated with it, as laid down in the various Egyptian *Books of the Dead*, persisted for well over 1,500 years after the end of pyramid building, so what happened to persuade the Egyptians that pyramid building was unnecessary is an interesting question.

See also SPHINX 440–44

If it rained knowledge, I'd hold out my hand; but I would not give myself trouble to go in quest of it.

Samuel Johnson (1709–84)

QUANTUM PHYSICS

399. Why do matter and energy adhere to Isaac Newton's classical mechanics in the macroscopic world, and yet, in the world of subatomic particles, they behave in a probabilistic manner?

When Newton was in charge of the universe, everything was so simple. You knew where everything was and how fast it was moving and you could work out, from his laws of motion, where everything would be in the future. Then Einstein, Heisenberg, Schrödinger, Dirac, Planck and all the other quantum physicists came along and told us first of all that we cannot know both where something is and how fast it is moving, and secondly that it is only a probabilistic wave function anyway, and the world only makes sense if we accept that it can be in two places at the same time.

In other words, the world of large objects seems to conform to the way we see things as behaving and think they ought to behave, but when we get down to the subatomic level, everything looks very different indeed. It is almost as though we are living in two radically different universes at the same time. As J.B.S. Haldane said in 1927, 'My own suspicion is that the universe is not only queerer than we suppose, but queerer than we *can* suppose.'

400. Why does Planck's constant have the value it has?

In 1900, while working on a problem concerning radiation, the German physicist Max Planck made the astonishing discovery that his theoretical predictions only matched the experimental data if one assumes that energy is not continuous, but rather comes in tiny chunks, which he called 'quanta'. This discovery led to the development of quantum physics, which changed the way we see the world. When Einstein showed the equivalence of mass and energy, it became clear that there are also discrete quanta of mass, and according to some theories there are even quanta of time.

Planck's constant, which is a measure of the size of quanta, is expressed in units of energy multiplied by time, and is equal to $6.62606896 \times 10^{-34}$ joule-second. In other words, it is equal to the energy of passing an electric current of one ampere through a resistance of one ohm for one second multiplied by a number written as a decimal point followed by 34 zeroes followed by 662606896.

The mass of all particles, including quarks and electrons, depends on Planck's constant. According to the latest theories, we can have particles with no mass, or a particle with a mass determined by Planck's constant, but nothing in between. There must be a reason for the size of Planck's chunks, which are the basic building blocks of the universe, but nobody knows what it is.

401. Is our universe the only one, or is it part of a multiverse?

The idea of stepping out of our universe into a parallel one is almost as old as science fiction itself, but it has gained a sort of respectability as a means of explaining some of the weirder parts of quantum theory. Take Schrödinger's cat, for example, a creature dreamt up in a 1935 thought experiment by the Austrian physicist Erwin Schrödinger: this unfortunate animal is both dead and alive at the same time until we take a peek and see which it is. There's no problem if you think of the experiment occurring in two universes, with a dead cat in one and a live one in the other, with no way of telling which you are in until you look at the cat.

String theory (→ PHYSICS 369) also predicts multiple universes. Well, actually there's only one, but it has ten dimensions, and our piddling little three-dimensional universe is just a slice of the real thing – and there are plenty more like it. Even the Big Bang, according to string theory, was nothing more than a collision between two slices of the universe. The idea may also help to explain dark energy (→ COSMOLOGY 108) if we see it as emanating from a force exerted on our universe by another one.

Whether we can ever envisage an experiment that would tell us if other universes exist, however, is another matter entirely.

402. If there are other universes, do they have the same physical laws as ours?

According to an idea called the 'anthropic principle', the laws of physics as we see them are only that way because we are here to see them. A number of laws and physical constants appear to be perfectly tuned to hold the universe together and create the conditions in which we have evolved. Without the inverse square law of gravity, for example, everything would fall apart; without the laws of conservation of energy and momentum, the stars and planets would not remain in their orbits. Even a small change in some of the physical constants would cause everything to disintegrate.

One way of looking at this is to say that God made it this way; a slightly more irreligious version would maintain that God had no choice in the matter if He wanted His universe to work. In contrast, adherents of the anthropic principle hold that things could have been different, but they would have been so different that we would not have been here to see them. Our view of the universe and the laws that govern it is heavily biased by our own perspective.

Whether one sees the ten-dimensional world of string theory as the one true universe of which we are but a slice, or a collection of all possible universes, or one of a number of multidimensional universes, or just a mathematical model that may explain some of the more puzzling aspects of our own universe is, until we learn a good deal more, just a matter of choice.

403. Why is there so little antimatter?

According to our current view of the universe, it all began in a Big Bang of energy, which transformed, according to Einstein's $E = mc^2$ equation, into matter. But both theory and experiment show that when energy transforms into matter, an equal amount of antimatter is created. Antimatter is just the same as matter, except in an antimatter atom, the negatively charged nucleus is orbited by positively charged positrons, while in matter, the atoms have a positively charged nucleus orbited by negatively charged electrons. Thus when matter meets antimatter, they annihilate each other and turn back into energy.

Just after the very beginning of the universe there must have been equal amounts of matter and antimatter, yet finding even the tiniest particle of antimatter is extraordinarily difficult. So where did it all go?

404. What happened in the first billionth of a second after the Big Bang?

The Big Bang happened at 1830 GMT on 28 March 1949. That at least was the precise moment when the astronomer Fred Hoyle, speaking on BBC radio, coined the term 'Big Bang'. Hoyle did not actually believe in the Big Bang theory, but was explaining the difference between the 'steady state' theory to which he subscribed and the alternative idea of a sudden creation.

In the time since 1949, more and more evidence has accumulated in favour of the Big Bang. In particular, measurements of the expansion of the universe and the speed at which galaxies are moving away from each other support the view that they all came from the same spot 13.7 billion years ago.

Theories about the creation of everything from fundamental particles to galaxies also tie in with the Big Bang theory. In fact, we can trace everything back to the tiniest fraction of a second after the Big Bang, and everything fits – but the first billionth of a second remains a Big Problem. The massive burst of energy must have created matter and antimatter in equal quantities (→ 403, 406), but something then happened to create an asymmetry, favouring the matter. The remaining antimatter was then annihilated by collisions with matter, creating the stream of energy known as the cosmic microwave background and leaving the surplus matter to form our universe. But what was responsible for the antimatter disappearing trick in that first billionth of a second is anyone's guess.

405. How do entangled particles communicate?

The idea of entangled particles, which has been confirmed by experiments, is one of the weirdest of all weird things in the weird world of quantum theory. Under certain circumstances, a pair of particles may be created that mirror each other's properties. The most common example is a pair of photons, which have a property known as 'spin' that may be either 'up' or 'down'. But if one of the pair is 'up' the other must be 'down', and this difference is maintained however far apart the particles are.

Actually, it's more complicated than that, as spin is one of those being-in-two-places-at-the-same-time sort of quantum properties that remain undecided until the particle is observed. So both the particles are in both 'up' and 'down' states until we measure them. And at that moment, as soon as the state of one is determined, so is the other.

It is almost as though the particles are communicating with each other, and experiments have shown that it happens instantaneously. Yet if information is being transmitted between the particles, it ought not to be able to travel faster than the speed of light. But it does. The optimistic view is that this may hold the key to instant intergalactic communications. The realistic view is that we don't have a clue what's going on.

406. Does antimatter come from other galaxies?

On its last trip, in May 2011, the US Space Shuttle *Endeavour* took a massive piece of equipment called the Alpha Magnetic Spectrometer to the International Space Station, where it is to be used for a variety of experiments, including the detection of dark matter and antimatter particles. In particular, it will be looking for an anti-helium nucleus which, if found, would support the theory that there may be galaxies made entirely of antimatter elsewhere in the universe. It would also lend support to the idea that antimatter particles – which have, on rare occasions, been detected on Earth – may have extragalactic origins.

407. How can we explain the wave-particle duality of light?

In classical physics, matter comes in particles while energy comes in waves. In the seventeenth century there was an intense debate over whether light was transmitted in waves or by tiny particles called corpuscles. Some aspects of light could only be explained by one, but other aspects favoured the other. In the twentieth century Einstein muddied the picture by showing that matter and energy could be transformed into each other, but this supported the highly convenient use of either particles or waves to explain physical phenomena, whichever did the job better. Especially in the subatomic world of quantum mechanics, the use of both waves and particles became not only common practice, but seemed to be essential.

One view is that matter and energy, especially light, can behave either as waves or particles (which we now call photons), but not both at the same time. Another view is that all this is deeply paradoxical and makes no sense. But it seems to work, and such paradoxes are not unusual in quantum theory.

See also FUNDAMENTAL PARTICLES 192–7, PHILOSOPHY 361, PHYSICS 369–71

REALITY

408. Is there such a thing as reality?

Plato took the view that all nouns refer to things that exist and are therefore real. Thus, because we have the abstract nouns Beauty and Good, for example, there must be real yet immaterial 'Forms' or 'Ideas' that embody these qualities in an absolute way, and of which examples of beauty or goodness that we experience in the world of the senses are mere shadows. For most thinkers, that is much too simplistic a view of reality. A noun, they would say, is merely our shorthand to describe our subjective experience or perception of something. The eighteenth-century Anglo-Irish philosopher Bishop George Berkeley took this further with the view that nothing exists unless it is perceived – and even Einstein questioned whether we can be sure the Moon is there if we cannot see it.

One of the fundamental questions of ontology (the study of the nature of being) is whether something can be said to have an existence independent of the way it is perceived. Quantum physics (→ 399–407) shows that the world is very different from the way we see and experience it, so where does that leave reality?

409. If so, how can we tell what is real?

In Daoist tradition there appears the following tale: 'Lao Tzu fell asleep and dreamt he was a butterfly. Upon wakening he asked, Am I a man who has just been dreaming he was a butterfly? Or a sleeping butterfly now dreaming he is a man?'

Looking on the Internet, we can find out how to tell diamonds from cubic zirconia, how to distinguish between real pearls and fake pearls, how to tell real fur from fake fur, and even how to tell real breasts from implants. But telling reality from illusion is a much bigger problem.

410. Are we living inside a computer simulation, as in the film *The Matrix*?

There is absolutely no way of knowing whether or not we are no more than virtual figments in a computer simulation, though in the absence of any suggestion of who is running the simulation, we tend to disregard this possibility. Perhaps the best argument against *The Matrix* hypothesis is the weirdness of the world and its physical laws. Surely nobody, even the most perverse of aliens, would have written a program incorporating such a bizarre universe. Unless, of course, it's a brilliant double-bluff.

411. Are the three spatial dimensions we perceive part of a ten- or eleven-dimensional reality?

We have mentioned before the mysterious ten-dimensional world of string theory (→ FUNDAMENTAL PARTICLES 192, PHYSICS 369, QUANTUM PHYSICS 401–2), but in fact the mathematics of the theory works equally well in ten or eleven dimensions. They are simply different formulations of the same theory. So if the maths works in either case, does it make any sense to talk of a ten-dimensional universe or an eleven-dimensional universe as 'reality', especially from our own very limited three-dimensional viewpoint?

ROME

412. What was the population of Rome at the time of the emperor Augustus?

It is frequently maintained that the population of Rome passed the million mark at the time of the birth of Christ, when Augustus was emperor, but there is precious little precise information on which this figure can be based.

According to Augustus' own census returns, there were 4,233,000 'citizens' in the Roman empire in 8 BC and 4,937,000 in AD 14, but that was in the whole empire, and we do not know who was counted as a 'citizen' anyway. The figure is thought to exclude slaves, women and children, and probably only included men available for military service. On the basis of these figures, an estimate of around 56 million has been given for the total population of the Roman empire.

As for the population of Rome itself, estimates have been made from the total size of the empire, from the area of Rome together with an informed guess at the population density, and from the figures for grain imports and consumption. These result in anything between 500,000 and 1,300,000.

For in much wisdom is much grief: and he that increaseth knowledge increaseth sorrow.

Ecclesiastes 1:18

SEX

413. How did sexual reproduction evolve?

The earliest organisms reproduced simply by splitting in two, so creating an identical copy of themselves. It's simple; it's effective; it allows for some introduction of genetic diversity through mutations; and it doesn't require the tiresome business of finding a member of the opposite sex, luring it into mating, and then successfully completing the mating process. Somewhere along the evolutionary line, sexual reproduction came into existence, but how it established itself successfully against the easier version is a bit of a puzzle.

Presumably, it has something to do with the vastly increased speed of genetic change when a mother and father both contribute half the genes to an offspring, which may have the effect of eliminating unsuccessful genes more quickly and enabling faster adaptation to changing conditions and newly emerging diseases. Yet nobody has convincingly demonstrated that such potential advantages outweigh the problems that sexual reproduction involves.

414. Is there a connection between sexual reproduction and death?

Very simple creatures can live forever. An amoeba, for example, reproduces by splitting in two; each half then becomes another amoeba, which can also split in two; and so the process continues – at least until something comes along and eats it. Even organisms that have a slightly more complex way of reproducing, which may involve merging with others before splitting into two, do not die. There is a theory that death began with the evolution of sexual reproduction.

Several creatures, from salmon to spiders, die almost immediately after contributing their sperm (in the case of males), or laying their eggs (in the case of females). The English evolutionary biologist Richard Dawkins famously wrote of the 'selfish gene', but the whole business may be even more selfish than he suggested. Once reproduction has been assured, the gene has little use for the body so is content to let it die. Perhaps we could live forever if we didn't have sex. A long life, if rather dull.

415. Why do African jumping spiders prefer to mate with spiders that have just eaten a mosquito that has gorged itself on mammalian blood?

Vampire spiders may sound like the stuff of rather lurid horror films, but in 2005 a species of spider was found in East Africa that seems to like the taste of blood. The *Evarcha culicivora* spider, however, is not likely to jump on you and sink its fangs into your neck. Not yet, anyway. Its taste for blood has so far been identified only in its preference for eating mosquitoes that have just gorged themselves on mammalian blood. Even more interesting is the fact that males of the species prefer to mate with females who have just eaten such a mosquito.

Experiments in 2009 confirmed this by wafting the smell of female spiders over males and seeing which ones seemed most attractive. The results showed that the male spiders definitely went for the females who had wolfed down the blood-gorged mosquitoes. Curiously, it didn't seem to be the smell of the blood that was attracting them: they were not at all interested in other males that had just eaten a blood-filled mosquito.

One theory is that a chemical reaction in the female's body while processing the blood may produce a chemical that attracts the male; another idea is that the smell of blood on a female may be taken as a sign of strength and breeding fitness. Further experiments are planned to test these hypotheses.

416. How and why is the sex of turtles determined by the temperature at which the eggs incubate?

Turtles lay eggs in holes they excavate on sandy beaches, and then leave them there to incubate. The eggs are very sensitive to temperature, and those that are incubated below 23°C or above 33°C are unlikely to hatch at all. When the temperature is between about 28 and 30°C, they hatch with a roughly equal rate of males and females, but when the temperature is between 23 and 28°C, the hatchlings are usually male, while for temperatures between 30 and 33°C, they are usually female.

Some birds and various other reptiles also display what is known as temperature-dependent sex determination, but neither the mechanism by which it happens nor its evolutionary significance is understood. It has been suggested that it allows the mother turtle to choose the sex of her young, but there is absolutely no evidence that female turtles do so.

417. Why are so many female albatrosses lesbian?

Albatrosses at a colony in Hawaii, according to a study published in 2008, are a model of successful lesbianism. According to the report, 31 per cent (39 out of 125) of the Laysan albatross pairs at the Kaena Point breeding colony in Oahu were female–female. Not only that, but sixteen chicks were hatched by the lesbian pairs, ten of which had been fathered by males who already had female mates of their own. 'Fathers of chicks in female–female pairs were located at varying distances from the nest and were not simply the nearest neighbours', the report continued, indicating some degree of selectiveness among the females in the matter of choosing the fathers of their offspring. Despite this, albatrosses are well known for their monogamous tendencies, and this also applies to lesbian couples, who tend to stay together for life.

Following the publication of the Hawaiian study, albatross

colonies elsewhere were examined for lesbianism, leading to a report of a similar pair of female albatrosses raising a chick together in New Zealand. The manager of the Taiaroa breeding colony was quoted as saying: 'It's an unusual situation because we've had a triangle with one male and two females for the past couple of years, and obviously that hasn't been terribly conducive to getting on with a breeding programme. This year the male left the trio, but obviously not before he had mated with one of the females. The same report also mentioned a nearby pair of male penguins who were incubating an egg together.

418. Why does the single-celled *Tetrahymena thermophila* have seven sexes?

The unicellular *Tetrahymena thermophila* is a simple creature. It is covered with a furry coat whose hairs, called cilia, wave back and forth, propelling it through the water in which it lives. And it has seven sexes, which researchers have very sensibly called I, II, III, IV, V, VI and VII.

Each of these sexes can mate with any of the other six, but proportions of the seven sexes are not equal in any large community. Naturally, this gives an individual greater choice in finding a mate, with roughly six out of seven of the community available compared with about 50 per cent in the more usual two-sex species. But there are some rather complex rules about what sex offspring can come from different pairings. Quite how such a simple creature evolved in such a sexually diverse way, or what the advantages of its doing so might be, have not yet been established.

419. Why do males ejaculate such a vast number of spermatozoa?

The average ejaculation of the human male contains around 180 million sperm, though the range has been estimated to be between

40 million and 1.2 billion. Yet it only takes one sperm to fertilize a female egg, so why are there so many – not just in humans, but in all mammals? The usual reason given is that it increases the chance of fertilization, but such a vast number looks like overkill. Fewer fitter and stronger spermatozoa would surely improve prospects more effectively.

Another reason that has been offered relates to sperm competition. The argument goes that if several males mate with the same female, each one wants to improve his chances of fertilizing her egg, and the best way to do this is by having the largest number of sperm in the competition. Yet fertilization does not take very long, and it would surely be a better strategy to be the first to mate with the female and then keep her away from other males for a short period afterwards. As it is, a vast number of sperm seem to be giving their lives in vain.

420. What (if it exists at all) is the biological root of sexual orientation?

Periodically, an announcement is made of the discovery of a 'gay gene', but this always seems to be followed by another study casting doubt on the earlier finding. Studies of twins seem to confirm the existence of a genetic component in homosexuality, while a large number of studies have claimed to identify biological differences between gay and straight people.

In no particular order, all the following have been associated with gay/straight differences: the size of certain parts of the brain; reactions to sex pheromones; responses to certain neurochemicals; ratio of limb-length to overall height; the functioning of the inner ear; the direction of hair whorls; left-handedness; finger-length ratios; ridge-density of fingerprints... and many others. Whether there is a single factor underlying all of these has yet to be discovered.

421. Was Queen Elizabeth I a virgin?

They named the state of Virginia after her, so she must have been, mustn't she? Well, not exactly. Her statesmanlike refusal to marry a foreign prince, to preserve England's independence, and her refusal to marry an English nobleman, for fear that her choice would cause discord, may have suggested a determination to preserve her chastity, but marriage and virginity have never been the same thing. There are, in fact, two prime candidates among those who may have been Elizabeth's lovers. Curiously, and perhaps coincidentally, she bestowed the title of Master of the Horse on both of them.

First there was Robert Dudley, Earl of Leicester, the childhood friend whom Elizabeth made Master of the Horse as soon as she became queen. She is said to have behaved in an extremely flirtatious manner towards him, but distanced herself from him when his wife died in suspicious circumstances (→ ENGLISH HISTORY 173). She later recommended that he marry Mary Queen of Scots, but the latter turned him down on the grounds that she would not take Elizabeth's discarded lover.

Then there was Robert Devereux, Earl of Essex, who became Master of the Horse in 1587. He also became a favourite of the queen, who is said to have loved his eloquence and keen mind. But he rather botched his job as Lord Lieutenant of Ireland, came home in disgrace, led a rebellion against the queen, and was executed.

422. Was Queen Christina of Sweden a man?

Queen Christina (1626–89) was an extraordinary woman – if she was a woman. When she was born, she was mistaken for a boy, apparently on the grounds of being very hairy and screaming with a hoarse voice. Her father, the king, who had wanted a son, gave orders that she should be brought up as a prince, and when she took the royal oath, it was as king, not queen.

Christina never married, never produced an heir to the throne, and when she abdicated in 1654 in favour of her cousin, she headed for the Danish border, changed into men's clothing and rode through Denmark as a man. Her masculine voice and general appearance were often remarked upon, and she had always shown a preference for men's clothing. In 1965 an examination of her remains reached no conclusion about her sex other than a suggestion that she may have been intersex, which is neither one thing nor the other, but by definition involves an atypical configuration of the elements that usually separate male from female.

See also GIRAFFES 216, SQUIRRELS 453, WORMS 481

SHAKESPEARE

423. What did William Shakespeare do between leaving school aged fourteen and marrying Anne Hathaway at the age of eighteen?

Almost nothing is known for certain about Shakespeare's early life, but it is generally accepted that he went to the King's New School in Stratford-upon-Avon from the ages of seven to fourteen. At the age of eighteen he married the twenty-six-year-old Anne Hathaway (some say in haste, as the marriage banns were read only once instead of the usual three times). But there is not a shred of evidence for anything he did in his formative years between the ages of fourteen and eighteen. Shakespeare's plays and poetry display not only an impressively wide vocabulary and an unequalled mastery of the English language, but also an accumulation of wisdom and knowledge in so many spheres that it is difficult to reconcile with the view that his formal education stopped at the age of fourteen. Yet no records survive to tell the tale of Shakespeare's teenage years.

424. What did Shakespeare do between 1585 and 1592?

Six months after the wedding, Anne gave birth to a daughter, Susanna. Two years later, twin children appeared: Hamnet, Shakespeare's son, and Judith, his daughter. They were baptized on 2 February 1585. After that, the trail of Shakespeare's life goes dead again until he is mentioned in accounts of the London theatre scene in 1592.

Shakespeare's 'lost years' from 1585 to 1592 have been the subject of intense speculation, with suggestions that he worked as a schoolmaster, or a theatre manager, or fled Stratford to escape prosecution for deer poaching. Such evidence as there is for any of these tends to be based on tales of people with a similar name to Shakespeare.

Shakespeare's son Hamnet died of unknown causes at the age of eleven in 1596, but we do not know whether his short life was always plagued by illness. If it was, perhaps Shakespeare spent much of this period looking after a sick child.

425. Who was 'Mr W.H.', to whom Shakespeare dedicated his sonnets?

'To the onlie begetter of these insuing sonnets Mr W.H. all happiness and that eternitie promised by our ever living poet.' So begins the dedication in the first edition of Shakespeare's sonnets, published in 1609. A few more words follow, ending with the initials T.T.

Those initials are assumed to stand for the book's publisher, Thomas Thorpe, but the identity of Mr W.H. has remained a mystery, though there has been no shortage of speculative suggestions. One of the candidates is William Herbert, Earl of Pembroke, on the grounds that he was also the dedicatee of the First Folio of Shakespeare's plays – but an earl would hardly have been addressed as plain 'Mr'. Other suggestions include William Hart (Shakespeare's nephew, who was only nine years old at the time); William Haughton, a dramatist; an actor named Willie Hughes (for whom no evidence exists that he even existed); Henry Wriothesley, Earl of Southampton (who was not only not a Mr but had his initials the wrong way round). Bertrand Russell suggested that W.H. might be a misprint for W.S. and refer to Shakespeare himself.

Frankly, all we know is that the dedicatee's initials were probably W.H. and that he was probably not a titled person. And to add to the problem, we do not even know what the word 'begetter' is meant to mean in this context. It could mean the author, but it could mean someone who inspired the sonnets, or someone who encouraged the writer to produce them.

426. Who was Shakespeare's Dark Lady?

Shakespeare's sonnets 127–152 concern a mysterious 'Dark Lady', who we learn has black hair and dusky skin. But who she was, or even whether she was a real person or an idealized figment of his imagination, is not known. Among the suggestions are Mary Fitton, who was a Maid of Honour to Queen Elizabeth and a mistress of William Herbert, Earl of Pembroke (who, you remember, may have been Mr W.H.), whose child she bore. Another candidate is Emilia Lanier, who was another mistress of a nobleman who had connections with Shakespeare, and who fitted the black-hair-and-dusky-complexion description perfectly.

Whoever the Dark Lady was, however, she would surely not have liked William Wordsworth's description of the sonnets written to her, which he thought were 'abominably harsh, obscure and worthless'.

427. Did Shakespeare really die on his birthday?

It has become conventional to celebrate the date of Shakespeare's birth as 23 April 1564 and the date of his death as 23 April 1616. There is a nice symmetry about it, especially as 23 April is also St George's Day. We know that was the day he died, but – as with most people at this period – Shakespeare's date of birth was not recorded, only the date of his baptism, which took place on 26 April. Being baptized three days after birth would not have been unusual at the time, so it is quite possible that he was born on 23 April, but there is no real evidence of it.

SLEEP

428. Why do we need to sleep?

All animals sleep. Even nematode worms sleep. Giraffes only sleep two hours a day, but they still sleep. Sleep must be very important, but we do not know why. One theory is that sleeping allows the body to repair damaged cells; another idea is that sleep allows us to replenish the molecules that are needed to transfer energy between our cells; a third idea is that sleeping is when our brains have a chance to clean out the junk that has accumulated in them during the day; and a fourth suggestion is that sleeping is necessary for our brains to be able to run through the information they have received during the day and file it away for later use.

The one thing we do know, however, is that sleep deprivation can have drastic consequences, including intense paranoia and even death. Surprisingly, we may have a good picture of what these consequences may lead to, but it still does not help us discover what sleep actually does.

429. What is the cause of the 'hypnic jerks' that sometimes occur as we are falling asleep?

Hypnagogia is the name for the state between wakefulness and sleep just as you are starting to nod off, and that is when you may experience one of those infuriating hypnic jerks, when your body jumps as though startled and may jolt you back into wakefulness. It is an involuntary muscle contraction called a myoclonic twitch. One theory is that changes in temperature, breathing and muscle relaxation may all cause the brain to think you are falling, so it sends a signal to your limbs to wake up. Another suggestion is that it is purely a muscle spasm and the brain has nothing to do with it. It's very irritating, whatever it is.

430. Why do koalas sleep so much?

Koalas sleep between eighteen and twenty-two hours a day. Even sloths are not that slothful. The reason seems to have something to do with their very slow metabolic rate and their diet. A koala eats mainly eucalyptus leaves, which are low in nutrition and very high in fibre, making them difficult to digest. A slow metabolism and a good deal of sleep may help provide the time for their digestive systems to extract all the energy they can from the leaves. But why they cannot do that while staying awake is puzzling. Cows and sheep have diets that are low in nutrition, but make up for it by spending a great deal of time eating. Koalas adopt the alternative strategy of sleeping. But falling asleep most of the time cannot be good for one's chances of survival.

431. Why do we dream?

Current theories of the role played by dreaming include the following:

(i) When we dream, we are rehearsing our behaviour in threatening situations; that's why so many dreams are horror stories.

(ii) Dreams are what happens when our brains are throwing out the rubbish from the day's experiences. That's why dreams are so disorganized.

(iii) Dreams are when our brains reset their connections in a more useful way.

(iv) Dreams are our own form of psychotherapy. As Sigmund Freud put it, dreams are 'disguised fulfilments of repressed wishes'.

(v) Dreams are just the result of our brains freewheeling after a hard day and mean nothing at all.

432. What is the connection between REM sleep and dreaming?

In the early 1960s a number of experiments were conducted that appeared to show that dreaming was just as important to us as sleep itself. The experiments were based on the belief that dreaming coincided with periods of so-called REM (rapid eye movement) sleep, when a fluttering of the eyelids indicates a darting about of the eyes while asleep. These early experiments concluded that waking people up when REM sleep began made them highly irritable – in fact noticeably more irritable than other people who were woken up just as often, but not when their eyes were flickering.

It was subsequently found that the association between dreaming and REM sleep was not so clear. People dreamt without REM and they showed REM behaviour when not dreaming. So dreaming may not be as vital as had been thought.

433. How does sleeping relate to learning?

In the 1950s some successful marketing was done around the theme of sleep-learning. You put on a tape with a lesson on it, fell asleep, and in the morning you would have learned at least some of the information on the tape. Detailed scientific investigations, however, thoroughly discredited the idea. You don't learn anything if you are really asleep. On the other hand, more recent experiments have suggested that sleep can consolidate knowledge.

One typical test involved teaching people something in the morning, then testing them twelve hours later. Their results were compared with a group who had learned the same thing at night, then had a good night's sleep and were tested in the morning, again twelve hours after the teaching. The results of the second group were 20 per cent better than the first group, though one could argue that it was merely being awake and doing something else that caused forgetfulness in the underperforming group. Similar improvements in performance, however, have also been found in animals that are taught something then allowed to sleep.

SMOKING

434. By what mechanism does smoking cause lung cancer?

We rely on our genes to ensure the smooth running of our body's normal growth processes. Any form of cancer involves a breakdown of those processes. In the case of smoking, our understanding is that the carcinogens in tobacco smoke convert to forms that react with DNA, and the altered DNA leads to the genetic changes that exist in human lung cancer. A great deal of work is now being carried out to fill in the details of this process.

435. Why do some long-term smokers develop lung cancer while others don't?

In the UK around 80 per cent of lung cancer cases are associated with smoking, and about 15 per cent of smokers develop the disease. So what prevents the other 85 per cent of smokers from developing cancer (although they may very well succumb to one of the many other fatal conditions caused by smoking)? And what causes the lung cancer in the 20 per cent of sufferers who do not smoke?

A good deal of evidence suggests that lung cancer runs in families, so the hunt for a genetic component of the disease has been intense. A number of candidates for a 'lung-cancer-susceptibility gene' have been discovered, while much attention has also focused on breakdown of the normal gene-repair mechanism that ought to prevent the disease developing. The extent to which a lung-cancer-susceptibility gene has a role in the development of the disease, or a lung-cancer-prevention gene protects against it, are questions that have yet to be answered.

The difference between what the
most and the least learned people know
is inexpressibly trivial in relation
to that which is unknown.

Albert Einstein (1879–1955)

THE SOLAR SYSTEM

436. How big is the Solar System?

The lack of clearly marked boundaries between one star's territory and another's makes this a difficult question to answer, but there are several other factors that make it even harder. The first problem is a matter of definition: where ought one to say that the Solar System ends? One answer is to say it ends where the Sun's gravitational effect is equalled by the gravitational pull of the rest of the galaxy. We cannot be sure where this is, but it is estimated to be about two light years away. The trouble is, we do not really know what is out there, two light years away, so we cannot calculate the overall gravitational pull.

The other definition of the edge of the Solar System is that it is where the solar wind ceases to have an effect. The solar wind is the stream of charged particles ejected from the Sun's upper atmosphere. It flows out across the region of space known as the heliosphere until it reaches an area known as the heliopause, where it meets equally strong solar winds from other stars. If we use that as our definition of the size of the Solar System, then estimates of its diameter vary between about 15 and 40 light hours, rather than two light years.

Even that is open to doubt, as measurements of cosmic wind by the *Voyager 1* spacecraft, which is now close to the heliopause, are significantly different from the predicted values, suggesting that we may have got it all wrong.

437. Why does space suddenly become very empty beyond the Kuiper Belt?

Travelling towards the furthest extremities of the Solar System, the last large object we know about is the planet (now reclassified as a dwarf planet) Pluto, which is one of the tens of thousands of bodies making up the Kuiper Belt. This region of the Solar System extends between about 30 and 55 AU from the Sun (an AU, or Astronomical Unit, is the average distance between the Sun and the Earth). After that, there is nothing – which is hard to explain. After all, the region beyond the Kuiper Belt is still well within the gravitational pull of the Sun, so one would expect some sort of space debris to have been captured in solar orbit.

One theory is that right at the edge of the Solar System, far beyond the Kuiper Belt, there is something called the Oort Cloud, composed mainly of frozen water, methane and ammonia. So far, the existence of the Oort Cloud is purely theoretical, with strong reasons to believe it is out there, but no definite observations or evidence to confirm it. Another theory is that we have missed one large object, sometimes known as Planet X, which may, through its own gravitational effect, have swept up all the material in the region beyond the Kuiper Belt.

Some have even equated Planet X with the planet Nibiru of ancient Sumerian mythology, which is destined to collide with Earth and bring about the end of the world. Naturally, that has been linked to the end of the world predicted for 2012 (→ INTRODUCTION) but astronomers consider that highly unlikely.

438. Why have the *Pioneer 10* and *Pioneer 11* space probes gone slightly off track?

The deep-space probes *Pioneer 10* and *Pioneer 11* were launched in 1972 and 1973 respectively, and are now both heading in opposite directions towards the furthest reaches of the Solar System. Their positions have been tracked throughout their journeys, and at first their courses went according to prediction, but since the early 1980s they seem to have been going off track in both direction and speed.

Various explanations have been offered, such as observational error, effect of the solar wind, the influence of dark matter, or gravitational effects from some large object we do not know about. It has even been suggested that there could be something wrong with our laws of physics. None of these seem entirely satisfactory solutions.

> # He must be very ignorant for he answers every question he is asked.
>
> Voltaire (1694–1778)

439. Has life on Earth spread to other places in the Solar System?

Just as the theory of exogenesis proposes that life on Earth originated elsewhere in the Universe and came here through space (→ EARTH 150), so the theory of panspermia proposes that life may exist elsewhere in the universe, having spread there from Earth. In 2000 NASA scientists announced their conclusion that single-celled organisms from Mars could theoretically have seeded the Earth with life, or vice versa. However, their calculations suggest that the transfer of microbes from one solar system to another is unlikely, but they did not rule it out. It would be a little disappointing, however, to find extraterrestrial life, only to discover that it had come from here in the first place.

See also THE MOON 311–2, THE PLANETS 374–81, THE SUN 454–5

THE SPHINX

440. By what name was the Great Sphinx known to the people who built it?

For all their hieroglyphics, the ancient Egyptians were very remiss when it came to leaving behind proper documentation of some of their finest achievements. The Great Sphinx of Giza is the largest monolith statue (carved from a single piece of rock) in the world, yet we do not even know what it was called.

The name 'sphinx' was given to it by the ancient Greeks around 500 BC, in reference to a Greek mythological beast of that name with a lion's body, a woman's head, and wings – though the Egyptian statue has no wings and the sex of its head is arguable. About a thousand years earlier the Egyptians had referred to it as Hor-em-akhet ('Horus of the horizon', Horus being one of the main gods of ancient Egypt), but the statue was originally made more than a thousand years earlier still, but during that millennium no record of any name has been found.

441. How old is the Sphinx?

The standard theory is that the Sphinx was carved around 2500 BC in the reign of the Pharaoh Khafra, yet this is mainly based on the location of the statue near the Second Pyramid of Giza, which has been connected with Khafra. There is no known inscription from the time of Khafra linking the pharaoh to the Sphinx. The evidence of certain parts of other constructions in the vicinity that appear to be pointing towards the Sphinx have been taken by some as indications that the Sphinx must have been there first, and may have pre-dated the reign of Khafra by two or three hundred years.

An even earlier date was suggested after signs of water erosion were detected on the walls of the Sphinx enclosure. It was said that this water erosion could only have been caused by long and extensive rain. Since Egypt has not had such heavy rainfall since the third millennium BC, that would argue that the Sphinx must have been built earlier, leading to one estimate of 3100 BC or earlier.

442. Which pharaoh was the Sphinx meant to resemble?

Some of those who linked the building of the Sphinx to the time of the Pharaoh Khafra suggested that its face was modelled on Khafra himself. Examinations and detailed measurements by a forensic anthropologist, however, cast doubt on that suggestion.

The author Robert Temple noticed a similarity between the Sphinx's face and that of the Pharaoh Amenemhet II, who reigned from 1929 to 1895 BC. Temple's idea was that the Sphinx was originally a statue of the Jackal god Anubis, but the face was re-carved at a later date.

443. Who destroyed the nose of the Sphinx?

All the evidence suggests that the metre-wide nose did not fall off by accident. Marks on the face suggest that chisels were hammered into the nose and used to pry it off in a deliberate act of vandalism. A wide variety of culprits have been accused of inflicting the damage, ranging from British troops and Egyptian Mamlukes to Napoleon's cannonballs. In one account, a medieval Muslim named Muhammad Sa'im al-Dahr is said to have hacked the nose off to punish Egyptian peasants for making sacrifices to the statue. All we know for sure, from a picture of the Sphinx drawn in 1737, is that the nose was already missing at that date. Which does at least exonerate Napoleon.

444. Is the Hall of Records in Ancient Egypt real?

The Roman writer Pliny the Elder described a cavity around and beneath the Sphinx, which has been linked to an ancient legend of the Hall of Records. This Hall of Records was said to contain a library of papyrus scrolls containing all the knowledge of the Egyptians, including a history of the lost continent of Atlantis.

There have been specific attempts to search for the Hall of Records, and passages of unknown origin have been located around the Sphinx, though Pliny said that the Egyptians believed that it was just the burial chamber of a king.

SPIDERS

445. Is *Aptostichus angelinajoleae* different from *Aptostichus stephencolberti*, or are they the same species?

What do Orson Welles, Harrison Ford, Angelina Jolie, Nelson Mandela, David Bowie and the comedian Stephen Colbert have in common? Answer: they have all had species of spider named after them. Actually Orson Welles had a whole genus of spiders named after him. There is some doubt, however, as to whether the trapdoor spider known as *Aptostichus angelinajoleae* is a different species from *Aptostichus stephencolberti*. The matter should be resolvable by analysing the DNA of both spiders, but since there is no general agreement on what precisely constitutes a species, the question may still remain open.

446. What do catatonic schizophrenics and moulting spiders have in common?

In the 1950s the Swiss pharmacologist Peter Witt began a remarkable series of experiments in which he showed that the patterns of webs spun by a certain species of spider could be altered by giving the spiders drugs. Not only that, but you could tell which drugs the spider had taken by making certain measurements on the resulting web.

One of Witt's early experiments involved the use of hallucinogens, which gave other researchers the idea of giving spiders extracts taken from the urine or the blood of hallucinating psychiatric patients to see whether that had a similar effect on the webs. The most striking result was reported by the Californian neuropsychiatrist Nicolas Bercel in 1959. In Bercel's experiment, a spider that had been fed with a dose of blood serum from a catatonic schizophrenic produced a totally straggly web with no shape or regularity.

Such a lack of shape had only ever been seen before in a web spun by a moulting spider. So to see what was going on, an extract from the body fluids of a moulting spider was then fed to another spider, which again spun a straggly web.

The clear conclusion is that there is something in both the blood of catatonic schizophrenics and the body fluids of moulting spiders that wrecks the patterns of spiders' webs. What it is and how it does the damage remain undiscovered.

See also COFFEE 91

447. What is it that makes spider silk so strong?

It is said that a thread of spider silk the thickness of a thumb would be strong enough to stop a jumbo jet travelling at a cruising speed of 900 kph (570 mph). Bulletproof jackets made of spider silk would only have to be a tenth of the weight of those made from Kevlar. In short, spider silk is one of the strongest substances known to science.

On the assumption that its strength must be due to a protein produced in the spider's spinning organ, genes from spiders have been transplanted into the mammary glands of goats to try to produce goat milk from which an ultra-strong substance could be made. Despite CIA funding and years of research, however, little progress has been made on the production of bulletproof jackets made from goat's milk.

448. How do tiny spider brains store the complex instructions needed to build webs?

Spiders vary in size from large and scary to almost microscopic, and the tiny ones must have really tiny brains. Working with *Anapisona simoni* spiders, which weigh only 1 milligram, William Eberhard of the University of Costa Rica investigated the hypothesis that tiny brains have less room to hold complex web-building information than larger brains.

Comparing the web complexity of the *Anapisona simoni* spiders and their ability to repair deformed webs with those of much larger orb-weaver spiders, Eberhard concluded that the balance of the evidence was that tiny brains are just as good at web-weaving as big brains. Not only that, but the tiniest spiders could design two different types of web, while the bigger ones had only one model.

Yet surely both the memory and processing capacity of tiny brains must be less than those of larger brains, so why is this not reflected in their web complexity?

It is good to love the unknown.

Charles Lamb (1775–1834)

449. Why are the eyes of the *Phintella vittata* spider so special?

In the wide spectrum of all possible electromagnetic radiation, there is a small range of wavelengths that we can detect with our eyes. Thanks to pigments in our retina, we can see wavelengths between about 400 (violet) and 700 (red) nanometres (billionths of a metre). At either end of that range, we have the ultraviolet and infrared parts of the spectrum, which humans cannot see.

We know that the vision of some animals extends into the ultraviolet (UV) range. Several fish, crustaceans, birds and mammals have the ability to see the part of the UV spectrum, known as UVA, which is closest to our own visible light. Between wavelengths of 270 and 320 nm is the UVB range, which is what we need to protect ourselves from when lying in direct sunlight, as UVB is absorbed in a way that can cause damage to our DNA and give rise to skin cancer.

Until recently, it was thought that no animals could see UVB, but in 2007 a team of researchers in Singapore discovered patches on the abdomens of the jumping spider *Phintella vittala* that reflected UVB light and seemed to be used in mating displays. To find out what was happening, an experiment was performed in which two groups of males were separated from females while performing their courtship dance. In one of the groups, the screen separating them included a UVB filter, allowing all light through except that in the UVB range. Result: while normally the females would go wild about the courtship dance, when the UVB filter was placed between them, they showed no interest at all.

Other creatures' eyes are known to be damaged by UVB, so if the female spiders are using their eyes to detect it, which seems very likely, they must in some way be protected. But why, alone of all animals so far investigated, can these spiders look where no other eyes have looked before? One theory is that this UVB detection has evolved as a private form of communication that other species cannot listen in on (so to speak). So what do these spiders have to say to each other that is so private?

450. Why are St Andrew's cross spiders so fussy about their choice of mate?

The St Andrew's cross spider, so-called from its habit of resting in its web with legs outstretched in an X-shape like a St Andrew's cross, has an unlucky sex life. Usually after mating, the male is eaten by the female, and they rarely if ever survive two matings. Despite this, the poor fellows have been seen to have strong preferences over whom they mate with. Experiments in Australia reported in 2004 showed that in the wild, males were strongly attracted to webs spun by laboratory-raised virgin females. Webs from non-virgin females did not seem to attract them at all. Virgin males also showed a preference for virgin females, but males that had previously survived mating did not care who they chose next time. Such a change in mate preference is very unusual, and what it is about the university-educated virgins they like so much also needs explaining.

451. To what extent is the web-planning of spiders a matter of chance, or can they control a web's location precisely?

When you see a spider's web spun in mid-air over some sort of chasm, you may have wondered how they get such a thing started. The answer is that they dangle a thread of silk until it is caught by a gust of wind that carries it over to the other side. With this rope ladder in place, they can then crawl along it, drop more threads, and build up the radii of the web. Then they lay down the sticky spiral of thread which is what catches their food, and right at the end they eat up those original threads that were only put down for construction purposes.

Going back to that first gust of wind, we have no way of knowing what part that plays in determining the precise location of the web.

Does the spider have a subtle feel for wind direction and choose where to dangle its first thread so it will be carried over to the precise point where it wants the web to be, or does it just dangle the thread, happy to build the web wherever the wind blows it?

See also SEX 415

SPONTANEOUS COMBUSTION

452. Has spontaneous human combustion ever occurred?

In his novel *Bleak House*, Charles Dickens gives a vivid description of the death of the rag-and-bone dealer Mr Krook by spontaneous combustion. When critics suggested that people do not suddenly burst into flames, Dickens fervently defended himself, and even added an account of a coroner's inquest supposedly proving that such things can and do happen.

Both historical accounts and even articles in medical journals, especially in the eighteenth century, have supported the idea of spontaneous human combustion, and in recent times bodies have been found after fires that display signs similar to those described in such accounts. One theory, called the 'wick effect', is that an initial flame can split the skin, releasing subcutaneous fat into the clothing, which acts as a wick in a burning candle. Yet no satisfactory explanation has been given of what could cause the initial flame to set off the process. The build-up of internal gases or a high alcohol level have both been suggested, but for spontaneous combustion to occur, either of these would have to be at impossibly high levels. A dropped cigarette still looks the most likely cause.

SQUIRRELS

453. Why do squirrels masturbate?

Nobody thought to ask that question until 2010, when a piece of research on a species of squirrel in Namibia appeared to confound the usual explanations offered to account for such behaviour. There are two standard reasons given for masturbation: it may act as a sexual outlet when a mate cannot be found; or it may (in the case of males) serve to increase the quality of sperm and the chance of fertilization by ejecting old and possibly dysfunctional sperm.

Either of those explanations would predict that masturbation would be most frequent among those who mated less frequently. In the case of the African ground squirrels whose behaviour was monitored in Namibia, however, precisely the opposite was the case: the most frequent masturbators were the males who had the most sex.

The biologist who carried out this research, Jane Waterman of the University of Central Florida, suggested that masturbation may serve as a form of genital grooming, possibly leading to a reduction in the chance of contracting a sexually transmitted infection – but a good deal more research would be needed to confirm that hypothesis.

THE SUN

454. What drives the twenty-two-year solar sunspot cycle?

In 1610, using his newly invented telescope, Galileo made the first observations of the black dots apparently on the Sun's surface known as sunspots. Ever since then, the number of such spots has been monitored and their cause speculated upon. The 'sunspot number' is calculated according to the number of individual spots and the number of groups of spots observed, and this number appears to follow a regular cycle, reaching a maximum every eleven years.

It is now known that sunspots are caused by bursts of intense magnetic activity, and that successive maxima have opposite polarity, so a complete cycle of sunspot activity lasts twenty-two years, but what causes that cycle is unknown. Neither do we understand the effect (if any) of sunspots on the Earth's weather, but that is another matter (→ WEATHER 473).

455. What is the cause of the many unidentified lines in the solar spectrum?

We can tell what elements are present in distant stars by examining the spectrum of light received from them. Any such spectrum includes dark features known as absorption lines, first discovered by the English chemist William Hyde Wollaston in 1802, rediscovered by the German Joseph von Fraunhofer in 1814, and almost fifty years later found to correspond, in many cases, to the emission lines of heated elements. The light spectrum from a star thus offers a celestial fingerprint of the elements present.

Yet Fraunhofer discovered 570 such emission lines in the Sun's spectrum, a figure that has since doubled, leaving a number far greater than the number of elements. The causes of many of the previously unidentified lines are now known, but there remain a large number unaccounted for.

TARDIGRADES

456. Why are the tiny creatures known as tardigrades found almost everywhere on Earth?

Wherever you go, you will not be far from a tardigrade. These microscopic, eight-legged creatures – also known as water bears or moss piglets – can live almost anywhere. No longer than 1.5 mm (3/50th in), they can survive temperatures close to absolute zero or as high as 151°C, and doses of radiation a thousand times the amount needed to kill most other animals. And they can go without water for ten years.

Tardigrades have been found deep in the oceans and high in the Himalayas, in the polar regions and at the Equator. They have even survived trips into space.

There are over a thousand species of tardigrade, but little is known of their evolutionary history. So different from almost everything else, their ubiquitous presence is evidence of a remarkable adaptability, which suggests an important role in evolution. Yet how they have managed to colonize almost everywhere on Earth is a mystery.

UNICORNS

457. Why were the people of the Indus Valley civilization so fascinated by unicorns?

Between 2600 BC and 1900 BC a great civilization flourished along the River Indus in what is now Pakistan and northwest India (→ WRITING SYSTEMS 493). This civilization was only rediscovered in the 1920s by Sir John Marshall, who was astonished by the evidence he found of their highly developed culture. They seem to have been a peaceful people, with no powerful or tyrannical rulers, no wars, no great displays of wealth or elaborate burial rituals, an advanced and efficient method of taxation, a decent sewage system, and a passion for baths – and unicorns. Over a hundred depictions of these fabled beasts have been found on Indus statues and ceramics.

Interestingly, the depiction of the unicorn as a mythological beast is a relatively modern phenomenon. Until the nineteenth century, the general view was at least open-minded as to whether they had existed. In ancient Greek and Roman writings, they appear in natural histories, not in mythology, with both Aristotle and Pliny the Elder indicating that they were to be found in India.

So were the Indus unicorns real? Sadly, no unicorn skeletons or fossils have been dug up in the region, but if they were not real, where did they get the idea from, and how did it establish itself so strongly in their culture?

THE UNIVERSE

458. Is there life elsewhere in the universe?

There are thought to be about 200 billion galaxies in the observable universe, each of which has about 200 billion stars. How many planets orbit how many of these stars is not known, but with numbers as vast as these, there seems to be a good chance that at least one of the 40,000,000,000,000,000,000,000 stars has a planet on which life has evolved. On the other hand, the more we look at life on Earth, the more we realize how delicately balanced the physical and chemical features have to be to allow life to come into existence.

Stars themselves, however, do not go on forever, and the right conditions for life may only exist for a short period of their existence, so while there may once have been life elsewhere in the universe, we may have missed it. With that number of chances, however, it seems very likely that there is some sort of life somewhere out there. Which brings us to the next question...

459. Is there intelligent life elsewhere in the universe?

In 1961, when the serious search for extraterrestrial intelligence was in its infancy, the American astrophysicist Frank Drake produced a famous equation to predict the chance of our making contact with intelligent life elsewhere in our galaxy, the Milky Way. His formula took into account the rate at which new stars are created, and the chances that they will have planets, that those planets will have the conditions to support life, that life will actually have formed, that it will develop intelligence, that its technology will be good enough to send out or receive radio signals, and that its civilization will not have died out. Multiply together all these factors, and you have the chance of our making contact.

The trouble with Drake's equation is that almost all the terms in it are a matter of guesswork, and the estimates it comes up with for the number of Milky Way civilizations we may contact range from about ten to around 10 billion. There is also, of course, the possibility that many of these may be far more advanced than we are, and may not want to talk to us anyway.

Given that the Milky Way is only one of some 200 billion galaxies, however, the chance of intelligent life somewhere out there, even if we have little hope of contacting it, must be very high – according to Drake's equation anyway. But we shall not know until we get a reply to one of our transmissions, or pick up one of theirs.

460. What is the Omega value of the universe?

In his book *The Phenomenon of Man*, written in the 1930s but not published until 1955, the French Jesuit priest, palaeontologist and philosopher Pierre Teilhard de Chardin (1881–1955) came up with the concept of an 'Omega Point' for the universe. If Alpha, the first letter of the Greek alphabet, represents the Creation then Omega is the end, which he defined as the state of maximum complexity towards which the universe is evolving.

When the Big Bang theory began to establish itself, Teilhard's Omega Point led to the idea of an Omega value for the universe that would predict its ultimate fate. The Big Bang led to all the matter in the universe sharing a massive amount of kinetic energy, which has been fuelling its expansion ever since. On the other hand, the gravitational pull of all the mass in the universe is working against this expansion by pulling everything back together again. The idea of the Omega value is to provide some sort of ratio between this kinetic energy and this mass, a ratio that will determine the ultimate fate of the universe. If Omega is less than 1, then the universe will continue expanding forever; if it is greater than 1, the expansion will come to an end before going into reverse and ending in a Big Crunch; if it is exactly equal to 1, then it will eventually approach a steady state.

Until recently, ideas of the matter-density of the universe predicted an Omega value very close to 1, leaving its fate still a three-horse race. Then came the theories of dark matter and dark energy, which have affected estimates of both the density and the expansion rate, making it more difficult than ever to predict what will happen at Teilhard's Omega Point. The smart money these days seems to be on an Omega less than 1 and eternal expansion, but that could all change with more cosmological discoveries.

461. What is the shape of the universe?

The question of the Omega value (→ 460) and the ultimate fate of the universe is tied in with its geometry and the question of whether Pythagoras' theorem works over vast distances. (Just in case you don't recall it, Pythagoras' theorem states that in any right-angled triangle, the square of the hypotenuse is equal to the sum of the squares of the other two sides.) Think of measurements made on the Earth's surface. Over short distances, Pythagoras works pretty well because the Earth is almost flat and so obeys the laws of Euclidean geometry. Over large distances, however, the curvature of the Earth comes into play and Pythagoras fails us.

Now try to imagine the same thing over the vast expanse of space. Considerations of the universe's expansion have led to the conclusion that if Omega is equal to 1, then the Universe is flat (in the sense that Pythagoras' theorem gives the right answers); if Omega is greater than 1, then space has positive curvature, rather like the surface of a sphere (though here we are actually talking about a hypersphere); and if Omega is less than 1, it has negative curvature and it is like taking measurements on a saddle.

Whatever the basic geometry, there is still an argument over the overall shape of the universe, with the debate focusing on whether it has been expanding at the same rate in all directions. Just as the Earth is not a perfect sphere but is a little squashed at the poles, the universe might not be spherical, but an ellipsoid. That would help solve some of the problems associated with the microwave background radiation (→ 462), but would introduce another problem of explaining how it got that way in the first place.

462. Why is the temperature of the microwave background radiation apparently uniform everywhere in the universe?

The cosmic microwave background radiation is a sort of afterglow of the Big Bang, the result of the initial massive surge of energy and heat being chilled by the expansion of the universe. Readings from NASA's Cosmic Background Explorer (COBE) satellite indicate a remarkable uniformity in this background radiation in every direction. Its temperature scarcely varies from a figure of about 2.76 degrees above absolute zero wherever one looks. Indeed, measured variations have only been around 0.001 per cent of the average figure.

This may seem all neat and tidy, but it is at variance with theories of how matter developed. Current theories predict changes in temperature according to the amount of matter in different regions. On the one hand, the almost perfect uniformity of cosmic background radiation is one of the strongest pieces of evidence supporting the Big Bang theory, but on the other hand, finding a way to account for its tiny fluctuations in terms of variations in the distribution of matter in the universe still poses great difficulty.

463. Is the universe finite or infinite in size?

The idea of a Big Bang and the limitations of the speed of light impose a limit on the size of the visible universe, but if the universe is expanding, that size is always increasing. Is there any limitation on the maximum size it could occupy?

Suppose a spacecraft takes off from Earth and travels in a straight line through space. Will it go on forever into the infinite universe, or will it, as some versions of the universe's geometry claim, eventually come back to its starting point? Such a finite universe is not out of the question, and claims have been made that it might explain ripples in the cosmic microwave background.

464. If string theory is right, how would we detect the influence of the other seven dimensions of the universe on our three-dimensional slice of it?

In Edwin Abbott Abbott's wonderful mathematical fantasy *Flatland* (1884), we meet a world of two-dimensional beings living on a flat plane who are visited by a sphere passing through their world. At first the sphere appears as a dot, then grows to a small circle, gradually increasing in size, but getting smaller as it continues its way through, before fading to a dot again then disappearing. Whether an analogous effect could be produced by a ten-dimensional inhabitant or piece of material of the ten-dimensional string-theory universe (→ PHYSICS 359) in passing through our three dimensions is an intriguing question.

Or perhaps we ourselves are in fact ten-dimensional creatures with the misfortune to be saddled with brains and sensory organs that can only recognize three of them. Spotting signs of the extra dimensions, however, seems to be a more difficult task for us than it was for the squares and triangles of Flatland.

465. Is the universe eternal?

Even Stephen Hawking seems to change his mind on this one. Not so long ago, he and other cosmologists were adamant that the Big Bang was the start of everything. Even asking 'What happened before the Big Bang?' was not a meaningful question. Now they are not so sure. And in the same way, 'What happens after the end of time?' may also be an acceptable question.

Whether or not the universe will go into reverse and end in a Big Crunch, we know that matter decays into smaller and smaller particles. With black holes sweeping up everything in their wake, one picture of the distant future has everything disappearing into a massive black hole containing all the energy in the universe.

In the past it was thought that nothing whatsoever could ever emerge from a black hole. Now it is believed that they can emit certain types of radiation, and radiation is energy, and energy is matter. This allows for a picture of an everlasting universe, acting on an unimaginably long time scale, pulsing between Big Bang creations and Big Crunch endings, into massive black holes which eventually explode again into another Big Bang. But we will have to wait a very long time indeed to know whether that scenario is correct.

466. How will it end if it isn't?

The old Norse legends had Ragnarok, other religions have Judgement Day or the Apocalypse, Wagner had *Götterdämmerung*, the twilight of the gods. Among more scientific theories, we have the Big Freeze, in which the temperature of everything approaches absolute zero. Alternatively, there is the theory of the Big Heat, where the laws of entropy bring everything into a state of maximum confusion and uniform temperature, with no free energy left to sustain life or any form of motion. The Universe would just stop. Then there is the Big Rip, when dark energy (possibly a kind of anti-gravity) tears everything apart, and the Big Crunch, where the universe collapses in on itself after the momentum of the Big Bang comes to an end and gravity reverses the process. Take your pick.

See also COSMOLOGY 106–14, PHILOSOPHY 367, QUANTUM PHYSICS 399–407

VENUS DE MILO

467. Who was the sculptor of the Venus de Milo?

Perhaps the most famous sculpture in the world, the Venus de Milo, was discovered in a cave on the Greek island of Milos in 1820. It was originally attributed to the master sculptor Praxiteles, which would have meant that it was made in the fourth century BC, but later a plinth was found that was said to fit the sculpture exactly and which included an inscription saying: 'Alexandros son of Menides, citizen of Antioch on the Maeander made this.' From the style of the lettering, this inscription would have dated the sculpture to around 100 BC, but some have suggested the inscription was not part of the original plinth but was only added later. To add to the confusion, the plinth quickly went missing after the statue arrived in Paris in 1821, and the only evidence we now have of the inscription is in a drawing made of the piece.

468. Who was the Venus de Milo meant to depict?

The general view is that she is most likely to be the goddess Aphrodite, whom the Romans called Venus and who was often portrayed half naked. There is even a suggestion that a missing piece of marble may have been an apple she was holding, making the statue suggestive of the Judgement of Paris. Others maintain that she is not Aphrodite but the sea goddess Amphitrite, who was venerated on Milos, where the statue was found.

469. What happened to the arms of the Venus de Milo?

In his memoir *Two Voyages to the South Seas*, the French explorer and sea captain Jules-Sébastien-César Dumont d'Urville (1790–1842) gave a thrilling account of his struggle with Greek brigands when transporting the Venus de Milo from Greece to France. In the fracas, he says, the statue was roughly dragged across rocks to the ships, resulting in both arms breaking off. The French sailors, eager to get away from the brigands, refused to return to search for them.

This whole story, however, appears to be pure fabrication, as other accounts and sketches indicate that the arms were absent when the statue was found. In either case, the missing arms have never been located. Nothing at all is known of what happened to the statue before or after it was hidden in the cave where it was found.

WATER

470. Where does the Earth's water come from?

This has always been a bit of a puzzle, as the Earth must have been much too hot in its early days to sustain any water on its surface. The usual theory is that water was deposited on the Earth from collisions with comets and asteroids in the planet's youth. Some investigations into the water content of such bodies has lent support to that idea by showing them to have much the same ratio as water on Earth of 'normal' hydrogen to deuterium (an isotope of hydrogen with a neutron in its nucleus). Other recent studies, however, notably of Comet Hale-Bopp, have led some to question the whole theory of the possible cometary origins of the Earth's water.

In 2007 Japanese scientists came up with an alternative hypothesis. In the early days, they suggest, the Earth had a great deal of hydrogen in its atmosphere, and this reacted with oxides in the Earth's mantle to form water. The heavy hydrogen cloud, they maintain, could also explain why the Earth's orbit round the Sun changed from an original elliptical shape as predicted by theory into the almost circular path we see today. While initially the water produced from their model might have been expected to be low in deuterium, their calculations also explain how it would have changed over time to the present amount.

471. Where did the water on the Moon come from?

In 2009 NASA crashed a lunar satellite into a crater on the Moon and announced that to their surprise they had found 'irrefutable' signs of significant quantities of water. But where did it come from? The scientists involved made all sorts of suggestions including solar winds, asteroids, comets, gases from the Moon's interior and grains of ice carried by intergalactic clouds. Or it may have come from the Earth. Or, in short, it might have come from anywhere.

Further lunar experiments are planned to get to the bottom of the mystery – or, as one scientist put it, to 'stuff the water back into the crater'.

472. How do ice crystals form?

We think of ice as a single entity: it's just frozen water after all, and water is water, right? Well, not really. Fifteen different forms of crystalline water have been identified. These different forms appear to result when freezing takes place in different conditions of temperature and pressure, but what precise conditions lead to which crystalline forms, and how changes in these conditions lead to differences in the geometry of the hydrogen bonds in the water molecules, are not yet completely understood. Only when we have achieved that understanding will we be able to explain the geometry of snowflakes.

473. What starts the process of ice formation in clouds?

The formation of ice droplets in a cloud has a highly significant effect on climate, influencing both the cloud's cooling effect in reflecting away the Sun's rays and its warming effect in trapping the heat radiating from the Earth. Yet we have very little understanding of how these ice droplets form.

When water is above a temperature of 0°C, it is liquid; when it is below –38°C, it will always be frozen; but between 0°C and –38°C it can be either. In this range, a water droplet needs a nucleus around which to freeze. Soot, mineral dust, meteoric particles, bacteria or pieces of ice may serve as this nucleus, but to what extent each different type of material performs this function, whether they are effective at different temperatures, and whether they lead to different crystalline formations of ice are uncertain. In 2009 a number of papers appeared supporting the view that biological particles such as bacteria play a strong role in the process, but research in Germany in 2010 claimed that dust was much more important. Until this is sorted out, we shall not know what to blame for the rain – which is, of course, what we notice when the ice crystals grow heavy enough to fall from the clouds, melting on their way down to the ground.

474. What is so special about water?

When two positively charged ions of hydrogen attach themselves to one negatively charged ion of oxygen to form a molecule of water, an additional factor that keeps them together is something called a hydrogen bond, which is the attractive force of the opposite charges.

Much of what we identify as the unusual properties of water seems to be dependent on the nature of the hydrogen bond: the fact that so many substances dissolve in water; the fact that water expands as it freezes; the surface tension of water. Life as we know it would be impossible without these special properties. Just think of the watery origins of life. If ice were heavier than water, it would sink to the bottom, leaving water at the top to freeze and sink again, until all life was extinguished from any body of water in sub-zero conditions. As it is, a layer of ice stays at the top, insulating the rest of the lake and allowing life to go on. And most of the salts and other chemicals that have led to the development of life have relied on water's solvent properties to get where they need to go.

Water is one of the most commonly encountered yet most unusual and least understood chemical compounds on Earth, and most of this seems to be due to the strange properties of the hydrogen bond.

WEATHER

475. How do tornadoes and tropical cyclones form?

'Cyclone' is a wonderful word. It signifies 'turning in a circle', just as the one-eyed Cyclops who gave Odysseus so much trouble might have done. Tropical cyclones are violent storms, including hurricanes and typhoons, which at their most dramatic exhibit the truly cyclonic, twisting behaviour which characterizes the tornadoes of North America. Such powerfully twisting storms seem to need several factors for their formation: warm water temperatures sustained to a considerable depth, high humidity, air rapidly cooling with height; consistent wind speed and direction, but otherwise disturbed atmospheric conditions. They also seem to need to be at least five degrees of latitude away from the Equator in order for the Coriolis force to deflect winds and create the turning effect. There is clearly something about them that we do not understand.

476. Is accurate long-range weather forecasting possible?

Short-term weather forecasting is based on taking measurements of current weather conditions, assessing where clouds and air masses are heading, and trying to work out what they will do when they get there. As computer systems become larger, and more detailed observations are fed into them, the results may become more accurate, but it seems that this accuracy is limited to a period of about five days.

The trouble is, weather is chaotic. When the American mathematician and meteorologist Edward Lorenz introduced the subject of chaos theory in 1972, he entitled his seminal paper 'Does the Flap of a Butterfly's Wings in Brazil Set Off a Tornado in Texas?' The whole idea of chaos theory is that it is possible to have a system whose behaviour is in principle totally determined by Newton's laws of motion, yet even the tiniest changes in the initial conditions can lead to completely different consequences. One set of conditions may lead to fine weather in Texas, but if you add one flap of a butterfly's wing in Brazil, you end up with a tornado. And even if your equipment is sensitive enough and your computer powerful enough to include the wing flaps of every butterfly on Earth, then the exhalation of an ant could still throw everything way off course.

One approach to long-range forecasting is to incorporate the unpredictability of chaos into computer simulations and run the data through several times, with slight changes to the initial figures.

If they all give the same result, one can be confident it is right (as long as the computer model is basically sound); but if they give different results, all one can do is offer a probabilistic estimate of the chance of different types of weather. And that, until we understand the weather much better and can better predict sea currents, air movements and their effect on one another, may be the best we can do for long-term forecasts.

477. What effect, if any, do sunspots have on our weather?

For more than a century, an argument has continued over the effect on our weather of sunspots (→ THE SUN 454). At various times, correlations have been published between the amount of sunspot activity and temperatures on Earth. The most striking example comes in data from the period 1645–1715, a period known as the Maunder Minimum after the English astronomer Edward Maunder (1851–1928) who first drew attention to it. This was a period of very low sunspot activity, which coincided with the severest part of the spell of prolonged cold weather known as the Little Ice Age. A link has long been suspected between the two events, but no convincing mechanism has been suggested to explain how sunspot activity could affect our weather. Other attempts to link sunspot activity to weather conditions have also failed to convince.

478. What is the cause of ball lightning?

Over the centuries there have been many accounts of glowing balls of fire appearing in the sky, usually during thunderstorms. These balls move through the air at a few metres per second, then either disappear or explode leaving a smell of sulphur. For long, such phenomena were dismissed as fantasies or hoaxes, but more recently the idea of ball lightning has been taken more seriously.

Vaporized silicon, aerodynamic vortices, large electrostatic charges and even black holes have been advanced as possible explanations, and scientists have produced in the laboratory effects that match accounts given of ball lightning. But there is still no way of knowing whether any of these laboratory-created phenomena are actually the same as those that take place in nature.

479. Why are noctilucent clouds becoming more frequent?

Noctilucent clouds, composed of tiny crystals of ice, are the highest clouds in the Earth's atmosphere. They are only visible when they reflect sunlight, especially as night draws on, which gives them their name, meaning 'night-shining'. Noctilucent clouds were first observed in 1885, two years after the massive eruption of Krakatoa, causing a suspicion that their existence may in some way have been due to volcanic debris in the atmosphere. Or it could be that the spectacular sunsets caused by the debris made people take more notice of what was going on in the sky.

In recent years noctilucent clouds have increased in frequency, which has led to a suggestion that their appearance is somehow connected to climate change. However, no mechanism has been suggested for such a link.

480. Will it rain next week?

The main thing we want to know from the weather forecast is whether it's going to rain. Up to about five days ahead, weather forecasts have a fair chance of being right (→ 476). A month or more ahead, a reasonable prediction of the chance of any particular type of weather may be made on the basis of past history. One week ahead falls uncomfortably between the two types of forecast. Frankly, your guess is as good as that of the next meteorologist.

See also CLIMATE 87–8

WORMS

481. What is the function of the hairs and bristles on the sperm of worms?

Making videos of tiny worms having sex under a microscope may seem an unusual way to spend one's time. Yet biologists in Switzerland have been doing just that with flatworms of the *Macrostomum* genus, their aim being to solve an old problem regarding the evolution of bristles and other adornments on the sperm of worms.

Macrostomum is an interesting little worm, about the size of a comma. They are completely hermaphroditic, having both male and female sex organs. When they mate, they curl together like two interlocking letter Cs, and the male organ of each enters the female organ of the other.

What the researchers were surprised to observe, however, was that after mating, each tried to remove the other's sperm by sucking it out. They conjecture that this is a method of sexual selection, choosing who they want to father their children not before mating, as is the common practice with many creatures, but after. They also suggest that the role of the bristles on the sperm of *Macrostomum* is to make it more difficult to suck out. Only making more videos of mating worms, of this and other genera, will confirm whether this is truly what happens.

> In other words, apart from the known and unknown, what else is there?
>
> Harold Pinter (1930–2008)

WRITERS

482. Who wrote *Beowulf*?

The epic poem *Beowulf* is the most important surviving work of Anglo-Saxon literature. Known only from a single manuscript called the Nowell Codex, it is a tale of heroic dragon-slaying exploits so potent that a translation of its 3,182 lines into modern English won Seamus Heaney the Whitbread Book of the Year prize in 1999. Yet we know almost nothing of the origins of *Beowulf*. The best that can be said is that it was written somewhere between the eighth and eleventh centuries. As for the identity of the writer, we have no idea at all. The story may, however, have existed for some time, being passed down in the oral tradition, before finally being written down.

483. Who wrote *Sir Gawain and the Green Knight*?

Unlike *Beowulf*, it is at least possible to draw some deductions about who wrote *Sir Gawain and the Green Knight*, and even to hazard a guess. A take recounting an adventure of King Arthur's youngest knight, who accepts a challenge from an unknown knight dressed in green, *Gawain* was written in the fourteenth century in a dialect of the northwest Midlands, a fact that is assumed to give a clue to the author's origins. Literary historians have also deduced that the author had a knowledge of French, Latin and theology, but was probably not a theologian himself.

The only name anyone has come up with is that of John Massey of Cotton in Cheshire, who is known to have written the poem *St Erkenwald*, which has some stylistic similarities with *Sir Gawain*. Massey's dates, however, are unsure, and there is even some doubt about whether he was alive when *Sir Gawain* was written.

484. Was Geoffrey Chaucer a rapist?

This question relates to an incident in the life of the author of *The Canterbury Tales* that has been a matter for intense speculation. On 4 May 1380 a woman called Cecily Chaumpaigne presented to the Chancery of Richard II a 'deed of release', which was copied into the court records. In it, she 'released' the poet Geoffrey Chaucer from 'all manner of actions such as they relate to my rape or any other thing or cause'. And that is essentially all we know of the case, except for a further suggestion that Chaucer paid Cecily £10.

Quite apart from the lack of any other information, the document was written in Latin, which has led to much argument about whether a rape was involved or not. The phrase '*de raptu meo*' could, according to some, have referred not to a rape, but more likely to a kidnapping or abduction.

To add to the mystery, the issuing of a 'deed of release' means that it was a civil case, not a criminal one. This, together with the £10 payment, suggests that Cecily did bring, or threaten to bring, a claim against Chaucer, and that he settled out of court. It is likely that we will never find out the full story behind these intriguing hints.

485. Who was the 'person from Porlock' who disturbed Coleridge in his writing of 'Kubla Khan'?

Samuel Taylor Coleridge claimed that the entire text of his poem 'Kubla Khan' (completed in 1797) had come to him in a dream, which he hastened to put down on paper on awakening. However, as he explained in an introduction when he first published the poem in 1816, a terrible thing then happened. (He refers to himself in the third person.)

On awakening he appeared to himself to have a distinct recollection of the whole, and taking his pen, ink, and paper, instantly and eagerly wrote down the lines that are here preserved. At this moment he was unfortunately called out by a person on business from Porlock, and detained by him above an hour, and on his return to his room, found, to his no small surprise and mortification, that though he still retained some vague and dim recollection of the general purport of the vision, yet, with the exception of some eight or ten scattered lines and images, all the rest had passed away like the images on the surface of a stream into which a stone has been cast, but, alas! without the after restoration of the latter!

So who was this 'person from Porlock'? Or was he just an invented excuse? One suggestion is that it was Coleridge's doctor, P. Aaron Potter, who regularly supplied the poet with laudanum (tincture of opium).

486. What did Edgar Allan Poe die of?

On 3 October 1849 the forty-year-old Edgar Allan Poe was found in great distress and a state of delirium on the streets of Baltimore, Maryland. He was taken to Washington College Hospital, where he died four days later, having never in that time been coherent enough to explain what had happened.

Poe had last been seen on 27 September, when he left Richmond, Virginia, on his way home to New York. No clear evidence of his whereabouts is known until he was found in Baltimore. During his four days in the hospital, he was kept in an area reserved for drunks, and was denied any visitors. On the night before he died, he is said to have repeatedly shouted out the name 'Reynolds'.

All medical records, including the death certificate, have been lost. Newspaper obituaries gave the cause of death as 'congestion of the brain' or 'cerebral inflammation', both being common euphemisms for alcoholism. Yet the doctor who treated him said there was not a trace of the smell of alcohol on his clothes or breath. Other suggestions include heart disease, epilepsy, syphilis, meningeal inflammation, cholera and rabies.

487. Why was Poe wearing someone else's clothes when he died?

To add to the mystery, when he was found in Baltimore, Edgar Allan Poe was apparently dressed in someone else's clothes, to judge from their shabbiness, which would have been most unlike him. The owner of the clothes was never identified, but has led to speculation that he might have been a victim of 'cooping', an electoral vote-rigging scam that involved seizing and drugging someone off the streets and turning up with them to vote at a number of polling stations. However, Poe was well known in Baltimore, and even shabby clothes might not have stopped him being recognized.

488. Why did Darwin delay so long before publishing *On the Origin of Species*?

Charles Darwin returned from his long trip on the *Beagle* in 1836, and by the end of 1838 told friends that he had the plans in place for his work on natural selection. Yet twenty years later, in 1858, he told Alfred Russel Wallace that he was not yet ready to publish. Darwin's great work, *On the Origin of Species by Means of Natural Selection*, did, however, come out the following year, in 1859, and was an immediate success. So why the delay of two decades?

One natural explanation could be Darwin's fear of upsetting his many friends in the clergy, or even his devout wife, Emma. He may even have feared religious persecution. All these may have played a part, but the most probable explanation could be that he was aware of the revolutionary impact his ideas would have, and was therefore determined to amass his evidence and polish his arguments to make sure he got it right.

The science historian and Darwin specialist John van Wyhe has suggested that the question needs no answer, as in Darwin's time twenty years would not have been seen as particularly long for a work of such magnitude. All the same, Darwin must have known of others' interest in the topic, and non-publication always ran the risk, even in the Victorian era, that someone else would get in first. There is good reason to believe that what eventually prompted Darwin's final decision to publish was a letter from Wallace outlining his own version of the theory of natural selection, with the implication that he was ready and prepared to publish it himself.

489. Was Émile Zola murdered?

Accident, suicide or murder? When in 1902 the sixty-two-year-old French novelist and political activist died of carbon monoxide poisoning caused by a blocked chimney in his home in Rue be Bruxelles, in Paris's seventh arrondissement, any of the three seemed possible. When Zola, in 1898, had written his famous front-page open letter to the president of the French Republic, headed with the words '*J'accuse!*' and charging the president with anti-Semitism and obstruction of justice in the Dreyfus case, he had made some powerful enemies. There had even been attempts on his life. His enemies, not unnaturally, celebrated his death and said, rather unconvincingly, that Zola had committed suicide on discovering that Dreyfus had been guilty after all (which turned out not to be the case).

Many years later a Parisian roofer, on his deathbed, is said to have confessed to blocking Zola's chimney 'for political reasons'. Yet that does seem a rather elaborate way of murdering someone, and the roofer did not say on whose orders he was acting.

490. Whatever happened to Ambrose Bierce?

Ambrose Bierce – journalist, satirist and author of *The Devil's Dictionary* – was seventy-one years old when he left Washington, DC, in October 1913 for a tour of Civil War battlefields. After that he is said to have joined Pancho Villa's army as an observer of the Mexican Revolution, and was in Chihuahua on Boxing Day 1913 when he wrote a letter to his friend Blanche Partington. He signed off with the words, 'As for me, I leave here tomorrow for an unknown destination.' He was never seen again.

One tale is that he was shot by a firing squad in Sierra Mojada, but others say he never went to Mexico at all. Despite several attempts, no trace of his movements has ever been found.

491. What became of the first draft of T. E. Lawrence's *The Seven Pillars of Wisdom*?

In 1919 Lawrence of Arabia had almost completed his first draft of *The Seven Pillars of Wisdom*, most of which he had written while attending the Paris Peace Conference. Around Christmas, back in England, he took the manuscript with him on a train journey that necessitated a change at Reading. While waiting for his connection, however, his briefcase, with the precious manuscript inside, went missing.

Some accounts say he left it on the train, others that he left it in the station buffet; some say it was stolen. All that remained in Lawrence's possession was a typescript of a few early chapters. The rest he rewrote from memory, and the book was published in 1921. The missing manuscript, and the briefcase, were never found.

Ignorance gives one a large range of probabilities.

George Eliot (1819–1880)

492. Why did Agatha Christie disappear for eleven days in December 1926?

Towards the end of 1926, the crime writer Agatha Christie, then aged thirty-six, was told by her husband Archie that he was in love with another woman and wanted a divorce. Not unnaturally, they quarrelled and on 8 December he left their house in Sunningdale, Surrey, to spent the weekend with his lover. That same evening, Mrs Christie left the house, leaving a note for her secretary saying that she was going to Yorkshire.

News of the disappearance mobilized Agatha Christie's army of fans, and a nationwide hunt was set up to find her. It took eleven days before she was identified at a hotel in Harrogate where she had checked in as 'Mrs Teresa Neele', using the same surname as her husband's lover. She never gave any account of what she had been doing for those eleven days, and suggestions have ranged from a nervous breakdown or a publicity stunt to an attempt to embarrass her husband or even have him framed for her murder.

See also SHAKESPEARE 423–7

WRITING SYSTEMS

493. Was the strange script of the Indus Valley civilization an unknown language, an accounting system, or what?

Serious excavations of the Indus Valley civilization, which thrived in what is now Pakistan and northwest India between 2600 and

1900 BC (→ UNICORNS 457), began only in 1920. But even before that, in the 1870s, a picture of a seal from the Indus people had been published, clearly showing their curious hieroglyph-like inscriptions. Since then, over 4,000 such seals or tablets have been found, providing a wealth of material but no long texts that might offer some information about the language. In fact, the typical tablet contains only five symbols, raising the possibility that it is not a language at all, but some sort of counting or messaging system. The longest inscription contains only seventeen signs.

Over the years, many have claimed to have deciphered the script, but no two experts seem able to agree even on what group the language of the Indus people might have belonged to, or what their symbols might mean. The only tentative conclusion that does have majority support is that the Indus script was written from right to left.

494. What did the symbols of the alphabet known as Linear A mean in ancient Crete, and what was the Minoan language they may have transcribed?

When Sir Arthur Evans excavated the palace of Knossos in Crete in the early 1900s, he discovered numerous clay tablets containing inscriptions in three different scripts. One consisted of hieroglyphs, the others he named Linear A and Linear B. In 1952 the English classical scholar Michael Ventris showed that Linear B was used to write an early form of Greek, but Linear A, though it contains some of the same symbols as Linear B, has never been decoded.

When our knowledge of the Linear B symbols is applied to Linear A, it produces words that appear to be unrelated to any known language. One suggestion is that this is the lost Minoan language, spoken in Crete before invasions by the Greeks around 1450 BC. Attempts to reconstruct this language and decipher the Linear A tablets have met with limited success at best. This may cast doubt on the assumption that the symbols shared by Linear A and Linear

B have the same syllabic values in each language, which would mean we would have to go back to square one in our attempts at decipherment.

As for the language that may have been behind Linear A, there is some evidence that it was Indo-European, or a pre-Indo-European precursor, though not enough to be sure. A form of pre-Greek has also been suggested, as has Luwian, an extinct language spoken in Anatolia. An archaic form of Phoenician is another idea, while Indo-Iranian and Tyrrhenian have also been proposed.

See also ANCIENT HISTORY 10

495. What is the language of the Voynich Manuscript, or is it an elaborate fake?

The Voynich Manuscript has been described as 'the world's most mysterious manuscript'. Others consider it likely to be one of the world's greatest hoaxes.

The beautifully illustrated manuscript is written in an unknown script and has defied all attempt by cryptologists to decode it, although the illustrations suggest it may have been some kind of pharmacopoeia or medical text. The manuscript – named after the book dealer Wilfrid M. Voynich, who acquired it in 1912 – has been carbon-dated to the first half of the fifteenth century.

The text consists of 170,000 characters, separated by narrow gaps, but with longer gaps dividing them into something resembling words. There are about twenty to thirty distinct characters that occur frequently, with about another dozen that make rare appearances. Statistical analysis suggests that the letter frequency resembles that of natural languages, but there are no very long or very short words. Its lack of clear resemblance to any particular language suggests a code, but, if that is the case, nobody has been able to crack it. It is not known where the manuscript originally came from, but it was in the possession of an alchemist in Prague in the seventeenth century.

If the Voynich Manuscript is a forgery, it is brilliant both in design and execution, which must have demanded the use of genuine fifteenth-century writing materials. If it is not a forgery, it is extraordinary that it has resisted every attempt – using all our knowledge of fifteenth-century coding methods and twenty-first-century computing power – to decipher it.

496. Where did our alphabetical order come from?

The Egyptians had hieroglyphs, which began as a form of pictogram and later came to represent sounds rather than objects. By 2700 BC the Egyptians had a sort of alphabet of twenty-two hieroglyphs representing the consonants in their language. The Phoenicians, around 1700 BC, were the first to come up with an alphabet that was beginning to look a little like ours, and the Greeks and Romans developed their alphabets from the Phoenician, keeping much the same order of letters as the Phoenicians had, but introducing letters of their own.

The Roman schoolteacher and grammarian Spurius Carvilius Ruga is credited with inventing the letter G, to avoid the confusion of C being used both for the 'k' and 'g' sounds. But why were the letters of the Roman alphabet (the one we use today) placed in a particular order, beginning with A?

The only answer seems to be that the Romans copied the Greeks, and the Greeks copied the Phoenicians, and nobody knows the process by which the Phoenicians arrived at their order.

See also EASTER ISLAND 154

Ignorance of one's misfortunes is clear gain.
Euripides (*c.* 450 BC–406 BC)

YETI

497. Is there any truth in the story of the abominable snowman?

The word 'yeti' is said to come from two Tibetan words meaning 'rocky place' and 'bear'. This bear from a rocky place captured the Western world's imagination when the Everest Reconnaissance Expedition of 1921 returned with tales of mysterious footprints in the snow. The Sherpa guides had said these must be those of the 'Wild Man of the Snows', for which they used an expression that was mistranslated as 'abominable snowman'. And the legend of the abominable snowman was born.

The yeti, however, had been part of local beliefs since before Buddhist times. He had been depicted as an apelike creature, making a whistling sound and carrying a large stone as a weapon. Around 1950, interest in the yeti peaked, following several claimed sightings and some unexplained footprints. The *Daily Mail* even sponsored a Snowman Expedition to find it. As recently as 2007 and 2008, more footprints have been sighted, and suspected samples of yeti hair found, but nothing has been confirmed, and the elusive beast has remained hidden. Some cryptozoologists like to think that the yeti is some kind of apeman or missing link, while the scientific community is inclined to believe that the footprints and sightings are more likely to have been of a bear – albeit a ' bear from a rocky place'.

498. What happened to the supposed finger and thumb of a yeti that the actor James Stewart helped to smuggle out of India in 1959?

In 1959 the Irish-born mountaineer Peter Byrne visited a lamasery in Pangboche, Nepal, where he hoped to examine something that was supposed to be the hand of a yeti. Having come prepared, Byrne stole a finger and thumb from the hand, replacing them with a human finger and thumb that he had brought with him. The supposed yeti parts were smuggled into India where Byrne bumped into the actor James Stewart and his wife Gloria, who agreed to help smuggle them to England. They are said to have wrapped them in underwear and carried them in their hand luggage. Sadly, this was in the days before DNA identification, so scientific tests on the digits were inconclusive. The samples subsequently vanished and have never reappeared. In May 2011 a replica of the missing yeti hand was returned to the monastery in Nepal as part of a 'Return the Hand' campaign. But the original yeti hand has still not turned up.

ZYMOLOGY

Zymology is the study of fermentation, in which, as you probably know, yeast plays an important part. Of course, the most interesting question of all about yeast is this:

499. Can yeast think?

Writing about the evolution of the brain in the *Sydney Alumni Magazine* in 2009, the molecular neurobiologist Professor Seth Grant posed the question 'Can yeast think?' His answer was rather surprising: 'At some level the answer to this is yes. Yeast cells make decisions in response to changes in their environment,' he said, and went on to explain how they detect changes in their environment and alter their growth or behaviour accordingly. That would not, of course, be considered 'thinking' by most people, but his view is supported by the discovery that the proteins used by yeast to make such changes are the same as some proteins found in the synapses of the human brain. So the origins of our own brain evolution may lie in the ancestral proteins of unicellular fungi such as yeast.

AND FINALLY...

500. Will there always be things we don't understand?

It certainly looks that way. The more we understand the more we realize we do not know – and the more we are inspired to find out more. As Benjamin Franklin put it: 'The doorstep to the temple of wisdom is a knowledge of our own ignorance.'

I hope this book will have given a useful lift towards that doorstep.

501. If there comes a time when we know everything there is to be known, will we recognize it?

...or will there come a time when the only thing we do not know is that we know everything?

ACKNOWLEDGEMENTS

Apologies and huge gratitude are due in about equal measure to all the academics and other experts whom I approached in the course of writing this work with requests that they tell me everything they didn't know. Responses varied from fascinating outpourings of ignorance to blank looks of incomprehension. I have decided against even trying to compile a list of all who helped, even by vaguely pointing me in promising directions, partly because the complete list would be too long, but also because I am sure I would offend someone by leaving them out. A particularly delightful Japanese lunch with Norman Lebrecht does, however, linger in the memory, and revealed to me the full mystery of Scriabin's shaving cut. For the rest of my anonymous guides, you may rest assured that I am truly grateful and the dark secrets of your ignorance are safe with me.

I must, however, thank Richard Milbank at Atlantic Books, for his unflagging interest in this project, his tolerance of my authorial foibles and the immense help he has given throughout in steering this work from concept to completion. I am also indebted to my editor, Ian Crofton, whose encyclopedia knowledge, and refusal to let me get away with vagueness or feeble attempts at humour have raised the respectability of this book at least a couple of intellectual notches. Any errors or bad jokes that remain, however, are all my own.

BIBLIOGRAPHY

To list all the books and journals I have consulted in the preparation of these 501 unknowns would probably result in a list longer than the rest of the book. So here is a selection of some of the references I have found most useful and interesting, for anyone in search of more detailed information. The references are indexed according to the number of the unknown item.

Introduction: Polak and Rashed (2010). 'Microscale laser surgery reveals adaptive function of male intromittent genitalia', *Proceedings of the Royal Society B Biological Science*

1. Yang, F. et al. (2003), 'Reciprocal chromosome painting among human, aardvark, and elephant (superorder *Afrotheria*) reveals the likely eutherian ancestral karyotype', *Proceedings of the National Academy of Sciences USA*

9. Bello, S.M. et al. (2011), 'Earliest directly dated human skull-cups', *PLoS ONE*

24. Andreasen, R.O. (2000), 'Race: biological reality or social construct?' *Philosophy of Science*

35. Ellington, C.P., van den Berg, C., Willmott, A.P., Thomas, A.L.R. (1996), 'Leading-edge vortices in insect flight', *Nature*

35. Buchwald, R. and Dudley, R. (2010), 'Limits to vertical force and power production in bumblebees (Hymenoptera: *Bombus impatiens*)', *The Journal of Experimental Biology*

36. Muller, H., Grossmann, H., Chitko, L. (2010), '"Personality" in bumblebees: individual consistency in responses to novel colours?' *Animal Behaviour*

37. von Frisch, K. (1946), 'Die Tänze der Bienen', *Österreichische Zoologische*

37. Su, S. et al. (2008), 'East Learns from West: Asiatic honeybees can understand dance language of European honeybees', *PLoS ONE*

37. Klein, B.A. et al. (2010), 'Sleep deprivation impairs precision of waggle dance signaling in honey bees', *Proceedings of the National Academy of Sciences USA*

44. Rovner, S.A. (2010), 'Recipes for limb renewal', *Chemical & Engineering News*

46. Klem Jr., D. (1989), 'Bird-window collisions', *Wilson Bulletin*

47. Heyers, D. et al. (2007), 'A visual pathway links brain structures active during magnetic compass orientation in migratory birds', *PLoS ONE*

48. Evans, C.S. and Evans, L. (1999), 'Chicken food calls are functionally referential', *Animal Behaviour*

49. Searcy, W. and Beecher, M. (2011), 'Continued scepticism that song overlapping is a signal', *Animal Behaviour*

59. Bickart, K.C. et al. (2010), 'Amygdala volume and social network size in humans', *Nature Neuroscience online*

60. Quian Quiroga, R. et al. (2005), 'Invariant visual representation by single-neurons in the human brain', *Nature*

72. Wells, D.L. and Millsopp, S. (2009), 'Lateralized behaviour in the domestic cat, *Felis silvestris catus*', *Animal Behaviour*

77. McGrew, W.C. and Marchant, L.F. (1999), 'Laterality of hand use pays off in foraging success for wild chimpanzees', *Primates*

90. Rogers, P.J. et al. (2010), 'Association of the anxiogenic and alerting effects of caffeine with ADORA2A and ADORA1 polymorphisms and habitual level of caffeine consumption', *Neuropsychopharmacology*

95. Neumayr, A. (1994), *Music and Medicine*, Vol. 1, Medi-Ed Press, Bloomington, Illinois

101. Damasio, A. (2010), *Self Comes to Mind: Constructing the Conscious Brain*, William Heinemann

111. Ellis, G.F.R. and Uzan, J.-P. (2005), 'c is the speed of light, isn't it?' *American Journal of Physics*

121. Baron-Cohen, S. et al. (1997), 'Is there a link between engineering and autism?' *Autism: An International Journal of Research and Practice*

128. Anandan, C. et al. (2009), 'Is the prevalence of asthma declining? Systematic review of epidemiological studies', *Allergy*

129. Johnson, C., and Eccles, R. (2005), 'Acute cooling of the feet and the onset of common cold symptoms', *Family Practitioner*

135. Rout, T.M., Heinze, D., McCarthy, M.A. (2010), 'Optimal allocation of conservation resources to species that may be extinct', *Conservation Biology*

136. Mascheroni, R.M., Senju, A., Shepherd, A.J. (2008), 'Dogs catch human yawns', *Biology Letters*

187. McKee, A.C. et al. (2009), 'Chronic traumatic encephalopathy in athletes: progressive tauopathy after repetitive head injury', *Journal of Neuropathology and Experimental Neurology*

190. Gelbart, N.R. (2004), 'The blonding of Charlotte Corday', *Eighteenth-Century Studies*

216. Coe, M.J. (1967), '"Necking" behavior in the giraffe', *Journal of Zoology*

222. Nelson, R. (1993), 'Understanding Eskimo science', *Audubon magazine*

222. Lin, R.C. (2004), 'Fractures of the radius and ulna secondary to possible vitamin D deficiency in captive polar bears (*Ursus maritimus*)', *Cornell University senior seminar paper*

223. Levermann, N. et al (2003), 'Feeding behaviour of free-ranging walruses with notes on apparent dextrality of flipper use', *BMC Ecology*

225. Forrester, G.S. et al (2011), 'Target animacy influences gorilla handedness', *Animal Cognition*

228. Gallup, A., Miller, M., Clark, A. (2009), 'Yawning and thermoregulation in budgerigars, *Melopsittacus undulates*', *Animal Behaviour*

228. Gallup, A.C. and Gallup, G.G. (2007), 'Yawning as a brain-cooling mechanism: nasal breathing and forehead cooling diminish the incidence of contagious yawning', *Evolutionary Psychology*

230. Panksepp, J. and Burgdorf, J. (2003), '"Laughing" rats and the evolutionary antecedents of human joy?', *Physiology & Behavior*

232. Miller, G.F. (2000), 'Evolution of human music through sexual selection', in Wallin, N.L., *The Origins of Music*, MIT Press

235. Setchell, J.M. et al (2009), 'Opposites attract: MHC-associated mate choice in an Old World primate', *Journal of Evolutionary Biology*

237. Brown, P. et al. (2004), 'A new small-bodied hominin from the late Pleistocene of Flores, Indonesia', *Nature.*

243. Bailey, N.W. et al. (2010), 'Acoustic experience shapes alternative mating tactics and reproductive investment in male field crickets', *Current Biology*

244. Maye, A. et al. (2007), 'Order in spontaneous behaviour', *PLoS ONE*

256. Mithen, S.J. (2005), *The Singing Neanderthals: the origins of music, language, mind and body*, Harvard University Press

260. Pullum, G. (1991), *The Great Eskimo Vocabulary Hoax and Other Irreverent Essays on the Study of Language*, University of Chicago Press

261. Herndon, J.M. (2007), 'Nuclear georeactor generation of the Earth's geomagnetic field', *Current Science*

264. Brody, S. (1945), *Bioenergetics and Growth*, Reinhold

264. White, C.R. and Seymour, R.S. (2003), 'Mammalian basal metabolic rate is proportional to body mass$^{2/3}$', *Proceedings of the National Academy of Sciences USA*

265. Reznikova, Z. and Ryabko, B. (2011), 'Numerical competence in animals, with an insight from ants', *Behaviour*

269. Crofoot, M.C. et al (2010), 'Does watching a monkey change its behaviour?' *Animal Behaviour*

270. Braithwaite, V.A. (2010), *Do Fish Feel Pain?* Oxford University Press

276. Manger, P.R. (2006), 'An examination of cetacean brain structure with a novel hypothesis correlating thermogenesis to the evolution of a big brain', *Biology Review*

277. Johnson, M.E. and Atema, J. (2005), 'The olfactory pathway for individual recognition in the American lobster *Homarus americanus*', *Journal of Experimental Biology*

277. Aquiloni, L. and Gherardi, F. (2010), 'Visual recognition of conspecifics in the American lobster, *Homarus americanus*', *Animal Behaviour*

282. Kaptchuk, T.J. et al. (2010). 'Placebos without deception: a randomized controlled trial in irritable bowel syndrome', *PLoS ONE*

287. Dawson, W. (1927), 'Mummy as a drug', *Proceedings of the Royal Society of Medicine*

313. Zegers, R.H.C., Weigl, A., Steptoe, A. (2009), 'The death of Wolfgang Amadeus Mozart: an epidemiologic perspective', *Annals of Internal Medicine*

334. Dickey, J. (2003), 'The structural dynamics of the American five-string banjo', *Journal of the Acoustical Society of America*

352. Ali, J. and Huber, M. (2010), 'Mammalian biodiversity on Madagascar controlled by ocean currents', *Nature*

362. Schmidt, H. (1978), 'Can an effect precede its cause? A model of a noncausal world', *Foundations of Physics*

382. Hutchinson, G.E. (1961), 'The paradox of the plankton', *The American Naturalist*

385. Kepr, F. et al. (2006), 'Methane emissions from terrestrial plants under aerobic conditions', *Nature*

385. Nesbit, R.E.R. et al (2009), 'Emission of methane from plants', *Proceedings of the Royal Society B: Biological Sciences*

386. D'Arrigo, R. et al. (2007), 'On the "divergence problem" in northern forests: a review of the tree-ring evidence and possible causes', *Global and Planetary Change*

396. Bauval, R. and Gilbert, A. (1994), *The Orion Mystery*, Cornerstone

415. Cross, F.R. (2009), 'How blood-derived odor influences mate-choice decisions by a mosquito-eating predator', *Proceedings of the National Academy of Sciences USA*

417. Young, L.C. (2008), 'Successful same-sex pairing in Laysan albatross', *Biology Letters*

446. Bercel, N.A. (1959), 'The effect of schizophrenic blood on the behavior of spiders', *Neuropsychopharmacology*

448. Eberhard, W. (2011), 'Are smaller animals behaviourally limited?' *Animal Behaviour*

450. Gaskett, A.C. et al. (2004), 'Changes in male mate choice in a sexually cannibalistic orb-web spider', *Behaviour*

453. Waterman, J. (2010), 'The adaptive function of masturbation in a promiscuous African ground squirrel', *PLoS ONE*

470. Genda, H. and Ikoma, M, (2007), 'Origin of the ocean on the Earth: early evolution of water D/H in a hydrogen-rich atmosphere', *Icarus*

481. Schärer, L. et al. (2010), 'Mating behavior and the evolution of sperm design', *Proceedings of the National Academy of Sciences USA*

499. Grant, S. (2009), 'From little things, big things grow', *Sydney Alumni Magazine*

PART 2

EVEN MORE THINGS
THAT NOBODY KNOWS

'To succeed in life you need two things:
ignorance and confidence.'

Mark Twain

CONTENTS

INTRODUCTION

'Real knowledge is to know the extent
of one's ignorance.'

Confucius (6th–5th century BC)

I have always found it much more enlightening listening to experts talking about what they don't know rather than what they do know. Only when we start peering over the boundaries of human knowledge do things begin to grow really interesting.

Every year, an estimated 1.5 million papers appear in academic journals. Each one of these pushes the boundaries of our knowledge a little further forwards. Just as important, it points the way into the unknown, giving us ideas for where our explorations should go next. The majority of the 501 unanswered questions in this book are about those areas where 'further research is needed', as the writers of those papers love to put it. Even if that is only a way of asking for their research grant to be renewed, it may also serve as a bright signpost into the unknown.

When I wrote the previous *Things That Nobody Knows* book in 2011, some readers were apparently disappointed that I did not give answers to the 501 questions posed. They both missed the point and clearly didn't read the title carefully: if I, or anyone else, were able to give the answers, the questions wouldn't have been in the book. These aren't the things that *most* people don't know; they are the things that *nobody* knows.

So here are another 501 unanswered questions. I hope you will find that my discussion of each of them is nonetheless enlightening, intriguing and in some cases even amusing.

William Hartston
Cambridge, 2015

AESOP

1. Was Aesop a fable?

The collection of stories known as Aesop's Fables dates back to around the sixth century BC, but whether Aesop himself was fact or fiction is still an open question. Herodotus, in the fifth century BC, and Aristotle in the fourth century BC both wrote of Aesop being a slave in Samos. Plutarch, some 300 years later, wrote of Aesop visiting Delphi on a diplomatic mission, annoying the locals and being thrown from cliffs to his death. Later still, probably around the first century AD, a work entitled *The Aesop Romance* appeared, putting together and further embellishing tales of Aesop's life.

Great doubt, however, has been cast on the accuracy of these tales, and in some cases the chronology simply does not add up. In 1965 the Aesop scholar Ben Edwin Perry concluded that much of what had been written about Aesop 'must be reckoned as literary fiction'. So the question of whether Aesop himself was a fable is still open.

'Ignorance is the softest pillow on which a man can rest his head.'

Michel de Montaigne

ALCHEMY

2. Who was Fulcanelli?

In the 1920s a Frenchman who called himself Fulcanelli gained the reputation in Paris of being the last of the great alchemists. His writing style and knowledge of Latin, Greek and several modern languages marked him out as a well-educated man and references in his writings to a wife suggest that he was married, yet no evidence has been found of his education or marriage. He disappeared in 1926, after which tales of alleged sightings have only added to the mystery surrounding his true identity.

Fulcanelli is said to have met with the Russian/French spy Jacques Bergier in 1937 to warn him of the dangers of atomic explosives, which he said alchemists had known of for centuries. He is also said to have told a pupil, Eugène Canseliet, the secret of transmuting lead into gold, and there is an account of Canseliet demonstrating the method successfully by turning 100 grams of lead into gold at the gasworks of Sarcelles in the north of Paris.

Canseliet was also responsible for ensuring the publication of Fulcanelli's great work, *Le Mystère des cathédrales*, which his master had left with him before he disappeared. It has been suggested that Fulcanelli was in fact Canseliet himself, which would of course have involved a deception of great ingenuity to stage the disappearance of a man who didn't exist.

Canseliet insisted that Fulcanelli survived the Second World War and that the two men had their last meeting in 1953, when Fulcanelli would have been in his eighties but was said to look about thirty years younger. Canseliet died in 1982 and, if one is to believe the tales about

Fulcanelli, the secrets of the Philosopher's Stone and eternal youth vanished with him.

SEE ALSO FRANCE 201; LONGEVITY 280; PHYSICS 372

ALCOHOL

3. Why does alcohol make women less fertile?

In 1998 a paper was published in the *British Medical Journal* with the title 'Does moderate alcohol consumption affect fertility?' Based on a study of 430 Danish couples who were trying to conceive their first child, it concluded, after correlating their conception rates with their drinking behaviour, that: 'A woman's alcohol intake is associated with decreased fecundability even among women with a weekly alcohol intake corresponding to five or fewer drinks.'

Previous research studies had shown lower conception rates among women who drank more than five units of alcohol a week, but most of them had not detected any such effects for moderate drinking. Another surprise was that: 'Among men no dose–response association was found after control for confounders including women's alcohol intake.' In other words, previous studies reporting low conception rates among male drinkers may have occurred because men who drink a lot may be more likely to have partners who drink a lot and whose conception rates suffer as a result.

Since then, many further studies have failed to reach agreement on whether low alcohol intake can decrease chances of conception. Alcohol has been associated with effects on the production of oestrogen and other hormones in women, but the mechanism by which this occurs is not properly understood.

A further complication was added in 2014 when a study in the USA reported that stress may diminish a woman's fertility. Measurements of the levels of an enzyme associated with stress showed that women with higher levels were twice as likely to be infertile. Since people may have a greater tendency to drink when they are feeling stressed, this finding raises the possibility that the alcohol effect reported in earlier studies may, at least in part, be explained by stress.

See also ATILLA 31; BIOLOGY 58; CANNABIS 87; WINE 494

ANATOMY

4. Why do we have pubic hair?

In the course of human evolution, we have shed a great deal of our bodily hair. With much of our heat loss occurring through the head, it makes sense to have retained hair there to perform a warming function, but armpit and pubic hair need a different explanation. Here are a few theories:

(i) Pubic hair has a similar warming or protective effect for our reproductive organs.

This is hardly convincing. The hair is not very well located to perform either of those functions in regions where it might be useful.

(ii) Hair reduces friction when love-making.

This is also unconvincing when one considers the amount of time people spend making love.

(iii) Hair acts as a protective barrier to prevent dirt and unwanted organisms from entering the vagina or penis.

This appears a more likely explanation, by analogy with the hairs in our ears and nostrils and on our eyelashes and eyebrows, but while pubic hair may perform a similar function for women, it would only have a limited effect in that respect in men. Indeed, a consideration of the relative amount of protection one might think necessary for the vaginal and penile openings, pubic hair might by now be expected to have survived only in women.

(iv) Pubic hair plays a role in mate selection through its ability to enhance bodily smells.

There is some evidence that smells created by secretions from glands near our genitals help us select sexual partners in a manner that is most likely to be evolutionarily successful. These apocrine glands secrete a fluid which only develops an odour when it meets bacteria on the surface of the skin. Our pubic hair is perfectly placed to absorb these fluids, thereby increasing the smell. Whether this theory, and our pubic hair, can survive the ever-increasing use of deodorants, however, is open to question.

5. How did the corpus callosum evolve?

The two halves of our brains are joined by a thick bundle of nerve fibres known as the corpus callosum, which provides the pathways through which the two hemispheres communicate with one another. However, not all animals with two cerebral hemispheres have a corpus callosum. In fact, every species of mammal that develops a placenta during pregnancy has a corpus callosum while non-placental mammals, including all marsupials, do not have one.

In 1863 the zoologist T. H. Huxley wrote: 'the appearance of the corpus callosum in the placental mammals is the greatest and most sudden modification exhibited by the brain in the whole series of vertebrated animals...' Over 150 years later, we still have no idea how the corpus callosum evolved or of any connection between having a placenta and having a corpus callosum.

Having a brain divided into two halves makes little sense unless something joins them, and in the non-placental animals, that function is served by more primitive structures called commissures. How the primitive corpus callosum evolved with the commissures already in place is a mystery.

6. Does the human appendix serve any useful purpose?

Until recently, the appendix was seen as some sort of vestigial organ which may have served some useful purpose in our evolutionary past, but now had no function other than to give people appendicitis. Surgeons would remove the appendix at the first signs of the disease, and sometimes it would be removed as a prophylactic measure when other stomach surgery was being performed.

In the last few years, however, the view has grown that the appendix may have a useful function after all. First, it was found to be a reservoir of useful bacteria that may play a part in the role white blood cells perform in our immune system, and then a comparison of human appendices with those of other animals suggested that there may be more to these organs than had been thought. A study in 2013 reported a hitherto unsuspected degree of evolution in the appendix, suggesting that it had evolved thirty times in its long history to perform varying functions in different animals according to their diets.

Quite what the human appendix does is still unclear, but it is looking more likely that it does have a useful function after all.

7. Why are the left sides of people's faces more expressive than the right sides?

A curious result that has been confirmed in numerous studies since the 1970s is that people find the left sides of other people's faces more expressive, more attractive and generally more fun than the right sides.

It has been conjectured that this may have something to do with the right hemisphere of the brain being more involved with emotions and also controlling the muscles on the left side of the face, but how this would work in shaping human preferences for left or right side is quite unclear and further complicated by the problems caused by mirrors transposing left and right. How can we find the left sides of our faces more expressive when we see them in a mirror, when the image is then on the same side as the right side of anyone we look at?

The closely related question of left–right preferences by painters and their portrait subjects is discussed later (→ ART 25).

See also BRAINS 78, CHINA 103, EARS 162, HUMAN EVOLUTION 237, LEGS 269

ANCIENT CITIES

Our knowledge of the ancient world is infuriatingly incomplete, with remains of many lost cities leaving few if any clues as to who were the people who built them or how they were constructed. Here are just a few such mysteries.

8. Who built the ancient Mexican city of Teotihuacan?

More than a thousand years before the Aztecs arrived in Mexico, the great city of Teotihuacan became one of the world's largest cities. It had an estimated population between 100,000 and 250,000, and its structures included the Pyramid of the Sun, which was one of the largest buildings in the western world.

We do not know who built it; we do not know what name they called it; but archaeological investigations have dated its beginnings to around 100 BC and believe that it reached its zenith between AD 250 and 650. When the Aztecs discovered the ruins of the city, they called it Teotihuacan, meaning 'place where the gods were born', as they believed it to be the place where the world was created.

For a long time, it was thought that the Toltec people built Teotihuacan, but the Toltec civilization did not become powerful until hundreds of years after the city was built, so this seems unlikely. The Totonac, who were another pre-Columbian, pre-Aztec people in Mexico, have also been suggested, and even claimed themselves to have built Teotihuacan, but whether their history goes back that far is also doubtful. When the city collapsed in the seventh or eighth century, so much of it was destroyed that modern archaeologists have been left with few clues as to its origins.

9. Why did Teotihuacan collapse?

Teotihuacan was by any standards, but particularly by those of the first millennium, a huge city, covering a vast area including massive pyramids, temples, canals and canoe traffic. It thrived for at least 500 years, but around AD 550 many of its major buildings were sacked and burnt to the ground, and the city appears to have been completely abandoned in the seventh or eighth century.

With no evidence of a war or of a successfully invading force taking the city over, it has been suggested that the collapse was caused by an internal uprising against the most powerful classes in the city, but again there is no evidence of any other group seizing power. Climate change, droughts and ecological disaster have also been suggested, but without enough supporting evidence to be convincing. With several other sudden collapses of cities and entire civilizations in the region, Teotihuacan serves as a reminder of how little we know about Central and South America in the era before the Aztecs.

10. Who built the city of Nan Madol and how did they do it?

On Pohnpei island in Micronesia in the Pacific Ocean lies the ruined city of Nan Madol. Built within a lagoon, it consists of a number of artificial islands linked by a series of canals, which have led to its being described as the 'Venice of the Pacific', but its origins are unknown.

According to local legend, Nan Madol was constructed by twin sorcerers Olisihpa and Olosohpa, who used a flying dragon to lift the stones used in its construction. Archaeological investigations have failed to support that view, with carbon dating indicating that Nan Madol's construction began around 1200, though the region may have been occupied since 250 BC.

The mortuary sector alone contains over fifty islets on which high walls surround the tombs. On the royal mortuary islet of Nandauwas, the walls are 5.5–7.5 metres (18–25 ft) high, raising the question of where the stones came from to enable all this construction and how they were moved there. A number of possible quarry sites on Pohnpei have been identified, but the exact origin of the stones has not been determined, nor has their method of transportation ever been explained.

11. How did the Incas build Puma Punku?

Like Teotihuacan in Mexico (→ 8 and 9), the Inca city of Puma Punku (or Pumapunku) in Bolivia was identified by a legend as the place the world began, and its age, together with the extraordinary precision of its construction, show why. At its heart, Puma Punku consists of a massive clay mound, decorated with polished metal plaques and brightly coloured fabrics and ceramics, and surrounded by massive stone blocks chiselled to fit together with astonishing accuracy.

Radiocarbon dating shows that the stonework was constructed around the seventh century, but chemical samples from the stones indicate that they came from a quarry 10 kilometres away. The largest of these stone blocks is 7.8 metres long, 5.1 metres wide, 1 metre thick, and weighs about 131 tonnes. The blocks are also said to be cut with such precision that they fit together in a way that would not allow even a razor blade to be inserted between them. The standards of engineering needed both to transport the blocks and particularly to carve them with the necessary precision must have been far in advance of those known to have been achieved by the Incas hundreds of years later.

See also BRAZIL 82; INCAS 247

ANCIENT HISTORY

12. Who built thousands of giant stone wheel-like structures in the Middle East?

In 1927 RAF pilot Percy Maitland was on a routine mail delivery flight in the Middle East when he spotted beneath him hundreds of wheel-like patterns up to 70 metres in diameter made of stone. When he asked local

Bedouin tribesmen about them, he reports that their reaction was fearful and all they would say was that they were 'the works of old men'.

Stretching from Syria to Saudi Arabia, they are only visible from the air and are now known to number well into the thousands. They depict a number of designs, the most common of which is a circle with spokes radiating from the centre, but the direction of the spokes seems to follow no clear pattern. Several conjectures have been made of their purpose, but none are more than guesses. They are thought to date back around 2,000 years, but who made them and why is totally unknown.

13. How did ancient Minorcans build the Taulas?

The Taulas is the name given to thirty-five huge stone megaliths on the island of Minorca. Their appearance is remarkably like the similar structures at Stonehenge in England, but rather than being together at one place, as they are at Stonehenge, they are scattered at various locations throughout the island. Each Taula (which takes its name from a Catalan word meaning 'table') consists of one or two stones over 3 metres high, with a stone of similar size placed horizontally across the top.

They are thought to have been constructed by the Talayot people, who are believed to have lived in Minorca for around 2,000 years until the Romans arrived in 123 BC, but their reasons for building them and the means by which they transported and lifted the huge monoliths are an even greater mystery than that of Stonehenge. The positions of the stones at the English site at least seem to be connected with the motion of the Sun, which indicates a purpose connected with astronomy or astrology, but the Minorcan stones offer nothing more than a weak hint in that many of them appear to be set in horseshoe patterns facing south.

One theory is that the Taulas were used to predict solar eclipses; another suggestion is that they formed part of a healing ritual; but we know so little of the Talayot people and their beliefs that evidence for such ideas is scanty.

See also ANCIENT CITIES 8–11; ANCIENT ROME 14; CHINA 99–103; EGYPT 168; INCAS 247; MAYANS 293; MESOPOTAMIA 305; MUMMIES 322; PREHISTORY 380–3; TURKEY 457

ANCIENT ROME

14. What happened to Spartacus?

We all know, even if only from the 1960 film starring Kirk Douglas, that Spartacus was a slave and gladiator who plotted an escape from his captors and led an uprising of his fellow slaves against the might of the Roman empire. Taken by surprise by Spartacus' forces, and hampered by the fact that many of their legions were taking part in other military operations, a number of Roman army camps were overrun, which enabled the slave army to grow to around 70,000 men in the years around 70 BC.

Spartacus' forces were finally defeated by the legions of Pompey and some Roman historians said that Spartacus was slain in the final battle, but his body was never found. Six thousand survivors were captured and crucified along the Appian Way, but Spartacus was not among them. Had he been captured or his body found, the Romans would no doubt have wished to make a spectacle of him, so precisely what happened to him is a mystery.

Another problem concerns the intentions of Spartacus in his battles against the Romans. His aim had always been to fight his way to freedom and lead his followers across the Alps and back to their homelands, but when that objective was in sight, he turned his forces back towards Rome and the final hopeless battle. Some of his men may not have joined this final march, but escaped over the Alps. There is a slim possibility that Spartacus did the same.

See also ENGLISH HISTORY 177; ITALY 258; NAMES 334

ANIMALS

15. Is the number of animal species on Earth increasing or decreasing?

Environmentalists and ecologists frequently warn us of the potentially negative effects of human activity on biodiversity. Hunting and deforestation reduce animal numbers, constantly driving more species to the verge of extinction. Yet while this is going on, new species are constantly being discovered, and we have no idea whether they have existed unnoticed for centuries or are recently evolved.

Around 1.3 million species have been named and catalogued, and each year another 15,000 or so are added to the list. Attempts to estimate the total number of species on Earth have varied between about 3 million and 100 million. In 2011 a paper was published using a new and apparently logical method, which came up with an answer of 8.7 million plus or minus 1.3 million. All estimates are based largely on the number of species that have already been identified and the rate at which new ones are being discovered. That, however, may be more a measure of human activity and interests than the true biodiversity that exists.

Research on flies and fleas and periwinkles and urchins and many other creatures has shown that animals evolve into new species to cope with environmental changes. Even changes wrought by human intervention may be creating as many new species as we destroy. Frankly, we have no idea.

16. Are there more species on land or in the oceans?

One of the problems of estimating species numbers is our relative lack of knowledge of life in the oceans, particularly at great depths. The research mentioned in the previous item estimated the number of species on Earth as 6.5 million on land and 2.2 million in the oceans, but those figures were based on what we know now. Yet 71 per cent of the planet is covered by seas and oceans, with only 29 per cent land. So why should we believe that there are three times as many species on land as in the water?

Perhaps because we live on the land ourselves, our researches have concentrated on that 29 per cent of the planet, for reasons of both convenience and anthropic self-interest.

17. How should a species be defined?

Before we can even try to answer the previous two questions, we need to come up with a good working definition of what a species is, and that is not as easy as it may seem. When Charles Darwin wrote *On the Origin of Species* in 1859, he spent some time trying to explain to the reader what he and others meant by the word 'species'. The nearest he came to a definition was this: 'I look at the term species, as one arbitrarily given for the sake of convenience to a set of individuals closely resembling each other.'

The words 'arbitrarily' and 'for the sake of convenience', however, are hardly what one is looking for in a rigorous scientific definition. When such a serious definition has been attempted, the scientific literature reveals over twenty versions, each different from the others in some small but significant way. Most such definitions are based on the idea of a population that can interbreed and produce fertile offspring. That introduces the immediate problem of how one expands the idea to include organisms that reproduce asexually, but even if we restrict our attention to sexual reproduction, problems emerge.

What about animals that can mate with each other, in the laboratory or in captivity, for example, but do not do so in the wild? What about three varieties of an animal, A, B and C, distinguishable by sight, of which members of A mate with members of B, and B with C, but A does not, or cannot, mate with C? Should we consider them all the same species?

Darwin himself questioned whether our concept of a species is something that exists in nature, or whether the boundaries between one species and another are too blurred for the word to have a precise meaning. Even now, scientists and philosophers struggle with the same problem. When we cannot even agree whether Neanderthals and *Homo sapiens* were the same species, the task of enumerating all the species on Earth is impossible.

18. Do animals suffer from depression?

In recent years, there have been reports of cats, rats and even goats showing signs of depression. Vets have increasingly been prescribing antidepressants for dogs, and in 2014 the Home Office in the UK was reported to be funding research into whether laboratory monkeys get depressed. The question of whether animals do, or even can, suffer from depression is not so easy to answer.

The problem is that the diagnosis of depression in humans depends on identifying symptoms that are subjective. Animals cannot directly communicate how they feel and the question of whether they can be said to have emotions at all is open. From that point of view, we would have to conclude that we cannot say whether animals suffer from depression.

On the other hand, research has associated certain physical symptoms, such as low serotonin levels in dogs and a shrinking hippocampus in rats, with apparently depressive animal behaviour. This may suggest that a diagnosis of depression for such animals is more than just anthropomorphism. Quite apart from the communication problem, however, we do not understand enough about depression in humans to draw clear conclusions from such evidence about depression in animals (→ PSYCHOLOGY 389).

19. Is there any species of animal in which homosexuality does not exist?

Ever since Darwin, the issue of homosexuality in animals has been contentious. The very idea of it seemed to run against the principles of evolution. It seemed even less compatible with the religious concept of intelligent design, and anyone who suggested that homosexuality might exist in the animal world ran the risk of being howled down by both homophobic and religious communities.

In 1999, however, the Canadian biologist Bruce Bagemihl blew the lid off the gay animal taboo by publishing his book *Biological Exuberance: Animal Homosexuality and Natural Diversity*, which gave a detailed analysis of just how widespread same-sex encounters are in the animal kingdom. Darwinists rationalized that a baby creature looked after by two lesbians could lead to better childcare, while having a gay uncle could also be of positive survival value.

Bagemihl's research indicated that homosexual behaviour had been identified in almost 1,500 species, from apes to worms, and was well documented in some 500 of them. In particular, lesbian albatrosses, gay giraffes and bisexual bonobos have attracted much attention. According to a recent estimate, homosexuality has been observed in around 10 per cent of all known species.

Twenty years ago, animals were generally considered to act by instinct, and instinct made them want to have sex in order to propagate their species. Having sex for fun was out of the question. Now, however, the question is not whether any animal can be considered truly homosexual, but whether some members of every species display such tendencies.

See also under names of individual animals: ANTS, BABOONS, BEARS, BEES, ETC.

ANTS

20. Do ants have personalities?

For social insects, ants can be very cruel to one another. There are over 15,000 known species of ant worldwide which vary considerably in aggression. Some species even live by making slaves of other species. Even within a single species, it has long been accepted that different colonies may display different 'personalities'. Some colonies seem naturally aggressive; others show a marked tendency to run away when threatened. The question of whether individual ants have personalities, however, has only recently begun to be addressed.

Research at the Johannes Gutenberg University in Mainz in 2011 reported that a single colony of ants may display a wide range of aggression in its individuals. Ants with high aggression were employed in fighting other colonies, while less aggressive ants were assigned to brood care. Further evidence for ant personalities was claimed by research at the University of Arizona in 2014, where individual ants of the same species were seen to show different behavioural traits when foraging for food.

It is an open question, however, whether such individual differences are merely the result of learnt behaviour or evidence of truly innate personality differences.

21. Which weighs more: all the people on Earth or all the ants?

In their book *Journey to the Ants* (1994), Wilson and Hölldobler assert that the weight of all the ants on Earth is equal to that of all the humans, but it is far from clear whether this is correct.

As of 2015, there are around 7.2 billion people on Earth with an average weight of about 62 kilograms. That gives a total weight of just over 446 billion kilograms for all the people. The weight of an average ant is estimated to be about 2 milligrams, so for the ants to equal the weight of all the humans, there would need to be 223,000 trillion of them. Nobody really has much idea of the true figure for the number of ants in the world, but estimates range from 100 trillion to 10,000 trillion. Even taking the higher figure, the ants would be well behind the humans in weight.

It has also been estimated, however, that there are twenty-seven times as many termites as ants in the world, and termites are generally bigger than ants, so if this is right, there is good reason to believe that all the termites weigh more than all of us.

See also BEES 47; PANGOLINS 354

ART

22. Who was Vermeer's *Girl with a Pearl Earring*?

Thanks to Tracy Chevalier's 1999 historical novel *Girl with a Pearl Earring* and the 2003 film of the same title starring Scarlett Johansson, Vermeer's painting of that name has become one of the world's best-known works of art, but nobody knows who the girl depicted in the painting was.

The work, originally entitled *Girl with a Turban*, is thought to have been painted around 1665–7, and one suggestion is that she could be Vermeer's eldest daughter Maria, who was eleven or twelve at the time. Apart from her being roughly the right age, however, there is no real evidence that she was the sitter.

Another suggestion is that she may have been Magdalena, the only daughter of Vermeer's patron Pieter van Ruijven. The only supporting evidence for that idea is that van Ruijven once owned the painting. In any case, if the girl really is either Maria or Magdalena, it would raise the question of why Vermeer painted her against a totally dark background. Some identification of either the person or the location might have been expected in the picture.

23. What is going on in Velázquez's painting *Las Meninas*?

Velásquez's 1656 painting *Las Meninas* ('The Ladies-in-Waiting') is one of the most enigmatic in the history of art. Velásquez himself is seen in the painting, working on a large canvas, but we cannot see what he is painting, as only the back of the canvas faces us. Behind Velásquez is a mirror in which we can clearly see King Philip IV and Queen Mariana of

Spain, but it is unclear whether the mirror reflects Velásquez's painting or is showing us the king and queen standing outside the painting and watching the scene as Velásquez paints someone or something else.

The other figures in the painting only add to the mystery. At the centre stands the five-year-old infanta Margaret Theresa, who is attended by two ladies-in-waiting, who are the Meninas of the title. On her right are two dwarfs, one of whom is nudging a large dog with his foot. Behind them, the infanta's chaperone may be seen talking to a bodyguard, who is the only figure in the painting who cannot be identified. Right at the back of the painting is the queen's chamberlain, Don José Nieto Velásquez, who is caught in a pose on a staircase with one foot on a higher step than the other. It is impossible to judge whether he is coming into the room or leaving it. It is also unknown whether this Velásquez was related to the painter or not.

Some say that Velásquez is painting the infanta, who at the time was the only child of the king and queen, and the function of the other characters in the painting was to keep the young child entertained while she sat for the painting. Meanwhile, her parents are watching, as seen in the mirror. Several of the characters, however, are seen looking out of the canvas directly at the viewer. Some have taken this to suggest that the whole painting depicts the viewpoint of the king and queen as they watch Velásquez painting their daughter. The fact that one of those looking directly out of the picture at us is Velásquez himself adds further mystery to the question of who is looking at whom. Perhaps the fundamental uncertainty is conveyed by the idea of looking at a painting and seeing the painter looking back at us.

No two art critics or historians seem to agree on their interpretation of this picture. All they agree on is that it is a masterpiece.

24. Did Thomas Gainsborough use skimmed milk in his *Study of a Cow*?

In the 1770s Thomas Gainsborough experimented with unusual innovative techniques to improve the pictorial quality of his drawings on paper. According to the 1772 Royal Academy exhibition catalogue, his drawings were 'in imitation of oil painting'. Gainsborough himself, in 1773, revealed 'my secret of making those studies' when using chalk for his drawing, telling how he would dip his paper in skimmed milk to adhere the white chalk to it, thereby building up layers of chalk and colour. Finally, he would complete the work with varnish or, as he put it, 'float it all over with Gum'.

The collection at Tate Britain includes Gainsborough's *Study of a Cow in a Landscape*, which it dates to 1758–9. This is a pencil drawing on paper which, according to the Tate's own description of the work, 'has been coated with a layer of fixative which has subsequently discoloured'. They go on to say: 'Gainsborough recommended "skim'd milk" for fixing chalk, but whether he used the same substance for fixing pencil is not known.'

Using skimmed milk to fix a drawing of a cow would have been somehow appropriate, but whether Gainsborough would have let such a thing influence him is unlikely.

25. Why do most portrait sitters incline their heads to the right?

Several studies of portraits have identified a significant bias in the way the face of the sitter is inclined. One comprehensive study of nearly 1,500 portraits painted in Europe over the last 500 years found that roughly 60 per cent showed the sitter favouring the left side of their face. Male portraits showed this tendency 56 per cent of the time, portraits of women 68 per cent. Later studies confirmed this finding, extending it back to the fourteenth century and American paintings. Paintings depicting the Crucifixion were found to display the left side of Christ's face more prominently an astounding 90 per cent of the time. A recent study showed that the same is true of selfie photographs: the left side of the face is preferred.

Why this should be so is not at all clear. One theory links it to the differences in function between the two sides of the brain. Emotions are said to be controlled by the right brain, which also controls the muscles in the left side of the face. This would tie in with other research reporting that the left sides of our faces are seen as more sensitive and generally pleasing. On the other hand, other studies have shown that when we look at other people's faces, we pay more attention to their right sides, which is odd if we think the left side is more sensitive and pleasing.

Such lateral preferences are often most simply explained by the fact that a large majority of people are right-handed, but the portrait results still seem to be true for left-handed painters. The main exception seems to be self-portraits, but as these were generally painted with the use of a mirror, even that may confirm the general finding.

The ambidextrous Leonardo da Vinci was one of the few painters who showed no left or right preference in his portraits, though it should be noted that the Mona Lisa, who is the subject of his most famous portrait, is indeed inclining the left side of her face towards the artist. And so is Vermeer's *Girl with a Pearl Earring* (→ 22).

See also AUSTEN 33; AZTECS 38; BIBLE 53; CODES 107; HITLER 232; HUMAN EVOLUTION 238; LEONARDO 273; MUSIC 330–1; OPERA 348

ASPARAGUS

26. Does asparagus make our urine smell?

The science of post-asparagus urine sniffing goes back to 1731 when the Scottish mathematician and doctor John Arbuthnot wrote that 'asparagus affects the urine with a foetid smell'. Marcel Proust said that asparagus 'transforms my chamber-pot into a flask of perfume', while Benjamin Franklin, in a letter to the Royal Academy of Brussels in 1781, wrote that 'A few stems of asparagus eaten shall give our urine a disagreeable odour'.

For almost 200 years, asparagus retained this reputation, until in the 1950s some research papers appeared suggesting that the effect of asparagus on urine was not universal – it was detectable in some people but not others. In 1980 a classic experiment was conducted in Israel in which subjects were asked to sniff not only their own urine but that of other subjects who may or may not have eaten asparagus.

The conclusion was that people differ not in the production of smelly post-asparagus urine but in the ability to detect the smell: 'Those who could smell the odour in their own urine could all smell it in the urine of anyone who had eaten asparagus, whether or not that person was able to smell it himself.' They also reported that 10 per cent of their subjects could detect the smell even at very low concentrations, which suggested that some people were hypersensitive to the odour.

In the 1980s research generally seemed to support the view that we all produced the smell, but only some of us could detect it, and chemists even identified a number of sulphurous compounds, including methanethiol, in post-asparagus urine that could be producing it. A study in 2011, however, reported that three out of thirty-seven subjects produced urine after eating asparagus in which the characteristic smell could not be detected by any of the other subjects.

Researchers seem to be coming round to the view that the ability to produce the smell and the ability to detect it are two distinct traits, probably genetically based. According to another report in 2011, 'excreting may be a simple one-gene character, with the allele for excreting dominant, but more work needs to be done'. The same report also concluded that 'There is no family data on the smelling/non-smelling trait… so more work needs to be done on this trait as well'.

ASTRONOMY

27. How do stars form in galaxies?

In the immediate aftermath of the Big Bang, the universe consisted of radiation and subatomic particles. Out of that were formed the stars, star clusters and galaxies we know today, but how that happened is a matter of intense dispute. Did the small particles clump together into bigger and bigger celestial bodies, or did the early universe consist of even huger bodies than we know today, which later split into galaxies?

On the one hand, everything is being brought together by the gravitational pull of every particle on every other particle; on the other hand, the energy of the expansion of the early universe is flinging everything apart. Our knowledge of what must have happened in the earliest moments after the Big Bang led astronomers to produce the idea of dark matter and dark energy, without which everything would indeed have fallen apart. The gravitational forces exerted by the mass we can detect is far too little to hold it all together.

The latest hope for progress on this question lies in the study of some recently discovered dwarf galaxies in the Milky Way which have appeared in regions thought to be free of dark energy. These may provide a clue to where stars come from and how they form.

28. Why do space probes change speed?

When space probes are sent on long missions, their routes are often calculated to take them via the regions of planets or moons in order to use the gravitational fields of those bodies to add to their momentum. Gravity accelerates their speed in the region of the body before they are catapulted out into space again.

For over twenty years, precise monitoring of such craft has revealed something known as the 'fly-by anomaly', which causes an unexpected variation in the craft's speed. In 1990 and 1992, when the Galileo space probe flew over Earth, its speed increased by a small but totally unexpected four millimetres per second on both occasions. In 1998 the spacecraft NEAR was measured to be going at thirteen millimetres per second faster than it ought to have been, and similar anomalies were found for Cassini in 1999 (whose speed was two millimetres per second less than expected), and for the Messenger and Rosetta probes in 2005.

In all these cases, the deviation from the expected speed was tiny, but it remains unexplained. Various theories have been put forward, including solar radiation, the influence of tides, magnetic fields, dark matter and a hypothetical gravitomagnetic field, but none of these has attracted great support, so the mystery remains.

29. Why is Betelgeuse shrinking?

Over the past twenty years, astronomical observations have shown that the star Betelgeuse seems to be getting smaller. Between 1993 and 2009 it was reported to have lost 15 per cent of its size, and nobody is sure why. Actually nobody is even sure whether these figures can be trusted or are just an illusion, but recent measurements from the Hubble Space Telescope seem to confirm that it is smaller than it used to be.

Betelgeuse, in the constellation Orion, is one of the brightest stars in our sky. It is a red supergiant 600 light years away; it is about 135,000 times as bright as our Sun, with a diameter about 700 times that of the Sun, and it is believed to be near the end of its life. Soon – which in astronomical terms means probably within a million years, and perhaps as soon as a thousand – it will explode into a massive supernova. In our skies, it will be as bright as the full moon, and it is possible that its decrease in size is part of its process of dying. It could also be due to a number of other factors:

(i) Red supergiants do not have a true surface. They are just a core surrounded by massive balls of gas, so we may be measuring something happening in the atmosphere of Betelgeuse rather than the star itself.

(ii) Betelgeuse is rotating but it is not spherical; it may have just turned and be presenting a smaller surface towards us.

(iii) There is evidence that such stars undergo an oscillation in their apparent size. Two such pulsations have already been identified for Betelgeuse. We may have just caught it in another slimming period which will be followed by one in which it regains its former size.

(iv) The whole thing may be an illusion caused by temperature differences in different parts of Betelgeuse's atmosphere.

A decent supernova has not been widely seen on Earth since 1054, and an explosion of Betelgeuse promises to be even brighter than that one. Those who hanker after great astronomical events would be delighted to hear that Betelgeuse's weight loss is a real sign of its impending death, but the truth is we just don't know.

30. What, if anything, was the Star of Bethlehem?

Now when Jesus was born in Bethlehem of Judaea in the days
of Herod the king, behold, there came wise men from the east to
Jerusalem, Saying, Where is he that is born King of the Jews? for we
have seen his star in the east, and are come to worship him.
Matthew 2:1–2 (King James Bible)

Was there really such a star, or is Matthew's tale just a piece of religious romanticism?

The birth of Christ is now dated at around 4 BC. It cannot have been later, for that was the date Herod the Great died and Herod is clearly identified as king at the time of the birth. So what was going on in the sky at that time? Anyone in search of astronomical verification of the star has a surprising number of candidates to choose from.

The only genuine star among those candidates is found in the records of Chinese astronomers which identify a new star being born in the constellation of Aquila in 4 BC. A new star, or nova, can be bright when it first appears, then fade, so it might have drawn the attention of the wise men. Whether one tiny new star could have been seen as sufficiently important to draw them to Jerusalem, however, seems unlikely.

A more visually striking candidate is not a star at all but a comet. In 5 BC a bright comet appeared in the constellation of Capricorn, which was again recorded by the Chinese. This would have appeared in the southern sky with its tail pointing upwards. This could be taken as a south-pointing signpost, and Bethlehem was due south of Jerusalem, so following the 'star' might have taken the wise men to the right place. One problem with this theory, however, is that comets tended to be associated with disasters or other destructive events.

A third idea rejects the star or comet hypotheses and suggests that the event was a triple conjunction of Jupiter and Saturn, which would have brought the Sun, the Earth and those two planets into close alignment in the sky on three closely spaced occasions. The appearance of two bright planets together in the sky would have made quite an impact on people who believed in astrological portents.

Finally, the Greek astronomer George Banos published a paper in 1979 suggesting that the 'star' was in fact the planet Uranus, which the

Magi had discovered some 1,800 years before William Herschel did so.

See also BIG BANG 54–6; BLACK HOLES 70–1; COSMOLOGY 117–26; ENERGY 172–4; MARS 285–6; MILKY WAY 315–17; OUTER SPACE 350; SOLAR SYSTEM 441–4; UNIVERSE 463–7; VENUS 479–80

ATILLA

31. How did Atilla die?

The Huns were a nomadic people who lived in eastern Europe and central Asia between the first and fifth centuries AD. Little is known about them until the fifth century when, under the leadership of Atilla, they became an unlikely threat to the Roman empire, both in the east and the west. His campaigns stretched from Persia to Constantinople to Roman Gaul and to Italy itself, all of which he attempted and failed to conquer. In 453, at the estimated age of forty-seven, Atilla died, though the cause of his death has never been clear.

The only contemporary account was by a chronicler named Priscus, who said that Atilla suffered a severe nosebleed at a banquet held to celebrate his marriage and choked to death in an alcoholic stupor. A later analysis of this story from a more modern medical viewpoint suggested that the nosebleed might have been a symptom of internal bleeding caused by a condition called oesophageal varices, which can be caused by heavy drinking. However, the Roman chronicler Marcellinus Comes, writing some eighty years later, reported that Atilla was stabbed by his wife.

For over 1,500 years, historians had only these two versions to choose from and most went for Priscus' account, despite the fact that other accounts of Atilla's life portrayed him as a man of simple tastes who did not drink excessively. Comes' account was generally viewed simply as a means of blackening Atilla's name.

In 2005, however, a new theory emerged in a book by the American philologist Michael A. Babcock called *The Night Atilla Died*. In his view, Atilla had made enough enemies during his rise to power and subsequent conquests for an assassination to be a distinct possibility. Indeed, there is evidence of a failed plot to have him killed a year or two earlier. A painstaking reconstruction of the politics of the time led Babcock to believe that Priscus' account was just a cover story for an assassination plotted by Emperor Marcian, ruler of the Eastern Roman empire in the 450s.

According to legend, after Atilla's death his body was placed in a triple coffin of gold, silver and iron, which was buried under a riverbed. The burial party were all killed when they returned, so that nobody would be able to find the body. Until it is found, however, there seems no hope of advancing our knowledge of how he died.

32. What language did the Huns speak?

Under Atilla, the Huns conquered much of Asia and a good deal of Europe to form a huge empire, yet we do not know what language they spoke. It is not even known if they had a script for writing their language, and the little we do know has come through the writings of others. All we have to go on are a few unidentified inscriptions on pots which may or may not have been part of the Hunnic language, and three words which are the only ones generally agreed to be Hunnic: *medos*, a drink possibly similar to mead; *kamos*, a drink made from barley; and *strava*, a word for a funeral feast. These words, together with the names of various Huns, have fuelled a long debate about the origins of the language, but there is no agreement on which other languages it may be related to, if any.

AUSTEN

33. What did Jane Austen look like?

Only two paintings of Jane Austen exist that were painted in her lifetime: both were by her sister Cassandra, and one is a back view. The other, an unfinished portrait, was painted in 1817, the year of Jane Austen's death, and depicts her looking pale and rather sickly. Her family reportedly declared the painting a bad likeness, and fifty years after her death her nephew James Edward Austen-Leigh commissioned an artist to paint a more flattering portrait of her.

His own account of his aunt, in his 1872 *Memoir of Jane Austen*, described her as 'very attractive' and went on to say:

> *Her figure was rather tall and slender, her step light and firm,*
> *and her whole appearance expressive of health and animation. In*
> *complexion she was a clear brunette with a rich colour; she had full*
> *round cheeks, with mouth and nose small and well-formed, bright*
> *hazel eyes, and brown hair forming natural curls round her face.*

In 2014 the forensic artist Melissa Dring was commissioned to produce a waxwork of Jane Austen based on that description. Austen lovers generally approved of the result, which was definitely more cheerful than Cassandra's portrait, but whether it looked more like her or was just an idealized chocolate-box type of image is open to debate.

34. What did Jane Austen die of?

In the last year of her life, Jane Austen suffered from increasing ill health. She described her illness as 'bile' and a form of rheumatism, but she found herself having difficulty walking or finding the energy to work. She died on 18 July 1817 at the age of forty-one.

For many years, her death was attributed to a chronic disorder of the adrenal glands now known as Addison's disease, but recently a number of alternative diagnoses have been made. One suggestion is Hodgkin's lymphoma, a type of cancer affecting the white blood cells. Another idea is bovine tuberculosis, which is now associated with drinking unpasteurized milk. And finally there is Brill–Zinsser disease, a recurrent form of typhus which she is known to have had as a child.

Unsurprisingly, there is little enthusiasm for the idea of exhuming Jane Austen's body and trying to settle the matter.

AUSTRALIA

35. When did the first Aboriginal people reach Australia?

Until about 12,000 years ago, Australia, New Guinea and Tasmania were joined by a land bridge and together formed a continent which has been called Sahul. The earliest colonization of Australia is thought to have been by settlers crossing this land bridge from New Guinea. These settlers would have been the ancestors of the Aboriginals, but when they first reached Australia has been hotly debated.

The traditional view, supported by carbon dating of various artefacts, puts their arrival at 40–45,000 years ago. Carbon dating, however, is considered an unreliable method in general for dating items more than 40,000 years old, so the first Aboriginals would be stretching it to its limits and the true answer could be further back in history.

More recently, thermoluminescence has been increasingly used for dating ancient objects. Like carbon dating, it is based on measurements of radioactivity, but it is not linked to the decay of an isotope of carbon, so is not subject to the same limitations.

A few sites in northern Australia have been dated by thermoluminescence to around 50,000 years ago, but recent finds in western Australia have been dated to 70,000 years ago, while reef deposits in Queensland have suggested that humans may have been there up to 100,000 years ago. The most extreme suggestion came in 1998 when data from a rock shelter in northern Australia were published suggesting that artefacts had been found in levels of sand that had been dated by thermoluminescence to between 116,000 and 176,000 years ago.

Until we have more confidence in the results of thermoluminescence as a dating method, or some more accurate method is developed, the debate will continue.

See also BIRDS 69; DOLPHINS 156; HUMAN EVOLUTION 240; KANGAROOS 265; MICE 313; PLATYPUS 374

AUTISM

36. Can vaccines cause autism?

In the 1990s huge debates erupted on the question of whether certain vaccinations that were routinely being given to children increased the chance of those children developing autism. In the USA the prime suspect was thimerosal, a preservative containing mercury that was often added to extend the shelf life of various vaccines. In the UK the argument centred on MMR vaccines against measles, mumps and rubella, which were thought by some to have an effect on the brain development of children.

Many studies followed on both sides of the argument, but the majority of medical opinion seems to support the view that vaccines do not cause autism and the entire scare resulted from the fact that the first symptoms of autism tend to occur in children around the same time as vaccines are administered. Nevertheless, in 1999 the American Academy of Pediatrics and vaccine manufacturers reached an agreement that thimerosal should be reduced or eliminated in all childhood vaccines for children aged six or younger.

Since then, further studies have been published showing that the rates of autism among children receiving thimerosal-containing vaccines are no worse than among children given thimerosal-free vaccines. Despite this, however, several courts in various countries have awarded damages to children for alleged vaccine-induced autism. In 2012 an Italian court ruled that a child's autism had been caused by the MMR vaccine; in 2014 a court in Milan awarded compensation to a child who was adjudged 'more likely than not' to have suffered brain damage and autism because of the neurotoxic mercury and aluminium in a vaccine that contained thimerosal.

Doctors and politicians may be convinced that vaccines do not cause autism, but the legal profession is clearly not so sure.

AVOCADOS

37. How did avocados survive the extinction of the giant sloth?

In order to reproduce successfully, plants need a method to disperse their seeds. Just dropping the seeds on the ground leaves them all competing for the same nutriment in a limited space. Sometimes the seeds are carried by the wind; sometimes they are carried by birds or insects which eat the succulent part of the plant, then excrete the seeds elsewhere. Avocados evolved in the age of giant fauna when huge creatures roamed the land – animals such as the rhinoceros-like *Toxodon*, *Glyptodon*, which was an armadillo the size of a family car, the gomphotheres, which were early four-tusked giant elephants, and *Megatherium*, the giant ground sloth as tall as a giraffe and weighing four tons.

In Mexico the ground sloth is thought to have been particularly effective in spreading avocado stones. Its mouth and digestive tract had no problems coping with a whole avocado, and when it had digested the soft fleshy part, it would excrete the stone. Around 13,000 years ago, however, giant sloths and the other megafauna died out, after which there were no animals capable of swallowing a whole avocado.

The Mexicans are known to have cultivated avocado trees from as long ago as 5,000 BC, but that still leaves a gap of 8,000 years since the giant sloths had become extinct. How the avocado survived during that period is a mystery.

AZTECS

38. Was Aztlan, the legendary original home of the Aztecs, a real place?

According to legend, Aztlan was the ancestral home of the Aztec people from which they emigrated to Mexico. According to traditional sources, the Aztec ancestors dwelled in the place of the seven caves called Chicomoztoc, where each cave corresponded to one of the Nahuatl tribes which would later reach the Valley of Mexico, but whether this is all an old myth or Aztlan really existed is unknown.

Some say Aztlan was in northern Mexico, but another idea is that it was in the southern United States. No real evidence has been found of its existence, though a cave painting was recently discovered in Utah that appears to be of an Aztec god. All that would show, however, is that early Aztecs visited Utah, though there is also claimed to be some similarity between the language of the Ute tribe of Native Americans and the Nahuatl language of the Aztecs.

39. Did the Aztecs use wheels for transport?

Although several examples have been found of Aztec toys with wheels on them, there is a curious lack of evidence that the Aztecs ever used wheels for transportation. It has been speculated that they used logs to move large stones when they built their pyramids, but even that is not clear.

There is a theory that the early Aztecs lived in regions that were mountainous or on an island in the middle of a lake. In the former case, carrying things may have been simpler than using a wheeled vehicle, while in the latter, most transportation would have been done by boat, so wheeled vehicles might have been seen as unnecessary. All the same, there must have been times when throwing something on the back of a cart would have been easier than carrying it.

See also ANCIENT CITIES 8–9; CHOCOLATE 105

BABOONS

40. Do baboons eavesdrop?

Baboons make a good deal of noise while having sex. The males grunt loudly and the females emit what have been described as 'long operatic calls'. And in 2007 an academic paper appeared claiming that other male baboons eavesdrop on them while they are doing it.

The experiment reported in the paper involved a group of free-ranging chacma baboons in Botswana. High-ranking male baboons were seen to dominate females and stay with them for up to a week. During that period, the experimenters played the sounds of male grunting and female copulatory squealing through separate loudspeakers. When the speakers were far enough apart, the effect was similar to the sounds associated with a baboon couple breaking up. However, it was not the couples that were being studied but the lower-ranking males.

These seemed to ignore the male grunt and concentrate their attention on the female squeals. Deducing that the female had been left by her lover, the male, who was previously a hopeful bystander, would then rush to approach her and, with luck, would mate with her himself. By eavesdropping, the low-status males were provided with a chance to mate.

It is unclear whether this behaviour can properly be described as eavesdropping or whether the males are simply excited by the sounds of sex. If we do call it eavesdropping, it raises the question of whether female baboons eavesdrop too.

BEARS

41. Why do bears pee in the woods?

American brown bears are known to mark their territory by leaving their scent on trees, either by rubbing against them or by urination. In 2013 research was published showing that, in one region of Canada at least, tree-marking behaviour varied according to food availability (specifically according to the amount of pink salmon in a nearby river). Interestingly, males marked more trees with their scent at times of low food availability, while females marked more trees when food availability was high.

Another research paper in the same year, however, reported that the criteria used by a bear in determining which trees to mark are primarily location, species and size. Bears, they found, will mark trees in often-visited areas and will select the largest trees and those of rarer species.

There appears to be more going through a bear's mind when it chooses which tree to rub against or pee on than one might have imagined.

42. Why do female grizzly bears have six nipples?

Male bears, like male humans, have two nipples, but the nipple count on female bears varies according to the species. Female polar bears generally have four nipples, though five or even six have been seen. Female black bears, grizzly bears and Kodiak bears all have six nipples.

In the case of Kodiak bears, this makes sense, as six is a normal litter size for newborn Kodiak bear cubs. Black bears tend to have two or three cubs, though a litter of six has been recorded. Grizzly bears, however, have six nipples and the most common number of cubs in a litter is two or three, though litters of four have been seen. Six nipples therefore seems surplus to requirements.

See also POLAR BEARS 377–8

BEES

43. Can bees count?

Since 1995 a growing amount of research has suggested that bees may be able to count but get into difficulties with numbers greater than four. In that year an experiment was performed in Germany in which bees were trained to find food left for them in a tunnel. As a clue to remembering where they had found the food, a series of 'landmarks' were placed in the tunnel with the feeder positioned between the third and fourth landmarks.

After learning where the food was, the bees would fly past the third landmark and then slow down and start looking for it. Even when the landmarks were placed closer together or further apart, the bees would start looking for the food between the third and fourth landmark. Some bees were seen to fly the same distance before hunting, but the majority seemed to be counting landmarks. When the number of landmarks was increased to five, however, the bees became confused.

In 2008 a similar result was reached by researchers in Australia, who then went on to give the bees a more demanding counting task. This involved the use of a Y-shaped tunnel at the start of which there was a sign at the bottom of the Y, and then two more signs where it branched into two paths. The signs all contained a number of dots and the bee would only find its food reward if it chose the branch with the same number of dots as had been displayed at the start of its flight.

The bees quickly mastered this task, and even when the shape, colour and pattern of the dots were altered, they still chose the path displaying the same number of dots as the starting sign. Again the bees showed the ability to distinguish between three and four dots, but distinguishing between four and five, or even four and six, was beyond them.

Whether the bees are doing something analogous to what we think of as counting is open to question, but the current conclusion seems to be that if bees can count, they can only count up to four.

44. Do bees always dance as well as they can?

Ever since 1967, when Karl von Frisch published his findings in which he decoded the 'waggle dance' of bees, there has been much research on this strange means of communication. By repeatedly running along a figure-of-eight pattern, the bee appears to communicate the quality of a recently discovered food source as well as its direction and how far away it is. Recent research, however, has cast doubt on both the degree of accuracy of the information imparted by the dance and the ability of other bees to follow it.

One interesting finding concerns the direction of the food source. This has been shown to contain an apparent inbuilt error, which grows larger when the food source is closer. One suggestion is that the dancing bee is not trying to convey accurately where the food is but just to give a vague idea in order to get other bees in the colony to forage in the same area in the hope of finding further sources of food. An Australian study published in 2014 suggested that the inbuilt imprecision in the dance may spread followers over a roughly constant area as distance increases and direction becomes more accurate. But are the dancing bees deliberately giving vague information in order to spread their colony members over a wide area, or is inaccuracy of information an inbuilt defect of the dance language itself? After analysing all the studies done on the topic, Kaitlyn Preece and Madeleine Beekman concluded: 'the bees dance as best they can.'

Until we know how much information is conveyed, how much is picked up, and what other means the bees have of communicating to one another the location of food sources, we cannot be sure they are dancing to the best of their abilities.

45. Why do bumblebees spend so long having sex?

In 2009 a study on the mating habits of bumblebees reported that when a male copulated with a queen, the average mating time was thirty minutes and most matings lasted between twenty and forty minutes. When a queen was only allowed to continue mating for between two and five minutes, however, there was only a 7.2 per cent chance on average that she would accept another mating. However, 'Incompletely mated queens... did not show significant difference from fully mated queens in production of new queens and males.' In other words, the longer mating times were found to convey no advantage. As the researchers put it: 'This study shows that colony development was not affected by short copulation duration.' So from an evolutionary perspective, we may well ask why they spend so long over it.

46. How does a single bee find its way home?

There has been a good deal of research on the navigational abilities of bees, but some of the results are contradictory. When a young bee leaves its hive for the first time, it makes a series of figure-of-eight flights of increasing size as though surveying its surroundings and getting its bearings. How it codifies the information it obtains, however, is far from clear.

In 2004 the results of a study into the homing behaviour of leaf-cutter bees was published showing that manipulations of devices forming geometrical figures surrounding a bee's nest could affect its ability to find its way home. 'Manipulations of the edges provided by the boundaries of the device... strongly impaired the homing performance.' Manipulating edges near their hive confused them more than changes to edges further away. 'These results suggest that bees learn the distances of the various edges from the goal.'

A paper in 1995, however, had suggested that, for honeybees, distances were something the bees were likely to ignore. In their paper 'Can honeybees count landmarks?' Chittka and Geiger reported how they trained some bees along a row of four identical tent-shaped landmarks leading from their hive to a feeder. After the training sessions were completed, the number and distance apart of the landmarks were changed. In subsequent trials, most of the bees were seen to fly greater distances when the number of landmarks was decreased and shorter distances when they were increased. Only a significant minority of bees were observed to be flying the correct distances. Similar results have been found for a bee's ability to find its way back to a hive when the landscape is altered.

47. Why are bees so sociable?

There is more to being social than just living together as a group. True sociality, known as 'eusociality', is defined by three features:

(i)   co-operative brood care rather than each creature caring for its own offspring;

(ii) an overlapping of generations so that the group may be sustained, with offspring assisting parents; and

(iii) a division of both labour and reproduction with not every individual reproducing equally in the group.

Almost all species in which eusociality has been found are ants, bees, wasps or termites. Bees are especially interesting because different species may show all or none of the above features, or anything in between.

Honeybees, in particular, are eusocial, but how this characteristic evolved is unclear. Analysis of the genomes of different species of bees has shown that eusocial behaviour depends on more than a hundred genes, and it has evolved at least eleven times. The problem is that the eusocial lifestyle involves a large number of individuals being sterile, and sterility is not generally an asset in passing on genes.

In his *On the Origin of Species*, Darwin described the existence of sterile worker castes in social insects as 'the one special difficulty, which at first appeared to me insuperable and actually fatal to my whole theory'. He did find ways of getting round the problem, but there is still no general agreement on how eusociality evolved and how solitary bees developed into eusocial bees.

BIBLE

48. Did the biblical cities of Sodom and Gomorrah exist?

The Book of Genesis tells of the cities of Sodom and Gomorrah being destroyed by fire and brimstone by a wrathful God, and the Qur'an also tells of miracles there, but the question of whether Sodom and Gomorrah were real places is still a matter of debate.

The Greek geographer and historian Strabo, who died around AD 24, wrote of 'thirteen inhabited cities in that region of which Sodom was the metropolis', but no archaeological evidence has been found to support that opinion. A number of excavations around the Dead Sea have found signs of ancient cities, and there have even been claims of signs of fire and sulphur, but nothing very convincing.

The account of fire and brimstone has been linked to a suggestion that the Dead Sea was devastated by an earthquake between 2100 and 1900 BC, which is plausible as the Jordan Rift Valley fault line runs through the region. Another suggestion, however, has been based on an analysis of a cuneiform tablet in the British Museum, thought to have been produced by an Assyrian scribe around 700 BC, which depicts a celestial body heading for Earth. Is this evidence that Sodom and Gomorrah were destroyed by an asteroid impact? Well, probably not, but we cannot rule it out.

49. Was the biblical King David a real person?

As the second king of Israel, David appears as a leading character in the Old Testament, yet there is little historical evidence of his existence. Perhaps this ought not to surprise us: most modern chronologies of the Old Testament story place King David around the tenth century BC, which would place him somewhere towards the end of the Bronze Age. This is not a period from which many documents have survived.

Until the 1990s it could have been fairly claimed that no evidence at all existed outside biblical sources of the existence of King David. In 1993, however, excavations at a site believed to be the ancient city of Dan revealed a victory stone including the letters 'dwd', which are thought to refer to the House of David. The stone has been dated to around 850–835 BC and another victory stone from the same period also contains references to a name that may be that of David.

In 1995 a stone structure was discovered in Jerusalem which it was claimed might have been David's palace, or possibly the Fortress of Zion which David was said to have captured, but the dating of the structure is in great doubt. In December 2014, however, the journal *Near Eastern Archaeology* published preliminary results of an excavation by a team from Mississippi State University indicating signs of a state already being formed in a region east of Gaza in the tenth century BC. If confirmed, this may show that the biblical account of King David has its foundations in fact, but there is still no evidence of how accurately the king himself was portrayed.

50. Who wrote the Book of Esther?

Much doubt exists over the authorship of many parts of the Bible, both Old and New Testaments, but the puzzle over the Book of Esther is greater than most. The book itself gives no hint as to its author and tells the tale of a Jewish girl who becomes queen of Persia and saves her people from genocide. Other than the Song of Songs, which is also of unknown authorship, it is the only book in the Bible which contains no explicit mention of God. There is also not a single act of worship. To add to the mystery, there is also an ancient tradition that the Book of Esther is displayed on a scroll which only has one roller on the left-hand side rather than the customary two, one on each side.

The Babylonian Talmud attributes the writing of Esther to the men of the Great Synagogue, but whoever the author was, he (or she) must have been Jewish with a detailed knowledge of Persian customs and culture. According to the Roman historian Josephus, it was written by Mordecai, who features in the book as the cousin and adoptive father of Esther. Whether Mordecai would have heaped praise upon himself the way the book does, however, gives rise to considerable doubt. The other main candidate for authorship is Ezra.

There is also the question of why this highly unusual book was selected to be included in the official canon of the Old Testament. Perhaps if we knew who wrote it, we would be in a better position to understand that selection.

51. Why did Nebuchadnezzar II go mad for seven years?

Nebuchadnezzar II was a Chaldean king of Babylon who reigned for over forty years until his death in 562 BC. The construction of the Hanging Gardens of Babylon has been ascribed to him, but he is best known through his portrayal in the Book of Daniel in which he is punished by God for his boasting by being driven mad and forced to live like an animal in the wild for seven years.

St Jerome was of the opinion that Nebuchadnezzar was suffering from hypochondriacal monomania, an extreme form of illness anxiety, but more modern writers have made different diagnoses. These include clinical lycanthropy, which involves a belief that one is turning into a wolf, and porphyria, which was the form of madness that was later to afflict King George III of Britain. A form of dementia associated with advanced cases of syphilis has also been suggested, but that is difficult to reconcile with Daniel's account of Nebuchadnezzar regaining his reason after seven years.

Another suggestion is that the biblical story mixes facts from the lives of two Babylonian kings, Nebuchadnezzar II and Nabonidus. A fragment of the Dead Sea Scrolls tells of Nabonidus being similarly smitten by God with a fever for seven years, and there is also an account of Nabonidus spending a long time in the desert. Details of this fever, however, are even more scanty than those of Nebuchadnezzar's lycanthropic madness.

52. Who wrote the Epistle of Mathetes to Diognetus?

In the early years of the Christian church, a group of writers emerged who used information and logical argument to defend the church against its critics and persecutors. These were called 'apologists' and the anonymous author of the Epistle of Mathetes to Diognetus has been called the first apologist.

The one thing we know about its author is that he wasn't called Mathetes, which is a word simply meaning 'disciple'. The identity of its intended recipient is also unclear. There was a tutor of the emperor Marcus Aurelius who was called Diognetus, but it is thought very unlikely that he would have been the person the epistle was directed at.

The epistle itself was found in a thirteenth-century manuscript collection but it was destroyed in a fire in 1870. Fortunately a printed version existed, dating back to 1592, so the text, apart from a couple of lines which were presumably illegible in the original, has been preserved. Written in Greek, it deals with the state of the world at the time of Christ, and the need for His coming, with one chapter on 'Why the son was sent so late'. The names 'Jesus' and 'Christ', however, are never used, with the writer preferring to call him simply 'the son'.

The language and style in which it was written have led to its being dated at some time in the second century, possibly as early as AD 130, which could mean that the writer was a contemporary of one or more of the gospel writers. Whoever he was, he describes himself as 'a disciple of Apostles', but no further clues as to who he was have ever been found.

53. How many wise men did Matthew think visited the baby Jesus?

Now when Jesus was born in Bethlehem of Judaea in the days of Herod the king, behold, there came wise men from the east to Jerusalem. Matthew 2:1

Matthew did not, please note, identify the number of the wise men, nor say that they were kings. The tradition of referring to the 'three wise men' came later and derived solely from Matthew's identification of three gifts: gold, frankincense and myrrh. The identification of the three as Caspar, Balthazar and Melchior, the kings of India, Arabia and Persia, dates only from around AD 500. Referring to them as kings may have its origin in Psalm 72, which predicted: 'all kings shall fall down before him.'

But whether they were kings or not, how many of them did Matthew think there were? One might well think that if there had only been three, he would have specified the number. By saying 'wise men from the east', he gives the impression of a rather larger group. Some early references in the eastern Christian churches referred to twelve Magi, which ties in with the feeling that three would have been too few for Matthew's account.

In Botticelli's 1475 painting *Visit of the Magi*, his sons were the models for the three visitors, so that number must have already been traditional. It was, however, only in 1857 that the number became irrevocably part of the Christmas story, for that was when the Episcopal bishop John Henry Hopkins (1820–91) of Vermont penned the carol known as 'We Three Kings' and that is the way they have been seen ever since – even if they weren't kings, and there were more than three of them.

See also ASTRONOMY 30; CAMELS 83; JESUS 259–63; LITERATURE 276

BIG BANG

54. What happened in the first 10^{-37} of a second after the Big Bang?

Most astronomers now agree that the universe began about 13.8 billion years ago with a huge burst of energy known as the Big Bang. This agreement is comparatively recent. Until about fifty years ago, the debate was over whether we live in a steady state universe or an expanding universe. Indeed, the term 'Big Bang' was coined in 1949 by the astronomer Fred Hoyle to mock those who suggested that the universe had grown from almost nothing.

Increasingly, however, evidence supported the expanding universe theory, and once it was seen that galaxies are moving further and further apart, it became possible to trace the expansion backwards to a point 13.8 billion years ago when it all began. Einstein had taught us the equivalence of energy and matter, and vast experiments, such as those taking place at the Large Hadron Collider at CERN in Switzerland, have increased our knowledge of how the massive explosion of energy at the Big Bang might have led to the creation of the universe as it is now.

Measurements of the cosmic microwave background (CMB), which is a sort of echo of the explosion of the Big Bang, and gravitational waves, whose existence is predicted by some models of what happened immediately following the Big Bang, have led to increasingly refined pictures of the very first moments of the universe.

It must have started with almost inconceivably high temperatures, pressure and energy density forcing rapid expansion and cooling. According to the model now most generally agreed, after about 10^{-37} of a second (that's a decimal point followed by 37 zeros and a 1), a phase known as cosmic inflation began when the universe grew exponentially. Elementary particles such as quarks and gluons began to appear, with the first protons and neutrons appearing at about a millionth of a second after the Big Bang. Electrons and positrons arrived after about one second, after which it took only about another 400,000 years before atoms formed.

But what was going on in that first 10^{-37} of a second before even the elementary particles had come into existence? And that question leads to the next one…

55. What was the nature of the energy that filled the universe at the time of the Big Bang?

When we run time backwards to the moment of the Big Bang, the big question is what happens when we get there. We can talk about the massive expansion that must have taken place when the universe was a tiny fraction of a second old, but when we take it back to time zero, we reach a single point of infinite density and infinite temperature where the laws of physics fall apart. Mathematicians know such an imponderable as a singularity, much like what you get when you try to divide something by zero.

Talking about what happened before the Big Bang makes no sense because we have to get through that singularity to get to a 'before', and all the maths suggests that time itself began at the moment of the bang, so there was no 'before' anyway.

There is no doubt that it all started in the burst of a massive amount of energy, but we have no way of knowing where that energy came from and what its nature was. All we can say is that some unknown form of energy made the young universe inflate at a rate that was faster than the speed of light. That is highly unsatisfactory, of course, but it's the best we can do at present.

56. What is the origin of the matter–antimatter imbalance?

The world of physics, which is the physical world as we understand it, is made up of matter and antimatter. Particles of antimatter have the same mass as their corresponding matter particles but the opposite electric charge. A positively charged positron, for example, is the antimatter equivalent of a negatively charged electron. When corresponding matter and antimatter particles come into contact with each other, the result is mutual annihilation, leaving only pure energy behind.

The same thing in reverse, starting with the energy of the Big Bang, ought to have resulted in an equal number of particles of matter and antimatter popping into existence, then immediately destroying each other and turning back into energy. Yet wherever we look, there seems to be a vast excess of matter over antimatter. From the tiniest life forms to huge galaxies, everything seems to be made out of matter. Even detecting a few particles of antimatter is a huge achievement.

At some moment very shortly after the Big Bang, something must have happened to result in a small excess of matter over antimatter. There is then enough matter to annihilate all the antimatter, with a bit of matter left over to grow into the universe as we know it. But the laws of physics are supposed to be symmetric: if the number of antimatter particles declined, the number of matter particles should have declined too.

Apart from being annihilated by their corresponding partners, particles can disappear through decay, and it is supposed that something must have caused more antimatter to decay than matter. But what that something was is unknown.

See also BLACK HOLES 71; COSMOLOGY 119, 122–4, 126

BIOLOGY

57. Do STAP cells exist?

In 2014 a debate erupted over the existence of a type of cell that would have answered biologists' dreams. Stimulus-Triggered Acquisition of Pluripotency, or STAP for short, was the name given to cells that, like stem cells, had the propensity to develop into any type of cell its organism required. The theory was that if the right stimulus could be found, a developed cell could be turned back into a type of stem cell that could develop into whatever was needed.

If this could be done, it could pave the way towards techniques for regeneration of lost limbs or other body parts, which explains the massive interest aroused by a paper in *Nature* in January 2014 announcing the development of STAP cells in Japan. Over the next few months, huge resources were poured into STAP cell research and a patent was even taken out for the process to produce them.

Then it all began to fall apart, beginning with some deep criticism of the original paper and ending with its retraction after a number of experiments had failed to reproduce its findings. One of its authors has since resigned; another has committed suicide.

None of this, however, proves that STAP cells cannot exist, just that the method claimed for their production has been shown to be wrong.

58. Why are some people so much more prone to drug or alcohol addiction than others?

There can hardly be any aspect of human behaviour that has been so intensively studied yet remains so poorly understood as addiction. Behaviour that starts as simple pleasure-seeking turns into a pathological malfunctioning of the brain's reward system to such an extent that drug-craving overrules the normal decision-making function. Even though the addict knows it is disastrous for him, he cannot give up the habit.

We know that drug dependence is connected to the release of dopamine and other chemicals in the brain which result in a positive emotional state. We know that continued use of drugs results in an increase in synaptic connections between the brain's neurons that strengthen the perceived need for the drug, though we do not know how this happens. We know that some people seem much more prone to addiction than others, though we cannot say why. We know that some addicts seem able to recover completely, while others are prone to a relapse, even long after all withdrawal symptoms have disappeared. In short, we are still some way from understanding the biological basis of addiction and why some people become addicts and others do not.

59. How do our circadian clocks keep time?

Most of us live most of our lives in a cycle in which the Sun rises every morning and sets every evening, leading to a regular rhythm of days of 24 hours in length. Our bodies are geared to that schedule, with our waking and sleeping hours more or less matching it. When something such as jet lag badly disrupts our sleep and waking schedule, our bodies react to it. What keeps us more or less in sync with the Earth's rotation is our circadian clock, which is our bodies' internal time-keeping.

The word 'circadian' comes from the Latin *circa diem*, meaning 'about a day', which is a brilliantly accurate approximation. For our body clocks work to a day length of about 24.5 hours. Why this is about half an hour longer than the real day is unclear. A mouse's body clock, by contrast, is only about 23.5 hours long. One can only speculate on why humans have evolved to feel comfortable about staying up late, while mice want to go to sleep earlier.

In practice, what happens is that our body clocks reset every morning when we wake up. Their operation, however, is not run by the cycle of light and dark. Even if we live in total darkness, or in artificial light providing an apparent day length different from 24 hours, the body clock still maintains its 24.5-hour cycle.

We now know the genes that control the body clock, but we don't know how the circadian clock itself keeps time or how the cells of the body all agree what time it is.

60. How many different proteins make up a human being?

If the human genome is the blueprint for building a human body, then proteins are the building blocks. Between them come the amino acids of which there are about twenty. Proteins are strings of amino acids of various lengths. Since amino acids can be strung together in arbitrary order and the longest known protein is close to 27,000 amino acids long, the number of potential proteins is enormous.

In 2014 two teams in the USA and Germany independently produced drafts for maps of the human proteome – the protein equivalent of the genome. The American team identified proteins encoded by 17,294 genes out of the 19,629 genes that had been predicted to encode proteins. They also found 193 new proteins that came from regions of the genome that had not been thought to code for proteins, so the 19,629 figure cannot be seen as an upper limit. The German team reported a similar result with around 400 unexpected proteins. They referred to 'potentially 20,000 protein-coding genes'.

Research on a large number of human genomes has identified around a million different proteins, while the total number in all terrestrial organisms has been estimated at over 10 million. However, with the most recent results suggesting that gene-counting may be giving a false picture, those figures are no more than an educated guess.

61. How do prions replicate?

First discovered in 1982, prions are quite unlike any other biological structures. Consisting mostly of proteins, they appear to behave like viruses, yet they are not alive, have no DNA or RNA, and therefore cannot reproduce more of their own kind. The do replicate, however, in a manner that can cause degeneration of brain tissue and death, as we have discovered in scrapie in sheep, BSE in cows and CJD in humans, all of which are prion-based diseases.

Prions come in two types: cellular prion proteins, which are normal and harmless, and infectious prions (their name comes from the opening and closing letters of **PR**oteinaceous infect**ION**). Normal prions are thought to have a role in protecting cells, primarily in the nervous system, but infectious prions have the capacity to refold into the infectious form. One factor that makes prion diseases so effective is the body's failure to recognize them as abnormal and thus its inability to produce an immune response.

The big question about their ability to replicate is how the abnormal prion recruits normal prion protein and causes it to convert to the abnormal form.

62. What triggers puberty?

To some extent, we know what triggers puberty in both boys and girls. The hypothalamus in the brain secretes a hormone GnRH (gonadotropin-releasing hormone), which stimulates the pituitary gland to emit luteinizing hormone and follicle-stimulating hormone. These prompt the sex organs to release oestrogen in females and testosterone in males, which lead to the usual signs of puberty in the body.

These signs usually start to appear in girls aged between eight and fourteen and boys aged between nine and fifteen. When they occur in a girl below the age of eight or a boy under nine, it is called 'precocious puberty', and it is such cases that suggest we still have much to learn about what really triggers puberty. In around 50 per cent of cases of precocious puberty in boys and 10 per cent in girls, a physiological or genetic cause can be identified to explain why it happened early, but in the remaining 50 per cent of boys and 90 per cent of girls, no cause can be found. Such cases are known as 'idiopathic precocious puberty', and 'idiopathic' in this expression just means we don't know what triggered it at all.

63. How do some loriciferans live without oxygen?

Until the twenty-first century, every multicellular life form known to man needed oxygen to survive. Even the molluscs known as giant tube worms found in the Pacific at depths of several miles were found to live by hydrothermal vents from which they obtained dissolved oxygen. From 2000 onwards, however, a team of researchers from Italy conducted expeditions to search for life in mud samples deep under the Mediterranean Sea.

Expecting to find only bacteria and viruses, they were surprised to discover signs of multicellular creatures, some of which were found to be still alive. Given the name Loricifera, from two Latin words meaning 'armour-bearing', these strange shelled creatures less than a millimetre long live in the spaces between marine gravel and have now been confirmed as the first multicellular life forms that live in environments totally free of oxygen. Besides a shell, they have a head, a mouth and a digestive system and are thought to live on primitive oxygen-free micro-organisms called hydrogenosomes.

Whether this discovery of loriciferans is the forerunner of similar findings in the oxygen-free deep sea is a matter of speculation, as is the question of whether such creatures could exist on other planets with no oxygen in their atmospheres.

BIRDS

64. Are birds the only creatures alive today that descended from dinosaurs?

The idea that birds descended from dinosaurs dates back to an 1870 treatise by Thomas Henry Huxley in which he pointed out similarities between the skeletal structure of birds and those of some dinosaur fossils. It was the discovery of an archaeopteryx in Germany in 1861 that had led Huxley to his idea, and over the next century further fossil discoveries supported it. Fused clavicles were identified as prehistoric wishbones; flexible wrist joints had much in common with birds' wing joints; and the three-toed feet of some dinosaurs were seen as precursors of birds' feet. Finally, in 1996, came the discovery in China of dinosaur fossils with feathers.

This settled the matter for most, leaving only a few still doubting the dinosaur ancestry of birds, but what is more open to question is whether birds are their only living descendants. What about crocodiles and other reptiles, which at least look more like our common image of dinosaurs than birds do?

Crocodiles are thought to have evolved around 200 million years ago in the Mesozoic era, which was a long time before dinosaurs became extinct, but the term 'dinosaur' (meaning 'terrible lizard') was never intended to apply to all prehistoric animals. Dinosaurs had four legs, an upright gait and lived on the land. Prehistoric crocodiles spent too long in the water and walked with their bodies too close to the ground to be considered dinosaurs. In fact, it is thought that crocodiles and dinosaurs had a common ancestor around 250 million years ago called the archosaur from which both groups evolved independently.

When the vast majority of dinosaurs became extinct, probably after an asteroid impact around 66 million years ago, the survivors included some avian dinosaurs and some species of small dinosaur that later evolved into birds. Turtles, snakes, lizards and about half the species of crocodiles also survived, presumably, in some cases, thanks to their living in the water, but also because of their small size and adaptable metabolisms.

Whether other animals alive today are direct descendants of small dinosaurs that survived the asteroid impact is an open question, though no fossil records have yet been found to allow such a link to be traced back for any modern species.

65. Are crows impatient?

Patience demands self-control and restraint, and until 2011 those aspects of behaviour were thought to be found exclusively in primates. In that year, however, research was published with evidence that crows and ravens could be patient too. The experiments involved giving the birds items of food and training them to wait before they were offered the opportunity to exchange the food for something they liked more.

The design was simple. The bird was placed in an enclosure and given the initial foodstuff. The superior food was in full view outside the enclosure. After a period of time had elapsed, a bell was rung and the bird was offered the chance to exchange the food it had for the one it preferred. It was denied the better food if it had already eaten the first piece, or if it tried to exchange before the bell was rung. The researchers found that crows and ravens could learn to wait for up to 5 minutes 20 seconds, restraining themselves from eating the food they had been given to preserve the chance of exchanging it for something better.

In 2014, however, this view of corvine patience was modified by another paper reporting a refinement of the result. What the new research revealed was that crows can wait for a superior foodstuff but not for a larger portion of the same food. They are patient enough to wait for quality but not for quantity.

In his *Devil's Dictionary* Ambrose Bierce defined patience as: 'A minor form of despair, disguised as a virtue.' For crows and ravens, it is clearly something more complicated.

66. Do female birds prefer intelligent males?

Research on a number of species of birds has shown that females prefer to mate with more intelligent males. Female songbirds choose males with more complex songs, and complexity of song is a sign of superior brain development. Female crossbills choose males who have shown the greatest prowess at foraging. Female bower birds go for males with the snazziest displays in their nests. Both female zebra finches and female bower birds have been shown to go for the males that perform best at problem-solving tasks.

With the exception of the crossbills, however, none of the females in the above studies saw the male performing a task that could be directly linked to intelligence. If we could ask the birds whether they preferred more intelligent males, we cannot tell if they would say 'yes'.

There is also the possibility that the male birds have simply learned how to attract females. If the girls like a pretty nest, or a nicely warbled song, the brighter males will give it to them. The females need not think of their chosen males as 'intelligent', merely as good home decorators or singers. An increasing number of studies seem to show that intelligent male birds achieve more copulations, but it may be a Machiavellian form of intelligence that is designed just to give the girls what they want.

In any case, intelligence may not be the best thing for males to have in all species of bird. Female African widow birds choose males with the longest tails, and long tails in widow birds have never been associated with a high level of intelligence.

> 'Learning, *n*. The king of ignorance distinguishing the studious.'
>
> Ambrose Bierce

67. Why do birds return to their nesting grounds in the summer?

Many species of birds escape winter climates by migrating, often over considerable distances. That makes sense. Energy demands increase in cold weather and food becomes scarce. How birds decide where to migrate to, and, even more, why they travel all the way back are puzzling questions.

A recent study on Eurasian spoonbills, for example, showed that the most popular places to spend winter were the most southerly of their common migration sites, which are found in Mauritius and Senegal. Those countries, however, surprisingly turned out to be among the places that had the lowest survival rates for the birds. The spoonbills that set up their winter homes in southern France or Spain tended to do better.

Equally, research on the migratory patterns of birds in North America has raised the question of why they bother to fly all the way back home to their original nesting grounds in the spring. The longer the return flight, the greater the energy expenditure and the greater the danger, so one might expect birds from the far north to move home, stopping at the first hospitable location they fly over in spring. In general, however, that does not happen and the birds fly all the way to the original home again.

68. Why do female boobies cheat on their mates?

How do female birds in basically monogamous relationships choose which males to be unfaithful with? According to the 'good genes' hypothesis, a female who is paired with a low-quality male might be expected to be less faithful (or have more 'extrapair copulations', as the researchers put it) than females with high-quality mates. Research on blue-footed booby seabirds, however, provided no more than very weak support for that idea.

Females with younger mates were found to be more likely to indulge in courtship behaviour with other males, but their choice of which males to copulate with following courtship was not found to be predicted by the age, size, condition or previous breeding success of the male. The female birds with the most attractive partners were found to be more likely to indulge in extrapair copulation with males whose blue feet had the strongest tinge of green. Unattractive females, however, were found to indulge in fewer extrapair copulations than attractive ones, suggesting that male choice may also have some effect on observed female behaviour.

The researchers concluded that 'EP [extrapair] interactions involve more complexity than originally envisioned'.

69. Do male songbirds try harder when singing at more attractive females?

In most songbird species of the northern hemisphere, only the males sing. In Australia and New Zealand, however, both males and females tend to sing. The ability of males and females to sing duets has been given as a reason for stronger pair-bonding in antipodean birds compared with the one-sided role of song in the north, where only the males use song to attract mates.

Research has shown that females are more attracted to longer and more complex songs, which may indicate superior fitness or control of greater territorial space in the singer. Male birds, however, have been shown to sing longer and more complex songs when there are rivals in the vicinity.

The question of whether male birds try harder in the presence of an attractive female was addressed in some research at the University of Wyoming. After placing male finches together with various females, they recorded and analysed the songs they sang and reported that both the quantity and the quality of the songs they performed to different females varied. Interestingly, they also found that songs performed at the start of each interaction were significantly more attractive than those they sang later. Whether this shows that they try harder with more attractive females, especially at the start of a potential relationship, is an open question.

See also EVOLUTION 180, 183; MUSIC 329; PANGOLINS 354; PLATYPUSES 375; SLEEP 423

BLACK HOLES

70. What happens to the information in black holes?

The traditional view of black holes was that anything swallowed up by them was lost for ever. Their huge mass all scrunched into an infinitesimal space had such a gravitational pull that even light itself could not escape. With nothing ever coming out, the information about anything that went in was irretrievably lost to the outside observer.

In 1975, however, Stephen Hawking showed that the laws of quantum physics meant that black holes would leak radiation which eventually, even though it might take trillions of years, would lead to the evaporation of the black hole itself.

The question then arose about what this Hawking radiation could tell us about the inside of the black hole. Does the radiation that comes out of a black hole depend on what went into it? If so, then the information contained in matter forming the black hole cannot be said to have been lost at all.

Scientific views have been split on the answer to that question ever since. The real problem was that general relativity insisted that the information that went into a black hole could never come out, while quantum theory said that the future of the hole, including the radiation that emerged from it, would depend on its past history, which would mean that the information it contained was not lost at all.

Even Hawking changed his mind about it, and new theories to reconcile the Black Hole Information Paradox appear every few years to sway the views of top physicists. But they are still completely split on the matter.

71. Can black holes turn into white holes?

In 2014 a radical new theory was proposed to resolve some of the problems posed by black holes. Just as black holes are regions that sucked material in which could never escape, the new proposal was that the exact opposite may also exist: a white hole that spews out massive amounts of matter in a Big Bang all of its own. Just as a black hole had a way in but no way out, a white hole would have a way out but no way back.

Based on the theory of loop quantum gravity, which maintains that the universe is composed of fundamental particles in the form of vibrating loops, the new theory predicts that a black hole will, under its own ever-increasing gravity, be crushed smaller and smaller until it reaches the size of these fundamental loops. It will then be unable to diminish in size and become subject to a force known as 'quantum bounce', which sends everything into reverse and all the energy and material that went into the black hole are flung out again.

The existence of white holes is still only a theoretical possibility as none have yet been observed. One suggestion is that they may have occurred but been mistaken for supernovas. Another is that they have not been observed because the white hole that a black hole turns into will be in a parallel universe.

See also COSMOLOGY 123; QUASARS 390–1; UNIVERSE 466

BONES

72. Why don't human males have penis bones?

- Humans and hyenas are the only carnivorous mammals that don't have one.

- Humans and spider monkeys are the only primates that don't have one.
- The walrus has a bigger one than any other animal.

We are talking, of course, about the baculum or penis bone, and the reason human males are missing it is lost in our evolutionary history.

The main advantage of having a penis bone is that it allows a male to have quick and frequent sex. Instead of having to wait for increased blood pressure to make the penis erect, creatures with a baculum can just push it from inside them into the penis and they are ready for action. One theory about its absence in humans suggests that our ancestor males were very good at sticking close to their chosen female, keeping her free from molestation from rival males while also ensuring that she was close whenever he wanted her. Result: the male could wait for an erection to occur in the knowledge that the female would still be there when he was ready.

Another suggestion links the bone's absence to the short length of primate penises relative to other mammals. Shorter penises led to shorter bones until, in humans, it eventually disappeared. Why almost all other primates have one, however, is unexplained.

Finally, there is the suggestion that the baculum was the 'rib' from which God created Eve out of Adam. This is advocated in a letter published in the *American Journal of Medical Genetics* in 2001, though the point of the letter may have been to suggest that the lack of a human penis bone was the origin of the story, rather than that the loss of the baculum dates back to the Garden of Eden.

73. Why do human bones become brittle in space?

One of the problems faced by astronauts on the International Space Station is a loss of bone mass. This begins within days of arriving in space and becomes severe between the second and fifth months. Long stays have resulted in loss of as much as 20 per cent of bone mass.

Increase in the amount of calcium found in the blood of astronauts confirms that the loss of bone mass is due to calcium in the bones being broken down and released into the bloodstream. This is known as 'disuse osteoporosis' and leaves bones weak and brittle. It is presumably caused by near-weightlessness in the microgravity of space, which leaves the bones free from their usual task of supporting the weight of the body.

NASA says that the mechanism causing this loss of calcium is unknown. One suggestion is that microgravity may cause bone to break down much faster than it takes to build up, but 'the exact trigger for this rate change has not been found'.

See also BIRDS 64; CAMELS 83; CANNIBALISM 88; CATS 91; DINOSAURS 137; ENGLISH HISTORY 176; HUMAN EVOLUTION 234, 239, 243; POLAR BEARS 378; SHIPS 421; SLOTHS 430-1; TYRANNOSAURUSES 461; WALRUSES 486

BRAINS

74. How do we recognize faces?

Our ability to recognize the faces of other people, even if we have not seen them for a long time, is one of the most remarkable feats of the human brain. The evidence suggests that we can remember up to 10,000 faces, and experiments have shown that we can generally recognize people even if we have not seen them for ten years or more.

The temporal lobe of the brain, the right fusiform gyrus, the anterior temporal cortex, the inferior occipital gyri, the superior temporal sulcus and the amygdala are all brain regions that have been associated with face recognition by various researchers, and studies of prosopagnosia, or face blindness, have shown that damage to the fusiform area can lead to inability to recognize faces.

With age and sex and emotions as well as identity being read from people's faces, our brains are processing a very large amount of data at a glance. How we can do all this so quickly is one of the most remarkable of our abilities and we really don't understand how we do it.

75. How does the brain put together information from the various senses?

We all know about the five senses of sight, hearing, touch, smell and taste, and some would add other senses such as balance, pain, temperature, body position and motion. However many senses you count, though, they were, until recently, seen as independent means of receiving information about the world, and the brain's task was to build up a complete picture from the various sensory inputs. We can perceive what something looks like, sounds like, feels like, smells like and tastes like; put them all together and we have the complete picture. Recent research, however, has shown that it's not so simple.

Both psychological studies and research on the brain itself have shown that the senses are not independent at all. One sense can influence others in surprising ways. Perhaps the clearest demonstrations of this have been given by the Oxford psychologist Charles Spence, who has produced astonishing results on how our sense of taste can be tricked by the other senses. Strawberries taste sweeter and better when served on white plates than on black. White wallpaper makes red wine taste worse. Different sounds can bring out different flavours in food. Away from the dining table, it has also been shown that what we think we hear can be changed by what we think we see.

Such findings have been supported by brain scans which have identified individual neurons that react to information perceived by more than one sense simultaneously. This ability seems not to exist at birth but to begin to develop at a very early stage of development. The brain doesn't just put information together, but by letting the senses overlap it somehow develops a wiring that lets them function together in a dynamic way automatically. But if senses can overlap and change one another, how this helps us draw up an accurate and consistent picture of what we perceive is quite unclear.

76. How is information coded in the brain?

There are many unanswered questions about the way the brain functions, but one of the most basic is the question of how information is encoded and transmitted from one brain region to another. Our brains are seen as massively complex networks involving connections between neurons, but how one neuron communicates with another is unclear. Measurement of fluctuation voltages at the membranes of neurons has suggested two basic components: the average rate of the pulses of the fluctuation and the timings of individual pulses.

After half a century of argument about which of these components was more important, a team in Germany suggested in 2010 that both pulses and timings could operate simultaneously. Then, in 2014, another German team proposed that resonance may also play a part, with different networks of cells having different frequencies which enable them to communicate with one another or inhibit the activity of other cells.

None of this gets us significantly closer to understanding what information looks like in the brain, or how one neuron knows what another is telling it, but at least we may be getting closer to understanding the mechanisms by which they communicate.

77. How does the brain pay attention to something?

In 1999 the psychologists Daniel Simons and Christopher Chabris conducted an extraordinary experiment on human attentiveness. Subjects were shown a film of six people practising on a basketball court. Three wore white and three wore black, and each team had its own ball which they passed to team-mates while wandering around the court. The subjects were asked to watch the film and count how many passes took place between members of the white team. Many came up with the correct answer of fifteen passes, but very few, when asked if they had seen anything unusual happening in the film, noticed that a man in a gorilla suit had walked right across the court, stopping in the middle to face the camera and beat his chest. In various trials the number spotting the gorilla varied from none at all to around 20 per cent.

The 'inattentional blindness' shown in this experiment is as clear a demonstration as one could wish for of the way our brains can miss something, however glaring, when they are looking for something else. On the other hand, it is important for our self-preservation that we pay attention to unexpected sounds and sights that could signal a threat. But how do our brains decide what is worth paying attention to?

This may be linked to other things we don't understand, such as free will and consciousness. All that is clear is that our brains can choose what to pay attention to and what to ignore before we are conscious of having had any influence on such decisions.

78. Why did our brains divide into two hemispheres?

All mammals and even fish have brains divided into two almost identical parts which constantly communicate with each other. This confirms that the evolution of the split brain occurred very early in our development, but what advantage it conferred is a matter of pure speculation.

Since the left side of the brain controls the right side of the body, and vice versa, it is generally assumed that the split brain must have something to do with lateral specialization, but why it should be an advantage for the two halves to be physically so strongly separated and joined only by a thick tube of fibres is unknown.

In 2000 an experiment was performed on unborn chicks to try to determine the advantages of a lateralized brain. One group of unhatched chicks was incubated in the dark, while another was exposed to light in a manner that had been previously shown to lead to brain lateralization in a number of visual tasks. When they hatched, the chicks were tested on two tasks at the same time, one involving pecking at seeds, the other detecting predators. It was found that the lateralized chicks performed the tasks better. This supported the theory that two half-brains are better than a single brain at the parallel processing required when doing two things at the same time.

To go from that single result to a theory of the evolution of the brain, however, is a large step for chick-kind, let alone humankind.

79. What goes on in the brain during hypnosis?

When a person is in a hypnotic trance, they may perform actions that they would not normally do, and when they come out of the trance, they are liable to have no memory of what they did. So what is going on in the brain to make this happen?

Most hard data on the question come from electroencephalographs measuring the brain waves of people under hypnosis. Some studies have revealed an increase in lower-frequency waves and a drop in higher-frequency, which is a pattern similar to sleeping and dreaming. Other studies have reported a lower level of activity in the left hemisphere of the cerebral cortex, accompanied by increased activity in the right hemisphere. This is in line with the idea that associates the left brain with conscious logic and deduction and the right brain with the subconscious mind and creativity; hypnosis is thus seen as subduing the subject's conscious inhibitions.

How someone enters a hypnotic state, however, remains unexplained. There is general agreement that the hypnotist does no more than relax and guide the subject to induce hypnosis, but how the subject then turns off the conscious mind without falling asleep is quite unknown. There is clearly a difference between the hypnotic state and the dream state, but it is unclear physiologically what that difference is.

80. Is morality hard-wired into the brain?

Eating, staying alive, having sex and caring for our children are basic instinctive desires that we are born with. Our brains are necessarily hard-wired for these things as essential to the survival of our species. From ancient philosophers to modern neurologists, however, people have long argued over whether the same applies to moral judgements and our views on the differences between what is 'good' and what is 'evil'. Are the rules of morality something that we acquire from our education and culture, or are they inbuilt in our brains?

Two dilemmas are often cited as arguments to support the hard-wired morality argument:

(i) You are a railway man standing by the side of a track on which a train is speeding out of control. If you do nothing, it will stay on the same track and run straight into a group of five people. You can avoid this by flicking a lever which will send it onto another track where it will kill only one person. What do you do?

(ii) A doctor is in charge of a ward where five people will die if they don't receive transplants immediately. A healthy stranger walks into the ward. If the doctor kills the stranger, he can harvest his organs and save all five patients. Should he do so?

The vast majority of people say that it is morally correct to flick the lever in the first case, but not to kill the stranger in the second, yet in both cases one person is sacrificed to save five. The fact that such a moral judgement appears to be universal has been claimed to support the idea that morality itself is universal and we are born with it.

On the other hand, one could say that flicking a switch is a very different type of decision to make than cold-bloodedly killing someone, and it is no surprise that different cultures reach the same moral conclusions by a rational rather than hard-wired process.

81. Why does the cerebellum have so many neurons?

The cerebellum (which gets its name from a Latin word meaning 'little brain') contains about half the total number of neurons in the human brain, yet it is only a tenth of the total size of the brain. Situated at the bottom of the brain, beneath the cerebral hemispheres, it used to be considered mainly as the motor centre of the brain, with an important role in maintaining balance and co-ordinating movements and motor learning. It was also known to play a part in certain cognitive functions such as language, which might also, at least for spoken language, be said to involve motor skills. In all these cases, the cerebellum does not initiate the movement but seems to be essential in carrying it out.

Recent research comparing a number of primate species has suggested that a fast expansion of the size of the cerebellum occurred when apes and monkeys diverged. It has even been suggested that a large cerebellum lies at the centre of human cognitive abilities. Its large number of neurons and vast number of connections suggest that the cerebellum plays a vital part in the brain's function, but we still have very little knowledge of what it does and how it does it. As anthropology professor Robert Barton of Durham University wrote in October 2014: 'Nobody really knows what all these neurons are for, but they must be doing something important.'

See also ANATOMY 5, 7; AUTISM 36; BIOLOGY 58, 61–2; BIRDS 66; CHOCOLATE 104–5; DISEASE 142, 144–6; DREAMS 160–1; EVOLUTION 178; EYES 185; HYPNOSIS 246; INTELLIGENCE 248–50; LANGUAGE 267; LOBSTERS 278; MAMMALS 283; MEDICINE 299; MUSIC 328; PHILOSOPHY 360, 363, 365; PLATYPUSES 375; PSYCHOLOGY 384–9; SEX 406; SEX DIFFERENCES 411–12; SLEEP 423–4, 426, 429; SPORT 446; WORMS 499

BRAZIL

82. Did Percy Fawcett find the lost city of Z?

In 1925 Colonel Percy Harrison Fawcett disappeared during an expedition to find a city he called 'Z' in the uncharted jungles of Brazil. After studying ancient legends and other records, he was convinced there was an ancient city in the Mato Grosso region which was possibly the fabled El Dorado. The last that was heard of him was a letter to his wife on 29 May 1925 saying that he was setting off into unexplored territory with his son Jack and one of Jack's old friends. They were never seen again. Many rumours followed about what had happened to him: that he had been killed by tribesmen; that he had been killed by animals; that he had become chief of a cannibal tribe. But no evidence of him or his remains was ever confirmed.

The lost city of Z, which Fawcett was seeking, had been described in 1753 by a Portuguese slave trader who gave a detailed description of the city but omitted to reveal its location. In January 2010, however, the journal *Antiquity* reported the identification, using Google Earth, of more than 200 massive earthworks in the upper Amazon basin near Brazil's border with Bolivia.

So Percy Fawcett might have been right after all, and he might even have found his lost city. He has, after all, been cited as a possible inspiration for the character of Indiana Jones.

> 'Not ignorance, but ignorance of ignorance is the death of knowledge.'
>
> Alfred North Whitehead

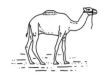

CAMELS

83. Did Abraham have camels?

And he entreated Abram well for her sake: and he had sheep, and oxen, and he asses, and menservants, and maidservants, and she asses, and camels. Genesis 12, 16

There are twenty-two mentions of camels in the Book of Genesis, and they led to a huge dispute between archaeologists and theologians in 2014. At the heart of it were excavations of copper mines between the Red Sea and the Dead Sea which had revealed some camel bones.

The bones, said the archaeologists, appear abruptly in the strata of the mines and thus give a clear indication of when domesticated camels arrived in the region. Radiocarbon dating, they claim, has allowed them to pinpoint that moment, which they say was around the ninth century BC.

According to the traditional Bible chronology, however, Abraham lived around 2000 BC, which was more than a millennium too early for the camels. The archaeologists say their findings show that a camel-based economy only became established after the rise of Egyptian power in the region, which was too late even for King Solomon and King David to have had camels.

In reply, theologians have questioned the reliability of radiocarbon dating, which has made mistakes in the past.

CANCER

84. How do blind mole rats resist cancer?

The blind mole rat lives underground, digs with its teeth, has skin over its eyes, survives with very little oxygen and no light, and has never been known to have a cancerous tumour. Even when treated with carcinogenic chemicals, it shows total resistance to cancer, which is one reason the sequencing of its genome in 2014 was seen as a possible step forward in understanding the disease.

The genetic adaptation that enables the blind mole rat to cope with very low oxygen levels is thought to be responsible for its highly effective defence against cancer. Whether this has applications in human cancer treatment has yet to be discovered, but the publication of the mole rat's genome will certainly lift the animal's status in medical research.

85. Why do some moles become cancerous?

Moving from blind mole rats to moles on the skin...

We used to call moles 'beauty spots' until their beauty became tarnished with the link to skin cancer. A mole, or nevus, is a benign (non-cancerous) pigmented skin tumour. Most moles never cause any problems, but sometimes they become cancerous, and it is not known why this occurs.

A number of factors have been identified that increase the chances of moles turning into cancerous melanomas. One risk factor is excessive exposure to sunlight, particularly in one's youth. The ultraviolet light from the Sun or from tanning beds, particularly UVB rays, can damage the DNA in skin cells and cancers can be caused by DNA changes. People with many moles seem more likely to develop cancers than people with only a few. A large, flat and often irregular type of mole called 'dysplastic' (or 'atypical') is known to be more likely to become cancerous.

Yet in all of these cases, we cannot tell whether a particular benign mole is going to develop into a melanoma until it happens.

86. How does physical activity affect cancer risk?

A study published in December 2011 estimated that about 1 per cent of cancers in the UK are linked to people doing less physical activity than is recommended in the government guidelines. Cases of bowel cancer in particular were seen to be significantly less frequent among people who indulged in most physical activity, as were cases of breast cancer in women.

Inactive lifestyles have been linked to many health problems, including stroke and heart disease, diabetes, osteoporosis and a range of problems associated with weight gain. Regular physical activity is claimed to have a protective effect against cancer, over and above its effect on bodyweight, but without better knowledge of the causes of cancer, we cannot be sure of such things. As statisticians often remind us, correlation does not imply causation. If inactive people are more likely to develop cancers, it could even be that proneness to cancer is a cause of an inactive lifestyle, rather than the other way round.

Physical activity has an effect on levels of insulin, some hormones and our hormone-like prostaglandins, all of which may have a role in fighting cancer, but that is a speculative explanation of how cancer and physical activity may be linked – if indeed they are connected at all.

See also AUSTEN 34; CHEMICALS 95; HENRY VIII 230; LONGEVITY 280; MEDICINE 295

CANNABIS

87. Does cannabis have a direct effect on men's sperm production?

An extensive study in 2014 reported that taking cannabis was the only factor found to have a negative effect on men's sperm production. Alcohol, smoking, obesity and even wearing tight underwear were found to have no effect on sperm quality, but taking cannabis was reported to double the chances of men under the age of thirty producing abnormal sperm.

However, the researchers admit that it is not known how or even whether cannabis has a direct effect on sperm production, or whether the correlation is caused by an association with another unknown factor. Also, the study was based on analysis of sperm samples from men who had attended fertility clinics, which may not be representative. Poor sperm quality is one of many possible reasons for attending a fertility clinic. One might say that the study showed that cannabis-taking had a beneficial effect on the other possible reasons for their attendance at the clinics.

See also MEDICINE 299

'We are all born ignorant but one must work hard to remain stupid.'

Benjamin Franklin

CANNIBALISM

88. Did the cannibal cavemen of Spain eat members of their own clan?

Most, if not all, accounts of cannibalism among early humans have either been associated with ritual killing and eating of selected body parts of enemies, or were thought to have taken place at times of famine. In 2010, however, bones were found in a cave in Spain which were claimed as evidence that cannibalism was just another meal to our ancestors 800,000 years ago.

Marks on the bones of around a dozen humans were seen as evidence that their flesh had been removed; decapitation and marks on the skulls suggested that their brains had been eaten; and smashed bones were taken as evidence that their marrow had been consumed.

The fact that the bones were found mixed up with those of bison, deer, sheep and other animals suggested that the human flesh was seen as nothing special among *Homo antecessor*, who are thought to be Europe's earliest humans. Furthermore, the region was thought to have been rich in food and water and to have had a mild climate, all of which would argue against cannibalism being a last resort in time of famine.

DNA studies of the bones in 2013 revealed that they were all from one family and included three men, three women, three teenagers and three children aged two to nine. Their relationship to the people who ate them, however, is not known, and there is some argument about how often human flesh was on the menu and whether people ate their friends as well as enemies.

See also BRAZIL 82; DISEASE 144–5

CARROLL

89. Why was Lewis Carroll so generous to Mr Dymes?

There has long been a mystery concerning the relationship between Lewis Carroll, author of *Alice in Wonderland*, and a Mr Dymes, whom he is believed to have met on holiday. Dymes had a large family and Carroll records having dinner with Mrs Dymes and taking his daughters to the theatre. He wrote an acrostic poem for Ruth Dymes and is known to have helped some of Dymes's older daughters get work.

In 2006 details of Carroll's bank account were found at a bank in Oxford. They reveal substantial payments to Mr Dymes between 1883 and 1885, a period during which Carroll himself was in constant financial difficulties. Not only did Carroll give or lend money to Dymes on various occasions (which was never repaid), but he even paid off Dymes's landlord when he was threatening to seize his furniture.

Carroll's own letters and correspondence suggest that he didn't like Dymes much, but saw him as a dull character always moaning about his misfortunes. He did not even seem to have strong feelings towards any of Dymes's family.

Carroll's giving Dymes money that he could ill afford can only be explained by his being a very generous man without much financial good sense, or by his having something to hide which he was paying Dymes not to reveal.

CATS

90. Why do cats sit in circles?

Towards the end of 2014, a sudden spate of pictures of cats sitting inside circles began appearing in the popular press and the Internet. Somebody had started the craze by noticing that if you make a circular shape on the floor of a room or on the ground outside with a piece of string, or electrical wire, or masking tape, or indeed almost anything, any cat in the vicinity will be liable to wander over, step into the circle, settle down and refuse to move. And it doesn't even have to be a circle: as many of the pictures showed, a square, a pentagon or almost any closed shape would do.

A range of possible explanations have been advanced to account for this newly discovered aspect of feline behaviour:

- The cat may be defending the territory marked out by the newly created boundary.
- The cat may see the boundary as a sort of wall offering it greater security.
- The cat may assume that the person who created the circle must have done so for a reason, so the circle must be important.
- The cat may like the feeling of being enclosed that the circle gives it.
- The cat may just be investigating something new in its environment.
- The cat may be attracted not by the circle but by the smell of whatever was used to create the boundary.

In short, nobody really has any idea why cats like to sit in circles.

91. Why do cats purr?

As all cat owners know, their pets purr when they are contented. But cats also purr when they are in pain or when they are nervous, so what is this purring all about?

One theory is that a cat's purr evolved as medically beneficial. A purr is a sound made at a frequency of between 250 and 150 Hertz, which has also been found to be the frequency of vibrations that help muscles and bones grow or repair themselves when damaged. Purring may thus have begun as a beneficial therapeutic process and then turned into a general expression of well-being and contentment.

Another theory is that purring is a form of communication. Cats have been shown to purr at similar frequencies to the crying of human babies when they want food, and it has been suggested that cats purr when they are hungry too. Or the purring of baby cats may be a way for the blind newborn kittens to locate and communicate with their mothers.

Or perhaps cats just purr because they like purring. We really don't know.

92. What happened to Peter the Great's Russian blue cat?

The earliest known example of the Russian blue breed of cat was a pet of the Russian tsar Peter the Great. His name was Vaska, a diminutive of the name Vassily, and he is said to have been looked after by the tsar's daughter Elizabeth.

Lenin used to tell the tale of Vaska the cat, living in the palace of the tsar and stealing food from the kitchen. The palace cook used to make appeals to the cat to refrain from its immoral banditry. The cat listened but went on eating.

Lenin cited this as an example of the futility of making moral appeals to the exploitative classes, but neither he nor anyone else seems to have told what eventually happened to Vaska.

See also ANIMALS 18; WALRUSES 486

CHAPLIN

93. When and where was Charlie Chaplin born?

Biographies of Charlie Chaplin all seem to agree that he was born in London on 16 April 1889. Chaplin himself confirmed that date, and until 2012 there seemed no reason to doubt it. In that year, however, newly declassified files from Britain's MI5 revealed considerable uncertainty about the star's origins.

In the 1950s MI5 had been asked by the FBI to investigate Chaplin, whom they suspected of having communist sympathies. Even J. Edgar Hoover himself was said to have denounced Chaplin in private as being 'one of Hollywood's parlour Bolsheviks'. What must have seemed a routine enquiry from the FBI, however, became a mystery when MI5 could find no record of Chaplin's birth. Their conclusion was: 'It would seem that Chaplin was either not born in this country or that his name at birth was other than those mentioned.' MI5 also found no evidence to support a theory that Chaplin was really a Frenchman named Israel Thornstein. The 1891 UK census does, however, record the two-year-old Charles Chaplin as living in London with his mother and elder brother.

At around the same time as the declassification of the MI5 files, another clue emerged in the form of a letter found in a locked drawer of a bureau that had belonged to Chaplin. Written by an Englishman named Jack Hill in the early 1970s, it told Chaplin that he had been born 'in a caravan belonging to the Gypsy Queen, who was my auntie', in a Roma community in Smethwick, near Birmingham, England. Chaplin's mother's maiden name was Hill.

CHEESE

94. Does Roquefort cheese have sex?

Until 2012 nobody had ever suggested that Roquefort cheese might be having sex, but in that year a paper appeared reporting a study in France suggesting that it could indeed be happening. 'Sex in cheese: Evidence for sexuality in the fungus Penicillium roqueforti' (by Jeanne Ropars and others) begins by saying that: 'Although most eukaryotes reproduce sexually at some moment of their life cycle, as much as a fifth of fungal species were thought to reproduce exclusively asexually', but goes on to say: 'recent studies have revealed the occurrence of sex in some of these supposedly asexual species.' Their study of reproduction in the Roquefort fungus 'revealed the existence of individuals of both mating types, even in the very same cheese', and they concluded that: '*P. roqueforti* underwent more or less recent sex events.' So the Roquefort fungus might be having sex after all.

See also USA 473

> 'Education is a progressive discovery
> of our own ignorance.'
>
> Will Durant

CHEMICALS

95. Is dimethyl sulfoxide good for you?

For more than fifty years, arguments have raged over the use of dimethyl sulfoxide (DMSO) as a medicine. Its supporters see it as a modern panacea with an unending list of potential applications, particularly in the realm of pain-killing, but ranging from the treatment of headaches to cancer. Others, however, including the US Food and Drug Administration (FDA), have severe doubts about both its efficacy and its safety. In fact the FDA has approved its use only for the relief of symptoms of interstitial cystitis and as a preservative for transplant organs.

A by-product of the wood industry, DMSO has been used as an industrial solvent since 1953. Over 40,000 articles in scientific journals have been written on its chemistry and over 10,000 on its potential medical applications. Two factors, however, interfered with research. One was its ready availability for industrial applications, which led to a good deal of unsupervised use; the other was that even when absorbed through the skin, it made people's breath smell of garlic. That made double-blind studies difficult to conduct, as researchers could always tell who had taken DMSO and who had not. The smell may also have put off drug companies from studying DMSO, as it was seen as difficult to market.

In 1965 a woman in Ireland died of an allergic reaction after taking DMSO and some other drugs. Although the precise cause of death was never established, clinical trials of DMSO were stopped and suspicion against the drug has persisted ever since.

Meanwhile, DMSO has continued to be produced and sold in private clinics, with good results claimed for its effect as a fast-working analgesic and as a slower-working treatment for chronic pain. But the garlic-smelling breath is still seen as a problem.

See also BIOLOGY 58; CANCER 84; CHOCOLATE 105; DISEASE 146; INTELLIGENCE 250; JUPITER 264; POLAR BEARS 378; SMELL 436; TERMITES 452

CHEWING GUM

96. Did General Santa Anna invent chewing gum?

General Antonio Lopez de Santa Anna (1794–1876) is best known for his success in leading the Mexican forces at the Battle of the Alamo in 1836 and for his subsequent periods in office as president of Mexico, but, according to some accounts, another of his greatest achievements may have been generally overlooked: the invention of chewing gum.

After being overthrown as president of Mexico in 1855, Santa Anna fled to Cuba where he lived in exile, trying to raise money to fund an army to take over Mexico City. In 1869 he visited Staten Island, New York, where he was hoping to sell the idea of using chicle, a sticky gum from trees, as a rubber substitute.

Like other similar gums, chicle was often chewed by Mexicans for its high sugar content, but Santa Anna never saw that as a potentially lucrative application. When in Staten Island, however, he met an inventor named Thomas Adams whom he hoped would join him in his rubber project. Adams bought a ton of chicle from him but was unable to produce a workable rubber from it.

Adams's son Horatio, however, saw its chewability and gave 200 balls of it to a drugstore owner who sold them at two a penny. The Adams family went on to create Adams Clove Gum, Chiclets and other chewing gums, the first of their type in the USA. Adams may have been the real inventor of chewing gum, but he would never have done it without the hero of the Alamo.

CHICKENS

97. Why do chickens count from left to right?

Research has shown that when people think of numbers, they arrange them on a mental number line (MNL) with lower numbers on the left and higher numbers on the right. A wonderfully designed experiment, the results of which were published in 2015, showed that three-day-old chickens do the same thing.

The chicks were first placed in an enclosure with a centrally placed panel on which a number of spots were visible. When one of the chicks walked round the panel, it was rewarded with food. After some time, the chicks got the hang of it and learnt to associate walking round the panel with receiving a reward.

When this had been reliably learnt, the experiment moved on to its second stage in which the single panel was now replaced by two panels, one on the left and the other on the right, at equal distances and angles from the chicks. The two panels had equal numbers of spots on them, but it was not the same number as had been there during training. The researchers held their breath and waited to see which panel was preferred by the chicks.

Remarkably, they found that when the number of spots was lower than had been there during training, about 70 per cent of chicks went to the left panel, but when it was higher, 70 per cent chose the right. The experiment was performed with varying numbers of spots, both during the initial training and the subsequent experiment, but the chicks always went left for lower numbers than had appeared in training and right for higher ones.

The fact that chickens and humans share this left–right bias in our number lines suggests that it may be something that occurred very early in our joint evolution. Why chickens think of numbers from left to right is an even bigger problem than the same question for humans.

See also FOOTBALL 199; GORILLAS 220; PANGOLINS 356

CHIMPANZEES

98. Is aggression in chimpanzees the result of human influence?

Chimpanzees and humans have often been described as the only species that wage war on their own kind. Other creatures, such as various spiders and certain insects, may kill their own kind when competing for sex or food, but humans and chimps get involved in a form of intergroup conflict that has been likened to primitive warfare. Bonobos, on the other hand, which are even more closely related to humans, are remarkably peaceful.

Ever since the anthropologist Jane Goodall reported on warlike chimpanzee behaviour in the 1970s, there has been a debate about whether this aggression is caused by human intervention or is innate and natural behaviour. In 2014 the journal *Nature* published a paper based on an extensive survey of 152 lethal attacks by chimpanzees on their own kind in eighteen chimpanzee and four bonobo communities over the past fifty years. The conclusion was that 'lethal aggression directed toward members of other groups is part of the natural behavioural repertoire of chimpanzees' and human intervention plays no part.

That finding, however, was immediately challenged by other anthropologists, particularly on its lack of a clear definition of 'human influence' and the statistical methods used to establish the root causes of chimpanzee aggression.

Interestingly, however, the study reported that, much as in human warfare, 92 per cent of the attackers and 73 per cent of the victims in the killings were male, and 66 per cent of them were the result of attacks on one community by another. Perhaps we have more in common with chimpanzees than we thought, and perhaps what we should really be studying is what makes bonobos so peaceful.

See also EBOLA 167; INTELLIGENCE 254; WALRUSES 486

CHINA

99. Where did the Tarim mummies come from?

Early in the twentieth century, various European explorers reported finding desiccated bodies at the eastern end of the Tarim Basin (now Xinjiang) in China. Many were tall or red-haired, indicating an origin more European than Chinese. The earliest mummies have been dated to around 1800 BC, and both their physiology and the textiles they wore support the theory that they had a European origin.

Pliny the Elder, in his *Natural History*, written around AD 77–9, mentioned a report from a Ceylonese ambassador to the Roman emperor Claudius of people in north-west China who 'exceeded the ordinary human height, had flaxen hair, and blue eyes, and made an uncouth sort of noise by way of talking'.

Until the discovery of the 'Tarim mummies', Pliny's description was viewed as fanciful, but recent DNA analyses have confirmed that they probably did have a European rather than Asian origin. How they got there and precisely where they came from, however, has never been revealed.

100. Who built the Longyou caves?

In 1992 a villager in Longyou County in China made an extraordinary discovery while pumping water from a cave. What he found was the first of a series of massive caves, with a floor of over 2,000 square metres and a height at its tallest point of over 30 metres. He went on to discover four more such caves and now twenty-four of them are known, all with wall carvings of horses, fishes and birds, which confirm that they were man-made. They are thought to date back to between 500 and 200 BC, and their scale is awesome. According to one estimate, almost 1 million cubic metres of rock must have been removed to build them.

Yet their origin is a complete mystery, with nothing known of who constructed them or why they were built. To add to that mystery, no reference to them has ever been found in historical records.

101. How did the hanging coffins of Sichuan get there?

From around AD 1000 to 1600, the Bo people of Sichuan in south-west China practised an extraordinary form of burial which involved placing bodies in coffins made of hollowed-out tree trunks that were then hung on limestone cliffs at heights between 10 and 130 metres above the ground. Over 300 such coffins are known in Sichuan, but the reasons behind the ritual and the methods used have long been a matter for speculation.

Presumably the location of the coffins was intended to protect the bodies, possibly from wild animals, or perhaps as part of a religious ritual to smooth their passage to an afterlife. The Bo people are known, from historical records, to have believed that coffins set high up were propitious, and the higher they were, the more propitious. But how did they get the coffins to such inaccessible places?

One idea is that they may have built earth ramps to allow the coffins to be lifted high, but that would have involved an immense amount of labour for each coffin, as the ramp would presumably be destroyed after each burial to keep the body safe. Another suggestion involves the building of timber scaffolds supported by stakes in the rocks, but no stake holes have ever been found that would support such a theory.

The idea that has attracted the most support is that the coffins were lowered on ropes from the cliff tops, and some signs that such ropes were used have recently been discovered, but that would not explain why some coffins are relatively close to the ground.

There is a similar mystery about the hanging coffins of the Guyue people on the cliffs of Dragon-Tiger mountain in Jiangxi. These include coffins big enough for ten bodies and they are hung in such inaccessible spots that some say they can only have been placed there with the aid of the immortals in heaven.

102. What is inside the tomb of China's first emperor?

China's first emperor, Qin Shi Huang, died on 10 September 210 BC and was buried in the most elaborate tomb complex ever known, a series of caverns the size of a city built in a hillside and guarded by an army of terracotta soldiers. So far, around 2,000 such soldiers have been uncovered, but there may be many more. Terracotta concubines are also thought likely to have been made to accompany the late emperor into the afterlife.

As for the central tomb, which is thought to contain a palace and the body of Qin Shi Huang, nobody has been inside for over 2,000 years and nobody is likely to in the near future. One problem is a reluctance of the Chinese government to disturb their first emperor, but there are also concerns about current excavation methods and the likelihood that these would damage the findings. When the terracotta soldiers were first exposed to air, their paint crumbled, and there is a natural fear that something similar would happen if the tomb were broken into.

There is also a little problem about mercury. According to ancient writing, the tomb is encircled with rivers of liquid mercury, which the ancient Chinese believed could bestow immortality. While he was alive, the emperor even took pills containing mercury, believing it would give him immortality. The resulting mercury poisoning is probably why he died at the age of thirty-nine. Soil samples from the area of the tomb have revealed very high levels of mercury contamination, which would make excavations very dangerous. So for the time being, the emperor may rest in peace.

103. How did the ancient Chinese get Neanderthal ears?

How do you recognize a Neanderthal? Well one way, until very recently, was to look in its ears. Neanderthal ears display an arrangement of the semicircular canals of their temporal labyrinth which is thought to have been a remnant from a primitive balance system. This arrangement was found in nearly all examinations of Neanderthal skulls and was thought to be unique to them.

In 2014, however, a re-examination of a 100,000-year-old skull that had been found in China thirty-five years earlier revealed the same arrangement. This came as a great surprise, as Neanderthals were thought to have lived only in Europe. The finding is thought to support the view that Neanderthals did not die out completely around 40,000 years ago, but interbred with other more modern human species. That would explain how a man in China acquired the gene responsible for Neanderthal ears.

See also EVOLUTION 183; INVENTIONS 255; SEX DIFFERENCES 411; USA 473

CHOCOLATE

104. Does chocolate consumption predict Nobel Prize winners?

In 2012 the *New England Journal of Medicine* published a paper showing a strong correlation between the number of Nobel Prizes a country has won and the amount of chocolate eaten per capita in that country. While accepting that correlation does not imply causation, Dr Franz Messerli, the author of the paper, said: 'since chocolate consumption has been documented to improve cognitive function, it seems most likely that in a dose-dependent way, chocolate intake provides the abundant fertile ground needed for the sprouting of Nobel laureates.' According to his calculation, a country's Nobel Prize score rises by one for each 0.4 kilogram rise in the average chocolate consumption rate per person per year.

Later research, however, raised some doubts about these conclusions. According to a paper in the *Journal of Nutrition* in 2013, the improvements in cognitive function mentioned above referred to benefits derived from cocoa flavanols, but national consumption rates of other flavanol-rich nutriments, such as tea and wine, do not show any correlation with Nobel Prize awards.

105. Is chocolate an aphrodisiac?

Belief in the aphrodisiac properties of chocolate date back to the days of the Mayans and Aztecs, with reports that the Aztec ruler Montezuma liked to drink fifty cups of chocolate elixir before visiting his harem. More recently, Casanova declared chocolate to be the world's second-best aphrodisiac, beaten only by champagne.

In the scientific age, chocolate's supposed aphrodisiac properties have been linked to its phenylethylamine (PEA) content, which is a chemical that has been shown not only to be present in the brains of people who are in love but also to release the same hormone as having sex. Chocolate has also been shown to produce natural opiates in the brain, which may have a general feel-good effect, while other chemicals in chocolate may have similar effects to marijuana in boosting dopamine production.

The only thing wrong with all this is that the levels of these chemicals in chocolate seem far too low to have any significant effect. Not only does the PEA from chocolate not remain long enough in our systems to have the desired effect, but according to the National Institute of Mental Health in the USA, an average person would have to eat 25 pounds of chocolate to perceive a marijuana-like effect.

See also SNAILS 438

CHRISTIANITY

106. Did Origen castrate himself?

One of the most prolific writers and theologians of the early Christian church was Origen, whose 6,000 works had a great influence on the development of Christianity itself. A profoundly devout man, he has been described as the first Christian theologian, but the question of whether he castrated himself has never been resolved.

According to the Roman historian Eusebius, who lived shortly after Origen, he so strongly believed in the doctrine of self-denial that he took the words of Matthew 19:12 literally:

For there are some eunuchs, which were so born from their mother's womb: and there are some eunuchs, which were made eunuchs of men: and there be eunuchs, which have made themselves eunuchs for the kingdom of heaven's sake.

Origen, Eusebius said, was one of the last group and that story was believed throughout the Middle Ages and until the nineteenth century. More recent historians, however, have suggested that the self-castration was malicious gossip by Origen's enemies, and that Origen himself had expressed strong views against a literal interpretation of Matthew's words given above.

See also ART 25; ASTRONOMY 30; BIBLE 52–3; JESUS CHRIST 259–63

CODES

107. What does the Shugborough inscription mean?

In the grounds of Shugborough Hall in Staffordshire, England, lies the Shepherd's Monument enclosed in a stone arch. The monument shows a reversed copy, in relief, of Poussin's painting *The Shepherds of Arcadia*, and below the carving are ten letters: D and M, placed low down and well separated, and above and between them, O U O S V A V V.

Charles Dickens and Charles Darwin are among those who were fascinated by the inscription and tried to work out what it might mean, but neither they, nor anyone else, has explained it. Theories include the initial letters of a new translation of various biblical phrases; a dedication of the monument to the late wife of the owner of the hall; a love message; a coded treasure map; and a coded anagrammatic sign-off by the stonemason.

In 2014 a spokesman for Shugborough Hall was quoted as saying: 'We get five or six people a week who believe they have solved the code so we are a bit wary of them now.'

108. What are the symbols on the Phaistos Disc?

The Phaistos Disc is a piece of clay found in 1908 on the site of the Minoan palace of Phaistos on Crete. It is thought to date back to around 1700 BC. Made of fired clay, it is a disc about fifteen centimetres in diameter with a spiral of symbols on both sides. The hieroglyphic symbols seem to have been made by pressing seals into the soft clay. There are 242 such symbols featuring forty-five different signs.

The number and distribution of the signs is tantalizing: there are enough of them to offer hope to someone trying to break their code, but not enough to give a realistic prospect of success when the context of their message is not known. The fact that different occurrences of the same sign are identical has led to the disc being described as one of the earliest known examples of movable type printing. Some scholars, however, think the whole thing is a hoax.

109. What is the secret of the Beale Ciphers?

In 1885 a pamphlet was published containing three coded texts said to relate to treasure buried by a man named Thomas J. Beale around 1820. The texts were alleged to have been found in a box given by Beale to a local innkeeper, who opened the box twenty-three years later; then, many years later still, passed it on to a friend before he died. In the meantime, Beale had disappeared, leaving the unnamed friend with the three coded messages. The first was said to give details of where the treasure was buried; the second contained a description of the treasure itself; the third lists the names of the owners of the treasure and their next of kin.

The friend is said to have spent the next twenty years trying to decode the texts, but managing to do so only in the case of the second, which described a treasure of over 35,000 troy ounces of gold, worth around $65 million at today's prices. There was also around $1 million worth of silver and various jewels. The code used to encrypt the second message, however, did not work for the first or the third.

A computer analysis of the coded messages in the late 1960s convinced one specialist that they were probably legitimate coded versions of an intelligible text, though later cryptographers have given their opinions that they are unlikely to be encoded versions of anything in English. Some of the language in the decoded second message has also been thought unlikely to date back to the 1820s as it is supposed to. Attempts to confirm the existence of Thomas J. Beale have not been successful.

There is, however, a Cheyenne legend dating back to around 1820 relating to gold and silver being taken from the west and buried in mountains in the east, which may help explain why so many treasure-hunters have been arrested for trespassing in Bedford County, Virginia, where some say Beale buried his treasure.

COFFEE

110. Can you tell whether coffee is roasted just by the sounds of its cracking?

The art of perfect coffee-roasting is said to be a skill acquired by using all five of one's senses. The colour of the bean, its smell, its taste, the cracking sound it makes during the roasting and its texture all provide information to the roaster. But can a perfect roast be achieved on the basis of sound alone?

That was the question addressed by Preston S. Wilson in his paper 'Coffee roasting acoustics' in 2014. After recording and analysing the sounds emitted by coffee beans during the roasting process, he identified three factors that might lead to an automated roasting process based on sound alone. The 'first crack' sounds emitted near the end of roasting are louder than 'second crack' sounds emitted later. First crack also emits more low-frequency energy than second crack. Thirdly, 'the rate of cracks appearing in the second crack chorus is higher than the rate in the first crack chorus'. All of these factors may be measured independently of other roasting noises.

Whether the results correlate with the excellence of the roast, however, has not been determined. Wilson also suggests that: 'Future work should include analysis of all the various types of green coffee beans of interest and different roasting processes and machines.'

See also DISEASE 143

COMETS

111. Why did comet P/2013 P5 have six comet-like tails?

On 27 August 2013 astronomers working in Hawaii announced the discovery of a puzzling body in the asteroid belt. Asteroids usually appear as a point of light, but this one was strangely fuzzy, so they used the Hubble Space Telescope to take a closer look. When the Hubble image arrived on 10 September, they became even more puzzled. Amazingly, it had six comet-like tails, and when Hubble looked again on 23 September, its appearance had changed even more, looking as though it had completely swung around.

Because of the tails, P/2013 P5 was classified as a comet, despite the fact that it was thought to be an asteroid, which is mainly rock, rather than a comet, which is mainly ice. Its tails are thought to consist of dust from its surface smudged out behind it by the pressure of solar radiation, with the multiple tails caused by different ejections of dust. It is also possible that the whole body is breaking up, possibly as a result of an increase in its rotational speed. But nothing like a six-tailed comet/asteroid has ever been seen before, so until further evidence of its progress is available, its tails remain a mystery.

112. Why is comet 67P/Churyumov–Gerasimenko singing?

When the Rosetta spacecraft succeeded in sending its robotic lander Philae down to the surface of comet 67P/Churyumov-Gerasimenko in November 2014, it made a strange discovery: the comet was singing. The 'song' takes the form of oscillations in the magnetic field around the comet, emitted at 40–50 millihertz. The frequencies would need to be multiplied by about 10,000 to be audible to the human ear, but they have been clearly identified by monitoring equipment on Rosetta.

The oscillations are thought to be caused by ionization of particles released by the comet, but such a thing has never been detected before and the physical process behind it is completely unknown.

113. What is the origin of the long-period comets?

Around 4.6 billion years ago, the Solar System is thought to have begun to form with the collapse of a vast molecular cloud. Most of this collapsing mass formed the Sun, with the planets forming from much of the leftovers. This still left a great deal of 'crumbs' (comparatively speaking) which are now thought to account for the comets.

These are much smaller bodies than the planets, with very eccentric orbits round the Sun, and they come in two types: short-period and long-period. The short-period comets take less than 200 Earth years to orbit the Sun and originate in the Kuiper Belt, which is a disc-shaped region of space, past the orbit of Neptune and about 30–100 astronomical units (AU) from the Sun. An AU is defined as the average distance between the Earth and the Sun, so 30–100 AU is a huge distance. The Kuiper Belt is named after the Dutch-American astronomer Gerard Kuiper, who predicted its existence in 1951, though his prediction was not confirmed until 1992. There are thought to be around 70,000 small, icy bodies in the Kuiper Belt, some of which become comets when they are flung by the gravitational force of other stars towards the inner Solar System.

The long-period comets are far more mysterious. These are thought to have orbital periods of between 200 and several million years, and they do not come from a reasonably flat disc like the Kuiper Belt, but have been seen to enter our skies from all directions. In 1950 calculations by the Dutch astronomer Jan H. Oort led to his prediction that these comets originated in a spherical cloud of up to a trillion rocks on the very fringe of the Solar System, surrounding the rest of it at a distance of perhaps 100,000 AU from the Sun, which is about half the distance to the nearest star.

The only problem with this is that no direct confirmation or observation of the Oort Cloud has ever been made. Evidence for its existence is based entirely on calculations of the motion of comets. So the generally held theory on the origin of long-period comets is still unconfirmed.

See also ASTRONOMY 30; COSMOLOGY 121; GEOLOGY 212; NAMES 336; SOLAR SYSTEM 442

COMPUTERS

114. Will computers ever be able to understand natural human speech?

Science-fiction films for decades have featured scenes in which a human carries on a conversation with a robot or the ship's computer. Progress on voice synthesizers and voice-recognition programs have made such a scenario appear ever more plausible, and rather stilted versions of such conversations have become possible, but there are huge problems to overcome before computers can be said to understand natural language.

The basic problem is that computers rely on logic and humans don't. Language, as we use it, is not just an application of a dictionary and the rules of grammar. Language is full of ambiguity and illogicalities such that effective linguistic communication depends on the shared culture of the speaker and listener. Asking a human 'Do you have the time?' may invite the answer 'Half past four', but a computer would be more likely to tell you that it had some time at its disposal and ask how much you needed. Even if you asked, more precisely, 'Can you tell me the time?', it would probably just say 'Yes'.

Of course, it is easy enough to program a machine to deal with specific questions such as these, but language is full of such imprecise sayings.

Understanding what someone really means demands a knowledge of the real world that is wide enough to cut through the imprecision of language. Giving a computer such knowledge seems unlikely to be achieved in the foreseeable future.

115. Will machine intelligence ever be impossible for humans to comprehend?

Computers can now play chess better than almost all humans, and it seems inevitable that 'almost all' will soon become 'all'. They can make more accurate predictions of the weather and are well on the way to making more reliable medical diagnoses. All of these achievements, however, are due to human programming combined with phenomenal calculating speed. We understand what they are doing because we told them how to do it, but their speed and accuracy in carrying out our instructions have led to better results than we can hope for on our own.

What would happen, though, if computers could write their own programs? There seems no inherent reason why we could not program a computer to increase its own efficiency by analysing its own program and improving it. Perhaps it could then move on to producing the design specifications for a better computer. Then the improved computer could produce an even better one, leading eventually to a self-programming machine whose program is beyond human understanding.

Whether a machine can move outside its own operating system to design a better one, however, is a highly speculative question which may depend on the next one.

116. Are there any limits to machine intelligence?

Since the 1950s scientists and science-fiction writers have written about the 'technological singularity' that could lead to the sort of machine-dominated world depicted in films such as the Terminator and Matrix series. Computers in such a world will have moved so far beyond human intelligence that they can not only perform at a level that we can no longer comprehend, but make their own decisions about what they do and therefore pose a threat to the human race.

In 2014 Stephen Hawking wrote about the prospect of developing true artificial intelligence (AI) to the extent that it not only surpassed human intelligence but became responsible for its own design: 'Success in creating AI would be the biggest event in human history. Unfortunately, it might also be the last, unless we learn how to avoid the risks.'

Quite what those risks might be, however, depends on the answer to the above question.

See also INTELLIGENCE 252; MILKY WAY 315–16; SCIENCE 403; SEX DIFFERENCES 411; SHAKESPEARE 415

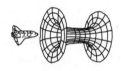

COSMOLOGY

117. Where do cosmic rays come from?

Every second billions of high-energy tiny particles moving at almost the speed of light bombard the Earth's atmosphere. These are called cosmic rays, though they are not rays at all but mostly the protons from hydrogen or helium atoms. Unlike the rest of the energy we receive from space, however, they do not come from the Sun. If they did, their concentration would presumably vary throughout the day as light and heat from the Sun do, but the energy from cosmic rays hitting the Earth seems constant throughout time and place.

Most cosmic rays are thought to come from outside our galaxy and may be the result of the massive explosions of supernovas. Some cosmic ray bursts have been linked to specific supernovas, but it is by no means clear that they all have such origins. The main problem is that the electrical charges of the particles make them susceptible to having their direction altered as they travel through space, and this makes it impossible to work out where they came from.

118. Why have we found so few dwarf galaxies?

By most standards dwarf galaxies are pretty huge. They include several billion stars and may be hundreds or even thousands of light years across, but compared with the 200–400 billion stars in the 100,000 light years of the Milky Way, they are real dwarfs – and the Milky Way isn't even a large galaxy. So far, just under thirty dwarf galaxies have been found in orbit around the Milky Way, but according to some estimates, there ought to be far more.

Galaxies in general are thought to have been formed in the early universe mostly by the interaction between gas clouds and dark matter. The trouble is that computer simulations of this theoretical galaxy formation predict around 500 dwarf galaxies forming around the Milky Way. One possibility is that the predicted dwarf galaxies are all there, but we cannot see them as they contain so much dark matter. Another theory is that larger galaxies have been eating up smaller ones in a way that we don't understand.

119. What is the origin of cosmic magnetic fields?

Throughout the known universe, magnetic fields are everywhere. Planets, stars, galaxies and the gas between stars all have a very small magnetic field. The generation of such fields requires huge amounts of electrically charged material or the motion of such masses of material, but whether the formation of galaxies was responsible for the creation of these fields or the magnetic fields played a vital part in the formation of the galaxies is unclear.

In 2015 it was shown that an instability in electromagnetic plasmas can create such a magnetic field, which ties in with the idea of the universe consisting mainly of plasma after its massive expansion following the Big Bang. That seems the best theory yet of how cosmic magnetic fields were formed.

120. What caused the blast of energy that hit the Earth in AD 770?

A good deal of evidence from widely spaced places on the globe points to the Earth's having been hit by a massive blast of radiation around AD 770. In Japan, examination of the carbon-14 in tree rings formed between 774 and 775 shows a 1.2 per cent increase over that year compared with the usual figure of 0.05 per cent. Such an increase, Japanese researchers say, can only have been caused by extremely high-energy cosmic rays hitting the Earth. Similar rises in carbon-14 have been found in trees in both America and Europe, while the cosmic ray theory is also supported by examination of Antarctic ice cores from 775. What might have caused this blast, however, is a matter of great dispute.

One theory suggests that it was a very energetic solar flare, but if that was the case, it would have been highly visible on Earth, yet there is no historical record of such a thing being observed. Another suggestion is that it was a supernova, but that would have left remnants that would be visible today, and no such remnants have been found.

The latest idea is a short gamma-ray burst caused by the collision of two neutron stars several thousand light years away. Such gamma-ray bursts, however, are thought to be very rare. They have been detected in other galaxies, but too little is known about them (see the next question) to test the theory that one may have hit the Earth in AD 775.

121. What causes gamma-ray bursts?

Gamma rays are a form of electromagnetic radiation of extremely high energy. They were first detected in 1900 and massively powerful gamma-ray bursts (GRBs) were first discovered in space in 1967 by US satellites that had been designed to detect secret tests of nuclear weapons. It has been estimated that a typical GRB releases as much energy in a few seconds as our Sun will in its 10-billion-year lifetime. Bursts can last from a few milliseconds to several minutes, and they are the brightest electromagnetic events in the known universe. All known GRBs have occurred outside our galaxy, sometimes billions of light years away. They are thought to consist of a narrow beam of intense radiation released during the collapse of a star or a cosmic collision.

It has been suggested that long-burst GRBs are released during a supernova when a star of high mass collapses to form a neutron star or a black hole, while short-burst GRBs may be the result of a collision or merger of binary neutron stars. Collisions between comets and neutron stars have also been suggested as a possible cause. Unfortunately for science, GRBs are very rare, with only a few taking place in any galaxy over a million-year period, so we really have too little evidence to determine their causes. This may be fortunate for us, as it has been estimated that a GRB pointing directly at Earth could result in a mass extinction of all life on our planet.

122. Do gravitational waves exist?

In 1916 Einstein predicted the existence of gravitational waves as a consequence of his theory of general relativity. He saw them as ripples in the space–time continuum transporting energy as gravitational radiation. In the century since then, however, neither gravitational radiation nor gravitational waves have been directly observed, though there is a good deal of indirect evidence for them.

One of the problems is that the ripples of gravitational waves, if they exist, are predicted to be very small, but in 2014 astronomers in the USA announced that they had identified a 'direct image of gravitational waves across the primordial sky'. Within months, however, doubts began to be expressed about this claim to have detected gravitational ripples caused by the Big Bang.

Further papers towards the end of 2014 and at the beginning of 2015 raised further doubts, so it seems fair to say that we still do not know whether Einstein's gravitational waves exist.

123. Is Roger Penrose's cosmic censorship hypothesis correct?

What happened before the Big Bang? What goes on inside a black hole? Questions such as these, and even whether it makes sense to ask such questions, raise almost philosophical problems for physicists. The problem behind them is connected with the idea of a singularity, where mathematics breaks down and the laws of physics no longer hold.

Tracing the universe back to its start or predicting the future of a huge collapsing star both run into the problem of a huge mass occupying an ever-decreasing volume. The density keeps increasing to a point when we find ourselves dividing by zero, which is mathematically impossible. In the case of the Big Bang, the problem is neatly side-stepped by saying that it marked the beginning of time itself, so asking what happened 'before' makes no sense. In the case of black holes, the question is again sometimes side-stepped by saying that information cannot ever escape from a black hole, so has effectively ceased to exist (→ BLACK HOLES 71).

Is it possible, however, for singularities to exist which do let us see what is going on? In 1969 the theoretical physicist Roger Penrose proposed some sort of cosmic censorship hypothesis – 'some sort of' because even Penrose did not seek to define precisely what he meant by the term. His idea was that there may be some sort of meta-law of physics guaranteeing that any singularity must be accompanied by an 'event horizon', like the outer reaches of a black hole, beyond which nothing can be known. Singularities would then become no-go areas for the usual laws of physics and the problems associated with them would be defined out of existence.

It's a nice idea, but nearly fifty years after Penrose raised the question, his cosmic censorship hypothesis has not only been neither proved nor disproved, but there is not even agreement on how it should be formulated.

124. When did cosmic acceleration begin?

Until comparatively recently, we had a nice simple picture of the universe: it had all started with a massive explosion of energy at the Big Bang, which flung everything outwards creating its own space and thus giving an expanding universe. The gravitational attraction of everything in the universe, however, would be bound to slow down that process, eventually bringing things closer together either to a steady state or to a 'Big Crunch', when everything would go back to the singularity whence it came.

In the 1990s, however, measurements of the motion of distant galaxies revealed that the rate of expansion of the universe was not decreasing but speeding up. We have already encountered the concept of dark matter – intangible and invisible, yet exerting gravitational pull by its mass; to this was now added dark energy, the name given to the all-pervading force that seemed to be behind the acceleration of the universe.

But if dark energy is pushing everything apart with more force than gravity can keep it together, how long has this been going on? Dark energy, or whatever is causing the unexpected acceleration, is seen as a property of space itself, so its density throughout space is thought to be constant. The density of matter, however, has been decreasing as it gets further spread out. Presumably, at some stage in the expansion of the universe, the total inward gravitational pull was greater than the outward force of dark matter, and only the outward energy of the Big Bang was stopping a Big Crunch. It was also the inward gravitational pull that allowed matter to be drawn together and stars and galaxies to form.

The question of when the effect of dark energy became greater than the effect of gravity may hold the key to our understanding of how the early universe formed and how it will eventually end.

125. Is there life on Gliese 581g?

In 2010 the discovery was announced of a planet orbiting the red dwarf star Gliese 581. The planet's distance from its star was only about one seventh of the distance between Earth and the Sun, but Gliese 581 is much weaker than the Sun. As a result calculations showed that Gliese 581g (as the planet was named) was in the range within which life and habitability might be possible.

With other information about Gliese 581 and its planets, such as their atmosphere and geology, also not ruling out the possibility of life, Gliese 581g was hailed as the first potentially habitable extra-solar planet to have been found. Since it is twenty light years away, and any probe launched from Earth would take about half a million years or more to reach it, it is unlikely that we will have an answer soon.

There is also a small further problem that later observations have cast doubt on whether Gliese 581g exists at all.

126. Can wormholes exist?

Wormholes are one of Albert Einstein's greatest contributions to the world of science fiction. When a sci-fi film-maker wants his starship commander to travel unimaginable distances at speeds faster than light, or flit between different time periods, or even travel to another universe, the solution is simple: take a short-cut through a wormhole. But are such things conceivable?

The idea of wormholes, which were given that name by the US physicist John Wheeler in 1957, stemmed from Einstein's equations of general relativity. These equations were found to have mathematically valid solutions that would permit short-cuts across the space–time continuum. No evidence of the existence of wormholes has ever been found, but that has not stopped some notable physicists from entertaining the concept. Even Stephen Hawking has suggested that travel through wormholes might not be impossible.

One mathematically justified idea is that wormholes might lead through black holes into parallel universes. Trying to travel through them, however, would presumably be fatal. Another idea for traversable wormholes involves their being stabilized by something called 'exotic matter' which has negative energy. Again, such exotic matter has not been found, but is not ruled out by the laws of physics. A third idea is the 'quantum foam' hypothesis, which is based on subatomic particles that formed the fabric of the universe at the moment of the Big Bang. These could have created tiny wormholes which, with the expansion of the universe, could now be big enough to travel through.

So the laws of physics do not absolutely rule out the existence of wormholes, but there is absolutely no reason to rule them in either.

See also ASTRONOMY 27–30; MILKY WAY 315–17; OUTER SPACE 350; SOLAR SYSTEM 441–4

COSTA RICA

127. What were the Costa Rican spheres for?

When the jungles of Costa Rica were being cleared in the 1930s to make room for banana plantations, workmen discovered a large number of stone spheres. Some of the stones were destroyed by the workers who thought they might contain gold, but around 300 remain, varying in size from a few centimetres to over two metres in diameter. The largest of them weigh up to two tons.

Known locally as 'Las Bolas', the stones are thought to have been made by the Precolumbian Diquis culture, which became extinct around 1530. The oldest of the stones may date back to AD 600. How the Diquis made them and what their function was supposed to be is completely unknown.

See also SLOTHS 432

CRICKETS

128. Is the courtship of crickets affected by traffic noise?

Many animals use mating calls to attract partners and a number of studies have shown that traffic noise and other human-generated sounds can disrupt this process. In 2014 a paper was published on research conducted to see if such an effect occurred in tree crickets in the USA.

After recording some road noise, the researchers played it back to see what effect it had on the production of sound by male crickets and the reception of the sound by females. Since acoustic signals by males are of low amplitude and easily masked by traffic noise, the playbacks were expected to lead to changes in their behaviour.

Surprisingly, they found that male tree crickets did not change the characteristics of their signals when the traffic noise was played, though they called less frequently. The behaviour of female crickets in response to the calls was not changed at all. The researchers suggest that: 'Because tree crickets often communicate in environments with many species of calling insects, tree crickets may be adapted to tolerate novel sources of acoustic interference.' In view of the unexpected result, however, it is clear that more research is needed.

CRIME

129. Did Frank Morris and his companions escape from Alcatraz in 1962?

The 1979 film *Escape From Alcatraz*, starring Clint Eastwood, was based on a genuine incident that happened in 1962. Alcatraz prison in San Francisco Bay was, at the time, widely seen as escape-proof. Almost all who had tried to escape were shot by guards or recaptured quickly. Only one is known to have reached the mainland and he was arrested almost as soon as he reached San Francisco.

On the night of 11 June 1962, however, a well-planned escape attempt was made by three men, Frank Morris and the brothers John and Clarence Anglin. After leaving dummy heads made of soap, toilet paper and hair in their beds to fool the guards, they crawled through holes dug with spoons in their cell walls, reached the roof through ventilation shafts, scaled a fence, made a raft out of raincoats and paddled away.

There is no evidence that they survived the strong currents to reach land and no confirmation that any of them were seen again. The FBI closed the case in 1979 after a seventeen-year investigation, concluding that the prisoners had drowned. But no bodies were ever found.

See also DEATH 131; GOLD 219; NAZIS 339; WORDS 497

CROCODILES

130. Does fruit benefit from being eaten by crocodiles?

Research published in 2013 produced two surprising revelations: first, that crocodiles eat fruit; and second, that this might be good for the fruit.

Until recently, crocodiles were assumed to be solely carnivorous and unable to digest vegetable proteins, but out of eighteen species of crocodile under observation, thirteen had been seen eating fruit. The interesting question of whether this might also benefit the fruit hinged on whether being eaten by crocodiles was an effective mode of seed dispersal.

Ingested seeds were often found to be retained in the crocodiles' stomachs for lengthy periods, regurgitated, or passed through the digestive tract and excreted. Despite not knowing what effect these processes had on the viability or the ultimate fate of the seeds, the researchers concluded that it was likely that crocodiles are effective agents of seed dispersal.

See also AVOCADOS 37; BIRDS 64; TYRANNOSAURUSES 461

DEATH

131. Does the death penalty have a deterrent effect?

This question has been the subject of dozens, perhaps hundreds, of studies by criminologists and statisticians, but huge variance in their conclusions ensures that the debate continues.

One argument often advocated by those claiming that there is no deterrent effect is the fact that US states with the death penalty have significantly higher murder rates than those without. Critics, however, would argue that the high murder rates are precisely why those states have chosen to keep the death penalty. Without it there would, they claim, be even more murders.

Some studies have even identified – or so they claim – precisely how many murders each execution prevents. The fact that their answers range from three to forty-two, however, suggests that they are at best based on imprecise methods.

In the UK the rates for unlawful killings have more than doubled since abolition of capital punishment in 1964, but whether this may be attributed even in part to that abolition is debatable, as the nature of society in general and crime in particular has changed dramatically over that period. Drug-related gun crime, for example, has greatly increased, as have stabbings and virtually motiveless killings in street fights. Domestic murders have decreased, possibly because divorce has become so much easier.

Statistics, it seems, will never answer this question, but without reliable information on the influence of the death penalty on the intentions of potential murderers, that is the only way we have of trying to find an answer.

132. Did Sigurd Eysteinsson really die after being bitten by a severed head?

Sigurd Eysteinsson, also known as Sigurd the Mighty, was the second Viking Lord of Orkney and a leader in the ninth-century Viking conquest of northern Scotland. According to the Orkneyinga saga, written by an unknown Icelandic author around 1230, the cause of his death was a bite from a dead man's head.

The saga recounts how Sigurd challenged a native ruler, Mael Brigte the Bucktoothed, to a battle with forces of forty men on each side. Sigurd treacherously brought eighty men, and after winning the battle beheaded Mael Brigte and strapped the head to his saddle to take it back as a trophy. On the ride back, however, his leg was scratched by Mael Brigte's buck-tooth. The wound became infected and killed him.

It's a great story and seems to have been generally accepted as true, but the Norse sagas are such a mix of historic truth, legend and romanticism that we shall probably never know.

133. Was King Harold shot in the eye with an arrow at the Battle of Hastings?

As everyone knows from the Bayeux Tapestry (which isn't a tapestry anyway, but an embroidery), King Harold II of England died at the Battle of Hastings in 1066 from an arrow shot into his eye. Or did he? Recently, increasing doubts have been expressed about this long-held view.

First, there is the matter of other accounts of Harold's death, the earliest of which was written long before the tapestry appeared. In the *Gesta Normannorum Ducum* ('Deeds of the Norman Kings') by William of Jumièges, which was written around 1070, Harold is said to have fallen 'covered with deadly wounds', but there is no mention of an arrow in his eye.

Second, there is evidence from the tapestry itself on which investigations have raised all sorts of questions concerning the horseman with an arrow in his eye. The words 'HAROLD REX INTERFECTUS EST' ('King Harold is killed') are inscribed above it, but they may refer to another character in the picture, particularly the soldier falling to the ground next to an axe. Also, it has been suggested that the 'arrow' was in fact a mistake in restoration of the embroidery, having originally been no more than a dotted line of stitch marks.

Towards the end of 2014, an even more surprising account was found in a twelfth-century document in the British Museum which claimed that Harold survived the battle and died quietly of old age some forty years later after living out his life in obscurity.

134. How did King Edward II die?

After a massively contentious and unsuccessful twenty-year reign, Edward II was forced to abdicate in 1327 by forces led by his wife, Isabella of France, whom he had married when she was twelve, and her lover Roger Mortimer. The king was imprisoned first at Kenilworth Castle, then moved to Berkeley Castle in Gloucestershire. On 23 September his son was informed that his father had died and he took the throne as Edward III. Over the next fifteen years very different accounts of how he died emerged.

Until 1330 such stories followed the official account that the king had died of natural causes, but after that date the suggestion that he had been murdered became common. Around 1340 accounts began to appear that the mode of murder had been by a piece of metal pushed up his anus through a horn to destroy his entrails while leaving no mark on the outside of his body. Early such accounts said the metal was a rod of copper, but this soon changed into a red-hot iron poker. Such a suggestion may have been made to draw attention to the king's long-term homosexual relationship with Piers Gaveston.

Most modern historians discount the red-hot iron story as a myth, but accept that he was murdered in September 1327. Recently, however, increasing attention has been given to evidence purporting to show that Edward II was still alive in 1330. There had certainly been attempts made to rescue him from his imprisonments, and it could be argued that if such a rescue had succeeded, it might have been in the interests of both his supporters and his enemies to pretend he was dead.

135. What happened to Antoine de Saint-Exupéry?

Antoine Marie Jean-Baptiste Roger, comte de Saint-Exupéry (1900–44) was an aviator, writer, poet and French aristocrat best known for his fantasy *The Little Prince*, which has been translated into 250 languages and is said by some to have been outsold, as a work of fiction, only by Tolkien's *Lord of the Rings*.

At the outbreak of the Second World War, Saint-Exupéry was flying planes on airmail routes in Europe and signed up for the French Air Force. When France capitulated to Germany, he travelled to the USA on a mission to persuade the Americans to join the war against the Nazis. During that period he wrote *The Little Prince*, but returned to join the Free French Air Force in North Africa, despite officially being well over the age limit for pilots.

Flying from Corsica on a reconnaissance mission in July 1944, he disappeared over the Mediterranean, vanishing without trace. In September 1998 an identity bracelet with the names of Saint-Exupéry, his wife and his publisher was found near Riou island, south of Marseilles. That, however, was a long way from his flight path and its authenticity was therefore disputed.

In May 2000 a diver found remains from a Lockheed P-38 Lightning spread over a large area again south of Marseilles. The remains were later confirmed to have come from the plane Saint-Exupéry was flying. None of the remnants bore any signs indicating that the plane had been shot down. Why it crashed and how it came to be found so far from its flight path remain open questions.

See also GUILLOTINES 224; SHEEP 417; SOCRATES 440

DINOSAURS

136. Why did some dinosaurs have such extravagant horns or crests on their heads?

Many large dinosaurs such as *Triceratops* had huge horns, crests or neck frills, but what was the function of these impressive structures? There have been many suggestions:

- They may have served to attract mates.
- They may have helped individuals to identify themselves to members of their own species.
- They may have served as weapons when fighting rivals.
- They may have acted as resonance chambers to increase the power of the creature's roar.
- They may have served a protective function.
- They may have had a thermostatic function to help control the creature's body temperature.
  We just don't know.

137. How did dinosaurs mate?

How did tyrannosauruses and other large dinosaurs have sex? In 2012 and 2013 that question was much discussed by palaeontologists, resulting in several conflicting theories. Some years earlier, English researcher Dr Beverly Halstead had said: 'All dinosaurs used the same basic position to mate. Mounting from the rear, he put his forelimbs on her shoulders, lifting one hind limb across her back and twisting his tail under hers.' Minnesota academic Kristi Curry Rogers was still of a similar opinion. Pointing out that a tyrannosaurus penis is estimated to have been almost four metres long, she said: 'The most likely position to have intercourse is for the male behind the female, and on top of her, and from behind. Any other position is unfathomable.'

Brian Switek, author of *My Beloved Brontosaurus*, pointed out, however, that females could not raise their tails because the bones at the top were fused. There was also the problem of lethal spikes on dinosaurs' backs which could be a fatal hazard. A computer reconstruction in Berlin led to the conclusion that a male *Kentrosaurus* mounting from behind would face castration.

Another point of view was put forward by US biologist Stuart Landry Jr in 1994. In his opinion, dinosaurs were too heavy to make love on land and would have fallen over if they tried. He suggested that they must have had sex in mud-holes or bodies of water.

Professor Switek identified one vital reason why there is such a mystery surrounding the question of dinosaur sex: 'Soft tissues are seldom preserved during fossilisation, so we have never found a fossilised phallus, but doing so would solve many mysteries.'

138. How fast did dinosaurs move?

There are three basic ways of trying to work out how fast dinosaurs moved, but none of them really works:

(i) *Morphological* This involves looking at the shape of skeletons of modern animals and the length of their limbs and any other bodily factors, such as stance and the angles at which the limbs attach to the torso, that we think may affect their speed of movement. Then we correlate these factors with the animals' known top speeds and use the results to predict the top speeds of animals the size of dinosaurs. The trouble with this method is that we have no way of knowing whether the results obtained on living animals would scale up to something the size of the large dinosaurs. We also do not know whether speed would have been as important in the evolution of dinosaurs as it is for present-day mammals.

(ii) *Biomechanical* This is pure engineering. If we knew the muscular structure of dinosaurs, we could estimate the power they could generate and a knowledge of their weight would then enable us to work out how fast they could travel. Getting a reliable estimate of the musculature of a 65-million-year-old fossil, however, is not easy.

(iii) *Footprints* By looking at the footprints left by dinosaurs and measuring how far apart they are, we can see what their stride length was, and comparing their stride length with the length of their legs would enable us to estimate the speed they were travelling at. This sounds the most reliable method of all – as long as we know that the fossil whose legs we are measuring was the same animal that left the footprints. Unfortunately, matching dinosaur footprints to dinosaur skeletons has never been possible.

The only thing we can say with a fair chance of being right is that the tyrannosaurus in the film *Jurassic Park* was running too fast.

See also BIRDS 64; NOSES 342; PANGOLINS 354; TYRANNOSAURUSES 459–61

DISEASE

139. Did seals bring tuberculosis to the Americas?

An intriguing theory was advanced in 2014 that seals had been responsible for transmitting tuberculosis (TB) to the Americas. Until then, the similarity between strains of TB from America and Europe had led to the conclusion that it had been contact with Europeans that brought it to America, but the new theory was based on palaeoanthropological detective work.

The technique involved the examination of all known strains of TB, seeing how much they differ from each other and estimating how long it would have taken for such differences to evolve. The results suggested that TB began in Africa around 70,000 years ago and that the modern

European variant is no more than 6,000 years old. Traces of TB have, however, been found in 1,000-year-old Peruvian mummies.

Putting these dates together reveals that TB reached America well before Columbus, but long after the land bridge between Asia and America had disappeared. It must therefore have arrived by sea, and according to the paper in *Nature*, it probably came from Africa to South America and the prime suspect is seals.

140. Why does Down syndrome happen?

Most people are born with forty-six chromosomes, twenty-three from the mother and twenty-three from the father. Babies with Down syndrome, however, have an extra copy of one of these chromosomes, chromosome 21. Usually this results in the baby having three copies of chromosome 21 instead of the usual two in every cell of the body, though far more rarely the extra chromosome may only be in some cells, or even be 'translocated' to a different chromosome and not appear as an extra chromosome 21 at all.

Only this last form, translocational Down syndrome, can be inherited. In all other cases, which is around 98 per cent, the extra chromosome is seen as a random event during cell division, early in the development of the foetus. We do not know what triggers such an event and we do not know what the connection is between the extra chromosome and the wide range of features, both physical and mental, that are commonly associated with Down syndrome.

141. What caused the Dancing Plague of 1518?

In July 1518 a dancing mania affected the people of Strasbourg in the Alsace. It began when a woman, Frau Troffea, began to dance fervently in the street, continuing to do so for between four and six days. Within a week thirty-four others had joined her, and within a month there were reported to be around 400 dancers, some of whom died from heart attacks, strokes or exhaustion.

Bizarrely, local physicians decided that the Dancing Plague was a 'natural disease' caused by hot blood and could be best treated by encouraging the dancers to continue dancing. Two guildhalls, a grain market and a specially constructed stage were set aside for that purpose, and musicians were paid to accompany them.

The cause of the dancing mania has never been explained.

142. What is the cause of Tourette's syndrome?

There is a group of specialized cells deep inside the brain called the basal ganglia, which are known to help regulate movement. They are also thought to play a part in decision-making and motivation, so when a person has a sudden urge to perform an action that the conscious mind neither wants nor can explain, as happens in Tourette's syndrome, the basal ganglia are thought to have something to do with it. The result is a verbal or physical tic, beyond the control of the sufferer, sometimes consisting of the repeated utterance of an irrelevant or rude word. But that's about as much as anyone knows.

The structure of the basal ganglia in Tourette sufferers has been seen to differ from normal, but whether that is the cause of Tourette's or a result of it is unknown. Studies on twins have shown that genetics may play a part, but no specific Tourette's gene has yet been identified.

143. To what extent can Alzheimer's disease be staved off?

'Three cups of coffee a day could stave off Alzheimer's disease', reported the *Daily Telegraph* in 2012.

'Meditation can help ward off Alzheimer's disease', said the *Daily Express*.

'Viagra could be used to stave off dementia', the *Daily Mail* reported.

'Nicotine patches may help fight Alzheimer's', insisted the *Daily Mirror*.

Other recent reports from sources ranging from reputable scientific journals to the popular press have put their anti-Alzheimer's money on fish and vegetables, red grapes, knowing a second language, or nuts, seeds and olive oil.

Much of the research leading to the above claims, however, has been studies on mice or fruit flies. Whether any of the above reduce a human being's chances of developing Alzheimer's disease, and if so, by how much, is a topic which – as they are so fond of saying – requires further research.

144. What is the function of prions?

We have already discussed the mystery of how prions reproduce (→ 61), but their function is also a puzzle. Prions are types of protein that have been found to be the cause of some devastating diseases in animals and humans alike. Scrapie in sheep, bovine spongiform encephalopathy (BSE, or 'mad cow disease') in cattle, and Creutzfeld–Jakob Disease (CJD) in humans have all been shown to be caused by prions. So was the disease called 'kuru', which was spread by cannibalism in New Guinea.

Prions have been found in the brains of all mammals that have been studied. Normally they present no problems, but when they go wrong, they can be highly infectious in a unique way. Like all proteins, prions are formed of strings of amino acids folded into a three-dimensional form. Rogue prions are misfolded, and despite not having the DNA or RNA usually essential for anything to reproduce, they have the capacity to hijack other proteins and cause them to misfold. The mechanics of how this happens is not understood, but it leads to fatal results when prions start attacking the neurons in their host's brain, which leads to the death of cells and the release of more prions.

The fact that all mammals have prions suggests that they must have evolved for a purpose other than to take over our brains and kill us, but what that purpose is has yet to be determined. Studies on mice have suggested that prions may have a role in helping neurons communicate. They may even have a role in delaying mental degeneration, but what that role is and how they perform it is unknown.

145. How many people are harbouring dormant CJD?

When an epidemic of BSE, or mad cow disease, hit Britain in the early 1990s and was linked to several cases of CJD in humans, research on prion diseases increased dramatically. Cattle had been fed on foodstuffs obtained by rendering sheep that had suffered from scrapie. It was known that scrapie could not be transmitted directly from sheep to humans, which led to the assumption that it could not be transmitted from sheep to humans via cows. The new version, vCJD, proved that assumption to be tragically incorrect.

Prion diseases are known to incubate in the brains of both animals and people for long periods. In 2006 a study was published based on cases in New Guinea of kuru, a prion disease thought to have been caused by the cannibalistic practice of eating human brains. That practice died out several decades ago, but cases of kuru continued to be reported. The conclusion was that its incubation period could be as long as forty years. Since incubation periods tend to be longer in diseases spread across species, it has been suggested that vCJD may lie dormant for fifty years before symptoms appear.

One report in 2006 suggested that 'millions' could be affected in the UK alone. The first case of vCJD was notified in 1996. By 2014 a total of 229 sufferers had been identified, 177 of whom were from the UK. In recent years, the number of new cases has gone down to about two a year. Whether that is a sign that few are harbouring it, or that it has a very long incubation period, only time will tell.

146. What causes schizophrenia?

Schizophrenia is a long-term mental illness that may lead to disordered thoughts and beliefs, delusions, and generally losing touch with reality, but its causes are unknown. There is strong evidence of a genetic link: while 1 per cent of people will suffer from schizophrenia in their lifetime, that figure rises to 10 per cent of people with a close relative who suffers from it. If that close relative is an identical twin, the chances of getting the illness rise to 50 per cent or more. It seems unlikely, though, that schizophrenia is caused by a single gene or a small set of genes.

Some progress has been made in identifying differences in the brains of schizophrenics, or in their brain chemicals, but if, as seems likely, schizophrenia is caused by an interaction of genes and psychosocial factors, we could still be a very long way from being able to predict whether an individual is likely to develop it or not.

147. What is the link between vitamin D and depression?

An extensive survey in 2013 revealed a strong statistical correlation between people's vitamin D levels and whether or not they suffered from depression. Low levels of the vitamin were found to be linked to depression and risk of depression. It is an open question, however, whether low levels of vitamin D cause depression, make it worse, or are a symptom of the depression itself. There is no known mechanism which can explain how vitamin D could relieve depression.

Since our bodies produce vitamin D when exposed to sunlight, an alternative explanation of the supposed link could simply be that the people who get the least sunlight are the most likely to suffer depression.

See also ANATOMY 6; AUSTEN 34; BIOLOGY 61; CANCER 84–6; EBOLA 165–7; HUMAN EVOLUTION 235; LONGEVITY 281; MUSIC 327

DOGS

148. Is it normal for dogs to chase their tails?

Until recently, tail-chasing in dogs was seen as perfectly normal and several reasons were offered for why they might do so: it could be boredom, or fleas, or a natural response to suddenly catching sight of something usually out of its line of vision. In 2012, however, researchers in Helsinki came up with another diagnosis: obsessive compulsive disorder.

Their study, conducted among 368 dog owners, showed that tail-chasing was associated with behaviours such as timidity and fear of loud noises. It was also found to be reduced by giving the dogs vitamin supplements. They concluded that tail-chasing could be a mental health issue but thought that a genetic component probably also played a part.

149. Can dogs make inferences?

The ancient Greeks argued about whether dogs were capable of reasoning. The logician Chrysippus (280–204 BC) suggested the case of a dog tracking its prey and reaching a point where the road branches into three. After sniffing two of the paths and picking up no scent, the dog takes the third path without sniffing, apparently reasoning that its prey must have gone that way because it didn't take either of the other two roads.

In 1615 King James I of England took part in a debate in Cambridge about logical ability in dogs, and the argument continues even today. In 2014 researchers in Japan published the results of a curious set of experiments with thirty-four pet dogs. Each dog was at first presented with two containers, only one of which contained food. The containers had also been sprayed to ensure they all had the same smell, so the dog could not detect which held the food. The experimenter then pointed to the container with the food. In general the dogs seemed to understand, and when left to choose, they went for the correct container. The second stage of the experiment again featured two containers, but this time the experimenter opened them to show which one had the food, closed them again and then pointed to the empty one. The final, third, stage was a repeat of the first stage.

When the responses of the dogs at the first and third stages were compared, it was found that significantly fewer dogs followed the experimenter's pointing at stage three than had done so at phase one. The researchers concluded that: 'dogs are highly skilled at understanding human pointing gestures, but also they make inferences about the reliability of a human who presents cues and consequently modify their behaviour flexibly depending on the inference.'

Or it could just be that by the time they arrived at stage three, the dogs were really confused. Further research is clearly needed.

150. Where were dogs first domesticated?

The genetic similarity between dogs and wolves confirms that they had a common ancestor, but when the species diverged, and when the first dog-wolves were domesticated, have long been contentious matters.

According to one theory, dogs and wolves first split somewhere in East Asia around 32,000 year ago, but another study concluded that dogs were only domesticated around 10,000 years ago, when the Agricultural Revolution led to scrap heaps of food waste which wolves started scavenging.

The latest study, based on analysis of mitochondrial DNA from dog and wolf fossils and comparison of that DNA with modern dogs and wolves, concluded that modern dogs are more closely related to European fossils than to those from Asia. They also concluded that most domestic dogs last shared a common ancestor 18,800 years ago, but they last shared a common ancestor with a wolf around 32,100 years ago. Domestication must have occurred sometime between those dates, but that still leaves a window of over 13,000 years for when it first happened.

The question is further complicated by a 32,000-year-old dog skull found in Goyet Cave in Belgium. It is quite unclear whether this came from an early domestication attempt and represents a species that died out, or whether it came from an unknown species of wolf.

Since most of the earliest European dogs fossils are thought to be about 15,000 years old and the oldest Asian dog fossils are no more than 13,000 years old, that still leaves many thousands of years in which we do not know what happened in canine domestication.

151. Are dogs social eavesdroppers?

People gain information about each other by watching how we behave with others. We are more likely to choose to interact with people we see being generous than with those who display signs of meanness. This is called 'social eavesdropping' and two recent studies came to different conclusions about whether dogs do the same in their dealings with people.

The first study, in 2011, involved dogs watching two researchers eating cereal from a pot that also contained sausages. A third researcher then entered the room and begged for some cereal. One of the cereal-eaters then shared his meal with the newcomer, the other shooed him away. When the dog was then let off its lead, it was found to be significantly more likely to approach the generous researcher, apparently in the hope of being given a sausage, which the researchers apparently had not been interested in eating themselves.

Curiously, however, the experiments showed that the dog was more influenced by the tone of voice of the two researchers than by the act of giving food away. The researchers concluded: 'We found that the dogs were capable of eavesdropping on human food-sharing interactions, and vocal communication was particularly important to convey the human's cooperative versus noncooperative intent.'

In 2014 a similar experiment was conducted in which the two experimenters swapped their positions, switching sides relative to the dog halfway through the experiment. The results showed that the side the person was sitting on was the critical factor affecting the dogs' choices, not the person. The conclusion was: 'The results of these experiments provide no evidence for social eavesdropping in dogs.'

152. Can dogs tell men's voices from women's?

Research has shown that dogs can distinguish between the sound of dogs barking and sounds made by other animals or other non-dog noises, but can they tell men's voices from women's? To try to answer that question, an experiment was conducted in which a man and a woman stood on either side of a speaker through which a male or female voice was played. A dog was placed facing the two people and the speaker, and the researchers observed whether the dog, on hearing the voice, inclined its head towards the man or the woman.

Some dogs' responses seemed to indicate that they could tell the sex of the voice, but others did not. As might have been expected, dogs living in households with three or more adults looked towards the 'correct' person far more frequently than dogs living with only one person. In such cases, the dogs made the right choice 80 per cent of the time. Yet for the other dogs, 71 per cent looked towards the wrong person. Perhaps dogs from single-person households are more suspicious of people and choose to look at the person they think was silent, while dogs from multi-person households choose to incline their heads towards the supposed source of the voice. Or it may not be the supposed sex of the voice they are responding to at all.

153. **Do dog owners have healthier children?**

Research conducted in various countries around the world has reported health benefits associated with owning a dog. The exercise involved in walking a dog, and the increased social interaction caused by dog-walking, have both been cited as benefiting health. In 2012, however, a more direct link between pet dogs and children's health was suggested by researchers in California after a study on respiratory disease in mice.

They found that mice which had been fed house dust from homes with dogs became protected from respiratory syncytial virus (RSV), a common cold strain associated with symptoms including mucus production and lung inflammation. RSV is a leading cause of bronchiolitis and can be fatal to premature or chronically ill infants.

As the researchers pointed out, mice are not the same as humans, but the result suggests that there may be a direct link between healthy children and germs associated with dogs. Previous research had suggested that children in dog-owning homes are less likely to suffer from asthma. The RSV connection may help explain why.

154. **How do dogs catch frisbees?**

A good deal of study has been done on how baseball players or cricketers catch balls. Essentially the task involves making a quick prediction of the speed and flight path of the ball and then selecting a route to run that will allow interception of the ball before it hits the ground. A study in 2004 suggested that dogs catch frisbees in much the same way.

The authors of the paper 'How dogs navigate to catch Frisbees', which appeared in *Psychological Science*, report that: 'Using micro-video cameras attached to the heads of 2 dogs, we examined their optical behavior while catching Frisbees. Our findings reveal that dogs use the same viewer-based navigational heuristics previously found with baseball players.' Specifically, they say that the dogs kept the target 'along a linear optical trajectory, LOT, with optical speed constancy' using 'simple control mechanisms that utilize invariant geometric properties'.

What the dog thinks it is doing is another question entirely, but cricketers and baseball players probably don't know what's going on in their heads when they catch a ball either.

See also ANIMALS 18; EBOLA 167; PSYCHOLOGY 389; SHEEP 417; WALRUSES 486

DOLPHINS

155. Why do whales and dolphins put up with remoras?

The relationship between remoras, which are also known as suckerfish, and dolphins and whales is difficult to explain. Remoras are fish which may be over seventy-five centimetres long and which are topped with long flat fins that look rather like the soles of running shoes. These form a gripping surface that enables them to attach themselves to whales or dolphins.

Very little is known of their lives before they find such a creature to stick to, but once they have done so, the benefits are clear: they suck blood from their hosts to provide food, they hitch a free ride, giving them increased opportunity for finding a mate, and their new home offers protection from sharks and other predators.

This raises the question of what's in it for the whales and dolphins. The remoras may help clean wounds, remove dead skin or clear parasites, but it is difficult to see how such benefits over a comparatively small area can be worth the irritation and drag they cause.

Remoras are far more frequently seen on young whales and dolphins than on adults, but it is unknown whether this is because remoras prefer younger hosts or because only older ones have worked out how to get rid of them.

156. Why do some dolphins use sponges?

Dolphins come in two varieties: spongers and non-spongers. This remarkable discovery was announced in 1997 when a group of bottlenose dolphins was observed off the coast of Australia carrying sponges in their mouths. Further investigations revealed that more than half the female dolphins in the area did this, and 'sponging' had first been seen in dolphins at least 160 years earlier.

One idea was that they carried the sponges in order to protect their noses from sharp rocks or stingrays or other hazards they might encounter while foraging for food, but more recently another theory has emerged: carrying the sponges may help them find food sources that non-spongers cannot reach.

Investigations of tissue samples from both spongers and non-spongers indicated that the two groups had totally different diets. It has been suggested that carrying sponges somehow helps the spongers to locate fish that live on the seafloor. Normally these are difficult for dolphins to find as their location impedes the proper functioning of the dolphin's echolocation system, but for some reason carrying sponges seems to help.

157. Why do dolphins go deaf?

A survey in 2010 reported that nearly half of all stranded dolphins turning up on beaches from Florida to the Caribbean were suffering from severe hearing loss. Whether they had been washed up on the beach suffering from exhaustion because their poor hearing had prevented them from finding food by echolocation, or whether deafness had damaged their navigational abilities, was not known.

The cause of the deafness is also not known. It could simply be age, but shipping noise and military sonar have also been suspected as possible causes.

DRACULA

158. Did Dracula ever live in Transylvania?

Bram Stoker's fictional vampire Dracula has often been associated with the historical figure of Vlad Tepes, or Vlad the Impaler, though the evidence is unconvincing that Bram even knew of the existence of Vlad, let alone based his character on him. In early versions of his manuscript, Stoker called him 'Count Wampyr' but changed it to 'Dracula' after reading that the name, in the Wallachian language, meant 'Devil'.

Whatever the reason for Stoker's choice, and whether or not he knew it, the name 'Dracula' was shared by Vlad Tepes. His father, Vlad II, ruler of Wallachia, was inducted by King Sigismund of Hungary into the knightly Order of the Dragon. That gave Vlad II a new surname, Dracul, which was the old Romanian word for 'dragon' (and later came to mean 'devil', as Stoker had read). As his son, Vlad Tepes, or Vlad III as he became, was known as 'Son of the Dragon', or 'Draculea'.

At the time of the younger Vlad's birth, thought to have been in 1431, his father definitely owned property in Sigisoara in Transylvania, where Vlad III is often said to have been born, but according to Florin Curta, a professor of medieval history and archaeology at the University of Florida, there is no real evidence that this was the case.

Vlad III also never owned any property himself in Transylvania, and Bran Castle – the modern tourist attraction in Romania also known as 'Dracula's Castle' – had no connection with him. According to Curta, Vlad III may well have been born in Targoviste, which was the royal seat of the principality of Wallachia, where Vlad II was a 'voivode', or ruler.

159. Where was Vlad Dracul buried?

One thing that is true about Vlad is that he was indeed an impaler. His favourite way of executing his enemies was by impaling them on long stakes, and the sight of 20,000 impaled corpses on the roadside was enough to persuade at least one rival leader not to confront him.

There have long been at least five versions of precisely how and where Vlad met his end, but until recently there was general agreement that he was killed in battle against the Turkish army at the end of 1476. One contemporary account reported that he was decapitated and his head sent to Constantinople.

In 2014, however, researchers from Estonia uncovered the headstone of a tomb in Naples which bore carvings of dragons and other images and symbols relating to Vlad Tepes. They point out that the graveyard of Piazza Santa Maria La Nova, where the headstone was found, is also where Vlad's son and daughter were buried. Their belief is that he was not killed by the Turks but captured and held for ransom, which was eventually paid by his daughter. They say this claim is supported by documentary evidence, and they have asked permission to investigate the grave.

DREAMS

160. What happens when we 'see' things in our dreams?

Some people say they dream in black and white while others claim to dream in colour. People who are blind often report seeing things in their dreams. But our eyes are closed when we are asleep, so what is this 'seeing' that we claim to be doing?

One factor that makes this difficult to answer is that we cannot report our dreams while we are dreaming. Our accounts of them are our conscious interpretations of the sensory stimulations and sensations generated while we were asleep. What we say we see in dreams we could not have seen at all, as our primary visual cortex was out of commission at the time. Our secondary visual cortex, however, which is where we interpret visual stimuli, is still working, trying to make sense of the images thrown up by our dreaming brains.

On the question of whether dreams are in colour or black and white, research has suggested that people's responses to that question are age-related: young people report dreaming in colour; the elderly dream in black and white. It has been suggested that this is related to the pictures on TV screens when one was growing up. Colours in dreams have also been linked to high emotions, but whether such colours were there at the time of the dream or have been painted in afterwards is not known.

161. Is dreaming a conscious state?

The trouble with consciousness was beautifully expressed by Stuart Sutherland in the *Macmillan Dictionary of Psychology* in 1989: 'Consciousness is a fascinating but elusive phenomenon: it is impossible to specify what it is, what it does, or why it has evolved. Nothing worth reading has been written on it.'

We all have a strong feeling that we know what it means, however, and it's something to do with being aware of the external world and disappears when we fall asleep. But where does that leave dreams? Our brains, during dreams, are using memories and knowledge of the world, albeit sometimes in a rather perverse way, to generate thoughts. We are not consciously aware of those thoughts at the time, but we can often reconstruct them when we regain consciousness.

And then there are questions about lucid dreaming, when we seem to be both conscious and dreaming at the same time, and hypnosis, when we react to the external world but not in a conscious way. We need to know a good deal more about the nature of consciousness itself to formulate answers to such questions as these.

See also BRAINS 79; SLEEP 423–9

EARS

162. How do our genes affect our earlobes?

Arguments about earlobe genetics are almost as old as genetics itself. In 1922 – just seventeen years after the word 'genetics' had been coined by William Bateson, in 1905 – a study was published giving a highly simplistic view of earlobes, based on a small and inadequate sample. The neat but fallacious conclusions of the study formed an earlobe myth that has persisted to the present day: that earlobes may be classified as either free (F) or attached (A), and that trait is controlled by a single gene with the two alleles F and A, of which F is dominant.

The study had indeed shown that among the families studied, all children of two A parents had attached earlobes, but there were no children in the study with two F parents, so there was insufficient evidence to say that the F allele was dominant.

An even greater problem lay in the classification of earlobes into those two categories. Any close inspection of a significant number of ears reveals a full spectrum of ear attachments, with the height of the attachment point (technically known as the 'otobasion inferius') varying from total lobe freedom given by attachment at the top right down to no freedom at all when it is attached at its lowest point (the 'subaurale').

Later studies identified many A offspring from two F parents, as well as many F offspring from two A parents. Researchers differ in the percentages quoted, but they all agree that earlobes cannot be controlled by a single gene.

Summarizing the results in 2011, the Delaware geneticist John H. McDonald wrote: 'While there is probably some genetic influence on earlobe attachment point, family studies show that it does not fit the simple one-locus, two-allele myth.' He then added the cautionary advice: 'You should not use earlobe attachment to demonstrate basic genetics.'

See also ANATOMY 4; CHINA 103

EARTH

163. Why is the Earth's magnetic field weakening?

In July 2014 data from European Space Agency satellites indicated a weakening of the Earth's magnetic field. While the field had strengthened in some areas mainly in the Indian Ocean, these were heavily outweighed by a decrease over most of North and South America and surrounding regions.

Previously it had been estimated that the Earth's magnetic field was weakening by about 5 per cent a century; the new results suggest that it could be ten times faster. The cause of this is unknown; some have suggested that a slowing-down of the liquid metal in the outer Earth's core beneath America is responsible, others that it is an indication that the Earth's magnetic poles might be about to flip, as has happened in the past. The Earth's magnetic polarity reverses every few hundred millennia, with the north and south poles swapping location, but what causes the flip or how long it takes is unknown.

164. When and where will the next super-volcano erupt?

Around 640,000 years ago, a massive volcanic eruption occurred in what is now Wyoming, ejecting more than 1,000 cubic kilometres of ash and lava into the atmosphere. It created a huge crater, called a 'caldera', in what became Yellowstone Park. For comparison, the biggest recent volcanic eruption was at Mount Pinatubo in the Philippines in 1991, which ejected only about 10 cubic kilometres of ash and lava. Pinatubo decreased the global temperature by 0.4 °C for a few months; a super-volcano eruption of the size that occurred in Wyoming is predicted to lead to a fall in temperatures of 10 °C lasting for a decade. In short, a super-volcano eruption is far worse than any natural phenomenon humans have ever experienced, but we know very little of where and when such a thing might happen.

Volcanoes are fuelled by underground chambers of molten rock called magma. When the pressure in these chambers grows too much, the rock is pushed upwards through fissures in the Earth's crust, exploding in an eruption. The magma chambers of super-volcanoes are much larger and much deeper, and their depth makes them difficult to detect and measure.

At the end of 2013 a study reported that the magma chamber beneath Yellowstone was two-and-a-half times the size previously thought. It is 55 miles long and 18 miles wide, runs at depths of between 3 and 9 miles, and is thought to contain at least as much magma as it did at the time of its last eruption. Other sites of ancient super-volcano eruptions have been identified around the world, but in most cases we do not know the size of their magma chambers or even if they still exist. We also do not know how they store such vast volumes of molten rock for so long, or what triggers an eruption.

See also ANTS 21; COSMOLOGY 120; EVOLUTION 181; GEOLOGY 212; GLOBAL WARMING 216; INTELLIGENCE 253; MARS 285–6; MERCURY 304; METEOROLOGY 308, 310; SALMON 399; SOLAR SYSTEM 443–4; WATER 488

EBOLA

165. Did Ebola pass from bats to humans, and if so, how?

Following the Ebola outbreak in West Africa in 2014, the disease became the subject of a great deal of research, but how it started is still a mystery. A year earlier, a toddler in Meliandou in Guinea died of an unknown disease. Soon after, his sister, mother and grandmother also died, and they are thought to have been the first victims of the epidemic. How the toddler caught Ebola in the first place is unknown, but bats are the prime suspect.

Several species of bat are known to survive experimental infection with the virus, and Ebola virus RNA has been found in at least three species of fruit bat. The toddler in Meliandou is known to have liked playing in a hollow tree in which bats roosted, but there is no evidence that he was bitten by a bat, and it is not known whether his family were in the habit of eating bats. Unfortunately, before researchers arrived in Meliandou, the tree burnt down, preventing any investigation of the bats beyond reports that a 'rain of bats' came from the burning tree and that they were a small smelly species with long tails.

166. How have some people managed to survive Ebola?

Ebola kills people by attacking their immune system. Not only does the virus deplete the white cells of the immune system, but it turns the immune system against itself, making it release inflammatory molecules, which cause tiny blood vessels to burst, leading in turn to a drop in blood pressure and multi-organ failure. Of all the people infected with Ebola, over half have died, but how the others survive has been a matter of urgent research.

One gene, known to be important in the functioning of the immune system, has been linked to Ebola survival, and another genetic mutation has been found to produce cells that resist Ebola infection in the laboratory. The majority of the survivors tested, however, display neither of the genes, so other as yet undiscovered factors must also be involved.

167. Why doesn't Ebola have any bad effects on pigs, bats and mice?

The Ebola virus has been detected in chimpanzees, gorillas, monkeys, antelopes, porcupines, rodents, dogs, pigs, bats and humans, but it is only fatal to primates. The other animals, bats in particular, seem to have developed an immune response to the virus which prevents it infecting host cells. What it is about their immune systems, or the nature of the Ebola virus itself, that has led to this response is not known.

EGYPT

168. When was the Great Library of Alexandria destroyed?

The Royal Library of Alexandria was founded in the third century BC by Ptolemy I Soter, a Macedonian general who was one of the successors to Alexander the Great. With a vast collection of papyrus scrolls, it was a major centre of scholarship and perhaps the largest library in the world.

The contents of the library are not known, and it is most famous today for its burning down, which resulted in the irretrievable loss of a great deal of ancient knowledge. When that destruction took place, however, has long been a matter of great speculation. Some say it burnt down as a result of Julius Caesar setting fire to his ships when he was besieged at Alexandria in 48 BC, while others say it was destroyed in AD 391 according to a decree by the Coptic pope Theophilus.

Some Arab sources, however, say the library, or at least some of it, survived until the Muslim conquest of Egypt in AD 640 or 641. For an event that has always been seen as a major intellectual tragedy, we know very little about the destruction of the Great Library at Alexandria.

See also MUMMIES 322; RELIGION 394; SEX 407; TECHNOLOGY 450

EINSTEIN

169. What happened to Einstein's illegitimate daughter?

In 1986, more than thirty years after the death of Albert Einstein, the discovery of letters between him and his first wife, Mileva Marić, revealed for the first time the existence of their daughter Lieserl, who had been born in 1902, the year before Einstein and Marić were married. Lieserl is mentioned several times in the correspondence in 1903, but then disappears and is never mentioned again.

One theory is that she was put up for adoption, another that she was brought up by a friend of her mother, but there is no clear evidence of what happened to her or whether she ever knew she was Einstein's daughter. In the book *Einstein's Daughter: The Search for Lieserl*, published in 1999, the novelist Michele Zackheim concludes that Lieserl died of scarlet fever when young, but others have suggested that she had Down syndrome or may have been blind.

170. How many illegitimate children did Einstein have anyway?

In *Einstein's Daughter: The Search for Lieserl*, Michele Zackheim suggested that Einstein suffered from syphilis and fathered an illegitimate son who lived in Prague, but another alleged love child is the subject of a different story.

In 2011 the death was announced in New York of Evelyn Einstein. Allegedly adopted as a baby by Hans Einstein, son of the great physicist, Evelyn had always maintained that she had actually been fathered by Einstein himself and was the result of his affair with a ballet dancer. She was, she said, brought up by his son to avoid any embarrassment. No DNA evidence was ever offered to support her claim.

See also COSMOLOGY 122, 126; ENERGY 172–3; MATHEMATICS 292; MILKY WAY 317; PHILOSOPHY 362–3

ELEPHANTS

171. Can elephants show insight when solving problems?

In 2006 the American Psychology Association reported a study on elephants under the heading 'Asian elephants do not show insight'. In 2011 another study appeared in the online journal *PloS ONE* with the title 'Insightful problem solving in an Asian elephant'. So do elephants show insight or not?

The earlier experiment involved training elephants to retrieve food from a bin. First the bin had no lid and the elephant was shown the food inside it, then it was trained to retrieve the food with its trunk. Then a lid was placed on the bin and the elephant was trained to throw the lid off and then retrieve the food. Finally the lid was placed on the ground a short distance from the bin. The elephant then walked over to the lid and threw it away before going to the bin and taking the food out. The conclusion was that the elephants were not learning through reasoning but were just following their training blindly and showing no insight.

The later experiment also involved elephants retrieving food, but this time with the use of tools and cubes which the elephant had to stack and climb on to accomplish the task. The animals' success in this was described as 'consistent with the definition of insightful problem solving'. Furthermore, the researchers suggested that: 'Previous failures to demonstrate this ability in elephants may have resulted not from a lack of cognitive ability but from the presentation of tasks requiring trunk-held sticks as potential tools, thereby interfering with the trunk's use as a sensory organ to locate the targeted food.'

See also AVOCADOS 37; HUMAN EVOLUTION 242; TECHNOLOGY 450; WHALES 492

ENERGY

172. What is energy?

Physicists, mathematicians and engineers have been making calculations involving energy for centuries. Stationary objects may have potential energy, which can be converted into kinetic energy. A rise in temperature increases an object's thermal energy, while the atoms in the object itself are held together by nuclear energy. We know, thanks to Einstein, that $E = mc^2$ and in general we know how to calculate the effect of turning one form of energy into another, but that does not help explain what energy itself is. Thinking of energy as a state or a condition helps get round this problem, but still leaves other questions such as...

173. How much energy does space contain?

Ever since the Big Bang the universe has been expanding. On the one hand, this expansion energy is forcing galaxies further apart; on the other hand, gravitational forces are drawing them together. In 1998 observations of distant galaxies from the Hubble Space Telescope revealed that the rate of expansion of the universe was increasing and had been doing so for about 7.5 billion years.

The only explanation was that space itself possessed a 'dark energy' that was forcing galaxies apart. However, when we try to calculate how much energy that consists of, we run into huge problems. If we calculate it according to Einstein's gravitational theory, we can work out the energy needed to account for the measured rate of expansion. Alternatively, we can use the quantum theory of matter in which the energy of space is provided by virtual particles which are constantly appearing and disappearing. The trouble is that the second of these methods gives an answer that differs by a factor of around 10^{120} from the answer given by the first method.

We shall return to this problem when we discuss the vacuum catastrophe (→ 371).

174. Does dark flow exist?

In 2008 an extensive survey of galaxy clusters reported a very surprising discovery: they were all heading in the same direction. Since shortly after the Big Bang, a flash of light known as the cosmic microwave background (CMB) has pervaded the universe. Relative to the CMB, all galaxies should, on average, show no preferred direction, but the new findings seemed to show evidence of an unexpected flow of clusters along a line joining the Solar System and a point between the constellations Centaurus and Hydra Vela.

Since the evidence for this 'dark flow' affecting the motion of galaxies was produced, several papers have appeared both challenging the original finding and confirming it. If dark flow exists, there is nothing that would explain it in terms of our current view of the universe. It has even been claimed as the first evidence of the existence of other universes, which provide the gravitational pull behind the dark flow. Like dark matter and dark energy, dark flow has left us in the dark.

ENGLISH HISTORY

175. Who were the green children of Woolpit?

Sometime in the twelfth century, two children described as brother and sister appeared in the Suffolk village of Woolpit. According to two English histories written in 1189 and 1220, they spoke in a language that could not be understood, they would only eat beans, and their skin was a greenish colour. They learnt to eat other food and lost their green colour, but the boy became ill and died. The girl grew up in the village, learnt English, and said that they had come from an underground land called St Martin's Land, where all the inhabitants were green.

The curious thing about this story is that the accounts of it date from only shortly after the events they describe. Fantasies, myths and legends usually date from 'long, long ago'. One theory giving a precise suggestion of the children's origin is that they might have been the offspring of Flemish settlers who had been killed in civil conflict, and that the 'St Martin's Land' they referred to may have been a reference to Fornham St Martin near Bury St Edmunds. If that were so, however, one would have expected someone to recognize the language they spoke.

176. What happened to the body of Alfred the Great?

On 26 October 899 Alfred the Great died. He was buried in the Old Minster in Winchester, but four years later his body was moved to the New Minster. In 1110 the monks of the New Minster were transferred to Hyde Abbey, along with Alfred's body and those of his wife and children.

The graves survived the dissolution of the abbey and demolition of the church in 1539 and were rediscovered by chance in 1788 during the construction of a prison by convicts. The coffins, however, were stripped of lead, and the bones were lost. In the mid-nineteenth century the prison was demolished and a number of bones were found which were said to be those of Alfred and were buried in an unmarked grave in a local church graveyard.

In March 2013 these bones were exhumed and were later radiocarbon-dated, but the results showed that they were from the 1300s and therefore not Alfred's. In 2014, however, a fragment of pelvis unearthed in a 1999 excavation of the Hyde Abbey site was radiocarbon-dated to the correct period. It is not known whether this was Alfred's, but in any case the location of the rest of his remains is unknown.

177. What happened to Queen Cartimandua?

All that we know about Cartimandua, queen of the Brigantes, comes from the writings of the Roman historian Tacitus. She ruled the Brigantes, who were a Celtic people of northern England, at the time of the Roman invasion and was one of the British rulers who announced loyalty to Rome.

Tacitus tells of the English chieftain Caratacus seeking sanctuary with Cartimandua after his defeat by the Romans, and Cartimandua putting him in chains and handing him over to the Romans, who rewarded her well. Despite that, Tacitus describes her behaviour as treacherous and criticizes her for leaving her husband Venutius and replacing him with his armour-bearer Vellocatus.

In AD 69 Cartimandua was overthrown by Venutius and left the area. Nothing is known of her after that date.

'It is a good morning exercise for a research scientist to discard a pet hypothesis every day before breakfast. It keeps him young.'

Konrad Lorenz

EVOLUTION

178. How did the brain evolve?

The trouble with brains is that they consist of soft tissue which does not survive fossilization. We can guess, from the size of their skulls, how big the brains of early animals were; we can also infer, from examining primitive organisms such as bacteria and sea sponges, similarities between their nervous systems and mechanisms in mammalian and human brains. Cells in bacteria communicate with each other through ion channels, which are similar to the channels through which neurons in the brain communicate. Sea sponges use chemical messengers similar to some of those in our brains to detect aspects of their environment. There is a long way to go, however, to fill in the gaps to get a picture of the entire evolution of the brain as we know it.

179. Where did angiosperms come from?

Charles Darwin once described the evolution of flowering plants as 'an abominable mystery'. At the time there seemed to be a sudden abundance of fossils of flowers in the geological record within a relatively short period of time with no evidence of where they had originated. We know a great deal more now, but there are still many questions.

Plants are divided into gymnosperms, which have no flowers or fruits and have unenclosed or 'naked' seeds on the surface of scales or leaves, and angiosperms, which produce flowers or fruit and have seeds enclosed within an ovary. Gymnosperms are unisexual and their seeds are spread by the wind; angiosperms require pollination to reproduce.

It is now known that, while angiosperms evolved significantly later than gymnosperms, they did not develop from them but evolved independently around 130 million years ago. Pollinating insects are thought to have evolved in parallel with them around the same time. While we now know that gymnosperms evolved from seed ferns during the Palaeozoic era, about 390 million years ago, there is still no agreement on what were the evolutionary predecessors of the angiosperms.

You could say that the evolution of flowering plants is still a mystery, though not quite as abominable as in Darwin's day.

180. How did wings evolve?

There is general agreement that wings must have been an example of exaptation, an adaptation of something that previously evolved for a different use. What that use was in the case of wings, however, is a matter of speculation. Suggestions include the following:

(i) Wings evolved from front limbs when quadrupeds started running on two legs, which left the front legs free to catch small prey.

(ii) Wings were an adaptation of front limbs which had been used to help animals leap into the air.

(iii) Wings evolved primarily for sexual display, with females preferring larger ones.

(iv) Wings evolved after scales had turned into feathers, which kept the animal warm, and flying evolved from gliding, which was an accidental bonus of the aerodynamic features of feathers.

181. To what extent has the evolutionary process been inevitable?

What would happen if we could rewind the universe to the moment of the Big Bang, or even the creation of planet Earth, and let it all run again? When Stephen Jay Gould raised that question in his 1989 book *Wonderful Life*, he had no doubt we would see a totally different world develop. The entire process of evolution is so dependent on random mutations and the occasional asteroid colliding accidentally with Earth, that anything could happen.

Certain features of evolution, however, appear inevitable. Life, we like to feel, was bound to happen sooner or later, and with the passage of time more and more complex organisms were likely to come into existence, culminating with the evolution of intelligent life. Believers in God and intelligent design will embrace that argument to explain how He created the world knowing that it would inevitably lead to the evolution of man in His own image.

Others, however, might ask whether mammals and man would ever have evolved and survived if an asteroid hadn't fortuitously wiped out the dinosaurs about 65 million years ago.

182. Why were sauropods so successful?

The sauropod dinosaurs of the Jurassic and Cretaceous periods were the largest terrestrial animals ever by a long way. They weighed up to 120 tons, could be over 30 metres (100 ft) long, and roamed the Earth for around 150 million years. Evolutionarily speaking, as no animal has grown to such dimensions in the 65 million years since, there must have been some environmental features in the Mesozoic era that were particularly favourable to animals of such huge dimensions, but it has proven difficult to pinpoint anything that could have been responsible. In 2011 a paper in the journal *Biology Review* suggested that the long neck, long tail and small head of the sauropods may have combined to allow more efficient food uptake than in other large herbivores. The fact that they didn't chew their food was also cited as a possible contribution to the large size of their bodies compared with their heads. Unfortunately the absence of chewing leaves a big gap in our understanding of their digestive systems, which would affect any calculations about their rate of extracting energy from food, so even this new theory brings us little closer to understanding how they got away with being so large.

183. Which came first: feathers or warm blood?

Two long-running arguments on which opinions have changed several times concern the blood temperature of dinosaurs and the question of whether they had feathers. If, as is now generally thought to have been the case, some of the smaller dinosaurs evolved into birds, they must have had feathers. That idea has been supported since 1980 by findings, particularly in China and Siberia, of feathered dinosaur fossils.

It has been argued, however, that large dinosaurs would have over-heated if they had had feathers. So large cold-blooded dinosaurs may have evolved into smaller warm-blooded, feathered dinosaurs, which became the first birds, but whether the warm blood or the feathers came first is not known.

In 2014 another theory emerged that dinosaurs may have had neither cold nor warm blood – it was somewhere in between. Where feathers fit into that theory is unclear.

184. How much interbreeding went on between ancient human species?

Recent studies of the DNA of Neanderthals suggest that at least two bouts of interbreeding went on between early *Homo sapiens* and Neanderthals. Modern Asians have more Neanderthal DNA than Europeans, which suggests that the interbreeding took place between different migrant groups at different times.

Neanderthals and *Homo sapiens*, however, were not the only species of early human. From *Australopithecus afarensis*, which lived in Africa between 3 and 4 million years ago, to the hobbit-like *Homo floresiensis*, which only died out about 17,000 years ago, fossil evidence has identified around twenty human-like species. The only one, apart from the Neanderthals, that *Homo sapiens* is known to have interbred with are the recently discovered Denisovans, of which fossils were unearthed in Siberia. Whether modern humans did, or even could, breed with other species is unknown.

See also ANATOMY 4, 6; ANIMALS 19; BEES 45; BONES 72; BRAINS 78; CHICKENS 97; DINOSAURS 136–8; FISH 190; GENETICS 210; GORILLAS 221; HUMAN EVOLUTION 234–43; HUMOUR 244; INTELLIGENCE 253; LANGUAGE 268; LEGS 271; LEOPARDS 274; MAMMALS 283; MOTHS 320; MUSIC 329; PANDAS 353; PANGOLINS 355–6; PSYCHOLOGY 386; SEX 408; SLEEP 424, 429; SNAKES 439; WHALES 492

EYES

185. How do we tell black from white?

Look up the terms 'Cornsweet illusion' and 'lateral inhibition' on the Internet and you are liable to be treated to a whole range of visual illusions in which black is made to appear as white, and vice versa. In one of the most striking examples, a portion of a checkerboard is displayed with a shadow cast diagonally across it. In the shadowed area, both the light and dark squares look darker. In fact, a light square in the shadowed area is exactly the same shade as a dark square in the unshadowed area, but our brains refuse to accept that. Even when we know what is happening, the shadowed light square looks much lighter.

This is due, in part at least, to 'lateral inhibition', which is the term given to the capacity of an excited neuron to reduce the activity of its neighbours. Put simply, black looks darker when surrounded by white. But some versions of the illusion cannot be explained by any physiological theory of perception. Telling the difference between black and white is not, as we may have thought, a simple matter of judging how much light they are reflecting.

186. Why do reindeer's eyes change colour in winter?

In 2013 a team from University College London and the University of Tromsø, Norway, announced their discovery that Arctic reindeer's eyes change colour in winter. Reindeer, like many animals, have a layer of tissue behind the retina in the eye called the tapetum lucidum, which reflects light back through it to enhance night vision. In the bright light of summer this layer is gold, but by winter it has turned blue.

The researchers can explain the advantages of this in helping the reindeer to see predators and find food in the murky winter light, but they are unsure how the colour change is accomplished. They suggest that it may be due to increased pressure caused by pupil dilation.

187. What colour were Eleanor of Aquitaine's eyes?

Eleanor of Aquitaine was one of the wealthiest and most powerful women in Europe during the twelfth century. She was wife first to Louis VII of France, then to Henry II of England, and was widely praised for her beauty. In her youth she was described as 'perpulchra' – more than beautiful; when she was thirty, the troubadour Bernard de Ventadour extolled her 'lovely eyes and noble countenance'; even in her seventies, the monk and chronicler Richard of Devizes called her 'beautiful'. Despite all this praise, however, nobody seems to have recorded the colour of her eyes or hair.

See also AUSTEN 33; CANCER 84; DEATH 133; DREAMS 160; HAIR 227; HENRY VIII 229; HUMAN EVOLUTION 239; LOBSTERS 278; SLEEP 425

FASHION

188. Who designed the tuxedo?

The suit known in the USA as a tuxedo and in the UK as a dinner jacket takes its American name from the Tuxedo Park Club, a social club for the New York gentry where the garment made its debut in 1886. One version of its origin gives the credit to Pierre Lorillard IV, a tobacco magnate and one of the developers of Tuxedo Park, who is said to have become irritated by the long tails of the frock coat that was the standard formal wear, so designed a shorter garment that did not interfere with sitting or dancing. It was not Pierre Lorillard but his son Griswold who is credited with being the first to wear it, when he shocked all at the 1886 Autumn Ball at Tuxedo Park by appearing with a group of friends dressed in the outrageous new garment.

Another version, however, gives the credit to James Brown Potter, a co-founder of the Tuxedo Club, who is said to have encountered the style in England when he was invited to Sandringham by the Prince of Wales (later King Edward VII). When he asked what he should wear, the prince sent him to the London tailors Henry Poole & Co. Unfortunately, the records of what Potter ordered have been lost, so we cannot be sure whether this was the dinner jacket which he later introduced to Tuxedo Park.

The archives of Poole & Co. do, however, show that the Prince of Wales himself ordered a 'short celestial blue evening coat' for informal dinners at Sandringham as early as 1865, and this is thought to have been the garment on which dinner jackets were based. Pierre Lorillard is also documented as a customer of Poole & Co. in the 1860s. In the absence of clear records for the designs, it is impossible to say whether the tuxedo, as introduced at Tuxedo Park, was created by Pierre Lorillard, Griswold Lorillard, James Brown Potter, the Prince of Wales or Henry Poole himself.

FISH

189. Why do goldfish like the colour blue?

In 1966 researchers trained goldfish to discriminate between blue, green and red painted panels and reported that all the discriminations were easily learnt by the fish. They also said: 'The results also suggest that the goldfish has a preference for blue.' Why this should be the case is unclear, particularly when seen in the light of later research which has shown that juvenile goldfish have great difficulty discriminating blue from both green and red.

190. Why did fish give up sex?

Recent research has shown that penetrative sex evolved much earlier than had previously been thought. Examination of fossils of a group of fish called antiarchs, which lived around 385 million years ago, has revealed them to have been the first vertebrates to evolve an organ for internal fertilization. Their front limbs are also thought to have been used to hold a mate while fertilization took place.

Antiarchs became extinct, but their descendants appear to have reverted to external fertilization, with penetrative sex evolving again a long time later. This apparently backward evolutionary step had previously been considered highly unlikely, if not impossible. The reasons fish gave up sex are still unknown.

191. Why do convict blennies take mouthfuls of their young and then spit them out?

The convict blenny is a curious eel-like fish that can grow up to sixty centimetres in length. It lives in tunnels or coastal reefs in the western Pacific and the adults seem unusually house-proud. While the young swim out of their nest during the day to feed on plankton, the adults feed in their tunnels and keep the place clean by gathering mouthfuls of debris which they then spit out of the nest.

Adults have also frequently been seen gathering up mouthfuls of their young and spitting them out again. The function of this curious behaviour is not known.

See also BRAINS 78; DOLPHINS 155; SALMON 399; SALT 400

FLORIDA

192. How did Edward Leedskalnin build his coral castle?

Edward Leedskalnin (1887–1951) was a gloriously eccentric Latvian immigrant to the United States who single-handedly built a massive monument in Florida known as the Coral Castle.

After spending six years working in various lumber camps in North America, he contracted tuberculosis and moved to Florida for his health. There, he spent the next twenty years building his Coral Castle, which he dedicated to the sixteen-year-old Latvian girl who had left him the day before their planned wedding.

The castle was made from around 1,000 kilograms of coral which Leedskalnin had quarried himself at night. His tools were basic, made from wood and parts of an old car, and when he was asked how he did it all on his own, he would reply, 'I understand the laws of weight and leverage and I know the secrets of the people who built the pyramids.'

See also DOLPHINS 157

FOOD

193. How should restaurant menus be set out?

In their splendid book *The Perfect Meal* on the science of food and dining, Charles Spence and Betina Piqueras-Fiszman devote fifteen pages to discussing the design of restaurant menus. How does the format of the menu affect diners' choices and, specifically, where should a restaurant owner place the details of an item he is particularly keen for them to order?

Much research has been conducted on how people scan menus and which areas they spend longest looking at. Apparently, the right-hand page of a menu, about a third of the way down the page, is the place that gets the most attention. Enclosing an item in a box is also known to draw people's attention to it. How this affects people's choices, however, is unclear. Spence and Piqueras-Fiszman give an example of a restaurant that applied those findings to the design of their menu, which featured two items in boxes on the supposedly most effective places on the menu. They report: 'This strategy had no effect whatsoever on the sales of the boxed items.' They go on to say: 'We guess that further research is needed here.'

194. Does food taste better when eaten with the fingers?

When I met Charles Spence, I asked him what else he didn't know about the psychology of food. Initially he seemed reluctant to disclose details of his forthcoming research, but then told me they were planning a study to discover whether food tastes better when eaten with the fingers.

Finding myself shortly after in a burger restaurant in which knives and forks were provided in a glass in the centre of each table, I asked a waitress what proportion of people chose to use them. She told me that it was about 50/50, but men are far more likely to eat with their fingers than women. Whether this is a matter of perceived taste or a question of relative size of hands and burger is, I feel sure, a question Professor Spence will address in his research.

195. Why do our taste buds dull in space?

Experience has shown that after a few days in space astronauts may start craving spicy foods much more than they did on Earth. This may partly be accounted for by evidence of a lessening of their sense of smell, which accounts for a good deal of our perception of taste. Why being in space should diminish smell or taste, however, is by no means clear.

One theory is that it may have something to do with weightlessness. In a gravity-free environment, the fluids in a person's body are no longer pulled downwards. This results in more fluids in the head, which apart from giving it a rounder appearance may result in a feeling of congestion similar to the feeling of having a cold. A sniffy inability to smell may then result.

196. Why does champagne from a magnum taste so different from champagne from a standard bottle?

There is general agreement among connoisseurs that champagne from a magnum tastes better than the same wine from a standard bottle. This is even found to be the case in blind tastings, so it cannot be due to a psychological effect of seeing the size of bottle it is poured from: the taste is definitely different and magnums generally taste better.

It must have something to do with the process of ageing in the bottle, and it has been suggested this is to do with the rate of oxidation and the relative surface area of liquid exposed to the air in the different sizes of bottle. What this effect consists of precisely, however, is not known.

197. What is the origin of the Yorkshire pudding?

The earliest recorded recipe for a Yorkshire pudding is to be found in the 1737 edition of a book entitled *The Whole Duty of a Woman*, with the author's name given only as 'A Lady'. The book calls it 'Dripping Pudding', but a very similar recipe appears under the title 'Yorkshire Pudding' in *The Art of Cookery Made Plain and Easy* by Hannah Glasse in 1747.

Cooked in the oven under a roasting joint of meat (the earlier book specifies a shoulder of lamb), this is clearly the model for today's Yorkshire pudding, but it seems to have been made all over Britain at the time and how it became associated specifically with Yorkshire is unknown.

198. Do the microbes in our foods affect the microbes in our guts?

Makers of probiotic foods have long claimed that microbes in the food we eat can have a beneficial effect on the microbes in our guts. Everyone has around 1.5 kilograms of gut bacteria, and it is known that it can affect our appetite, health and even brain function, but there is far less evidence to support the idea that microbes in our diet can affect the microbe content of our guts.

For this to happen, the live bacteria in our foods would first have to survive being eaten and passing through the stomach, which is highly acidic. They would then have to survive and breed in the gut. Ideally, they would also have to have a real effect on our health.

The most that has so far been proved is that live bacteria from probiotic products can survive their passage to the stomach, but unless one keeps taking them, they get flushed out of the system and do not establish a long-term presence. The European Food Safety Authority has therefore ruled that makers of such products may claim, in their advertising, that they can have a short-term medical effect, but any claim of long-term health benefits must await better evidence.

See also BEARS 41; BEES 43–4; BIRDS 65; DOLPHINS 156; ELEPHANTS 171; HUMAN EVOLUTION 235; MARS 286; MEERKATS 301; MONKEYS 318–19; PLATYPUSES 374; RATS 393; WHALES 492; WILD BOAR 493

FOOTBALL

199. Do soccer referees have a rightward bias?

Research has shown that speakers of languages that are written from left to right tend to think of events unfolding from left to right. There is therefore a propensity to be more suspicious of events that are seen as happening from right to left. In 2010 a study was published on whether this has an effect on soccer referees when deciding whether a foul has been committed. This was based on an experiment in which referees were shown pictures from real football matches and asked to rule on whether the picture displayed a foul being committed. The referees were found to call more fouls for pictures of left-moving events than for right-moving events.

The research has, however, only been done on referees whose native language is written left to right. Whether Arabic-speaking referees have a right-to-left bias is unknown. If they are found to share the rightward bias of the referees in the study, it would suggest that, like chickens (→ 97), the rightward bias is innate rather than language-based.

200. Does sacking the manager help an unsuccessful soccer team?

Statisticians have long debated the evidence for and against sacking the manager of a poorly performing soccer team. A survey of the academic literature in 2012 reported that, of nine studies from six countries, five concluded that replacing a manager does improve a club's results, while four found that hiring a new manager did not improve team performance on average.

In 2013 the Dutch economist Dr Bas ter Weel compared the results of teams doing badly that changed their manager and teams doing badly that did not change manager. His conclusion was: 'Changing a manager during a crisis in the season does improve the results in the short term, but this is a misleading statistic because not changing the manager would have had the same result.'

In 2014, however, a ten-year study of sixty managerial changes among the thirty-six clubs in the English Premier League between 2003 and 2013 reached the opposite conclusion, at least as far as teams struggling to avoid relegation were concerned. The question of whether it is beneficial for a football team to change manager is therefore still open.

FRANCE

201. Who was the comte de Saint-Germain?

Scholar, linguist, violinist, composer, alchemist, philosopher, diplomat, dandy, braggart and probable impostor, the comte de Saint-Germain – the Count of St Germain – was one of the most extraordinary figures of eighteenth-century society, wherever he went in Europe, yet nobody knows who he was or where he came from.

He claimed to be the son of Francis II Rákóczi, the Prince of Transylvania, and was clearly well educated and rich enough always to appear well dressed and often festooned with jewels. Horace Walpole wrote in praise of his abilities in diverse fields, but also described him as a 'great Pretender'. He thought Spanish or Portuguese was his native language, though he also spoke French and Italian and understood Polish. Casanova described him as a 'learned impostor' and said: 'Notwithstanding his boastings, his bare-faced lies, and his manifold eccentricities, I cannot say I thought him offensive.'

Saint-Germain made a laboratory for Louis XV of France and travelled to Holland in 1760 to try to open negotiations between Britain and France during the Seven Years' War, though neither side had commissioned him to do so. According to different accounts, he told people he was either 300 or 500 years old and had solved the secret of eternal life. He died in 1784 and nobody has ever discovered his true identity.

202. What was the relationship between Marie Antoinette and Count Axel von Fersen?

The Swedish count Axel von Fersen (1755–1810) is celebrated for distinguishing himself on the battlefield during the American War of Independence and for his defence of the royal family during the French Revolution, but most of all, he is remembered for the mystery concerning his relationship with Marie Antoinette.

The two met at the Paris Opera in 1774, and within a few years he had become a member of her intimate circle of friends. Thanks to her influence, he became a colonel in the German infantry and later a colonel in the Royal Swedish Regiment. Their secret correspondence shows the strength of the feelings between them, and he once wrote to his sister telling her that he would never marry as 'I cannot belong to the one person whom I would truly wish to be mine'.

After the French Revolution began, he organized the flight of the royal family to Varenne in 1791, but when Marie Antoinette was guillotined in 1793, he wrote: 'I have now lost everything that I had in the world.' But how close they really were we shall probably never know.

See also DEATH 134–5; EYES 187; MURDER 323; RELIGION 394; SEX 407

FROGS

203. What killed the frogs in Windham, Connecticut, in 1754?

On a dark night in June 1754, the residents of the town of Windham, Connecticut, were woken by a hideous, shrieking roar. Some thought they were being attacked by Indians; others thought it must be Judgement Day. Many fired their muskets in the direction of the noise, but none dared venture to see what it was.

By morning the noises had died away and the source of the din gradually became clear: the shores of the mill pond and the stream leading from it were covered with the bodies of hundreds, perhaps even thousands, of dead bullfrogs. Since then, the event has been known as the Windham Frog Fight (or Windham Frog Fright) and is now commemorated by many sculptures of frogs in the town.

The cause of it all was probably a drought in the region which had left the local frog population desperate for water, but what had drawn so many of them to one small pond in Windham, and whether there was indeed a huge battle or whether they died from exhaustion and dehydration, is still rather unclear.

FUNDAMENTAL PARTICLES

204. Is the particle discovered at CERN really a Higgs boson?

In 2012 there were great celebrations at the Large Hadron Collider (LHC) at CERN in Switzerland when it was announced that they had discovered the elusive Higgs boson, the elementary particle said to account for why some particles have mass and others do not. But was it really a Higgs boson they discovered?

Shortly after the announcement of the discovery, scientists at CERN admitted that the particle they had discovered was totally in accordance with predictions about the Higgs boson, but they could not rule out the possibility that it was in fact some other particle with similar properties. The other main suspect is a particle known as the techni-higgs. A crucial difference between the Higgs and the techni-higgs is that the Higgs is an elementary particle, which means that it cannot be broken down into smaller particles; the techni-higgs, however, is made up of techni-quarks which are thought to be elementary.

Finding out whether the particle they discovered is indeed a Higgs boson is one of the tasks on the agenda for the recently upgraded LHC.

205. Do protons decay?

One of the difficulties in finding a Grand Unified Theory (GUT) that would explain all the fundamental forces known to physics is that the universe does not seem to behave quite the way it should. Any GUT would rely on a symmetry between the various fundamental particles and the various forces. We have matter and antimatter, electrons and anti-electrons, neutrinos and anti-neutrinos and anything-else-you-care-to-name matched by an anti-anything-else-you-care-to-name. In particular, the strong force ought to be equivalent to the weak force, and baryons, such as protons and neutrons, ought to be equivalent to leptons, such as electrons and neutrinos.

For the most part, such symmetry seems to exist, but the proton presents an apparent anomaly. According to most ideas of how a GUT would work, a proton should eventually decay into a positron and a pion. The trouble is that no evidence of proton decay has ever been observed. If protons do decay, however, calculations suggest that it could take a very long time: an average of around 10^{33} years in fact. Since the universe has only been in existence for just over 10^{10} years, it could simply be that there has not been enough time for more than a very few protons to decay, but the search for a decayed proton continues.

206. Is there anything smaller than quarks and gluons?

A century ago, atoms were thought to be the smallest components of matter. The very word 'atom' was borrowed from the ancient Greek philosophers who had argued that there must be a limit beyond which matter could not be divided (the word 'atom' is from the Greek meaning 'that which cannot be divided'). Then, in 1917, Ernest Rutherford built on the theoretical work of contemporaries such as J. J. Thomson and split the atom.

The world of subatomic physics began with protons, neutrons and electrons, of which atoms were thought to be composed. Then, in the 1960s, by which time the zoo of subatomic particles had a bewildering plethora of different types, Murray Gell-Mann introduced the idea of quarks, which came in six varieties and were shown to be the building blocks of other particles.

But are quarks themselves indivisible? There is no direct evidence that quarks are composite, but in 1974 the theoretical physicists Jogesh Pati and Abdus Salam conjectured the existence of a particle called the preon. Their calculations showed that several problems in particle physics could be explained if, as they suggested, quarks were themselves made of preons.

The preon has, since then, been in a position similar to that of the quark from the mid-1960s until around 1980: its existence would solve several problems, but there was no hard evidence that it existed at all. For the time being, therefore, the quark is the smallest particle. But nobody could rule out the existence of a smaller one.

207. What is the mass of a neutrino?

Neutrinos are among the most puzzling of all subatomic particles. Trillions of them pass unnoticed through our bodies every second, some dating back to the Big Bang, others more recently generated by nuclear reactions in the Sun. Neutrinos are very similar to electrons but carry no electric charge.

According to the Standard Model of elementary particles, the neutrino should have no mass, but in the 1980s it was discovered that neutrinos could oscillate, which suggested that they had mass, and in 1998 it was indeed confirmed not only that neutrinos had mass, but that the three known types of neutrino had different masses. These masses, however, are so small as to be almost undetectable and attempts to discover precisely how much a neutrino weighs have not yet produced an answer.

See also ASTRONOMY 27; BIG BANG 54–6; BLACK HOLES 71; COSMOLOGY 117, 119–22, 126; ENERGY 172, 174; GRAVITY 223; PHILOSOPHY 363; PHYSICS 372; UNIVERSE 463, 467

GAMES

208. Can video games improve intelligence?

Playing video action games has long been shown to increase people's speed of perceptual processing and reactions, but research in 2013 concluded that it may also lead to a more general improvement in cognitive function.

Subjects, who were selected specifically for their relative lack of video-gaming experience, were divided into three groups. One group played an easy version of an action game; another played a more complex version of the same game; the third group engaged in another video-game activity which placed little or no demand on memory or tactical skill.

All groups played for forty hours spread over six to eight weeks, after which they were tested on various problem-solving tasks. The results showed that the participants who had been trained on the complex action game did better than the players of the simple game, and players of the simple action game did better than those who had been engaged in the even less challenging game.

The researchers conclude that playing video action games can enhance cognitive flexibility and performance. They do, however, point out that all seventy-two participants in the experiment were female students at the University of Texas, as they could not find any male students who had the required low experience of video games. There is also the question of whether the observed improvement in performance is temporary or long-lasting.

209. Is playing good for us?

Research at Oxford in 2014 concluded that children who played video games for up to an hour a day were happier and more sociable, had fewer emotional problems, and were less hyperactive than those who didn't play at all. It has also been claimed that playing video games can reduce addictive cravings in other areas. Other research, however, has concluded that players can become obese, lazy, slovenly, unproductive, aggressive, antisocial and addicted to the games themselves.

Clearly further research is needed before we can decide whether the benefits or drawbacks are greater.

See also INTELLIGENCE 252; PSYCHOLOGY 385

GENETICS

210. Can fear be inherited?

Before the work of Darwin led to the development of the science of genetics, there was a general belief in the inheritance of acquired characteristics, or Lamarckism as it came to be known. The French naturalist Jean-Baptiste Lamarck (1744–1829) believed that evolution functioned through changes that took place during a creature's lifetime being passed on to its offspring. As the science of genetics grew, this idea was abandoned, but since the 1990s the new science of epigenetics has produced increasing evidence that – to some extent at least – Lamarck may have been correct.

A striking example was given in an experiment in 2013 in which mice were conditioned to associate a particular smell with an electric shock and therefore to show signs of fear when the smell was perceived. The conditioning was performed before the mice mated and the resulting offspring were subsequently found to be liable to exhibit signs of fear when exposed to the same smell, and so were the grandchildren of the original mice. The offspring were also found to have more receptors for the smell in their brains and therefore to be more sensitive to it.

While an acquired characteristic, such as fear of a particular smell, cannot alter the DNA of an animal, it seems that it can alter the way genes express themselves. Whether humans can acquire fears from their parents and grandparents in a similar way is unknown.

211. Is there a genetic secret to a long life?

Research has shown that living to an old age seems to run in families. Studies on twins have even reported that 40 per cent of longevity is genetic, but the quest to identify the genes responsible has not been successful.

In 2014 the genomes of seventeen supercentenarians (110 years old or more) were sequenced to explore the genetic basis for longevity. No significant evidence was found that their genes differed from those of a normal population. In common with other elusive genetic traits, it appears that longevity is not controlled by a single gene, or even a simple combination of genetic factors.

See also ASPARAGUS 26; BIOLOGY 62; CANCER 84; DISEASE 142, 146; DOGS 148, 150; EARS 162; EBOLA 166; HAIR 226; HUMAN EVOLUTION 234, 237–9; LONGEVITY 279; MEDICINE 298; MICE 313; PANGOLINS 355; PREHISTORY 383; SALAMANDERS 398; SEX 406; SMELL 435

'One of the greatest joys known to man is to take a flight into ignorance in search of knowledge.'

Robert Staughton Lynd

GEOLOGY

212. What caused the Permian mass extinction?

Around 252 million years ago, at the end of the Permian period, an estimated 93 to 97 per cent of all species became extinct. It was the most intense extinction event ever known and has been called the 'Great Dying'. Various theories have been put forward to explain this near-extinction of life on Earth, including glaciation, global warming, volcanoes, an asteroid or comet impact, catastrophic methane release from the ocean floor, or a massive drop in oxygen levels.

In other words, in terms of identifying the cause for certain, we are still at the stage of rounding up the usual suspects.

See also COSMOLOGY 125; EVOLUTION 179; RUSSIA 397; TURKEY 457

GERMANY

213. Who was Kaspar Hauser?

In May 1828 a teenage boy wearing tattered clothing was found wandering in a public square in Nuremberg, Germany. He was clutching an envelope with two letters in it but seemed unable to read or write anything other than his name, which he gave as Kaspar Hauser. The only sentence he spoke was 'I want to be a cavalryman, as my father was', and in reply to questions he would just say 'Don't know'. When offered food and drink, all he would eat was bread and water. Later he claimed to have been brought up alone in a cell and to have never seen another person until he was set free in Nuremberg. The letters were allegedly from his mother and a man who had taken care of him, but both seemed to be in the same handwriting and many thought that Kaspar Hauser had written them himself.

This mysterious boy attracted international attention and the British nobleman Lord Stanhope later gained custody of him. Stanhope paid his living expenses and made considerable efforts to find out where he had come from, but later declared it his duty 'openly to confess that I had been deceived'. In December 1833, when Hauser was about twenty-one years old, he appeared with a deep stab wound in his left breast and a story that he had been attacked by a stranger. He died of his wound shortly after.

Some theories at the time suggested that he was an heir of the grand ducal House of Baden, but recent DNA investigations have failed to confirm this (though they do not totally rule it out). Another theory is that he was a pathological liar. The truth has never been discovered.

214. What is the Salzburg Cube?

In 1885 an employee named Reidl at a foundry in Austria discovered a mysterious hunk of metal in a seam of coal estimated to be 20 million years old. Roughly cubic in shape, with rounded sides and a deep groove apparently cut into it, the Salzburg Cube, as it came to be known (it was also called the Wolfsegg Iron after the place the coal had come from), aroused great interest.

At first, it was thought to be an ancient meteorite, but later investigations showed it to have been artificially manufactured and to be made of iron. The question of how it found its way inside a 20-million-year-old coal seam produced several theories:

- It may have come from a lost human civilization.
- It may have been left by alien visitors.
- It may have fallen from an alien spacecraft.

Or it may all have been a hoax, which seems the most likely explanation. But who the hoaxers were and why they did it have never been explained.

See also BIRDS 64; NAZIS 338–40; SLOTHS 434; USA 477

GLOBAL WARMING

215. Why is atmospheric methane rising?

Most efforts to control global warming have concentrated on reducing carbon dioxide emissions, but recent years have seen a rise in levels of methane in the atmosphere, which is a considerably more potent greenhouse gas.

Several causes of methane emissions are known, but puzzlingly measurements of the changes in atmospheric methane levels do not seem to correlate with known changes in emissions. Coal production, for example, is known to produce methane emissions, yet between 2000 and 2006, when Chinese coal production was known to be increasing at 7 per cent a year, there was no change in methane levels. It could be that the increased methane from Chinese coal has been balanced by a reduction in methane emissions from wetlands, which are a major source of the gas, but there are no global figures to verify that idea.

Since 2007 atmospheric concentrations of methane have been rising quickly, but whether this is due to fossil fuel emissions, or the melting of Arctic ice leading to an increase in the area covered by wetlands, or high rainfall having the same effect in tropical regions is unknown.

216. What is the relationship between global warming and oceanic anoxic events?

The geological record shows that mass extinctions in the Earth's history have frequently coincided with oceanic anoxic events (OAEs), which occur when the oceans become depleted of oxygen. These OAEs in turn have been associated with global warming. The logic is simple: not only is oxygen less soluble in warmer water, but warming decreases the density of the surface water, leading to greater stratification and less mixing of the surface layers, which have high oxygen content, with the deeper levels where the oxygen is lower.

Research in 2014 revealed anomalies that cast doubt on this process. While the oxygen content of the oceans was found to have decreased between 1990 and 2010 when the waters were warming, it increased from 1950 to 1990, which was equally a period in which the waters were getting warmer. Measurements in the North Pacific suggested that another process was occurring which had the opposite effect from the conventional theory.

The argument was that the old theory ignored the effect of winds on the production of phytoplankton which consume the oxygen. A heavy concentration of such organisms at the surface of the water decreases the amount of oxygen underneath. Phytoplankton production is increased by strong winds because they result in the availability of more nutrients from deeper waters. This theory was supported by measurements of oceanic oxygen content, which were found to be higher during periods of high trade winds.

Although such winds have been higher since 1990, global warming is predicted to lead to weaker trade winds in the future and thus to an increase, not a decrease, in oceanic oxygen levels.

See also GEOLOGY 212; METEOROLOGY 306–7

GOLD

217. Who discovered gold in the Klondike?

On 16 August 1896 gold was discovered in the Klondike region of north-west Canada, which led to a stampede of prospectors from all over North America. The team credited with the discovery comprised George Carmack, his wife Kate Carmack, who was a member of the Tagish Native American tribe from the Yukon region, her brother Skookum Jim, and their nephew Dawson Charlie. They had been travelling south of the Klondike river on a recommendation from Robert Henderson, another prospector.

It has never been clear who was first to make the discovery. The group apparently agreed to list George Carmack as the discoverer, as it was feared that mining authorities would not approve a claim made by a Native American. Robert Henderson's basis for advising the group on where to look has also never been explained, so it is possible that he was indeed the first to discover the Klondike gold.

218. Where are the 93 tons of gold moved from Romania's National Bank to Russia in 1916?

During the First World War, when Romania was occupied by Germany, the Romanian government decided to move a collection of national treasures, including an estimated 120 tons of gold coins, ingots and objects, to Russia for safekeeping. A deal was signed that the Russians would keep the treasures safe until the end of the war.

After the Russian Revolution of 1917, however, the new Soviet government severed diplomatic relations with Romania and confiscated the treasures. Since then, successive governments of Romania have tried to recover the treasures and the gold, but with only very limited success. In 1935 and 1956 almost 40,000 artworks were returned among the treasures in seventeen railway wagons, but most of the gold was not among them. Some of the crates were also found to have been tampered with. What happened to the gold has never been discovered.

In 2012 Romania tried to raise the matter in the Council of Europe, but Russia was reported to have 'expressed regret' over Romanian attempts to raise the issue and called on Bucharest not to 'stir up the past'. The Council said that such a return could start with the return of the National Bank of Romania's gold reserves consisting of 93.4 tons of gold. Russia responded by saying that the subject of Romanian gold should be consigned to history.

219. Does Yamashita's gold exist?

Since the end of the Second World War, many treasure-hunters have travelled to the Philippines in search of the so-called Yamashita treasure, but nobody is even sure whether it has ever existed.

The story behind the alleged treasure concerns the Japanese general Tomoyuki Yamashita, who commanded Japanese forces in the Philippines from 1944. Yamashita is said to have been in charge of a massive campaign of looting which involved people ranging from the Japanese imperial family to gangs of Yakuza gangsters; valuables were looted from banks, commercial buildings, private homes and even religious institutions to finance the Japanese war effort. The loot is said to have initially been concentrated in Singapore but later moved to the Philippines, though no clear evidence of its existence was ever found.

Yamashita himself was convicted of war crimes and executed by the US Army in 1946, and others said to have been involved were killed during the war. In 1988, however, an extraordinary case was heard in a court in Hawaii brought by a Filipino treasure-hunter Rogelio Roxas against Ferdinand Marcos, former president of the Philippines, and his wife Imelda. Roxas claimed that he had discovered the Yamashita gold but had it stolen from him by Marcos.

The court found that Roxas had indeed found a treasure which had been stolen by Marcos, but ruled that they were not required to determine whether this particular treasure was the legendary Yamashita's gold. In 1992 Imelda Marcos claimed that the basis of her late husband's fortune (Ferdinand Marcos died in 1989) was indeed Japanese gold which he had found at the end of the Second World War. She was quoted as saying: 'I understand there was some Yamashita gold.' Marcos kept it secret, she said, because the amount was so large 'it would have been embarrassing'.

Many others, however, have dismissed the whole story of the Yamashita gold as a myth.

See also ALCHEMY 2; BIBLE 53; CODES 109; COSTA RICA 127; HITLER 232; TREASURE 455; USA 470

GORILLAS

220. Is there an albino gorilla Amomongo hiding in the Philippines?

The British have the Loch Ness Monster, North Americans have the Sasquatch or Big Foot, the Nepalese have the Yeti, and the Filipinos have Amomongo. Described as a man-sized ape or albino gorilla with long nails, Amomongo is said to live in caves near the foot of the Kanloan volcano.

Generally considered to be a mythical creature, Amomongo was the subject of renewed interest in 2008 following reports of at least two sightings, including one at which the creature was said to have attacked goats and chickens and eaten their entrails. There were also reports of its having attacked humans, one of whom was said to have needed treatment for scratches at various places on his body.

221. Are gorillas predominantly right-handed?

Why most human beings are right-handed has long been debated, and evidence from the teeth of Neanderthals suggests this preference dates from an early time in our evolution. To find out how early, a good deal of research has been done on handedness in apes and monkeys. Chimpanzees, gorillas and bonobos have been reported to have right-handed tendencies, while orangutans have been found to be predominantly left-handed.

Several studies have reported that gorillas are the closest to humans in this respect, with about 90 per cent of them exhibiting right-handedness, but some doubts have been raised about this claim. Most of the studies have been on captive gorillas, while observation of gorillas in the wild has generally been less convincing in demonstrating a right-hand preference. It has been suggested that the captive gorillas being studied are not showing a natural hand preference, but are simply mimicking the hand usage of the experimenters or their keepers.

We eagerly await a study conducted only on gorillas brought up by left-handed zoo-keepers to resolve this matter.

See also BRAINS 77; EBOLA 167; WALRUSES 486

GRAVITY

222. What is the strength of gravity?

More than 300 years ago, Isaac Newton discovered the law of gravity: any two objects in the universe attract each other with a force proportional to the product of their masses divided by the square of the distance between them:

$F = Gm_1m_2/r^2.$

All that remained was to calculate the value of G in the formula, and scientists have been arguing about it ever since. Research into the values of other scientific constants has followed a pattern of getting better and better estimates, allowing the answer to be known with ever-increasing accuracy. Different experimenters, however, have obtained, and continue to obtain, values for G that differ by more than can be explained by the limitations of their experiments. In some cases, the identical experiment performed at different times has given slightly different results.

In 2010 the International Council for Science gave a new figure for its recommended value of G, while also increasing the margin of uncertainty about the figure.

223. How can quantum theory and gravity be reconciled?

The biggest problem in physics is explaining why there seem to be different sets of rules governing the world at the scale we are used to dealing with it and the micro-world of atoms and subatomic particles. First we had Newton, explaining the macro-world with his theory of gravity; then came Einstein, who modified Newton's ideas with the theory of relativity; but soon after that quantum theory arrived to explain the micro-world in terms not of tangible objects and certainties but of waves and probabilities.

Any theory of everything, or Grand Unified Theory (GUT), will need to come up with something that reconciles the physics of Newton and Einstein with that of quantum mechanics. In particular, it needs a single theory that brings together all the fundamental forces. The trouble is that the electromagnetic, strong nuclear and weak nuclear forces are all best described by quantum mechanics, but the much weaker gravitational force is explained within the framework of classical physics.

See also ASTRONOMY 28; BLACK HOLES 71; BONES 73; COSMOLOGY 124; FOOD 195; MILKY WAY 317; PHYSICS 371; SLOTHS 431; UNIVERSE 465–7

GUILLOTINES

224. Did Dr Guillotin know about the Halifax gibbet?

In the sixteenth century the Lord of the Manor in the town of Halifax in Yorkshire had the right to sentence any criminal who had stolen more than 13½ pence worth of goods to be summarily executed by decapitation. Until the mid-seventeenth century, the sentence was carried out by means of a device consisting of an axe-head fitted to a wooden block that ran in grooves between two tall uprights. The block and axe-head were raised by means of a rope, then allowed to fall on the hapless victim's neck.

In 1791, as the French Revolution progressed, the French physician Joseph-Ignace Guillotin was a campaigner against capital punishment, but accepting that it would not be abolished, he advocated that the death penalty should be carried out as humanely as possible. The result was the device that became known as the guillotine – a nice feminization of his own name. Its similarity to the Halifax device is striking, but whether Dr Guillotin knew of the earlier device is unknown.

See also FRANCE 202

GUINEA-PIGS

225. To what extent do guinea-pigs have personalities?

Guinea-pig owners, to judge from many websites, are generally convinced that their pets have distinct personalities, but animal behaviourists are less sure. To show personality, an animal would have to exhibit forms of behaviour that distinguished it from others of its species and were also stable over time. Research in 2013 investigated the social behaviour and emotionality of adult male guinea-pigs on two occasions eight weeks apart. Comparison of their behaviour on the two occasions revealed that there was individual stability with respect to social behaviour, but none with respect to emotional behaviour.

The researchers said their results 'suggest that the concept of animal personality is applicable to domestic guinea-pigs'. Without the factor of emotionality, however, guinea-pig personality may seem limited.

HAIR

226. How do hair whorls influence handedness in humans?

In 2003 the geneticist Amar Klar published a study relating the clockwise or anti-clockwise direction of a person's hair whorl at the back of their head and whether they were left-handed or right-handed. He reported that in a normal sample of mainly right-handed people, only 8.4 per cent had anti-clockwise whorls, while in a sample of people who were left-handed or ambidextrous, 44.9 per cent had anti-clockwise whorls.

This finding led to a theory that a single gene is responsible for both the direction of hair whorl and determining whether a person is left- or right-handed. Later attempts to reproduce Klar's results, however, have met with only limited success. Of six studies performed between 2005 and 2010, only two reported a significant correlation between whorl direction and handedness. Putting all the studies together, however, does reveal a slight tendency for left-handed people to have anti-clockwise whorls.

227. Do hair whorls influence cattle development?

Research at the University of Colorado has identified several factors relating to cattle that appear to correlate with aspects of the location and direction of their hair whorls. In 1995 the researchers found that spiral hair whorl position on the forehead may be associated with a calm temperament, while whorls above a bull's eyes indicated excitability. In general, the odder and more untidy a whorl looked, the more likely the animal was to be unmanageable.

Research at the University of Limerick in Ireland in 2008 also found that horses with clockwise hair whorls were significantly more likely to move toward the right, or start trotting with their right-sided hooves.

It has been suggested that whorl development is associated with brain development in both animals and humans, but more evidence is clearly needed.

See also ANATOMY 4; CHINA 99; CRIME 129; EYES 187; NAPOLEON 337; PANGOLINS 354; SLOTHS 432; WAITRESSES 484

HENRY VIII

228. What was the illness that killed Henry VIII's elder brother Arthur?

Arthur Tudor, eldest son of Henry VII of England, was born in 1486, married in 1501 and died in 1502. A contemporary account of the illness that killed him refers to 'a malign vapour which proceeded from the air'. This may have been the mysterious 'sweating sickness' that killed thousands in the 1480s, but at the time of Arthur's death had not been heard of since 1492.

His wife Catherine had also been suffering from the illness, but she recovered and seven years later married Arthur's younger brother, who became Henry VIII. That marriage didn't work out very well for her either.

229. Did Catherine of Aragon and Prince Arthur consummate their marriage?

On Sunday 14 November 1501 the sixteen-year-old Catherine of Aragon married fifteen-year-old Prince Arthur, heir to the English throne. What happened that night, however, has been argued over for more than 500 years.

Sir Anthony Willoughby, who was a 'body servant' to the young prince, later testified: 'I made the said prince ready to bed and with others conducted him clad in his nightgown unto the princess's bedchamber often and sundry times when he entered and then continued all night.' The following morning, the prince emerged from his wife's bedchamber and said: 'Willoughby, bring me a cup of ale, for I have been this night in the midst of Spain.' Twenty-six years later, however, the question of whether the marriage had indeed been consummated became a major issue for both church and state.

Arthur had died in 1502 and Catherine had subsequently married his brother Henry. She bore him six children, all but one of which died, leaving only Mary. Henry saw an explanation for this in Leviticus 20:21, which says, 'And if a man shall take his brother's wife, it is an unclean thing: he hath uncovered his brother's nakedness; they shall be childless.' Henry sought an annulment of the marriage on the grounds that it went against biblical teaching. Catherine, however, maintained that her marriage to Arthur had never been consummated and it was therefore that marriage which was automatically dissolved, making her marriage to Henry perfectly legitimate in the eyes of both the state and the church.

Despite his strong efforts to have his marriage annulled, however, Henry VIII never stated that Catherine was not a virgin on their wedding night.

230. Was Catherine of Aragon poisoned?

When Catherine died at Kimbolton Castle in 1536, rumours were rife that she had been poisoned by friends of the king or Anne Boleyn. When her body was being prepared for burial, the chandler at Kimbolton reported that all her organs were normal except her heart, which had a large black and hideous growth.

On hearing of this, the Spanish ambassador, Eustace Chapuys, wrote to the emperor of his suspicions at no doctor or surgeon having been present at the opening of the body. Chapuys also quoted the queen's physician as saying that he was in no doubt that the queen had been poisoned, as she became ill after drinking a glass of Welsh beer.

However, the black growth on the heart could also be taken as a description of a cancerous tumour. Cancer was not recognized in those days, but making a reliable diagnosis after 500 years is not possible.

See also EYES 187; SHAKESPEARE 415; SHIPS 421

HITLER

231. How many testicles did Hitler have?

Surprisingly, the British wartime song 'Hitler has only got one ball' (sung to the tune of 'Colonel Bogey') may have had some basis in fact. Medical records confirm that during the First World War Hitler was wounded at the Battle of the Somme. A man who was a German army doctor at the time is on record as saying that he saved Hitler at the battle and saw that he had a groin injury and had lost a testicle.

In 1970 the Soviet autopsy on Hitler's body was released, revealing that 'the left testicle could not be found either in the scrotum or on the spermatic cord inside the inguinal canal, or in the small pelvis'. On the other hand, Hitler's personal physician and another doctor who had treated him while he was alive are on record as saying there was nothing wrong with his testicles.

232. What happened to Hitler's gold?

In 2013 a collection of 1,500 paintings said to be worth almost £1 billion was found in an apartment in Munich. The collection, reported to include works by Picasso, Matisse and Chagall, had been hidden by Cornelius Gurlitt, the eighty-year-old son of an art dealer trusted by the Nazis to dispose of plundered artworks.

That, however, was only a very small part of the loot plundered by the Nazis which they are thought to have hidden as defeat in the war became inevitable. Hitler is known to have had a personal diamond collection which is thought to have gone missing, together with the entire gold reserves of the Reichsbank.

233. Who was Hitler's paternal grandfather?

Adolf Hitler was the son of Alois Hitler Sr, who was born Alois Schicklgruber, but there is great doubt over who Alois Schicklgruber's biological father was. At his baptism, the space for his father's name was left blank and the priest recorded that he was illegitimate. When Alois was five, his mother married Johann Georg Hiedler. By the age of ten, however, Alois had been sent to live with his stepfather's brother, Johann Nepomuk Hiedler, but he continued to use the surname Schicklgruber. At the age of thirty-nine he applied to change his surname to that of his family, which (perhaps through a mishearing of 'Hiedler') was recorded as 'Hitler'.

Who Alois's real father was has always been a mystery. When he applied to change his name, he said that Johann Georg Hiedler was his biological father, but it has been suggested that the real father was Johann Nepomuk Hiedler, which would explain why he was sent to live with him.

Finally, another rumour centres on a story that Alois's mother, Maria Schicklgruber, became pregnant while working for a Jewish family in Graz. That account names the prime suspect as Leopold Frankenburger, the heir to the family's wealth. No evidence has ever been produced to support this story, which may have been invented solely to support a claim that Adolf Hitler was one-quarter Jewish.

See also NAZIS 338, 340

HUMAN EVOLUTION

234. Who were the Palaeo-Eskimos?

DNA evidence was found in 2014 of a previously unknown race of people which inhabited the Arctic north of America for more than 4,000 years before they died out about 700 years ago. These Palaeo-Eskimos, as they have been dubbed, were not related to the Native Americans, who were there before them, nor to the Inuit, who arrived later.

These three groups are all thought to have reached North America from Siberia across the Bering Strait, but the genetic evidence shows that the Palaeo-Eskimos lived in total isolation and did not reproduce with the other groups. Such long-lasting isolation and the apparent stability of their culture make them quite unlike any other group of humans of the past few thousand years.

Curiously, what we now know about them is similar to an ancient Inuit myth of a magical giant race called the Tunit, who are said to have lived in isolation, making no contact with others.

There is also no evidence to explain why the Palaeo-Eskimos died out.

235. What happened to the Neanderthals?

There is evidence that Neanderthals lived in Eurasia around half a million years ago. According to the latest estimates based on carbon dating, they died out about 40,000 years ago. Why they died out has long been a subject of dispute, but many theories link their extinction to the arrival of modern man in Europe between 45,000 and 43,000 years ago. Possible theories include the following:

- Violence: *Homo sapiens* and *Homo neanderthalensis* just didn't get on and the brighter *Homo sapiens* killed off their rivals.
- Disease: it was the diseases that *Homo sapiens* carried that wiped out the Neanderthals, who had little resistance to them.
- Food shortage: *Homo sapiens* had superior animal-hunting technology which resulted in their Neanderthal cousins being left with insufficient food to survive.
- Interbreeding: *Homo sapiens* and *Homo neanderthalensis* got on so well together that they interbred and the two species simply merged, with the result that the Neanderthal genes became diffused and the pure Neanderthals disappeared.

On the other hand, it could be that *Homo sapiens* had very little to do with it. There is much evidence of climate change around 40,000 years ago which resulted in severe cooling. This would have resulted in less food being available and the Neanderthals may have simply been unable to adapt their hunting methods to the demands of the new conditions.

236. Why do we have five fingers?

For the past 340 million years or so, the vast majority of land mammals have had five digits on their limbs. Before that, there is evidence of six-, seven- or eight-fingered animals, especially in the sea, but evolution seems to have settled on five as the best number. But why five? Might not four or six be preferable under certain circumstances?

The mechanics behind finger formation was discovered in 2014 and outlined in a paper with the rather forbidding title 'Digit patterning is controlled by a Bmp-Sox9-Wnt Turing network modulated by morphogen gradients'. Taking an idea originally proposed by the mathematician and code-breaker Alan Turing, the authors of the paper showed that there are three groups of molecules, called Bmp, Sox9 and Wnt, which interact with each other and turn each other on and off to control the growth of fingers in an embryonic hand. Between them, Bmp and Sox9 are responsible for the growth of fingers, but importantly, Wnt is responsible for the spaces between them, blocking Sox9 from having an effect where another finger would just get in the way.

The final number of fingers thus becomes dependent on the size of the hand. If our hands were 20 per cent larger, we would grow another finger, which is why around one in 500 people is born with an extra finger or toe. The mechanism controlling the formation and number of a creature's fingers seems firmly set to such an extent that even if a sixth finger were an advantage, its evolution might be ruled out. Pandas have shown the need for a thumb to help them grasp bamboo, but instead of evolving a sixth, opposable finger, they adapt a wrist bone into a pseudo-thumb to help them in that task.

James Sharpe, one of the authors of the paper mentioned above, described the question of why our bodies have evolved to give us hands with room for exactly five fingers as 'the ultimate meta-problem on top of everything', and he goes on: 'I often say that if we understood why five, we'd probably understand everything.'

237. When did human speech evolve?

The trouble with language is that it leaves no fossils. All evidence of the origins of language must therefore be indirect, relying on anatomy, genetics or calculations based on linguistic diversity, none of which can give a definitive answer.

The anatomical approach is based on the evolution of the vocal tract. Before this evolved, we lacked the apparatus necessary to make the sounds associated with language. Between 100,000 and 50,000 years ago changes are known to have taken place in the shape and capabilities of the human mouth, tongue, pharynx and larynx, which had profound effects on our abilities to produce a wide range of sounds, but whether our sound production could have supported a primitive language much earlier is disputed. There is even considerable uncertainty about the position of Neanderthals' larynxes, which would have strongly affected the question of whether they spoke or not.

The figure of 50,000 to 100,000 years ago for the origins of speech was recently supported by a study of the diversity of modern languages. Using a statistical technique for estimating the time-scale on which linguistic changes take place, a similar figure was reached for the appearance of the earliest proto-languages.

Different approaches, perhaps taking a more lenient view of the question of when grunting turned into talking, have come up with figures of up to 1.75 million years ago. The recent discovery of the FOX2P gene, which plays an important part in language formation, and the fact that chimpanzees possess a similar gene, have been cited as evidence that human language skills date back to soon after our divergence from chimps. Another recent study of blood flow in the brain has claimed to show that the mental processes associated with language evolved in parallel with the evolution of tool use.

So the best answer we can give to the question of when human speech evolved is somewhere between 1.75 million and 50,000 years ago, which is a very wide range indeed.

238. What sparked Upper Palaeolithic culture in human evolution?

From 40,000 to about 11,000 years ago, Upper Palaeolithic culture transformed Europe and the world. The people at the start of that period were skilled hunters, but the stone tools they used developed not only great diversity but began to show ornamentation in their designs. This was also the period of the earliest ivory carvings and rock paintings, which date back to around 35,000 years ago. At the end of the period, the era of agriculture began, in which humans began to take control of their environment.

What was responsible for these huge advances is unknown. Human brain size had not increased and no specific genetic changes have been identified that could account for it.

239. What did the Denisovans look like?

In March 2010 it was announced that a fragment of a finger-bone had been discovered in the remote Denisova Cave in the Altai Mountains in Siberia, a cave which was also known to have been inhabited by Neanderthals and modern humans. Analysis of the DNA of the bone revealed that it was genetically distinct from both those groups.

Further investigations, and the discovery of similar DNA in specimens from northern Spain, led to the conclusion that modern humans, Neanderthals and Denisovans, as this newly discovered human species was called, had shared a common ancestor around a million years ago. The Denisovans broke away from the Neanderthals about 400,000 years ago.

The coldness of the cave in which the finger-bone fragment was found was responsible for preserving the DNA, which has allowed scientists to build up a detailed picture of the evolutionary history of the Denisovans. This, however, tells us very little about their lifestyle or appearance. Indeed, with only a bit of bone to go on, together with two teeth that were discovered later, the only conclusion reached is that the female from whom the finger-bone came probably had brown eyes.

240. Who did the Denisovans mate with?

By comparing the genomes of Neanderthals, Denisovans and modern humans, much has been learnt about the inter-group mating patterns. We know that the Denisovans are more closely related to Neanderthals than to modern humans; and we know they must have made their way to South-east Asia, as their DNA shows signs of interbreeding with Melanesian and Aboriginal populations of New Guinea and Australia. But their genes also show evidence of their having bred with an even older human species than the Neanderthals.

Nobody knows who these mysterious early humans were who seemed to co-exist with Neanderthals and Denisovans. No fossils or other evidence of their existence have yet been found, other than the DNA they passed on, even to several groups of people alive today, via the Denisovans.

241. What was the most recent ancestor of both Neanderthals and modern humans?

Examination of the DNA of different species has revealed a great deal about the evolutionary path of mankind, but one question that has never been resolved is the nature of our evolutionary relationship to the Neanderthals. *Homo heidelbergensis*, *Homo erectus* and *Homo antecessor* have all been suggested as the common ancestor from which *Homo sapiens* and *Homo neanderthalensis* developed; some have even classified *Homo neanderthalensis* as a subspecies of *Homo sapiens*, but recent research has cast even greater doubt on the closeness of the relationship.

In 2013 a study was made of the shape of the teeth of various human species. In all, approximately 1,200 molars and premolars taken from thirteen hominid species were compared, and none of the three species mentioned above was found to have teeth compatible with the shape expected of an ancestor of both *Homo sapiens* and *Homo neanderthalensis*.

According to the writers, the evidence of the teeth suggests that Neanderthals diverged from modern humans as much as a million years ago, which is more than twice as long as had previously been thought. If this is right, then perhaps our search for a common ancestor has been in the wrong time period.

242. How many kinds of humans co-existed 100,000 years ago?

Homo sapiens first appeared around 200,000 years ago and by 100,000 years ago had begun to dominate other species of human. At that time, *Homo neanderthalensis* was still around and *Homo erectus* was probably not yet extinct. *Homo heidelbergensis* may also not have completely died out.

That had been the picture generally accepted for some time when remains of *Homo floresiensis* were found on the Indonesian island of Flores in 2003. Nicknamed 'Hobbit' because of its small stature, *Homo floresiensis* was found to have made stone tools, hunted dwarf elephants and large rodents, and even coped with predators such as Komodo dragons. He may also have used fire.

Some have suggested that *Homo floresiensis* may have been a dwarf species of *Homo erectus*, but the comparative recency of this discovery raises the question of whether there are other species of humans yet to be discovered which were around when *Homo sapiens* began throwing his intellectual weight around.

243. Why don't humans have tails?

Monkeys have tails; apes don't. The existence of the coccyx, or tail-bone, at the end of our spines is strong evidence that we lost our tails at some point in our evolution, but what crucial factor was responsible for the loss is a matter of speculation.

Animals with tails put them to a variety of uses: tails can swat flies, aid locomotion, act as a rudder while swimming, help preserve balance, and (if the tail is prehensile) enable its owner to swing from a branch while keeping its hands free. It has been suggested that we ceased to need a tail when we started walking on two legs instead of four, but it could equally be argued that having a tail would have been a useful aid to balance when we were becoming bipedal.

The advantages of having a tail may seem small for a modern human, but the disadvantages of having one seem to be even smaller. Why we lost it therefore seems to require some explanation.

See also ANATOMY 4, 6; ANIMALS 19; BONES 72; BRAINS 78; CHICKENS 97; EVOLUTION 181; GORILLAS 221; HUMOUR 244; INTELLIGENCE 253; LANGUAGE 268; LEGS 271; MUSIC 329; NOSES 344; PSYCHOLOGY 386; SEX 408; WORDS 498

HUMOUR

244. What are the evolutionary origins of humour?

There are three main theories that are commonly given to explain the existence of humour:

- Relief: humour is based on the alleviation of tension. A joke or humorous situation begins by setting up an unresolved conflict between two ideas; the resolution of that conflict in a non-damaging way results in relaxation.

- Superiority: humour is a way of asserting or emphasizing one's superiority over others. It thus has a social function of uniting or strengthening the bonds in a group by making others, who are the subject of the humour, look silly.
- Incongruity: an aspect present in almost all forms of humour is an unexpected outcome or a form of behaviour that goes against previous experience. The perception of incongruity may be advantageous in daily life to detect threats. It could be argued that humour helps develop that ability.

Such a categorization, however, seems more to be an attempt to analyse the content of humour than to explain its evolution. It could be argued that life is sufficiently full of stress without creating more tension and laughing at it; asserting one's own superiority could be potentially damaging as well as bond-strengthening; and laughing at incongruity could be seen as encouraging a tendency to take signs of potential threats insufficiently seriously.

In short, no convincing case has yet been made for the evolutionary benefits of humour.

245. Do animals have a sense of humour?

Much research on the topics of humour and laughter treats the two topics as two sides of the same phenomenon: humour is a cognitive reaction to a situation; laughter is our physical reaction to it, or our means of communicating that reaction. Research on humour in animals suffers from a similar confusion.

Young animals of various species have been observed having play-fights and making high-pitched laughter-like sounds as they do so. Rats have been shown to produce a giggling sound when tickled that is similar to the noise they make when they appear to be enjoying themselves. Apes have been documented apparently playing tricks on both their keepers and other apes and apparently laughing at the results.

In all such cases, however, we do not know whether there has been a cognitive humour response that led to the laughter. Indeed, we do not even know if it can be called 'laughter'. Some researchers have concluded that many animals have a sense of humour, but more cautious ones will only say that the animal's response to a situation has been a positive display indicating pleasure.

HYPNOSIS

246. Is hypnosis a distinct state of consciousness?

Consciousness and sleep are two states everyone recognizes. In addition there are trance states that may be induced by meditation, and there are drug-induced states. All of these may be detected by both behavioural and physiological signs. Whether hypnosis is a distinct state or is simply a heightened or lessened version of those already mentioned is something that even hypnotists have argued about for more than a century.

One theory is that hypnosis enables (or causes) people to divide their consciousness into two parts, one responding to the outside world, the other observing but not participating. By turning off the part that responds, the hypnotic subject may, for example, not consciously feel pain.

Another theory is that hypnosis can be explained by an individual's suggestibility. Good hypnotic subjects, this theory maintains, are simply people with high suggestibility who therefore behave as they believe they are expected to, even if that involves not feeling pain.

Supporters of the hypnotism-is-a-state hypothesis point to effects produced in subjects under hypnosis which can be neither explained nor replicated by other means. Their opponents, however, point to a lack of neurological evidence that hypnosis differs from other states. They also point to experiments that have demonstrated that when asked to simulate hypnosis, subjects can be even more consistent in producing hypnosis-like results.

This seems to be another of those questions that will not be resolved until we know much more about the functioning of the brain.

See also BRAINS 79; DREAMS 161

INCAS

247. Why did the Incas build Machu Picchu?

In the middle of the fifteenth century, the Incas built the magnificent city of Machu Picchu on a mountain ridge surrounded by a turbulent river in Peru. A century later, at the time of the Spanish conquest, it was abandoned and was not discovered again until 1911. Having no written language, the Incas left no record of their reasons for building the city or what it was used for.

One early theory was that it was a nunnery devoted to worship of the Sun. This idea now seems unlikely since investigation of remains from Machu Picchu in 2000 revealed that there had been about equal numbers of males and females.

Another theory is that it was a royal retreat, but this idea is based on a sixteenth-century Spanish document that mentions a royal estate called Picchu, but it is known that the Spanish never discovered the city.

Two more theories suggest that Machu Picchu had religious significance, either as a re-creation of a creation myth or simply as a place to honour the sacred landscape in which it was built. With around 500 buildings in a remote and generally inaccessible location, it must have had some special significance and purpose, but there is too little evidence to say what they were.

See also ANCIENT CITIES 11

INTELLIGENCE

248. What is intelligence?

We are all happy in our use of the word 'intelligent', but arriving at a definition of it is not so easy. Are problem-solving ability, learning ability, verbal fluency, spatial ability and a good memory all separate components of intelligence, or are they different ways of demonstrating some underlying trait? Early in the twentieth century, the psychologist and statistician Charles Spearman proposed the existence of a factor which he called 'g' that lay behind any human ability. This theory led to the development of intelligence tests which were designed to measure that factor. Anyone with a high g score might be expected to be good at any mental task as long as he had the specialist skills appropriate to that task, while anyone with low g would face difficulty whatever mental task he set his mind to.

Later the psychologist Raymond B. Cattell proposed that there are two types of intelligence which he called 'fluid' and 'crystallized'. Fluid intelligence is a measure of one's capacity to think logically and analyse and solve new problems; crystallized intelligence is the ability to use acquired knowledge, skills and experience.

More recent research, based on brain scans taken during mental tasks, suggests that there may be even more types of intelligence, but whether Spearman's g factor underlies them all is still a matter of debate.

249. Are we getting cleverer?

In 1984 the political scientist James Flynn published his research comparing intelligence test results in a wide range of studies throughout the world. His results showed that people's average IQ scores were rising by about three points per decade in whatever country one looked at. This observation, which has become known as the Flynn effect, has been cited as evidence that human beings are getting more intelligent.

This conclusion, however, is by no means the only possible explanation. Whatever intelligence tests measure, it can hardly be denied that above all they measure the ability to do intelligence tests. As such tests have become more common, one might expect people to become more attuned to them and able to perform better at them. Before asserting, from this evidence, that people are becoming more intelligent, one would need to be able to separate pure intelligence (whatever that is) from the 'intelligence' measured by intelligence tests, and that is something we have been unable to do.

250. Can plants be intelligent?

Researchers in the field they call plant neurobiology have shown that plants can react in a manner that would be called intelligent if it was done by animals. Plants, of course, do not have brains or neurons, so the expression 'plant neurobiology' is a bit of an oxymoron, but they do gather sensory information and react to it in a logical manner.

In one recent experiment, plants were played a recording of a caterpillar chewing on leaves. The plants responded by secreting anti-caterpillar defensive chemicals. Somehow, the plants 'heard' the sounds, associated them with the caterpillar threat and took appropriate action. Another controversial experiment seems to show that mimosa plants can learn from experience.

Finding a definition of intelligence that excludes plants is not as easy as it may once have seemed.

251. Are sea lions brighter than primates?

Sea lions have been taught to perform tricks and even to recognize a sign language, but over the past twenty years experiments on sea lions in California have shown that they are capable of more unusual feats of logic. In one experiment, sea lions had to choose between two symbols, one of which was a number, the other a letter. The numbers from 0 to 9 and the letters from *a* to *j* were used, so there were ten of each. If the sea lion pressed the number with its nose, it was given a fish; if it pressed the letter, it received nothing. The sea lion soon learnt to discriminate between the winning symbols (the numbers) and the losing symbols (the letters).

When it was consistently displaying a high level of accuracy, the experimenters played a mean trick on the animal: they reversed the condition. Now it was the letters that won a fish and the numbers that received nothing. Naturally, the sea lions started making the wrong decision, but after a time they realized what had happened: everything that had previously won now lost and vice versa. They could now be shown a number and a letter that they had not seen since the rule reversal, and they would make the right decision and pick the letter. The only animals that had previously shown this ability to swap entire classes were humans and pigeons.

In another experiment, a sea lion was taught to associate a picture of a crab with a picture of a tulip and then to associate a tulip with a radio. The sea lion then showed that it associated the crab with a radio. In mathematical terms, this is the law of transitivity:

If A = B and B = C, then A = C.

The sea lion is the first non-human animal to show that it understands this law. Whether other primates have the same logical skills is unknown.

252. Can human minds influence machines?

For the last thirty years the Princeton Engineering Anomalies Research Laboratory has been conducting research on whether the human mind can influence computers. In particular, experiments have been performed with random number generators (RNGs) to determine whether humans can make the numbers they generate less random than they ought to be.

The earliest results suggested that such machines produced subtly different results when attended by a human than when left alone. Further experiments suggested a small but significant difference in their output when humans were asked to concentrate and will them to produce higher numbers or lower numbers.

A scientific basis for this phenomenon, if it really exists, has been suggested in a possible interaction between the electrical fields generated by the human and the machine, but there are no suggestions of quite how that would work. The subject is particularly interesting to gamblers, as RNGs are at the heart of all computerized card games and slot machines. Research will no doubt continue into this subject.

253. If there is intelligent life elsewhere in the universe, why haven't they got in touch?

Everything we know about the evolution of intelligent life on Earth suggests that there should be intelligent life elsewhere in the universe. It may need very special conditions for life to develop, and it may take a long time for intelligence to develop, but there are billions of galaxies each containing billions of stars, many of which will have planetary systems. The Solar System itself is only about 4.6 billion years old, compared with the 13.8 billion years since the Big Bang, so even if we are only talking about life in Earth-like conditions, there is every reason to believe that intelligent life should have evolved in plenty of places.

Such an argument led the great physicist Enrico Fermi in 1950 to pose the question that subsequently became known as the Fermi paradox: 'Where is everybody?' Suggested answers include the following:

- They have been in touch with us, but we are too stupid to understand their messages.
- They know all about us but think we're insufficiently advanced to be worth contacting.
- They are higher-dimensional beings and we're too three-dimensional to notice that they are here.
- They all developed long ago and destroyed each other in intergalactic wars.
- What we think of as intelligent life is just a short phase in the development of matter and the alien life forms moved on billions of years ago.
- We've got it all wrong and we are alone in the universe after all.

254. Are bonobos cleverer than chimpanzees?

In 2011 scientists at Antwerp Zoo conducted a puzzle-solving contest between a group of chimpanzees and a group of bonobos. Each group was posed six timed tests, all involving puzzle boxes which required the use of tools to obtain the walnut rewards. The bonobos won the contest by four to two, thanks largely to the star of their team, a female named Djanoa, who is said to have concentrated on the puzzles while the chimpanzees were getting involved in fights with one another over dominance.

Chimpanzees, however, have long been known to be more aggressive than bonobos and to resolve conflicts in their male-dominated society by fighting, while the matriarchal bonobos resolve problems by having sex. The Antwerp contest therefore hardly adds to our knowledge on which species is cleverer. If Djanoa had not been particularly hungry or had not liked walnuts so much, the result could have been very different.

See also BIRDS 66; COMPUTERS 115–16; EVOLUTION 181; GAMES 208; WAITRESSES 484

INVENTIONS

255. Where were mechanical clocks invented?

From the ancient Egyptians around 1600 BC until the thirteenth century, time-keeping relied on the clepsydra, or water-clock. By allowing water to drip into a container at a constant rate, the passage of time could be measured to an accuracy up to about fifteen minutes a day, which was good enough for most purposes for almost three millennia.

The replacement of such devices by mechanical clocks was more a slow evolution than a sudden invention, which is why dates given for the invention of the first mechanical clock vary from AD 723, when the Chinese mathematician and monk I Hsing is credited, to 1344, when the Italian doctor, astronomer and clock-maker Jacopo de' Dondi (also known as Jacopo dell'Orologio) installed a clock in the tower of the Palazzo Capitaniato in Padua. The French architect Villard de Honnecourt is also sometimes mentioned as the inventor of the mechanical clock, while other sources claim that it was invented in England in 1275.

Part of the reason for the confusion lies in the development of the escapement, which is the clicking weight- or spring-driven wheel or pendulum that gradually replaced dripping water as the clock's essential time-keeper. From China in the eighth century to Europe in the thirteenth, several hybrid clocks appeared, still driven by water but using the ticking escapement for time-keeping. In Europe the first purely escapement-driven time-keeper was Villard de Honnecourt's astronomical device that tracked the Sun's motion across the sky.

For a real clock, however, we need a dial and hands as well as an escapement, and these first appeared in many places in Europe in the early fourteenth century so close to each other in time that it is impossible to say which place was first.

256. Who invented the door-knob?

On 10 December 1878 the black American inventor Osbourn Dorsey was granted US patent No. 210,762 for his 'Door-holding device'. On the basis of this, Dorsey is often credited with being the inventor of the door-knob, but around 100 door-knob patents had been issued in the forty years before Dorsey's device. Even earlier, glass door-knobs had been popular, while the French and English had used ceramic ones before cast-metal knobs and knobs made of potter's clay began to appear.

The *Oxford English Dictionary* dates the earliest recorded use of the word 'door-knob' to a US patent of 1847, but Dorsey's may indeed have been the first door-knob that had more than a decorative use and could actually be turned to close and open a door.

See also CHEWING GUM 96; SEX 407

IOWA

257. What was the Van Meter Visitor?

For several days in 1903, the town of Van Meter, Iowa, was terrified by nightly visits from a creature described as half-man, half-animal with enormous bat wings. It was first spotted flying over the roofs of buildings, and the sightings were by respected and reliable people, including a doctor and bank cashier. The creature was reported to have let off a powerful stench and shot a blinding light from its horned head.

On the third night, the townsfolk armed themselves and followed it to an abandoned coal mine, where it let out a noise 'as though Satan and a regiment of imps were coming forth for battle'. They chased it down the mine and it was never seen again.

The story has no doubt been embellished over the years, but it seems certain that something was seen in Van Meter over those days. More than a century later, however, there is still no idea of what it might have been.

ITALY

258. How and why were the tunnels at Baiae built?

In the early 1960s the British amateur archaeologist Robert Paget started to investigate a mysterious doorway in the rocks at the old Roman resort of Baiae on the Bay of Naples. It had been discovered about a decade earlier after having been left undisturbed and hidden for around 2,000 years. The doorway was narrow and led to a pitch-black, fume-filled passageway which had deterred anyone from venturing inside. Paget and an American colleague Keith Jones, however, started investigating the passageway, which turned out to reveal an astonishingly complex system of tunnels.

The initial passageway ran exactly east–west, which suggested a ritual purpose probably connected with the equinox. For its first 400 metres it had a slow incline downwards, with niches every metre or so, probably for oil lamps. There followed a much steeper passageway downwards, leading to an S-bend which revealed an underground stream filled with hot, sulphurous water. An ascending passage on the other side of the stream led to an ante-chamber from which hidden staircases led to the surface.

How the ancient Romans could possibly have built an underground complex on such a scale is one mystery, but even greater is the question of how they could possibly have known of the existence of the underground stream which seems to have been the justification for the work. One suggestion is that whoever built it may have modelled its construction on myths of Hell, with the underground stream representing the River Styx, which was the boundary of the underworld, or the River Phlegethon in Hell itself. Or perhaps they even believed that they had discovered a real entrance to Hades. It was not until the 1970s that it was finally discovered that the stream led not to Hell but out into the Gulf of Naples miles away at Cape Miseno.

See also ATILLA 31

'Beware of false knowledge: it is more dangerous than ignorance.'

G. B. Shaw

JESUS CHRIST

259. How did Joseph and Mary, the parents of Jesus Christ, die?

The New Testament is very sparing in the details it gives about the lives of Joseph and Mary. The last we hear of Joseph is when Jesus was twelve years old and went missing on a trip to Jerusalem and was found by Joseph and Mary in the temple. According to the 'Story of Joseph the Carpenter' in the Coptic Apocrypha, Joseph died at the age of 111, on 20 July AD 18 or 19. St Epiphanius gave his age as ninety when he died and the Venerable Bede wrote that he was buried in the Valley of Josaphat. Their sources for these claims are unknown. It seems reasonable, however, to assume that Joseph had died before the Crucifixion, or Jesus would not have entrusted his mother to John's care.

Mary's death is also not recorded in the scriptures, but both the Catholic and Orthodox churches say that she was taken bodily into heaven and did not die at all. According to the seventh- or eighth-century writer Hippolytus of Thebes, she lived for eleven years after the Crucifixion and died in AD 41.

260. Did the manuscript of Jesus' sayings known as Q ever exist?

The Gospels of Matthew and Luke have much in common. Their writers are thought to have both used Mark's Gospel as a source, but they also share a good deal that is not in Mark. Much of this consists of the sayings of Jesus which, it has been conjectured, they obtained from a hypothetical document known as Q (from *Quelle*, German for 'source').

Whether Q was an actual document or just represented the oral tradition of the early Christian church has been argued since about 1900. Opponents of the theorized existence of Q say that no direct evidence of such a document has ever been found and such an important piece of writing would never have been allowed to disappear. Supporters of the Q theory, however, point to the close similarity of a large number of references in Matthew and Luke, which would have been very unlikely to occur if they were relying on spoken and remembered accounts.

261. How many brothers and sisters did Jesus have?

Both Matthew and Mark tell us that Jesus had four brothers – James, Joseph, Simon and Judas – and they also mention that he had sisters, but neither names them nor tells us how many. When Matthew (13:56) reports Jesus' followers asking in the synagogue, 'His sisters, are they not all with us?', the use of the word 'all' would seem to imply that he had at least three.

Some have argued, however, that the words 'brothers' and 'sisters' may refer to the children of Joseph by a previous marriage, or the cousins of Jesus rather than later children of Joseph and Mary.

262. Did Jesus ever work as a carpenter?

There is an eighteen-year gap in the Gospels in their account of Jesus' life between the ages of twelve and about thirty. All we are told of that period is that he 'advanced in wisdom and stature, and in favour with God and men' (Luke 2:52). One suggestion is that he entered the family business and learnt the skills of a carpenter from Joseph.

In Mark 6:3 the question is asked, 'Is not this the carpenter, the son of Mary', which suggests that Jesus was recognized as a carpenter, while Matthew 13:55 poses the same question as: 'Is not this the carpenter's son?' This suggests that Jesus was recognized at best as an apprentice to his father, or even as 'the kid we used to see playing at the carpenter's place'.

There is also a problem about the word 'carpenter', which is a translation of a Greek work signifying a more general type of handyman than we now associate with the word 'carpenter'.

263. How many contemporaries of Jesus were direct descendants of King David?

Both Matthew and Luke make a point of establishing that Jesus was a direct descendant of King David whose own genealogy is traced back to Adam. Both give very similar lists from Adam to David, but they diverge considerably in the way they trace the family tree from David to Jesus. Matthew's list gives twenty-seven generations from one to the other, Luke gives forty-two generations. When you do the maths, however, this ought not to be surprising, for there would probably have been many ways to trace back Jesus' ancestry to David.

Tracing anyone's ancestors will reveal two parents, four grandparents and, in most cases, eight great-grandparents. The number of great-grandparents may be lower if inbreeding took place. As we go further and further back, the numbers of direct ancestors will continue growing until we reach a stage when almost everybody is an ancestor. The only exceptions will be those in closed communities who never married outside, and those who never had children or whose lines of descendants died out.

The population of the Holy Land at the time of Jesus was about a million, and calculations based on a plausible mathematical model of reproduction show that King David would have been a common ancestor of the entire population of the Holy Land somewhere between twenty and thirty-five generations after his own. So almost everyone alive in the Holy Land at the time of Jesus would have been able to claim David as an ancestor.

See also ANATOMY 7; ASTRONOMY 30; BIBLE 52–3

'Research is what I'm doing when I don't know what I am doing.'

Werner von Braun

JUPITER

264. Why are Jupiter's clouds so colourful?

From an artistic point of view, Jupiter is beautiful. From the Great Red Spot in its atmosphere to the wide range of colours in its clouds, from white to yellows and ruddy browns, and even occasional hints of green and blue, it presents an ever-changing technicolour rainbow. From a scientific point of view, however, it is a mystery, because we do not know about the chemistry that is producing these colours.

Jupiter's atmosphere is known to be mostly frozen ammonia, but ammonia ice is white and cannot account for the colours. There are plenty of chemicals which might, but theories about how the colours are produced do not match the data obtained from either the Infrared Space Observatory in the 1990s or the Cassini fly-by of Jupiter in 2000/1.

Even the Great Red Spot is unexplained, as this indicates the presence of something absorbing blue light and we do not know what it is.

See also ASTRONOMY 30; SOLAR SYSTEM 441

KANGAROOS

265. Were giant kangaroos too big to hop?

Until about 30,000 years ago, a species of giant kangaroo called sthenurines roamed Australia, but how exactly they did the roaming is a matter of some dispute. Research on modern kangaroos has shown that hopping is for them the most energy-efficient means of locomotion at speeds of more than 29 km/h. Giant kangaroos, however, were three times the weight of even the largest species of kangaroo today, and a recent study of the bones of both modern and extinct species has suggested that the giant kangaroo might have swaggered rather than hopped.

The authors of the study suggested that the muscles used to flex the spine in giant kangaroos were too small to allow efficient hopping. Their conclusion was that as kangaroos grew larger, they started to walk on two legs rather than bending down to bounce. If that is all true, however, it raises the question of how the kangaroos managed in the first place to evolve to a size that interfered with their primary means of locomotion.

See also MAMMALS 283

KISSES

266. Who was the first to use X as a symbol for a kiss?

According to the *Oxford English Dictionary*, the earliest recorded use of an X to signify a kiss was in 1763, when the naturalist and cleric Gilbert White ended a letter: 'I am with many a xxxxxxx and many a Pater noster and Ave Maria, Gil White.'

It is not clear, however, whether Gilbert White's Xs signified a string of kisses or Christian blessings. An X had long symbolized the Crucifixion as well as being the first letter of 'Christ' in Greek, so when a cleric strung several together in conjunction with a Pater noster and an Ave Maria, it could be that he wasn't thinking of kisses at all.

In any case, some have derived the use of X to symbolize a kiss back to a much older practice of illiterates signing documents with an X and then kissing the X to show sincerity. Some say that an X is simply designed to suggest the coming together of two puckered-up lips, while perhaps the most romantic idea of all is that a letter-writer might place a kiss at the end of the script, then add an X over the kiss to let the recipient know where it was so they could place it to the lips and receive the kiss. But when the practice began seems not to be known.

LANGUAGE

267. Is language ability hard-wired into our brains?

In the 1960s the US philosopher/linguist Noam Chomsky popularized the idea that language is hard-wired into the human brain. His idea was not that we are pre-programmed to understand and speak a particular language but that we are all equipped with what he called a 'universal grammar', which is the underlying structure behind all languages.

The idea that language ability is innate has been argued for half a century, and papers continue to appear both for and against Chomsky's view. Supporters of the innateness theory cite evidence of the way children learn languages, apparently picking up and generalizing rules without needing to be taught them. Opponents, however, have questioned the existence of a universal grammar, and, after comparing the structure of different languages, have concluded that there is nothing they all have in common. They also claim that the so-called innate linguistic abilities of children are not language-specific at all, but are simply examples of our general innate skills of concept formation and pattern recognition.

268. Did every language evolve from a single primitive mother tongue?

Similarities between different languages have led to the conclusion that some must have had a common origin. We know that many English words had their roots in Latin and Greek, while others were borrowed from French or Germanic languages. Pursuing the trail further back has led to the belief that all those languages, together with Hindi, Gaelic, Russian and a host of other tongues, had a common ancestor in an unknown ancient language known as Proto-Indo-European.

Similar comparisons between language groups have led to notional languages from which all others, including those that have now died out, evolved. Knowledge of human evolution suggests that the physical ability to utter sounds dates back to the earliest days of *Homo sapiens*. Even Neanderthals had the basic anatomy needed for speech, so it seems likely that some sort of language may have existed before the earliest modern humans emerged from Africa. Tracing the fifty or so proto-languages back to a single common ancestor, however, has so far been no more than pure guesswork.

See also ATILLA 32; AZTECS 38; COMPUTERS 114; ENGLISH HISTORY 175; HUMAN EVOLUTION 237; MARRIAGE 284; MEERKATS 302; PREHISTORY 383; WORDS 498

LEGS

269. Why do centipedes have so many legs?

Centipedes may have more than 300 legs or fewer than twenty, but the evolutionary advantages of having so many is unclear. A large number of legs is no doubt helpful in letting them move quickly, or in using some legs to hold captured prey while using others to grab more, but numerous legs are also liable to get in each other's way and at the best of times their co-ordination will take up considerable mental resources.

Interestingly, millipedes, which have more legs, move more slowly than centipedes, so the question of why they have so many is even more difficult to answer.

270. Why do centipedes never have a hundred legs?

A centipede's body is divided into segments and each segment has two legs. The number of legs is therefore always even, but the number of segments is always odd, so the number of pairs of legs is odd. This may be explained by the way the centipede's body grows. It does this by adding segments, and each time it adds a segment, that segment divides into two. This leaves an even number of pairs of legs on the added segments, which becomes an odd number when we include a pair of legs on the head segment which are used as pincher-legs.

Whether the pincher-legs are formed on a segment that divides, however, is not known. If that is the case, another reason would need to be found why the number of pairs of legs is odd and why a centipede with exactly 100 legs (i.e. fifty pairs) is impossible.

271. Why did apes start walking on two legs instead of four?

Writing about the evolution of bipedalism in 1871, Charles Darwin said that the early hominids walked on two legs in order to leave their hands free. He said that 'the hands and arms could hardly have become perfect enough to have manufactured weapons, or to have hurled stones and spears with a true aim, as long as they were habitually used for locomotion'.

This sounds plausible enough, but later evidence showed that apes started walking on their hind legs about 7 million years ago, which was about 4.5 million years before the earliest stone tools came into use.

Another theory has linked bipedalism with environmental changes leading to deforestation, when walking on two legs across open country could have been more energy-efficient. It has also been suggested that bipedalism evolved alongside monogamy, enabling males to carry food back to females who were looking after the young.

Until further evidence is found of early hominids and the environments they lived in, the origins of their bipedalism will remain a mystery.

See also DINOSAURS 138; MEDICINE 300; SLOTHS 431

LEMURS

272. Why do fat-tailed dwarf lemurs hibernate?

The fat-tailed dwarf lemur of Madagascar is the only primate known to hibernate. According to research published in 2013, it is also the only animal known to fall fully asleep while hibernating and was the first tropical mammal known to hibernate. Other animals when hibernating enter a state of torpor when metabolism almost stops. Lemurs fall properly asleep and metabolism continues. Unlike other animals that hibernate because of the cold, the behaviour in lemurs seems to be an adaptation to drought, when food and water are scarce. During their six- or seven-month hibernation period, they live off the fat stored in their tails. Even more unusually, their body temperature does not stay low during the hibernation period, but fluctuates quite dramatically.

Other lemurs have recently been found to hibernate, but their hibernation is more like that of other mammals. How the fat-tailed dwarf lemurs of Madagascar evolved this unique behaviour and what triggers it when they decide to curl up in a tree trunk and fall asleep for half the year are not yet known.

LEONARDO

273. Were Leonardo da Vinci's catapults ever used in battle?

In the 1480s Leonardo da Vinci made at least two detailed sketches of designs for catapults. Although gunpowder had already been introduced to Europe, da Vinci is known to have been concerned about its safety and general unreliability and believed that there was still a need in military battles for more traditional weapons such as catapults.

One of his designs features a single-arm catapult using a ratchet system to move the swing arm into a position from which it could unleash a projectile with great power. The other design was for a double-arm catapult which used gears to allow the throwing arm to be drawn back. Both designs featured improvements on anything that had been seen previously.

Da Vinci is known to have touted his ideas to kings and noblemen, who we may assume would have been very interested in any device that might have enhanced their prospects on the battlefield or the defence of their castles. There is no evidence, however, whether or not da Vinci's catapults were ever even made during his lifetime, let alone used in battle.

Later reconstructions have confirmed that they may have been difficult and expensive to construct at the time, but would almost certainly have been effective if someone had taken the trouble to do so.

See also ART 25

LEOPARDS

274. Why do leopards kill their young?

A recent survey covering a thirteen-year period in South Africa's Kruger National Park revealed that of 280 dead leopard cubs recorded by the researchers, forty-five had been killed by male leopards which then ate them. There have also been accounts of female leopards eating their own babies, but that is much rarer. So what is the evolutionary advantage of such behaviour? There are several theories:

   (i) They may be driven to it by a food shortage.

   (ii) They may do it to keep the family to a manageable size.

   (iii) They may be driven to it by stress, possibly caused by human behaviour.

   (iv) They may just be aggressive animals, with the cubs just collateral damage from fights between adults.

   (v) Males may be killing off babies of a potential mate to give their own future offspring a better chance.

In view of the fact that most such killings are done by males, the most likely of these is the last, with the eating of the babies just a nutritional, opportunistic by-product of the killing, but the other explanations seem equally possible if females are simply less inclined towards infanticide.

LITERATURE

275. Was Wordsworth's Lucy a real person?

Between 1798 and 1801, when William Wordsworth was living in Germany, he wrote a series of five poems expressing his love for 'Lucy', an English girl who 'dwelt among th' untrodden ways beside the Springs of Dove' and who died young. The passionate melancholy in these verses about the 'maid whom there were none to praise, And very few to love' is very striking, but the question of whether Lucy was a real person or an idealized figment of Wordsworth's imagination has never been resolved.

The poet himself never revealed any details about Lucy, leaving others to speculate on her possible identity. It has been suggested that Lucy represented his childhood sweetheart Peggy Hutchinson, who died young in 1796. Wordsworth later married Peggy's sister Mary, but it has also been suggested that Lucy in fact was based on his own sister Dorothy, who went on to live to the age of eighty-three.

276. Did the Book of the Wars of the Lord ever exist?

The King James Bible, in Numbers 21:14, refers to the 'Book of the Wars of the Lord' and goes on to quote lines from a song and sayings of poets, without making it clear whether these quotations are taken from the same Book of the Wars of the Lord.

It has been conjectured that the book referred to may have been a collection of victory songs or poems, or it may have been a military history. It has also been suggested that the phrase 'Book of the Wars' was not the title but only a quotation from the book, but since no trace of the book has ever been found, it may not have existed at all.

277. What does the first word of *Beowulf* mean?

The opening words of the epic poem *Beowulf*, which begins 'Hwæt! We Gar-Dena in gear-dagum...', are usually translated 'Listen! We have heard of the might of the kings...', but there has long been dispute over the meaning and significance of the opening word.

In 1837 Jakob Grimm (one of the brothers Grimm, who collected fairy tales when not pursuing their linguistic researches) wrote that 'Hwæt' was purely an interjection. For many it was seen simply as a way of telling the reader or listener to take notice, which later writers translated as 'Listen!' or 'Attend!' or even 'So!' (which was the choice of Seamus Heaney in his acclaimed 2000 translation).

In 2013, however, Dr George Walkden of Cambridge University gave a very different view based on an analysis of 141 other clauses using the word 'Hwæt', combined with general evidence of the Anglo-Saxon use of exclamation marks. His conclusion was that 'Old English *hwæt* (as well as its Old Saxon cognate) was not an interjection but an underspecified wh-pronoun introducing an exclamative clause'. In other words, 'hwaet' is not an exclamation on its own, but only becomes one when taken in conjunction with the words that follow. The translation he suggests for the opening line was: 'How we have heard of the might of the kings.'

Some 1,200 or 1,300 years after *Beowulf* was written, we are still arguing about what its first word means.

See also TROY 456

LOBSTERS

278. How long can a lobster live?

Lobsters have very long lives. For a long time, some people even believed they were immortal. They do not even seem to age, and lose neither strength nor reproductive abilities as they grow older. The reason for this seems to lie in the lobster's habit of discarding its shell quite frequently and growing a new one, which enables it to grow while renewing the parts of itself that might be considered susceptible to ageing.

The same process, however, makes it very difficult to assess the age of a lobster. Unlike both trees and other animals, it does not have obvious growth rings, such as have been found in dinosaur bones and fish scales, marking the years of its development. The best way to judge a lobster's age until recently was from its size: multiply its weight in pounds by four, add three and you have an approximation of its age in years.

In 2012, however, a more scientific way of estimating a lobster's age began to be developed. Although moulting destroyed the exoskeleton and all the hard parts of a lobster which would normally be relied upon to bear the marks of ageing, growth rings were found in their eye-stalks and the gastric mills in their stomachs which are used to grind up food. The build-up of neurolipofuscin in their brains was also found to give an indication of age. The reliability of such measures continues to be investigated in order to establish whether the metabolic age, as measured by such ring-counting, correlates with chronological age.

Since shedding their shells demands increasingly large amounts of energy as lobsters get bigger, eventually they stop shedding and die, so they are definitely not immortal, but how long they can live is still not known. In 1977 a lobster weighing over 20 kilograms was caught in Nova Scotia, which, by the old formula, would have made it at least 179 years old. But nobody counted the rings on its eye-stalks at the time.

'Is an intelligent human being likely to be much more than a large-scale manufacturer of misunderstanding?'

Philip Roth

LONGEVITY

279. How long can humans live?

In 2004 BBC News reported a story under the headline: 'We will be able to live to 1,000.' The story centred on the SENS (Strategies for Engineered Negligible Senescence) project which consisted of 'a very detailed plan to repair all the types of molecular and cellular damage that happen to us over time'. The Cambridge geneticist Aubrey de Grey was quoted as saying: 'I think the first person to live to 1,000 might be 60 already.'

Some other scientists dismissed such claims as more fantasy than science, but in 2013 the *Daily Mail* published a report of research in California under the heading: 'Could humans live to 500 years old? Scientists believe genetic tweaks could significantly extend our lifespan.' The research, however, was on worms, not humans. By modifying the genes of *Caenorhabditis elegans* lab worms, the researchers had been able to increase their lifespans by a factor of five. If a similar technique could be applied to long-lived humans, the newspaper report said, we could live to the age of 400 or 500. 'The next step is to investigate if the effects occur in mice,' it said.

Today worms, tomorrow mice, maybe one day humans, but in the meantime our worldwide life expectancy is still 68.5 years for males and 73.5 years for females.

280. Is human immortality out of the question?

Is death an inevitable part of life? Ever since alchemists started looking for an elixir of immortality, that question has been asked and the comparatively recent discovery of telomeres is the nearest we have yet come to an answer. Telomeres are chains at the ends of our DNA molecules which become shorter every time the cell replicates. When the telomere becomes too short, the cell loses its vital DNA code, its ability to replicate is damaged, and the process of dying begins.

The number of times a cell can divide without damage is called the Hayflick limit, after US anatomist Leonard Hayflick, whose study of cell reproduction in 1961 put an end to the belief that human cells were in principle immortal. Later it was found that the Hayflick limit correlated with telomere length, and the quest for immortality began to concentrate on looking for ways to prevent the shortening of telomeres with each cell division.

The good news in that regard is an enzyme called telomerase which can turn telomere production on and off. You might say that telomerase is potentially the elixir of immortality for our cells. The bad news, however, is that telomerase is precisely what makes cancer cells keep reproducing. Thanks to telomerase, cancer cells are, in fact, the nearest thing we have to immortality. Anything that increases our production of telomerase, boosting our telomeres and maintaining the reproduction of our cells, will also lead to an increase in cancers.

Immortality by this route would therefore seem to need something that blocks the action of telomerase on cancerous cells while not interfering with its action on normal cells.

281. Are short telomeres a sign of ageing or a cause of ageing?

In 2002 a study at the University of Utah confirmed that shorter telomeres in humans are associated with shorter lives. People with shorter telomeres were three times more likely to die within the next year from heart disease and eight times more likely to die from infectious disease. In healthy people, however, it has been shown that telomeres do not shrink significantly until old age thanks to the production of telomerase. The net shortening of telomere length seems to be caused by a combination of cell division and lessening telomerase production.

The 2002 study showed that only 37 per cent of the variation in the risk of dying among the over-sixties was accounted for by a combination of age, gender and telomere length. The other 63 per cent was attributed to other causes such as oxidative stress and glycation, caused by our intake of oxidants and glucose, which can damage DNA, proteins and fats.

Ageing and shortened telomeres undoubtedly go together, but which is the cause and which is the effect remains unproven. Mice, after all, have much longer telomeres than humans, but live much shorter lives.

282. How long do fangtooths live?

Members of the ugly fang-toothed Anoplogastridae family – commonly known, appropriately enough, as 'fangtooths' – are among the least-known fish in the oceans. There are two species, the common fangtooth and the short-horn fangtooth; they live at depths of up to 5,000 metres (but more often at 500–2,000 metres), growing to just over eighteen centimetres in length, and have no known close relatives.

Fangtooths have very poor sight and seem to locate prey through their chemical receptors, latching on to it with their huge teeth when they bump into it. The upper parts of their mouths have holes in them through which their lower fangs slot to enable them to close their mouths.

The depths at which they live have hampered attempts to find out more about them. All that is known about their mating behaviour is that females seem to deposit eggs in the water at the same time as males deposit sperm. And nobody seems to have any idea how long they live.

See also GENETICS 211; SHARKS 416

'Science... is made up of mistakes, but they are mistakes which it is useful to make because they lead little by little to the truth.'

Jules Verne

MAMMALS

283. Why do only placental mammals have a corpus callosum?

Mammals come in three varieties: monotremes, such as the platypus and echidna, which lay eggs; marsupials, such as the kangaroo and koala, which have pouches; and placental mammals, such as humans and rats, in which the mother nourishes the foetus within a placenta until it is fully developed. As mentioned earlier (→ 5), all the placental mammals, and only the placental mammals, have brains divided into two halves joined by a thick bundle of neural fibres called the corpus callosum.

The evolutionary split of mammals into these three classes is thought to have occurred between 65 and 100 million years ago, which is roughly when the corpus callosum is thought to have evolved. So was the evolution of the placenta in some way connected to the evolution of the corpus callosum?

Nobody has yet suggested a way the two might be connected, but the fact that all mammals have either both or neither seems to demand an explanation.

See also ANATOMY 5; BONES 72; BRAINS 78; DINOSAURS 138; DISEASE 144; EVOLUTION 178, 181; HUMAN EVOLUTION 236; LEMURS 272; PANDAS 353; PANGOLINS 354; PLATYPUSES 375; RATS 393; SALAMANDERS 398; SLEEP 423–4; WALRUSES 486

MARRIAGE

284. When and where did the first marriage ceremony take place?

The earliest recorded formal marriage ceremonies between a man and a woman took place in Mesopotamia about 2350 BC. In the language of the Sumerians of southern Mesopotamia, the word for 'to love' was even a compound verb connected with the marking-off of land, suggesting that the concept of love and marriage had a primarily legal aspect. Indeed, in the Code of Hammurabi, which around 1750 BC laid down 283 laws and punishments for breaking them, more than fifty were concerned with the legal rights and wrongs of marriage, polygamy, dowries and adultery.

With such long and detailed regulations surrounding the concept of marriage, it seems reasonable to suppose that the idea of it had already been around a long time before the Mesopotamians formalized it so precisely. Very early human societies are thought to have consisted of communal groups in which women and responsibility for children were shared, so they would have had little use for marriage. How these societies developed from promiscuity to pair-bonding is not known, but it must have happened long before the Mesopotamians had advanced enough to draw up copious laws and procedures related to it.

See also ATILLA 31; HENRY VIII 229; SHAKESPEARE 414

MARS

285. What turned Mars into a dry planet?

Evidence from space research has revealed water vapour in Mars's atmosphere as well as a vast amount of ice and even a freshwater lake on the planet's surface. The planet is now predominantly desiccated, but around 4 billion years ago, when the Solar System was in its infancy, Mars is thought to have been kept warm by a thick atmosphere and to have had rivers flowing into lakes and seas. NASA's Mars Atmosphere and Volatile Evolution (MAVEN) orbiter is currently trying to get to the bottom of the question of what dried Mars out when it seemed to be firmly on the path to producing life in a way similar to what happened on Earth.

One idea is that the Martian atmosphere may, over billions of years, have been blown away by the solar wind. The reason this has not happened on Earth is that we have a global magnetic field to protect us. Mars has just a few areas similarly protected by its own magnetic properties.

Another suggestion is that the greenhouse gas carbon dioxide (CO_2) may have been absorbed by the planet's surface with a resulting cooling effect. It is hoped that MAVEN will be able to measure the rate of escape of CO_2 and other gases and extrapolate the figure backwards to get an idea of what has been going on for the past 4 billion years.

286. What is the source of the methane on Mars?

Ever since 1909 we have known there is a small amount of methane in Mars's atmosphere. This cannot be the remains of ancient methane because methane molecules last only 300 or 400 years in Martian air before they are broken down by sunlight. So the planet must still be releasing methane. In December 2014 the Martian methane question became still more intriguing when NASA's *Curiosity* rover reported the discovery that Mars was periodically belching out clouds of methane from its surface.

On Earth most methane is produced as a waste gas from the consumption of food by living organisms, so the Martian methane was seen as a possible hint of life on the planet. It could also be produced by the remains of long-extinct organisms being heated in the Martian interior and vaporized.

There are plenty of ways, however, that methane could be produced that do not involve life of any form, and the gas on its own will never be enough to prove that there is or is not life on Mars. Nevertheless, investigation of the rocks on Mars and the gases in its atmosphere may suggest or rule out other possible causes for the methane.

See also MERCURY 304

MATHEMATICS

287. Does a perfect cuboid exist?

Given any three positive integers, we can imagine a cuboid (that's a rectangular box) whose length, breadth and height are given by those integers. Pythagoras' theorem lets us work out the lengths of the diagonals on the faces of the box, and if the lengths of all three such diagonals are also integers, the cuboid is known as an 'Euler brick' after the great eighteenth-century Swiss mathematician Leonard Euler.

The first such Euler brick was discovered in 1719, with sides of lengths 44, 117 and 240 (where the diagonals work out at 125, 244 and 267 exactly). But what about the internal diagonal, from the bottom, front, left corner to the top, back, right? Can that have an integer length too?

What we're looking for is three integers, a, b and c (the side lengths), for which not only are $a^2 + b^2$ and $b^2 + c^2$ and $c^2 + a^2$ (the squares of the diagonals) perfect squares, but $a^2 + b^2 + c^2$ (the square of the internal diagonal) is also a perfect square. If such numbers can be found, then the result is called a 'perfect cuboid', but so far nobody has either discovered one or proved that none can exist.

288. Can every sufficiently large number be expressed as the sum of six cubes?

One cubed = 1 x 1 x 1, which is 1, two cubed is 2 x 2 x 2, which is 8, and we can go on with the sequence of cubes: 27, 64, 125, 216, 343, 512, 729...

What happens, though, if we try to express any number as the sum of positive cubes? It was proved about a century ago that every number can be expressed as the sum of at most nine cubes, and the only numbers that required nine were 23 (= 8 + 8 + 1 + 1 + 1 + 1 + 1 + 1 + 1) and 239 (= 125 + 27 + 27 + 27 + 8 + 8 + 8 + 8 + 1). Later it was proved that, apart from these, the only numbers needing at least eight cubes were 15, 22, 50, 114, 167, 175, 186, 212, 231, 238, 303, 364, 420, 428 and 454, so it follows that any number greater than 454 can be expressed as the sum of at most seven cubes.

But can we make a similar statement about six cubes? Is there a number beyond which we can say that any larger number is the sum of at most six positive cubes?

289. Are there infinitely many Fermat primes?

The great French mathematician Pierre Fermat, who died in 1665, spent much effort looking for a formula that would generate prime numbers. The nearest he got was the so-called Fermat primes, which are numbers of the form $2^{(2^n)} + 1$.

Fermat conjectured that all such numbers were prime, and for the first few values of n, he was right. The first five values given by the formula are 3, 5, 17, 257 and 65537, and these are indeed prime numbers. Unfortunately, as Euler discovered in 1732, the next number in the series, 4294967297, is equal to 641 x 6700417.

Since that time, no Fermat prime apart from the first five has ever been discovered, yet whether there are any more, or even possibly an infinite number of them, is still unknown.

290. Does the number 10 have any friends?

Think of a number; find all the numbers (including itself) that divide into it exactly; add them all together and divide by the number you first thought of. Now try to find another number that gives you the same answer if you do the same thing. If you find one, then the two numbers you started with are called 'friendly'. For example, 30 and 140 are friendly:

The sum of the divisors of 30 is

$1 + 2 + 3 + 5 + 6 + 10 + 15 + 30 = 72.$

Dividing that by 30 gives 72/30, which equals 12/5.

The sum of the divisors of 140 is

$1 + 2 + 4 + 5 + 7 + 10 + 14 + 20 + 28 + 35 + 70 + 140 = 336.$

Divide that by 140 and we get 336/140, which (dividing top and bottom by 28) equals 12/5.

If we start with the number 10, we get $(1 + 2 + 5 + 10)/10 = 9/5$, and nobody has ever found another number that gives the same result. Nobody has ever proved that no such number exists, however, so we do not know whether 10 has any friends or not.

291. Is there a 3 x 3 magic square all of whose entries are distinct perfect squares?

A magic square is a square array of numbers, all of whose rows, columns and diagonals add up to the same number. Here's an example in which they all add up to 15:

4	9	2
3	5	7
8	1	6

Here's another more complicated example devised by Euler in 1770:

4624	841	1681	1369
289	961	6241	1024
3481	783	529	3721
121	5929	64	2401

But Euler was not just fooling around with large numbers, for his square has a really magical property: not only do all lines add up to 8515, but all sixteen numbers in it are themselves squares.

The question is, can the same trick be done with a 3 x 3 square? Does a magic square of that size exist that is made up of nine different square numbers? Nobody has ever found one or proved that no such square exists.

292. Why is mathematics so effective at explaining the world?

Why do two bodies, according to Newton's law of gravity, attract each other with a force proportional to the product of the masses of the bodies and inversely proportional to the square of the distance between them?

Why do Maxwell's equations tell us all we need to know about electricity and magnetism?

Why does $E = mc^2$?

In short, as Einstein put it: 'How is it possible that mathematics, a product of human thought that is independent of experience, fits so excellently the objects of physical reality?'

According to mathematical Platonists, maths is a pure and idealized language that is in effect the mother tongue of the real world and everything must yield to its power or make no sense. According to non-Platonists, maths is, as Einstein said, a product of the human mind, a mental construct that can at best give a rigid approximation to what is really happening.

Mathematics, even the non-Platonists must agree, has made a pretty good job of explaining the world, but many of the unanswered questions in this book could be cited as evidence that its explanations are never complete.

See also BIG BANG 55; COSMOLOGY 123, 126; JESUS CHRIST 263; NUMBERS 346; SOLAR SYSTEM 444; UNIVERSE 464

MAYANS

293. What caused the collapse of the Mayan civilization?

In the ninth century the Mayan empire stretched right across Central America. Their cities had large populations and were ruled by a strong and dominant elite. Its temples and stone carvings were evidence of a thriving culture. Even long-distance trade was flourishing. Yet within about 150 years, everything fell apart, leaving the cities in ruins and abandoned. So what happened?

One theory suggests a natural disaster, an earthquake or volcano, or terrible disease perhaps, but while the collapse was fast, it was too slow to suggest a dinosaur-like sudden extinction. Another idea is warfare: perhaps the various Mayan city-states went to war and wiped each other out. But that hardly explains what happened to the victors in such wars.

It could have been famine; it could have been environmental change; it could have been floods; it could have been drought; but there is little evidence of any of these.

It may have been a combination of any or all of the above that destroyed the Mayans, but the lack of evidence suggests that there is something we have not yet discovered.

See also CHOCOLATE 105

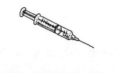

MEDICINE

294. Does acupuncture work?

Supporters of acupuncture cite studies in which subjects suffering from pain or depression or other conditions are treated with acupuncture and report a significant level of improvement. Opponents of acupuncture insist that the results in such studies are no better than those achieved with placebos.

In 2009 and again in 2012, analyses were published assessing the results of numerous studies in different countries in which the effects of no acupuncture, acupuncture and sham acupuncture were compared. In the last of these, the patient is 'treated' by having needles inserted into him acupuncture-style, but the places they are inserted are randomly chosen rather than being placed at the so-called 'meridian points' advised in traditional acupuncture. The results showed a very small difference between acupuncture and sham acupuncture, and a rather larger difference between no acupuncture and acupuncture (real or sham).

Supporters of acupuncture say it proves what they've been saying all along, as acupuncture proved itself significantly better than no acupuncture. Opponents point out that the differences between the trials involving acupuncture and no acupuncture are exactly what one would expect from what we know about placebos, and while the differences between real and sham acupuncture may be *statistically* significant, that is mainly because the sample sizes, when the various studies are all taken together, are so large that a tiny difference may account for it. For a treatment to be worth employing, it needs to be *clinically* significant, which is a different matter entirely. In any case, the effect of the person conducting the trials, who would normally be a trained acupuncturist, can influence the results.

So on the question of whether acupuncture works, we would have to say that the jury is still out.

295. Are bacteria good for us?

We have already touched on this subject when discussing probiotic foods (→ 198), but there is far more to it. We like to think of our bodies as nice all-human entities, but our non-human cells outnumber our human cells by about ten to one (though admittedly the non-human ones are much smaller). The question is whether this co-habitation agreement is to our benefit.

Our non-human microbiota, which are mostly bacteria, have an important part to play in the regulation of our health, but not all of this is good. To take one example, there is a bacterium called *Heliobacter pylori* which is known to cause ulcers and has also been implicated in the development of stomach cancer. Zapping it with antibiotics was a standard treatment until a study in 2011 showed that it may also have a role in warding off asthma.

Such findings, suggesting that even the 'bad' bacteria may be good for us, make it difficult to form a definitive view on whether our bacteria are good for us.

296. How do antidepressants decrease pain?

Antidepressants, as the name suggests, were created in order to treat depression. In cases of depression caused by chronic pain, however, a surprising benefit – that the drugs appeared to reduce the pain as well – was discovered. So antidepressants started to be prescribed for the treatment of pain when normal analgesics were having insufficient effect.

Since then, a vast number of papers have appeared in the medical literature on the question of whether antidepressants are effective in treating pain. Even those who are convinced of the efficacy of antidepressants in this respect, however, are liable to disagree on the details of which particular antidepressants are effective against which types of pain.

One of the underlying problems is that we do not know how antidepressants perform their function as analgesics. Those most generally used are serotonin uptake inhibitors (SUIs), which lead to increased concentrations of the neurotransmitter serotonin. Since serotonin is associated with feelings of well-being and happiness, it is easy to see how it could treat depression, but reasons for SUIs to be effective in treating pain are more elusive.

In a 2008 report, Sansone and Sansone say 'multiple mechanisms are likely to be involved' and go on to mention 'adjunctive thera-peutic influences through histamine receptors', 'modulation of sodium channels' and mechanisms exerting their effects on the neurotransmit-ters serotonin and norepinephrine, 'particularly along the descending spinal pain pathways'.

Or, to put it more simply, we don't know.

297. How do placebos work?

For hundreds of years both medical practitioners and quack doctors have known that if patients think their condition is going to improve, then it is liable to do so. For this reason, whenever a new drug or other treatment is introduced, its effect on one group of subjects is compared with the results on another group given a harmless placebo. Neither the subjects nor the doctors administering the treatments know who is getting which. On average, about 30 per cent of the subjects receiving the placebo treatment will report an improvement in their condition, so for a new treatment to be considered effective, it has to outperform that figure.

But why are those 30 per cent getting better? For a long time it was thought that the improvement was only in the mind. People were being treated; they expected to get better; so they reported improvements. Later studies, however, showed that in many cases they really were getting better. Patients with stomach ulcers who were given placebos were found to recover more quickly than those who received no treatment. Patients given a placebo which they were told would raise their heart rate and blood pressure were found to have higher heart rates and blood pressure, and the reverse effect was found in patients who were told the same placebo would lower their blood pressure and heart rate.

Clearly our bodies' defence mechanisms can be stimulated into performing more effectively by our believing that they will do so. Most curiously, one study has even reported a placebo effect in patients who were told they were being given a placebo, but perhaps they did not believe what the experimenters had told them.

If placebo treatments can lead to real improvements in health, as seems to be the case, potentially it would be very beneficial to know how they work, but we really have no idea.

298. Why are autism rates rising?

In the 1970s and 1980s, around one in 2,000 children in the USA was diagnosed with autism. Now the figure is about one in 150. This raises two important questions:

Is autism really rising, or do the statistics merely reflect a growing awareness of the condition and a recent tendency to refer to an 'autistic spectrum' ranging from mild Asperger's syndrome to severe autism?

If autism is rising, as seems to be the case, what is causing the increase? Is it diet, genetics, environmental changes, or some unsuspected medical treatment, all of which have come under suspicion?

299. Does marijuana reduce pain?

In the USA, under the Controlled Substances Act, marijuana (cannabis) is a Schedule I drug, the strictest classification, yet several states have legalized the medical use of marijuana for pain relief, and more are likely to follow. The Food and Drug Administration (FDA) classification is based on the drug's high potential to lead to abuse, addiction or other harm, but are they right in saying that it has 'no currently accepted medical use'?

Supporters of legalized marijuana point to the pain reliever Sativex, which is based on a natural extract of marijuana, or the drug Marinol, which is used to treat nausea in cancer patients and contains a synthetic form of a cannabinoid known as THC, which is found in marijuana. Both of these have been approved by the FDA, so how can there be doubts about marijuana's effectiveness?

The doubters, however, were supported by a study in Oxford in 2013 based on brain-imaging scans to see exactly what effect cannabis had. The results showed that the drug did not affect the areas of the brain that interpret pain to any significant degree, as conventional pain medicines do. The areas cannabis affected were those that are responsible for the emotional reaction to pain. In other words, cannabis does not reduce pain, it just makes it more bearable.

300. What is the cause of muscle cramps?

Muscle cramps, which tend to occur at night and wake us up in sharp pain, are sudden spasms or tightening, usually in the calf muscles of the leg, which may last anything from a few seconds to several minutes. They tend to occur just as you are falling asleep or waking up; they are sometimes associated with recent exercise, or dehydration, or pregnancy, or blood-flow problems, or mineral deficiency, or simply sleeping in an awkward position.

But sometimes they just happen, and we really do not know what causes them.

See also CHEMICALS 95; NAPOLEON 337; PANGOLINS 356; SOCRATES 440

'The doorstep to the temple of wisdom is a knowledge of our own ignorance.'

Benjamin Franklin

MEERKATS

301. Why do meerkats stop begging?

Young meerkat pups make begging calls to which adults respond by bringing them food. Eventually, the young meerkats stop begging, the adults stop bringing them food, and the young go and find their own. Three reasons have been suggested for the young stopping their begging:

(i) The adults think it's time for the young to become self-sufficient, so stop responding to the calls.

(ii) The young decide they'd prefer the wider choice they might get if they took charge of the foraging.

(iii) The young simply lose the ability to make the begging calls.

A study in 2008 showed that adults who had ceased their food delivery service could be induced back into it by being played a recording of pups begging. This suggested that the initiation of the pups' foraging was not forced on them by the adults. The experimenters also found acoustical differences in pups' begging sounds as they grew older and showed that adults responded better to sounds made by younger pups. They concluded: 'We suggest that older pups are unable to produce stimulating begging calls.'

302. What do meerkats talk about?

Meerkats have a variety of about thirty sounds with which they communicate with each other. They chatter, they squeak, they growl and they purr. They seem to purr when content, growl when looking for food, chatter when anxious, and squeal when danger threatens. They have also shown signs of being able to recognize each other's voices.

They also communicate by scent and posture, but with at least thirty words in their language, and recorded utterances apparently having between one and four syllables, they must have the capacity to convey reasonably detailed information. We just haven't learnt their language yet.

MERCURY

303. What caused the Pantheon Fossae in the Caloris Basin on Mercury?

When the Messenger spacecraft went into orbit around Mercury, the pictures it sent back revealed a huge set of grooved valleys radiating outwards from a central crater. It was first informally dubbed 'The Spider', but the International Astronomical Union later officially named it 'Pantheon Fossae', as the pattern of its grooves or ditches (*fossae* is Latin for 'ditches') resembled the dome of the Pantheon in Rome. They also named the central crater 'Apollodorus', after the architect of the Pantheon.

What caused the grooved pattern is still a matter of debate, as is the question of whether its formation is connected with the Apollodorus crater at all. With the crater not at the exact centre of the radial grooves and some evidence that the crater was formed later than the grooves, it may be just a coincidence that they are in the same place.

304. Why is the planet Mercury so dense?

We know the size of Mercury and we know, from calculation of its gravitational pull, what its mass is. These figures allow its density to be calculated and the result is much higher than that of Venus, Earth and

Mars. The conclusion is that the planet's metal-rich core must account for about 60 per cent of its mass, which is twice as much as the other three planets.

For this to have occurred, Mercury must have lost some of the lighter elements early in its formation. It could be that solar nebular gas dragged off the lighter silicates before Mercury was formed, leaving mainly the heavier metallic elements. It could be that when Mercury was in its early stages of formation, the heat from the Sun vaporized part of its outer layers. It could be that Mercury was once similar to the other planets, but was the victim of a giant impact that stripped off its crust.

Each of these theories would predict a different composition of the rocks on Mercury's surface, and it is hoped that information from the Messenger orbiter will be enough to identify which of them is most likely to have occurred.

MESOPOTAMIA

305. What was the purpose of the Baghdad batteries?

In 1938 the German archaeologist Wilhelm König made an intriguing discovery when working just outside Baghdad. The object he dug up consisted of a thirteen-centimetre-high clay jar containing a copper cylinder with an iron rod inside it. Tests indicated that an acidic liquid such as lemon juice or wine had been inside the cylinder.

König decided this must have been a voltaic cell, leading to the suggestion that the ancient Mesopotamians had invented the battery almost 2,000 years earlier than the Europeans. It is not clear how many of these 'Baghdad batteries' were unearthed, but some estimates put the number at around twelve.

Replicas of these objects that have been made in recent years show that they could, with lemon or grape juice in the jar, have generated a current of between 0.5 and 2 volts. They could, König suggested, have been used for electro-plating, though later it was found that the objects he thought might have been treated in such a manner were in fact fire-gilded with mercury.

Hardly anyone believes the ancient battery theory now, but the only other suggestion relies on their similarity to storage vessels found at a nearby location. Those vessels, however, lack the outside clay jar.

See also MARRIAGE 284; PREHISTORY 382

METEOROLOGY

306. Why are US tornadoes occurring on fewer days than they used to?

In 2014 the National Oceanographic and Atmospheric Administration in the USA published a survey of weather data stretching back over fifty years. Their analysis revealed that the number of tornadoes hitting the US each year had not changed much over that period: it was always about 1,200. But, mysteriously, the number of days on which tornadoes struck had decreased. In fact, the figures showed that during the 1970s the number of days on which thirty or more tornadoes were recorded had been around six a year, but in the past twenty years it was only about three. In other words, there have been about the same number of tornadoes, but they tend to occur more closely together in time.

It has been vaguely suggested that this may have something to do with global warming or atmospheric changes due to pollution, but the mechanism causing the change is unknown.

307. What is the effect of polar warming on mid-latitude regions?

In 2012 research was published suggesting that the melting of the Arctic ice-cap could lead to very cold winters in mid-latitude regions in the northern hemisphere. The argument was that rapid melting of the sea ice could bring about changes in the flow of the jet stream, driving it further south and bringing colder temperatures and longer-lasting winters to more southern regions.

The argument was supported by some data on Arctic ice cover and changing paths of the jet stream, but the authors agreed that further details were needed and it was still only a hypothesis.

The research was immediately leapt on by representatives of both sides of the global warming debate. Sceptics said it was just more evidence that the global warming doom-mongers could twist anything to support their theory: whether it gets colder or hotter, they can say it's due to global warming. Adherents of the global warming hypothesis, however, criticized the research as unconvincing, saying that far more evidence was needed before we could justify any conclusions about the effect of polar ice melting on the motion of the jet stream.

So whether the melting of polar ice brings hot or cold weather to mid-latitude areas is still an open question.

308. Is there a connection between space weather and Earth weather?

The region of space surrounding the Earth is constantly being bombarded by a flow of electrons and protons from the Sun known as the solar wind. The Earth's magnetic field protects us from most potentially harmful effects by deflecting the solar wind, but changes in the Sun's activity have been linked to effects measured on Earth. Geomagnetic storms can disrupt technological systems and solar flares can disrupt long-range radio communications. The effect of such space weather on terrestrial weather, however, is less clear.

From about 1645 to 1715 observations of the Sun indicated a significant decrease in the number of sunspots (patches of relative coolness on the Sun's surface). This period is now known as the

Maunder minimum and coincided with a period known as the Little Ice Age, which was characterized by a cooling of the Earth's climate. The Sun is now known to have a magnetic cycle of around twenty-two years which is responsible for an eleven-year sunspot cycle. For more than a century it has been conjectured that sunspot activity affects the Earth's weather, but this has never been convincingly demonstrated.

Changes in the Sun's magnetic field seem to affect sunspot activity and will presumably also affect the solar wind. One suggestion is that changes in cosmic ray flux caused by the solar wind may cause changes in the amount of cloud formation, which would have a direct effect on the weather. But convincing evidence for this has not yet been demonstrated.

309. How do climate change and land vegetation affect each other?

The relationship between climate change and land vegetation is a complex one. On the one hand, plants absorb carbon dioxide (CO_2) from the atmosphere, which has a cooling effect; on the other hand, they convert the CO_2 into food, releasing energy and water into the atmosphere by transpiration, which has a warming effect. This warming effect is short-term, but the cooling effect is long-term.

Recent research suggested that the amount of water lost through transpiration by plants decreases as CO_2 rises, which would mean that the warming effect was not as large as it might be. However, this issue is again complicated by the fact that different types of plant respond differently to rising CO_2 levels.

Then there is the question of plants growing in regions where snow and ice have melted. That will make the surface less reflective and absorb more heat, which will have a warming effect. And then there is the question of the effect of greenhouse gases on the soil, which will also affect plant growth.

How the various warming and cooling effects balance out and which one comes out on top is the subject of continuing debate.

310. How does lightning happen?

Any elementary science book will explain the cause of lightning. An electrical charge builds up in clouds with the positive charge at the top and the negative charge at the bottom: this is called ionization. The negative charge then attracts positively charged particles on Earth, and the force between them eventually becomes so big that it overcomes the insulating properties of the air between them. Result: a flash of lightning as the positively charged particles from the ground rush up, at the speed of light, to meet the negatively charged lower side of the cloud.

It's when you start reading the small print that you realize it's not that simple. First, there is no real explanation of how the clouds become ionized other than a rather vague suggestion that water and ice droplets bump into each other and dislodge electrons that fall to the bottom of the cloud. Secondly, measurements of electrical charge within clouds often yield anomalous results that do not support the simple picture given above. And thirdly, large thunderstorms, when viewed from above, have been seen to emit other electrical phenomena called transient luminous events (TLEs), which have been given suitably exotic names such as 'red sprites' (large but weak red flashes), 'blue jets' (sudden cones of blue light) and 'elves' (large expanding glowing discs of light lasting only a thousandth of a second). None of these have been explained at all.

311. What causes bends in the jet streams?

The jet streams are fast-moving narrow currents of air flowing west to east high in the atmosphere which are known to have a huge influence on the motion of weather systems. They follow meandering paths known as Rossby waves, which sometimes flatten out and sometimes become more intense. When these waves are flatter, it leads to high pressure and more settled weather.

To add to these meandering waves, the jet streams themselves seem to move north or south in an unpredictable manner. In recent years, the motion of the northern polar jet stream has been closely mapped and shown to correlate with extreme weather patterns. In particular, floods in Britain in 2007 were attributed to an unusually southerly jet stream bringing depressions across the country. In the same period, however, the same jet stream was shown to exhibit a slow annual drift northwards, which suggested that the weather in Britain was caused by an unusually big bend in the stream's meandering path.

A connection has long been suspected between climate change and changes in the paths of jet streams, particularly that of the northern jet stream, but whether jet streams are causing climate change or climate change is changing the jet streams' paths is unknown. In either case, the possible role of human activity in the changes is also a matter of speculation.

See also GLOBAL WARMING 215–16

MEXICO

312. How did Gil Pérez get to Mexico City?

On 24 October 1593 Gil Pérez was on duty as a guard at the governor's palace in the Philippine capital Manila. The governor, Gómez Pérez Dasmariñas, had been killed by Chinese pirates the previous night and the guards were awaiting the appointment of his successor. Pérez is said to have leaned against a wall to rest. When he opened his eyes, however, he was in an unfamiliar place which turned out to be Mexico City's Plaza Mayor.

Pérez was reported to be still wearing the uniform of the palace guards in Manila and he told the Mexicans about the assassination of the governor. Thinking him to be a madman, a deserter or a servant of the devil, the Mexicans put him in jail. Two months later, they freed him when a ship arrived from the Philippines with news of the governor's death. Pérez was taken back home on the ship and is not known to have instantly teleported again.

This story is presumably all an urban myth, but it has been around since the seventeenth century and is allegedly backed by accounts in both Mexico and the Philippines.

See also ANCIENT CITIES 8; AVOCADOS 37; AZTECS 38; CHEWING GUM 96; VOLCANOES 482–3

MICE

313. Did the house mouse reach Australia on convict ships?

James Cook claimed Australia as part of the British empire in 1770 and British convict ships started arriving at Botany Bay in 1788. Dutch explorers, however, had discovered 'New Holland' long before in 1606, so was it the British or the Dutch who brought house mice with them? Or did the mice arrive from Asia before the Europeans came?

In 2011 a study was made of the mitochondrial DNA of mice in Australia, Britain and the Netherlands, and the results were compared with each other and with Japanese mice. Australian mice were found to have far greater similarities with European mice than with Asian mice, and there were strong indications that they came from British strains rather than Dutch ones.

The analysis, the researchers said, 'does not fully exclude the Netherlands as a possible source area for the Australian house mouse', but 'pending larger sample sizes and more detailed genetic data, a British Isles origin of Australian mice is the most reasonable interpretation of our results'.

It must also be possible, I suppose, that British mice found their way onto Dutch ships and travelled to Australia on them before the British fleet arrived.

314. Do mice like excrement?

Or, to put it less crudely, do wild mice have the luxury of avoiding faeces? That was the question posed by a research paper in 2013 which examined whether wild mice took steps to avoid the potential health risks of proximity with the faeces of others of their own species. Laboratory animals have been observed to stay away from such faecal droppings, but there has been little research of the same phenomenon in the wild.

Contact with faeces can spread parasites and lead to infection. However, the presence of faeces may also be a guide to successful foraging or finding a safe nesting place as it indicates that other members of the same species have already visited the area.

The results of the research suggested that in contrast to their laboratory cousins, wild mice do not demonstrate faecal avoidance. In fact, they preferred being near faeces and did not even distinguish between parasite-ridden and uninfected samples.

Staying healthy is clearly a good behavioural strategy, but finding a good place to eat or nest seems to count for more as far as faeces avoidance is concerned.

See also BIOLOGY 59; DISEASE 143–4; DOGS 153; EBOLA 167; GENETICS 210; LONGEVITY 279, 281; PSYCHOLOGY 389; WALRUSES 486

'The difference between stupidity and genius is that genius has its limits.'

Albert Einstein

MILKY WAY

315. When will the Milky Way collide with Andromeda?

Until recently, astronomers were unsure about a predicted collision between the Milky Way and the Andromeda Galaxy. Some said it would happen in 2 billion years; others said that it might not happen at all. The two galaxies were definitely moving closer together, but Andromeda also had a transverse component to its velocity that could make it pass by the Milky Way without a collision. Assessing this transverse component accurately was difficult until 2012, when pictures from the Hubble telescope measured it and allowed a computer simulation to be made of the galaxies' future progress. The new prediction was that the Milky Way and Andromeda would definitely collide in about 4 billion years' time.

Some reports, possibly feeling that the figure of 4 billion sounded a bit vague, said it would happen in 3.75 billion years. Others pointed out that the two galaxies would only make contact in 4 billion years and would take another 2 billion to merge completely.

Since then, however, the universe has been found to be expanding faster than had been thought, and mysterious discoveries such as the so-called Great Attractor and the Sharpley Supercluster have been found to be attracting all galaxies in our Local Group. Also, in 2015, a massive hydrogen cloud was found to be heading this way which could collide with our galaxy in about 30 million years, adding extragalactic material to the Milky Way.

Observations may still be in alignment with the predictions based on the 2012 prediction based on Hubble, but a good deal could happen in the next 4 billion years to change our minds about its conclusion.

316. What will happen when Andromeda and the Milky Way collide?

The computer simulation by NASA based on observations by the Hubble telescope shows the two galaxies passing through each other and slowing down during the collision, then being drawn back towards each other by their mutual gravitational pull. This oscillation will continue until they have merged. The stars, they say, will be thrown into different orbits around the new galactic centre. To reassure us, NASA say that 'our solar system will probably be tossed much farther from the galactic core than it is today'. They also say that 'although the galaxies will plough into each other, stars inside each galaxy are so far apart that they will not collide with other stars during the encounter'.

While it may be true that any individual star has a very small chance of hitting another, there are around about a trillion stars in Andromeda and 300 billion in the Milky Way. A rough calculation indicates that the distance between stars is similar to ping-pong balls 3 kilometres apart. The chance of two specified ping-pong balls hitting each other is therefore very slim, but with a trillion going in one direction and 300 billion in the other, the chance of a stellar collision somewhere must surely be high.

317. Did the Milky Way collide with Andromeda 10 billion years ago?

In 1981 the Israeli physicist Mordecai Milgrom suggested that some of the major problems in cosmology could be solved by making a small adjustment to Newton's second law of motion. Milgrom's Modified Newtonian Dynamics (MOND) theory suggests that gravity behaves differently on a very large scale, and if we apply his theory, it becomes unnecessary to hypothesize the existence of dark matter, which has still not been confirmed, to explain anomalies such as the rotational speed of galaxies.

In 2013 a group of European astronomers applied the MOND theory to calculate the motion of galaxies in the Local Group to which the Milky Way and Andromeda belong. Their calculations suggest that 10 billion years ago these two galaxies had a close encounter. According to the conventional Newton–Einstein theory together with the dark matter hypothesis, they would have merged, but Milgrom's methods suggest they would have passed through each other harmlessly. They could now be on the way back, heading for another collision, but the results of it could be very different from those predicted by Newton–Einstein.

See also ASTRONOMY 27; COSMOLOGY 118; QUASARS 390

MONKEYS

318. Do capuchin monkeys pay for sex?

In a classic experiment at Yale in 2005, capuchin monkeys were taught to exchange tokens for food in order to see if they could grasp the concept of money. Not only could they grasp the concept, but they were shown to take economic decisions as sensibly as humans.

One of the researchers, however, reports seeing a monkey exchanging a money token for sex. As further evidence that the monkeys knew what they were doing, the female who accepted the money then traded it in for a grape.

Sadly, this line of research was not pursued as the researchers felt that turning the monkey laboratory into a brothel might not reflect well on their research ethics. This remains the only known instance of monkeys paying for sex.

319. Why do capuchin monkeys tell lies?

In 2009 an experiment was conducted to see if capuchin monkeys will lie to other monkeys in order to get more food. Specifically, the researchers wanted to see if the monkeys would make deceptive alarm calls in order to lure more dominant monkeys away from the dinner table so that they could then grab more of the food.

Giving the monkeys access to plates of banana pieces, then counting their alarm calls, the experimenters predicted:

(i)   there would be more deceptive alarm calls by subordinates than by dominants;

(ii) alarm calls would be more frequent when the food was placed in a smaller number of locations (making it more liable to be contested);

(iii) calls would be more frequent when less food was available;

(iv) calls would be made when the caller was in a good position to grab the food.

All the predictions were supported except (iii), for which the results were not statistically significant.

The researchers conclude: 'These results generally support the hypothesis that alarm calls are used by capuchins to reduce the effects of feeding competition. Whether this is intentional on the part of the caller requires further investigation.' In other words, we don't really know if they are lying deliberately or not. Whether capuchins would lie about paying for sex (→ 318) is a complex question that only future research can resolve.

See also ANIMALS 18; BONES 72; BRAINS 81; EBOLA 167; GORILLAS 221; HUMAN EVOLUTION 243

MOTHS

320. Why do moths fly towards a light?

Most attempts to explain this suggest that it is something to do with navigation by the stars or Moon. Several insects are known to navigate by a process called transverse orientation by which they keep a constant angle to a distant light source. When the light source is close, however, it is said to throw them completely off course. If you try to keep the angle constant between yourself and the Moon or stars, you'll more or less go in a straight line, but if you do the same with a light-bulb, you'll go round in circles.

This explanation, however, runs into trouble when we consider the evolutionary implications. Light-bulbs may be a relatively modern invention that moths haven't had time to adapt to, but people have been lighting camp-fires for 100,000 years or so. Flying towards a fire is a sure path to extinction, one would have thought.

Another rather bizarre theory was suggested when it was discovered that female moths' pheromones are slightly luminescent. Could it be that male moths are attracted to light because it reminds them of female moths' sex hormones? Are moths trying to mate with our candles and light-bulbs? Perhaps if the pheromones glowed at the same frequency as such artificial light sources, it might suggest that something of the sort was going on, but the frequencies are totally different, so it seems very unlikely.

See also SLOTHS 433

MOUNTAINEERING

321. Where is the body of Andrew Irvine and what can his camera tell us?

In 1924 Andrew Irvine and George Mallory died while attempting to be the first people to climb Mount Everest. They were last sighted only a few hundred metres from the summit, and it has never been clear whether they conquered the mountain and died on their way down or whether they never got to the top. Mallory's body was found in 1999; Irvine's has never been discovered.

The pair are known to have been carrying two VPK (Vest Pocket Kodak) cameras, which suggests that Irvine would probably have had charge of one of them. Photographic experts have said that if the camera is ever found, there is a good chance that printable images could be obtained from its film, as it has been frozen all the time it has been missing. The camera might not tell us how they died, but it would at least offer the prospect at last of finding out whether they reached the top.

MUMMIES

322. How did Egyptian mummies get traces of tobacco and cocaine in them?

In 1992 analysis of samples taken from Egyptian mummies revealed traces of cocaine, hashish and nicotine. Two of these substances are derived only from American plants, so how did they get to Egypt so long before Columbus? Various theories were proposed by critics of the research findings:

(i)   There was no evidence that the drugs were in the mummies before their death.

(ii) The drugs may have been absorbed into the mummy tissue from visitors to the museums where they were housed.

(iii) The mummies may have been recent fakes.

(iv) Chemical effects may have taken place in the mummies to produce substances similar to the drugs mentioned.

(v)   The drugs may have been introduced by people who had handled the mummies.

On closer examination, however, none of these suggestions seemed likely, which leaves only two possibilities:
(vi) The ancient Egyptians conducted trade with the pre-Columbian Americans.
(vii) Nicotine and cocaine existed in ancient Egypt but became extinct.
Neither of those seems very likely either.

See also CHINA 99; DISEASE 139

MURDER

323. Who killed Arthur I, Duke of Brittany?

Arthur of Brittany had a short but eventful life. Born in 1187, he was the son of Geoffrey Plantagenet, the fourth son of Henry II of England. Arthur was born after Geoffrey had died, and when he was two years old, Richard I became king of England. When Arthur was three, in 1190, Richard named him his successor before setting off on a crusade. In 1199, however, Richard changed his mind on his deathbed and named his own brother John his successor instead. This led to some friction between Arthur and his uncle John, but a great deal more between the French barons, who supported Arthur, and the English, who accepted John.

In 1202, at a battle north of Poitiers between the forces of King John of England and Philip II of France, Arthur was captured and imprisoned at Falaise. What happened then is unclear. According to one story, which Shakespeare seized on for his play *King John*, the English king ordered Hubert de Burgh, who was in charge at Falaise, to have Arthur blinded and castrated to remove him as a rival, but de Burgh refused.

Arthur was then moved to Rouen under the charge of William de Braose, who was the man who had captured him and delivered him to John in the first place. Arthur disappeared at the end of March 1203. Some say he was killed by de Braose; some say he was killed by John himself in a drunken rage. In Shakespeare's version, however, Arthur is killed when leaping from the castle battlements while trying to flee from his wicked uncle.

324. Who was the 'boy in the box' murdered in Philadelphia in 1957?

In February 1957, in the Fox Chase neighbourhood of Philadelphia, the body of a boy aged between four and six was found in a cardboard box, naked and battered. The body was wrapped in a plaid blanket and the box was from the JCPenney department store chain and had once contained a baby's cradle.

The police took the boy's fingerprints and were hopeful that his identity could quickly be established. Even when pictures of the boy were sent to every home in Philadelphia, however, no information was ever received. The case is still open.

325. Who killed the Black Dahlia?

In January 1947 the investigation of one of the most gruesome murders in American history began when the body of Elizabeth Short was found in a Los Angeles parking lot. It had been sliced in half at the waist, drained of blood and washed; her face had been slashed from the corners of her mouth to her ears; and the two halves of the body were placed about a foot apart with her intestines neatly tucked beneath her buttocks. There were multiple cuts on other parts of her body and ligature marks on her neck, wrists and ankles. The case, not unnaturally, attracted a great deal of interest in the press, which began referring to the victim as the 'Black Dahlia' after the 1946 film noir *The Blue Dahlia*.

The notoriety of the case led to at least fifty people confessing to the murder, but none was considered plausible. In 2014 a retired police detective named Steve Hodel was reported to have found evidence that his father, George Hodel, who had died in 1991, was a serial killer whose victims may have included Elizabeth Short. Apparently, however, he is not the only person to have suggested a relative as the murderer.

The case is still unsolved and no charges have ever been filed.

326. How does gun availability affect firearm homicide rates?

The number of homicides worldwide is estimated to be around half a million a year and 42 per cent of them are committed with a firearm. The US gun lobby say that the right to bear arms acts as a deterrent to potential killers; their opponents say that the more people have guns, the more are going to be shot. So who is right?

In 2011 the *American Journal of Criminal Justice* published a reassessment of the relationship between gun availability and homicide which showed that the situation is highly complex and in particular 'the relationship between gun availability, gun homicide and homicide is not stable across nations'. Gun availability, they found, made gun homicide more likely in Western developed nations and Latin American nations, but exhibited a small negative effect in Eastern European countries. 'Perhaps Western citizens view guns as a defence mechanism against the aggression of others,' they suggest, 'rather than a tool to be used with the intent of causing great bodily harm or death.' In Latin America, however, the figures suggested that the opposite was the case.

Socio-historic and cultural factors, economic inequality, and urbanization were all found to have effects on firearm homicide rates, but those effects could be very different in different countries. The authors conclude that the relationship between gun availability and gun homicide does not operate uniformly across nations.

An earlier study in the US reported that murders were more numerous in areas with more firearms, but whether it was the rise in gun ownership that led to the murders or the high murder rate that drove up gun ownership by people feeling a need to defend themselves was not answered.

See also DEATH 131, 134; NAPOLEON 337; SHIPS 420

MUSIC

327. Do vuvuzelas spread disease?

The plastic horns known as vuvuzelas achieved worldwide renown during the 2010 World Cup soccer tournament in South Africa. While most people either rejoiced in or protested at their loud honking noise, one group of researchers from London became worried by their possible propensity to spread disease by expelling aerosol particles at great intensity.

They accordingly asked eight healthy volunteers to blow vuvuzelas and to shout. In both cases, their expelled air was measured by a particle counter, and the velocity of the air and the duration of vuvuzela-playing were also measured. The results showed that vuvuzelas emit 178 times as many particles as shouting. The writers say that further research is needed 'to assess the potential of the vuvuzela to contribute to the transmission of aerosol-borne diseases' but recommend, as a precautionary measure, that 'people with respiratory infections should be advised not to blow their vuvuzela in enclosed spaces'.

328. Does the human brain have a pitch centre?

Much research has been done in recent years on how our brains perceive sound in general and music in particular. Sound is, after all, only vibrations in the air. These are picked up by our tympanic membrane (eardrum), amplified by the three small bones in our inner ear, and changed by the cochlea into neurological signals. Then it is up to the brain to react to the various structural elements of the sound, which include pitch, timbre, amplitude, duration and location, and of all these, pitch seems the most complex.

611

At its most basic, pitch is what enables us to tell whether one note is higher or lower than another. It is how we recognize a tune. A small percentage of people have perfect pitch (also known as absolute pitch), which enables them to recognize and remember any note without the benefit of another note to compare it with. An equally small percentage are totally tone-deaf and cannot recognize tunes at all or even say whether one note is higher or lower than another.

All sorts of brain scans, from PET (Positron Emission Tomography) to fMRI (functional Magnetic Resonance Imaging) to TMS (Transcranial Magnetic Stimulation), have been employed to try to see what's going on in our brains when we analyse pitch, but it seems that the more we look, the more complex it becomes.

Until a few years ago, a part of the auditory cortex called the lateral Heschl's gyrus was thought to be the general pitch centre. Then it was found that several other parts of the brain were, under different conditions of timbre and tonality, involved in the assessment of pitch. It has also been found that left-handers have a better short-term memory for pitch than right-handers, and ambidextrous people are best of all. Studies on absolute pitch have also failed to locate a brain region that may be responsible. Some even suggest that absolute pitch results from the suppression of activity in certain areas of the brain rather than the activation of others.

Music may be one of the most complex functions the brain performs.

329. Did human music evolve as a courtship display?

In his book *The Descent of Man*, published in 1871, Charles Darwin wrote:

> *it appears probable that the progenitors of man, either the males or females or both sexes, before acquiring the power of expressing their mutual love in articulate language, endeavoured to charm each other with musical notes and rhythm.*

The argument is simple: human evolution, like that of other animals, has been driven either by natural selection (which is survival of the fittest) or sexual selection (aids to reproduction). Since art in general and music in particular have no discernible survival value, their role, like birdsong or the croaking of frogs in the mating season, must have been to help attract a suitable mate.

In 2000 the evolutionary psychologist Geoffrey Miller wrote in support of Darwin's theory:

> *Consider Jimi Hendrix, for example. This rock guitarist*
> *extraordinaire died at the age of 27 in 1970, overdosing on the drugs*
> *he used to fire his musical imagination. His music output, three*
> *studio albums and hundreds of live concerts, did him no survival*
> *favours. But he did have sexual liaisons with hundreds of groupies,*
> *maintained parallel long-term relationships with at least two*
> *women, and fathered at least three children in the U.S., Germany,*
> *and Sweden.*

One Jimi Hendrix, of course, does not make a scientific theory, but Darwin's idea is probably the only one we have for the origin of human music-making.

330. What happened to Jacques Duphly and his harpsichord?

Jacques Duphly (1715–89) was a French composer and harpsichordist greatly esteemed as a performer and teacher. He published four volumes of harpsichord pieces, but shortly after the last of these, which appeared in 1768, he mysteriously disappeared from public life.

He died the day after the storming of the Bastille, on 15 July 1789, in a small apartment at the Hôtel de Juigné on the Quai Malaquais in Paris, having apparently not been heard of for twenty years. He was surrounded by his books, but there was no harpsichord in his apartment.

To add to the mystery, another man, who also lived at the same address, left Paris on the day Duphly died. This was Antoine de Sartine, ex-chief of police, ex-minister of the navy and patron of the arts, after whom Duphly had named one of his earlier harpsichord pieces.

331. Was Wagner a cross-dresser?

There are several stories about the life of Richard Wagner that suggest a strong interest in women's clothing. He is known to have ordered pink silk underwear and to have enjoyed wearing silk next to his skin, if only because he suffered from erysipelas, a condition that could lead to painful skin rashes. Yet the stories suggest that his affection for women's clothing may have been more than for medical reasons.

In 1864 it was said that Wagner escaped from creditors in Vienna dressed in women's clothes. In 1869 he placed an order with a dressmaker for a black satin costume that could be worn outside or indoors as a negligée. In 1874 he sent an order to Milan for a bodice with 'a high collar, with a lace jabot and ribbons; close-fitting sleeves; the dress trimmed with puffed flounces – of the same satin material ...' His description continues with more and more precise instructions.

Of course, he could have been ordering all these things for his wife Cosima, but she was a prolific diarist and never recorded having received any of them.

See also DISEASE 141; SUICIDE 449

MYANMAR

332. Are there any British Spitfires buried in Burma?

Since the end of the Second World War, a rumour has circulated that the British had buried between twenty and sixty unassembled Spitfires in the Burmese (now Myanmar) jungle as the war was reaching its end. In 2012 a project was initiated to try to find and recover these planes and permission was obtained to dig for them. With security concerns and bad weather hampering the excavations, however, and the two-year exploration contract running out, the search was abandoned in 2014.

No hard evidence has ever been found for the planes, but there have been accounts by British, American and Burmese eyewitnesses who say they saw them being buried. Documents detailing deliveries of aircraft parts to the RAF in Burma during the war, however, appear not to mention any Spitfires.

MYTHOLOGY

333. Where did Geoffrey of Monmouth get his stories of King Arthur from?

King Arthur, according to legend, was a British leader who fought against the invading Anglo-Saxons in the late fifth or early sixth century. The earliest known mention of him may have been in the ninth-century Latin historical compilation called *Historia Brittonum*, but the bulk of the Arthurian legend as we know it comes from Geoffrey of Monmouth's *Historia Regum Britanniae* ('History of the Kings of Britain'), written in 1135.

Geoffrey of Monmouth's work was later embellished by Chrétien de Troyes and Thomas Malory, but where Geoffrey got his story from in the first place is unclear. He claimed that he was merely copying a 'very ancient book written in the British language' he had in his possession, but he may have invented most of it, though its roots perhaps lay in Celtic myth. The ancient book referred to by Geoffrey of Monmouth has never been identified.

See also AZTECS 38; ENGLISH HISTORY 175; GORILLAS 220; HUMAN EVOLUTION 234; INCAS 247; ITALY 258; PREHISTORY 382; TROY 456

NAMES

334. What does 'Britain' mean?

Pliny and other ancient Roman writers referred to the island as 'Britannia' and the British Isles as 'insulae Britannicae', and the modern name of Britain probably stems from these, but the earlier history of the name is obscure.

One theory is that it derives from the Old Welsh 'Priten', which was the name the British called themselves. This in turn may derive from an old Celtic word 'pryd' meaning 'countenance', 'image' or 'beauty', though it has also been suggested that 'Priten' or 'Priton' may have some connection with the practice of tattooing or body art. Explanations for how the initial P changed into a B are rather vague, however, ranging from complex discussions of phonological shifts in Celtic to a possible mishearing by the Romans.

Another suggestion is that the name of Britain has nothing at all to do with Welsh, Celtic, beauty or tattooing, but derives from a word for 'tin' in a Middle Eastern language, perhaps used by Phoenician traders to describe Britain, as tin was the most important commodity brought from Britain.

335. How did Mongolia get its name?

Mongolia seems to have taken its name from the word the inhabitants used for themselves – Mongol – but where that word came from is highly uncertain. Suggestions include the following:
- It was the name of a mountain.
- It was the name of a river.
- It was an abbreviation of a phrase *Mongkhe-tengri-gal*, meaning

'Eternal Sky Fire'.
- It comes from a word *mong*, meaning 'brave'.
- It derives from the name *Mugulu*, a fourth-century tribal leader.

The *Oxford English Dictionary* just says 'of uncertain origin', which sounds a pretty good summary.

336. How did Edmond Halley pronounce his surname?

Hailey, Hawley or Halley (to rhyme with 'valley')? The argument about how to pronounce the name of the discoverer of Halley's Comet seems to have gone on since his own time. He lived from 1656 to 1742, and contemporary accounts are recorded referring to him as Hailey, Hayley, Haley, Haly, Halley, Hawley and Hawly.

Modern historians tend to favour the 'Hawley' pronunciation (to rhyme with 'poorly'); others, perhaps influenced by the rock singer Bill Haley and his backing group 'The Comets', rhyme it with 'daily'; while the Royal Astronomical Society in 1910 came down firmly in favour of the third possibility in a drinking song:

> *Of all the comets in the sky,*
> *There's none like Comet Halley.*
> *We see it with the naked eye*
> *And periodically.*
> *The first to see it was not he,*
> *But still we call it Halley.*
> *The notion that it would return*
> *Was his originally.*

'Real knowledge is to know the extent of one's ignorance.'

Confucius

NAPOLEON

337. How did Napoleon get arsenic in his hair?

In his will, written three weeks before he died aged fifty-one, Napoleon Bonaparte wrote: 'I die before my time, murdered by the English oligarchy and its assassin.' This accusation, coupled with the later finding of traces of arsenic in Napoleon's hair, fuelled the suspicion that the French emperor had been deliberately poisoned by his captors on St Helena. When his body was exhumed in 1840 for reburial in Paris, its remarkable state of preservation supported the theory of arsenic poisoning: arsenic is known to be toxic to the micro-organisms that cause decomposition. In Napoleon's time, however, deliberate poisoning was far from the only way to get arsenic into someone's system:

- An arsenic-laced paste was commonly used to hang wallpaper, and a sample of the wallpaper at Napoleon's prison home of Frogmore was found in 1980 to contain arsenic.
- Arsenic was also an ingredient commonly used in weed-killers, fly-paper and rat poison.
- Arsenic was commonly used to treat a number of ailments including syphilis, from which Napoleon was known to suffer.
- Even as late as the 1950s, arsenic was a common ingredient of various medicines and skin creams.

In 2008 a team of scientists in Italy compared hairs taken from Napoleon's head at various times in his life and found that the arsenic level barely changed between his boyhood in Corsica and his death on St Helena. Similarly high levels were found in the hairs of his son Napoleon II and his wife Josephine. They concluded that the results 'undoubtedly reveal a chronic exposure that we believe can be simply attributed to environmental factors, unfortunately no longer easily identifiable, or habits involving food and therapeutics'.

See also OPERA 348

NAZIS

338. Who planted Germany's swastika forests?

In 1992 a cluster of larch trees in the shape of a swastika was observed from the air growing in a forest in the German state of Brandenburg. For most of the year the larches blended in with the pine forest, but for a few weeks in spring and autumn their leaves turned bright yellow and their swastika formation stood out. Invisible from the ground and in an area only occasionally flown over by private planes, it went unnoticed for over fifty years. Then various stories emerged about its possible origins.

A local farmer said that he had been paid a small amount by a forester for planting the larch seedlings as a child. Another tale told of a member of the Hitler Youth planting the larches, possibly in tribute to Hitler on the Führer's birthday in the late 1930s. More mundanely, a Berlin newspaper reported that the trees were planted in gratitude to the Reich Labour Service for building a street in Zernikow.

Other swastika forests were later found in the German towns of Jesberg, Wiesbaden and Neukirchen, and one was even discovered near the edge of the Himalayas in Tash-Bashat, Kyrgyzstan. One theory of the swastika grown on Soviet territory was that it was planted as an act of secret defiance by German prisoners of war.

Between 1995 and 2000 the trees forming the swastika in Brandenburg were uprooted. Whether more such formations remain to be discovered, and whether they were originally planted as local tributes to Nazism or under orders from the party or the German government, are questions that have yet to be answered.

339. Who betrayed Anne Frank to the Nazis?

On the morning of 4 August 1944 a car carrying an Austrian officer and members of the Dutch Nazi Party arrived outside the warehouse and office at 263 Prinsengracht in Amsterdam. The occupants of the car went into the building brandishing a gun and demanded to know where the Jews were hiding. As a result, eight arrests were made including that of Anne Frank. They were all sent to Auschwitz and the only one to survive the war was Anne's father Otto Frank, who subsequently published Anne's meticulously kept diaries.

An investigation in 1948 into who betrayed them reached no conclusion. Anne, in her diaries, reports their wariness about the new warehouse manager Willem van Maaren, who had been very curious about the rooms at the back of the warehouse where they had been hiding throughout the war.

A cleaner at the warehouse, Lena van Bladeren-Hartog, was also suspected, having allegedly been heard gossiping with another woman about Jews hiding in the building. There was also a rumour that the call to the Gestapo betraying the Franks had been made by a woman.

Then there was Tonny Ahlers, a vicious anti-Semite known to have betrayed several Jews during the Occupation and to have been arrested for other crimes. In 2002 Ahlers' son Anton said that he believed his father, who died in 2000, had been guilty of the betrayal.

As a result, the case of who betrayed Anne Frank to the Nazis was reopened in 2003, but the investigation concluded that, while the case against Ahlers was strong, all evidence was circumstantial and, along with the other suspects named above, his name was cleared.

340. Was Fritz Todt's death an accident?

In the early years of the Second World War, Fritz Todt was one of Hitler's leading strategists. An Oberführer in the Nazi Party, he founded the Organisation Todt, which supervised the building of the West Wall, later known as the Siegfried Line, a 630-kilometre line of bunkers, tank traps and tunnels built to defend Germany from assault from the west.

While remaining close to Hitler, whom he warned against letting his army get bogged down in the Russian winter, Todt found himself increasingly in disagreement with army commanders, particularly Hermann Göring, and party chief Martin Bormann.

In 1942, shortly after taking off from an airfield on the Eastern Front, a plane carrying Todt exploded in mid-air and all on board were killed. He was buried in Berlin and decorated with the Deutscher Orden, the first person to receive this award for 'duties of the highest order to the state and party', but the circumstances of the crash that killed him have always raised speculation of an assassination plot. Albert Speer, who succeeded him as Minister of Munitions, had cancelled plans to travel on the same flight shortly before it took off.

The official Germany Air Ministry inquiry into the plane accident ended abruptly with the words: 'The possibility of sabotage is ruled out. Further measures are therefore neither requisite nor intended.'

See also DEATH 135; HITLER 231–3

NORTH DAKOTA

341. Why does the Great Seal of the state of North Dakota look the way it does?

Since the inauguration of the US state of North Dakota in 1889, its constitution has contained the same description of its Great Seal:

A tree in the open field, the trunk of which is surrounded by three bundles of wheat; on the right a plow, anvil and sledge; on the left, a bow crossed with three arrows, and an Indian on horseback pursuing a buffalo toward the setting sun; the foliage of the tree arched by a half circle of forty-two stars, surrounded by the motto 'Liberty and Union Now and Forever, One and Inseparable'; the words 'Great Seal' at the top; the words 'State of North Dakota' at the bottom; 'October 1st' on the left and '1889' on the right.

The date was when the voters approved the state's constitution, but research has failed to reveal the reasons behind the choice of the symbols.

The tree could be an elm, but the elm did not become the state tree until 1947. It has been conjectured that the three bundles of wheat may represent the three branches of government: executive, legislative and judicial. The plough, anvil and sledge may make reference to the agricultural background of the state and its work ethic, while the bow and arrows, buffalo, the Indian on horseback, and the setting sun could be reminders of its history, but, without any official explanation, all of this is speculative.

To add to the mystery, the seal is adorned with forty-two stars, which is curious as North Dakota was only the thirty-ninth state of the Union. Either they miscounted, or they were making a guess at how many other states would have joined by the time the seal was produced.

NOSES

342. Why did the hadrosaur have a big nose?

In 2014 a new species of hadrosaur (or duck-billed dinosaur) was discovered which was promptly names *Rhinorex*, meaning 'King Nose', because of its truly enormous nose. One report even referred to it as the 'Jimmy Durante of dinosaurs'. Most hadrosaurs have a bony crest extending from the skull, but not *Rhinorex*. This one has a huge nose instead, but what it did with that nose is completely unknown.

Terry Gates, a palaeontologist from North Carolina State University who was one of the team that discovered it, said:

The purpose of such a big nose is still a mystery. If this dinosaur is anything like its relatives then it likely did not have a super sense of smell; but maybe the nose was used as a means of attracting mates, recognizing members of its species, or even as a large attachment for a plant-smashing beak.

They are still trying to sniff out the answers.

343. Why do we pick our noses?

According to a study published in the *Journal of Clinical Psychiatry* in 2001, only 4 per cent of students in Wisconsin never pick their noses. Half of them pick their noses four or more times a day and about 7 per cent say they do it twenty or more times a day. Of the nose-pickers, 80 per cent use their fingers, while the rest are divided equally in their use of tweezers and pencils.

Excessive nose-picking, or rhinotillexomania as it is technically known, is generally viewed as an example of obsessive-compulsive disorder, but if 96 per cent of us do it, does that mean we are almost all mildly obsessive-compulsive?

Because almost all cultures consider nose-picking impolite, or at least something that should only be done in private, most nose-pickers feel a sense of shame in doing it, yet we go on picking, even if we only do so when alone. The simplest explanation is that unblocking our nasal passages opens our airwaves and helps breathing. We do not always have a handkerchief to hand, so we pick our noses. According to the research mentioned above, only 50 per cent of students said they picked their noses to unclog nasal passages or to relieve discomfort or to relieve itching, while 11 per cent did it for 'cosmetic reasons' and another 11 per cent picked their noses for pleasure. Curiously, in view of the social stigma of nose-picking, practices were found to be the same across all social classes.

There is, however, one other aspect of nose-picking that could contribute towards an answer to this question...

344. Is it healthy or unhealthy to eat our nose-pickings?

In 2004 a report appeared on the Ananova news wires quoting an Austrian doctor saying that eating nose-pickings was good for us and recommending that society should change its attitude and encourage children to take up the practice. Eating nose-pickings, the report claimed, boosts our immune system by transferring bacteria which our nose traps into our stomach, where they can perform a useful function.

This report was widely quoted as a piece of bizarre news, and some even suspected it of being an April Fools' joke. There was no evidence cited in support of the argument other than an unsupported claim that 'people who pick their noses with their fingers were healthy, happier and probably better in tune with their bodies'. In 2013, however, Scott Napper, a biochemistry professor at the University of Saskatchewan, Canada, was reported to be investigating the 'health benefits of boogers'. His argument, however, was not that eating nose-pickings transferred useful bacteria to our stomachs but that it was a way of training our immune system by exposing it to germs. His theory follows others that have suggested that improved hygiene may have led to an increase in allergies and auto-immune disorders.

Professor Napper has even suggested a way to test his idea: put some sort of molecule in the noses of a group of volunteers, half of whom pick their noses and eat it, while the other half don't. Then look for immune responses to the molecule and see if they're higher in the booger-eaters. Perhaps, if the experiment is ever conducted, the researchers could consider getting subjects to eat each other's nose-pickings as well, to see if that is equally, or perhaps even more, effective.

If eating nose-pickings is indeed beneficial for us, however, it reflects badly on the evolution of our cultural taboos which, according to the study mentioned in the previous item (→ 343), have led to only 4.5 per cent of nose-pickers eating their pickings.

345. What is the purpose of the 'nose' of the Pinocchio frog?

In 2010 a new species of tree frog was found in Papua. It has not yet been given a scientific name as its genus has not been confirmed, but it has informally been dubbed the 'Pinocchio frog' because of a strange protuberance on the end of its nose. When making energetic calls, the male frog has the ability to inflate the nose and point it upwards, while deflation takes place and the nose points downwards when the males are less excited.

Whether the nasal shape and gymnastics have any effect on its sense of smell or ability to attract a mate, or whether they have some other function, has yet to be determined.

See also ATILLA 31; AUSTEN 34; DOLPHINS 156; INTELLIGENCE 251

$$\pi = 3.1415$$
$$92653589793$$
$$238462643383$$
$$279502884197169$$

NUMBERS

346. Is pi (π) normal?

The idea of normal numbers is one of the most infuriating in mathematics: we know that almost all numbers are normal, but we hardly know any that definitely are. The formal definition of a normal number is a little off-putting but the idea is quite simple.

Let's start by taking any number expressed as an infinite decimal expansion. One seventh, for example, is 0.142857142857142857...

The only digits this contains are 1, 2, 4, 5, 7 and 8, each of which, as we go on counting further into the expansion, approaches a total of one sixth of the digits counted. For a number to be normal, its digit count must be the same for all possible digits. In the case above, it's the same for 1, 2, 4, 5, 7 and 8, but 0, 3, 6 and 9 don't appear at all, so the number is not normal.

We can do better with 0.0123456789012345678901234567 89... where all the digits from 0 to 9 appear equally often, but even that won't fulfil the stern demands of normality, because in its full definition it demands not just an equal number of each of the single-digits but an equal number of all the double-digit and triple-digit numbers too. The number above clearly fails that test as every 1 is followed by a 2, so the numbers 11, 13, 14, 15 and so on are never seen.

So how about .0123456789101112131415 16 .... and so on, just going through the positive integers in increasing order? Now we're nearly there, for it has been proved that the above number does what is asked for. As we continue further and further down the decimal expansion, not only do all the single-digits approach the limit of one-tenth of all the digits counted, but any double-digit number approaches one-hundredth of all double-digit numbers counted, all triple-digit numbers approach one-thousandth of their type, and so on.

But we're not quite there yet. The trouble with the above is that everything we've discussed so far is expressing numbers to base 10. The last number we mentioned is called 'normal to base 10', but what if we had worked out the same number to base 2, as a string of 1s and 0s? Would there be an equal number of them? Or to base 3, or 5, or 47?

For a number to be considered normal, it must be normal to any base one chooses. It is known that if it were possible to pick a number at random, it would almost certainly be normal, but no test is known by which we could discover whether any particular number is normal or not. Indeed, only very few normal numbers have been discovered and they are all numbers that have been created by exotic and laborious procedures.

An examination of the first 6 billion digits of pi makes it highly credible that it is normal to base 10, though even that has not yet been proved. To prove that it is normal to every base is beyond all known mathematical techniques.

See also BEES 43; BIBLE 53; CHICKENS 97; HUMAN EVOLUTION 236; INTELLIGENCE 251–2; MATHEMATICS 288–91; PHYSICS 370–1

OCTOPUSES

347. How do octopuses recognize each other?

When two octopuses meet for the first time, they touch each other with the suction caps on their arms. If the same two octopuses meet again shortly after, they stay away from each other. In 2011 a study was published using this behaviour to see if octopuses recognized each other.

The first stage of the experiment was to keep octopuses in pairs in tanks. They would approach each other as expected, feel each other with their arms, then move apart. The next day, the octopuses were again placed in pairs, but some were with the same octopus as they had met the day before while others were with a different octopus. Those placed with a new tank-mate were found to be much more likely to approach it and feel it than those that were with the same octopus as on the previous day. Those with a new companion were also found to be more likely to squirt ink, which is a sign of feeling threatened.

The conclusion was that octopuses can indeed recognize other octopuses whom they have previously met, but how they do so is not known. Interestingly, the sense of touch appears to play a strong part in getting acquainted, but no part in the recognition. The researchers suggest that touch, sight and smell may all have a role to play.

OPERA

348. What happened to Baron Sciarpa, on whom Puccini's Scarpia in his opera *Tosca* was based?

The most villainous of all operatic villains is surely Baron Scarpia, the police chief who lusts after the opera singer Tosca, whose lover Cavaradossi, a painter, he arrests and tortures so that he can have his evil way with her. For all his melodramatic villainy, however, Scarpia appears to have been modelled on a real person.

In 1798, when Napoleon was marching against the various pre-unification Italian states, King Ferdinand IV of Naples had been deposed and was fighting to regain his throne against the Republicans. One of his strongest supporters was Cardinal Ruffo, who brought together various outlaw bands to fight for the king. The most powerful of these outlaws was a mercenary soldier Gherardo Curci, who was known as Sciarpa and had been the chief of the palace guard. When he was dismissed from that post, he raised his own army and offered their services to the French. When they turned him down, he adopted a career of pillaging, but was then brought back on the king's side by Ruffo.

When Ferdinand was restored to the throne, he not only granted a pardon to Sciarpa but rewarded him with estates, a valuable annuity and the title of baron. Sciarpa then oversaw a campaign of revenge against former Republicans, who would have included artists and politicians such as Cavaradossi and Angelotti, whom the painter is trying to help in the opera.

What happened to Sciarpa after that is unknown, but he is unlikely to have been stabbed to death in his own study by an opera singer. The opera, incidentally, was based on the play *La Tosca* by Victorien Sardou, which was written as a star vehicle for Sarah Bernhardt.

See also FRANCE 202

OTTERS

349. What do otters talk about?

An acoustical analysis of the vocalizations of giant otters in 2014 reported 'a sophisticated vocal repertoire' consisting of twenty-two different sounds made by adult otters and eleven by newborn otters. They bark, howl, whistle, growl or hum and make sounds identifiable as begging, or mating calls, or isolation calls (when separated from the group). The sounds made by newborn otters were seen as 'precursors of the adult repertoire' or 'babbling bouts'.

Comparing the vocalizations of otters with those of other sea or river creatures, the researchers concluded that 'the giant otters' social complexity seems to be reflected in their vocal complexity'. Their analysis of the different sounds seemed mainly to provide a general association of types of sound with types of social behaviour, rather than offering more precise insights into the nature of otter vocal communications.

With twenty-two sounds, they might be expected to be able to communicate a good deal to each other, but we still don't really know what they talk about.

OUTER SPACE

350. Why is outer space roaring at us?

In 2009 NASA scientists discovered a radio signal from outer space that was six times louder than it should have been. At the time, they were trying to explore the oldest parts of the universe by monitoring emissions from the furthest galaxies. The further away in the universe you look, the further back in time you see, owing to the time light takes to travel. Owing to the continuous expansion of the universe, however, the wavelengths of light from the most distant parts are stretched by the time they reach us and are detected not as light but as radio waves. They can therefore be heard, rather than seen, by radio telescopes.

What was actually heard when they trained their telescopes at the furthest stars, however, was a strong hiss six times louder than expected. After eliminating equipment error as the cause of the surprising power of the hiss, the scientists have been at a loss to explain why it is happening. Nothing in the known universe has the potential to generate a radio signal of such power. The space roar, as it has been called, is one of the great unsolved mysteries of cosmology.

See also COSMOLOGY 117–26

PALAO

351. When and why were the great stone faces in Palao carved?

The island group of Palao in the western Pacific is home to thirty-seven massive carved ancient monoliths, many of which have carved faces. Who built them and what they were built for is completely unknown. To add to the mystery, the stone they are made from does not appear to be from Palao, so it must have been imported over a large distance from somewhere else, but how it was brought to Palao is unknown.

The sculptures are thought to date from around AD 100. One theory is that they were part of a large construction being built for the gods or demigods which was never completed. Another legend is that they were part of a construction built by the gods themselves.

PANDAS

352. Did the giant panda in Edinburgh Zoo have a miscarriage in 2014?

On 13 April 2014 Tian Tian, the giant panda in Edinburgh Zoo, was artificially inseminated. In August it was announced that a scan had confirmed that she was pregnant and a cub was expected at the beginning of September. On 1 September, however, it was announced that she did not seem to be pregnant at all and must have suffered a miscarriage.

On 22 September the announcement came that all hope of her giving birth had gone and there was now no evidence of her ever having been pregnant in the first place. Panda specialists said they had been misled by the data on which they had relied. There was even a suggestion that Tian Tian had faked her hormonal level in order to obtain more comfortable living conditions.

So what was going on? The previous year, a similar thing had happened after a supposedly successful mating had taken place. Tian Tian was declared pregnant; then, just as the cub was due, her hormone levels had gone back to normal and she was declared to have suffered a miscarriage. Later she was said not to have had a miscarriage but to have 'reabsorbed the foetus', which is apparently something pandas sometimes do.

If the data can mislead, right up to the time the baby is due, about whether she is pregnant or not, how can it be relied upon to tell whether she has miscarried, reabsorbed a foetus, or was never pregnant in the first place?

353. How long is a giant panda's gestation period?

Another strange thing about panda pregnancy is 'delayed implantation'. Unlike the pregnancy of almost every other mammal, a fertilized egg of a giant panda does not immediately implant in the mother's uterine wall but may stay in her reproductive tract without developing for two months or more. Because of this, we cannot say that we know precisely the length of the giant panda's actual gestation period. All we can say, from observations of successful panda births, is that the time from mating to birth ranges from 95 to 160 days.

See also HUMAN EVOLUTION 236

PANGOLINS

354. What was the evolutionary origin of a pangolin's scales?

Birds have feathers, reptiles have scales, mammals have hair or fur. So where does that leave the pangolin? Apart from being one of the cutest and most endangered animals in the world, the pangolin is also one of the most mysterious, for it is the only mammal whose body is covered with scales. The scales come in very handy as a defence mechanism, for they enable the pangolin to curl up into a ball when threatened, leaving its body totally covered by an impenetrable shell of sharp, overlapping scales. The name 'pangolin' actually comes from the Malay word *pengguling*, which means 'something that rolls up'. Where its scales came from in evolutionary terms, however, continues to be a matter of speculation.

Feathers, scales and hair are all composed mainly of types of keratin. So are nails, claws and beaks. Birds' feathers are thought to have developed from the scales of dinosaurs, and it has been suggested that pangolin scales were the result of a reverse form of that evolution. Since pangolins are neither birds nor reptiles, however, the idea of them developing scales, then turning into mammals, or turning into mammals while keeping their scales, which no other mammals did, seems to require some sort of explanation.

Examination of the types of keratin in the scales of pangolins has led to the alternative suggestion that they came not from compressed feathers but from nails or claws, but again this raises the question of why the pangolin was the only mammal that performed this trick.

355. Is the pangolin descended from the stegosaurus?

The American geneticist Eugene M. McCarthy offers a radically different theory of the pangolin's scales on his <u>macroevolution. net</u> website. He starts by challenging the common view of what a stegosaurus looked like. 'The familiar image of *Stegosaurus*', he says, 'shows a creature with spikes tipping its tail and upright angular plates sheltering its spine', but he goes on to point out that such an image is a reconstruction based on scattered remains and guesswork. 'Suppose… the plates actually did lie flat on the skin in an overlapping fashion', he says, pointing out that such a formation would offer better defence against predators. Suppose too that the 'tail' spikes were not on the tail, but instead were huge claws on the feet. 'How would such an animal look?' he asks, and then gives us the answer: 'Clearly, it would closely resemble extant pangolins.'

The stegosaurus had very small teeth and the pangolin has no teeth at all, and both of them digest food by grinding it up in their stomachs. He lists other similarities too, but the nicest point of all is that the smallest stegosaurus ever found was only slightly bigger than the largest pangolin fossil. Perhaps the stegosaurus did not become extinct at all: it just became smaller, surviving as a dwarf species which became the animal we now call the pangolin.

356. Do pythons often eat pangolins?

Quite apart from such evolutionary questions, there are many other things we do not know about pangolins:

- How many still survive in the wild?
- What is the normal male–female ratio?
- What is their gestation period?
- How do the answers to all these questions vary among the eight known species of pangolin?
- And which came first anyway, the Asian pangolins or the African?

In 2007, at the National University of Singapore, a start was made at finding out more about this elusive creature. For his Master of Science degree, Norman T-Lon Lim captured twenty-one Malayan pangolins (also known as the Javan or Sunda pangolin), fitted them with radio transmitters, and put them back in the wild. Unfortunately, seventeen of the transmitters fell off or were otherwise got rid of by the pangolins, leaving only a sample of four that were tracked throughout the project.

One of the seventeen discarded transmitters was later tracked to the stomach of a reticulated python. The presence of pangolin scales in the same stomach indicated that the snake had eaten the poor thing. Lim writes: 'it is unclear whether pythons are able to coil around and constrict a curled-up pangolin.' Citing an earlier piece of research based on an examination of the stomach contents of 1,070 reticulated pythons in Sumatra, he says that 229 contained identifiable remains, of which only six were remains of pangolins, compared with 148 field rats, thirty-one long-tailed giant rats, eleven silvered leaf monkeys and eight domestic chickens. Conclusion: 'It is unclear whether python predation on pangolin is a common event in the wild.'

In fact, the most common predators by far – which has resulted in all eight species of pangolin being listed as endangered – are human beings, illegally trapping pangolins to sell to Vietnam, where their meat is prized as a delicacy, or to sell their scales to the Chinese for use in their medicines.

PARAPSYCHOLOGY

357. Is beginner's luck real?

When performing an activity for the first time, whether it is gambling at a roulette table, or cooking a soufflé, or playing on a putting green, or anything else where luck may play a part, people are often struck by the fact that their later attempts never seem to match the promise of the first. The good start is put down to 'beginner's luck' and no more is said about it.

One of the most consistent results in parapsychology experiments, however, seems to suggest that beginner's luck may be real. Reports of experiments on telepathy or psychokinesis or demonstrations of other supposedly psychic abilities have frequently reported subjects performing significantly above chance at the start of the experiments, but falling back as the session continues.

Those who believe in such things say that extrasensory abilities work best when the normal senses are suppressed. The early trials were therefore more successful because the subject had low expectations and wasn't really trying. Once effort came to be put in, the extrasensory abilities were overruled and ceased to function.

Or it may be that the experimenters are just more likely to remember the cases in which beginner's luck seemed to be operating.

See also SCIENCE 405

PENGUINS

358. Why do crested penguins kick their first egg out of the nest?

Crested penguins lay two eggs of which the second-laid egg is usually the larger. If they are both allowed to hatch, the second typically hatches first or at the same time as the other and produces a bigger chick. More often than not, however, the first-laid egg is kicked out of the nest by the adults before hatching time.

In the case of the erect-crested penguin, the second egg is on average 81 per cent larger than the first egg, and nearly all pairs get rid of the smaller first egg around the time the second egg is laid. What the point of the first egg is and what evolutionary quirk resulted in this phenomenon are not known. Perhaps, at some stage, the penguins' eggs were vulnerable to predators and laying a spare egg was a good survival strategy, but we have no evidence that this was ever the case.

PHILOSOPHY

359. What can a body do?

In his philosophical masterpiece *Ethics*, published in the year of his death, the Dutch philosopher Baruch Spinoza (1632–77) wrote: 'no one has hitherto laid down the limits to the powers of the body, that is, no one has as yet been taught by experience what the body can accomplish solely by the laws of nature.'

The French philosopher Gilles Deleuze (1925–95) posed that statement more succinctly as a question: 'What can the body do?' As usual with twentieth-century postmodern French philosophers, Deleuze's discussion is metaphysical and unintelligible, so let us continue with Spinoza's account:

> No one hitherto has gained such an accurate knowledge of the bodily mechanism, that he can explain all its functions; nor need I call attention to the fact that many actions are observed in the lower animals, which far transcend human sagacity, and that somnambulists do many things in their sleep, which they would not venture to do when awake: these instances are enough to show, that the body can by the sole laws of its nature do many things which the mind wonders at.

> Again, no one knows how or by what means the mind moves the body, nor how many various degrees of motion it can impart to the body, nor how quickly it can move it.

We know much more now about how muscles control the body and how our minds control the muscles by sending nerve impulses, but Spinoza's basic statement remains true: we still do not know how our minds limit the potential of what our bodies could achieve.

360. How can we know that other people have minds?

The history of robots in the movies exemplifies the philosophical idea behind this question. At the start, robots such as Robby in *Forbidden Planet* or C-3PO in *Star Wars* looked like robots and everyone knew they were robots. Then came Ash in *Alien* and Arnold Schwarzenegger in the first three *Terminator* films when robots (or cyborgs, as they were often called) looked and, when they wanted to, behaved so like humans that they could fool people. Finally, there were robots, such as David in *AI* and Marcus Wright (played by Sam Worthington) in *Terminator*

Salvation, who not only fooled everyone but actually believed they were human.

It all comes down to the question of 'philosophical zombies': how can we tell whether a human-like creature we meet has consciousness and sentience? Is it possible in theory to program a robot to behave in a manner totally indistinguishable from that of a human being?

Metaphysical solipsists will argue that we can only ever know about our own minds. The knowledge that one has a mind is a personal conscious experience, so trying to prove that someone else has a mind is futile. Physicalists, however, may say that the brain is a physical object and the mind is a product of the workings of the brain, so the mind and consciousness will one day be detectable as physical processes. Then we'll be able to tell whether the person we're talking to has a mind or not.

361. Can we experience anything objectively?

Everything we know, everything we believe, everything we think comes to us through our senses and is followed by a supposedly logical analysis of that sensory input. The analysis may be objective, but the data it is applied to must be subjective.

Plato, in his theory of forms, argued that the highest and most fundamental reality is the non-material abstract, not the material world of change we perceive through our senses. Platonic idealism involves a belief in a world of ideas that is objective, unchanging and absolute. We experience the world subjectively and abstract the objective reality from our experiences.

The opposite point of view is expressed in the Buddhist concept of 'emptiness', which, according to the Dalai Lama, is 'the true nature of things and events'. Nothing exists in the way we think it does. He also warns us 'to avoid the misapprehension that emptiness is an absolute reality or an independent truth'. In other words, we can't even experience emptiness objectively.

362. Is time an illusion?

According to Einstein, 'the dividing line between past, present, and future is an illusion'. In other words, there is no objective reality to the concept of 'now'. One of the fundamental ideas behind his theory of general relativity is that one observer may see various things happening at the same time while another sees the same things happening one after the other. My 'now' may be your past, present or future.

Until Einstein came along, we were all happy with the idea that we lived in a three-dimensional space with time ticking along happily at the same rate for all of us. Einstein showed that the passage of time may be different for all of us, though that difference may only be noticeable when we are moving at speeds close to that of light.

To resolve this apparent anomaly, Einstein changed our view of the world. It was no longer a three-dimensional entity moving through time, but a four-dimensional space–time continuum. There is no difference between what we see as a fixed past, a real present and an open future; they are all the same. We humans, however, are doomed to travel through the world along a one-dimensional, no-going-back timeline, which gives us the very reasonable illusion that time is real. It may be real to us, but time may appear to have a different reality for someone else.

Whether the flexible, personal nature of time makes the whole concept of time an illusion is a much deeper philosophical question.

363. Is reality an illusion?

As if it were not bad enough Einstein telling us that time was an illusion, the pioneers of quantum mechanics then suggested that reality itself might be an illusion. First, we were treated to particles that could be in two places at the same time. Then we realized that they might not be particles at all but sometimes were better seen as waves. Then we learnt that they might not be anywhere at all until we observed them. And now the string theorists tell us that what we think of as solid matter may actually consist of vibrating ten-dimensional wiggly things.

Once life evolved, our senses developed in a way that best enabled us to cope with the world. It looks increasingly as though the world that we perceive is just a construction – a hologram, if you like – created in our brains. It's not quite as bad as the plight of Neo in the *Matrix*, but quantum mechanics has forced all of us to take at least a small dose of the red pill that shows us what reality is really like.

364. Did David Hume believe in God?

In his book *Dialogues Concerning Natural Religion*, the Scottish philosopher David Hume (1711–76) employed a highly readable way of discussing the question of whether God exists. The form of the book is a series of discussions about the existence and nature of God among three characters named Demea, Philo and Cleanthes.

Demea argues that God exists but is incomprehensible; Philo agrees that God is incomprehensible but says that if you look at the evidence, you'd have to agree that He may be morally corrupt; while Cleanthes says that the evidence of nature confirms God's existence. For each of these characters, Hume argues their position so well that it is impossible to deduce what his own views were.

Hume's enemies often charged him with atheism, saying that his refusal to admit it was simply through a fear of the problems such an admission could cause for his career. On the other hand, throughout his life Hume argued against allowing human reasoning to overreach itself, so he may well have felt equally hostile to those who maintained that God definitely did not exist and those who were sure He did.

Perhaps the strongest conclusion we can reach is that Hume was opposed to traditional theistic views, but did not rule out the existence of a god absolutely.

365. Are free will and determinism incompatible?

Philosophers have been arguing this question for over 2,000 years and they are still no nearer to agreeing on an answer. Part of the problem lies in defining precisely what is meant by the terms 'determinism' and 'free will', but however one defines them, there seems to be an argument over whether they are compatible.

The incompatibilist line is simple: determinism means that everything in the universe is predetermined, either because God already knows what is going to happen and there's nothing we can do to change it, or because the laws of physics, including those we haven't discovered yet, determine everything in the world, including the actions of the particles in our brains that we use to make decisions. So you can't have both free will and determinism.

Compatibilists, however, will denounce the religious argument on the grounds that God, if He exists, knows everything, including what we're going to decide with our free wills. As for the laws of physics, the ancient compatibilists see no problem: the decisions we make with our free will are bound to be influenced by our upbringing, what we had for breakfast, our state of mind and all sorts of other things in the past. If I'd had three rashers of bacon instead of two with my fried egg, I might well have made a different decision later in the day. I call that free will, you call it the laws of physics. Modern compatibilists have it even easier: quantum theory, after all, is non-deterministic and has a good deal of inherent randomness.

We haven't the faintest idea, however, how quantum randomness could affect the operation of free will.

See also ANIMALS 17; BRAINS 80; COSMOLOGY 123; FRANCE 201; FUNDAMENTAL PARTICLES 206; LANGUAGE 267

PHYSICS

366. Do tetraneutrons exist?

In 2002 researchers at the Large Heavy Ion National Accelerator in Caen, France, fired beryllium-14 nuclei at a small carbon target. This was not just for fun, but to see whether they could create a tetraneutron. The beryllium-14 ion has a halo of four neutrons which were expected to break away when it smashed into the carbon.

Theory predicts that when that happens, it should produce a beryllium-10 nucleus and four separate neutrons. Instead of the four neutrons, however, only one signal was detected, suggesting that the four neutrons had bound together into a single tetraneutron.

The trouble is that according to current models of nuclear forces, a tetraneutron ought to be impossible. Attempts to replicate the Caen findings have not so far been successful and some doubts have been raised over its detection methods. There are, however, another four or five reports of tetraneutrons being produced in other experiments, so the jury is still out on whether they are possible or not.

367. Why don't moving bicycles fall over?

In a celebrated scene from the 1949 French film *Jour de Fête*, the blunder-prone postman François, played by Jacques Tati, is seen chasing his runaway bicycle as it winds its way riderless down a country road. Twisting right and left, the bicycle rolls a surprising distance without falling over. It looks like an excellent piece of trick photography, but that is what bikes do: when they start to veer off in one direction, their front wheels auto-correct and send them back the other way.

Since the film came out, various suggestions have been proposed to explain what causes this effect. Some said it was the gyroscopic effect of the rotation of the wheels that was keeping the bike upright; others said it was like the castors on a shopping trolley automatically turning the right way when the trolley was steered. The same explanations had also been advanced to account for the remarkable stability of moving bikes with riders on them.

In 2011, however, a team at Cornell University designed an experimental bicycle that had all its gyroscopic effects cancelled out by a system of counter-rotating wheels. It still stayed upright when rolling along on its own. The researchers admitted that this does not solve the problem of why bikes don't fall over, but it does rule out some possible answers.

368. Can magnetic monopoles exist?

Any magnet has a north pole at one end and a south pole at the other. Cut it in half and you get two magnets, each with a north pole and a south pole. And you can go on cutting it in half, eventually arriving at an atom with a north pole at one end and a south pole at the other. You just cannot get down to a single monopole.

Maxwell's equations for electromagnetism were even thought to show that monopoles were impossible, but in 1896 Pierre Curie pointed out that they may be possible. In 1931 the great physicist Paul Dirac proved that monopoles could only exist if electric charge was quantized (i.e. electric charge came in discrete chunks), so when that was later found to be true, interest in monopoles was renewed.

Recently, the existence of magnetic monopoles has been predicted by string theory and the search for them has intensified. In January 2014 it was widely reported that magnetic monopoles had been created in a lab in the US, but the reports proved to be exaggerated. What had been created was not an actual monopole but a physical system exhibiting the magnetic field that a monopole would produce. So we still do not know if they exist, but it is looking more likely than it did a few years ago.

369. Is there a general theory to describe the dynamics of turbulent flow?

The Nobel Prize-winning physicist Richard Feynman described turbulence as the most important unsolved problem of classical physics. Feynman died in 1988 and we are still a long way from solving it. Turbulence affects the flow of gases or liquids, turning a smooth flow into something choppy and unpredictable. It spills our tea, it makes our washing-up bowls splash all over our clothes, it terrifies plane passengers, and it even has to be taken into account in the design of artificial heart valves.

Whether we are talking about the water flowing out of a tap or a plane moving through air, everything may start smooth, then – as velocity or resistance increases – suddenly become disordered and turbulent. And once turbulence starts, it can take some time to die down, even after whatever caused it in the first place is reduced.

Despite a great deal of research and volumes of intensely complicated mathematics, we are still unable to make reliable predictions of when turbulence will occur.

370. What is responsible for the value of the fine-structure constant?

Another of Richard Feynman's 'greatest damn mysteries of physics' is the value of the fine-structure constant known as α (alpha). It's one of the fundamental constants of physics that make the universe what it is and governs the strength of the force between electrically charged particles and the energy levels of atoms.

To calculate α, you take the square of an electron's charge, divide it by the speed of light and Planck's constant, then multiply by 2π (pi), and the answer is 0.007297, or about 1/137. The extraordinary thing, though, is that if it differed from that figure by as little as 4 per cent, either higher or lower, then the nuclear reactions in stars that lead to the production of oxygen and carbon would not take place and we carbon-based life forms would not exist. Why α has this particular life-supporting value is a complete mystery.

As Feynman said: 'All good theoretical physicists put this number up on their wall and worry about it.'

371. How is the vacuum catastrophe explained?

Think of a number. Add 107 zeros onto the end of it. The difference between the number you started with and the one you now have is a measure of the so-called 'vacuum catastrophe'.

It's all to do with the energy of empty space, which is a problem we raised earlier (→ 173). According to quantum field theory, the energy of space is not zero and the theory enables us to calculate what it should be. However, when the Voyager spacecraft came to calculate its real value by measuring the gravitational pull of empty space, it came up with a much lower number. Very much lower: in fact, a number differing from the theoretical value by as much as the same number with 107 zeros on the end of it.

This has been described as the worst theoretical prediction of all time. If we were to estimate that the entire universe consisted of one atom, it would be closer than this prediction. Something is going very badly wrong here, either with quantum field theory or with our understanding of gravity, and we do not know what it is.

372. Can negative mass and negative energy exist?

In the seventeenth century, alchemists were puzzled by the fact that some things gained weight when they were burnt. We now know, of course, that burning often involves combining with oxygen, which accounts for the weight gain. Not knowing about oxygen, the alchemists came up with the 'phlogiston' theory. When something is burnt, it loses phlogiston, and phlogiston has negative mass.

After oxygen was discovered in the 1770s, the idea of negative mass disappeared for around two centuries, but it has returned recently through the work of theoretical physicists exploring the more exotic implications of physical laws. If we allow negative mass and negative energy, it could, some say, explain why we have not yet discovered gravitational waves (which could be absorbed by a combination of positive and negative mass), and it could provide an explanation of how wormholes might exist.

For many years, there was a bit of a problem that negative mass was thought to break one of the fundamental assumptions of Einstein's general relativity. In 2014, however, physicists at Montreal University found a solution to Einstein's equations that allowed mass to take a negative value.

So in theory, negative mass might exist after all, though we have no evidence for it, nor any clear idea of how it might have been produced in the first place.

See also BIG BANG 54–6; BLACK HOLES 70–1; COSMOLOGY 123, 126; ENERGY 172–4; FUNDAMENTAL PARTICLES 204–7; GRAVITY 223; PHILOSOPHY 365; UNIVERSE 463–7

PLANTS

373. How long can seeds live?

Gardeners know that if seeds are kept cold and dry, they can last for years, but in 2005 scientists in Israel announced that they had grown a date palm from a seed which carbon dating had revealed to be 2,000 years old. Around ten years earlier, a Chinese lotus plant was reported to have been grown from a seed dated to be 1,288 years old.

The date-palm seed had been dug up during excavations, so it had been kept cold and away from the sun and air, while the lotus seed had been preserved in peat. The lotus germinated easily but its seedlings grew up deformed, probably because of damage caused by radioactivity in the soil.

Examples such as these show that seeds can indeed live a long time, but exactly how long remains completely unknown.

See also AVOCADOS 37; EVOLUTION 179; INTELLIGENCE 250; METEOROLOGY 309; NAZIS 338

PLATYPUSES

374. Why are Tasmanian platypuses much bigger than North Australian platypuses?

Tasmanian platypuses are significantly larger than platypuses in mainland Australia, but in general platypuses in the north of mainland

Australia are smaller than those in the south. Why this should be so is important for a large range of animals, not just platypuses.

In 1847 the German biologist Carl Bergmann proposed that as a general rule for any species, members of that species coming from colder climates are smaller than those from warm climates. This would seem to explain the difference between mainland platypuses and Tasmanian platypuses, but the difference in size of animals in different regions of the mainland seems to go in the wrong direction. In 1986 the Ukrainian-born US environmentalist Valerius Geist suggested that Bergmann's rule was spurious. It wasn't temperature that mattered but food availability during the growing season.

In 2012, however, a study comparing platypus size in different locations came to the conclusion that the main factor affecting it was rainfall, with larger-sized individuals typically found in lower-rainfall environments. Evidently the effect of environment on platypus body size is more complex than had been thought.

375. Why do ostriches sleep like platypuses?

When most mammals or birds sleep, they exhibit two different states: slow-wave sleep (SWS) and rapid eye movement (REM) sleep. SWS is characterized by slow, high-amplitude brain waves; REM sleep has fast, low-amplitude waves accompanied by rapid eye movements. However, the egg-laying mammals, platypuses and echidnas, have only a single sleep state that combines elements of both SWS and REM sleep.

In 2011 ostriches were found to have a sleep pattern all of their own. Episodes of REM sleep were accompanied by the usual rapid eye movements, similar to those observed in other birds and mammals, but at the same time their forebrain activity would flip between the high-amplitude waves of REM sleep and SWS-like slow waves, much like the platypus.

How two animals as different as the ostrich and the platypus came to be the only ones with such brain activity while asleep is a mystery.

POKER

376. Do poker faces help poker players?

Wearing an emotionless expression has long been considered a key to success at poker, but some research in 2010 cast doubt on the value of a 'poker face'.

Subjects played a simplified version of Texas Hold 'Em poker against an opponent whose face they could see on-screen. The faces were taken from a database and each was modified by computer into three versions designed to be seen as trustworthy (smiling and optimistic), neutral (poker face), or untrustworthy (scowling). In each hand the opponent bet first and the subject had to decide whether to fold or match the bet. The decisions were correlated against the type of face depicted on the screen to see which was most effective.

'According to these results,' the experimenters concluded, 'the best "poker face" for bluffing may not be a neutral face, but rather a face that contains emotional correlates of trustworthiness.' Whether this finding will influence the facial expressions of poker players, however, is doubtful.

POLAR BEARS

377. Do male polar bears find mates by following females' smelly feet?

Polar bears are solitary animals and how they find each other for the purposes of mating has long been a matter of speculation. Males have been known to follow a female's trail for 160 kilometres or more during the mating season, and it has been presumed that scent plays a part in their ability to do so. A study published in 2015 revealed that smelly feet may be very important in this process.

Swabs were taken from the feet of polar bears and presented to a number of polar bears in zoos. Female bears in particular were found likely to approach the scent of smelly feet during the spring. Males were found to differentiate scent donor by sex and reproductive condition.

Whether smelly feet are the main guide males use to pick mates, however, is an open question.

378. Are polar bears' penises weakened by pollutants?

In 2015 a paper on the possible effect of pollutants on the density of the bone in polar bears' penises set off a wave of headlines in the popular press. 'Is pollution destroying polar bears' penises?' they asked. 'Chemical pollution is causing polar bear penises to break' or 'Polar bear penises are wilting', they stated. But is it true?

What the research behind the paper had identified was a negative correlation between the density of the bacula (penis bones) of polar bears and levels of organic chemicals known as PCBs in the bears' fat. No mechanism was suggested to explain how the chemicals might affect bone density, nor was there any evidence to suggest that bones of lower density were more likely to break. No examples of broken penis bones were found in the investigations.

See also BEARS 42

> 'What is research but a blind date with knowledge.'
>
> Will Harvey

PORPOISES

379. Do porpoises choose their friends?

Porpoises are not known to be particularly social animals, and a report in 1999 suggested that mother–calf pairs were probably the only stable social unit. That finding, however, had been based on observations of porpoises on the surface of the water, and it was challenged in 2011 by some research that monitored their underwater behaviour.

The diving behaviour of six finless porpoises was recorded to see whether they exhibited any patterns indicating preferences in which of the group they dived with. Two pairs in particular were found to dive together more frequently than other possible pairings, and later dives by such pairs were found to last longer. One of these pairs was an immature female and an adult male, the other was a young male and an adult male.

The researchers concluded that 'certain individuals form associations even if they are not a mother and calf pair'. With only six porpoises involved in the research, however, more work is clearly needed before we conclude that porpoises choose their friends.

PREHISTORY

380. What were the Carnac stones for?

Around the village of Carnac in Brittany, a collection of over 3,000 huge standing stones were erected, cut from local rock during the Neolithic period between 4500 and 3000 BC. Although many of the stones have been moved or destroyed, it is clear that they were arranged in patterns generally consisting of straight lines, with the stones increasing in height as one moves down the line.

Artefacts including axes and arrow-heads have been found in the region of the stones, as well as pearls and other gems and probable human graves and tombs. It has been speculated that the stones were arranged in some astronomical alignment to serve as a primitive observatory, but despite the large number of stones, nothing has been confirmed about the reasons for this massive construction.

381. Did something crash into the Baltic Sea 140,000 years ago?

In 2011, while looking for a shipwreck in the Baltic Sea between Sweden and Finland, a Swedish team discovered a strange formation on the sea bed. Described as looking like 'rough granite', it was round, about 60 metres in diameter, and stood on a 9-metre-tall pillar at a depth of 85 to 90 metres. A staircase and a round black hole going directly into the structure were reported on a later investigation. Also a long rough path, reminiscent of a skid mark, was seen leading up to the object.

Samples of either the object itself or rocks that had formed around it were brought to the surface and subsequently found to be around 14,000 years old (or possibly 140,000 years ago, depending which account you read). A host of theories have emerged to explain it:

- It may be a natural rock formation, though its shape looks man-made.
- It may be something that formed around a sunken German Second World War U-boat.
- It may be a meteorite.
- It may be an alien spaceship (its shape is a bit like that of the Millennium Falcon in *Star Wars*) which crashed into the Baltic during the last ice age.

382. Who or what were the lizard men of al-'Ubaid?

In 1919 the Egyptologist Harry Reginald Hall began excavations at a site called Tell al-'Ubaid in the region of ancient Mesopotamia. Among the artefacts that were dug up were a number of figurines with human-like bodies and lizard heads. Each of the figures has its own individual pose, with the strangest of them showing a naked female suckling a baby which also has a lizard head.

The figurines have been dated to around 7,000 years ago, which was when the Sumerian culture was reaching its peak in Mesopotamia. They were found predominantly at grave sites, so they are thought to have had some ritual significance. While snakes are known to have had mystic significance for the Sumerians, lizards are not thought to have featured highly, if at all, in their mythology.

Perhaps they were placed in graves to ensure safe passage to the underworld, but with no known links to what we know of Sumerian culture, any such suggestions are pure guesswork.

383. What is the origin of the Basque people?

There are two main ways of trying to find out where the Basque people of southern Europe originated: from the Basque language, which is unlike anything else spoken in Europe, or from an analysis of their DNA. Neither method has so far yielded more than tantalizing theories.

While the Basque language includes some borrowed words from Latin-based languages, it is mostly so different from other languages that it is thought to have developed from a proto-Basque that was spoken before Indo-European languages even arrived in the region. One theory is that Basque is the only survivor of a number of similar languages that were spoken in the Palaeolithic era around 16,000 BC. This is generally linked to a theory that the Basque people spread to Europe from Africa after the European climate warmed at the end of the last ice age.

DNA studies have revealed a number of markers the Basques share with other European peoples, but they seem to point in several different directions. Studies concentrating on the Y chromosome have related the Basques to the Celtic, Welsh and Irish; one study of mitochondrial DNA suggested that they have shared some features with the rest of Europe since prehistoric times; studies in Spain in 2007 and 2010 concluded that the Basques have a DNA profile indistinguishable from the rest of the Iberian peninsula; while another general DNA study in

2012 said that they have unique features in their genetic profile that do distinguish them from other groups.

See also ANCIENT CITIES 8–11; ANCIENT HISTORY 12–13; BIRDS 64; DINOSAURS 136–8; TYRANNOSAURUSES 459–61

PSYCHOLOGY

384. What is the explanation of foreign accent syndrome?

On 2 October 2014 the UK newspaper the *Daily Mirror* ran a story under the headline: 'Woman is diagnosed with Foreign Accent Syndrome after "waking up speaking Italian".' Well, perhaps 'waking up speaking Italian' was a little sensationalist, as anyone reading further would have discovered that her speech was only distorted in a manner that made some people think she was talking with an Italian accent, while others described it as French, Japanese, Polish or Lithuanian. But foreign accent syndrome (FAS), though rare, is a well-documented condition.

First described in 1907, there have been fewer than seventy cases of FAS reported in more than a century since then. They usually follow a stroke, head injury or migraine attacks and are presumed to result from damage to parts of the brain involved in speech production, or possibly to the tongue or jaw or the muscles that control them.

Despite various types of brain scan being performed on people suffering from FAS, however, no specific area of the brain has been found to be associated with the syndrome.

385. Do we make better decisions when we're hungry?

Many studies have shown that predators take greater risks when hunting for food if they are hungry. That makes sense, but the question of whether hunger generally increases risk-taking, particularly in humans, has produced contradictory results.

In 2010 a study at University College London was conducted on two groups, one of which had eaten shortly before the experiment, while the other had fasted. Subjects in both groups were asked to select lottery tickets marked with potential prizes of various sizes and the odds against winning them. The higher prizes offered lower chances of winning. The experimenters reported that the subjects who had fasted were more likely to go for the high-prize, low-chance lotteries. In other words, hunger increases risky behaviour.

In 2014, however, a study in the Netherlands reached almost the opposite conclusion. Their experiment compared the behaviour of well-fed and hungry groups at a gambling game and reported that 'hungry participants performed better in this complex task with uncertain outcomes'.

Whether one should eat before taking decisions still seems to be an open question.

386. How much of our behaviour reflects our evolutionary past?

This question underlies the recently developed subject of evolutionary psychology. An ordinary (non-evolutionary) psychologist will take the line that as conscious, thinking beings, we learn from experience. We may be born with certain skills and elementary patterns of behaviour, but as we grow, we learn about the world and other people, and our interactions with them result in our forming likes and dislikes and patterns of behaviour that make us what we are as individuals.

Evolutionary psychologists take a rather different view. Our brains and minds, they say, have evolved in a similar way to our bodies. For 99 per cent of the history of *Homo sapiens*, we were hunter-gatherers living in small groups in Africa. Many of our behavioural traits, in their view, stem from behaviour that evolved during that long period. People are afraid of snakes because that was a key to survival for our distant ancestors. Our social skills have developed from life in those hunter-gatherer groups.

Some evolutionary psychologists will even say that most of the problems of modern mankind stem from conflicts between the modern world and our evolutionary heritage. All our social skills, sexual impulses and aggression may be the result of our long evolution. On the other hand, they may be the result of our conscious, thinking ability to adapt and solve problems in real time rather than waiting for evolution to do the job for us. The question is: how much of our behaviour do we owe to evolution and how much to the man-made social structures of the world we live in?

387. At what stage does free will enter our decision-making process?

A study in 2008 raised perplexing questions about the nature of free will. Subjects were placed in front of a button and asked simply to decide whether to press it with their left hand or right hand. Before they pressed the button, they were also asked to watch a screen on which an ever-changing stream of letters was displayed and to remember which letter was shown at the moment they took the decision which hand to use for the button-pressing. While this was going on, the subjects were attached to brain-scanning equipment.

The remarkable finding was that the brain scans not only revealed which hand the subject chose, but by monitoring the scans, the researchers could predict which hand they would choose up to ten seconds before the subjects thought they had made the decision.

We like to think that we take decisions consciously after thinking about the alternatives. This simple experiment, however, seems to show that we may first make a decision subconsciously, then our subconscious tells our conscious mind about it. Where that leaves free will is very puzzling.

388. What causes déjà vu?

The only thing all scientists seem to agree about déjà vu is that it is very difficult to study in the laboratory. The feeling, when seeing something for the first time, that you have encountered it before is not only fleeting, but difficult to reproduce to order. Several theories have been advanced, but there is very little evidence to support any of them:

(i)   It is caused by the split-second delay in transferring information from one side of the brain to the other: both sides may see something, then one side tells the other about it, with the result that one side gets the information twice and thinks it has seen it before.

(ii) Just as our muscles may twitch unexpectedly, so do the neurons in our brain; déjà vu is nothing more than a brain twitch.

(iii) Any face has much in common with any other face; any room is, to some extent, like any other room; déjà vu results from our brains detecting such similarities before they start concentrating on the differences.

(iv) Sigmund Freud said it was a result of paramnesia – a confusion between fact and fantasy caused by repressed memories.

In fact, around forty different explanations have been offered to explain déjà vu. I shall spare you the other thirty-six. We just don't know.

389. What is the connection between depression and serotonin?

We have already touched on this subject a couple of times when talking about depressed dogs (→ 18) and antidepressants (→ 296), but the real nature of the connection is highly elusive. One of the problems is that we can accurately measure serotonin levels in the blood, but there is no simple way of assessing serotonin levels in the brain and we do not know whether levels in the bloodstream reflect the levels in the brain. Many studies have shown a correlation between low blood serotonin levels and depression, but whether low serotonin causes depression or depression causes serotonin depletion is not known.

In 2014 research on mice threw another spanner into the workings of serotonin. To discover more about the serotonin–depression link, the researchers developed a strain of mice that lacked the ability to produce serotonin in their brains. Behavioural tests showed the mice to be compulsive and extremely aggressive, but they showed no signs of depression. Even when put under stress, the mice behaved the same as normal mice. The researchers concluded that serotonin may not play a major role in depression at all – in mice anyway.

See also BRAINS 75, 77; DREAMS 161; ELEPHANTS 171; FOOD 193–4, 196; INTELLIGENCE 248; MUSIC 329; SEX 410; SEX DIFFERENCES 412

QUASARS

390. What powers quasars?

Quasars, which is short for 'quasi-stellar radio sources', were first detected in the 1950s as sources of radio waves, but were soon shown to be immensely bright and compact regions at the centre of massive distant galaxies. In fact, barring such explosive events as supernovas, quasars are the brightest objects in the universe, emitting more energy than seems possible. The energy output of one quasar may be many times that of the entire Milky Way galaxy.

The most plausible current theory is that every quasar is powered by the existence of a supermassive black hole at its centre. The black hole is surrounded by a large, rotating cloud of gas which is hugely heated as it falls into the black hole. The gas emits thermal radiation, which may be the source of the quasar's energy.

Whether all quasars have black holes at their centre, however, is unknown, as is the way such supermassive black holes would have come about. The reason they are hypothesized as the power source of quasars is more by default than through evidence: nobody has come up with any other suggestion of a sufficiently powerful power source to do the job.

391. Where have all the quasars gone?

As far as we know, every quasar is very distant from us. More than 200,000 quasars have been detected, but the closest is about 600 million light years away. This suggests either that quasars stopped being formed about 600 million years ago, or that they ran out of fuel at that time as their black holes sucked up all the gas that was providing their power source. There could, in fact, be no quasars in the universe today, and what we detect of them is just a trace of the ancient universe that has taken more than half a billion years to reach us.

RATS

392. Does tickling a rat make it optimistic?

The science of rat-tickling began in the 1990s when research in Massachusetts revealed that rats emit an ultrasonic vocalization akin to human laughter when they seem to be enjoying themselves. This naturally led to the question of whether rats laughed when tickled and whether this was the same laughter as when they were having fun. Experiments seemed to show that they did and it was.

The next stage was to see if the positive emotions associated with laughter affect rats in the same way as people. In particular, does laughter make rats more optimistic? In 2012 an ingenious experiment was set up to explore this question.

First, the rats were trained to distinguish between two sounds. In either case, after hearing the sound, the rat was presented with a lever to press. For one sound, pressing the lever earned them a reward of food; for the other sound, they received a painful electric shock if they pressed the lever. Then the rats were divided into two groups: those in one group were tickled; those in the other group were handled but not tickled. Finally, the rats were returned to the set-up with the sounds and the lever, but now they were played a sound that was halfway between the two on which they had been trained. Would they then take the optimistic point of view and press the lever or be pessimists and not press it?

The results showed that the tickled rats pushed the lever significantly more often than the non-tickled group. This was seen as evidence that tickling and laughter induce optimism in rats, though other explanations are also possible. It could be, for example, that the tickled rats placed greater trust in the experimenters while the handled rats distrusted them. Further research and rat-tickling are clearly needed on this matter.

393. Why do kangaroo rats not come out on moonlit nights?

According to the 'moonlight avoidance theory', small mammals do not come out at night to forage for food when the Moon is bright. This seems to make sense: the darker it is, the less likely they are to be spotted by predators. In fact, it made so much sense that nobody bothered to test it until recently, when the results showed that matters are not so simple.

A study in 2013 in the Great Basin Desert in the USA revealed that most small mammals were just as active on bright moonlit nights as at other times. The only mammal that seemed to subscribe to the moonlight avoidance theory was the kangaroo rat, a giant rodent that hops around on two legs.

One theory is that kangaroo rats, being bigger than other rodents, generally beat the others to any food that's going. They therefore have the luxury of being able to stay at home on moonlit nights while the others, having run out of food, have to go out anyway, whatever the risk. Another suggestion is that the predators of small mammals are themselves preyed on by larger animals, so they too avoid bright nights to avoid being spotted, which makes it safe for the small mammals to come out after all.

Studies in other places such as New Mexico, however, have suggested that kangaroo rats come out more frequently on moonlit nights than on dark ones. Evidently the effect of moonlight on rodents' behaviour is much more complicated than had been thought and depends on many more factors than just the lighting.

See also ANIMALS 18; HUMOUR 245; MAMMALS 283; PANGOLINS 356; SEX 410; WALRUSES 486

RELIGION

394. What happened to the Ark of the Covenant?

According to the Book of Exodus, God told Moses to build the Ark of the Covenant to hold the two tablets on which were inscribed the Ten Commandments. The Ark and its powers are then frequently mentioned in the Old Testament until King Josiah of Judah (in 2 Chronicles 35) orders the caretakers of the Ark to return it to the temple in Jerusalem.

After that, the picture is confused. In the New Testament, Paul, in his Letter to the Hebrews, mentions that as well as the Ten Commandments, the Ark also contained Aaron's rod, a jar of manna, and the first Torah scroll, written by Moses. The Ark is also mentioned in Revelation as being in heaven, but since Moses' ark was meant to be a copy of one in heaven, the one mentioned in Revelation may be the original rather than Moses' copy.

According to the non-canonical Book of Maccabees, the prophet Jeremiah, after being warned by God of the Babylonian invasion, buried the Ark in a cave on Mount Nebo near the east bank of the River Jordan, where it would remain until God gathered his people together again. More recent accounts have placed the Ark in France, the USA, Rome, Egypt (including one version that had it in the tomb of Tutankhamun), the UK or Ireland.

The most detailed claim comes from the Lemba people of South Africa and Zimbabwe, who have said that their ancestors carried the Ark south. Arabic sources have maintained that it was first taken to Yemen, where the Lemba found it and brought it to Africa. According to Lemba oral traditions, the Ark self-destructed on arrival in their homeland and their priests constructed a new one from a piece of the original.

The interesting thing is that a German missionary found this alleged replica in the 1940s. It was taken to a museum in Harare, where it was carbon-dated to around 1350, which was about the time of the end of the Great Zimbabwe civilization.

395. Who was the Cretan Snake Goddess?

When the British archaeologist Arthur Evans discovered the Minoan civilization of Crete in 1903, he unearthed the first examples of ceramic Snake Goddess figurines. Several more were found later, all depicting a bare-breasted woman holding a snake in each hand, usually wearing a crown and having an owl on her head.

The figurines date back to around 1600 BC and stand out in a culture that appears to have produced very little art or sculpture. There is no other evidence of a snake goddess in Minoan beliefs, and while several other cultures had snake goddesses, nothing is known that would relate them to the Minoan version. Snakes were often used as a symbol of rebirth because of their habit of shedding their skins, and it has been suggested that the figurines represented some sort of Earth goddess, but there is no evidence that the Minoans worshipped such a goddess.

See also ANIMALS 19; ASTRONOMY 30; CHINA 101; CHRISTIANITY 106; GOLD 219; INCAS 247; JESUS CHRIST 259–63; PHILOSOPHY 364–5; SCIENCE 405; TURKEY 457; UNIVERSE 464

RIDDLES

396. What is the answer to Bishop Samuel Wilberforce's riddle?

Samuel Wilberforce, bishop of Oxford, is now best remembered for three reasons: his fervent opposition to Charles Darwin; the nickname

'Soapy Sam' given to him by Benjamin Disraeli, who described his manner as 'unctuous, oleaginous, saponaceous'; and the riddle that was found among his papers after he died in 1873:

> *Sweetest of sound, in orchestra heard,*
> *Yet in orchestra never have been,*
> *Bird in light plumage, yet less like a bird,*
> *Nothing in nature has ever been seen,*
> *On earth I expire, in water I die,*
> *Yet I run, swim and fly,*
> *If I cannot be guessed by a boy or a man,*
> *A girl or a woman I certainly can!*

A number of possible solutions, including 'whale' and 'mermaid', have been proposed, but none fits the description well enough for all to agree on what Wilberforce intended, so the riddle is generally considered still unsolved. Perhaps the most likely suggestion is 'a siren'.

RUSSIA

397. What created the Patomskiy crater in Siberia?

In 1949 the Russian geologist Vadim Kolpakov, exploring a region of Siberia near Irkutsk, discovered a massive convex cone made of limestone with a huge crater in its top and a rounded hill in the crater. Its appearance resembled a huge bird's nest with an egg in it, which is why the local people call it the 'Eagle's Nest'.

The cone is 80 metres tall with a diameter of 150 metres at its widest, and the depth of the inner circle crater is around 10 metres; it is thought to be about 250 years old, but that figure could be well out. More than sixty years after its discovery we still do not know what caused it. The obvious explanation is a meteorite impact, but no meteorite fragments have ever been found. Other theories include the following:

(i) It was caused by a secret nuclear test – which is unlikely as radiation levels are normal.

(ii) It is an ancient slag heap – unlikely as there is no evidence of a sizeable population ever having been in the region.

(iii) It could have been caused by a volcanic eruption – only there are no known volcanoes nearby.

(iv) It may have been built by aliens – which is a solution for some people to anything out of the ordinary.

As well as the mystery over its origin, the crater changes shape, rising and falling periodically, and trees near it are said to grow particularly fast, which also has not been explained.

See also CATS 92; GOLD 218

SALAMANDERS

398. How do adult salamanders regrow their limbs?

If an adult salamander loses a limb or even its tail, it can grow a new one. Salamanders are the only vertebrates that can regrow limbs in such a manner. In recent years, a great deal of research has gone into trying to discover what makes them so special, but we are not quite there yet.

When a human embryo is developing in the womb, its stem cells develop into specific types of cell for the various parts of the body. Soon after birth, however, we lose the ability to create all-purpose cells which can be sent to the region of any missing part and grow into whatever is necessary. Essentially that is what the salamander does and it is a very complex procedure. Not only must the animal send a supply of all-purpose cells to the affected area, but when they get there, they must recognize where they are in order to know what to grow into.

Recently something called the ERK pathway was discovered to play a vital role in this process. The ERK pathway acts as a communications highway between a cell's surface and the nucleus, which contains the cell's genetic material. Not only is the ERK pathway not fully active in adult mammals, but if it is turned off in salamanders, they lose the ability to regenerate limbs.

How salamanders keep the pathway turned on while we humans cannot must be a key question in accounting for their regeneration ability.

SALMON

399. How do salmon find their way back to their place of birth to spawn?

After being born in a river, salmon may swim to the open sea and spend two or three years there before returning to their original home to spawn. How they manage to find their way back has long been a puzzle. In 2013 a study at Oregon State University showed that the Earth's magnetic field may have something to do with it.

Their study involved looking at fifty-six years of fisheries' data monitoring sockeye salmon returning to the Fraser River in British Columbia. To reach the river, they must choose which way to go around Vancouver Island. Whether they chose the northern or the southern route was found to correlate with changes in the Earth's magnetic field. What was probably happening, the researchers concluded, was that some sort of map of the magnetic field was imprinted on the salmon on their outward journey and they were selecting the route that most closely resembled it. At what distance from their goal the geomagnetic data are useful, however, is unclear, and it is thought likely that the salmon also use the Sun as a compass, as well as tracking waves breaking on the beach with infrasound and using smell.

See also BEARS 41

SALT

400. Can we predict El Niño from sea-salt levels?

Every few years, the usual climate patterns of the western Pacific Ocean are thrown off balance by the phenomenon known as El Niño. In a normal year the trade winds blow westward, pushing warm surface water near Australia and New Guinea towards the western Pacific. The build-up of this warm water forces nutrient-rich cold waters to rise up from the deeper ocean off the west coast of South America. This colder nutrient-rich water fosters the growth of the fish population, much to the joy of the South American economy.

In an El Niño year, however, the trade winds weaken, warm waters are not pushed westward, cold water is not forced to the surface, and the fish stay away. Also, the warmer waters may add to the problems of the region by leading to heavy rain.

Forecasting when El Niño is going to strike is not an easy task. All we know is that it happens every three to seven years. The salinity of ocean water, however, is known to play an important part in determining its capacity to store and transport heat. Greater salinity results in an increase in ocean density, which affects the circulation of the waters. Since 2010 the NASA Aquarius satellite observatory has been monitoring ocean salinity from space to see how salt levels might be used to predict El Niño events.

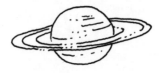

SATURN

401. Why is there a hexagonal cloud pattern around the north pole of Saturn?

In 1981–2 the Voyager spacecraft sent back pictures of a hexagonal cloud pattern around the north pole of Saturn. In 2006 the Cassini mission confirmed that it was still there. The sides of the hexagon measure about 13,800 kilometres (8,600 miles), and it rotates with a period of 10 hours 39 minutes 24 seconds, which is the same as the period of the radio emissions from Saturn's interior.

The only hint at what might cause this regular geometric pattern is some research showing that regular polygons may appear in areas of turbulent flow between two fluids rotating at different speeds. The atmospheric winds of Saturn and the planet's rotation may create the conditions for such a pattern.

402. What is responsible for the anomalous surface temperatures on Saturn's moon Mimas?

William Herschel discovered Saturn's moon Mimas in 1789, and it was long thought to be a small and uninteresting piece of celestial rock and ice. In 2010, however, measurements from the Cassini spacecraft indicated that the temperatures on the surface of Mimas were very strangely distributed. As on Earth, temperatures at various places might have been expected to correlate with how much light was received from the Sun, but a very different pattern was observed.

A wide difference in thermal conductivity across the surface could account for the unexpected pattern, leading to some surface regions being heated directly by the Sun, while at others the solar heat soaks into the surface. The coldest regions are around the huge crater known as Herschel, but whether the crater has something to do with the temperature differential is not known.

See also ASTRONOMY 30; SOLAR SYSTEM 441

SCIENCE

403. Who built the Antikythera mechanism?

At the end of 1900 Greek divers found the wreck of an ancient ship off the coast of the island of Antikythera. Further investigations of the wreck revealed fragments of a clockwork mechanism made of at least thirty bronze gears, of which the largest was about fourteen centimetres in diameter and originally had 223 teeth.

After reconstruction, the Antikythera mechanism, as it was dubbed, was found to be a device for calculating the positions of the Sun and Moon, the cycles of the Olympic Games, and perhaps even the locations of the planets. The complexity and astonishing accuracy of its calculations have led to its being described as 'the world's first analog computer'.

According to recent estimates, the device dates back to 205 BC, but it seems reasonable to assume that its construction must have evolved from less complex instruments. Remarkably, however, nothing quite like it has ever been found. After the ship carrying it sank, it seems that the relevant technology was lost, and it was a long time before the Greeks rediscovered the ideas behind it.

404. Is science methodical?

Those who practise science take great pride in the scientific method: we form hypotheses, make predictions based on these hypotheses, then perform experiments to see if the predictions are correct. This scientific method dates back to Descartes, who established its framework in 1619 and later wrote that its essence was

> *never to accept anything for true which I did not clearly know to be such; that is to say, carefully to avoid precipitancy and prejudice, and to compromise nothing more in my judgment than what was presented to my mind so clearly and distinctly as to exclude all ground of methodic doubt.*

The great twentieth-century philosopher Karl Popper pointed out the cracks in this framework. A hypothesis, he said, is only worth considering if it is falsifiable. You form a hypothesis, make a prediction, test the prediction, and if it doesn't work, then you reject the hypothesis. So you can never actually prove that anything is right, you can only prove it wrong. When the experiment conforms to the prediction, it may increase your belief that the hypothesis is correct, but you can never be sure.

Even worse, the hypothesis-prediction-testing procedure may seem methodical, but there are no rules, or set procedure, or algorithm for coming up with hypotheses in the first place. So perhaps there's no real 'method' behind science at all.

405. Can science, pseudo-science and non-science be distinguished?

When is a science not a science? Closely connected to the previous question is what Karl Popper called the 'demarcation problem': what distinguishes a science from a pseudo-science or a non-science? Why is chemistry a science when alchemy wasn't? In what way does astronomy differ from astrology? Alchemists and chemists both performed experiments and built up theories based on their results; astrologers and astronomers both observed the motion of celestial bodies and looked for their effects.

In Popper's view the crucial difference was falsification: scientists formulate a hypothesis and design experiments which will test whether the hypothesis makes incorrect predictions; pseudo-scientists only perform experiments designed to verify their theories. Alchemy and astrology survived for so long because they were formulated in a way that was so vague as not to allow them to be disproved.

Popper's rival Thomas Kuhn, however, pointed out that a historical approach showed that this wasn't how scientists behaved at all. Far from following Popper's rules, they were liable to ignore falsifying data unless the evidence was overwhelming. Kuhn proposed that the essential ingredient of science is puzzle-solving. 'Normal science', as he called it, consists in solving puzzles posed by the existing theory. Only very rarely, after the theory had been found to create too many anomalies, did scientists turn to Popper's falsification methods.

Later writers on the philosophy of science have suggested that both Popper and Kuhn were too limited in their views and that there is no universal rule for what constitutes a science or where the boundaries are to be drawn between science, pseudo-science and non-science. So the scientific status of homeopathy, psychoanalysis, parapsychology and perhaps even religion may still depend on whom you are talking to.

SEX

406. Is there a gay gene?

In 1990 research was published purporting to show a small difference in the brain between gay and straight men. In 1993 it was widely reported that a gay gene had been discovered. Actually even the scientist responsible for the research never claimed to have found a gene for homosexuality. It was only a linkage between a small stretch of DNA on the X chromosome and homosexuality in males, but such an idea was too complex for the press to report.

In 2005 researchers at the University of Illinois identified several stretches of DNA on other chromosomes that occurred more often in gay men. They concluded that there is no single gay gene but that 'sexual orientation is a complex trait'.

In 2014 a study – claimed to be the biggest ever – of 409 pairs of gay brothers identified five genetic markers pointing to homosexuality, but stressed that other factors, both genetic and environmental, played a part in determining sexual orientation. Again, the study identifies only regions on chromosomes rather than specific genes. As one of the lead authors said: 'until somebody finds a gene, we don't know.'

The issue is further complicated by various studies showing that men with older brothers are more likely to be gay. There is also the question of gay women, for whom no genetic markers have been identified.

407. Who invented condoms?

The early history of condoms is shrouded in mystery. Some claim that a cave painting in France dating back 12,000 to 15,000 years depicts condom use, but that is disputed. People in ancient Egypt, Rome and Greece are all known to have practised birth control, but only female methods are well documented. There are some references to men taking responsibility for contraception, but these are short on detail and it is unclear whether they suggest condom use or simply coitus interruptus. Egyptian and Greek men are known to have worn very sparse loincloths, doing little more than covering the penis, but whether they kept these on during sex is arguable.

According to one legend dating back to the second century AD, King Minos of Crete was the victim of a curse that made his semen contain scorpions and snakes. He is said to have used a goat's bladder to keep his sexual partners safe, but that was probably as a female pessary rather than a male condom.

After the fall of the Roman empire, there seems to be no reference to contraception in Europe until the Middle Ages, when a few references appear about soaking the penis in tar or soaking it in onion juice to lessen the chance of conception.

The first clear reference to a condom appears in a treatise on syphilis, *De morbo Gallico*, written by Gabriele Falloppio (after whom the

Fallopian tube is named), which was published in 1564. His condoms were linen sheaths soaked in a chemical solution, left to dry, then attached to the penis with a ribbon. Falloppio claimed they were his own invention. Even then, however, the condom was seen as a device to guard against syphilis rather than contraception. The first definite reference to condoms being used to prevent pregnancy did not appear until 1655.

408. Why do females have orgasms?

The biological function of the male orgasm is easy to explain: men need to spread their seed to have a chance of procreating. Why females have orgasms, however, is less easy to explain. There are essentially three theories:

(i) It's part of the pair-bonding process: a good orgasm helps females select a suitable mate and bonds the male and female together to ensure that an offspring has two parents.

(ii) Female orgasms involve uterine contractions that help suck sperm into the uterus.

(iii) Female orgasms actually serve no functional purpose but are an evolutionary by-product of male orgasm. The erectile and nervous tissue necessary for female orgasm is effectively the same as the sperm delivery system in men and is no more use than male nipples, which are a similar evolutionary by-product.

Which of these is correct is hotly disputed.

409. Do poor and hungry men prefer women with bigger breasts?

Two interesting studies on men's preferences in female breast size were reported in 2013. The first study was conducted on men of varying socioeconomic status in Malaysia. The men were shown figures of women with varying breast size and the results revealed that the lower the economic status of the subject, the bigger the breasts he preferred. The second study showed the same female figures to men in Britain, but this time the difference between the subjects was that one group had recently been fed while the others had not eaten for some time.

The results this time showed that hungry men like bigger breasts.

The researchers suggested that the results showed that men's attractiveness ratings were influenced by resource security: poor and hungry men see larger breasts as a source of security.

Earlier research, however, had suggested that preference for larger female breasts was associated with tendencies to be sexist, to objectify women and to be hostile towards women. So an alternative explanation of the Malaysian result could be that men who are lower on a socioeconomic scale are more likely to be sexist.

410. Do aphrodisiacs work?

Scientific studies on the effects of items claimed as aphrodisiacs are almost unanimous in their view that they do not have a significant physiological effect to support the claims. They also agree that even if such items did have a genuine effect, it would be far less than the psychological results given by a placebo effect.

Cucumbers and bananas, sometimes touted as aphrodisiacs, probably owe their reputation to their similarity in shape to a penis. Avocados even take their name from an Aztec word for testicles. Chillies and Spanish fly may irritate the urinary tract, which may feel like sexual arousal.

More promisingly, in 2005 researchers in Miami and Naples announced to the American Chemical Society the results of a study of oysters and other bivalve molluscs. This included the discovery of two amino acids which had previously been found to trigger the production of the sex hormones testosterone in male rats and progesterone in female rats.

However, the research on the rats involved injecting the amino acids directly into their bloodstream, and it is not known if humans eating them would have a similar effect. The quantities involved are also so small that we would expect to have to eat a lot of oysters to have any noticeable effect. So perhaps Casanova's recommendation of fifty oysters for breakfast had some sense to it after all.

See also ANIMALS 17, 19; BABOONS 40; BEES 45; BIOLOGY 62; BONES 72; CHEESE 94; CHOCOLATE 105; DINOSAURS 137; FISH 190; INTELLIGENCE 254; MONKEYS 318; MUSIC 329; SQUID 447

SEX DIFFERENCES

411. Are women better than men at multitasking?

There has long been a popular belief that women are better than men at multitasking, but is this really true or has it arisen simply because women are more often seen to be responsible for doing more than one thing at the same time? Until recently, very little research had been done on this. Indeed, the word 'multitask' was first seen only in 1965, when it was used not of humans but of computers. In 2013, however, a study appeared which was reported to show that women are indeed better at multitasking than men, though that statement was heavily qualified.

The word 'multitasking' can be used in either of two senses: doing two or more things at the same time, or dealing with multiple demands while not necessarily having to do more than one at any given moment. The research supported the notion that women are better than men at the second type but not the first. They concluded: 'More research on this question is urgently needed, before we can draw stronger conclusions and before we can differentiate between different explanations.'

Four years earlier, in 2009, a study in China had also reported that women were better at multitasking but warned that their tests might not reflect real-life multitasking. They also advised that further research was required. A Swedish study in 2013, however, found that men actually outperformed women at handling multiple tasks simultaneously, with the performance gap being correlated to the female menstrual cycle.

Meanwhile, a study in France in 2009 reported that the structure of our brains' frontal lobes stops us from doing more than two things at the same time anyway, while a study in the USA in 2014 reported that only 2 per cent of people can truly multitask, in the sense of doing two things at the same time without it affecting performance at either of them.

412. Is there an innate difference between male and female brains?

Opinions on this question differ dramatically, and each side can advance strong arguments in support of its cause.

On the one hand, it is known that hormones have a strong effect on brain development. Boy babies are exposed to much higher levels of testosterone in the womb than girl babies, which may lead to greater analytic skills but lower social skills. On the other hand, differences between males and females are not consistent across cultures, which would suggest they are culturally influenced rather than innate. Also, maps of the neural connections in women's brains display a very different pattern from those in men's, but that distinction only begins to appear several years after birth, which is another argument for environment and conditioning rather than innate differences. A classic experiment in support of the innateness side, however, involved offering Barbary macaque monkeys the choice between dolls or toy trucks. The girls took the dolls; the boys favoured the trucks.

I once asked some psychologist friends, all of whom had young children, whether their personal experiences as parents supported or clashed with their academic views on this question. They all laughed and said that while their academic view was that boys' and girls' brains are innately the same, their own experience confirmed an innate difference. One mother of a boy and a girl, who had resolutely tried to bring them up unisex, said that when they went into the garden and found a stick, the boy used it as a weapon while the girl cuddled it. 'There is no doubt', said another, 'there is a gun receptor on the Y chromosome.'

The evidence seems to suggest that we may start with small innate differences, which are then exaggerated hugely by culture and upbringing.

SHAKESPEARE

413. Why did Shakespeare use the word 'all' less frequently than his contemporaries?

A study in 2013 of word frequencies in the plays of William Shakespeare, Thomas Middleton, Ben Jonson and John Fletcher revealed that Shakespeare used the word 'all' significantly less frequently than his contemporaries, but he used 'will' as a noun more frequently than the others.

Jonson was the writer who most often used the word 'any'; Fletcher had a fondness for 'have'; while Middleton liked 'master', 'gentleman' and 'widow' more than the other writers.

Middleton's city comedies may account for his extensive use of his favourites, but why Shakespeare kept away from the word 'all' is difficult to explain.

414. Did William Shakespeare love his wife?

We know very little about the relationship between Shakespeare and Anne Hathaway. They married when he was eighteen and she was twenty-six; they had their first child, Susanna, six months later; she stayed living in Stratford while he went to work as a playwright in London; and when he died, he left her his second-best bed. The rest of their life together – or apart – raises far more questions than answers.

Presumably it was Anne's pregnancy which led to the hurried marriage, but was it so hurried that a registrar got her name wrong when the banns were announced? One record in the Episcopal Register names the woman to marry Shakespeare as Anne Whateley. Was this another woman whom Shakespeare really wanted to marry before Ms Hathaway told him she was pregnant, or was it just a mistake? It has even been suggested that Anne Hathaway was a widow who had previously married a man named Whateley.

When Shakespeare, after about seven years' marriage to Anne, went to London, did she come to visit? How often did he return to Stratford to see her? Was it a separation or just a necessary business arrangement?

And was that 'second-best bed' line in his will just an innocent bequest or a piece of posthumous rudeness? It has been suggested that a wife would have been entitled to a sizeable portion of the estate, so the bed could have been just an extra loving touch. The bulk of the estate mentioned in the will, which must have included the best bed, went to his daughter.

415. How much of *Cardenio* did Shakespeare write?

In May 1613 Shakespeare's theatre company, The King's Men, performed a set of six plays at court including one called *The History of Cardenio*, based on a section in Cervantez' *Don Quixote*, which had first been translated into English in 1612. The company performed the same play later the same year for the ambassador of the Duke of Savoy, but it seems not to have been published at the time and all manuscripts of it have been lost.

In 1653 *Cardenio* was registered for publication and the authors were given as William Shakespeare and John Fletcher, which is very plausible as they had worked together before, notably on the play *Henry VIII*. If the play had survived, no doubt scholars would still be arguing about which parts were by Shakespeare and which by Fletcher. Instead, all we are left with is a trail of clues which have further complicated the matter.

In 1727 the playwright and Shakespearean editor Lewis Theobold announced that he had found the missing *Cardenio* manuscript and improved it to produce his own play *The Double Falsehood*. The manuscript Theobold claimed to have found is said to have been left in the Covent Garden Playhouse in London, which burnt down in 1808. There is no record of anyone else ever seeing the manuscript.

To confuse the issue still further, a play called *The Second Maiden's*

Tragedy, dating from 1611 and known only in manuscript, has also been claimed to have strong connections with *Cardenio*. The manuscript bears no author's name, but it also takes its theme from *Don Quixote* and is generally thought to have been written by Thomas Middleton. In 1994, however, a handwriting expert identified the calligraphy as Shakespeare's hand.

We are left with a play by Theobold allegedly based on a manuscript by Fletcher and Shakespeare, which may itself have had its origin in a play by Middleton copied out by the Bard. Extensive computer analyses have been performed to try to identify the parts of all this that are genuine Shakespeare, but how much credence can be placed on the results is unclear.

See also MURDER 323; THEATRE 453

SHARKS

416. How long do great white sharks live?

Telling the age of sharks is notoriously difficult. Attempts have been made by counting growth bands in their vertebrae, but it is not even known if these bands are deposited annually. Sharks in captivity are also known to have a considerably shorter lifespan than in the wild, so little useful information on longevity is gained from studying them. Tracking sharks for long periods has also proved difficult as they cover such large areas, though this has improved a little with the use of satellite data and GPS tracking.

Until very recently, estimates for the lifespan of great white sharks varied between just under thirty years and about forty. In 2013, however, a new technique involving radiocarbon dating indicated that great whites might live much longer than had been thought.

The new method is based on comparing radiocarbon values in the vertebrae of sharks with chronologies documenting the marine uptake of a radioactive carbon isotope produced by atmospheric testing of thermonuclear devices. Measurements on four male and four female sharks from the north-west Atlantic produced estimates of forty years of age for the largest female and seventy years for the largest male. If those figures are correct, some male sharks might be expected to reach the age of 100 or more.

SHEEP

417. Do sheep put on weight when they die?

In 1901 Dr Duncan MacDougal of Massachusetts conducted a bizarre experiment to determine the weight of a human soul. His idea was to weigh six patients just before and after the moment of death. The difference would be the weight of the soul, which had departed the body at the moment of death. In charge of a ward for terminally ill tuberculosis patients, he recognized when they were only two hours from death, then moved their beds onto an industrial scale.

Dr MacDougal discounted five of the six experiments because of 'technical difficulties', but the other patient, who was the first of the series, was found to have lost three-quarters of an ounce at the moment of death. MacDougal therefore proudly announced that three-quarters of an ounce was the weight of the human soul. He later performed the same experiment on dogs, for which he detected no weight loss. He took that as evidence supporting the belief that dogs have no souls.

In 2001 Lewis Hollander of Redmond, Oregon, repeated MacDougal's experiment, not on humans and dogs but on sheep and a goat. He reported that:

Twelve animals (one ram, seven ewes, three lambs and one goat) were studied... At the moment of death an unexplained weight gain transient of 18 to 780 grams for 1 to 6 seconds was observed with seven adult sheep but not with the lambs or goat.

In other words, sheep gain weight when they die, but lose it again within a few seconds. Three possible explanations suggest themselves:
(i) Sheep's souls have a negative weight.
(ii) The cessation of, or change in, biomechanical processes at the moment of death may result in a small change in recorded weight.
(iii) Both MacDougal's and Hollander's experimental set-ups were insufficiently precise to measure what they claimed to.

The film *21 Grams*, directed by Alejandro González Iñárritu and made in 2003, was inspired by MacDougal's experiment. The title is the metric equivalent of his three-quarters of an ounce.

See also BIOLOGY 61; CAMELS 83; CANNIBALISM 88; DISEASE 144–5

SHELLFISH

418. Do crayfish worry?

Until 2014 crayfish were seen as ancient and simple creatures incapable of experiencing emotions. Then an experiment was reported that seemed to show there might be much more to them.

First, some crayfish were subjected to electric shocks for about twenty minutes to induce stress. Then they were placed in a cross-shaped tank in which two arms of the cross were brightly lit and two dark. The crayfish were seen to avoid the well-lit areas and instead stay in the dark.

Other crayfish that had not been given the electric shocks explored all areas of the cross-shaped tank, both light and dark. However, when these crayfish were injected with serotonin, they started behaving like the others, staying out of the lit areas. Serotonin is a neurotransmitter associated with anxiety in humans and the stressed crayfish were found to be producing it naturally. When they were treated with drugs used to treat anxiety in humans, their apparent fear of the well-lit areas disappeared.

The experiment does not show that crayfish get worried, but it certainly indicates that their responses to stress have many similarities with those of humans.

SHIPS

419. What happened to Captain Gray of the SS *Great Britain*?

In 1872 the captain of the most celebrated ship in the British merchant fleet disappeared. John Gray had been captain of the SS *Great Britain* for eighteen years. Six feet tall and weighing nearly seventeen stone, he was a huge man, very popular with his passengers and enjoying a reputation and record no other captain could match. While Brunel's ship was under his command, it took some 13,000 people from Britain to start a new life in Australia, as well as transporting a large number of convicts there.

On the night of 25 November 1872, while the ship was returning to Liverpool from Melbourne, Gray vanished. He had retired to his cabin early, complaining of pains in his bowels, which nobody took seriously as he had a reputation for being a bit of a hypochondriac. A steward checked on him later and found him writing a letter and, in the steward's words, 'as sensible as ever'. The next morning his cabin was found to be empty and Gray could not be discovered anywhere on board. The only clue was an open transom window in the lower saloon at the stern of the ship, which another steward had screwed shut the previous night.

The manner of his disappearance suggested suicide, but no good reasons to support that explanation have ever been given.

420. What happened to Sir Cloudesley Shovell?

Admiral of the fleet Sir Cloudesley Shovell (1650–1707) was one of the most successful ship's captains in a long career in the English navy and became a favourite of Queen Anne for his heroic victories.

In 1707, after an attack on Toulon which had ended in the French scuttling their own fleet, Shovell's ship HMS *Association* hit the rocks near the Scilly Isles and sank in only three or four minutes. None of the 800 men on board survived. Shovell's body was later found at Porthellick Cove in the Scillies, some seven miles from where the wreck took place, near the bodies of his two stepsons, suggesting that they had escaped from the *Association* in a lifeboat, but the manner of his death has become a subject of much debate and various legends.

According to one story, he reached the shore barely alive and was murdered by a woman for the emerald ring he was wearing. In 1709, two years after the disaster, it was reported that Shovell's body had first been found by two women, stripped of his shirt and with his emerald ring missing. Some thirty years later, a woman, on her deathbed, was reported to have confessed to a clergyman to having killed the admiral. She is said to have produced the ring, but there is no evidence of that. Another story – for which no evidence has ever been produced – was that a sailor on *Association* warned Shovell that they were off course and the admiral had him hanged for inciting mutiny.

Whatever happened to Sir Cloudesley Shovell, it had one good and lasting effect: a large prize was offered by the British government for a reliable method of calculating longitude, and it resulted in improvements in navigation that must have saved thousands.

421. Did poor communication sink the *Mary Rose*?

On 19 July 1545 Henry VIII's flagship the *Mary Rose* sank in the Solent. The only eyewitness account of the sinking reported that she was executing a tight turn when she was caught by a gust of wind, but various theories about contributory factors have been put forward.

The French claimed she had been hit by their cannon, but when the ship was finally raised in 1982, there was no evidence of that. Overloading, with soldiers or guns, has been suggested, but the ship had crossed the Channel successfully, so why should she sink in the comparatively calm Solent? A more likely explanation is that water rushed in through the open gun-ports on one side of the ship, an idea that has often been associated with possible human error by the captain. In 2008, however, a new theory emerged from a Canadian criminologist.

Lynne Bell had examined bones and teeth from human remains of the *Mary Rose* crew and was surprised to find that the evidence suggested that many of them were not British but may have been from Spain. 'The reason the *Mary Rose* sank', she said, 'is because there was very poor communication between the crew because you have this really large foreign contingent.' It wasn't so much a careless crew failing to close the gun-ports in the heat of battle as a foreign crew failing to understand their captain's order to do so.

422. What happened to the crew of *Kaz II*?

On 18 April 2007 a helicopter pilot flying over Australia's Great Barrier Reef spotted a catamaran apparently drifting and out of control. He reported it and the maritime authorities reached the boat, called *Kaz II*, and boarded it on 20 April. What they found was mystifying: everything about the boat seemed normal but there was no sign of the three-man crew. Food was set on a table, a computer was on, the engine was running, all the life jackets were in place and untouched, and all the emergency systems were in good working condition. The only sign of anything untoward was a big rip in one of the sails. A video camera was also found with footage of the crew close to the time they disappeared. The men looked relaxed and nothing out of the ordinary was recorded.

At a hearing to determine what had happened to the men, the state coroner said that the men must be presumed to have died but said that he 'cannot be so definitive about the circumstances in which the deaths occurred'. In his opinion, the most likely scenario was that one of the men had fallen overboard trying to deal with a problem with the fishing lure and the other two perished trying to save him.

No explanation was offered for what caused the rip in the sail, why nobody put on a life jacket or called for help over the radio, how it all happened when they were about to sit down for a meal, and why the engine was turned on. All three men were experienced and cautious sailors, and no plausible explanation of what happened to them has ever been given.

See also DOLPHINS 157; MEXICO 312; MICE 313; PREHISTORY 381; SCIENCE 403

SLEEP

423. Can birds sleep while they fly?

When birds are observed in their nests or at ground level, we can see that they sleep, but some birds remain on the wing for days or weeks or even longer. Can they sleep while they are flying? Birds, like mammals – as we mentioned when discussing ostriches and platypuses (→ 375) – exhibit two types of sleep: slow-wave sleep (SWS) and rapid eye movement (REM) sleep. The first of these may occur in both hemispheres of the brain at the same time, or in just one hemisphere. While each of a mammal's eyes is connected to both halves of the brain, a bird's left eye connects to its right brain and its right eye to its left brain. So a bird can, in theory, keep one eye open watching the sky while the other eye sleeps. REM sleep, however, can only occur in both halves of the brain at the same time and is usually accompanied by a loss of muscle tone, making it unlikely that this type of sleep is compatible with flying at all.

Until recently it was supposed that birds on the wing obtained enough rest from slow-wave sleep, alternating halves of the brain until they reached their destination, then recovering with an extensive REM sleep. In 2013, however, alpine swifts were tracked on a long migratory flight to Africa and thereafter, and it was found that they remained in the air for 200 days without touching down. Since their main diet is airborne insects, of which there are far more in Africa than in their northern summer residences, all the food they need is in the air. How they survive for 200 days without proper sleep will only be understood when electroencephalogram recording devices are developed that can monitor the birds' brains over long periods and long distances.

424. When did sleep begin in animal evolution?

From an evolutionary perspective, it is not easy to see why we, and all other mammals, sleep. There is no doubt that our bodies perform a number of essential recuperative functions while we sleep, such as repair of cells, consolidation of memories and restoration of energy, but why these functions demand a cessation of conscious activity is unknown.

While we sleep, the risk from predators and from being unaware of our surroundings would seem to be a great survival threat. Even some primitive organisms are known to exhibit circadian rhythms that make them alternate between periods of activity and periods of rest, and it seems likely that sleep evolved from these rest periods.

Mammalian sleep, to judge from electroencephalogram (EEG) readings, is far more complex than the sleep-like states of reptiles and fishes, but it is still difficult to see the evolutionary advantages of a period of total loss of consciousness or to tell whether early mammals exhibited our type of sleep or whether it developed much later. Perhaps sleep, as we know it, only arose when the mammalian brain had evolved sufficiently for it to design safe sleeping places.

425. Do centipedes sleep?

In 2014 the genome of a species of centipede was sequenced for the first time. *Strigamia maritima* is a venomous and carnivorous centipede found on the coast of the Moray Firth in Scotland, and is a representative of a group that evolved over half a billion years ago. Its genome indicates that it has no genes related to vision and must have lost its eyes at least 200 million years ago. It also has no genes relating to the circadian clock, which regulates an animal's sleep.

Since they live underground, these centipedes have no need for light receptors or eyes: this may explain the lack of a circadian clock, which usually relies on light input to tell day from night. But how the centipede sleeps, and indeed if it sleeps at all without a circadian clock to tell it when to do so, remain open questions.

426. Why does sleep deprivation provoke epileptic seizures?

A link between epilepsy and sleep deprivation has been suspected for well over 2,000 years. Around 400 BC Hippocrates advised sufferers from epilepsy to 'spend the day awake and the night asleep. If this habit be disturbed, it is not so good... worst of all when he sleeps neither night nor day.'

Over the past fifty years a great deal of research has been done on the subject, but we still cannot claim to understand the nature of the link. Some epileptics seem to have seizures predominantly while asleep or at the point of falling asleep or waking. Some people have had their only epileptic seizure when sleep-deprived. In others, the occurrence of seizures seems to have no connection with their sleep cycle.

Since sleep deprivation is also usually caused by a disorder, it could be that the same disorder is responsible for triggering the seizure directly, rather than the seizure being caused by the sleep deprivation. Sleep certainly results in changed electrical activity in the brain, and changed electrical activity is strongly associated with epileptic seizures, but the precise connection between the two is still unknown.

427. Do women need more sleep than men?

Over the past few years many pieces have appeared in both academic journals and the popular press claiming to compare the amount men sleep and the amount women sleep. Some say that men sleep more; others say that women sleep more. The *United Kingdom 2000 Time Use Survey* reported that women sleep longer, particularly in the 30–60 age group. A survey in the USA in 2005, however, reported that women do sleep longer than men but complain more about their sleep quality. Other reports say that women spend longer in bed, but take longer to get to sleep, and when they do, the sleep is more disturbed, all of which results in them actually sleeping less than men. More recently, there have been claims that women need more sleep than men, whether they get it or not.

The vast majority of all this is anecdotal, or at best speculative, but a clear suggestion of a possible difference in quality of male and female sleep came in a study of physiological stress in 2013. Based on research at the University of California, it measured blood levels of C-reactive protein (CRP), which is known to rise in response to inflammation. The research showed that the strongest single factor correlating with an increase in CRP for women was their taking longer than half an hour to fall asleep at night. The conclusion was that women are not only more likely than men to suffer from insomnia, but also more likely to suffer the effects of physiological stress associated with it.

428. What is the function of REM sleep?

We have already discussed rapid eye movement (REM) sleep briefly in the context of platypuses (→ 375) and birds (→ 423), but the real function of REM sleep is still a puzzle. Shortly after it was first identified in 1953, REM sleep was thought to be strongly associated with dreaming. Subjects woken up when they began the characteristic rapid eye fluttering tended to report strong memories of dreams they had been having. Later, the dreaming–REM connection was found to be weaker as non-REM dreaming was also found to exist. REM sleep, however, still seems to be accompanied by more vivid and lifelike dreams.

Adults spend 20 to 25 per cent of their sleeping time in REM sleep; the figure is higher in infants. We have four or five sleep cycles a night, each with a few minutes of REM sleep. People with depression have less REM sleep than others; we are more likely to snore during REM sleep; the activity of the brain's neurons is more intense, but the body stops releasing the neurotransmitters that are responsible for stimulating our motor neurons and our muscles become paralysed.

Even with such physiological effects identified, however, we cannot really claim to understand what the function of REM sleep is. One theory is that REM sleep is the period during which our brains consolidate memories. Another idea is that it is when our brains repair themselves and build the neural connections that are essential for conceptual thought and creativity. This may help explain why infants have longer periods of REM sleep as their brains grow and develop.

Because our brains are so active during REM sleep, it is sometimes called 'paradoxical sleep', but we need to know much more before all its paradoxes are resolved.

429. Why do some animals sleep longer than others?

Giant armadillos sleep for around eighteen hours a day. Some species of bats sleep for almost twenty hours. Lions sleep for nearly fourteen hours, humans and rabbits both sleep around eight hours, but cows get by on four hours and horses manage on less than three. So what is responsible for these wide variations?

The size of an animal, the amount of time it spends eating, its brain size as a percentage of body size, its metabolic rate and its risk from predators have all been suggested as factors determining how much sleep it gets. The time spent in short naps rather than one long sleep may also play a role. Some studies have suggested that an animal's evolutionary past may play a highly significant part, but we have too little evidence of the sleeping patterns of long-extinct animals to be sure.

See also BIOLOGY 59; BRAINS 79; DREAMS 160–1; HYPNOSIS 246; LEMURS 272; MEDICINE 300; PHILOSOPHY 359; PLATYPUSES 375

SLOTHS

430. From which ground sloth species did three-toed sloths evolve?

Until around 10,000 years ago, giant sloths roamed South America. The fossil record has now revealed over 100 genera of giant sloths since the first skeleton was discovered in 1796. Now the only species that remain are the two-toed *Choloepus* and the three-toed *Bradypus*.

A detailed analysis of the bones of ancient and modern sloths has indicated that *Choloepus* is allied with extinct members of the family Megalonychidae, but where *Bradypus* came from is far more difficult to say. The results of the analysis suggested that the split between the two varieties of modern sloth may date back 40 million years, with *Choloepus* evolving from known species of giant sloth, with whom *Bradypus* probably had an unknown common ancestor even further back. The habit of hanging upside down in rainforest canopies, which the much larger ground sloths were of course too big to do, would then have evolved independently in each species.

431. How fast could a giant ground sloth run?

Modern sloths, as their name suggests, are very slow at moving around on the ground. Their front and hind legs have evolved to make them perfectly designed for hanging upside down from branches in the forest canopy and when necessary scampering along in the same upside-down position. At ground level the best they can do is drag themselves along slowly with their front claws, but that was not always the case.

The giant ground sloth was about the size of an elephant and is thought to have walked around rather like a bear, either on all fours or on its hind legs. Having little or nothing to run away from, it seems to have been built more for stability than speed, with thick bones in its short hind legs and its thick tail giving it a low centre of gravity. Its front legs were long and strong for both weight-bearing and stretching to help it strip vegetation from high branches of trees.

The giant sloth's large claws would have meant that it had to turn its feet inwards to walk, and while some examples of fossil footprints confirm that they sometimes walked bipedally, the prints are not far enough apart to suggest that they were running. What speed these animals did or could move at remains unknown.

432. Why do sloths have orange patches on their backs?

One of the many projects at the Sloth Sanctuary of Costa Rica is to try to discover why male three-toed sloths have evolved bright yellow or orange patches on their backs. The patch, known as a speculum, begins to develop around the age of three as the sloth reaches sexual maturity. The patch is divided by a central black stripe and other black markings that are unique to each sloth. Unlike the rest of the sloth's fur, the orange patch has no algae growing in it, and it has a different texture from its other hair. It is also covered with an oily secretion which, when rubbed off, takes the yellow or orange pigment with it.

Whether the patch has some significance in mate selection is unknown, but with the rest of the animal so well camouflaged against the rainforest background, it seems very odd to display a bright patch of orange.

433. Why do three-toed sloths poo on the ground?

Three-toed sloths climb down from their trees once a week to urinate and defecate on the ground, then slowly climb back up again. Some two-toed sloths do the same, but others don't bother to make the energy-consuming climb but just let their bodily waste fall downwards through the tree.

In 2014 a link was established between a sloth's lavatorial habits and its nutrition. Sloth fur is covered in algae and moths. When the sloth relieved itself on the ground, moths were found to lay eggs in its poo, and when the eggs hatched, the newborn moths would hop back into the sloth's fur. Sloths' stomachs were also found to contain samples of nutritional algae which they had presumably licked from their fur. The tree-climbing habit gave the three-toed sloths a higher concentration of moths than their two-toed, poo-where-you-hang cousins; more moths correlated with a greater concentration of nitrogen, and more nitrogen meant more algae to lick.

On the other hand, climbing down a tree represents an immense expenditure of energy for the sloth. Whether it represents a greater expenditure of energy to climb a tree with only two toes is unknown, but that could, perhaps, tip the balance and be the reason why *Choloepus* stays hanging in the canopy while *Bradypus* makes the long trip down on poo-days.

434. How do sloths communicate?

We know very little about how sloths communicate with one another or how often they do it. Generally they are very solitary creatures; some mutual grooming has been observed, but only between mothers and infants. Although they are usually silent, sloths sometimes emit sounds. An infant separated from its mother will emit a loud bleat which may last around a minute. A defensive hiss has also been noted, though their distress call is low-pitched, which ties in with a finding that the sloth's ear picks up low-frequency sounds best.

Little research seems to have been done into the range of sloth sounds or what they may mean, but these animals must have some sort of communication. In 2012 a male sloth named Leander arrived in London from Germany in the hope that he would mate with London Zoo's resident female Marilyn. In 2013 zoo-keepers announced with some astonishment that Marilyn was pregnant. Not only had the keepers not known that they had mated, but they did not even think the pair had acknowledged each other's existence.

See also AVOCADOS 37

SMELL

435. Why do we like some smells and not others?

It is undeniable that people's reactions to smells differ. Some people may quite enjoy a smell that others find repulsive. Even the smell that a skunk emits in defence is liked by some people.

People's abilities to detect certain smells also differ and such traits are determined genetically, but until recently our smell preferences were widely thought to be formed through culture and experience. In 2014, however, research at Duke University, North Carolina, indicated that our personal smell preferences depend on some extremely fine tuning of our amino acids. Around 400 genes are known that code for smells, and the difference of a single amino acid on a single gene can lead to a difference in our smell perception. By comparing the scent receptors of different people and seeing their reactions to a variety of odour molecules, the researchers found that the receptors of any two individuals differ by about 30 per cent.

The conclusion is that we are born with the potential specifically to like or dislike particular smells. What we don't know is how our personal smell preference profile emerges in the first place, and what the connection is between the sensory perception of a smell and the emotional appreciation of it.

436. How does the smell of a queen bee influence the behaviour of others in the hive?

A queen bee emits a substance known as queen mandibular pheromone (QMP), which is a cocktail of pheromones that have different effects on members of the hive. About a week after hatching, the queen goes on a mating flight during which she passes through colonies of drones (though we do not know how she finds them) where her QMP attracts them to fly after her. Back in the hive, they queue up politely awaiting their turn to mate with her, then drop off her and die shortly after. Once mating has been completed, the QMP starts performing its second main function, which is to suppress the reproductive systems of the workers in the hive, thereby ensuring that the queen is the only reproductive female.

Identification of the chemicals in QMP has allowed it to be synthesized, and when the synthetic version is sprayed in the hive, it has been seen to achieve the same effects, even when the queen is absent. Precisely how the chemicals achieve their results is unknown.

See also ANATOMY 4; ASPARAGUS 26; BRAINS 75; CATS 90; CHEMICALS 95; COFFEE 110; DOGS 149; EBOLA 165; FOOD 195; GENETICS 210; NOSES 342, 345; OCTOPUSES 347; POLAR BEARS 377; SALMON 399

SNAILS

437. Are left-handed snails better off than right-handed snails?

Most snails in South-east Asia are right-handed. That is to say, their shells coil in a clockwise direction. This can make life difficult for left-handed snails, for mating between left-handed and right-handed snails is very difficult, if not impossible. There is, however, one big potential advantage conveyed by left-handedness for a snail, which was found by examining the teeth of a group of snakes known as pareatids.

Being quite partial to an occasional mouthful of snail, these snakes have evolved in a manner that is best suited to extract a snail from a right-handed shell. Their tooth arrangements and hunting strategies both find southpaw snails trickier. Research has confirmed that there are, in fact, higher proportions of left-handed snails in regions with the highest populations of pareatid snakes.

What gave rise to the preponderance of right-handed snails in the first place, however, is not known. Nor is it known how long it will take for specialist left-handed-snail-eating snakes to evolve.

438. Does chocolate improve the memory of snails?

In 2012 researchers at the University of Calgary performed an interesting experiment on two groups of snails. The snails in one group were put in ordinary pond water; those in the other group were placed in pond water to which the flavonoid epicatechin, which is present in chocolate, had been added.

The snails then underwent thirty-minute training sessions to teach them to keep their breathing tubes closed in deoxygenated water. Snails usually breathe through their skins, but when oxygen levels are low, they stick their breathing tubes above the surface of the water to increase the oxygen supply. For this experiment, the researchers tapped the snail's breathing tube if the snail tried to open it above the water. The snails therefore quickly learnt to keep their breathing tubes shut.

The next day the snails were put back in the deoxygenated water to see if they remembered the lesson. In general, the snails that had been in normal pond water did not remember the lesson but stuck their breathing tubes out of the water to breath, but the snails in the epicatechin-spiked water kept their breathing tubes closed.

Later experiments concluded that chocolate does not improve memory in humans, but the result on snails has been neither confirmed nor contradicted.

SNAKES

439. Are snakes right-handed?

Talking of handedness in creatures that have no hands may sound strange, but research published in 1999 suggested that garter snakes are not totally symmetric and may prefer one side of their body to the other.

Male snakes possess one testis, one hemipenis and one kidney on each side of its body and these are not symmetric. In particular, the right hemipenis and testis are both larger than their counterparts on the left. When garter snakes mate, only one hemipenis enters the female and the males tend to alternate between them. There are advantages in using the right, however, particularly at the conclusion of mating, when the male deposits a gelatinous 'mating plug' that prevents, or at least delays, the female from mating with any other snake. It may therefore be of evolutionary advantage for the male to prefer his right side as it would give a better chance of procreation.

At high body temperatures the male was also found to prefer using the right hemipenis when mating, which the researchers suggest may have something to do with the ability to make 'subtle postural adjustments'. They conclude, however, that their inferences are speculative:

> *We have no direct evidence to show that a larger hemipenis... is actually a more effective copulatory device than a smaller unit. The nonrandom patterns in hemipenis usage suggest that the asymmetry is not a trivial one, however, and further work to clarify these issues would be of great interest.*

See also BIRDS 64; PANGOLINS 356; PREHISTORY 382; PSYCHOLOGY 386; RELIGION 395; SEX 407; SNAILS 437

SOCRATES

440. Was Plato's account of Socrates' death honest?

When the Greek philosopher Socrates was found guilty both of corrupting the minds of the youth of Athens and of not believing in the gods of the state, he was condemned to death by drinking hemlock. His pupil Plato, in his dialogue *Phaedo*, gives a touching account of Socrates' willingness to take the poison and accept his death, but there has long been argument over whether this account was factual or a fictional romanticization of what happened.

After Socrates had taken the poison, Plato tells of a numbness slowly creeping over him from the feet upwards, with the philosopher remaining calm and lucid until it reached his heart and killed him. This has long been criticized, however, as it is not how hemlock works at all. Hemlock is a neurotoxin which attacks the central nervous system and leads to a very gruesome and nasty end. Defenders of Plato, on the other hand, argue that the effects of hemlock were well known in ancient Greece and it would have made no sense for Plato to tell anything other than the truth. Furthermore, the word 'hemlock' may then have been used for a wide variety of drugs.

Experts from the world of medicine have generally been critical of Plato's account, while experts on the Greek language have sprung to his defence. We shall probably never know the truth.

SOLAR SYSTEM

441. Why does the minor planet Chariklo have rings?

Until 2013 the only bodies in the Solar System known to have ring systems were the large planets Saturn, Jupiter, Uranus and Neptune. Then a fifth ring system was found around the minor planet Chariklo, which orbits the Sun between Saturn and Uranus. Chariklo has an estimated diameter of about 250 km, which had been thought far too small to support a ring system. The rings consist of two bright, narrow bands about 7 and 3 km wide, separated by a distance of about 9 km.

They orbit Chariklo at a distance of about 400 km, but what they are, how they got there and how long they are likely to stay there have all yet to be ascertained.

Since the gravitational pull of Chariklo is thought to be too weak to hold the rings in place for more than a few million years, either they are very young or they are held in place by so-called 'shepherd moons', which have not yet been discovered. The likeliest cause of such rings is that they are debris from a collision, but whether it was something colliding with Chariklo, or with an unknown moon of Chariklo which possibly no longer exists, is unknown.

In 2015 it was announced that Chiron, an even smaller minor planet, is also suspected of having a ring system.

442. Why is there a rapid fall-off in astronomical objects in the Kuiper Belt after a certain distance?

After Pluto was discovered in 1930, orbiting the Sun at a greater distance than any of the previously discovered planets, astronomers began to speculate about what else might be out there. In 1951 the Netherlands-born US astronomer Gerard Kuiper suggested the existence of a disc of objects in the outer regions of the Solar System. Many of his assumptions were later shown to be incorrect, but when such a region of small bodies was later confirmed, it was given the name Kuiper Belt. Consisting mainly of comets, it is thought to contain more than 100,000 objects greater than 100 km in diameter in a region between 30,000 and 50,000 astronomical units (AU) from the Sun. Since one AU is the distance from the Earth to the Sun, that is a very long way out.

Over 1,000 large Kuiper Belt objects have now been discovered, but once we get beyond 50 AU from the Sun, the number suddenly falls off. This distance is known as the Kuiper Cliff, and none of the theories of how the Kuiper Belt was formed accounts for it. The rapid decline is known not to be caused by observational bias. The most likely suggestions are that material at that distance was too scattered to form large objects, or that something happened to remove or destroy such objects as were formed. The only other suggestion is that the gravitational pull of an undiscovered massive object has rid the region of material.

443. Did the Earth collide with a planet known as Theia in the early Solar System?

The fact that the Moon's orbit around the Earth always keeps the same side facing us supports the view that the Earth and the Moon were once a single body. This theory goes on to suggest that the Earth collided with an astronomical body the size of Mars about 4.5 billion years ago, which was very early in the life of the Solar System. That hypothetical body has been given the name Theia, after the Greek Titan who gave birth to the Moon goddess Selene.

The impact, if it happened, is supposed to have destroyed Theia, one part of which merged with the Earth, another with part of the Earth which broke away to form the Moon, and another that spun off into space. While some comparisons between the composition of the Earth and the Moon support the suggestion that they were once together, other measurements are difficult to reconcile with the 'giant impact hypothesis', as it is known.

A major problem in assessing the truth of the hypothesis is that the same findings have often been interpreted either in support or in opposition to it. Differences in Moon rocks and Earth composition are cited by some as evidence that they were never the same body, while others see it as evidence that Theia contributed the un-Earthly parts of the Moon. Equally, similarities between the Earth and the Moon may be seen either as evidence that they were once together or as evidence of an absence of any contribution by Theia.

444. What is the probability that the Sun will rise tomorrow?

In the eighteenth century, the French mathematician Pierre-Simon Laplace raised this question as an early example of applied probability theory. His approach to the problem was to apply his 'rule of succession', which was a way of modifying one's initial expectations after subsequent observations. If we have seen one sunrise, we may be open-minded about whether the Sun will rise again tomorrow, but when it continues rising day after day, we become more certain that it will rise tomorrow. Taking a creationist reading of the Bible, which put the age of the Earth at 6,000 years, Laplace calculated that we had had about 6,000 x 365 = 2,190,000 sunrises, so he estimated the chance of the Sun rising tomorrow as 2,190,001/2,190,002 = 0.9999995.

With our modern scientific knowledge, however, we might insist on a different means of calculating. We could, for example, ask what would stop the Sun rising. Since what we see as sunrise is caused simply by the Earth's rotation on its axis, the only reasons the Sun wouldn't rise would be the Sun blowing up or the Earth ceasing to rotate. The latter could only happen if something very large collided with the Earth before morning, which we think is not going to happen. But we may have missed something. What are the chances that something very large slipped past the Hubble telescope without our noticing? What are the chances that our entire theory of astronomy since Newton is all hopelessly wrong and the Sun is going to explode before tomorrow? Is our faith in the development of scientific knowledge subject to the same rule of succession as Laplace's probability calculations?

Working out the probability of the Sun rising tomorrow is not as easy as it may seem.

See also COMETS 113; ENERGY 174; INTELLIGENCE 253; MARS 285; MILKY WAY 315–17; VENUS 479

SPIDERS

445. How do spiders find their way home at night?

The male Namib Desert spider goes for long walks at night searching for females and always finds its way home. How it navigates, however, is unclear. Research in 2003 showed that they can wander long distances in erratic paths over featureless dune surfaces, then walk back in a straight line to their burrows.

Further research in 2007 showed that they do not use their sense of smell to find their way home, but computer-tracking in 2012 reported that they make learning walks on exiting their burrows. By making stereotyped movements in an unfamiliar area, they seem to learn the appearance of their home. But we still don't know how they tell one patch of sand from another or how they unerringly navigate their way home from a distance.

See also CHIMPANZEES 98; MERCURY 303

SPORT

446. How do we decide how to catch a ball?

How does a fielder in cricket or baseball decide how to run in order to catch a ball? Several researchers have attempted to answer this question by tracking the movements of sportsmen trying to make a catch. Their experiments have reached a surprising conclusion: what sportsmen do is run at a speed and along a path that keeps the acceleration of the tangent of the angle of elevation of gaze to the ball equal to zero.

This strategy will not tell the fielder where or when the ball will land, or send him on an optimal trajectory to intercept it, but it will take him on a path that ensures that he runs through the place where the ball is at catching height at the moment when the ball arrives there. Specifically, what the fielder does is wait about half a second watching the ball, then start to run, accelerating until the acceleration of the tangent of the angle of elevation of gaze to the ball is equal to zero – in other words, until the rate of change of the tangent of the angle is constant. Only in the final moments will the fielder change strategy, but he will then be in the right position to catch the ball.

This is all very surprising, because most of the subjects in the experiment would probably not know their tangent from their cosine, let alone know how to measure its rate of change. Clearly, when we run to catch a ball, our brains are making complex calculations, but they are not telling us what they are.

See also DOGS 154; TENNIS 451

SQUID

447. How do squid get pregnant?

Well, a girl squid finds a boy squid whom she really likes, and then... it all gets a bit complicated, because squid sex is one of the most mysterious things in the animal world. One thing that makes it unusual is that the female does not have a vagina. Another is that the male's penis does not touch the female. Instead, the penis extrudes needle-like structures called spermatophores into its own body. It then reaches in with one of its arms, called a hectocotylus, to retrieve the spermatophores which it places on or inside the female's body. The spermatophores then ejaculate, leaving a sticky substance called spermatangium on the female skin. Sometimes, the spermatangium seems to burrow its way into the skin.

What happens next is up to the female squid, for she keeps the spermatangia in special receptacles until she is ready to fertilize an egg. She may even store the spermatangia of a number of different males, then select which she wants to use. However, the sperm in a spermatangium must first migrate to parts called spermathecae before it can be used to fertilize an egg.

Nobody knows how the female chooses which of her stored sperm to use for fertilization, or how she gets it to the egg, or whether she uses the spermatangia or the spermathecae. The fact is that no female squid has ever been observed at the task of sperm-picking or sperm-moving, so it is even possible that the sperm makes its own way to the egg.

See also WHALES 490

SQUIRRELS

448. Why do squirrels approach rattlesnakes?

In California the greatest threat to ground squirrels is posed by rattlesnakes. So why, when a squirrel sees a rattlesnake, does it walk straight towards it and hold its tail high?

Observations of squirrel–snake interactions show that rattlesnakes are often deterred from striking a squirrel when it performs its tail-flagging display. It is also liable to leave the area and try its luck elsewhere. It could be that the rattlesnake has learnt that its chances of catching a squirrel are far greater if the squirrel has not seen it, so the display may be taken as meaning 'I know you're there and I'm ready to run away if you come a step closer'. The tail-flagging may also serve as a warning signal to other squirrels, which may be what persuades the rattlesnake to try somewhere else. All the same, walking up to your greatest enemy and waving your tail still seems a rather dangerous policy.

SUICIDE

449. Did Jeremiah Clarke toss a coin before committing suicide?

Jeremiah Clarke (1674–1707) was organist at the Chapel Royal and one of England's leading composers. He is most famous for his 'Prince of Denmark's March', commonly known as the 'Trumpet Voluntary'. He is also well known for an often-repeated story about his suicide in 1707.

The tale, as recounted by the eighteenth-century musical historians Sir John Hawkins and Dr Richard Burney, tells of Clarke 'falling into a hopeless passion for a lady of high position' who was 'so far above his own social station as to remain forever unattainable'. As a result, he fell into a state of melancholy and resolved to kill himself. After riding to a field where he saw a pond, he is said to have been quite unable to decide whether to hang himself or drown himself, so he tossed a coin. The coin landed on its side in the mud, so he went home and shot himself.

Clarke definitely shot himself at his home, but the indecision and coin-tossing may be a romantic embellishment of the story. According to a contemporary account, he apparently spent the day very 'Chearful and Merry' at home, where he was visited by his father and friends and was 'Playing on his Musick for a considerable time'. After his father left, however, he went to his room and later the fatal shot was heard.

See also BIOLOGY 57; SHIPS 419; TERMITES 452

TECHNOLOGY

450. How did the ancient Egyptians put their obelisks up?

The Egyptian obelisks represent one of the major technological feats of the ancient world. From 2300 to 1300 BC they erected around a hundred of these massive monuments. From a square base, they were made with a single piece of stone, tapering upwards to the top which was usually surmounted with a small pyramid shape. Some were over 30 metres (100 ft) high and weighed almost 500 tons. Unfinished or fallen obelisks of over 1,000 tons have also been discovered. The standing obelisks were not embedded in the ground, but simply stood on their bases, and some are still standing after 4,000 years.

Various theories have been suggested concerning how these structures were erected. Some have suggested that elephants may have been used, which is very unlikely as elephants were not known in Egypt at the time, and cow-power has also been proposed, but it is generally thought that humans must have done most of the pulling.

In the 1990s attempts were made, for a US TV series, to emulate the ancient Egyptians by erecting a 25-ton obelisk using only technology available to the ancient world. The first two attempts, in 1994 and 1999, ended in failure. The third attempt involved dragging the obelisk up a gravel-and-stone ramp. In the middle of the ramp a pit was dug and filled with dry sand. By pulling on ropes tied to the obelisk, it was dragged into the pit and lifted, then the sand in the pit was slowly removed.

Modern technology was used for some of the process, but experiments convinced the late twentieth-century obelisk-erectors that it could have been done using manpower alone. That, however, was only a 25-ton obelisk. The Lateran Obelisk, now in Rome but originally erected at the Temple of Karnak, weighs 455 tons. Even with the almost unlimited manpower available to the Egyptian pharaohs, putting that up cannot have been easy.

See also COMPUTERS 116; HUMAN EVOLUTION 235; METEOROLOGY 308; SCIENCE 403; WINE 494

TENNIS

451. Are left-handers innately better than right-handers at tennis?

It has often been claimed that there are disproportionately many left-handers at the top of world tennis. One recent report even claimed that 40 per cent of top tennis players are left-handed, compared with only 12 per cent of the general population. If that is true (and some statistical surveys have challenged the finding), there are two plausible explanations: either lefties are at an advantage because righties are less used to playing against them, or being left-handed somehow conveys an innate advantage.

Rafael Nadal, a great left-handed champion, was quoted in 2012 as dismissing the innate advantage theory:

> The thing that everybody say, 'Well, you have your forehand against the backhand of the righty'... But the righty have the forehand against the backhand of the lefty. The outside slice, outside serve against the backhand, the righty have the same on the deuce. Seriously, the only thing is probably you play less times against lefties than righties. That's the only advantage.

In 2006, however, a study in Australia reported that left-handers are faster at conveying information between the two halves of the brain. On a task involving matching letters displayed to the left and right visual fields and thus involving both hemispheres in detecting a match, left-handers were on average 43 milliseconds faster than right-handers. That may not sound much, but a tennis ball served at 100 mph can travel six feet in forty-three milliseconds.

TERMITES

452. How do exploding suicide termites synthesize toxic crystals?

By far the best suicide bombers in the insect world are *Neocapritermes taracua* termites. Older members of this species have been found to carry a backpack of toxic chemical crystals of two types. These older termites are sent into battle, and when they are attacked by members of another species, their backpack explodes, the two types of stored crystals mix, the termite's body wall ruptures, and a chemical reaction is created that results in the enemy termites being sprayed with a toxic mess.

How the crystals are synthesized and how the two-component explosive defensive system evolved in this species are both unknown.

See also ANTS 21; BEES 47

THEATRE

453. Who was the first English professional actress?

Until 1660 the acting profession was considered unseemly for a woman to enter and it was illegal for women to appear on the stage. Who was the first to do so, however, is unclear and there are several claimants to the title.

The first recorded instance of women on stage in England was in 1629, when a troupe of French players, male and female, gave performances at Blackfriars. Their names are not known, but they were not well received. According to a letter written to the bishop of London, the French actresses were 'hissed, hooted, and pippin-pelted from the stage', and the writer said he 'did not think they would soon be ready to try the same again'.

In May 1656 a respectable married English woman referred to only as 'Mrs Coleman' appeared in the first performance of *The Siege of Rhodes* by Sir William Davenant in a private theatre at Sir William's home, Rutland House, in the City of London. Despite the fact that it was a private theatre, it was played to a paying audience, so Mrs Coleman has some claim to be considered England's first professional actress.

That title, however, is most commonly given to Margaret Hughes, who is thought to have appeared as Desdemona in a performance of *The Moor of Venice* (a reworking of Shakespeare's *Othello*), given by The King's Company on 8 December 1660. Margaret Hughes went on to great stage success as well as being famous as the mistress of the English Civil War general and later Restoration admiral, Prince Rupert of the Rhine.

It is not totally clear, though, that Margaret Hughes did indeed play the part of Desdemona on the first night of that play on 8 December, as The King's Company had two other actresses who also appeared in that role during the run. Anne Marshall certainly appeared as Desdemona in some of the performances, while Katherine Corey has also been suggested as a possible casting for the first-night Desdemona. Many commentators, however, have rather ungallantly suggested that Corey's lack of physical beauty would have made her unsuitable for the role.

See also CARROLL 89; SHAKESPEARE 415; USA 482

TIME

454. Does time slow down during a frightening event?

An experiment in 2007 attempted to investigate whether there is any scientific basis for the belief that time slows down when you are frightened. To create the frightening event, subjects were dropped from a Suspended Catch Air Device (SCAD) at an amusement park. After falling backwards 30 metres (100 ft), they landed safely in a net.

Two measurements were taken of possible time dilation. The simpler one was to ask them how long they thought the fall had taken and to compare their answers with their estimates of the time other subjects' falls had lasted when they saw them on video. The second measure involved a device strapped to their wrists while they fell. This displayed a dot-matrix image which alternated between showing the number 4 and its reverse image (with the dots forming the 4 now unlit and the others lit). The speed of alternation was gradually increased until the viewer could not distinguish between the two images, which now appeared as a continuously lit screen. The cut-off alternating speed at which that happened was compared with the cut-off previously found before the subject went on the SCAD.

The results were inconclusive. On the one hand, subjects judged their own falls as lasting on average 36 per cent longer than other people's, which would support the hypothesis of time slowing down. On the other hand, the alternating displays in the flashing screen merged together at exactly the same rate of alternation during the fall as earlier.

The researchers concluded that 'subjective time is not a single entity that speeds or slows, but instead is composed of separable subcomponents'. In other words, in some ways time seems to slow down, but in other ways it doesn't.

See also BIG BANG 55; BIOLOGY 59; COSMOLOGY 123, 126

TREASURE

455. Is there a Money Pit on Oak Island?

Just a couple of hundred metres from the shore of Nova Scotia in Canada lies Oak Island, the site of a mystery dating back more than 200 years. The story began in 1795, when eighteen-year-old Daniel McGinnis saw lights coming from the island and, when he went to investigate, found a circular depression in an area cleared of trees. There was also a block and tackle attached to a tree branch that overhung the depression. With the help of friends, he excavated the area to a depth of nine metres and reported finding a wooden platform every three metres. There was also talk of them finding a large flat stone covered with inscriptions, which some say mentioned a £2 million treasure buried below.

The pit subsequently flooded. Later attempts at excavation over the next 150 years reached depths of over fifty metres but revealed only enough evidence to fuel all sorts of rumours. Among these are suggestions that the pit may have been used by the pirates Captain Kidd or Blackbeard to bury their plundered treasure, or French gold, or Marie Antoinette's jewels, or even the Holy Grail. There are even tales of evidence of chests at a great depth along with human remains, but what the pit was originally used for, and whether any of it is still there, remain an enigma.

See also CODES 107, 109; GOLD 218–19

TROY

456. Was the myth of the Trojan War based on fact?

Homer's *Iliad* is perhaps the greatest of all early works of literature. It is thought to be the culmination of a long period of story-telling transmitted orally. Its theme of a struggle between men and gods is the stuff of myth, but was the story based on real events?

Until the 1870s Homer's tale was generally seen as pure fiction, but Heinrich Schliemann's archaeological excavations at Hisarlik in Turkey were then seen as evidence that the city of Troy might actually have existed. We now know that there were at least three Trojan wars and that Troy was destroyed at least twice between 1300 and 1000 BC. We know that the kingdoms of the Mycenaeans and the Hittites were expanding during that period, and Troy may have been caught between them. We know there was a great palace at Mycenae, which could have been the model for Agamemnon's kingdom.

From having no evidence at all to support the claim that the *Iliad* was based on a real war, we now have almost too many possible scenarios to choose from. While many of the archaeological remains support the view that the stories may have been based on historical events, however, nothing has ever been found that can clearly be identified as identical with Homer's account.

TURKEY

457. Why and by whom were the stone circles at Göbekli Tepe built?

Six thousand years before Stonehenge was built, long before the Egyptian pyramids or any signs of approaching civilization, thousands of years before the wheel was even invented, stone age man constructed the amazing stone circles at Göbekli Tepe in Turkey. These consist of dozens of massive limestone pillars, cleanly carved and decorated with sculptures of gazelles, snakes, scorpions, foxes and other animals. The pillars are arranged in circles, each pillar fitting neatly into a slot carved into the rock beneath it.

The stone circles were discovered in 1994, since when excavations have revealed more and more pillars, with geological surveys indicating that hundreds more remain underground. When they were made, people are thought to have lived in small communities living in huts, yet the scale of Göbekli Tepe is massive and must have required large numbers of people for its construction.

No signs of living accommodation have been found nearby, however, and there is no evidence of any source of drinking water closer than three miles away. How they dragged the stones there, without domesticated beasts of burden or even the wheel, is a mystery. The entire site is massively bigger than any other man-made construction known on Earth at the time, and the level of co-operation required to build it is far beyond anything known to exist in human groups so long ago.

The meticulousness and sheer size of the stone circles at Göbekli Tepe suggest that it was some sort of temple, perhaps the world's first, which in turn suggests that religion may have been the driving force behind the development of civilization. But how small nomadic groups came together to share the common vision behind the construction remains unexplained.

See also TROY 456

TURTLES

458. Are roads bad for turtles?

Campaigns have been run at various places in North America to help turtles cross roads. One study even reported that some drivers swerve their vehicles in order to run over a turtle. Yet in 2014 a survey in Canada came to the paradoxical conclusion that, despite all the figures for turtle road-kill, roads may not be bad for turtles after all.

The study was based on analysis of the figures for the sizes of painted turtle populations at twenty ponds in eastern Ontario. Ten of the sites were selected as close as possible to high-traffic roads while the other ten were as far away as possible from such roads. The researchers reported:

There was no significant effect of roads on painted turtle relative abundance. Furthermore, our data do not support other predictions of the road mortality hypothesis; we observed neither a higher relative frequency of males to females at Road sites than at No Road sites, nor a lower average body size of turtles at Road than at No Road sites.

They suggest that although roads can cause substantial turtle mortality, other factors may act in the opposite direction. Many types of turtle predator, for example, may tend to avoid roads, thus making the near-road locations safer. They stress, however, that the findings should not be extrapolated to other species of turtle.

See also BIRDS 64

TYRANNOSAURUSES

459. How big was a newborn tyrannosaurus?

Our knowledge of tyrannosauruses is greatly hampered by the extreme rarity of their young in the fossil record. Furthermore, no tyrannosaurus eggs have ever been discovered. As if that weren't bad enough, there is the confusion caused by *Nanotyrannus lancensis*. For a long time fossils of *Nanotyrannus* were thought to be examples of young tyrannosauruses, but in 2010 close examination of the skull of a *Nanotyrannus* identified clear differences, suggesting that it was a different species.

So now, quite apart from the problems of assessing the ages at which tyrannosaurus fossils died, in many cases we cannot even be sure that the fossils previously classified as young tyrannosauruses were members of the species at all.

460. What did tyrannosauruses do with their arms?

Even a tyrannosaurus would probably admit that for the huge size of the creature, its arms were ridiculously short. What it used those arms for continues to be a matter of debate. One suggestion is that it used its arms to hold its mate during love-making. Another idea is that the arms were used to hold prey. A third suggestion is that their main function was to provide lift to help the tyrannosaurus stand from a seated position – though we have no evidence that tyrannosauruses made a habit of sitting down.

Studies on the shape of the bones and possible muscle layout may help with this question, but perhaps the most likely answer is that the forelimbs were as near useless as made no difference.

461. How long did tyrannosauruses live?

In the early years of dinosaur study, it was thought that dinosaurs must have been long-lived creatures, some estimates of their lifespan even suggesting 100 to 200 years. Such guesses were based on the general rule that large reptiles live longer than small ones and on a comparison between tyrannosauruses and modern crocodiles.

In the 1980s, however, growth lines were found in some dinosaur bones which allowed far more precise estimates to be made from their skeletons of the number of years these creatures had lived. Conclusions were also drawn about the growth rates of tyrannosauruses by comparing the sizes of animals that had died at different ages. One result of all this was a drastic reassessment of a tyrannosaurus's lifespan down from about 100 years to something closer to thirty.

The trouble is that we have no way of comparing the size of a tyrannosaurus at one age with the size of the same animal some years later. The conclusions about growth rates have been reached by comparing one animal with another and assuming they would have been about the same size at the same age. We simply do not have enough specimens of tyrannosauruses to know how valid that assumption is.

See also DINOSAURS 137

UNITED KINGDOM

462. Who wore the Allerton Cope?

In 1858, at the bottom of a chest in Chapel Allerton Church in Somerset, was found an exquisite piece of medieval embroidery now known as the Allerton Cope. The embroidery portrays the Assumption of the Virgin Mary, with the details of cherubs' tiny faces beautifully worked around it. The fabric of the cope and the silver threads of the embroidery mark it as an object that must have been highly valued, but its history is completely obscure.

The cope (which is a word for a mantle worn by a priest or other churchman) has been dated to around the end of the fifteenth century, and one suggestion is that it was given to Chapel Allerton Church by John Gunthorpe, dean of Wells Cathedral from 1472 to 1498. Why it should have been given to such a relatively insignificant church, however, is a mystery. Chapel Allerton was not even important enough to be dignified with the name of a saint. However, Gunthorpe had purchased the parish of Chapel Allerton shortly before his death. It is possible that his cope found its way there and was later hidden in the chest at the time of the Dissolution of the Monasteries.

Yet that did not happen until some forty years after Gunthorpe died, and there is no known mention of the cope at Allerton during that period.

See also ANIMALS 18; AUTISM 36; CANCER 86; CHAPLIN 93; DEATH 131; DISEASE 145; FASHION 188; PSYCHOLOGY 384; RELIGION 394; SLEEP 427

UNIVERSE

463. Is the universe unstable?

One of the things that the discovery of the Higgs boson has done is to increase our belief that the universe may be unstable. According to the Standard Model of particle physics which led to the prediction of the existence of the Higgs boson, the vacuum occupied by the universe is not empty but full of particles and antiparticles that pop into existence and annihilate each other in tiny moments of time. As long as they do it quickly enough, this constant creation and annihilation does not contradict any laws of physics. The question is whether this mayhem-rich vacuum is stable.

According to our understanding of the Standard Model, the necessary condition for vacuum stability is that our universe exists at a minimum of potential energy. A good guide to whether that is the case is given by the masses of two fundamental particles, the Higgs boson and the top quark. Current estimates of those masses suggest that it is too close to call. Both appear to be very close to the limit required for the universe to be stable. So it could be that a random quantum fluctuation might lead to a vacuum bubble sweeping through space and destroying the universe – in which case the Sun will not rise tomorrow (→ 444). But even if that is the case, it will probably not happen for several billion years.

464. Did the universe have a beginning?

Our current view of the beginning of the universe dates it back to about 13.8 billion years ago when it all started with a Big Bang. Specifically, it was a massive explosion of energy from a single point which has fuelled the expansion of the universe ever since. The figure of 13.8 billion years comes from calculations of the separation of galaxies. Tracing their movements, we can not only predict where they will go in the future but we can work out where they have come from, and the figures seem to show that they were all in the same place 13.8 billion years ago.

And this is where the mathematics breaks down. Going back to the moment of the Big Bang, we reach a singularity: all the energy in the universe is in the same place, time itself stops, and all the laws of physics stop working. There are several ways round this problem:

(i) Religion: in the beginning God created... That's what we've always said. We're glad you scientists at last agree with us. And His 'Let there be light' is just your Big Bang.

(ii) Multiversal: that Big Bang stuff only applies to our three-dimensional universe. There were probably plenty of other universes before ours came along. String theory says we're probably just a slice of a ten- or eleven-dimensional universe anyway, so what's the problem?

(iii) No boundary: just like the surface of the Earth, space–time itself is finite in extent but has no boundary. The universe had a beginning, but its beginning was determined by the laws of physics. The singularity is not a problem.

(iv) Actually, we've got it slightly wrong and everything wasn't quite at the same place at the same time. If we trace the galaxies back properly, they just miss each other. There never was a singularity.

465. Can we experimentally obtain evidence of higher spacial dimensions?

Superstring theory says there are ten space–time dimensions. It originated from the more fundamental M-theory, which was based on eleven dimensions. If the extra dimensions that these theories require exist, they must be hidden from us by some physical mechanism. One suggestion is that the extra dimensions may be 'curled up' at such tiny scales that they are effectively invisible. If there is no measurable effect of these extra dimensions, how can we ever test whether they exist?

In the early years of string theory, this posed a philosophical problem. If it made no testable predictions, the theory failed Karl Popper's condition of falsifiability ($\rightarrow$ 404), which it had to satisfy in order to qualify as worthy of consideration as a scientific hypothesis. More recently, however, superstring theory has appeared to be the most likely candidate to produce a Grand Unified Theory to explain all the fundamental forces of physics. The problem with this has always been the weakness of gravity compared with the other forces, but if our gravity is viewed as a pale, three-dimensional component of a ten- or eleven-dimensional force, it could explain why it is so weak in our slice of the universe. The extra dimensions could then be revealed by variations in gravity within the part of the universe we can test.

This idea has been around for more than a decade now, but we still have not found any real evidence for further dimensions. But it may not be out of the question.

466. Do we live in a cyclic universe?

The universe is not only expanding, but that expansion is accelerating. We do not know what causes that acceleration, so we do not know how long it will continue, but it has made the old picture of a cyclic universe less likely. In that scenario, the expansion continued until it ran out of energy, after which it would start shrinking as gravity drew all the matter closer together. In the end, just as at the Big Bang, it would finish in a Big Scrunch. This gave rise to a cyclic universe theory, with all the matter, now sucked up into one massive black hole, exploding outwards again in another Big Bang, with the cycle of Bangs and Scrunches endlessly repeating.

One problem with this idea was that it seemed to contradict the second law of thermodynamics, which demands a continuous increase in entropy or disorder. As the universe gets more and more disordered, it cannot get back to the state of perfect order that existed at the Big Bang.

More recently, amended theories of a cyclic universe have appeared with all the matter in the universe spreading ever more thinly and decaying until everything is energy. When that happens – according to whose theory you read – there will be either another Big Bang, or a huge series of Big Bangs, each creating its own universe. In either case, the time taken for each cycle will be in the region of a trillion years.

467. Is the rapid expansion in the early universe related to its current expansion?

In the tiniest fraction of a second after the Big Bang, the universe is thought to have expanded at an unbelievably fast rate, probably faster than the speed of light. One proposal for the mechanism fuelling this is a hypothetical field called the 'inflaton field', caused by as yet undiscovered particles called 'inflatons'. The inflaton field created a form of dark energy which was the driving force behind the early expansion. Subsequent changes in the inflation rate may have been caused by the interaction of this inflaton field with gravity and the residual momentum from the Big Bang.

The dark energy which has been credited with the current acceleration in expansion could be the same energy field that fuelled the original expansion.

See also ASTRONOMY 27; BIG BANG 54–6; BLACK HOLES 71; COSMOLOGY 118–19, 121, 123–4, 126; ENERGY 173–4; EVOLUTION 181; FUNDAMENTAL PARTICLES 205; GRAVITY 222; INTELLIGENCE 253; MILKY WAY 315; OUTER SPACE 350; PHILOSOPHY 365; PHYSICS 370; QUASARS 390–1

USA

468. What caused the Great Chicago Fire of 1871?

On Sunday 8 October 1871 a fire started in the barn of Patrick and Catherine O'Leary in Chicago. By the time the fire was put out a day and a half later, it had destroyed property valued at $192 million, left 100,000 people homeless, and 300 others had lost their lives. A long inquiry was held into the cause of the fire, but it eventually reported that 'whether it originated from a spark blown from a chimney on that windy night, or was set on fire by human agency, we are unable to determine'.

According to a popular nineteenth-century belief, the fire was caused by Mrs O'Leary's cow knocking over a lantern, but there is no more evidence for this than countless other suggestions explored at the Inquest. Might the fire have been caused by a man named Regan, who had been visiting the O'Learys that evening, whose peg leg could have slipped on the floor of the barn and caused him to drop his pipe? Might he have tripped over the feet of his companion Daniel Sullivan? We shall probably never know, but the cow story is as good as any other.

469. How big is the Lost Sea in Tennessee?

In 1905 a thirteen-year-old boy named Ben Sands discovered an underground lake in Sweetwater, Tennessee, after crawling through a muddy opening 90 metres (300 ft) underground. He was amazed to find himself in a huge cave half-filled with water. When he went back with his father some time later, the entrance to the lake had become hidden and it was some years before it was rediscovered and proper explorations of the lake began.

In 1974–5 a survey reported depths of over 30 metres in the lake, which in one cavern occupied an area 240 metres long and 67 metres across. A later exploration added another 460 metres to the length of various passages from the lake. Its full extent is still unknown, though it is already classed as the world's second-biggest non-glacial underground lake, after Dragon's Breath Cave in Namibia.

470. Where did all the Confederate gold go?

As the American Civil War was nearing its end in 1865, a large amount of gold held by the Confederates went missing. Originally it was probably taken away by train from New Orleans. Some say the train was robbed and the gold hidden by a variety of plantation owners; others say it was taken by a group of deserters from both sides who divided it up.

There is hardly an area of the USA where some legend or other does not say the gold is buried. Its value is also unknown, with estimates varying between about $500,000 and $2 million at today's prices.

471. Why does the city of Taos in New Mexico hum?

The town of Taos in New Mexico has, since the 1990s, been famed for its hum. When this hum of unknown origin was first researched, around 2 per cent of the town's inhabitants claimed to have heard it. Sensitive devices were set up in the homes of several hearers but nothing unusual was detected. Secret government mind-control experiments, underground UFO bases, hippies and an assortment of paranormal phenomena were suspected of causing the hum, but further investigations suggested that there might be more than one sort of hum, as some called it a 'whir' and others a 'buzz', as well as the usual 'hum' description.

Whether there really is a hum at all must be open to doubt, in which case the question is how the rumour started in the first place.

472. Is the stovepipe hat in the Abraham Lincoln Presidential Library and Museum authentic?

Two American institutions possess items that claim to be stovepipe hats worn by Abraham Lincoln. There is no doubt about the hat at the Smithsonian: it is the size 7⅛ hat Lincoln put on to go to Ford's Theatre on the night he was assassinated. After he was shot, the hat was found on the floor beside his chair and was taken to the War Department. With permission from Lincoln's widow Mary, the department gave the hat to the Patent Office, which in 1867 transferred it to the Smithsonian Institution.

There is some dispute about the other hat, however, which may be seen at the Abraham Lincoln Presidential Library and Museum in Springfield, Illinois. Lincoln is said to have given it to William Waller, a farmer and political supporter in Jackson County, Illinois, whose family kept it for decades. It was later sold to a collector and donated to the library.

In 2013, however, a member of the board that oversees the library was quoted as saying, 'I think we have a credibility gap with this hat', and the Illinois State Police were asked to conduct DNA testing of the hat to see if Abraham Lincoln ever really wore it. The hat size is also 7⅛, and like the Smithsonian hat, it also carries the mark of Lincoln's usual hat-maker. The trouble is that there is no clear evidence, other than the Waller family's assertions, that the hat really was Lincoln's.

The Lincoln Library curator has described the proposal to DNA-test the hat as 'even worse than a bad idea' and ridiculed the suggestion that it be vacuumed for traces of Lincoln's dandruff.

473. Did Benjamin Franklin ever make tofu?

The United States owed a great deal to Benjamin Franklin in its early years. Lightning rods, rocking chairs and bifocal spectacles were all his idea, and he is also credited with the introduction of tofu. The earliest-known mention of tofu by an American is in a letter written by Benjamin Franklin, who was in London, to John Bartram in Philadelphia dated 11 January 1770. The letter included a sample of soya beans, and with them what he called 'Father Navarrete's account of the universal use of a cheese made of them in China'.

This 'cheese', he said, so much aroused his curiosity that he took steps to find out how it was made, and he went on to describe the procedure to Bartram. The method involved adding 'some runnings of salt' to water, then adding the soya beans 'to turn it to curds'. And the curds, Franklin said, 'are what the Tau-fu is made of'.

Whether Franklin took the recipe on trust, however, or made his own tofu with it before passing it on to Bartram, is not known.

474. Which speech did Lincoln deliver at Gettysburg?

Seven score and twelve years before this book was written, Abraham Lincoln brought forth, in Gettysburg, Pennsylvania, one of the greatest speeches ever uttered. There are, however, five known copies of the speech in Lincoln's handwriting, each with a slightly different text, and nobody knows which was the one delivered by Lincoln.

Two of the copies are thought to have been written before the speech was made and three were written as responses to people who asked him for copies later. The text of the speech on the walls of the Lincoln Memorial in Washington is taken from the copy Lincoln gave to Colonel Alexander Bliss for use as a fundraiser for soldiers. It is the only copy signed and dated by Lincoln. This is, however, the last copy Lincoln is known to have made, so it cannot be the one he read from at the time. Perhaps the best candidate for that description is the copy he gave to White House assistant John Hay, which is thought to be the second draft of the speech as it includes some handwritten changes by Lincoln.

He could, however, have made some spontaneous changes while delivering the speech, so the versions written afterwards may be more accurate accounts of what he actually said. They all differ only by a few unimportant words, but it is sad there is no definitive version of such a momentous speech.

475. Did Pocahontas save John Smith?

The story of the young Native American girl Pocahontas intervening to save the life of the pioneer settler John Smith has become one of the great American legends, but what really happened?

The essence of the story is that John Smith, a leader of the settlement in Jamestown, Virginia, was captured with two others by a group of Native Americans led by a chief called Powhatan. Two of them were later killed, but Smith was allowed to live until Powhatan decided that the moment for his execution had arrived. When Powhatan was about to cudgel him to death, however, the chief's daughter Pocahontas came between them and put her head on Smith's. This brave act of humanity and benevolence led to peace breaking out between the settlers and the natives.

That's the story, but the only corroboration for it comes in Smith's own account written some seventeen years after the event. He had already given two other accounts without mentioning it at all. There are three theories:

(i)   It happened exactly as Smith said.
(ii) It was actually an elaborate ritual for pardoning Smith and letting him live with the tribe, but Smith totally misunderstood what was going on.
(iii) It was a self-serving invention by Smith to enhance his reputation and identify himself with a girl who had now become a prominent woman.

The first version is the one the Disney organization chose to believe, and even then they turned Pocahontas from a ten-year-old into a young lady to make a better romance of it all.

476. Did Betsy Ross sew the first American flag?

The story goes that, one day in 1776, George Washington and two others from a congressional committee called on Mrs Betsy Ross, an upholsterer and seamstress, to ask for her help sewing a flag. Washington took a sketch from his pocket showing thirteen red and white stripes and thirteen stars representing the thirteen colonies and soon-to-be states. When asked if she could do it, Ross replied, 'I do not know, but I will try.' Her only immediate suggestion, which the men agreed to, was to change the stars from six-pointed to five-pointed.

But did any of this really happen? The evidence for it is so scanty as to be almost non-existent. The earliest-known account of the story dates from more than 100 years later when Betsy Ross's grandson William Canby said he'd heard it from Betsy herself. Canby said that Washington was a family friend who had often visited Betsy's shop.

There is, however, no written evidence of any business between Washington and Ross, nor do congressional records contain any reference to a committee in 1776 going out to make a flag. Congress passed a law about the flag on 14 June 1777, which mentioned thirteen red and white stripes and thirteen white stars on a blue field, but there is no evidence of a flag committee a year earlier.

On the other hand, one of the men accompanying Washington in the story is named as George Ross, who was the uncle of Betsy's husband. Also, in May 1777, records suggest that Betsy was paid for making flags for the Pennsylvania State Navy. Still, that is a long way from making the first one for George Washington a year earlier, especially as Washington was not a member of Congress at the time but commander-in-chief of the Continental Army.

477. Did George Washington cut down his father's cherry tree?

The uplifting tale of the young George Washington admitting to cutting down his father's cherry tree was something all Americans were brought up on in the nineteenth century at least. The story was first related in print by Mason Locke Weems (1759–1825), an itinerant preacher known as 'Parson Weems', in his bestseller *The Life of Washington*, which went through dozens of editions after its first publication in 1800.

The tale, as he wrote it, was that the six-year-old George Washington had received a present of a hatchet which he gleefully tested in his garden. When his father returned, he found the bark of his favourite cherry tree had been hacked away and asked who had 'barked' (not cut down) the tree. The young George then replied, 'I can't tell a lie, Pa; you know I can't tell a lie. I did cut it with my hatchet.' 'Run to my arms, you dearest boy,' cried his father in transports, 'run to my arms; glad am I,

George, that you killed my tree; for you have paid me for it a thousand fold. Such an act of heroism in my son is more worth than a thousand trees, though blossomed with silver, and their fruits of purest gold.'

Weems said that he had been told the story by 'an aged lady who was a distant relative [of Washington]', but much suspicion later grew that he had made it all up. In 1896 future president Woodrow Wilson, in his own biography of Washington, described it as a fabrication, saying, 'Of its factual truth there is no evidence whatsoever.' Other writers called it 'idle quip and irreverent jest', 'pernicious drivel' or a 'slush of plagiarism and piety'.

In 1912, however, US historian Carl Anthony came across a long-forgotten earthenware mug, made in Germany no later than 1790, which shows a young man standing beside a fallen tree along with a large hatchet; it is marked by the date 1776 and the initials 'G.W.'. It seems that the story was around at least a decade before Weems used it, so perhaps he did not make it up after all.

See also FASHION 188; FRANCE 202; IOWA 257; MURDER 325; NORTH DAKOTA 341

VANUATU

478. What is the explanation of the headless bodies buried in Vanuatu?

Between 2003 and 2009 archaeologists on the Pacific islands of Vanuatu, about 1,750 kilometres east of Australia, excavated an extraordinary ancient cemetery. In all, they dug up seventy or seventy-one skeletons, all of which had their skulls missing. Two of the bodies were buried with three skulls each, though none of the heads belonged to the body.

724

The bodies are thought to have been placed in their graves about 3,000 years ago and are believed to have been buried with their heads. Only after the flesh rotted away were the heads removed. A number of ritualistic procedures seem to have been enacted during the burials, but the rituals appear to have differed at different levels of the burial site. The only common feature was that all the heads were removed.

Nothing seems to be known about what all this signified, where the people came from or anything else about their culture.

VENUS

479. Are there any live volcanoes on Venus?

Of all the planets in the Solar System, Venus has by far the most volcanoes. Over 1,600 major volcanoes or volcanic features have been identified, and estimates of the number of smaller volcanoes vary between around 100,000 and 1 million. While Venus is much the same size as Earth, its surface temperature is much higher, its atmosphere is very different, and its air pressure is much higher. It also seems to have no plate tectonics, which is what causes most earthquakes and volcanic eruptions on Earth. All of these features could greatly influence the frequency and types of volcanic activity.

One big question, however, is whether any of the Venusian volcanoes are still active. No volcanic activity has ever been recorded, but we have so little data about what is going on there that it is impossible to rule it out.

480. Why are the winds on Venus getting stronger?

The atmosphere on Venus is very dense and rich in carbon dioxide, which leads to the planet being covered by a blanket of yellowish cloud. Tracking the movement of this cloud has revealed extremely powerful high-altitude winds around 70 kilometres above the planet's surface.

These winds have been observed and measured both by spacecraft and directly from Earth, but the latest observations from the Venus Express have revealed some surprising features. After cloud movements had been monitored for ten Venusian years, wind speeds were found to change according to the time of day and latitude, but the most remarkable finding was that overall these super-hurricane-force winds have been speeding up.

What is driving these strange atmospheric patterns is completely unknown.

See also MERCURY 304

VIKINGS

481. Where exactly was Erik the Red's Vinland?

The discovery and exploration of North America by the Vikings Leif Eriksson and Erik the Red were written about in two Icelandic sagas, the *Greenlanders' Saga*, written around 1200, and *Erik the Red's Saga*, which appeared about fifty years later. Both sagas are thought to form part of the oral history of the Icelanders dating back some 200 years before the sagas were written down.

According to the *Greenlanders' Saga*, North America was first sighted by Bjarni Herjolfsson, who was blown off course on his way from

Iceland to Greenland in 985 or 986. He did not go ashore, but Leif Eriksson decided to follow up on his sightings. With a crew of thirty-five, Eriksson landed first at a place that he called Helluland, the 'Land of Flat Stone'; then went to 'Markland' ('Forest Land'); then landed on an unnamed island; and finally, in autumn 1001, reached Vinland, which means either the 'land of the vine' or the 'land of the pastures'.

All the sagas tell us about the location of Vinland is that Eriksson reached it by following a river that led to a lake and that the mouth of the river was on the west of a large peninsula pointing north. A number of places in North America have staked their claims to have been part of Eriksson's Vinland. There are mysterious symbols on a rock at Dighton, Massachusetts, that may be Norse carvings; there is a tower in Rhode Island that may be the remains of a Norse church; there are depressions at Cape Cod which could mark where Eriksson left his ship. Or was it at L'Anse aux Meadows on the north-eastern tip of Newfoundland, where remains of a Norse settlement were found in the 1960s? None of these places offer more than a tantalizing glimpse of where the true discoverers of America may have been.

See also DEATH 132

VOLCANOES

482. Where was the volcano whose eruption killed thousands in London around 1258?

In 1258 a volcanic eruption wiped out a third of the population of London and we have no idea where the volcano was. That was the conclusion reached from what began as an ordinary archaeological investigation in 2012 on the site of the ancient St Mary Spital church in

East London. The archaeologists knew that the church had a cemetery, so they were not surprised to unearth a number of skeletons, but the more they dug, the more skeletons appeared, until they numbered over 10,000. With more of the cemetery inaccessible under the nearby market, the total number of bodies was estimated at 18,500, which was more than a third of the total population of medieval London.

Carbon dating indicated that the skeletons dated from around 1250, which was too early for them to have been victims of the Black Death or the Plague, but investigations of chronicles of the period gave strong clues to what had happened. They spoke of a failure of crops, 'unendurable cold' and a winter that never abated. It was the sort of cataclysm that can only be caused by a massive volcanic eruption, spewing out sulphurous clouds that block out the Sun. Other references do indeed mention a massive volcanic eruption, but where it happened is unknown. The most likely culprits are thought to have been El Chichón in Mexico, Quilotoa in Ecuador or the Samalas volcano in Indonesia, but really it could have been anywhere on Earth.

483. Did the same volcano trigger the onset of the Little Ice Age?

Throughout the Middle Ages, the world climate went through a period known as the Little Ice Age. Some put its start at around 1650, others say 1350, but the most recent evidence suggests that what triggered it was a series of major volcanic eruptions between 1250 and 1300. Radiocarbon dating of dead plant matter in the Arctic indicates that something happened in this period that killed off vast numbers of plants, probably by freezing. Measurements of Icelandic glaciers also indicate that the ice grew quickly in thickness by a large amount at the same time.

The massive eruptions of the volcanoes in Ecuador, Mexico and Indonesia mentioned above (→ 482) all occurred in the late 1250s, as did the disastrous deaths in London in 1258. All these things could be linked.

See also EARTH 164; GEOLOGY 212; MAYANS 293; VENUS 479

WAITRESSES

484. Why do blonde waitresses get bigger tips?

There seems to be no doubt about it: a number of studies have reported that blonde waitresses get bigger tips than brunettes. Whether a change in hair colour is effected by dyeing the hair or by wearing a wig, blondes' tips are on average about 8 per cent higher. One study reported that blondes get higher tips even if their dark roots are showing.

While they all agree on the results, however, a number of different explanations have been offered. The obvious suggestion is that it ties in with other research showing that men give higher attractiveness ratings to women if their hair is blonde. Some of the tipping research also suggests that the higher tips received by blondes are mostly due to the behaviour of male customers.

Another possibility, however, is linked to a finding that blonde women are perceived as less intelligent than brunettes. This perceived stupidity may lead to a lower expectation of good service, so the blonde waitress has only to perform at an average level to exceed expectations and earn a larger tip.

Finally, it could be that having blonde hair changes the behaviour of the waitress, perhaps by increasing her confidence, or perhaps by increasing her flirtatiousness with customers.

See also FOOD 194

WALES

485. What happened to Owain Glyndŵr after 1412?

Owain Glyndŵr was the last native Welshman to hold the title Prince of Wales. In 1400 he instigated the Welsh Revolt against the rule of Henry IV of England. Initially very successful, the uprising gained control of large areas of Wales, but the superior resources of the English eventually drove Glyndŵr out of his strongholds. In 1409 he fled and avoided capture. The last documented sighting of him was in 1412.

Glyndŵr was twice offered a pardon from the new king Henry V of England, but ignored them. Despite large rewards offered for his capture, he was never betrayed to the English. Various theories have emerged concerning where he may have hidden after 1412, but no convincing evidence has ever been found to support them. His death was reported by a former follower to have occurred in 1415, but there is no corroboration of that either.

WALRUSES

486. Why do walruses have such large penis bones?

Humans and hyenas are in a very small minority of mammals that do not have a penis bone. This bone, also known as a baculum, is present in dogs, cats, bats, rats, mice, bears, weasels, lions, sea lions, chimpanzees and gorillas, among others. It is located in the tip of the penis and ranges in size from only a few millimetres in gorillas and mice to around eight centimetres in large dogs. And the largest of all is the sixty-centimetre-long baculum of the walrus.

Why does the walrus have such a long one? The function of the bone is unclear. Presumably it helps the male maintain an erection and it may help move the penis inside the female. It may also have a role to play in directing the male's ejaculate, but humans seem to have survived perfectly well without bacula, so why the walrus has evolved such a long one is a puzzle.

See also BONES 72

WATER

487. Why does warm water freeze more quickly than cold water?

In the fourth century BC, Aristotle noticed that hot water may freeze more quickly than cold water. In the seventeenth century, Francis Bacon and René Descartes also noticed it. The first scientific investigation of the phenomenon, however, did not happen until the 1960s, when a Tanzanian student named Erasto Mpemba was making ice-cream in a cookery class and noticed that a warm mix of ingredients froze faster than a cold one.

This 'Mpemba effect' was then confirmed in some properly conducted scientific experiments. In fact not all the experiments confirmed it, but nobody could explain what the difference was between the successful and unsuccessful versions. Suggestions have included:

- evaporation, which is an endothermic reaction, taking heat away from water;
- insulation, caused by the formation of frost on the top of the lower-temperature water;
- convection currents in the warmer water causing more rapid cooling;
- dissolved solids and gases in the water having different effects on freezing at different temperatures.

The latest idea is based on the possible energy released by a loosening of the hydrogen bonds in the water molecules, but there is still no general agreement on which explanation is correct.

488. How much water is in the Earth's interior?

Most of what we know about the interior of the Earth comes from the investigation of seismic waves caused by earthquakes. By monitoring the waves at the surface and detecting their speed at various depths, conclusions may be drawn about the nature of the material they pass through. In 2014 a study of over 500 earthquakes by 2,000 seismometers revealed a massive ocean about 700 kilometres below the Earth's surface containing around three times as much water as all the seas and oceans we can see.

This finding throws new light on the question of where the Earth's oceans came from and how they have stayed the same size for millions of years. The investigation, however, only relates to water beneath the United States. It could extend all the way round the planet occupying a region between the upper and lower parts of the Earth's mantle. The total amount of water down there could easily be enough to submerge the planet if it were on the surface.

489. Can water remember?

In 1988 the French immunologist Jacques Benveniste published a paper that was immediately seized on by homeopaths as complete justification of their views. The core of Benveniste's claims was that when something is dissolved in water, then diluted so many times that not even a single molecule of the original substance is present, the water still retains a 'memory' of its having been there. Specifically, his claim was that the configuration of the molecules of water is 'biologically active' in a way that makes it change when something is dissolved in it and retain that change after dilution.

Benveniste's paper aroused intense debate, ranging from huge support from believers in homeopathy to utter condemnation by those who criticized it as pseudo-science at its worst. Attempts to repeat Benveniste's experiments, however, were generally unsuccessful and the topic of 'water memory' fell under a cloud until the debate was reignited by research conducted by the Nobel Prize-winning virologist Luc Montagnier in 2010.

Montagnier's claim was that bacterial DNA dissolved in water created electromagnetic signals from which the entire DNA sequence could be obtained. Again the results were viewed with exultation by homeopaths and incredulity by most of the scientific community. Montagnier himself, however, went no further than suggesting that his result indicated that water may contain an information storage-and-retrieval property and that one 'cannot extrapolate it to the products used in homeopathy'. Attempts to replicate Montagnier's experiments, however, have not been successful.

See also ANIMALS 16; BIRDS 64; DINOSAURS 137; FROGS 203; GLOBAL WARMING 216; INVENTIONS 255; LEMURS 272; MARS 285; METEOROLOGY 309–10; PHYSICS 369; RIDDLES 396; SALT 400; USA 469

WHALES

490. How do sperm whales catch squid?

Every year, sperm whales eat half a million tons of squid, but how they manage to catch them is a bit of a mystery. Squid are faster and much more manoeuvrable than whales, so how the larger, lumbering creatures catch them so frequently and apparently so easily is a puzzle.

One old theory was that the whales stunned the squid with a sudden burst of sonar clicks, but research has shown that squid seem impervious to such whale sounds, even when played at very high volume through loudspeakers. Another idea is that the whales tend to catch the squid at great depths where the coldness of the water may make them sluggish, while yet another idea is that the squid may be lured into the whale's mouth by the pale pigmentation of its interior.

Whales have been seen vacuuming up squid from a few feet away with a powerful sucking action, but even so, one might expect the squid to see the whale coming and get out of the way.

491. Why has the song pitch of blue whales been getting lower?

From the northern Pacific to the Southern Ocean, the song of male blue whales, which is believed to play a role in their searching for mates, has been deepening. Scientists who have monitored whale song for over forty years have reported that their voices have deepened by some 30 per cent over that period.

One theory is that it is a result of competition in mate selection. Female blue whales are known to prefer larger males. A deep voice may indicate a bigger whale, which would convey a survival benefit to deeper-voiced males.

Another idea is that it may be the result of a recovery in the population of blue whales following bans on hunting them. That would result in their being less sparsely distributed, so the males would expect to find females a shorter distance away and would not need to sing so loudly. Since it is easier for whales to sing loud at higher frequencies, the need to sing high would therefore have diminished.

492. Why are whales so big?

The blue whale is the biggest animal that has ever existed. Bigger than the biggest dinosaur and thirty times as heavy as an elephant – indeed, a whale's tongue alone can weigh as much as an elephant – whales are enormous, but it's not easy to see why.

From an evolutionary standpoint, being large is not always an advantage. It may help in battles against competitors, but larger animals need more food to stay alive. When resources become scarce, it is the bigger animals that die out, as was the case with the several varieties of megafauna that became extinct around 10,000 years ago (→ AVOCADOS 37).

How whales have become so large is easier to explain than why they have done so: Arctic krill, which have formed the main part of the diet of many whale species, have long been plentiful, and whales can take huge mouthfuls of them. Floating at sea also requires far less energy than lumbering around on land. A creature the size of a whale would simply be too big to survive out of water: its legs would be unable to support its bulk.

All the same, once a creature has reached a size that enables it to dominate potential predators, the evolutionary advantages of growing even bigger seem to be outweighed by the disadvantages.

See also DOLPHINS 155; RIDDLES 396

WILD BOAR

493. Why do wild boar scatter their acorns?

When animals hoard their food, the threat of its being stolen by others of their species gives them essentially two options: larder-hoarding or scatter-hoarding. The first of these involves hiding all the food together in one cache, the second involves having a number of smaller caches. Wild boar like to scatter-hoard their acorns, but it is not clear that this is the best strategy.

In 2014 an experiment was conducted in which researchers buried a fixed number of acorns over a fixed number of patches within a fixed area, varying cache size and cache depth. They then recorded how successful wild boar were at finding and pilfering acorns from the various caches. As expected, they found that the time wild boar needed to stumble across the first cache and steal the acorns was shortest for scatter-hoarding, but the time needed to pilfer all the caches was slightly longer for scatter-hoarding than for larder-hoarding. Overall the rate of pilferage did not differ between scatter-hoarding and larder-hoarding.

The question of why the wild boar bother to scatter-hoard, which takes longer and involves greater expenditure of energy than larder-hoarding, is therefore still open.

WINE

494. Are screw-caps good for red wine?

Cork or screw-cap? The question of how best to seal a wine-bottle has aroused intense debate over the past couple of decades. A common view is that screw-tops are fine for most white wines, but many say that good red wines that need long ageing in the bottle require corks. But is this just the view of wine snobs, or is such a belief justified?

It all comes down to the question of how airtight one wants the bottle to be. On the one hand, there is a need to prevent air from entering the bottle and spoiling the wine; on the other hand, a small amount of oxygen may help the wine develop. The cork was long seen as the perfect way to keep the wine safe from degradation while letting enough oxygen seep through to improve it over the years. Screw-caps, however, are completely resistant to the mould that sometimes affects corks.

In the early years of screw-cap bottles, the seal was seen as too absolute to allow wines to age. More recently, types of screw-cap have been developed which allow the wine to be exposed to a small amount of oxygen to aid the ageing process. This technology, however, is too recent to be able to judge whether such screw-caps allow the wine to mature as well as corks.

It is also worth mentioning that whatever the quality of the wine, the sound made by a cork being pulled is unlikely ever to be matched by that of a screw-top being opened.

See also BRAINS 75; CHOCOLATE 104; FOOD 196; MESOPOTAMIA 305

WITCHES

495. Where were the Salem witches buried after their executions?

In 1692, in the town of Salem, Massachusetts, over 200 people, mostly women, were arrested on suspicion of witchcraft. The resulting trials later the same year ended in the execution of nineteen of them by hanging. But where the hangings took place and where the victims were buried is unknown. According to court records, the hangings took place at 'Gallows Hill'. There is a location in Salem now known by that name, but there are some good reasons for doubting that it is the right place. For one thing, the hill is too steep for the cart supposedly going to fetch the bodies to have made its way up to the supposed point of the hangings; and for another, the son of one of the victims was said to have rowed a boat to the base of the hill after the burials to exhume his mother and give her a proper Christian burial. Yet there is not, and never has been, a waterway leading to the present Gallows Hill. Other smaller hills in the area have been suggested as the location of the original Gallows Hill, but without any convincing evidence.

All the court records tell us is that the bodies were buried in an unmarked, shallow grave because of their association with the Devil. Their unstated desire to keep the precise location a secret has been successful up to the present day.

496. Why did the women in Salem behave like witches?

The arrests, trials and hangings at Salem were the culmination of a witchcraft hysteria that began with some decidedly odd behaviour from three girls, Abigail Williams, Betty Parris and Ann Putnam Jr. Their various antics included hallucinations, shouting out in church, having fits, making strange sounds, and feeling as if they were being pricked and poked. When physicians could find no cause for this, it was put down to the work of Satan and the girls were encouraged to reveal who was controlling them.

One of those accused was a slave girl called Tituba. She confessed to seeing the Devil, who appeared to her 'sometimes like a hog and sometimes like a great dog'. She also confessed that a conspiracy of witches existed in Salem, and the arrests began. But what made the three girls behave the way they did in the first place? There are several theories:

(i) Mental illness causing hysteria and delusions – though for that to have affected three girls simultaneously is unlikely.

(ii) Puritanism: it may all have been a reaction to the strict Puritan lifestyle. The restrictions imposed on the girls may have caused them to behave in the way they did, then blame it on possession by the Devil.

(iii) Ergot poisoning: ergot of rye is a plant disease causing a poisonous fungus which can bring on convulsive fits, muscle spasms, nausea, vomiting and hallucination.

(iv) It may all have been a plot by the girls' parents to have their own enemies denounced as witches.

WORDS

497. What does the 'drawn' in 'hanged, drawn and quartered' refer to?

From 1351 until it was finally removed from the statute book in 1870, the crime of high treason under English law could carry a penalty of being hanged, drawn and quartered. Specifically, the full sentence was:

> *That you be drawn on a hurdle to the place of execution where you shall be hanged by the neck and being alive cut down, your privy members shall be cut off and your bowels taken out and burned before you, your head severed from your body and your body divided into four quarters to be disposed of at the King's pleasure.*

This has led to a long-running dispute over the function of the word 'drawn' in the phrase 'hanged, drawn and quartered'. As the word is used in the description above, 'drawn' means 'dragged along behind a horse', but that punishment is surely 'drawn, hanged and quartered'.

Because the words, in the phrase as it is usually seen, are ordered as they are, some take 'drawn' to refer to the drawing out of the intestines or disembowelment. The confusion is well expressed by the *Oxford English Dictionary*, which says:

> *in many cases of executions it is uncertain whether this [evisceration], or sense 4 [To drag... to the place of execution], is meant. The presumption is that where drawn is mentioned after hanged, the sense is [evisceration].*

498. Is 'Huh?' a word?

What is the difference between a word and a grunt? Those who study linguistics attempt to differentiate between the two by defining 'word' as 'a lexical, conventionalised form that has to be learnt'. One cannot, for example, know that 'word' means a word without having learnt it; it is just a convention among English-speakers that that's what it means. 'Ow!', on the other hand, is just an involuntary expression of pain whose meaning is clear without having been learnt. So where does this leave 'Huh?'?

In 2013 researchers in the Netherlands examined the use of 'Huh?' as a 'repair initiator' – a comment indicating a problem in hearing or comprehension inviting the speaker to repeat or explain – in ten unrelated languages, in all of which recognizable versions of 'Huh?' are used with similar meanings. They say that its use 'is so common as to be practically universal, and yet calibrated to specific language systems such that it qualifies as a word'.

This leaves two possibilities: 'Huh?' is similar across languages because it is an innate grunt; or the similarity is a result of convergent evolution. In other words, we say 'Huh?' the world over because we all ran up against the same problem in similar conditions, as communication evolved, when it came to indicating a need for clarification. Some, however, may view the argument in favour of this latter explanation with a strong 'Huh?'.

See also SHAKESPEARE 413

WORMS

499. Is knowledge edible?

In the early 1960s a remarkable series of experiments was performed on flatworms to test a new theory of memory. The theory predicted that every new memory corresponded to a new molecule of RNA which could be reproduced and stored throughout the body. It was tested on planarians (a kind of flatworm) which were conditioned to behave in a certain way, then cut in half and allowed to regenerate, and then cut in half again and allowed to regenerate again; the result of all this was a worm none of which had been present for the original conditioning. Remarkably, it still seemed to retain knowledge of what it had learnt. More remarkably still, later experiments seemed to confirm that if a worm was taught something, then minced and fed to another worm, the worm that ate it could ingest the knowledge. Sadly, the RNA theory of memory was then shown to be wrong, so the worm experiments were abandoned and other explanations were found to explain why knowledge had appeared to be edible.

In 2013, however, knowledge came back on the menu – for worms anyway – in experiments on stem cells at Tufts University, Massachusetts. The focus of this research was less on the mechanics of memory storage than on the way a worm can regenerate its head and brain when it has been cut in half. How does a cell know when and how to grow into a brain? The research did, however, confirm one finding from the work done half a century earlier: if you teach a worm something, then cut its brain off, it will remember what it learnt once the brain has grown back. In other words, the memory must be stored somehow in its ordinary cells rather than in the brain itself. Which raises again the question of whether a memory can be taken from the body of one creature and transplanted into another, possibly even by eating. Knowledge may be edible after all.

500. How old is the oldest flatworm?

Research at Nottingham University in 2012 was reported to have shown that the ability of worms to regenerate over and over again with no sign of ageing may indicate that they could live forever. After creating a colony of 20,000 worms from one original by successive division and regeneration, they reported that the evidence showed that the worms could be immortal.

If this is correct, it would suggest that we cannot hope to tell the age of a flatworm: it can regenerate over and over again and stay just as young as it was at the start. It follows that we cannot know how old the oldest flatworm is.

See also ANIMALS 19; BIOLOGY 63; LONGEVITY 279

ZEBRAS

501. Why do zebras have stripes?

When I was at school long, long ago, everyone knew why zebras had stripes: obviously it was for camouflage in the long grass. Actually that theory had been dismissed even in Darwin's time. There was simply not enough long grass around for it to be credible. Darwin himself had suggested that the beautiful stripes might be for mate selection, while Alfred Russel Wallace suggested that the stripes acted as a defence against predators. 'In twilight,' he wrote, '[zebras] are not at all conspicuous, the stripes of white and black so merging together into a grey tint it is difficult to see them at a little distance.'

Recently, two more theories have emerged. In 2014 a report was published showing that the amount of striping on zebras in different parts of Africa correlated with the prevalence of biting flies. The stripes, the researchers concluded, are there to confuse the flies. In 2015, however, another study appeared suggesting that the stripes had a valuable function helping the zebra keep cool in the African heat. The definition of the stripes on a zebra's back did not correlate with the number of tsetse flies at all, but with temperature and rainfall. Light and dark stripes heat up at different rates, and this may generate cooling currents of air across the zebra's skin.

Whether these currents really occur, however, has yet to be experimentally tested, so for the time being we just have to accept that the question of why zebras have stripes is just another thing that nobody knows.

ACKNOWLEDGEMENTS

Finding another 501 questions that nobody knows the answers to would have been impossible without the help and tolerance of all the people I have pestered to tell me their expert ignorance and those who have steered me towards unexpected troves of ignorance. I cannot name you all, partly for reasons of space, but also because I have forgotten many of your names, but my forgetfulness does not diminish my gratitude.

Of those whose names I can remember, I am particularly grateful to Prof Charles Spence for telling me about the joys of eating with one's fingers, and to my work experience student Kazio Bakowski for revealing his unexpected knowledge of Romanian gold.

My work has also been considerably eased by the increasing availability of several scientific journals on the Internet, of which I should give special mention to PLoS ONE (www.plosone.org) and Animal Behaviour (available online at: http://www.sciencedirect.com/science/journal/00033472), which have been an endless source of the latest findings and the latest areas in which we realize that further research is needed.

Most of all, though, I am indebted to all at Atlantic Books for having confidence in me to come up with another *501 Things That Nobody Knows*, particularly to James Nightingale for being so understanding when, as usual, I was late with the manuscript. Many thanks also to my editor, Ben Dupré, for his meticulous work in correcting my errors and suggesting areas where improvements were needed. Any mistakes that remain, however, are all my own work.

BIBLIOGRAPHY

This is just a selection of references that may be useful and interesting as sources of further information on the topics discussed. The references are ordered according to the number of the question in the preceding material.

7. Blackburn, K., Schirillo, J. (2012), 'Emotive hemispheric differences measured in real-life portraits using pupil diameter and subjective aesthetic preferences', *Experimental Brain Research*

15, 16. Mora, C. et al. (2011), 'How many species are there on Earth and in the ocean?', *PLoS Biology*

19. Bagemihl, Bruce (1999), *Biological Exuberance: Animal Homosexuality and Natural Diversity*, St Martin's Press

21. Hölldobler, B. and Wilson, E. (1994), *Journey to the Ants: A Story of Scientific Exploration*, Harvard University Press

26. Lison, M. et al. (1980), 'A polymorphism of the ability to smell urinary metabolites of asparagus', *British Medical Journal*

28. Acedo, L. (2014), 'The flyby anomaly: a case for strong gravitomagnetism?', *Advances in Space Research*

40. Crockford, C., Wittig, R. M., Seyfarth, R. M. and Cheney, D. L. (2007), 'Baboons eavesdrop to deduce mating opportunities', *Animal Behaviour*

41. Clapham, M., Nevin, O. T., Ramsey, A. D. and Rosell, F. (2013), 'The function of strategic tree selectivity in the chemical signalling of brown bears', *Animal Behaviour*

41. Clapham, M., Nevin, O. T., Ramsey, A. D. and Rosell, F., 'Food availability affects the scent marking frequencies of wild brown bears', in preparation for submission to *Animal Ecology*

43. Gross, H. J. et al. (2009), 'Number-based visual generalisation in the honeybee', *PLoS ONE*

44. Preece, K. and Beekman, M. (2014), 'Honeybee waggle dance error: adaption or constraint? Unravelling the c omplex dance language of honeybees', *Animal Behaviour*

45. Ruhul Amin, Kyi Kyi Than, Yong Jung Kwon (2009), 'Copulation duration of bumblebee Bombus terrestris (Hymenoptera: Apidae): impacts on polyandry and colony parameters', *Journal of Asian-Pacific Entomology*

68. Kiera, L. M. and Drummond, H. (2014), 'Extrapair behaviour reveals flexible female choosiness and mixed support for classic good genes in blue-footed boobies', *Animal Behaviour*

69. Heinig, A. et al. (2014), 'Male mate preferences in mutual mate choice: finches modulate their songs across and within male–female interactions', *Animal Behaviour*

72. Gilbert, S. F., 'Congenital human baculum deficiency: the generative bone of Genesis 2:21–23', *American Journal of Medical Genetics*

78. Rogers, L. J. (2000), 'Evolution of hemispheric specialization: advantages and disadvantages', *Brain and Language*

86. Parkin, M. et al. (2011), 'The fraction of cancer attributable to lifestyle and environmental factors in the UK in 2010', *British Journal of Cancer*

94. Ropars, J. K. et al. (2012), 'Sex in cheese: evidence for sexuality in the fungus *Penicillium roqueforti*', *PloS ONE*

98. Wilson, M. L. et al. (2014), 'Lethal aggression in *Pan* is better explained by adaptive strategies than human impacts', *Nature*

104. Messerli, F. H. (2012), 'Chocolate consumption, cognitive function, and Nobel Laureates', *New England Journal of Medicine*

104. Maurage, P., Heeren, A. and Pesenti, M. (2013), 'Does chocolate consumption really boost Nobel award chances? The peril of over-interpreting correlations in health studies', *Journal of Nutrition*

110. Wilson, P. S., (2014), 'Coffee roasting acoustics', *Journal of the Acoustical Society of America*

128. Costello, R. A. and Symes, L. B. (2014), 'Effects of anthropogenic noise on male signalling behaviour and female phonotaxis in Oecanthus tree crickets', *Animal Behaviour*

130. Platt, S. G. et al. (2013), 'Frugivory and seed dispersal by crocodilians: an overlooked form of saurochory?', *Journal of Zoology*

139. Bos, K. I. et al. (2014), 'Pre-Columbian mycobacterial genomes reveal seals as a source of New World human tuberculosis, *Nature*

147. Anglin, R. E., Samaan, Z. et al. (2013), 'Vitamin D deficiency and depression in adults: systematic review and meta-analysis', *British Journal of Psychiatry*

148. Tiira, K. et al. (2012), 'Environmental effects on compulsive tail chasing in dogs', *PLoS ONE*

149. Takaoka, A. et al. (2014), 'Do dogs follow behavioral cues from an unreliable human?', *Animal Cognition*

151. Marshall-Pescinia, S. et al. (2011), 'Social eavesdropping in the domestic dog', *Animal Behaviour*

151. Nitzschnera, M. et al. (2014), 'Side matters: potential mechanisms underlying dogs' performance in a social eavesdropping paradigm', *Animal Behaviour*

152. Ratcliffe, V. F. et al. (2014), 'Cross-modal discrimination of human gender by domestic dogs', *Animal Behaviour*

154. Shaffer, D. et al. (2004), 'How dogs navigate to catch frisbees', *Psychological Science*

171. Foerder, P. (2011), 'Insightful problem solving in an Asian elephant', *PLoS ONE*

171. Nissani, M. (2006), 'Do Asian elephants (*Elephas maximus*) apply causal reasoning to tool-use tasks?', *Journal of Experimental Psychology*

180. Sander, P. M. et al. (2011), 'Biology of the sauropod dinosaurs: the evolution of gigantism', *Biological Reviews*

186. Stokkan, K.-A. et al. (2013), 'Shifting mirrors: adaptive changes in retinal reflections to winter darkness in Arctic reindeer', *Proceedings of the Royal Society B*

189. Muntz, W. R. A. and Cronly-Dillon, J. R. (1966), 'Colour discrimination in goldfish, *Animal Behaviour*

190. Long, J. A. et al. (2015), 'Copulation in antiarch placoderms and the origin of gnathostome internal fertilization', *Nature*

193. Spence, C. and Piqueras-Fiszman, B. (2014), *The Perfect Meal*, Wiley

199. Kranjec, A. et al. (2010), 'A sinister bias for calling fouls in soccer', *PLoS ONE*

208. Glass, B. D., Maddox, W. T. and Love, B. C. (2013), 'Real-time strategy game training: emergence of a cognitive flexibility trait', *PLoS ONE*

210. Dias, B. G. and Ressler, K. J. (2013), 'Parental olfactory experience influences behaviour and neural structure in subsequent generations', *Nature*

211. Gierman, H. J. et al. (2014), 'Whole-genome sequencing of the world's oldest people', *PLoS ONE*

216. Deutsch, C. et al. (2014), 'Centennial changes in North Pacific anoxia linked to tropical trade winds', *Science*

225. Zipser, B. et al. (2013), 'Dimensions of animal personalities in guinea pigs', *Ethology*

236. Raspopovic, J. et al. (2014), 'Digit patterning is controlled by a Bmp-Sox9-Wnt Turing network modulated by morphogen gradients', *Science*

241. Gómez-Robles, A. et al. (2013), 'No known hominin species matches the expected dental morphology of the last common ancestor of Neanderthals and modern humans', *Proceedings of the National Academy of Sciences*

251. Kastak, C. R. et al. (2001), 'Equivalence classification by California sea lions using class-specific reinforcers', *Journal of the Experimental Analysis of Behavior*

265. Janis, C. M. et al. (2014), 'Locomotion in extinct giant kangaroos: were sthenurines hop-less monsters?', *PLoS ONE*

274. Balme, G. A. and Hunter, L. T. B. (2013), 'Why leopards commit infanticide', *Animal Behaviour*

296. Sansone, R. A. and Sansone, L. A. (2008), 'Pain, pain, go away: antidepressants and pain management', *Psychiatry*

301. Madden, J. R. et al. (2009), 'Why do meerkat pups stop begging?', *Animal Behaviour*

307. Francis, J. A. and Vavrus, S. J. (2012), 'Evidence linking Arctic amplification to extreme weather in mid-latitudes', *Geophysical Research Letters*

311. Screen, J. A. and Simmonds, I. (2014), 'Amplified mid-latitude planetary waves favour particular regional weather extremes', *Nature Climate Change*

313. Gabriel, S. I. et al. (2011), 'Of Mice and "Convicts": origin of the Australian house mouse, *Mus musculus*', *PloS ONE*

314. Walsh, P. T. et al. (2013), 'Faecal avoidance and selective foraging: do wild mice have the luxury to avoid faeces?', *Animal Behaviour*

319. Wheeler, B. C. (2009), 'Monkeys crying wolf? Tufted capuchin monkeys use anti-predator calls to usurp resources from conspecifics', *Proceedings of the Royal Society B*

322. Balababova, S. et al. (1992), 'First identification of drugs in Egyptian mummies', *Naturwissenschaften*

327. Lai, K.-M. et al. (2011), 'Propagation of respiratory aerosols by the vuvuzela', *PLoS ONE*

343. Andrade, C. and Srihari, B. S. (2001), 'A preliminary survey of rhinotillexomania in an adolescent sample', *Journal of Clinical Psychiatry*

347. Tricarico, E. et al. (2011), 'I know my neighbour: individual recognition in *Octopus vulgaris*', *PLoS ONE*

349. Mumm, C. A. S and Knörnschild, M. (2014), 'The vocal repertoire of adult and neonate giant otters', *PLoS ONE*

374. Furlan, E. et al. (2012), 'Is body size variation in the platypus (*Ornithorhynchus anatinus*) associated with environmental variables?', *Australian Journal of Zoology*

375. Lesku, J. A. et al. (2011), 'Ostriches sleep like platypuses', *PloS ONE*

376. Schlicht, E. J. et al. (2010), 'Human wagering behavior depends on opponents' faces', *PLoS ONE*

377. Owen, M. A. et al. (2015), 'An experimental investigation of chemical communication in the polar bear', *Journal of Zoology*

378. Sonne, C. et al. (2015), 'Penile density and globally used chemicals in Canadian and Greenland polar bears', *Environmental Research*

379. Sakai, M. et al. (2011), 'Do porpoises choose their associates? A new method for analyzing social relationships among cetaceans', *PLoS ONE*

385. Symmonds, M. et al. (2010), 'Metabolic state alters economic decision making under risk in humans', *PLoS ONE*

385. de Ridder, D. et al. (2014), 'Always gamble on an empty stomach: hunger is associated with advantageous decision making', *PLoS ONE*

392. Rygula, R. et al. (2012), 'Laughing rats are optimistic', *PLoS ONE*

406. Sanders, A. R. et al. (2014), 'Genome-wide scan demonstrates significant linkage for male sexual orientation', *Psychological Medicine*

409. Swami, V. and Tovee, M. J. (2013), 'Resource security impacts men's female breast size preferences', *PLoS ONE*

411. Stoet, G. (2013), 'Are women better than men at multi-tasking?', *BMC Psychology*

417. Hollander Jr, L. E. (2001), 'Unexpected weight gain transients at the moment of death', *Journal of Scientific Exploration*

418. Fossat, P. et al. (2014), 'Anxiety-like behavior in crayfish is controlled by serotonin', *Science*

423. Rattenborg, N. C. (2006), 'Do birds sleep in flight?', *Naturwissenschaften*

433. Pauli, J. N. (2014), 'A syndrome of mutualism reinforces the lifestyle of a sloth', *Proceedings of the Royal Society B*

437. Hoso, M. et al. (2010), 'A speciation gene for left–right reversal in snails results in anti-predator adaptation', *Nature Communications*

438. Fruson, L. et al. (2012), 'A flavonol present in cocoa enhances snail memory', *Journal of Experimental Biology*

439. Shine, R. et al. (1999), 'Are snakes right-handed? Asymmetry in hemipenis size and usage in gartersnakes', *Behavioral Ecology*

440. Bloch, E. (2001), 'Hemlock poisoning and the death of Socrates: did Plato tell the truth?', *Journal of the International Plato Society*

445. Nørgaard, T. et al. (2012), 'Nocturnal homing: learning walks in a wandering spider?', *PLoS ONE*

446. McLeod, P. and Dienes, Z. (1996), 'Do fielders know where to go to catch the ball, or only how to get there?', *Journal of Experimental Psychology*

454. Stetson, C. et al. (2007), 'Does time really slow down during a frightening event?', *PLoS ONE*

458. Dorland, A. et al. (2014), 'Do roads reduce painted turtle (*Chrysemys picta*) populations?', *PLoS ONE*

484. Jiang, C. and Galm, M. (2014), 'The economic benefit of being blonde: a study of waitress tip earnings based on their hair color', *Journal of Behavioral Studies in Business*

493. Suselbeek, L. et al. (2014), 'Scatter hoarding and cache pilferage by superior competitors: an experiment with wild boar, *Sus scrofa*', *Animal Behaviour*

498. Dingemanse, M. et al. (2013), 'Is "Huh?" a universal word? Conversational infrastructure and the convergent evolution of linguistic items', *PLoS ONE*

499. Ziegler, R. A. (1963), 'Is knowledge edible? A study of conditioned responses in *Planaria*', *Worm Runner's Digest*

499. Shomrat, T. and Levin, M. (2013), 'An automated training paradigm reveals long-term memory in planaria and its persistence through head regeneration', *Journal of Experimental Biology*

501. Caro, T. et al. (2014), 'The function of zebra stripes', *Nature Communications*

501. Larison, B. et al. (2015), 'How the zebra got its stripes: a problem with too many solutions', *Royal Society Open Science*

INDEX

Entries are followed by item numbers, Part 1 items (**1**/) followed by Part 2 (**2**/).

A NOTE ABOUT THE AUTHOR

William Hartston graduated in mathematics at Cambridge but never completed his PhD in number theory because he spent too much time playing chess. This did, however, lead to his winning the British Chess Championship in 1973 and 1975 and writing a number of chess books and newspaper chess columns.

When William and mathematics amicably separated, he worked for several years as an industrial psychologist specializing in the construction and interpretation of personality tests. After ten years writing a wide variety of columns for the *Independent*, he moved to the *Daily Express*, where he has been writing the Beachcomber column of surreal humour since 1998. In addition to writing about chess, he has written books on useless information, numbers, dates and bizarre academic research, including sexology.

Recently, his skills at sitting on a sofa watching television have been appreciated by viewers of the TV programme *Gogglebox*, but he has still not decided what he wants to be when he grows up.